Research in Psychology

Methods and Design

Research in Psychology

Methods and Design

C. James Goodwin

Wheeling Jesuit College

John Wiley & Sons, Inc.

New York Chichester Brisbane Toronto Singapore

ACQUISITIONS EDITOR   Karen Dubno
MARKETING MANAGER   Rebecca Herschler
PRODUCTION MANAGEMENT   Ingrao Associates/Erin Singletary
TEXT DESIGNER   Michael Jung
MANUFACTURING MANAGER   Susan Stetzer
PHOTO RESEARCHER   Lisa Passmore
ILLUSTRATION COORDINATOR   Jaime Perea
COVER IMAGE   Marjory Dressler

This book was set in 11/12 Bembo by Digitype and printed and bound by RR Donnelly/Crawfordsville Press. The cover was printed by Phoenix Color.

Recognizing the importance of preserving what has been written, it is a policy of John Wiley & Sons, Inc. to have books of enduring value published in the United States printed on acid-free paper, and we exert our best efforts to that end.

The paper on this book was manufactured by a mill whose forest management programs include sustained yield harvesting of its timberlands. Sustained yield harvesting principles ensure that the number of trees cut each year does not exceed the amount of new growth.

Library of Congress Cataloging in Publication Data:
Goodwin, C. James,
    Research in psychology : methods and design / C. James Goodwin.
        p.   cm.
    Includes bibliographical references and indexes.
    ISBN 0-471-59385-0 (alk, paper)
        1. Psychology—Research.   2. Psychology—Research—Methodology.
    3. Psychology, Experimental.   I. Title.
    BF76.5.G64   1995
    150'.72—dc20   94-41288
                                                                              CIP

Printed in the United States of America

10 9 8 7 6 5 4 3 2

To Susan

PREFACE

Teaching the research methods course over the years has reminded me often of the opening sentence from *A Tale of Two Cities* by Charles Dickens. In "the best of times," it can be an exhilarating experience. Every instructor remembers moments when a student developed a creative idea for a study that was a perfect next step from the experiment being discussed in class. It is truly rewarding to hear a student arguing in the hall with a peer and saying things like "OK, but let's see some data;" and of course when the occasional student comes in after lab and asks about graduate programs in experimental psychology (and their first question is *not* "Can you get a job that way?"), it is a moment to be treasured. On the other hand, in "the worst of times," the course can be very frustrating to teach. Semester after semester there are always students who view the course as boring, obtuse, unnecessary ("I'm going to be a counselor."), and seemingly designed to destroy the quality of their lives.

For the interested, dynamic, creative students, a poor textbook can dampen their enthusiasm; for the bored group, resistant from the outset, it can confirm their worst fears. Thus it is important in experimental pscyhology that a text engage as well as instruct students. My goal in writing this book is to confirm the beliefs of the interested student and convince the uninterested student that experimental psychology can be intriguing, relevant, understandable, and even fun.

To accomplish this goal, I have attempted to provide some insight into the excitement that research in psychology can generate and I have tried to give students things to do other than just read the text. For example, I have tried to enhance the understanding of how specific methods work by including numerous "case studies"—detailed descriptions of actual research. Most are recent, but some are classics. I have also included several first-hand accounts of research, highlighting the passion that research psychologists have for their work. In addition, to keep students actively involved and to help them develop and appreciate scientific thinking in psychology, I have placed numerous "Applications Exercises" at the end of each chapter.

The book is organized into 12 chapters and 4 appendices. The introductory chapter lays the groundwork for all that follows by thoroughly explaining the scientific way of thinking; the final chapter returns to the theme and provides closure. Chapter 2 is devoted to research ethics. It concerns how the American Psychological Association's code of ethics is applied to research with both human and animal subjects. Scientific fraud is also discussed. Chapter 3 examines the question of how ideas for research originate and explains the continually evolving relationship between theory and research. Issues related to measuring behavior and statistical analysis are the focus of Chapter 4. The following three chapters explore the experimental method, the Cadillac of research methodology. There is a basic introduction to the experimental method (Chapter 5), a discussion of control problems in experimental reserach (Chapter 6), and an extensive treatment of experimental design (Chapter 7). Descriptions of other traditions in psychological research follow in subsequent chapters. These include correlational research (Chapter 8), applied research (Chapter 9), research using "small N" designs (Chapter 10), and several varieties of descriptive research (Chapter 11). The appendices describe how to prepare the (in)famous APA-style research report in accordance with the most recent *Publication Manual* (1994) and how experimental psychologists use statistical analysis for decison-making purposes.

At various points in the text, boxed sections highlight three distinct topics. *Origins* boxes supply interesting information about the historical roots of experimental psychology and show how various research concepts and methods, such as maze learning, have evolved over the years. *Classic Studies* boxes describe well-known experiments, such as the Bobo doll studies, that illustrate particular research designs and methodological issues. Finally, *Ethics* boxes deal with controversial problems of concern to researchers, such as the issue of whether some psychological research invades privacy.

For the student, there are several features designed to facilitate learning. First, there is a built-in study guide: Each chapter ends with a Student Review, which includes fill-in and multiple-choice questions. These sample test items are not just definitional; they ask students to apply some of the concepts learned in the chapter. The Student Review also includes the previously mentioned Applications Exercises. Second, because chapter summaries should always be read before the chapters themselves, I have placed them at the *beginning* of each chapter and called them "Chapter Overviews." Reading and studying the Chapter Overviews gives the student an idea of what's to come and provides a general framework for the chapter. Third, although there is a separate Glossary that includes every term that is boldfaced in the text, the Index is also structured to make it easy to find key descriptions of concepts. Thus the Index includes the following:

Counterbalancing   **169**–177, 196–198, 204, 274

This entry indicates that (a) counterbalancing is a glossary term, because one of the page numbers is boldfaced in the index, and (b) page 169 contains the place in the text where the term appears in boldface and is defined.

To help instructors prepare and teach the methods course, the accompanying *Instructor's Manual* includes detailed chapter outlines and an extensive test bank of multiple-choice, fill-in, and essay questions. It also includes numerous "Course Enhancements"—lecture/discussion/demonstration ideas—for each chapter. Finally, the instructor will find detailed descriptions of 18 data collection exercises that give the student (with proper guidance) hands-on experience in doing research in psychology.

For instructors, I hope this book will make your difficult task easier. For students, I hope the text will either affirm your excitement about research in psychology or at least lead you to develop an understanding of and an appreciation for it. For both instructors and students, I hope this book will help make the course in research methods among the best of times for you.

Acknowledgments

This book would not have been started, much less completed, without the encouragement and support of many people. The hundreds of students who have passed through my research methods course over the years have been my principle source of inspiration—many of them have told me to stop complaining about the textbook and write my own. I would especially like to acknowledge three students. Michelle Koloff and Nan Armstrong served arduously as "in house" reviewers for me and although they seemed to take more pleasure than was really necessary in wielding the red pencil, they improved the book's ability to communicate to students. Aimee Faso was the leader of a group of students interesting in cognitive mapping and was the senior author of the sample study on that topic in Appendix A.

To Darryl Bruce, my dissertation director, I owe a great debt. He first showed me just how exciting research in psychology can be. Through our (somewhat) annual three-hour APA breakfasts, he continues to be a mentor (his latest communication made it clear that with the text finished, I should get back to work). I would also like to thank two of my APA Division 2 colleagues, Wayne Weiten and Steve Davis. Both were instrumental in convincing me that I actually could write a text and both provided much support and encouragement along the way.

Thanks also go to the stalwart reviewers for the text, who include:

Clark Burnham
University of Texas-Austin

Thomas Critchfield
Auburn University

Wayne Donaldson
University of New Brunswick

Michael Firment
Kennesaw State College

Joel Freund
University of Arkansas

Donald Jenson
University of Nebraska

Dennis Keefe
California State University-Fullerton

John Lyons
Northwestern University

Ken McGraw
University of Mississippi

Arthur Markman
Columbia University

Michael Perone
West Virginia University

Michael Reich
University of Wisconsin-River Falls

Elaine Scorpio
Rhode Island College

Ellen Susman
Metropolitan State College

Ron Taylor
University of Kentucky

Paul Wellman
Texas A & M University

Finally, the editors and staff at John Wiley are the best in the business; they made the entire production process a breeze (or at least much less onerous than I had any right to expect). A special thanks goes to Acquisitions Editor Karen Dubno, who had complete faith in the project long before sufficient evidence warranted it.

CONTENTS

CHAPTER **4**

Measurement, Sampling, and Data Analysis *89*

CHAPTER **5**

Introduction to Experimental Research *127*

CHAPTER **6**

Control Problems in Experimental Research   *157*

CHAPTER **11**

Other Research Methods *331*

CHAPTER **12**

Epilogue: Doing Research in Psychology *361*

APPENDIX A

Communicating the Results of Research in Psychology *375*

APPENDIX B

Using Statistics *405*

APPENDIX C

Statistical Tables *427*

APPENDIX D

Answers to Student Review Questions and Selected Exercises *437*

Research in Psychology
Methods and Design

CHAPTER 1

Scientific Thinking in Psychology

Chapter Overview

- ### Why Take This Course?

  The research methods course is at the very core of the psychology curriculum. It should be taken by all psychology majors because it provides the foundation for doing any research in psychology, serves as a basis for other content courses in psychology, makes one a more critical consumer of information, is essential for admission to graduate studies, and teaches scientific thinking.

- ### Attributes of Scientific Thinking in Psychology

  Research psychologists assume that human behavior is lawful and predictable and that the regularities in behavior can be discovered by using scientific methods. They use objective measures of behavior and ask that conclusions about the causes of behavior be data based. They ask empirical questions and attempt to answer them scientifically. The scientific approach to knowledge can be contrasted with other ways of knowing such as relying on authority.

- ## Creative Thinking in Science
  Creative scientists combine normal scientific thinking with the ability to see connections between things that others don't ordinarily see. Wide-ranging knowledge is the foundation for scientific creativity, but this knowledge can also hinder the creative process by limiting the scientist's vision.

- ## Can Psychology Really Be a Science?
  It is sometimes argued that psychology cannot be scientific because (a) it does not have the precision of a "real" science like chemistry, (b) unlike other sciences, there is no clear separation between the observer and what is being observed, and (c) every person's uniqueness precludes the possibility of establishing general laws of behavior. However, it is argued that precision is a matter of degree, that a separation indeed occurs when behavior is the basic datum, and that uniqueness does not rule out being able to study a phenomenon systematically.

- ## The Goals of Research in Psychology
  Research in psychology aims to describe behavioral phenomena, to be able to predict behavior with some probability and to provide adequate explanations of behavior. The results of psychological research can also be applied to change behavior directly, which makes the control of behavior a fourth goal.

- ## The Excitement of Psychological Research (Part 1)
  As a relatively young discipline, psychology has more questions than answers, so doing research in psychology can be enormously rewarding. The joy of research can be seen in the research lives of famous psychologists such as Eleanor Gibson and B. F. Skinner.

In the preface to his weighty two-volume *Principles of Physiological Psychology,* first published in 1874, the German physiologist Wilhelm Wundt boldly and unambiguously declared that his text represented "an attempt to mark out a new domain of *science*" (Wundt, 1874/1904, italics added). Shortly after publishing the book, Wundt established his now famous psychology laboratory at Leipzig, Germany, attracting students from all over Europe as well as from the United States. American universities soon established their own laboratories, about twenty of them by 1892 (Sokal, 1992). In that same year the American Psychological Association (APA) was founded, and before long it ratified a constitution identifying its purpose as "the advancement of Psychology as a *science.* Those who are eligible for membership are engaged in this work" (Cattell, 1895, p. 150, italics added). Thus for psychology's pioneers, both in Germany and in the United States, the "new psychology" was to be identified with science. It gradually separated itself from physiology and philosophy to become the independent discipline it is today.

For the early psychologists, the new psychology was to be a science of mental life, the goal being to understand exactly how the mind was structured and how it worked. In order to study the mind scientifically, however, generally agreed upon methods had to be developed and taught. Hence, students of the new psychology found themselves in laboratories learning the basic procedures for studying the mind. Although the methods have changed over the years, today's psychology departments continue this long tradition of teaching the tools of the trade to psychology majors. From the very beginning of psychology's history, then, teaching research methodology has been the heart and soul of the psychology curriculum. Of course, today's students tend to be suspicious of the argument that they should take the experimental psychology course because "we've always done it that way." There are several other reasons to justify taking the course.

Why Take This Course?

The most obvious reason for taking a course in research methods is to begin the process of learning how to do research in psychology. My ideal scenario would be for you to become fascinated by research, decide that you'd like to do some, get your feet wet as an undergraduate (e.g., collaborate with a professor on some research projects and perhaps read a paper at an undergraduate research conference), go to graduate school and complete a doctorate in psychology, begin a career as a productive researcher, and eventually be named recipient of the APA's annual award for "Distinguished Scientific Contributions!" Of course, I'm also a realist and know that most psychology majors have interests other than doing research, most don't go on to earn doctorates, most who earn doctorates don't become productive researchers, and *very few* productive scholars win APA awards. If you won't be a famous research psychologist some day, are there still reasons to take this course? Absolutely.

For one thing, a course in research methods provides a solid foundation for other psychology courses in more specific topic areas (social, cognitive, developmental, etc.) The difference between the methods course and these other courses is essentially the difference between process and content. The methods course teaches a *process* of acquiring knowledge that is then applied to all of the specific *content* areas represented by other courses in the psychology curriculum. A social psychology experiment in conformity may be worlds apart in subject matter from a cognitive psychology study on short-term memory, but their common bond is method—the way in which the knowledge about these phenomena is acquired. Fully understanding textbook descriptions of research is infinitely easier if you know something about method.

To illustrate, take a minute and look at one of your other psychology textbooks. Chances are that virtually every paragraph makes some assertion about behavior that either includes a specific description of a research study or at least makes reference to one. On my shelf, for example, is a social psychology text by Myers (1990) that includes the following description of a study about the effects of violent pornography on male aggression (Donnerstein, 1980). Myers wrote that the experimenter "showed 120 . . . men either a neutral, an erotic, or an aggressive-erotic (rape) film. Then the men, supposedly as part of another experiment, 'taught' a male or female confederate some nonsense syllables by choosing how much shock to administer for incorrect answers. The men who had watched the rape film administered markedly strong shocks—but only toward female victims" (Myers, 1990, p. 393). While reading this description, someone unfamiliar with experimental design might get the general idea, but a researcher would also be registering that the study was at the very least a 2×3 between-subjects factorial design resulting in a type of interaction effect that usually makes any main effects irrelevant, that only one of the two independent variables was a manipulated variable, thereby affecting the cause and effect interpretations of the results, and that the "victims" were not really shocked but were clued in to the purposes of the study (i.e., they were confederates).[1] Also, the thoughts "I wonder what would happen if there was more of a delay between the film and the learning part of the study?" or "I wonder how female subjects would react in a replication of the study?" might also float through the mind of someone in tune with the kind of "what if?" thinking that accompanies a knowledge of method.

A third reason for taking experimental psychology is that even if you never collect a single piece of data after the course is completed, knowledge of research methods will make you a more informed and critical consumer of information. We are continually exposed to claims about human behavior from sources ranging from the people around us who are amateur psychologists (i.e., everyone) to media accounts ranging from the sublime (an account in a reputable magazine about research on the relationship between TV watching and aggressiveness) to the ridiculous (the headlines you read while waiting in line to pay for groceries). While the latter can be dismissed without much difficulty (for most), the TV study might have been penned by a professional writer unaware of the important distinction between experimental and correlational research. Consequently, the article might describe a correlational study in cause and effect terms, a mistake you'll have no difficulty recognizing once you've finished Chapter 8. Another example might be a claim that while under hypnosis, people can be transported back to the moment of their birth, thereby gaining some great insight into the origins of their problems. What you will learn in Chapter 3 about what are called "parsimonious" explanations will make you suspicious about such a claim and enable you to think of several alternative explanations for the reports given by patients about their alleged birth experiences.

Fourth, there is a very pragmatic reason for taking a methods course. Even if you have no desire to become a research psychologist, you might like to be a professional practitioner of psychology some day. As is the case for researchers, practitioners also must earn an advanced degree, preferably the doctorate. Even for future clinical psychologists, counselors, and school psychologists, graduate school almost certainly means doing some research, so a course in methodology is an obvious first step to learning the necessary skills. Furthermore, your chances of getting into *any* type of graduate program in the first place are improved significantly if you (a) did well in undergraduate research methods and statistics courses, and (b) were involved in doing some research as an undergraduate.

---

[1]All of the jargon in this sentence will be part of your everyday vocabulary by the time you finish the methods course.

Once you become a professional psychologist, your research skills will be invaluable. Even if you aren't an active researcher yourself, you'll need to keep up with the latest research and you'll need to be able to read research critically. Also, if you work for a social service agency of some kind, you may find yourself dealing with accreditation boards or funding sources who will want to know if your psychological services are effective. As you will learn in Chapter 9, research evaluating program effectiveness touches the lives of most professional psychologists.

Finally, a course in research methods introduces you to a particular type of thinking. As mentioned earlier, other psychology courses deal with specific content areas and concentrate on what is known about topic X. The methods course, however, focuses more on the process by which knowledge of X is acquired. That process is centered on scientific thinking and it is deeply ingrained in all research psychologists. The idea requires some elaboration.

Attributes of Scientific Thinking in Psychology

We acquire our knowledge about human behavior in a number of ways and this part of the chapter will focus primarily on the scientific approach to this knowledge. First, however, let's consider some of the other ways in which we come to know things and believe them to be true, using a scheme first outlined by the American philosopher Charles S. Peirce in 1877. In an essay called "The Fixation of Belief" (reprinted in Tomas, 1957) Peirce described four ways in which we achieve certainty in our beliefs—tenacity, authority, the a priori method, and science. Peirce believed that the first three methods were widespread but flawed, and that science was the best way to achieve true knowledge.

Nonscientific Ways of Knowing

Peirce's first method, **tenacity**, is similar to a blind faith that is stubbornly held, motivated by a fear of uncertainty. The person maintaining a belief tenaciously is impervious to contrary evidence and only pays attention to information supporting the belief. Peirce did not describe how these beliefs developed initially, except to say that they are usually simplistic and result from the "instinctive dislike of an undecided state of mind" (Tomas, 1957, p. 15), but once they do develop they are held rigidly. Such beliefs will be of great comfort to the holder of them, but they of course will be seriously flawed by personal bias. To a modern-day social psychologist, tenacity sounds very much like the phenomenon of "belief perseverance," a closed-minded unwillingness to consider any evidence that is contrary to a strongly held belief (Anderson, Lepper, & Ross, 1980). The phenomenon contributes to the strong emotional component of prejudice; people who are highly prejudiced hold their beliefs tenaciously and cannot be persuaded otherwise. For the person convinced that all people on welfare are diabolically cheating the system and unwilling to work, the long history of research by social scientists disproving this notion makes no impact whatsoever.

Peirce's second method of fixing belief is to follow **authority**. He was referring primarily to the authority of the state, which tries to "keep correct doctrines before the attention of the people, to reiterate them perpetually, and to teach them to the young" (Tomas, 1957, p. 16). More generally, however, the influence of authority is felt in a number of ways. As children we are influenced by and believe what our parents tell us (at least for a while), as students we generally accept the authority of textbooks and professors, as patients we take the pills prescribed for us and believe they will have beneficial effects, and so on. Of course, relying on the authority of others to fix our beliefs overlooks the fact that authorities can be completely wrong. Parents often pass along prejudices to their children, textbooks and professors are sometimes wrong or their knowledge is incomplete or biased, doctors can miss a diagnosis or prescribe the wrong medicine, and the fact that governmental authority is often misguided hardly needs elaboration.

On the other hand, we do learn important things from some authority figures. In particular, it is usually a good idea to listen to the views of experts in particular fields. Also, it doesn't stretch the concept of authority to consider the giants of the arts and literature as authority figures who can teach us much about human behavior. Who can read Shakespeare or Dickens or Austen without gaining valuable insights about human nature?

Peirce believed that tenacity and authority were seriously flawed as ways of knowing. They provide solace, and perhaps some occasional insights, but they very easily lead to error. His third method of "fixing belief" was an improvement over tenacity and authority but problematic in its own way. Peirce described it as the outcome of rational discussion between people with different ideas who "gradually develop beliefs in harmony with natural causes" (Tomas, 1957, p. 20). The beliefs that result from this process are said to be "agreeable to reason" (Tomas, 1957, p. 20). This third approach, then, relies on the use of reason and a developing consensus among those debating the merits of one belief over another. Peirce called this the **a priori method** because it is based more on argument and logical deduction than direct experience. Beliefs are deduced from prior assumptions ("a priori" translates from the Latin as "from what comes before"). With just a hint of sarcasm, Peirce pointed out that the a priori method was favored by metaphysical philosophers who could reason eloquently to reach some truth only to be contradicted by other philosophers who reasoned just as eloquently to the opposite truth (on the question of whether the mind and the body are one or two different essences, for instance). The result is that beliefs go in and out of fashion; in metaphysics for instance, Peirce observed that "the pendulum has swung backward and forward between a more material and a more spiritual philosophy, from the earliest times to the latest" (Tomas, 1957, p. 24).

The most reliable way to develop a belief, according to Peirce, is through the **method of science**. Its procedures allow us to know "real things, whose characters are entirely independent of our opinions about them" (Tomas, 1957, p. 25). That is, its chief advantage lies in its objectivity. Before discussing scientific thinking, however, and before you get the impression that scientists somehow are "above" others in avoiding the problems associating with the other ways of knowing, let me assure you that scientists are not immune to tenacity and authority; also, the rules of logic that underlie the a priori method are used by scientists.

Concerning tenacity, scientists sometimes hold onto a pet theory long after others have abandoned it and they sometimes seem to be less than willing to entertain new ideas. Indeed, Charles Darwin once wrote that it would be a good idea "if every scientific man was to die when sixty years old, as afterward he would be sure to oppose all new doctrines" (cited in Schultz & Schultz, 1992, p. 20). Also, scientists are susceptible to the influence of authority. The "authorities" are usually other scientists, and experts are more likely to be reliable sources than not, but a researcher should know better than to assume automatically that something is true simply because a reputable scientist said it was true. Finally, the a priori method is frequently found in science to the extent that scientists argue with each other and try to reach a rational consensus on some issue (e.g., whether to use the computer as a useful metaphor for the brain). As you will discover in Chapter 3, they also use the rules of logic and inductive/deductive reasoning to develop ideas for research and to evaluate research outcomes. But scientific thinking at its best has a number of distinct attributes; it is to those that we now turn.

Scientific Ways of Knowing

The way of thinking that characterizes scientists in general and research psychologists in particular involves a number of interrelated assumptions and features. First, researchers assume that events in the world, including the world of human behavior, follow certain rules and are therefore orderly and predictable. That is, they make the assumptions of **determinism** and **discoverability**, the ideas that events have causes and that these causes can be discovered by using scientific methods. This does not necessarily mean that events can be predicted with 100% certainty, however. It simply means that psychological phenomena occur with a regularity that is not random and that those regularities can be investigated successfully. Let us examine the assumption of determinism in greater detail.

Determinism

Students are often confused after reading that psychologists regard human behavior as "determined." They sometimes assume this means "predestined" or "predetermined." It doesn't. A believer in absolute predestination believes that every event is determined ahead of time, perhaps by God, and develops a fatalistic belief that one can do little but accept life as it presents itself. However, the traditional concept of determinism contends simply that all events have causes. Some philosophers argue for a strict determinism, which holds that the causal structure of the universe enables the prediction of all events with 100% certainty, at least in principle. Others, however, influenced by twentieth century developments in physics, take a more moderate view that could be called a probabilistic or **statistical determinism**. This approach argues that events can be predicted, but only with a probability greater than chance. Most psychologists take this position.

Yet the concept of determinism, even the "less than 100%" variety, is troubling because it seems to require that we abandon our belief in free will. If every event is caused, so the argument goes, then how can one course of action be freely chosen over another? The psychologist would reply simply that if determinism is not true at least to some degree, how can we ever know anything about human behavior? Imagine for a moment what it would be like if human behavior was completely unpredictable. How could you decide whether to marry Ed or Ted? How could you decide whether or not to take a course from Professor Jones?

Of course, there are multiple factors influencing human behavior and it is difficult to know for sure what someone will do at any one moment. Nonetheless, human behavior follows certain patterns and is clearly predictable. For example, because we know that children often do things that work effectively for them, it is not hard to predict a tantrum in a crowded toy store if that behavior has yielded toys for a child in that setting in the past.

Concerning the matter of free choice, at least one philosopher of science has argued that free choice is a meaningless concept *unless* determinism is true, because choices should be made on some reasonable basis and there can be no such basis for a choice unless the world is lawful to a degree. According to Rudolph Carnap, without "causal regularity, . . . it is not possible to make a free choice at all. A choice involves a deliberate preference for one course of action over another. How could a choice possibly be made if the consequences of alternative courses of action could not be foreseen?" (1966, p. 220). In short, Carnap argued that the idea of free choice is meaningless unless determinism is in fact true! Thus deciding between Ed or Ted as a marriage partner only makes sense if you know certain things that are predictable about them (e.g., Ed is more reliable). Deciding whether to take professor Jones might hinge on her reputation for being predictably fair in treating students.

Most research psychologists believe that the existence of free will cannot be answered one way or the other by science, but that it is a matter of belief. However, in order for choice to have any meaning for humans, events in the world must be somewhat predictable. Thus, when the psychologist investigates human behavior and discovers regularities, this does not eliminate or even limit human freedom. Indeed, if Carnap is correct, such research may actually enhance our ability to choose by increasing our knowledge of the alternatives.

Objectivity

A second characteristic of scientific thinking, the attribute that Peirce found most appealing about science, is its relative **objectivity**. However, to be objective does not mean to be devoid of human biases and preconceptions. Rather, an objective observation is simply one that can be verified with some degree of certainty by more than one observer. In science this usually takes the form of defining the terms and research procedures precisely enough so that any other person could repeat the study, presumably achieving the same observable outcome.

This process of repeating a study to determine if its results occur reliably is called "replication" (see Chapter 3, pp. 79–80); as results are replicated, confidence in the reality of some psychological phenomenon is increased. On the other hand, questions are raised when results cannot be replicated. Outcomes that consistently fail to replicate are eventually discarded, which makes science a self-correcting discipline. As you will see in the next chapter, a failure to replicate is also how scientific fraud is sometimes uncovered.

Of course, in order to repeat a study, one must know precisely what was done in the original one. This is accomplished by means of a prescribed set of rules for describing research projects. These rules are described in great detail in the *Publication Manual of the American Psychological Association* (American Psychological Association, 1994), an invaluable resource for anyone reporting research results or writing other psychology papers. Appendix A, a guide to writing research reports in APA format, is based on the manual.

Data Driven

A third attribute of scientific thinking in psychology is that researchers are **data driven**. That is, they expect conclusions about human behavior to be supported by the evidence of objective data gathered through a systematic procedure. Furthermore, researchers try to judge whether the data given to support a claim are adequate for the claim to be made. For example, if someone asserts that excessive TV watching reduces creativity in children, the scientist immediately begins to wonder about the type and amount of data collected (How was creativity measured? How large was the data set?), the procedures used to collect the data, and the type of statistical analysis that was done.

This attitude can be detected easily in research psychologists; they even find themselves thinking about how data might bear on the problems they encounter in daily living. Even a neighbor's offhand observation about the tomato crop being better this year might generate in the researcher's mind a host of data-related questions to test the claim (How exactly did you count the tomatoes during the past two years? Did you measure the number picked per day or the number ripened per day? How did you determine "ripe?"). Of course, there are certain hazards resulting from this kind of thinking, including the possible loss of a neighbor's friendship. Sometimes the driven (as in compelled) part of the term data driven seems to be the operative term!

A personification of this data-driven attitude taken to extremes can be found in the life of Sir Francis Galton, a nineteenth-century British jack-of-all-sciences whose interests ranged from geography to meteorology to psychology. Galton was positively obsessed with the idea of collecting data; for instance, he once measured interest in various theater productions by counting the number of yawns that he could detect during performances! For more on his penchant for collecting data on virtually every imaginable topic, read Box 1.1, which describes his attempt to collect data on the mental abilities of as many Britishers as possible.

Empirical Questions

Empiricism is a term that refers to the process of learning things through direct observation or experience. **Empirical questions** can be answered through the kinds of systematic observations and experiences that characterize scientific methodology. They are precise enough to allow specific predictions to be made. As we'll see in Chapter 3, question asking is the first step of any research project. How to develop a good empirical question will be one theme of that chapter.

We can begin to get an idea about what constitutes an empirical question, however, by contrasting them with questions that cannot be answered empirically. For example, recall that Peirce used the mind–body question to illustrate what he called the a priori method. Philosophers argued both sides of the question

Box 1.1

ORIGINS—*Much Ado About Data: Sir Fancis Galton*

Sir Francis Galton (1822–1911) was someone who took the idea of "data driven" seriously. The cousin of Charles Darwin, he is known for arguing that intelligence was inherited not learned, for developing the idea of calculating correlations between variables, for being the first person to use questionnaires extensively, for convincing Scotland Yard that fingerprints provided a useful tool for identifying people, and for developing a series of tests that were designed to measure basic mental capacity (Fancher, 1990). Using these tests, he hoped to collect data on the abilities of as many people as possible. In 1884, he set up an "Anthropometric Laboratory" in London. For three pence, Britishers could run through Galton's tests, which included such things as reaction time, color vision, hearing tests, height, weight, and "breathing power." During a six-year period, Galton collected data on more than 9,000 people (Schultz & Schultz, 1992)! Although his choice of tests for "mental" ability may seem odd to us today, he believed there was a connection between simple sensory abilities and intelligence—if our knowledge of the world originally comes to us through our senses, then people with sharp minds must have sharp senses as well.

Galton's fascination with data was a bit extreme but not significantly different from the kind of attitude held by a typical research psychologist today. The attitude is perhaps best summed up in B. F. Skinner's observation about the process of doing research: "When you run into something interesting, drop everything else and study it" (Skinner, 1956, p. 223).

for many years (they're still at it!), consensus changed many times, and Peirce wasn't optimistic about the question ever being resolved. Whether the mind and body are two separate essences or one is simply not an empirical question. However, there are a number of empirical questions to be asked that *are* related to the issue. For instance, it is possible to ask about the effects of mental activity (mind) on physical health (body) by investigating the effects of psychological stress on the immune system. Also, it is possible to look at the body's influence on mental states by investigating how physical fatigue affects problem solving ability in some task.

Although psychologists tend to believe that the scientific approach is the ideal way to answer questions, it is worth pointing out that there are many questions in our lives that science cannot answer adequately. These questions include such things as whether a deity exists or whether people are basically good or evil. These are certainly important questions, but they cannot be answered scientifically. Of course, it *is* possible to investigate empirically such things as the factors that lead people to believe in a deity or that lead them to do good or bad things.

In summary, I would describe research psychologists as "skeptical optimists." They are open to new ideas and optimistic about using empirical methods to test these ideas, but at the same time they are tough minded—they won't accept claims without data. Also, researchers are constantly thinking of ways to test ideas scientifically and they are basically confident that some truth will emerge by asking and answering empirical questions. Furthermore, those who are especially good at science add creativity to their skeptical optimism and to their normally logical thinking, which brings us to the issue of creativity in science.

Creative Thinking in Science

The German psychologist Hermann Ebbinghaus is justifiably famous for his pioneering research on memory and forgetting (Ebbinghaus, 1885/1913). He wanted to study the formation and retention of brand-new mental associations between ideas, so he needed stimuli that would combine to form meaningless sequences. His solution was the invention of "nonsense syllables," three-letter combinations of consonant–vowel–consonant (hence, its other name: CVC), such as QOM. Showing great perseverance and perhaps a complete absence of any social life, Ebbinghaus spent several years studying and recalling lists of these stimuli. Historians consider his invention of the nonsense syllable to be a truly creative event, and there has been considerable speculation about how he originated them. According to one account (Shakow, 1930), Ebbinghaus was visiting England at a time when Lewis Carroll's poem "Jabberwocky," a parody of the English language using nonsense words (e.g., "Twas brillig, and the slithy toves did gyre and gimble in the wabe"), was popular. It is a short step from nonsense words to CVCs.

If the Ebbinghaus story is true, it is a good example of scientific creativity at its best and what Louis Pasteur meant when he said that "chance favors the prepared mind" (cited in Myers, 1992, p. 335). **Creative thinking** in science involves a process of recognizing meaningful connections between apparently unrelated ideas. Such thinking does not occur in a vacuum, however, but in the context of some problem to be solved. Thus, faced with the problem of how to develop learning materials that would be meaningless, Ebbinghaus perhaps read "Jabberwocky," saw the connection to his dilemma, and created nonsense syllables. However, note carefully that Ebbinghaus had the "prepared mind" that Pasteur described. That is, he knew a great deal about the topic at hand, associations, and was actively searching for a way to study their formation. His openness to the use of an apparently unrelated ("chance") event, a poem, to the problem he was confronting, made the episode a good illustration of creative thinking. Numerous other examples can be found that follow this pattern, including the manner in which the first animal maze learning study was created (see Box 1.2 for the story). A scientist has considerable knowledge in some area, is dealing with a difficult and seemingly intractable problem, and encounters something that seems at first glance to be unrelated to the problem. For the creative scientist, however, a connection between the random event and the problem at hand is made and the problem is solved.

On the other hand, it is worth noting that although a thorough knowledge of

Box 1.2

CLASSIC STUDIES—Creating the First Maze Learning Experiments

Ask psychologists to name famous pieces of research equipment and mazes will be at or near the top of the list. Although the maze reached its peak of popularity in the period of 1920–1940, it is still used as an important tool to study such topics as learning and spatial behavior.

Literally hundreds of maze studies have been completed over the years and one might ask how it all started. Credit is sometimes given to Sir John Lubbuck, a nineteenth century Darwinian who used a crude Y-shaped maze to study ant behavior in the 1870s. Then in the 1890s, the American psychologist E. L. Thorndike observed chicks escape from simple mazes created by placing books on end. Credit for the first maze learning study with rats belongs to Willard Small of Clark University, however.

How did Small get the idea to put rats in mazes? Along with his laboratory colleague, Linus Kline, he was interested generally in rat behavior, in particular the rat's "home-finding" tendencies. In a discussion with Edmund Sanford, director of Clark's lab, Kline described some tunnels he had observed "made by large feral rats to their nests under the porch of an old cabin. . . . These runways were from three to six inches below the surface of the ground and when exposed during excavation presented a veritable maze" (Miles, 1930, p. 331). Sanford suggested that Kline build a maze himself. In particular, he proposed using as a model the Hampton Court Maze, England's most popular people-sized labyrinth. At the time of their conversation, Sanford had just returned from England and may have been at Hampton Court.

With other projects underway, Kline passed along the idea to Small, who built a 6-by-8-foot wire mesh maze, changing the Hampton Court maze's trapezoidal shape to rectangular, but keeping the design the same (see Figure 1.1). The story is another good example of scientific creativity. Apparently unrelated events (Kline's recollections of rats tunneling under a porch), combined with a breadth of knowledge (Sanford's familiarity with the Hampton Court maze), solve a problem at hand (how to study a rat's home-finding tendencies). Small published his findings at the turn of the century (Small, 1900) and began a rats-in-mazes tradition that continues to the present day.

Incidentally, while critics sometimes refer to the maze as an example of the "artificiality" of laboratory research in psychology, it is worth noting that Small's original intent in using the maze was not to create a sterile environment but one close to the rat's real world, or as Small (1900) put it, to create "as little difference as possible between the conditions of experiment and of ordinary experience" (p. 209).

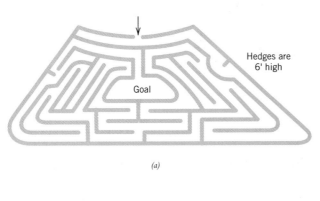

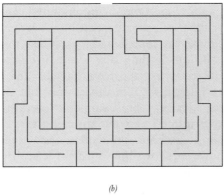

FIGURE 1.1   (*a*) Design of the Hampton Court Maze
and (*b*) Small's adaptation of the Hampton Court design for
his pioneering study of maze learning in rats.

one's field may be a prerequisite to creative thinking in science, the blade is double edged; this knowledge can sometimes create rigid patterns of thinking that inhibit creativity. Scientists occasionally become so accustomed to a particular method or so comfortable with a particular theory that they fail to consider alternatives (does this remind you of Peirce's "tenacity"?). Consider Ebbinghaus again.

The Ebbinghaus research began a tradition in memory research that continues today, more than one hundred years later. It is a laboratory approach that involves presenting subjects lists of stimuli (e.g., CVCs) and then testing memory for the information. More recently, however, some psychologists began arguing that memory researchers became so immersed in the Ebbinghaus tradition that they failed to look at how memory works outside of the laboratory. Everyday memory situations don't normally involve learning lists of words or nonsense syllables. Ulric Neisser (1978), for example, advocated a new strategy now called the "ecological" approach, meaning the emphasis would be on studying memory problems in more naturalistic settings than the laboratory and studying memory for real events in one's past rather than arbitrary lists.

As an illustration of this strategy, consider Neisser's (1981) analysis of the memory of former White House chief counsel John Dean, who blew the whistle on Richard Nixon's cover-up of illegal activities. Dean's actions precipitated the Watergate scandal in the early 1970s and led to the resignation of President Nixon. He testified before a Senate committee and read a 245-page account of dozens of Oval Office meetings that was so detailed that some reporters referred to him as a human tape recorder (Neisser, 1981). Of course, it was later revealed that the meetings had in fact been tape recorded by the White House, allowing Neisser to evaluate Dean's supposed photographic memory. Dean's memory wasn't so perfect after all. He was generally correct about the gist of the meetings, but he was usually wrong about details such as when a particular thing was said. The point is that memory researchers in the Ebbinghaus tradition, their thinking limited to tried and true laboratory procedures, might never have thought to study John Dean's memory. Sometimes tradition can limit one's vision.

Other examples of scientific creativity being inhibited can be found in research areas with procedures or types of apparatus that have become "standard." Consider mazes, for instance. The maze has contributed a great deal to our understanding of learning, and as you recall from reading Box 1.2, its invention illustrates scientific creativity at its best. However, the apparatus has also led to many dead ends. Perhaps the famous behaviorist E. C. Tolman was only half serious when he closed his 1937 APA presidential address by professing that "everything important in psychology . . . can be investigated in essence through the . . . analysis of the determiners of rat behavior at a choice-point in a maze" (cited in Hilgard, 1978, p. 364). His comment, however, shows how apparatus can shape scientific thinking. The origins of scientific equipment like mazes may reveal creative thinking at its best (e.g., Sanford's idea to use the Hampton Court model), but innovation can be dampened once an apparatus becomes established.

Can Psychology Be a Science?

Thus far in the chapter you have been reading about experimental psychology as if there is no question about its scientific status. You may be wondering about this, because you might have heard doubts expressed about whether psychology can be a science (perhaps your roommate is a physics major), or you might have some initial doubts yourself. Certainly, research psychologists fully acknowledge psychology's status as a science and for them there is indeed no question about it, but the issue has been a matter of some debate over the years, so it's worth looking at some of the arguments involved.

Claims that psychology cannot be scientific fall into three general categories. First, it is sometimes said that psychology is at best a soft science, that it lacks the precision and the high predictability of a hard science like physics or chemistry. The behavior of a ball rolling down an incline can be predicted almost perfectly, it is said, but whether or not a person would be inclined to roll down a hill cannot be known as easily. This is the easiest argument to counter. If one defines "scientific" in terms of a set of agreed-upon methods, an attempt to establish lawful and predictable relationships between events, and as a reciprocal relationship between theories and systematic empirical observations, then the difference between psychology and physics is simply a difference in degree, not a difference in kind. In terms of how they go about trying to uncover truth, research psychologists and physicists do basically the same things. The soft versus hard distinction doesn't amount to much.

Second, it is sometimes said that psychology cannot be scientific because it fails to separate the observer from the observed and is therefore inherently subjective. Again a comparison is sometimes made with physics. The physicist as an observer is separated from the ball rolling down the incline and can therefore make an observation that can be verified by another physicist watching the same ball. In psychology, the argument goes, the observer studying the human mind is not separated from what is being observed. The observer and the observed reside within the same person. The psychologist rolling down an incline can provide a self-observation of the experience — a description in terms of such things as dizziness and a series of perceptual events, but a second psychologist watching the first one cannot verify the rolling psychologist's self-observation.

In response to this, the experimental psychologist would say two things. First, the second psychologist could also roll down the hill to see if the experience matched that of the first psychologist. Although limited in some ways, verbal reports of experiences are acceptable as data. Second, and more important, it could be pointed out that historically, the problem of self-observation is the reason why psychology eventually shifted its definition of itself from the science of immediate conscious experience to the science of behavior.

In the late nineteenth and early twentieth centuries, psychologists were interested in studying the contents and the functions of conscious experience and a common technique was called **introspection**. This procedure varied considerably from one laboratory to another, but it was basically the kind of self-report just discussed. Participants in an experiment would undergo some task, then provide a description of their conscious experience of the task. To give you some sense of what introspection was actually like, read Box 1.3 before going any further. It provides an example of a verbatim introspective account of an experiment on attention and shows how scientific thinking early in the century included introspective analysis.

The problem with introspection was that although introspectors had to undergo rigorous training that attempted to eliminate bias in their self-observations, the method was fundamentally subjective (I cannot verify your introspections and you cannot verify mine). The problem motivated psychologists like John B. Watson to argue that if psychology was to be truly scientific, it needed to measure something that was directly observable and could be verified objectively. Behavior fit the bill, and Watson is usually identified as the founder of behaviorism for his vigorous arguments that the basic data of psychology ought to be observable behaviors.

With behavior as the basic data then, two psychologists could roll down a hill and a third psychologist could (a) record how long it took for the rolling behavior of each to be completed and (b) measure dizziness by having the psychologists get

Box 1.3

ORIGINS—A Taste of Introspection

The following introspective account is from a 1913 study by Karl Dallenbach dealing with the phenomenon of attention. Introspectors were instructed to listen to two metronomes set at different speeds and to count the number of beats between coincident beats (i.e., both metronomes hitting at the same instant). While counting, they were also asked to perform some other task, such as continuously adding numbers. Needless to say, the tasks tested the limits of attention. After finishing a session, one introspector reported:

> The sounds of the metronomes, as a series of discontinuous clicks, were clear in consciousness only four or five times during the experiment, and they were especially bothersome at first. They were accompanied by strain sensations and unpleasantness. The rest of the experiment my attention was on the adding, which was composed of auditory images of the numbers, visual images of the numbers, sometimes on a dark gray scale which was directly ahead and about three feet in front of me. . . . When these processes were clear in consciousness, the sound of the metronomes were very vague or obscure. (Dallenbach, 1913, p. 567)

When discussing the researcher's tendency to think in terms of data on page 9, I used the example of thinking about a neighbor's tomatoes in empirical terms, illustrating that scientific thinking doesn't just disappear when the scientist leaves the lab. In the same way, introspectionists didn't leave their way of thinking in the lab. In their letters to each other, for example, they would often reflect on some recent experience in introspective terms. For example, in a letter to Cornell's E. B. Titchener, Edmund Sanford of Clark University described his experience of violent thunderstorms in an introspective fashion. His experience included "organic and other sensations unpleasantly colored and, on the cognitive side, a cramp of apperception toward a small group of ideas related to the thing dreaded with certain resultants in instinctive act and thought" (Sanford, 1910).

up quickly at the bottom of the hill and walk a straight line accurately. In short, studying observable behavior satisfies the scientific criterion of objectivity.

A third reason for denying the scientific status of psychology follows from the observation that every person is a completely unique human being. All electrons may be essentially alike, so laws in physics aren't hard to find, but if every person is different from all others, how can general laws of behavior be derived? The Cornell introspectionist E. B. Titchener answered this problem beautifully in his 1909 *Text-Book of Psychology*. As a way of criticizing Titchener's attempts to analyze consciousness into its basic components, the famous American philosopher/psychologist William James had likened conscious awareness to a stream. According to James, no two events in consciousness are exactly alike, just as the water moving in a stream is never the same for any two moments. Both flow continuously. Titchener agreed that the same conscious event never repeats itself exactly, but went on to say that

> we can observe a particular consciousness as often as we wish, since mental processes group themselves in the same way, show the same pattern of arrangement, whenever the organism is placed under the same circumstances. *Yesterday's high tide will never recur, and yesterday's consciousness will never recur; but we have a science of psychology, as we have a science of oceanography.*"
> (Titchener, 1909, cited in Schultz & Schultz, 1992, p. 130, italics added)

For Titchener psychology was the science of consciousness, but his analogy works just as well for psychology as the science of behavior. Even though no two behaviors are exactly alike, patterns of behaviors can be studied by the experimental psychologist in the same way that patterns of individually unique waves can be studied by the oceanographer.

Ultimately, you will have to decide whether you agree with psychological researchers about the scientific nature of psychology and you should be able to reach that conclusion by the time you finish this course. If you are saying to yourself that you're a bit skeptical at this point and want to see some further evidence (perhaps some data) before making a decision, that's just fine. It means you're already starting to think scientifically!

The Goals of Research in Psychology

Research in psychology has four interrelated goals. Researchers hope to have complete descriptions of behaviors, to be able to make predictions about future behavior, and to be able to provide reasonable explanations of behavior. Furthermore, they assume that the knowledge derived from their research will be applied so as to benefit people, either immediately or eventually.

Describing Behavior

To accomplish a good **description** in psychology is to identify regularly occurring sequences of events, with these events including both stimuli or environmental events and responses or behavioral events. For example, a description of aggressive behavior in some primate species might include a listing of the situations in which fighting is most likely to occur (e.g., over food), the forms of the threat signals that might precede actual combat (e.g., baring teeth), and the form of the fight itself (e.g., attacks directed at nonvital areas like shoulders and haunches). Description also involves classification, as when someone attempts to classify various forms of aggressive behavior (e.g., fighting vs predation). Providing a clear and accurate description is an obvious yet essential first step in any scientific endeavor; without it, predictions cannot be made and explanations are meaningless.

Predicting Behavior

To say that behavior follows **laws** is to say that regular and predictable relationships exist between variables. The strength of these relationships allows for **predictions** to be made with some degree of confidence. After describing numerous primate fights, for example, it might become clear that after two animals fight over food and one wins, the same two animals won't fight again. If they both spot a banana at the same time, the winner of the initial battle might display a threat gesture and the loser of the first fight will probably go away. If that series of events happened often enough, the researcher could make predictions about future encounters between these animals and more generally, between animals who are winners and losers of fights.

Explaining Behavior

The third goal of the research psychologist is **explanation**. To explain some behavior is to know what caused it to happen. The concept of causality is immensely complex, and its nature has occupied philosophers for centuries. For our purposes, it can be thought of as the type referred to by Aristotle as *efficient* causality. That is, we'll say that we believe X is causing Y to occur if we conduct an experiment in which we systematically vary X, control all outside factors that could affect the results, and observe that Y occurs with some probability greater than chance and that variations of Y can be predicted from the variations in X. That is, X and Y are said to *covary*, or occur together, and because X occurs first, it is said to be the cause of Y. Furthermore, we'll have confidence in our causal explanation to the extent that we can rule out other possible explanations for Y occurring.

Explanation in psychology also involves developing theories about why things occur the way they do, and testing those theories in empirical research. The process of theory building and how research is derived from theory will be elaborated in Chapter 3. For now, simply be aware that causality is a complicated process involving covariation, a time sequence with cause preceding effect, the ruling out of alternative explanations, and a theoretical structure.

Controlling Behavior

This goal is sometimes controversial because it creates an unfair impression of psychologists deliberately and perhaps diabolically controlling other people's lives

(Box 10.3 in Chapter 10 examines the issue in more detail). Actually, **control** refers simply to the various ways of applying those principles of behavior discovered through psychological research. Psychologists assume that because of knowledge derived from the research they do, it is possible for people's lives to change for the better. Hence, research on the factors influencing depression enables therapists to help depressed people, research on aggression can help parents raise their children, and so on. This goal is seldom the immediate purpose of any particular study, but it is an underlying goal for all researchers.

The Excitement of Psychological Research (Part 1)

This chapter began by listing a series of reasons why the experimental psychology course is essential for the student of psychology. Besides tradition and the obvious fact that the course is the first step on the road to becoming a researcher in psychology, these reasons include helping you understand other psychology courses better, making you a critical consumer of research information, improving your chances of getting into graduate school, and giving you an appreciation for scientific thinking. All of this is fine, but in my opinion, the single most important reason to learn how to do research in psychology is that doing research is fun. It is challenging, frustrating at times, and the long hours in the lab can be tedious, but few researchers would exchange their careers for another. What could be more satisfying than getting an idea about behavior, putting it to the test of a research study, and having the results come out as predicted? Who could not be thrilled about making some new discovery about human behavior that could improve people's lives?

This attitude of seeing a research career as an ideal life is apparent in the final paragraph of a chapter written by E. C. Tolman (you met him earlier, in the discussion about maze learning) for a series about various theoretical approaches to psychology. The chapter was among the last papers he wrote; it was published the year he died, 1959. After describing his theory of learning, Tolman concluded by saying, in part,

> The system [his theory] may well not stand up to any final canons of scientific procedure. But I do not much care. I have liked to think about psychology in ways that have proved congenial to me. Since all the sciences, and especially psychology, are still immersed in such tremendous realms of the uncertain and the unknown, the best that any individual scientist . . . can do seems to be to follow his own gleam and his own bent, however inadequate they may be. In fact, I suppose that actually this is what we all do. *In the end, the only sure criterion is to have fun. And I have had fun.* (Tolman, 1959, p. 152, italics added)

Let me finish the opening chapter with two brief examples of how experimental psychologists become almost obsessively devoted to their work and find great satisfaction in it.

FIGURE 1.2   Eleanor Gibson receiving the National Medal of Science in 1992.

Eleanor Gibson

On June 23, 1992, Eleanor Gibson was awarded the National Medal of Science by then-president George Bush (Figure 1.2). It is the highest honor a president can confer on a scientist. Gibson, then 82, was honored for a lifetime of research in developmental psychology, studying topics ranging from how we learn to read to how depth perception develops. She is perhaps best known to undergraduates for her "visual cliff" studies.

Gibson is a prototype of the devoted researcher who persevered even in the face of major obstacles. In her case, the burden was sexism. This she discovered upon arrival at Yale University in 1935, eager to work in Robert M. Yerkes' primate lab (Yerkes was famous for his work both in comparative psychology and in mental testing). She was astounded by her first interview with him. As she later recalled, "He stood up, walked to the door, held it open, and said, 'I have no women in my laboratory'" (Gibson, 1980, p. 246).

Undaunted, Gibson eventually convinced the great behaviorist Clark Hull that she could be a scientist, and finished her doctorate with him. Then in the late 1940s she went to Cornell University with her husband James Gibson (another famous name, this time in perception research). Eleanor labored there as an unpaid[2] "Research Associate" for 16 years before being named Professor. It was during this period of uncertain status that she completed her work on perceptual development. A sense of her excitement for this research is evident from her description of how the visual cliff experiments first came about.

Briefly, the project evolved out of some perceptual development research with rats that she was doing with Cornell colleague Richard Walk. They were both curious about depth perception: In the army, Walk had studied training programs for parachute jumpers and at Cornell's "Behavior Farm," Gibson had observed newborn goats avoid falling from a raised platform. She also had a "long-standing aversion to cliffs, dating from a visit to the Grand Canyon" (Gibson, 1980, p. 258). With a lab assistant, Gibson

> . . . hastily put together a contraption consisting of a sheet of glass held up by rods, with a piece of wallpaper under one side of it and nothing under the other side except the floor many feet below.
>
> A few rats left over from other experiments got the first try. . . . We put a board about three inches wide across the division between the surface with flooring and the unlined glass, and put the rats on the board. Would they descend randomly to either side?
>
> *What ensued was better than we had dared expect.* All the rats descended on the side with textured paper under the glass. We quickly inserted some paper under the other side and tried them again. This time they went either way. We built some proper apparatus after that, with carefully controlled lighting and so on, to be ready for our dark-reared animals. *It worked beautifully.* (Gibson, 1980, p. 259, italics added).

Gibson and Walk (1960) went on to test numerous species, including of course young infants. The visual cliff studies, showing the unwillingness of 8-month olds to cross the "deep side," even with Mom on the other side, are now familiar to any undergraduate taking introductory psychology.

B. F. Skinner

If you ask students to name a famous psychologist but not Freud, many will say B. F. Skinner (see Figure 1.3), who is perhaps psychology's most famous scientist. His work on operant conditioning created an entire subculture within experimental psychology called the experimental analysis of behavior. Its philosophy will be explored in Chapter 10.

Skinner's three-volume autobiography provides a marvelous glimpse of his life and work. The following excerpt illustrates his almost childlike fascination with making a new discovery about behavior. It is from a period when Skinner had just completed his doctorate at Harvard and was staying on as a "Research Fellow," supported by a grant from the National Research Council. In early 1932 he was

---

[2]Cornell did not pay her a salary during this time, but she was paid salaries via the many successful research grants that she wrote (e.g., the Rockefeller Foundation, NSF, U. S. Office of Education).

FIGURE 1.3   B. F. Skinner.

studying a number of different conditioning phenomena, including experimental extinction. In his words,

> Pavlov had studied a process that was in a sense the reverse of conditioning and took place more slowly. He called it 'extinction.' In my early notes I sometimes called it 'adaptation,' because it resembled the slow disappearance of the unconditioned response to a click. My first extinction curve showed up by accident. A rat was pressing the lever in an experiment on satiation when the pellet dispenser jammed. I was not there at the time, and when I returned *I found a beautiful curve.* The rat had gone on pressing although no pellets were received. . . .
>   The change was more orderly than the extinction of a salivary reflex in Pavlov's setting, *and I was terribly excited.* It was a Friday afternoon and there was no one in the laboratory whom I could tell. All that weekend I crossed streets with particular care and avoided all unnecessary risks to protect my discovery from loss through my accidental death. (Skinner, 1979, p. 95, italics added).

Throughout the remainder of this book, you'll be learning the tools of the experimental psychology trade and will be reading about the work of other psychologists who are committed researchers in love with their work. My greatest hope is that by the end of this book, when you'll encounter another discussion about the excitement of psychological research (Part 2), you will be hooked on research and want to contribute to our growing collection of knowledge about what makes people behave the way they do.

Chapter Review

At the end of each chapter you will find two types of review materials: fill-in the blanks and multiple choice. You should study the chapter thoroughly before attempting to answer both types. For the fill-ins, each answer will be a key term (i.e., in the chapter it was printed in **bold**) that can also be found in the glossary at the end of the book. Sometimes the sentences will be similar to the definitions for the terms, but usually the sentences will ask that you apply the terms properly. The second type of review exercise will be a sample of multiple choice questions.

The answers for both types of review items can be found in Appendix D. This appendix also provides references back to the appropriate chapter page for further information about each item.

Glossary Fill-Ins

1. John strongly believes that people on welfare are not interested in working; his dismissal of evidence to the contrary shows how his thinking is influenced by what Peirce would call_____.

2. TV commercials trying to persuade you to buy a product because nine out of ten doctors recommend it are asking you to rely on_____ as a way of coming to believe something.

3. Someone who concludes that mind and body are one essence by arguing that the mind ceases to operate at the moment of the body's death is using Peirce's _____ method.

4. As psychologists use the term,_____ simply means that events occur regularly enough to be predicted with some degree of certainty.

5. Ed says he has a headache. His description is an example of an_____. Because only he can experience it, his observation lacks_____.

6. The following is a bad example of an_____. "Is there life after death?"

Multiple Choice

1. Concerning the issue of *determinism,* most psychologists take the following position:
    a. Every individual is unique, so no general laws of behavior are possible.
    b. Human behavior can be predicted with probabilities greater than chance.
    c. Everything that you will do in life has been determined from the moment of your birth.
    d. Because determinism is true, it is not really possible for us to make choices.

2. What does it mean to say that scientific thinking includes the characteristic of *objectivity?*

   a. It means that true scientists never let human biases affect their work.

   b. It refers to measurements that are made by some mechanical instrument, thereby eliminating human influence entirely.

   c. It refers to an observation that can be verified by two or more observers.

   d. It refers to psychologists' near obsession with the idea of answering questions by referring to data.

3. Of Peirce's nonscientific ways of knowing, which one would a research psychologist consider to be the furthest removed from scientific thinking?

   a. Tenaciously maintaining a belief in the face of contradictory data.

   b. Relying on the authority of experts.

   c. Arguing a case using the a priori method.

   d. Experimental psychologists never do any of the above.

4. According to the text, there are four goals of scientific psychology. Which of the following activities falls under the category of "describing" behaviors?

   a. Accurately categorizing several varieties of schizophrenia.

   b. Establishing laws so that estimates can be made about what people will do in certain circumstances.

   c. Identifying the causes of aggression in young children.

   d. Using the results of eyewitness memory research to train police to interview witnesses more efficiently.

5. Which of the following is true about the origins and development of mazes as instruments in psychological research?

   a. They were first invented to see if rats could adapt to situations completely unlike anything in their natural environment.

   b. Because rats are so totally unlike humans, interest in maze learning did not last very long in psychology.

   c. The idea for building people-sized mazes (e.g., Hampton Court) first occurred to researchers after observing rats learn mazes.

   d. The idea for the first maze was creative, but creativity was sometimes inhibited once mazes became established as standard instruments.

Applications Exercises

In addition to student review exercises, the end of each chapter will include "applications" exercises. These will be problems and questions that encourage you to think like a research psychologist and to apply what you've learned in a particular chapter. Answers to some of the exercises can be found in Appendix D.

Exercise 1.1 — Asking Empirical Questions

For each of the following nonempirical questions, think of an empirical question that would be related to the issue raised and lead to a potentially interesting study.

1. Is God dead?
2. Are humans naturally good?
3. Is the mind separate from the body? Or are they one and the same?
4. Do we get what we deserve in life?
5. What is beauty?

Exercise 1.2 — Data Based Conclusions

One attribute of scientific thinking is the tendency to insist that conclusions be supported by data and that the conditions of the study be precisely defined. For each of the following assertions, identify (a) which terms need to be defined more precisely, (b) the kinds of data that could be used as evidence to support the assertion, and (c) any questions that must be answered before a scientific study could proceed. That is, before any of these assertions could be put to an empirical test, what else needs to be known? For example, an assertion that "people go crazy when there is a full moon" requires (a) a definition of crazy in terms of measurable behavior and (b) a comparison of this crazy behavior on full and non-full moon nights. Differences between the two types of nights could support the assertion. But questions remain before the study could be run properly. If it's a full moon on Tuesday, May 2, at exactly what time do you begin measuring craziness? Sunset? Only after the moon is up? All of May 2? The night of May 2 and all day May 3? Also, there are only 12 full moons per year. How do you select comparison days? Randomly? Or the opposite of a full moon?

Go through this same process of identifying questions to be answered for the following assertions:

1. My toothpaste works better than yours.
2. Most people don't understand the true meaning of Christmas.
3. The astrological predictions in the tabloid newspapers are remarkably accurate.
4. Bad things come in threes.

Exercise 1.3 — Stimulating Creative Thinking

The following exercise is designed to stimulate your creative thinking abilities. It is based on the idea that if creative thinking involves the ability to see connections between apparently unrelated concepts, then a system for "forcing" connections might result in a creative product. The technique is similar to one called "morphological forced connections" by Koberg and Bagnall (1974) and begins by building a simple matrix that has two different dimensions in the rows and columns. For example, the columns could represent different sensory processes and rows could be forms of entertainment. Each cell then becomes a "forced connection" that could potentially be a creative idea. Cells A and B have already been invented. Silent movies were replaced by the "talkies" (A) in the 1920s and as children I'm sure you all read at least one scratch and sniff book (B).

	Seeing	Hearing	Smelling	Tasting	Feeling
Movies		A		1	
Books			B		2
Games					
Sports				3	

Can you think of some creative ideas to fill in some of the other cells? How about cells 1, 2, and 3?

To come up with ideas for research projects, try placing some topics from your general psychology book in the columns and some research apparatus in the rows:

	Perception	Learning	Therapy	Memory	Creativity
Mazes					
Reaction time					
Inkblot test					
Lie detector test					

From any of the above cells, create three research ideas.

CHAPTER 2

Ethics in Psychological Research

Chapter Overview

- ### Developing the APA Code of Ethics
  In keeping with psychology's habit of relying on data-based principles, the American Psychological Association developed its ethics code empirically, using a critical incidents procedure. The code was first published in 1953 and has been revised periodically since then, most recently in 1992.

✓ - ### Ethical Guidelines for Research with Humans
  The APA code for research with human subjects provides guidance for the researcher in planning the study. This includes weighing the scientific value of the research against the degree of risk imposed on research participants. The code also assures that participants are informed volunteers and are well treated both during the experiment and after it has been completed.

- ## Ethical Guidelines for Research with Animals
  APA guidelines for research with animal subjects concern the care and humane treatment of animals used for psychological research, provide guidance in deciding about appropriate experimental procedures, and cover the use of animals both for research and for education. The issue of animal rights is addressed and it is argued that animal research is justified and important.

- ## Scientific Fraud
  Manufacturing or altering data, rather than collecting it honestly, is the most serious form of scientific fraud. Although fraud is often discovered because of repeated failures to replicate unreliable findings, fraud may remain undetected because (a) the fraudulent findings are consistent with legitimate outcomes or (b) the sheer mass of published work precludes much replication. The academic reward system creates pressures that occasionally lead to scientific fraud.

A system of **ethics** is in essence a set of principles for behaving in a way that is morally correct. That is, to behave ethically is to do what is right. When doing research in psychology, the scientist's ethical obligations encompass several areas. The scientist must (a) treat human research participants with respect and in a way that maintains their dignity, (b) care for the welfare of animals when they are the subjects of research, and (c) be scrupulously honest in the treatment of data. This chapter will elaborate on each of these topics, introducing you to a set of principles that guide researchers in the planning and execution of their research studies. The topic is presented early in the text because of its importance—I will be referring back to the topic many times throughout the remainder of the book.

Before beginning to read about the code of ethics of the American Psychological Association, see Box 2.1, which describes one of psychology's best known and most ethically infamous studies. The Little Albert experiment is often described as a pioneering investigation of how children develop fears, but it also serves well as a lesson in dubious ethical practice.

Developing the APA Code of Ethics

Psychologists in the United States did not publish their first code of ethics until 1953 (American Psychological Association, 1953). This 171-page document was the outcome of about fifteen years of discussion within the APA, which created a temporary committee on "Scientific and Professional Ethics" in the late 1930s. The committee soon became a standing committee to investigate complaints of unethical behavior (usually concerned with the professional practice of psychology) that occasionally would be brought to its attention. In 1948, this group recommended the creation of a formal code of ethics. Under the leadership of Nicholas Hobbs, a new committee on Ethical Standards for Psychology was formed and began what became a five-year project (Hobbs, 1948).

Box 2.1

CLASSIC STUDIES—Scaring Little Albert

The February 1920 issue of the *Journal of Experimental Psychology* contained a brief article called "Conditioned Emotional Reactions." Although it included several methodological weaknesses and attempts to replicate it in the 1920s failed (Harris, 1970), it became one of psychology's best known and most often cited case studies. The authors were the behaviorist John B. Watson and Rosalie Rayner, a graduate student of Watson's and soon to be his second wife. The study used just one participant, an 11-month old boy given the pseudonym of Albert B. The purpose of the study was to see if Albert could be conditioned to be afraid.

The Little Albert study was part of Watson's project to study emotions. He already knew that infants were "naturally" afraid of little except loud noises and loss of support (he discovered this empirically; guess how). By early childhood, however, they develop a number of fears: of the dark, of spiders, of snakes, and so on. As a behaviorist, Watson believed these fears were products of life's experiences and he wished to see if deliberately influencing events could produce a learned fear.

In brief, Watson and Rayner determined that Albert (a) had no natural fear of a white rat, (b) would react with a strong fear response if a steel bar was struck with a hammer just behind his head (!), and (c) would come to fear the rat if the loud nose was paired with the animal. The following is what happened on the first trial:

> White rat suddenly taken from the basket and presented to Albert. He began to reach for rat with left hand. Just as his hand touched the animal the bar was struck immediately behind his head. The infant jumped violently and fell forward burying his face in the mattress. (Watson & Rayner, 1920, p. 4)

After several trials, the loud noise was no longer needed—Albert had developed a powerful association and was terrified of the rat. Because of generalization to similar stimuli, he was also afraid of a rabbit, a fur coat, and cotton wool.

Of course, it is difficult to hold Watson and Rayner responsible for ethical guidelines that were published 33 years after Albert appeared in their lab. It is clear, however, that they were aware some might object to the study, that "a certain responsibility attaches to such a procedure" (Watson & Rayner, 1920, p. 3). They decided to proceed because Albert seemed like a strong, healthy child, "on the whole stolid and unemotional. His stability was one of the principal reasons for using him. . . . We felt that we could do him relatively little harm by carrying out such experiments" (pp. 1–2). Watson and Rayner also justified the study by arguing that such fears would be learned by Albert *anyway*, "as soon as [he] left the sheltered environment of the nursery for the rough and tumble of the home" (p. 3).

Although Watson made no effort to remove Albert's fear, he gave a talk at Vassar College several years later that inspired a student in the audience to make such an attempt. Mary Cover Jones was the listener and she went on to demonstrate that a child's learned fears could be extinguished. Her successful elimination of the fear of a rabbit in a young boy (Jones, 1924) is often described as the pioneering use of the behavior therapy technique of systematic desensitization.

As you read about the APA ethical guidelines in this chapter, you should ask yourself whether the Little Albert study could be carried out today. If not, why not? If so, with what safeguards and changes in procedure?

We've seen in Chapter 1 that psychologists are trained to think scientifically. What is noteworthy about the Hobbs committee is that, in keeping with psychology's penchant for relying on data as much as possible, it opted for an empirical approach to forming the code. Using a procedure called the **critical incidents** technique, the committee surveyed the entire membership of the APA (there were about 7,500 members then) and asked for examples of "incidents" of unethical conduct that they knew about firsthand and "to indicate what [they] perceived as being the ethical issue involved" (American Psychological Association, 1953, p. vi). The request yielded over 1,000 replies and included some incidents involving the conduct of research. The committee organized the replies into a series of several drafts that were published in the *American Psychologist,* the Association's primary

TABLE 2.1   *General Principles of the APA Code of Ethics*

Principle A: Competence
   Psychologists "recognize the boundaries of their particular competencies and the limits of their expertise" and maintain competence through ongoing education.
Principle B: Integrity
   Psychologists are scrupulously honest in "the science, teaching, and practice of psychology" and are "honest, fair, and respectful of others."
Principle C: Professional and scientific responsibility
   Psychologists "uphold professional standards of conduct" and "accept appropriate responsibility for their behavior."
Principle D: Respect for people's rights and dignity
   Psychologists avoid treating people in a biased manner and respect their basic human rights "to privacy, confidentiality, self-determination, and autonomy."
Principle E: Concern for others' welfare
   Psychologists "seek to contribute to the welfare of those with whom they interact professionally" and do not "exploit or mislead other people during or after professional relationships."
Principle F: Social responsibility
   Psychologists "apply and make public their knowledge of psychology in order to contribute to human welfare."

Source: APA, 1992.

TABLE 2.2   *Categories of Ethical Standards in the 1992 Cade*

Category	Sample Standards
1. General standards [27]	1.02 Relationship of ethics and law
	1.11 Sexual harassment
	1.27 Referrals and fees
2. Evaluation, assessment, or intervention [10]	2.03 Test construction
	2.05 Interpreting assessment results
	2.08 Test scoring and interpretation services
3. Advertising and other public statements [6]	3.01 Definition of public statements
	3.04 Media presentations
	3.06 In-person solicitation
4. Therapy [9]	4.02 Informed consent to therapy
	4.05 Sexual intimacies with current patients or clients
	4.09 Terminating the professional relationship
5. Privacy and confidentiality [11]	5.02 Maintaining confidentiality
	5.05 Disclosures
	5.07 Confidential information in databases
6. Teaching, training supervision, research, and publishing [26]	6.03 Accuracy and objectivity in teaching
	6.06 Planning research
	6.23 Publication credit
7. Forensic activities [6]	7.02 Forensic assessments
	7.04 Truthfulness and candor
	7.06 Compliance with laws and rules
8. Resolving ethical issues [7]	8.02 Confronting ethical issues
	8.05 Reporting ethical violations
	8.06 Cooperating with ethics committees

Note: The full text of all 102 standards can be found in the December, 1992, issue of American Psychologist (pp. 1597–1611).

journal. The APA's Council of Directors accepted the final version in 1952 and published it the next year.

Over the years, the code has been revised several times, most recently in 1992. It currently includes a set of six general principles, which are summarized briefly in Table 2.1, and 102 standards, clustered into the eight general categories listed in Table 2.2. The general principles are "*aspirational* goals to guide psychologists toward the highest ideals of psychology (American Psychological Association, 1992, p. 1598, italics in the original), while the standards "set forth *enforceable* rules for conduct as psychologists" (American Psychological Association, 1992, p. 1598, italics in the original). In this chapter, we'll examine the standards concerning research with both human and animal participants.

Ethical Guidelines for Research with Humans

In the 1960s, one of the principles of the original code was itself elaborated into a separate code of ethics for research with human participants. An APA committee modeled on the Hobbs committee and headed by a former member of it, Stuart Cook, used the same critical incidents procedure and published an ethics code specifically for researchers in 1973; it was revised in 1982 (American Psychological Association, 1982) and again as part of the general revision of 1992. It contains a number of standards that can be arranged conveniently into three general categories—those having to do with planning the study, those concerning the voluntary status of participants, and those concerned with treating participants well.

Planning the Study

All research with human participants imposes some degree of burden on those participating as subjects in the study (experimental psychologists often use the term **subject** to refer to any participant, human or animal, whose behavior will be measured in some way in the study being conducted). At the very minimum, people are asked to spend time in an experiment when they could be doing something else. At the other extreme, people are sometimes placed in potentially harmful situations. In the name of psychological science, human subjects have received electrical shocks, have been told they failed some apparently easy test, and have been embarrassed in any number of ways. That such experiences can be distressing to subjects is clearly illustrated in one of social psychology's most famous series of studies, the obedience research of Stanley Milgram (1963, 1974).

In the guise of a study on the effects of punishment on memory performance, Milgram induced subjects to obey commands from an authority figure, the experimenter. Playing the role of "teachers," subjects were told to deliver what they thought were high voltage shocks (no shocks were actually given) to another subject (actually a professional actor) who was trying without much success to learn a sequence of word pairs. Milgram described one participant's experience as follows: "I observed a mature and initially poised businessman enter the laboratory smiling and confident. Within twenty minutes he was reduced to a twitching, stuttering wreck, who was rapidly approaching a point of nervous collapse" (Milgram, 1963, p. 377). As you might guess, Milgram's research has been controversial. He has been sharply criticized for exposing subjects to extreme levels of stress, for producing what could be long-term adverse effects on subjects' self-esteem and dignity, and because of the degree of deception involved, for destroying subjects' trust in psychologists (Baumrind, 1964).

The basic dilemma faced by Milgram and every other researcher is to weigh the value of the study being planned against the degree of intrusion on those participating as subjects. On the one hand, experimental psychologists believe strongly in the need to conduct psychological research on a wide range of topics. Indeed they believe that to fail to investigate some topic is to abdicate one's responsibility as a scientist. If the ultimate goal is to improve the human condition, and if knowledge about human behavior is essential for this to occur, then it is obviously essential to learn as much as possible. On the other hand, as we've just seen, research places demands on subjects. Thus when planning a research study, the experimenter always faces the conflicting requirements of (a) producing meaningful research results that could ultimately increase our knowledge of human behavior and (b) respecting the rights of the study's participants. Clearly, Milgram reached the conclusion that the potential value of his research outweighed the potential dangers of his procedures. He was motivated by questions about the Nazi Holocaust (Milgram was Jewish) and deeply concerned about the problem of obedience. Did the Holocaust reflect some basic flaw in the German psyche? Or is the tendency to obey authority to be found in all of us?

APA standards 6.06 through 6.08 deal with the researcher's problem of planning a study in order to balance the need to discover the basic laws of behavior with the need to protect subjects. The guidelines as the APA describes them are as follows:

6.06. *Planning Research*

(a) Psychologists design, conduct, and report research in accordance with recognized standards of scientific competence and ethical research.

(b) Psychologists plan their research so as to minimize the possibility that results will be misleading.

(c) In planning research, psychologists consider its ethical acceptability under the Ethics Code. If an ethical issue is unclear, psychologists seek to resolve the issue through consultation with institutional review boards, animal care and use committees, peer consultations, and other proper mechanisms.

(d) Psychologists take reasonable steps to implement appropriate protections for the rights and welfare of human participants, other persons affected by the research, and the welfare of animal subjects.

6.07. *Responsibility*

(a) Psychologists conduct research competently and with due concern for the dignity and welfare of the participants.

(b) Psychologists are responsible for the ethical conduct of research conducted by them or others under their supervision and control.

(c) Researchers and assistants are permitted to perform only those tasks for which they are appropriately trained and prepared.

(d) As part of the process of development and implementation of research projects, psychologists consult those with expertise concerning any special population under investigation or most likely to be affected.

6.08. *Compliance with Law and Standards*

Psychologists plan and conduct research in a manner consistent with federal and state law and regulations, as well as professional standards governing the conduct of research, and particularly those standards governing research with human participants and animal subjects.

Standard 6.06 insures that researchers appreciate the importance of making ethical considerations central to the original planning of the study. Right from the outset, the balance between the scientific importance of the study and the rights of the participants needs to be uppermost in the researcher's mind. Furthermore, the recommendation to seek advice (6.06.c) reflects the difficulty of making some of these decisions. This advice-seeking usually takes the form of presenting the research plan to a committee, called the Institutional Review Board (IRB). This group is a mixture of at least five people, usually faculty members from several departments and including at least one member of the outside community and one member who is not a scientist (Department of Health and Human Services, 1983). IRBs have to be in place for any college or university receiving federal funds for research. They became especially prevalent in the decade of the 1980s.

Part of the planning stage for a study involves determining the degree of risk to be encountered by participants (implied in 6.06.d). Sometimes there is no risk, as when experimenters observe public behavior and do not intervene in any way. At other times, subjects may be "at risk" or "at minimal risk." The distinction is not razor sharp; it is based on the degree to which subjects find themselves in situations similar to "those ordinarily encountered in daily life or during the performance of routine physical or psychological examinations or tests" (Department of Health and Human Services, 1983, p. 297). Hence, participants facing routine situations involving little or no stress are considered "at minimal risk." If the risks are greater than that, they are said to be "at risk." For instance, subjects would be at minimal risk in a memory study, which investigated whether training in visual imagery techniques led to better performance than the absence of such training. However, if that same study investigated whether the improvement due to training in imagery could be enhanced by having subjects ingest low or moderate doses of marijuana, the degree of risk would obviously be higher.

When subjects are at minimal risk, IRB approval is usually routine. However, when subjects are clearly at risk, the experimenter must convince the IRB that the value of the study justifies the risk to subjects and must scrupulously follow the remaining guidelines to ensure that subjects are informed of their rights and well treated.

Standard 6.07 makes it clear that the ethical guidelines must be followed not just by the principal investigator. Although the principal investigator bears primary responsibility for any research project, it is nonetheless true that everyone connected with the experiment must follow the guidelines and must be properly trained. This standard is especially relevant for you as a student researcher. Your instructor has the primary responsibility for any studies that you conduct in the research methods course, but you also bear an obligation to protect the people who participate as subjects for you. Also, before you collect any data for this course, you should be given thorough instructions (6.07.c).

Standard 6.07.d provides for research involving "special" populations. This applies to any category of research participant with particular features that should be taken into account in designing the study. For example, research in a mental institution with those suffering from schizophrenic disorders requires special training for researchers or consultation with those who have expertise in the disorder.

Standard 6.08 goes without saying, but reminds researchers to be aware of laws or regulations pertaining to their projects. For instance, a few paragraphs ago you read about the concept of risk as applied to subjects and you probably noticed a reference to a set of federal regulations from the Department of Health and

Human Services. The mandating of IRBs in institutions receiving federal funds is another example of a regulation that researchers need to follow.

Assuring That Subjects are Volunteers

A second important consideration for researchers concerns the volunteer status of participants in the study and centers around the issues of informed consent, deception, and the right of subjects to withdraw from the study at any time. Standards 6.10 through 6.12, and standard 6.15 are especially pertinent:

6.10. *Research Responsibilities*
Prior to conducting research (except research involving only anonymous surveys, naturalistic observations, or similar research), psychologists enter into an agreement with participants that clarifies the nature of the research and the responsibilities of both parties.

6.11. *Informed Consent to Research*
(a) Psychologists use language that is reasonably understandable to research participants in obtaining their appropriate informed consent. Such informed consent is appropriately documented.
(b) Using language that is reasonably understandable . . ., psychologists inform participants of the nature of the research; they inform participants that they are free to participate or to withdraw from the research; they explain the foreseeable consequences of declining or withdrawing; they inform participants of significant factors that may be expected to influence their willingness to participate (such as risks, discomfort, adverse effects, or limitations on confidentiality, except as provided in Standard 6.15, Deception in Research); and they explain other aspects about which the prospective participants inquire.

6.12. *Dispensing with Informed Consent*
Before determining that planned research (such as research involving only anonymous questionnaires, naturalistic observations, or certain kinds of archival research) does not require the informed consent of research participants, psychologists consider applicable regulations and IRB requirements, and they consult with colleagues as appropriate.

6.15. *Deception in Research*
(a) Psychologists do not conduct a study involving deception unless they have determined that the use of deceptive techniques is justified by the study's prospective scientific, educational, or applied value and that equally effective alternative procedures that do not use deception are not feasible.
(b) Psychologists never deceive research participants about significant aspects that would affect their willingness to participate, such as physical risks, discomfort, or unpleasant emotional experiences.
(c) Any other deception that is an integral feature of the design and conduct of an experiment must be explained to participants as early as feasible, preferably at the conclusion of their participation, but no later than at the conclusion of the research.

These standards can be considered together and center on the issues of informed consent and deception in psychological research. Standards 6.11 and 6.12 describe the principle of **informed consent**, the notion that in deciding whether to participate in psychological research, human subjects should be given enough information about the study to decide if they wish to volunteer. Subjects experience **deception** (6.15) when they are not told complete details of the study prior to participation or when they are misled about the procedures. How can these apparently contradictory concepts be reconciled?

One could argue that truly informed consent can never allow subjects to be deceived about the purposes of the study. Some (e.g., Greenberg, 1967) have suggested eliminating deception in all experiments and substituting a simulation procedure in which subjects are told the complete purpose ahead of time, and are then asked to role play someone who did not know the purpose ahead of time. However, studies (e.g., Miller, 1972) evaluating this idea have not been very supportive. There is a difference between behaving naturally and acting like you think you are supposed to act; consequently, it's not surprising that role-playing subjects and naive subjects behave differently.

Furthermore, there is evidence that subjects who are fully informed ahead of time about the purpose of an experiment involving deception behave differently from those who aren't informed. For instance, a study by Gardner (1978) looked at the effects of noise as a stressor for some subjects who were fully informed and others who weren't. The usual finding is that noise disrupts concentration and reduces performance on a variety of tasks, especially if the noise is unpredictable. But Gardner found that noise failed to have adverse effects for subjects who were first given complete information about the study, including the explicit direction that they could leave the study at any time. Apparently, the information increased the subject's *feelings of control* over the situation; other research (e.g., Sherrod, Hage, Halpern, & Moore, 1977) has shown consistently that an increased perception of control over one's fate generally acts to reduce stress. Thus, in order to investigate fully the variables influencing the relationship between noise as a stressor and performance on some task, it appears that some degree of deception is needed.

Milgram's obedience studies provide a further illustration of why psychologists sometimes withhold information at the beginning of the experiment. We've seen that Milgram told his subjects he was investigating the effects of punishment on learning. Teachers (the real subjects) would try to teach a list of word pairs to a learner (the apparent subject), believing they were shocking him for errors. Of course, Milgram was not really interested in learning; he wanted to know whether subjects would (a) continue to administer apparent shocks of increasing voltage to a learner who was in obvious discomfort and clearly not learning much or (b) disobey the experimenter and stop the experiment at some point. The outcome: Few subjects disobeyed orders. In the original study, 26 out of 40 continued shocking the learner even when the voltage level reached 450 and *nobody* disobeyed until it reached 300 volts (Milgram, 1963)! If Milgram had informed his subjects that he was interested in seeing whether they would obey unreasonable commands, would the same results have occurred? Almost certainly not. Blind obedience to authority is not something that people value very highly, so subjects told ahead of time they are in a study of obedience will surely be less compliant than they otherwise might be. The key point is that researchers want subjects to take the task seriously, to be thoroughly involved in the study, and to behave as naturally as possible. For that to happen, deception is sometimes necessary.

Standard 6.11.b makes it clear that subjects, even after they have consented to participate in a study, should be aware that they can leave the experiment at any time without penalty. If the code had been operative when Milgram was planning his study, he probably would have been asked by an IRB to modify certain portions of his procedure. During the sequence of learning trials, for instance, if the teacher showed any hesitation about continuing to administer shocks (and almost all subjects did), the experimenter said things like "The experiment requires that you continue," or "it is absolutely essential that you continue" (Milgram, 1963, p. 374),

One last point about informed consent, deception, and freedom to withdraw is that not all research participants are capable of giving consent, due to such factors as age or infirmity. In these circumstances, consent is obtained from parents or legal guardians. Nonetheless, the researcher has a special responsibility to monitor experiments using these populations, and to stop the experiment if it appears that undue stress is being experienced. For example, a parent may give consent for a study on the effects of TV violence on children's aggressive behavior, but the parent won't be in the room when the film is shown. It is up to the researcher to be sensitive enough to remove the child from the task at hand (and repair the damage) if stress levels are too high. Also, if consent is given but during the course of the experiment the child says "stop," then the experiment must stop. Finally, those in a subordinate status (e.g., prisoners) may feel coerced into giving assent by being rewarded with extra privileges if they participate. The investigator must be especially careful to make participation truly voluntary when studying such "captive" populations.

The most extraordinary instances of failure to obtain informed consent occurred in Germany and its occupied territories during World War II, in medical research using concentration camp inmates as subjects. In the name of medical science, Nazi doctors such as Josef Mengele completed a horrific series of studies. To measure how long humans could survive, inmates were immersed in ice water, injected with gasoline, or deliberately exposed to infectious and deadly diseases, among other things. Such abuse is to some degree ironic because in the early 1930s, Germany was a pioneer in developing consent guidelines for research using humans (Faden & Beauchamp, 1986). At their Nuremberg trials, the doctors defended their actions by arguing that voluntary consent didn't really exist in any medical research of the time. Their argument failed, they were convicted, and the tribunal convicting them wrote what was called the Nuremberg Code. It became the basis for all subsequent codes of medical research ethics as well as the consent portion of APA ethics code, establishing the principle that consent must be informed, competent, and voluntary, and that the person giving it must be able to comprehend the situation involved (Faden & Beauchamp, 1986).

Although the experiments performed on concentration camp victims are the most dramatic and appalling examples of consent violations, problems with consent have occurred in the United States as well. See Box 2.2 for brief descriptions of two cases from the field of medical research, in which (a) severely retarded children were infected with hepatitis in order to study the development of the illness,

Box 2.2

ETHICS—Informed Consent (?) in Biomedical Research

The research activities of doctors in the Third Reich are unprecedented in their degree of callousness and cruelty. Nonetheless, there are cases in the United States of medical research projects that have provoked intensely critical reaction and have invited comparisons, albeit remote, to the Nazi doctors. Two famous examples are the Willowbrook hepatitis study and the Tuskegee syphilis study (Faden & Beauchamp, 1986; Jones, 1981).

At Willowbrook, which housed children with varying degrees of mental retardation, a series of experiments began in 1956 and continued into the 1970s in which approximately one in ten new admissions were purposely infected with hepatitis. Parents were told of the procedure and agreed to it, but it was later shown that parents may have felt pressured into giving consent. Also, the study violated the principle that research using the mentally disabled as subjects should not be done unless it "related immediately to the etiology, pathogenesis, prevention, diagnosis, or treatment of mental disability itself" (Beauchamp & Childress, 1979, p. 182). The Willowbrook study was aimed at investigating hepatitis, not mental disability.

The study was initiated because hepatitis was rampant at the institution, partly due to a high proportion of severely retarded children who could not be toilet trained. At one point in the 1950s, there were 5,200 residents; of those, 3,800 had IQs lower than 20 and more than 3,000 were not toilet trained (Beauchamp & Childress, 1979). Even with the staff's best efforts, conditions were generally unsanitary and led to the spread of the disease. By deliberately infecting new admissions and placing them in a separate ward but not treating them, the researchers hoped to study the development of the disease under controlled conditions. Those in charge of the project defended it on the

and (b) poor Southern blacks with syphilis were left untreated for years and misinformed about their health, also for the purpose of learning more about the time course of the disease.

Finally, look at Figure 2.1, which displays an example of a typical consent form. Note that it has several features. Potential subjects agree to participate voluntarily after learning the purpose of the study, the general procedure, and the amount of time it will take. In addition, subjects understand that full information about the study may not be immediately forthcoming, that they can leave the study at any time without penalty, that strict confidentiality will be upheld, and that if there are any lingering questions about the study or complaints to be made, there is a specific person to contact. Furthermore, subjects confirm that effective debriefing occurs at the end of the study.

same grounds that Watson defended the Little Albert study (Box 2.1)—the children would almost certainly contract the disease anyway, so why not have them contract it in such a way that more could be learned about how to prevent it? Indeed, while the study has been criticized on consent grounds, it did contribute greatly to our knowledge of hepatitis and undoubtedly improved future treatment of the disease. Do you think this contribution offset the ethical problems with the study?

The Tuskegee study was designed to examine the physical deterioration of those suffering from advanced cases of syphilis. Beginning in the early 1930s, about 400 poor black men from the rural South were diagnosed with the disease and deliberately left untreated. They were never informed about the nature of the disease, nor were they told its name; doctors simply informed them that they had "bad blood." Also, local physicians were told of the study and agreed not to treat the men. Given the poverty level of the participants, it was not difficult to induce them to visit the clinic periodically (free rides and a hot meal), where blood tests and other examinations were done. The project continued into the early 1970s, even though it was clear by the late 1940s that, compared to a control group, subjects were dying at twice the rate and were developing significantly more medical complications (Faden & Beauchamp, 1986). Defenders of the study argued that when it began in the 1930s there was no effective treatment for the disease and little knowledge of it. Like Willowbrook, the Tuskegee study contributed to our knowledge of a serious disease. Do you think this contribution offset the ethical problems with the study?

With the clarity of hindsight, it is easy to criticize research that fails to satisfy current-day concepts of informed consent. Yet the motives of the chief investigators in both the Willowbrook and the Tuskegee study were quite different from whatever moved the doctors in the Third Reich. In both studies there was a sincere desire to learn as much as possible about two devastating diseases, hepatitis and syphilis. Nonetheless, the two studies are instructive examples of how the desire to advance science can sometimes conflict with the rights of individual research participants.

Treating Subjects Well

The last portion of the ethical code ensures that subjects are treated fairly and with respect, that they receive complete information about the study at its conclusion, that any stress they encounter is relieved, and that their participation be kept in confidence. In the words of the guidelines:

6.18. *Providing Participants with Information about the Study*
   (a) Psychologists provide a prompt opportunity for participants to obtain appropriate information about the nature, results, and conclusions of the research, and psychologists attempt to correct any misconceptions that participants may have.
   (b) If scientific or humane values justify delaying or withholding this

Procedure

- ✓ Experimenter describes the general nature of the study and asks the individual to consent to participate.
- ✓ Individual reads over the form, asks questions perhaps, then signs or doesn't sign.
- ✓ After debriefing, the participant signs the final part of the form.
- ✓ The participant is given a copy of the form.

An Experiment on Cognitive Mapping

The purpose of this research is to determine how accurately people can point to geographic locations. If you participate, you will be asked to move a compass-like object so that one arm of it points toward a series of locations. You will also be asked to indicate how confident you are about your decisions. The exercise will take approximately 15 minutes. The exact predictions that are being made in this study will be explained to you at the conclusion of your participation. If you have any questions or concerns about your participation or about the study in general, you may contact me as follows: _____

****

I have read the description of the experiment on cognitive mapping and I voluntarily agree to participate. I understand that I will be asked to point to the locations of a number of geographic places and that the full purpose of the study will be explained at the conclusion of my participation. I understand that I can quit the experiment at any time, without penalty, and that my participation and the record of my performance will be kept strictly confidential.

When the entire experiment has been completed, I [circle one]:

would   would not

like a brief summary of the overall results.

_____   _____
Signature of participant   Date

****

At the end of the experiment, I was given a full explanation of the study and any questions that I had were answered adequately.

_____   _____
Signature of participant   Date

FIGURE 2.1   A version of a consent form for human subjects research.

information, psychologists take reasonable measures to reduce the risk of harm.

6.19. *Honoring Commitments*

Psychologists take reasonable measures to honor all commitments they have made to research participants.

5.02. *Maintaining Confidentiality*

Psychologists have a primary obligation and take reasonable precautions to respect confidentiality rights of those with whom they work or consult, recognizing that confidentiality may be established by law, institutional rules, or professional or scientific relationships.

6.17. *Minimizing Invasiveness*

In conducting research, psychologists interfere with the participants or milieu from which data are collected only in a manner that is warranted by an appropriate research design and that is consistent with psychologists' roles as scientific investigators.

We've already seen that the research psychologist must make an estimate of the amount of risk to subjects, with greater amounts of risk creating a greater burden to justify the study. This problem of risk and potential harm is addressed again in the standard relating to deception (6.15) and once more in standard 6.18, which makes it clear that responsibility does not end with the conclusion of the study. The researcher must attempt to alleviate any stress experienced during the experiment and follow-up with subjects to insure their continued well-being. For instance, whatever one might think of the appropriateness of Milgram's study on obedience, he was clearly sensitive to the emotional well-being of his subjects. After the study was completed, he sent participants a questionnaire about their experience (84% said they were glad they had participated) and a five-page report describing the results and their significance. Also, he did a 1-year follow-up study in which a psychiatrist examined 40 former subjects and found "no evidence . . . of any traumatic reactions" (Milgram, 1974, p. 197).

Studies surveying research participants have found that fears of excessive harm in psychological research are exaggerated; subjects seem to understand and accept the rationale for deception (Christensen, 1988). One survey even found that students were considerably more lenient than professional psychologists in their judgments about the ethical appropriateness of four hypothetical studies involving such things as experimentally produced stress and alterations of self-esteem (Sullivan & Deiker, 1973). For example, Table 2.3 shows how psychologists and students differed when asked about a study in which subjects would be given a supposedly valid personality test and would be told "they had rather serious and deep-seated personality problems" (Sullivan & Deiker, 1973, p. 588). As you can see, the psychologists were more concerned about the appropriateness of the study than were the students. Other research shows that objections by subjects about participating in psychological research seem to center more on their concern about being bored than being harmed (Coulter, 1986).

In evaluating the problem of deception, it is important to keep in mind that the vast majority of psychological research involves tasks that are considerably less dramatic and deceptive than self-esteem manipulations or procedures like Milgram's.

TABLE 2.3   *Responses of Psychologists and Students about the Ethical Acceptability of a Study Designed to Lower Self-Esteem*

Questions	Psychologists answering "yes" (%)	Students answering "yes" (%)
1. Would subjects volunteer knowing details of study?	45	80
2. Is the deception unethical?	67	23
3. Are any other aspects unethical?	54	8
4. Was the deception justified?	32	84

Source: Sullivan & Deiker, 1973, p. 589

In fact, in most studies involving deception, subjects are not exposed to elaborate cover stories. Rather, the deception is often quite minor, involving such things as a memory task in which subjects studying and recalling a sequence of four or five word lists aren't told about a final recall of all the lists. With the exception of research in areas like social psychology, elaborate deceptions are the exception.

Standard 6.18 introduces debriefing, a postexperimental session in which all aspects of the research are thoroughly discussed with the participant. Debriefing serves two general purposes, referred to by Holmes (1976a, 1976b) as dehoaxing and desensitizing. Dehoaxing means revealing the true purpose of the experiment to participants, and desensitizing refers to the process of reducing any stress or other negative feelings experienced by participants.

There are several parts to a typical debriefing session, and the amount of time occupied depends on the complexity of the study, the presence and degree of deception, and the level of potential distress felt by the subject. In a study involving deception, a debriefing session typically begins by asking subjects if they thought the study had another purpose from the one initially described. This enables the experimenter to determine if the deception was effective and it also provides a lead-in for the experimenter to reveal the true purpose of the study. It is also at this time that the experimenter tries to justify the deception (e.g., emphasizing the importance of getting one's true reactions) and begins to alleviate any stress involved. Subjects "taken in" by the experiment's cover story should be assured that their behavior reflects the effectiveness of the cover story, not any personal weakness on their part. Furthermore, subjects in many studies can be assured that the situation they experienced had powerful effects on their behavior, that their reactions don't reflect any individual inadequacies, and that other subjects reacted similarly (Holmes, 1976b).

One result of an effective debriefing is that skilled experimenters can better understand their current studies and improve their future ones. Subjects can be asked for their input about revising the procedure in order to learn more about the problem being studied. In many cases their descriptions of what they were thinking about during the experiment are of immense help in interpreting the data and planning the next study.

At the final part of a debriefing, subjects should be given the opportunity to receive a description of the results when the study has been completed and should be told who to contact if they have further questions or any concerns about their participation (refer again to the consent form in Figure 2.1).

A properly conducted debriefing often lasts longer than the experimental session itself. Several studies have shown that subjects who are thoroughly and properly debriefed evaluate the research experience positively, and one study even showed that, compared to nondeceived subjects, those in deception studies actually rated their experiences higher in both enjoyment and educational value, apparently because the debriefing was more extensive (Smith & Richardson, 1983). The importance of leaving subjects with a good feeling about their research participation cannot be overstated. They have invested their time and their intellectual and emotional energy for us. We owe them a great deal.

We also owe them privacy: Subjects should be assured (5.02) of complete confidentiality in the experiment. That is, subjects should be confident that their identities as research participants will not be known by anyone other than the experimenter. The basic right to privacy is also the concern of standard 6.17, which applies particularly to research outside the laboratory that might affect people in daily living situations. We'll see in the next chapter, when laboratory and field research are compared, that concerns over invading the privacy rights of people going about their daily business keep many researchers within the protected confines of the laboratory.

Ethical Guidelines for Research with Animals

As you recall from your course in general psychology and from the Chapter 1 discussion of maze learning, psychologists occasionally use animals as research subjects. Although some people have the impression that psychologists seem to study rats more than people, the truth is that animal research is only a very small proportion of the total research done in psychology—about 7%–9% (Gallup & Suarez, 1985b).

Animals are used in psychological research for both methodological and ethical reasons. Procedurally, their environmental, genetic, and developmental histories can be easily controlled; ethically, most experimental psychologists take the position that animals can be subjected to procedures that could not be used with humans. Consider Gibson's visual cliff research again (Gibson & Walk, 1960). Thirty-six 6- to 14-month old infants were placed in the middle of the apparatus and although they were quite willing to crawl around on the "shallow" side, they hesitated to crawl onto the glass surface over the "deep" side. This shows they were able to perceive depth and apparently were aware of some of the consequences of depth. Does this mean depth perception is innate? No, because these infants had from 6 to 14 months worth of learning experience with distance perception. To control for experience, it would be necessary to raise these infants in complete visual isolation, a procedure that is obviously out of the question. Such a procedure *is* feasible with animals, however, and the isolation does not have to be very long—animals develop the ability to move through their environments very quickly, often in a matter of hours. So Gibson and Walk tested a variety of species from rats to kittens to lambs,

Box 2.3

ORIGINS—Antivivisection and the APA

Considering the high visibility of the animal research controversy, you might think it is a fairly recent development. Not so. Actually it has a long history, as documented nicely by the comparative psychologist and historian Donald Dewsbury (1990).

The term vivisection derives from the Latin *vivus*, or "alive," and refers to surgical procedures on live animals, usually done for scientific purposes. The antivivisection movement developed in nineteenth-century England, where activists' efforts contributed to the passage of England's "Cruelty to Animals Act" in 1876, a code similar in spirit to modern APA guidelines for animals. The movement quickly spread to the United States—the American Antivivisection Society was founded in 1883 in Philadelphia. Antivivisectionists and animal researchers (including physiologists and early experimental psychologists) engaged in the same arguments that are heard today, with claims of unspeakable torture on one side and justifications on scientific grounds on the other.

One especially controversial series of studies concerned John B. Watson (again). In order to determine which senses were critical for maze learning, Watson did a series of studies in which he surgically eliminated senses one at a time to examine the effects on rats in mazes (Watson, 1907). The study caused an outcry when reported in the *New York Times* on December 30, 1906, and Watson was satirized in a cartoon (see Figure 2.2) (from Dewsbury, 1990).

The American Psychological Association established its first code for regulating animal research in the 1920s, well before creating a code for research with humans. A committee chaired by Robert Yerkes was formed in 1924 and in the following year the APA adopted its recommendations. The committee proposed that laboratories create an "open door" policy, in which "any accredited member . . . of a humane society . . . [could] be permitted to visit a laboratory to observe the care

isolating them from birth until they could move around, and testing them on the apparatus. They discovered that depth perception, at least as measured by the visual cliff, is built into the visual system for those species who rely on vision.

The use of animals in all kinds of research (not just psychological) has become an emotional and highly controversial issue, however. Animal rights activists have denounced the use of animals in research ranging from medical research to cosmetics testing. In some cases, research laboratories have been vandalized and animals released. During the decade of the 1980s, for example, animal rights extremists vandalized approximately 100 research facilities housing animals (Adler, 1992). The problem was severe enough to produce federal legislation, the Animal Enterprise Protection Act of 1992, specifically outlawing such vandalism and setting stiff penalties.

FIGURE 2.2 Antivivisectionist cartoon of Watson on the operating table, from Dewsbury (1990).

of animals and methods of experimentation" (Anderson, 1926, p. 125), that journals require authors to be clear about the use of humane procedures in their research, that psychologists defend the need for animal research, both in the classroom and publicly, and that the APA maintain a standing committee on "precautions in animal experimentation" (Anderson, 1926, p. 125).

Even moderate supporters of animal rights, granting the need for medical research, have targeted animal research in psychology as wrong. Activists routinely picket the annual meeting of the American Psychological Association and occasionally disrupt sessions featuring reports of animal research. Despite the recent high visibility of this issue though, you should know that the controversy is an old one, dating at least to the last century. Before continuing, look at Box 2.3, which details some earlier conflicts between "antivivisectionists" and researchers such as John B. Watson.

What is the case against the use of animals as research subjects? At the extreme, some argue unequivocally that humans have no right to consider themselves superior to any other "sentient" species, that is, any species capable of experiencing feelings and in particular, pain. To do so is to practice **speciesism**, a prejudice said to be no different in principle from racism or sexism (Singer, 1975). Animals are said to have the same basic rights to privacy, autonomy, and freedom from harm as humans and therefore cannot be subjugated by humans in any way. Nonsentient species are excluded, perhaps to avoid the frequent dilemma of how to deal with ants and mosquitoes. Of course, taking the "absolute rights" argument to its logical conclusion creates significant problems for humans. Advocates must be vegetarians, cannot wear clothes derived from animals (e.g., fur, leather, wool, suede), and cannot keep pets (no slavery). It is even possible that baseball should be avoided because of the sport's dependence on cows for its defining piece of equipment.

Moderates among animal rights groups recognize the need for some medical research, but reject other research on the grounds that researchers have inflicted needless pain and suffering on animals when alternative approaches to research would yield essentially the same conclusions. The impact of this argument has been quite salutary in reducing unnecessary research on animals by the cosmetics industry (e.g., injecting injurious dyes into the eyes of rabbits to improve eye care products), but the argument has been applied to research in psychology as well. Psychological research with animals has been described as needlessly repetitive and concerned with trivial problems that have no practical human benefit. Critics have suggested that instead of using animals in the laboratory, researchers could discover all they need to know about animal behavior by observing animals in their natural habitats, by substituting nonsentient for sentient animals, or by using computer simulations.

In short, some animal rights advocates argue that no research at all should be done with animals on the grounds that animals have rights analogous to human rights; others argue that some medical research with animal subjects is acceptable, but that psychological research is not. How do research psychologists respond?

Using Animals in Psychological Research

Most psychologists flatly reject the argument that sentient animals have rights equal to those of humans. While granting that humans have a strong obligation to respect and protect nonhuman species, psychologists believe that humans can be distinguished from nonhumans because of our degree of awareness, our ability to develop culture and to understand history, and especially our ability to make moral judgments. Although animals are remarkable creatures capable of complex cognition, they are "incapable of being moral subjects, of acting rightly or wrongly in the moral sense, of having, discharging, or breaching duties and obligations" (Feinberg, 1974, p. 46). Of course, differentiating between human and non-human species does not by itself allow for the use of the latter by the former. Psychologists argue, however, that the use of animals in research does not constitute exploitation. Rather, the net effect of such research is beneficial rather than costly, both for humans *and* for animals.

The most visible defender of animal research in psychology has been Neal Miller, a noted experimental psychologist whose research on topics ranging from basic processes in conditioning and motivation to the principles underlying biofeedback earned him the APA's Distinguished Scientific Contributions Award in 1959 and its Distinguished Professional Contributions Award in 1983.

In "The Value of Behavioral Research on Animals" (1985), Miller argued that (a) activists grossly overstate the harm done to animals in psychological research, (b) animal research provides clear benefits for the well-being of humans, and (c) animal research clearly benefits animals as well. Concerning harm, Miller cited a study by Coile and Miller (1984), which examined 5 years' worth of published research in APA journals, 608 studies, and found *zero* instances of the forms of abuse claimed by activists. Also, examining the abuse claims shows that at least some of the alleged "abuse" may not be that at all, but merely seems to be because of the inflammatory language used. For instance, Coile and Miller cited several misleading statements from activist literature including: "[The animals] are deprived of food and water to suffer and die slowly from hunger and thirst" (Coile & Miller, 1984, p. 700). This evidently refers to the common laboratory practice in conditioning experiments of depriving animals of food or water for 24 hours. Animals then placed in a conditioning procedure are motivated to work for the food or the water. Is this abuse? Perhaps not, considering that veterinarians recommend that most pets be fed just once a day (Gallup & Suarez, 1985a)

Miller argued that situations involving harm to animals during the research procedures are rare, only occur when less painful alternatives cannot be used, and can be justified by the ultimate good that derives from the studies. This good applies both to humans and to animals and the bulk of his 1985 article was an attempt to document the kinds of good that derive from animal studies. First, he argued that while the long history of animal conditioning research has taught us much about general principles of learning, it also has had direct application to human problems. An early example of this was a device developed and tested by Mowrer and Mowrer (1938) for treating enuresis (excessive and uncontrolled bedwetting) that was based explicitly on the classical conditioning work contributed by Pavlov's dogs. Teaching machines and several forms of behavior therapy are likewise grounded in conditioning principles. More recently, animal research has directly influenced the development of behavioral medicine, the application of behavioral principles to traditional medical practice. Disorders ranging from headaches to hypertension to the disabilities following strokes can be helped with behavioral procedures such as biofeedback.

Finally, Miller argued that animal research provides direct benefits to animals themselves. Medical research with animals has improved veterinary care dramatically, but behavioral research has also improved the welfare of various species. The study of animal behavior has led to the improvement of zoo environments, aided in nonchemical pest control, and discouraged coyote attacks on sheep by using taste conditioning as a substitute for lethal control. Behavioral research can even help preserve endangered species. Miller used the example of imprinting, the tendency for young ducklings and other species to follow the first stimulus that moves (usually the mother). Research on imprinting led to the procedure of exposing newly hatched condors to a puppet resembling an adult condor rather than to a normal human caretaker, thereby facilitating the bonding process for the incubator-raised bird.

One final point about using animals in psychological research is that despite the arguments of some animal rights groups, most people seem to think that animal research is of value. Very little research exists on the question, but it appears that although people surveyed are concerned about the pain and suffering that might be experienced by animals, they believe that animal research, including research in psychology, is justified and necessary (Gallup & Beckstead, 1968; Fulero & Kirkland, 1992).

The APA Code for Animal Research

Standard 6.20 of the 1992 code sketches out the ethical guidelines for animal use and the elements of the code are elaborated in an earlier document (American Psychological Association, 1985). The guidelines deal with (a) the proper acquisition and care of animals (during and after the study), (b) the need to justify the study adequately when the potential exists for some harm to occur, and (c) the use of animals for educational rather than research purposes. The main theme revolves around the issue of balancing the scientific justification for a particular project with the need to care humanely for the animals. Here are the highlights.

Caring for the Animals

The research supervisor must be an expert in the care of the animals to be used, must carefully train all those who will be in contact with the animals, and must be fully aware of federal regulations about animal care. To further ensure proper care, a veterinarian must check the facilities twice annually and should be on call as a general consultant. The animals should be acquired from legitimate suppliers or bred in the laboratory. If wild animals are being studied, they must be trapped humanely. Analogous to the IRB for human research, there should be a "local institutional animal care and use committee" (American Psychological Association, 1985, p. 4).

Once an experiment is over, alternatives to destroying the animals should be considered. However, euthanasia is sometimes necessary, "either as a requirement of the research, or because it constitutes the most humane form of disposition of an animal at the conclusion of the research" (American Psychological Association, 1985, p. 8). In such cases, the process must be "accomplished in a humane manner, appropriate for the species, under anesthesia, or in such a way as to ensure immediate death, and in accordance with procedures approved by the institutional animal care and use committee" (American Psychological Association, 1985, p. 8).

Justifying the Study

Just as the researcher using humans must weigh the scientific value of the research against the degree of risk to participants, the animal researcher should be able to make the case that the "scientific purpose of the research [is] of sufficient potential significance as to outweigh any harm or distress to the animals used" (American Psychological Association, 1985, p. 5). The "scientific purpose" of the study should fall within one of three categories. The research should "(a) increase knowledge of the processes underlying the evolution, development, maintenance, alteration, control, or biological significance of behavior, (b) increase understanding of the species under study, or (c) provide results that benefit the health or welfare of humans or other animals" (American Psychological Association, 1985, p. 4).

The longest section of the guidelines concerns the range of procedures that can be used. In general, researchers are told that their requirement for a strong justification increases with the degree of discomfort to be experienced by animals. In addition, they are told that appetitive procedures (i.e., use of positive reinforcement) should be substituted for aversive procedures as much as possible, that less stressful procedures should be preferred over more stressful ones, and that surgical procedures require special care and expertise. Field research procedures should disturb the animals living in their natural habitat as little as possible.

Using Animals for Educational Purposes

The guidelines are designed primarily to aid researchers who use animals, but animals are often used educationally to demonstrate specific behaviors, to train students in animal research procedures, and to give students firsthand experience in replicating well-known phenomena such as operant conditioning principles. Unlike the research situation, however, the educational use of animals does not result directly in new knowledge. Consequently, the educator is urged to use fewer rather than more animals to accomplish a given purpose and to consider a variety of alternative procedures. For example, instead of demonstrating the same principle (e.g., shaping) to an introductory psychology class with a new rat each semester, the instructor might do it once, then videotape the procedure for future classes.

Sometimes computer simulations of various phenomena can be substituted for live procedures; several excellent simulations of both classical and operant conditioning procedures exist. These simulations can be effective (and are necessary in smaller schools, which cannot keep up with federal regulations for the proper care of animals), but shaping a schematized rat to bar press is not quite the same as shaping a real rat. Students often experience a deep insight into the power of reinforcement contingencies when they witness them firsthand. Direct experiences with animals in undergraduate learning laboratories have motivated more than one student to become an experimental psychologist (Moses, 1991).

In summary, most psychologists defend the use of animals in behavioral research while recognizing the need to closely scrutinize the rationale for every animal study that is conducted. Animal research has contributed mightily to our understanding of human behavior and promises to help in the future search for solutions to AIDS, Alzheimer's disease, mental illness, and countless other human problems.

Scientific Fraud

There has been much discussion in recent years about fraud in science, with specific cases sparking debate about whether they represent merely the occasional "bad apple" or, more ominously, the "tip of the iceberg." Obviously, scientists in general and research psychologists in particular are expected to be scrupulously honest in all their scientific activities. Principle B of the 1992 general code unambiguously states that psychologists "seek to promote integrity in the science, teaching, and practice of psychology" (American Psychological Association, 1992). Furthermore, several of the specific standards of the 1992 code directly concern fraudulent research practices. This last section of the chapter addresses the following questions: What is scientific fraud?; How prevalent is it and how can it be detected?; Why does it happen?

TABLE 2.4 *On Data Falsification and Plagiarism: Text of APA Standards*

Standard 6.21 → Reporting of Results

a. Psychologists do not fabricate data or falsify results in their publications.

b. If psychologists discover significant errors in their published data, they take responsible steps to correct such errors in a correction, retraction, erratum, or other appropriate publication means.

Standard 6.22 → Plagiarism

Psychologists do not present substantial portions or elements of another's work as their own, even if the other work or data source is cited occasionally.

Source: American Psychological Association (1992). Ethical principles of psychologists and code of conduct. *American Psychologist, 47,* 1597–1611.

The dictionary defines fraud as "a deception deliberately practiced in order to secure unfair or unlawful gain" (*American Heritage Dictionary,* 1971, p. 523). The two major types of fraud in science are (1) **plagiarism**, that is, deliberately taking the ideas of someone else and claiming them as one's own, and (2) **falsifying data**. In the 1992 code, plagiarism is specifically condemned in standard 6.22 and data falsification receives similar treatment in standard 6.21 (See Table 2.4 for the text of the standards). Plagiarism is a problem that can occur in all disciplines but falsifying data is a problem that only happens in science and it will be the major focus here.

Data Falsification

If there is a mortal sin in science, it is the failure to be scrupulously honest in managing data, the foundation stones on which the entire enterprise is built; if the foundation fails, all else collapses. Thus, the integrity of data is an issue of pivotal importance. This type of fraud can take several forms. First and most extreme, a scientist might fail to collect any data at all and simply manufacture it. Second, some collected data might be altered or omitted to make the overall picture "look better." Third, some data could be collected, but "missing data" could be "guessed at" and created in order to have a complete set of information. Fourth, an entire study could be suppressed because it "came out the wrong way." In each of these cases the deception is deliberate and the scientist presumably "secures an unfair or unlawful gain" (e.g., publication).

The traditional view is that fraud is rare and easily detected because faked results won't be replicated (Hilgartner, 1990). That is, if a scientist produces a result with fraudulent data, the results won't represent some "empirical truth." Other scientists, intrigued or surprised by this new finding, will try to reproduce it in their own labs, will fail to do so, and the fraudulent findings will be discarded eventually.

In addition to replication failures, fraud may also be detected (or at least suspected) during the normal peer review process. Whenever a research article is submitted for journal publication, or when a grant is submitted to some agency, it is reviewed by several experts whose recommendations usually determine whether or not the article will be published or the grant funded. On the assumption that there is strength in numbers, it is believed that anything that seems odd will be detected by at least one of the reviewers.

A third way of detecting fraud is when a researcher's collaborators suspect a problem. This happened in the 1980s in one of psychology's most notorious cases. In a series of studies that apparently made a breakthrough in the treatment of hyperactivity in retarded children, Stephen Breuning produced data showing that stimulant drugs could be effective for treating the problem. However, a colleague suspected the data were faked, a charge that was upheld after a 3-year investigation by the NIMH (National Institute of Mental Health), which had funded some of Breuning's research. In a plea bargain, Breuning pled guilty to two counts of submitting false data to NIMH; in exchange, NIMH dropped a charge that Breuning committed perjury during the investigation (Byrne, 1988).

One of the great strengths of science is the self-correction resulting from the replication process, peer reviews and the honesty of colleagues. Indeed, this system has detected fraud numerous times, as in the Breuning case. But what if peers fail to notice something awry or what if some fraudulent result is consistent with other, nonfraudulent findings (i.e., it replicates)? If the bogus results "fit" with other legitimate research outcomes, there is little reason to question them and the fraud may go undetected. Something like this might have occurred in one of psychology's best known cases of apparent fraud.

The case involved one of Great Britain's most famous psychologists, Cyril Burt (1883–1971), a major player in the debate over the nature of intelligence. His twin studies are often cited as evidence in support of the idea that intelligence is mostly inherited from one's parents. One of Burt's results was that genetically identical twins had virtually the same IQ score even if they were given up for adoption at birth and raised in different environments. His data went unchallenged for years and became assimilated into the literature on the heritability of intelligence. However, careful readers eventually noticed that in different publications describing the results with different numbers of twins, Burt kept reporting the *exact* same statistical results (identical correlation coefficients). Such an outcome is highly unlikely mathematically. Detractors accused him of manufacturing the results to support his strong hereditarian beliefs, while defenders argued that he collected the data but became a forgetful and careless reporter with increasing age. It was also said in his defense that if he were intent on fraud, he surely would have done a better job of disguising it (e.g., making sure the correlations weren't the same). There is no question that something is "odd" about Burt's data, but the question of how much was deliberate fraud and how much was oversight may never be determined, partly because after Burt's death, his housekeeper destroyed several chests containing notebooks and data (Kohn, 1986).

Analyzing the Burt affair has become a cottage industry in itself (Green, 1992; Samelson, 1992), but for our purposes the point is that "bad data," whether it be the result of error, oversight, or deliberate distortion, may fail to be noticed if it fits with other findings (i.e., if it is replicated elsewhere). This was certainly the case with Burt; his data were quite similar to other twin studies (e.g., Bouchard & McGue, 1981).

It is worth mentioning that recent commentators (e.g., Hilgartner, 1990) believe that while falsified data might go undetected because it replicates "good" data, it may not be detected for two other reasons as well. First, the sheer mass of studies being published these days makes it easier for a bad study to slip through the cracks, especially if it isn't reporting some notable discovery that attracts attention. Second, the reward system in science is structured so that new discoveries pay off, but scientists who spend their time "merely" replicating other work aren't seen as very creative. Consequently, the academic rewards elude them.

The reward system is also believed to be part of the reason why fraud occurs in the first place. This brings us to the final question about fraud—why does it occur? Explanations range from the individual (some character weakness) to the societal (a reflection of general moral decay in late twentieth century), with the reasons relating to the academic reward system somewhere in the middle. Productive scientists are promoted, tenured, win grants, and influence people. Sometimes the attendant "publish or perish" pressures overwhelm the individual, and lead the researcher (or the researcher's assistants) to cut some corners. It might begin on a small scale—adding a few pieces of data to achieve the desired outcome—but expand over time.

What does this mean for you as a student researcher? At the very least it means that you need to be compulsive about data. Follow procedures scrupulously and *never* succumb to the temptation to manufacture even a single piece of data. Likewise, never discard data from a subject unless there are clearly prescribed procedures for doing so (e.g., subject doesn't follow instructions, experimenter doesn't administer the procedure correctly). Finally, keep the raw data, or at the very least, the data summary sheets. Your best protection against a charge that your results "look funny" is your ability to produce the data.

The importance of being aware of the ethical implications of the research you're doing cannot be overstated: It is the reason for placing this chapter early in the text and it won't be the last you'll hear of the topic. On the immediate horizon, however, is a chapter that considers the problem of how to begin developing ideas for research projects.

Chapter Review

Glossary Fill-Ins

1. A debriefing session that makes the true purpose of a study clear but leaves the participant embarrassed and humiliated has succeeded at _____ but failed at _____.

2. The first APA ethics code was developed empirically, using the _____ procedure.

3. Potential participants who receive enough information for them to make a reasonable decision about whether to volunteer for the study have satisfied the ethical requirement for _____.

4. Most experimental psychologists reject the idea that animals have rights equal to those of humans; thus, they are likely to be charged with _____ by animal rights extremists.

5. The most serious type of fraud that is unique to science is _____.

6. In the past, research participants were sometimes called "observers." Today they are usually referred to as _____.

Multiple Choice

1. John Watson might have difficulty today if he presented a proposal for the Little Albert study to an IRB. Why?

   a. Studying emotions in eleven-month olds would not be acceptable because they cannot give informed consent.

   b. He would be proposing a potentially harmful procedure without making any provision to remove the harm.

   c. He did not have an adequate system for dehoaxing Albert once the study was completed.

   d. The study would involve a violation of confidentiality, since Watson revealed the child's name.

2. As part of the informed consent procedure, subjects are told

   a. That the experiment will not include deception of any kind.

   b. That they have a choice of whether to participate or not, but once they agree to be in the experiment, they are obligated to complete the study.

   c. Whether or not electrical shock will be used in the study.

   d. The general nature of the research, unless deception is involved—then they are told *nothing* about the study ahead of time.

3. Research on the use of deception in psychological research shows that

   a. It isn't needed; subjects asked to role play produce the same results.

   b. Students are more likely to judge a deception experiment as unethical than are psychologists.

   c. It is indeed harmful; many of Milgram's subjects needed counseling after going through the obedience study.

   d. Subjects fully informed about the purpose of a study often behave very differently from those deceived about the purpose.

4. All of the following are included in the APA code for the use of animals in research except

   a. Psychologists are discouraged from using animals for educational purposes.

   b. Pain is allowable if the value of the research outweighs the risk to the subjects.

   c. Just as an IRB judges proposals for research with humans, there should be an analogous group to evaluate animal research.

   d. If the animals are to be euthanized after the research or as part of the design, it must be carried out painlessly.

5. Which of the following is true about the falsification of research data?
    a. Fraud will always be discovered in the end, because the results won't be replicated.
    b. It is defined as making up all or most of the data for a study; just altering one or two data points does not constitute fraud.
    c. It may remain undetected if it produces results similar to other data.
    d. It is quite rare, partly because the academic reward system is structured so that no real benefits result from manufacturing data.

Applications Exercises

Exercise 2.1 — Thinking Empirically About Deception

From the standpoint of a research psychologist who is thinking empirically, how would you assess these claims about deception? That is, what kinds of empirical data would you like to have available in order to judge the truth of the claims?

1. Deception should never be used in psychological research because once people have been deceived in a study, they will no longer trust any psychologist.
2. Deception could be avoided by instructing subjects to "imagine" they are in a deception study; they are then asked to behave as they think a typical person would behave.
3. Psychologists are just fooling themselves; most subjects see right through their deceptions.

Exercise 2.2 — Defending the Urinal Study to an IRB

The effects of crowding on stress were investigated in an unusual fashion in a controversial study by Middlemist, Knowles, and Matter (1976). A number of studies show that people don't like to have their personal space invaded and will take steps to avoid intrusions. For instance, if someone stands too close to us we tend to back away. Middlemist et al. (1976) wanted to investigate this phenomenon more thoroughly by studying the physiological manifestations of personal space intrusions. They reasoned that an intrusion would upset people and their distress would be reflected in some physiological way. One such physiological indicator concerns urination. Under stress, people find it difficult to begin urination even when they have to go, and they also will stop urinating faster when stressed.

Middlemist et al. (1976) predicted that in a men's room with three urinals, subjects standing at urinal 1 would experience greater personal space intrusion (therefore stress, therefore the effects of stress on urination) if another person entered the room and stood at urinal 2 (right next to 1) than at urinal 3 (one removed from 1). Rather than simply wait for these events to occur naturally, the researchers used "confederates" who followed a subject into the men's room; if the subject was alone and standing at 1, the confederate stood either at 2 or 3 (or didn't enter, in a control condition), as determined randomly. Subjects were unaware that they were participating in the study. The amount of time it took for the subject to begin to urinate and the total time spent urinating were recorded by a researcher hidden in one of the stalls using a periscope, stopwatches, and acute hearing in ways that I'll leave to your imagination.

What ethical issues are raised by this study? As an exercise, develop a defense of the study on ethical grounds as if you were presenting it as a proposal to an IRB.

Exercise 2.3 — Avoiding Plagiarism

A student is doing a paper on lying and reads a book called "Telling Lies," by Paul Ekman (1985). The student comes across the following passage about a situation in which someone is actually telling the truth but is very nervous and therefore appears to be lying:

. . . Another equally important source of trouble, leading to disbelieving-the-truth mistakes, is the Othello error. This error occurs when the lie catcher fails to consider that a truthful person who is under stress may appear to be lying. . . . Truthful people may be afraid of being disbelieved, and their fear might be confused with the liar's detection apprehension. . . .

I have called this error after Othello because the death scene in Shakespeare's play is such an excellent and famous example of it. . . . (Ekman, 1985, pp. 169–170)

The student's term paper on lying includes this paragraph:

Disbelieving-the-truth mistakes are another kind of problem in the accurate detection of lying. Sometimes the person trying to catch someone else lying doesn't take into account that a truthful person under stress may seem to be lying. This is known as the Othello error. Sometimes you could be telling the truth, yet afraid that nobody will believe you. As a result you would seem to be nervous about being detected.

When the paper is returned, the student is shocked to learn the professor has made a charge of plagiarism. Do you think that plagiarism is involved here? If so, why? If not, why not?

CHAPTER 3

Developing Ideas for Research in Psychology

Chapter Overview

- ### Varieties of Psychological Research

  Basic research in psychology aims to discover fundamental principles of human behavior; applied research is undertaken with specific practical problems in mind. Both basic and applied varieties of research can take place either in the laboratory or in a field setting. Laboratory research allows greater control, but field research can more closely approximate real life situations.

- ### Asking Empirical Questions

  The initial step in any research project is to formulate an empirical question—one that can be answered with the evidence of objective data. Empirical questions include terms that are defined precisely enough (i.e., operationally) to allow for replication to occur.

● Developing Research from Observations and Current Problems

Some research ideas derive from reflection on everyday observations, especially of events that are unusual enough to attract one's attention. Serendipity is the act of discovering something by accident and serendipitous results often yield ideas for further research. Specific problems to be solved also lead to research; much of applied research in general and program evaluation research in particular develops this way.

● Developing Research from Theory

There is a reciprocal relationship between theory building and research. Empirical questions can be deduced from theory. The conclusions of the completed experiment then either support or refute the theory. Theories cannot be proven to be true. Technically, they can be disproven after the failure of a single prediction; actually, however, a theory is discarded only after a consensus develops that it is consistently failing. Theories are useful to the extent that they generate research that increases our knowledge of behavior. Good theories are parsimonious and precise enough to be falsified.

● Developing Research from Other Research

Researchers in experimental psychology seldom think in terms of isolated experiments. Instead, they produce programs of research, series of interrelated experiments within a specific topic area. They continually see the results of experiments as starting points for the next experiment.

● Reviewing the Literature

Empirical questions occur more frequently to the investigator who knows the research literature in some particular area. There are several standard sources available and the chapter ends with a discussion of how to use them to search for background material on a particular research topic.

As one of the requirements for this course, or perhaps as an independent project, you may find yourself being asked to develop a research proposal. You might react to this type of assignment with a feeling that the screen has gone blank, accompanied by a mounting sense of panic. Take heart—this chapter has come along just in time. When you finish it you may not find ideas for research projects flowing freely into your mind, but you should at least have some good ideas about where to start. Before looking at the sources of ideas for research, however, let us categorize the varieties of psychological research.

Varieties of Psychological Research

Research in psychology can be classified in several ways. For example, one distinction can be made between basic and applied research. Second, research can be categorized in terms of its setting.

Basic versus Applied Research

Most research in psychology concerns describing, predicting, and explaining fundamental principles of behavior, and this activity is referred to as **basic research**. On the other hand, **applied research** is so named because it has some direct and immediate relevance to the solution of a real-world problem. To illustrate the distinction, consider memory research. A basic research study might investigate the organization of memory by having subjects study a list of words, recall the list, study it again, recall it again, and so on through several trials (e.g., Tulving, 1966). The idea would be to see if the words gradually came to be recalled in the same groupings, thereby indicating how the words were being organized in subjects' minds. The study would have no obvious practical application, but would be done simply to learn more about the basic processes of memory organization. The results would presumably contribute to a developing body of knowledge about the inner workings of memory. On the other hand, an example of an applied research study in memory might be one concerned with eyewitness memory, in which subjects would see a film of an accident, then later try to recall what they saw as accurately as possible (e.g., Loftus & Palmer, 1974). This study would have some obvious applicability to the problem of eyewitness memory, an issue of importance to the legal system. The discussion in Chapter 1 about the traditional Ebbinghaus approach to memory and Neisser's ecological approach is in part a question of basic versus applied research.

It is sometimes believed that applied research is more valuable than basic research, because the former seems to concern immediately relevant problems. It could be argued, however, that a major advantage of basic research is that the principles can potentially be used in a variety of applied situations. Nonetheless, basic research is a frequent target of politicians, who bluster about the misuse of tax dollars to fund research (through grants from federal agencies like the National Science Foundation) that doesn't seem very "useful" for anything. The charges are easy to make and tend to resonate with voters; after all, a major component of the American national character is the high value we place on what is practical.

The difficulty is that much if not all applied research depends on a solid background of basic research; without this background, some applied projects would never have been imagined, much less carried out. A good example is a study by Egeland (1975) on reading. The purpose of the experiment was to evaluate a method for training preschool children to differentiate letters that are similar (e.g., R and P). The method involved showing children cards like the ones in Figure

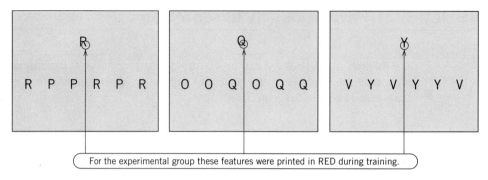

For the experimental group these features were printed in RED during training.

FIGURE 3.1   Stimulus cards similar to those used by Egeland (1975).

3.1. The task was to select each of the letters in the row of six that matched the single letter at the top of the card. Egeland highlighted the distinctive feature of the letter (e.g., the \ in R distinguishes it from P) by printing it in red. With successive trials, the red color was gradually faded to black. Compared to subjects whose letters were printed all in black for every trial, the training group made fewer errors. They also performed better in a follow-up test a week later.

For our purposes, what is notable about the Egeland study is that the procedure is based on the idea that letter recognition is affected by the perception of individual components or features of the stimuli. At the time of Egeland's study, this feature theory was the prevailing idea about how pattern recognition occurs and there was a great deal of basic research investigating various aspects of the theory. For example, an early study by Neisser (1963) had subjects scan arrays of letters like the ones in Figure 3.2. They were to respond as soon as they identified the target letter. As you can see from the arrays, Neisser varied the degree of similarity in the features making up the letters. The letter O took longer for subjects to iden-

```
1. Find the letter O:        2. Find the letter O:
      G  Q  Q  U                  A  X  A  N
      Q  S  G  G                  L  A  N  X
      U  Q  G  S                  X  X  N  L
      S  G  O  Q                  A  N  O  A
      U  Q  S  U                  L  L  X  A
      G  G  S  U                  A  L  A  N

3. Find the letter K:        4. Find the letter K:
      G  Q  Q  U                  A  X  A  N
      Q  S  G  G                  L  A  N  X
      U  Q  G  S                  X  X  N  L
      S  G  K  Q                  A  N  K  A
      U  Q  S  U                  L  L  X  A
      G  G  S  U                  A  L  A  N
```

FIGURE 3.2   Stimulus array from Neisser's (1963) study of feature detection.

tify when embedded in the letters Q, U, S, and G than when embedded within X, A, N, and L, presumably because the O shares more features with letters like Q than letters like X.

Although Egeland never mentioned the Neisser study or others like it, it is clear that the solid foundation of research on feature theory contributed to the development of the training program in reading. This is a process repeated many times in psychological research. Basic researchers investigate some psychological phenomenon solely for the sake of learning about it, a body of knowledge is created, and that body serves as a foundation for applied research dealing with specific problems.

If it is true that basic research often leads to applications, it is also the case that applied research outcomes frequently have relevance for basic research, providing evidence that either supports or refutes theories. Supporting a feature theory of pattern recognition was not Egeland's goal, but the study did just that. Similarly, the research mentioned earlier on eyewitness memory is applied research, but its findings have also contributed to basic theories about the nature of long-term memory.

The Setting: Laboratory versus Field Research

Another way of classifying studies is by location; the distinction hinges on whether the study occurs inside or outside the lab. The advantage of **laboratory research** is the greater degree of control it allows the researcher: Conditions of the study can be specified more clearly and subjects can be selected and placed into conditions more systematically. On the other hand, the advantage of **field research** is that the research settings more closely match the situations we encounter in daily living and the results of these studies might generalize more easily than lab studies. Although field research is often applied research and lab research is often basic research, you should be aware that some basic research takes place in the field and some applied research takes place in the lab.

A good example of a study that combines both laboratory and field research within a single series of studies is a project by Dutton and Aron (1974). They were interested in testing a hypothesis from a two-factor theory of romantic love: People experiencing strong physical arousal might sometimes misinterpret that arousal as "love" (the two "factors" in the theory are physiological arousal and a cognitive interpretation of the arousal). They created a situation in which male subjects experienced different degrees of what normally would be considered fear, then were exposed to an attractive female. Dutton and Aron hoped to see if part of the arousal connected with fear would be misinterpreted as physical attraction for the female. In the field part of their study, they used two locations over a river in British Columbia, Canada. One was a swaying, 450-foot long suspension bridge featuring a 230-foot drop to the river. The other was a solid wooden bridge just 10 feet over the river. In both locations attractive female confederates approached males and asked them for help with a psychology project on how scenic attractions could influence creativity. Agreeable subjects were given a supposed test for creativity and were also given the female's phone number, in case they had further questions about the project. Compared to males encountered on the "safe" bridge, who presumably experienced little fear, males on the suspension bridge had more sexual imagery in their test results and were more likely to call the female confederate.

These suspension bridge results came out as predicted from two-factor theory, but Dutton and Aron (1974) were rightly concerned that the results could have other interpretations. Perhaps the males on the suspension bridge were just more adventurous types of people than the other males. To account for this possibility, two additional studies were carried out, one of them a laboratory study. Briefly, Dutton and Aron recruited males for a study on the effects of electrical shock on learning. Also in the lab was an attractive female who appeared to be another subject but was actually a confederate. The subjects were led to believe they would be experiencing either strong or mild shock, with the former expected to produce greater physiological arousal than the latter. This apparently happened because Dutton and Aron found that males in the strong shock condition were more physically attracted to the female than those expecting a weak shock. Thus the lab study reinforced the findings of the field study that males could misinterpret fear arousal as physical attraction. Together, the studies supported the two–factor theory of love.

Although the Dutton and Aron (1974) study shows how lab and field research can supplement each other, it is sometimes argued that field research should be preferred because it more closely approximates real life. However, a case can be made that there are more important considerations than similarity to daily living. The social psychologist Eliot Aronson (1992) makes a distinction between mundane and experimental realism. **Mundane realism** refers to how closely the experiment mirrors real-life experiences. **Experimental realism** concerns the extent to which an experiment "has an impact on the subjects, forces them to take the matter seriously, and involves them in the procedures" (Aronson, 1992, p. 411). It's the experimental realism of the study that counts according to Aronson. If subjects are involved in the study and taking it seriously, then the researcher can draw valid conclusions about their behavior. The Milgram experiments on obedience, discussed in the last chapter, don't have much mundane realism—we seldom find ourselves delivering electrical shocks as consequences for someone's failure to learn a word list. Milgram's subjects were clearly involved, however, and his studies have strong experimental realism. We've seen that Milgram's research has been controversial, but there is no question that it shed important light on the factors influencing the general phenomenon of obedience to authority.

One final point about the decision of where to locate a study concerns ethics. Besides increased control, researchers often prefer the laboratory over the field because of problems with informed consent and privacy. In laboratory research, it is relatively easy to stick closely to the ethical code. In the field, however, it is difficult and sometimes impossible to provide informed consent and debriefing and in some situations the research procedures might be considered an invasion of privacy. Consequently, field studies can face a greater challenge from an Institutional Review Board and field researchers must show that the importance of their study justifies some of the risks involved. For a closer look at this question, read ethics Box 3.1, which considers the question of privacy invasions in field research.

Box 3.1

ETHICS—A Matter of Privacy

Unlike the laboratory situation, field research sometimes causes problems with informed consent, freedom to leave the study, debriefing, and invasions of privacy. An interesting study by Silverman (1975) illustrates why researchers are sometimes hesitant about doing field studies. He gave descriptions of ten published field studies to two lawyers and asked them to judge whether the procedures might violate any laws or if there seemed to be any invasion of privacy. The procedures included having a confederate fall down in a subway car to see if anyone would help, leaving cars in different places to see if they would be vandalized, going to shoe stores and trying on many pairs of shoes, and asking for small amounts of money from passersby.

The two lawyers gave almost the *opposite* responses. Lawyer 1 believed that intent was the key factor. The studies were designed for the ultimate good of increasing our knowledge of human behavior and not for the personal gain of the scientist. He believed that if charges were brought against the psychologist, the judge would "seek a balance between degree of annoyance and degree of legitimate purpose" (Silverman, 1975, p. 766). Lawyer 2, however, felt that several of the ten studies would be grounds, not just for a civil suit on the part of subjects not wanting to be subjects (i.e., invasion of privacy), but for criminal action on the grounds of harassment, fraud, criminal trespass, and even disorderly conduct!

Silverman was disconcerted enough by the contrast in responses to bring the descripton of the subway helping behavior study to a judge for his considered opinion about whether civil or criminal charges could be brought. In general, the judge sided with lawyer 1, at least on the issue of criminal charges, but he also pointed out that experiments in the field might have unforeseen consequences that could result in a negligence suit. In short, for the psychologist considering doing research in the field, there are some serous risks that don't occur in the laboratory.

By the way, you might be interested to know that laywer 1 was a successive criminal lawyer accustomed to seeing his clients acquitted. On the other hand, lawyer 2's specialty was in medical law; he usually "defended the legal rights of patients and subjects in medical practice and research" (Silverman, 1975, p. 767).

Asking Empirical Questions

Whether a research project (a) concerns basic or applied problems, or (b) occurs in the lab or the field, it always begins with a question. As you recall from Chapter 1, these are called empirical questions. They have two important features: They must be answerable with data and their terms must be precisely defined.

We've seen in Chapter 1 that questions like "Are people good or evil?" and "When we die, will we be reincarnated?" are interesting and individuals can reach their own conclusions about them and perhaps convince others using Peirce's a priori method. However, the questions are not answerable with the evidence of empirical data. Of course, there are some questions related to good, evil, and reincarnation that *are* empirical questions. These include the following:

✓ What is the relationship between belief in reincarnation and fear of death?
✓ Does belief in the afterlife influence pain thresholds for terminally ill patients?
✓ What is the effect of having an altruistic sibling on one's tendency to donate blood?

Notice that each of these questions allows for data to be collected in one form or another. Before such data can be collected, however, these questions must be refined even further. This task can be referred to as operationalizing the terms in the question. The process of defining terms precisely is the second feature of an empirical question.

Operational Definitions

The term **operationism** originated in the 1920s in physics, with the publication of *The Logic of Modern Physics* (1927) by the Harvard physicist Percy Bridgman. Bridgman argued that the terminology of science must be totally objective and precise and that all concepts should be defined in terms of a set of operations to be performed. These types of definitions came to be called **operational definitions**. The length of some object, for instance, could be defined operationally by a series of agreed upon procedures. In Bridgman's words, the "concept of length is therefore fixed when the operations by which length is measured are fixed; that is, the concept of length involves as much as and nothing more than a set of operations" (Bridgman, 1927, p. 5).

Given the tendency of experimental psychologists to emulate the older sciences, it is not surprising that operationism was embraced by the psychological community when it first appeared. A strict operationism did not last very long in psychology, however, in part because equating a concept with a set of operations creates an arbitrary limitation on the concept. For psychologists the problem with operationism boiled down to how to accomplish it in practice when dealing with such complex psychological phenomena as aggression, creativity, depression, and so on. For the physicist it may not be difficult to agree on a set of operations for measuring the length of a line, but how does one operationalize a concept like aggression? Even if social psychologists can agree that the term refers to a behavior that reflects some intent to harm (Aronson, 1992), exactly what behaviors are to be measured? In the aggression literature, the term has been operationalized as behaviors ranging from the delivery of electrical shocks to horn honking at intersections to pressing a button (making it difficult for someone to complete a task). Are these behaviors measuring the same phenomenon?

Despite this problem with the *strict* use of operational definitions, the concept has been valuable to psychology by forcing researchers to be clear about defining the terms of their studies. This is especially important when you consider that most research in psychology concerns concepts that are open to numerous definitions. For instance, suppose a researcher is interested in the effects of hunger on maze learning. Hunger is a term that can mean several things and is not easily determined in a rat. How can you tell if a rat is hungry? The solution is to operationalize the term. You could operationally define it in terms of a procedure (not feeding the rat for 24 hours—it's reasonable to assume this operation would produce hunger) or in terms of some behavior (creating some situation in which the rat has to work hard to earn food—it's reasonable to assume a nonhungry rat wouldn't perform the task).

One important result of the precision resulting from operational definitions is that it allows for an experiment to be repeated. As you know from Chapters 1 and 2, replication is an important feature of any scientific research. Also, research psychologists are not greatly troubled by the limitations imposed by having to define terms narrowly because in the long run the requirement for precision increases our confidence in the accuracy of theories about human behavior. Psychologists use the concept of **converging operations** to refer to the idea that our understanding of some behavioral phenomenon is increased when a series of investigations, all using slightly different operational definitions and experimental procedures, nonetheless "converge" on a common conclusion. Thus, if the results of several studies on the effects of hunger on maze learning reach the same conclusion, even though each defined hunger with a different set of operations, then confidence is high that a lawful relationship between hunger and maze learning has been established.

Developing precise empirical questions is a skill that takes some practice and involves a gradual narrowing from a broad to a more specific question. These questions can have several origins. They might evolve out of (a) everyday observations or some immediate practical problem, (b) attempts to support or refute some theory, or (c) some unanswered questions from a study just completed.

Developing Research from Observations and Current Problems

Observations can lead to research in two ways. First, the scientist might be wrestling with some research problem and a chance observation of some apparently unrelated event might accidentally provide the key. We've seen in Chapter 1 that creative scientists quickly grasp the significance of these events; the creation of nonsense syllables by Ebbinghaus after encountering Jabberwocky and the invention of rat mazes by Small after hearing about tunnels under porches are two examples that come to mind.

Another type of accidental outcome can occur when something goes wrong in an experiment, such as an apparatus breakdown, leading to some unanticipated re-

Box 3.2

ORIGINS—Serendipity and Edge Detectors

Some of the most important research in this century on the physiology of the visual system was triggered by a serendipitous finding in the Harvard laboratory of David Hubel and Torsten Wiesel. They were investigating the behavior of single neurons at various points in the visual pathway, seeing if the neurons could be made to fire in response to certain stimuli. Their experimental set-up consisted of a screen on which various stimuli could be projected and seen by a cat with its head held stationary and an electrode implanted within a single cell of its visual system. (Even in the 1960s, procedures were precise enough to isolate the activity of single neurons.)

Hubel and Wiesel were hoping the neuron would fire in response to black or white dots that were being projected to the cat's retina. Their first efforts were frustrating:

> The position of the microelectrode tip, relative to the cortex, was unusually stable, so much so that we were able to listen in on one cell for a period of about nine hours. We tried everything short of standing on our heads to get it to fire. (Hubel, 1988, p. 69)

Hubel and Wiesel persevered, however, eventually concentrating on one area of the retina. Passing the dot over that area sometimes produced neuron firing, but not reliably:

sult. The uncreative scientist sighs, tries to fix the problem, and tries the experiment again, while the creative scientist sees the accident as perhaps an opportunity to develop a new research idea. The term **serendipity** is sometimes used to refer to the kind of accidental observations that lead to creative ideas for research. Skinner's experience with extinction curves following an apparatus breakdown (see Chapter 1) is a good example of a serendipitous finding. Another involves the accidental discovery of feature detectors in the brain. This research was part of the basic research mentioned earlier as the foundation upon which Egeland (1975) developed the idea for making features salient in order to teach reading. To examine the origins of the research that led eventually to a Nobel Prize for David Hubel and Torsten Wiesel, read Box 3.2.

A second way for observation to produce research occurs when the scientist simply observes some event that leads to questions about its cause(s). All of us can think of experiences that have led us to reflect about the reasons behind human behavior. We read about a motorist stranded on the highway for hours and wonder why nobody stopped to help. We wonder about the nature of memory when we

> After about five hours of struggle, we suddenly had the impression that the glass [slide] with the dot was occasionally producing a response, but the response seemed to have little to do with the dot. *Eventually we caught on: it was the sharp but faint shadow cast by the edge of the glass as we slid it into the slot that was doing the trick.* We soon convinced ourselves that the edge worked only when its shadow was swept across one small part of the retina and that the sweeping had to be done with the edge in one particular orientation. Most amazing was the contrast between the machine-gun discharge when the orientation of the stimulus was just right and the utter lack of a response if we changed the orientation or simply shined a bright flashlight into the cat's eyes. (Hubel, 1988, pp. 69–70, italics added)

The unexpected discovery that cells ("edge detectors") in the visual system were specialized to respond to edges and contours set at specific orientations was just the beginning. Hubel and Wiesel went on to develop an extensive research program identifying the types of stimuli that would trigger cells at all levels of the visual system; it won them the Nobel Prize in 1981. Their work also reflects the excitement of doing research that was illustrated in Chapter 1 with the work of Gibson and of Skinner. In discussing the years spent studying receptive fields for vision, roughly 1950 to 1980, Hubel wrote:

> I count myself lucky to have been around in that era, a time of excitement and fun. Some of the experiments have been arduous, or so it has often seemed at 4:00 a.m., especially when everything has gone wrong. But 98 percent of the time the work is exhilarating. There is a special immediacy to neurophysiological experiments; we can see and hear a cell respond to the stimuli we use and often realize, right at the time, what the responses imply for brain function. (Hubel, 1988, p. vii).

notice that our grandfather can describe his experiences in World War II quite vividly, yet cannot recall what he did two days ago. We see a news story about an eight-year old concert pianist and wonder about the origins of genius. These observations, combined with the natural curiosity of the researcher, can lead to any number of experiments. One specific example comes from the social psychological research on helping behavior, which developed out of several well-publicized cases of failures to help. Most notable among them was the Kitty Genovese case in 1964, in which a woman was attacked several times and eventually murdered in New York in the full view of numerous witnesses, none of whom even made an anonymous phone call to the police. As John Darley, one of the leading researchers in the area of altruism and helping behavior, recalled later:

> Certainly the precipitating event for us all was the murder of a young lady in New York, the now famous Kitty Genovese case the *New York Times* picked up. A young lady was murdered, but sadly that's a rather typical incident. What was atypical was that thirty-eight people in her apartment building

watched out their windows while this happened, and none of them did much in the way of helping. Bibb [Latané, Darley's co-worker] and I were having dinner together one night shortly thereafter. Everybody was talking about it and so were we. . . . We probably sketched out the experiments on a tablecloth that day. (Krupat, 1975, p. 257)

The Kitty Genovese case led Darley and Latané to conduct a series of experiments showing that unresponsive bystanders aren't simply uncaring; they often assume that someone else will help if there are other people around (Darley & Latané, 1968). The study of helping behavior is now well established, as you can tell by looking at any modern social psychology text, which invariably includes an entire chapter on the topic.

Besides resulting from reflections on everyday observations, research can also derive from specific problems that one may be trying to solve. This is especially true of applied research and of the type of applied research that is called program evaluation research. I'll describe the latter more fully in Chapter 9, but an example will illustrate the point. Suppose a college wants to undertake a freshman studies program. Empirically thinking administrators might establish a research project that compares a group of freshmen in a pilot program with a comparable group of freshmen not in one. The outcome would be evaluated empirically to determine program effectiveness.

Developing Research from Theory

In Chapter 1, there was a brief discussion of the goals of scientific psychology, and one of those goals was said to be finding explanations for human behavior. The process of developing these explanations is, in essence, the process of theory building and theory testing. In this section, we'll look at what a theory is, the reciprocal relationship between theory construction and data collection, and how you can distinguish useful from useless theories.

The Nature of Theory

A **theory** in psychology is a set of statements about some behavioral phenomenon that (a) best summarizes and organizes existing knowledge of the phenomenon, (b) provides a tentative explanation for the phenomenon, and (c) serves as the basis for making predictions about behavior. It is considered to be a working truth, subject to revision pending new findings.

Theories differ in terms of their scope. Some aim to cover broad expanses of behavior and to be general theories—Erikson's stage theory of how our personality is developed and operates is an example. More frequently, however, a theory is narrowly focused on some specific aspects of behavior. For example, in social psychology, equity theory concerns how people relate to each other in terms of rewards, costs, and fairness; in abnormal psychology, learned helplessness theory attempts to account for psychological depression.

As a case example of how theories originate and evolve and to illustrate several important features of theories, let's consider the learned helplessness example in more detail. This is a theory that developed out of animal learning research and has been applied to the human problem of depression. It is also another example of a serendipitous finding: The first experimental demonstration of learned helplessness occurred unexpectedly. Here's how it happened.

Martin Seligman and his colleagues were interested in the transfer of a classically conditioned response to an operant escape situation. First, they conditioned a dog to fear a tone by pairing the tone with shock. This is a Pavlovian conditioning procedure in which a dog is restrained in a device called a Pavlovian hammock. A tone is sounded and the animal is briefly shocked. Before long the tone becomes a conditioned stimulus and the dog will be afraid of it. After the initial conditioning, Seligman placed a dog in a two-sided-chamber called a shuttlebox. He planned to train it to jump from side A to side B when it was shocked on side A and eventually to jump when it heard the tone that had been paired with the shock earlier. To Seligman's surprise, when the animal was shocked in Side A, it did not respond as a dog normally does (i.e., by running around and eventually escaping to side B). Rather, after some brief random activity in side A, the dog

> lay down and quietly whined. After one minute of this we turned the shock off; the dog had failed to cross the barrier and had not escaped from shock. On the next trial, the dog did it again; at first it struggled a bit, and then, after a few seconds, it seemed to give up and to accept the shock passively. On all succeeding trials, the dog failed to escape. (Seligman, 1975, p. 22)

Seligman named the phenomenon "learned helplessness—a learned unwillingness to avoid trauma after experiencing repeated failures to control unavoidable negative events (Seligman, 1975). In the Pavlovian harness, the dog learned that shock could not be avoided, regardless of its efforts. It learned to stop trying. The discovery led Seligman and his colleagues to investigate further and they eventually developed a theory of psychological depression centering on the idea that depression was the result of someone repeatedly experiencing unavoidable and uncontrollable aversive events.

I pointed out earlier that a theory summarizes and organizes knowledge, introduces possible explanations, and provides a basis for making predictions. Let's see how Seligman's theory fits these characteristics.

After making the initial discovery, Seligman set about to investigate the phenomenon more fully, eventually accumulating a great deal of data on the various factors influencing the kind of behavior shown by his dogs. He then built a theory consistent with this growing body of research (i.e., it summarized what was known). The theory's basic components are described by Seligman (1975, p. 47) in the following way:

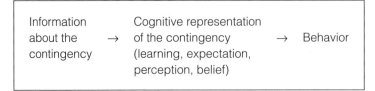

The process begins with the animal acquiring information (through experience) about the relationship (contingency) between its responses and the outcomes of those responses. Seligman proposed that learned helplessness can develop when the animal learns that the outcome is unrelated to the response. This produces a "cognitive representation of the contingency." For example, the individual is said to develop an expectation that what it does and what happens are independent of each other. That is, regardless of its efforts to escape the harness, it will be shocked. This expectation leads to the behavior of helplessness.

The "expectation" is an example of what psychologists call a **construct**. This is a hypothetical factor that cannot be observed directly but is inferred from certain behaviors and assumed to follow from certain circumstances. The construct called expectation was the central explanatory component of Seligman's original theory, "the causal condition for the motivational, cognitive, and emotional debilitation that accompanies helplessness" (Seligman, 1975, p. 48). As an explanatory construct, this expectation could be (a) inferred from the animal's behavior of failing to even attempt an escape and (b) assumed to follow from repeated experiences of having no control over events.

An important feature of any theory is its continual evolution in light of new data. No theory is ever complete and as you will learn in a few pages, Seligman's was no exception. Its development nicely illustrates the reciprocal relationship between theory and data and demonstrates a theory's third attribute—its ability to make predictions that lead to new research. This requires some elaboration.

The Relationship Between Theory and Data

The move from theory to data involves the logical process of **deduction**, reasoning from a set of general statements toward the prediction of some specific event. With regard to theory, deduction takes the form of the scientist reasoning that if my (general) theory is accurate, then (specific) I can predict that event X should occur with some greater than chance probability. The predictions about specific events that are derived this way from a theory are called **hypotheses**, which in general can be considered educated guesses about what should happen under certain circumstances. These hypotheses then lead to the design of a study, which produces the predicted results or doesn't. In the former case, the theory is supported, and in the latter it is not. If supported by a large body of research, confidence is high that the theory is a good one or, to put it another way, you could say that inductive support for the theory increases when individual experiments keep coming out as predicted by the theory. **Induction** is the logical process of reasoning from the specific (individual experimental outcome) to the general (theory).

Of course, experiments don't always come out as expected. The experiment might not be a good test of the hypothesis, it might have some methodological flaws, or it might just be the odd experiment that didn't work. Also, measurements of psychological phenomena are usually imperfect; a failed experiment could be the result of some form of measurement error. Consequently, one unexpected result seldom calls a theory into question. If results repeatedly fail to support the theory, however, confidence in it wanes quickly and the theory may be discarded or radically altered.

Note that in the previous two paragraphs, I have avoided saying things like "a successful prediction 'proves' a theory" and "a bad outcome 'disproves' a theory." This is because scientists hesitate to use the words "prove" and "disprove" when discussing theories and data, both on logical and practical grounds.

On strictly logical grounds, it is impossible to prove a theory to be true, while it is possible to disprove a theory. To understand why requires a brief side trip into the rules of conditional (if . . . then) logic. Suppose I make the assertion that I *always* play golf on Friday. This statement can take the conditional form "If it is Friday, then it is certain that I will be playing golf." Now suppose someone sees me playing golf. Can it be concluded that "therefore it must be Friday?" No, because it could be that I play golf on other days as well (actually, writing this text has created serious problems, golfwise). To conclude that it must be Friday is to commit the logical fallacy known as "affirming the consequent." The situation can be summarized as follows:

Logical fallacy of affirming the consequent:
If it's Friday, then he's playing golf.
He's playing golf.
Therefore, it's Friday.

On the other hand, suppose it is determined that I am not playing golf (and let's continue to assume it is true that I *always* play on Friday). Can you conclude that "therefore it cannot be Friday?" Yes, because it has been asserted that a Friday never passes without golf. In conditional logic this conclusion is known as a "modus tollens." Thus:

Logically correct modus tollens:
If it's Friday, then he's playing golf.
He's not playing golf.
Therefore, it's not Friday.

This distinction between affirming the consequent and a modus tollens can be applied directly to theory testing. The if . . . then statement takes this form: "If theory X is true, then event Y can be expected to occur." Consider learned helplessness theory again. Suppose I make this prediction: "If the learned helplessness theory of depression is true, then therapies that reduce depression in humans should also reduce helplessness behaviors in dogs." I then design a study in which some of the dogs conditioned to be helpless are given antidepressant drugs. My reasoning is that if these drugs help depressed humans, and if learned helplessness is the reason for depression, then drugs that work with depressed humans should work with the dogs. I run the study and discover that the treated dogs begin behaving normally (i.e., they are no longer helpless), an outcome that indeed occurred in a study like this by Porsolt, LePichon, and Jalfre (1977). If I now conclude that learned helplessness theory has been "proven" to be true, I am affirming the consequent:

> If the theory is true, then the antidepressants will work.
> The antidepressants worked.
> Therefore, the theory is true.

I think you can see that the conclusion about the theory being true (i.e., proven) cannot be made. The antidepressants may have worked for some reason having nothing to do with the learned helplessness theory. What can be said, and the careful scientist will never say more than this, is that the experiment "supports" or "is consistent with" the theory.

What if the antidepressants don't work and the animals show no lessening of the learned helplessness? On logical grounds, this would be a modus tollens and the theory could be considered not true (i.e., disproven):

> If the theory is true, then the antidepressants will work.
> The antidepressants didn't work.
> Therefore, the theory is not true.

Please note, however, my earlier comment that when discussing research results, scientists don't usually say things like "prove" and "disprove" on both logical and *practical* grounds. We've seen that to conclude that learned helplessness theory is proven because the drugs worked is to commit the fallacy of affirming the consequent. To conclude the theory is disproven because the drugs failed to work might be technically correct (i.e., a modus tollens) but would be a most imprudent decision to make. As mentioned earlier, single experiments can fail to come out as predicted for any number of reasons and to abandon a theory after just one problematic study is to throw the baby out with the bath water. Theories are indeed discarded in psychology, but only after scientists lose confidence in them; this only occurs after predictions have been repeatedly disconfirmed.

Theories may be supported, and theories may be discarded, but what happens most frequently is that they evolve as research accumulates. This is exactly what happened in the learned helplessness case. A number of studies with human subjects forced a reformulation of the theory to take additional cognitive factors into account (Abramson, Seligman, & Teasdale, 1978). For example, one feature of the new version is a construct called "explanatory style." Those experiencing failures who exhibit a pessimistic explanatory style are more likely to show learned helplessness effects than those who fail yet maintain optimistic styles. Pessimists "blame themselves and expect failure to recur over a longer period of time and in more situations" (Seligman & Schulman, 1986). Optimists blame circumstances, not themselves, and although they may be just as deluded as pessimists, they don't get depressed.

Like the original theory, the revised version makes predictions that must be tested with data. An example is an interesting field study using life insurance sales agents (Seligman & Schulman, 1986), chosen in part because they experience failure much more often than success. The agents were evaluated with a question-naire that measured explanatory style; the researchers found that agents with optimistic styles were more productive (i.e., sold 37% more policies over 2 years) and were about twice as likely to stay with the job than were more pessimistic agents.

Attributes of Good Theories

Some theories are judged by history to be more effective than others. Those judged to be good are characterized by several features. The most obvious one is that they advance knowledge by generating a great deal of research, a trait that clearly can be applied to learned helplessness theory. Two other attributes of good theories, falsification and parsimony, require some elaboration.

Falsification

A popular misconception about theories is that the ultimate goal is to produce one that will be so good that it will explain every possible outcome. In fact, a theory that appears to explain everything is actually a seriously flawed theory. To under-stand why, we need to look at an approach to testing theories first advocated by philosopher of science Karl Popper (1959) and clearly implied in what was said earlier about "proving" and "disproving" theories.

According to Popper, science proceeds by setting up theories and then attempt-ing to disprove or falsify them. Theories that are continually resistant to **falsifica-tion** are accepted as possibly true (with the emphasis on "possibly"). Recall my earlier comment that confidence in a theory increases as inductive support accu-mulates. This confidence never becomes absolute, however, because of the limits of induction. One hundred specific examples of birds could be found that would in-ductively support the conclusion "All birds can fly," yet it takes just a single nonfly-ing bird (a kiwi, for example) to destroy the general conclusion. Similarly, one hundred predictions derived from a theory could support a theory, but one dis-confirmation could disprove it, by way of modus tollens reasoning. Of course, we've already seen that on practical grounds, one disconfirmation won't lead to a wholesale abandonment of a theory. Nonetheless, Popper's argument suggests that disconfirmation carries greater weight than confirmation. At the very least, it re-quires that disconfirmations be investigated thoroughly.

If Popper is right, then theories have to be stated in such a way that the hy-potheses derived from them are capable of disproof. That is, there must be some possible outcome to the experiment that could disprove the hypothesis. In prac-tice, this requires the kind of precision in defining terms that was mentioned ear-lier, but it also requires that theories take the risk of being falsified.

A good example of a theory that failed the criterion of falsifiability is the nine-teenth-century pseudoscience of phrenology.[1] This was the first serious attempt to

---

[1] For more on phrenology in particular and the difference between science and pseudoscience in general, see Chapter 12.

assign specific functions to clearly identified areas of the brain, but it was eventually found to have picked the wrong functions and located them in the wrong places. The core of the theory was that the brain could be divided into a number of so-called faculties (e.g., different types of abilities and personality characteristics), that each faculty was associated with a different part of the brain, and that the strength of a faculty would be reflected proportionately in brain size (Boring, 1950). The strength of faculties could be measured by examining skull contour. So a person with a protruding skull in the area just above both ears would be said to have a great deal of the faculty of "destructiveness." Why destructiveness? Because a number of murderers and boxers (they both like to destroy things) had protruding skulls in that area.

At first glance, this seems to be a theory that would be easy to falsify: just find a murderer with a skull that is very narrow above the ears. If such a person were found, however, a phrenologist would discount the apparent disproof by pointing out that while the person might indeed be deficient in destructiveness, the problem was more than offset by other faculties that were strong, such as amativeness (sex drive), combativeness, firmness, and imitation (perhaps he's a copycat murderer). The point is that every possible type of person could be explained *after the fact* by some unique combination of faculties. While this might sound ideal at first glance, it is easy to see why the theory fails as soon as you ask it to make a single prediction. If Fred has a large faculty of destructiveness, will he be destructive? Maybe, maybe not. By providing for all possible outcomes, the theory failed to predict *any* single outcome.

A problem with Popper's falsification approach is that it doesn't take into account the psychology of doing research, in the sense that most researchers in the midst of their programs of research develop a sense of ownership and tend to look for evidence in support of their theories. Experimenters clearly recognize the importance of a falsification strategy, however. Even though they always hope to find support for their own theories, researchers are always trying to design experiments that rule out one explanation or another.

A typical strategy is to take some phenomenon that might have several competing explanations for it and run a series of studies that systematically rules out one explanation at a time while providing support for a remaining explanation. In Seligman's learned helplessness studies with dogs, for example, there were typically two treatment groups. In the first, dogs received shocks in the Pavlov hammock but could turn them off by pressing their nose against a panel. In the second group, each animal was paired with a dog from group 1 in the sense that it received exactly the same number of shocks, lasting the same amount of time, and in the same pattern, but could not turn them off. This, of course, is the situation presumed to produce learned helplessness. But could it be that just simply being shocked was enough to create helplessness? No. The fact that the dogs in group 1 showed no learned helplessness enabled Seligman to *rule out* (i.e., falsify) the idea that the helplessness effects were just due to the shock received.

A classic example of a falsification strategy involves the investigation of a famous horse with alleged mathematical and reading abilities. Take a moment and read Box 3.3, which chronicles the case of Clever Hans, a horse with intellectual skills more apparent than real.

Box 3.3

CLASSIC STUDIES—Disproof and Der Kluge Hans

In Berlin, Germany, at the turn of the century, the best show in town, except perhaps for the recently opened subway, could be found in the courtyard adjacent to a stable on Griebenow Street. There the spectator would encounter a horse (Figure 3.3) that appeared to have remarkable intellectual powers. When asked by his owner, Wilhelm von Osten, to multiply 4 × 4, the horse would tap his front hoof 16 times, then stop. Adding, subtracting, multiplying, and dividing didn't challenge the remarkable animal, known to the German public as Clever ("Kluge" in German) Hans. Even fractions and decimals were no problem. When asked to add 2/5 and 1/2, the horse would tap out 9 for the numerator and 10 for the denominator (Sanford, 1914). The horse could also read and spell, using a system of tapping that translated letters into numbers.

If you've been developing your scientific thinking skills, I assume you're a bit skeptical about this horse which read and did math better than some of your friends. Skeptics existed back then too and one of them, Oskar Pfungst, provides us with a wonderful example of Popper's falsification strategy. That is, Pfungst set out to see if

FIGURE 3.3   Clever Hans at work.

he could rule out intelligence as an explanation for the behavior of the horse, while at the same time trying to find a more reasonable explanation for what the horse was actually doing.

Although a special commission including scientists and animal trainers concluded that von Osten was not a fraud, Pfungst suspected that the owner might be giving the animal some subtle cues about how to respond. He reasoned that if that was the case, then the horse would be correct only if the questioner knew the answer. The horse's special skills in math might be related to the fact that von Osten was a mathematician.

To test the hypothesis that the horse wouldn't know the answer unless the questioner did was easy. Pfungst simply set up several tests in which the questioner knew the correct answer some of the times but did not know the answer other times. For example, Pfungst had questioners hold up a card with a number on it. When the questioner was allowed to see the number before holding it up, the horse tapped out the number correctly 98% of the time. However, if the questioner was not allowed to look at the card before the horse did, Hans was correct only 8% of the time (Fernald, 1984). So much for mathematical ability. In a series of similar tests, Pfungst was able to rule out (falsify) the idea that Hans could use language.

Thus, Hans was clearly getting information about the correct answer from the person asking the question. How this occurred was still a puzzle that was eventually solved by Pfungst. To make a long story short, he was able to determine that the horse was responding to very slight visual cues from the questioner. Whenever someone would ask a question, that person would bend forward ever so slightly without really being aware of it. Hans learned that the movement was a signal to begin tapping. When Hans would reach the correct answer, the person would straighten up, again just slightly and without awareness, but enough to signal Hans that it was time to stop.

The Clever Hans case illustrates two other points besides the falsification strategy of Pfungst. By showing that the horse's abilities were not due to a high level of intelligence but could be explained in terms of the simpler process of the horse learning to respond to two sets of visual cues (when to start; when to stop), Pfungst provided a more *parsimonious* explanation of the horse's behavior. Second, if von Osten could be giving subtle cues that influenced behavior, then perhaps experimenters in general might subtly influence the behavior of subjects when the experimenter knows what the outcome should be. We'll return to this point in Chapter 6; it's an example of *experimenter bias*.

Parsimony

Besides being stated so as to be potentially falsified, good theories are also **parsimonious**. This means ideally that they include the minimum number of constructs and assumptions that are necessary to adequately explain and predict. If two theories are equal in every way except that one is more parsimonious, then the simpler one is generally preferred.

In psychology, the idea originated with the late nineteenth-century British comparative psychologist Conwy Lloyd Morgan. He lived at a time when the theory of evolution was prompting naturalists to look for evidence of mental processes in animals (such as intelligence in horses like Clever Hans), in order to support the Darwinian notion of continuity between species. This search produced a number of excessive claims, including the notion that moths approach candles because they are curious and ants are in the "habit of keeping domestic pets" (Romanes, 1886, p. 83). Morgan argued that animal behavior should be explained in the simplest terms possible. His famous statement, which came to be known as Lloyd Morgan's Canon, was that "[i]n no case may we interpret an action as the outcome of the exercise of a higher psychical faculty, if it can be interpreted as the outcome of the exercise of one which stands lower in the psychological scale" (Morgan, 1903, p. 53). Instead of attributing reasoning to the dog that lifts a latch to get out of the yard, Morgan would explain the behavior more simply (i.e., more parsimoniously) as an example of trial and error learning.

In psychology, a good illustration of parsimony is a comparison of Freudian and behaviorist theories about why 4-year-old boys imitate their fathers. The Freudian explanation requires acceptance of a large number of assumptions and constructs, including the ideas of the unconscious control of behavior, infantile sexuality, Oedipal feelings, castration anxiety, repression, and identification with the aggressor. Briefly, the young boy is said to sexually desire the mother, but fears being castrated by the father if the desire is discovered. Consequently, he represses the desire into the unconscious, and identifies with the aggressive father. Learning theory simply assumes that (a) behaviors that are reinforced will tend to occur again in similar situations in the future and (b) parents are likely to notice and reinforce imitative behaviors. Learning theory is clearly more parsimonious than its Freudian counterpart in this instance, while still providing an adequate explanation and a basis for predicting further outcomes.

Developing Research from Other Research

To some extent, this final section on developing ideas for research is an extension of what was described earlier about the continuing relationship between theory and data, but research deriving from other research occurs even when theory development is not the prime focus. Sometimes researchers simply wish to investigate some phenomenon in order to discover regular and predictable relationships between variables (i.e., to discover laws of behavior) and are not very concerned about theory building. Skinner's operant conditioning research (Chapter 10) falls in this category.

I believe the most common sources of ideas for research in psychology are unanswered questions from a study just completed. Psychologists do not conduct individual experiments that are separate from each other; they build **programs of research**, a series of interrelated studies. You won't find someone doing a study on helping behavior, then switching to do a study on aggression. Rather, researchers become involved in a specific area of investigation and conduct a series of investigations in that area that may last years and may extend to many other researchers with an interest in the topic. The conclusion of one project invariably leads to another because while experiments answer some empirical questions, they also raise new ones. Seligman's work on learned helplessness is a good example of a research program.

One unmistakable indication of how research leads to other research can be seen by scanning any issue of a recent journal of psychology. Look at the authors of a specific publication, then look to see if those same names appear in the reference sections of the publication as authors of similar studies. As an illustration, in the first three issues of the *Journal of Experimental Psychology: Learning, Memory, and Cognition* for 1992, there are 52 different research articles. The authors of the articles reference other work by themselves in 48 of the 52 articles. Although some of this may be a normal human tendency to cite one's own work, for the most part it reflects the fact that researchers simply don't do single experiments—they establish systematic programs of interconnected experiments. Experiments lead to more experiments.

Research Teams and the 'What's Next?' Question

If you asked research psychologists to describe their day-to-day existence, you would get a wide variety of answers, but one general principle would emerge: Few researchers work by themselves. Rather, they assemble **research teams** within their laboratories. Typically, the team will include a senior researcher, Dr. X., several graduate students who are working for Dr. X., and perhaps one or two highly motivated undergraduates who have convinced Dr. X. of their interest and willingness to work odd hours and perhaps clean animal cages. This team will have several experiments going at once and team members will spend long hours in the lab collecting data and analyzing it while drinking coffee. Also, they will often find themselves sitting around a table in the greasy spoon across the street, discussing research projects in various stages of completion (and drinking more coffee). When discussing completed projects, they will use what could be called "what's next?" thinking: Given the outcome of this study, what should we do next? At some point in the conversation, someone will get an idea and ask the single most frequently heard question in conversations among research psychologists: "What do you think would happen if we did this?" The "this" refers to the idea for a study and the "what do you think would happen?" is a request for predictions about the outcome. The question will lead to a lively discussion in which the group will refine the idea or perhaps decide it is unworkable and think about the next "what next?" question that comes up. If the idea is pursued, some procedure will be created, tried in the next few days in trial runs that are sometimes called **pilot studies**, refined further (additional coffee involved here), and eventually shaped into a tightly designed study that is then completed.

Thus, research in psychology (a) usually involves a continuous series of interrelated studies; (b) is often a communal effort, combining the creativity and critical analysis of several people who are immersed in the same narrowly specialized research area; and (c) is very unstructured in its early creative stages. This lack of structure was noted some time ago by a panel of distinguished experimental psychologists, brought together in 1958 by the Education and Training Board of the APA and charged with making recommendations about graduate training in experimental psychology. They described "the process of doing research—that is, of creating and building a science of psychology—[as] a rather informal, often illogical and sometimes messy-looking affair. It includes a great deal of floundering around in the empirical world, sometimes dignified by names like 'pilot studies' and 'exploratory research'" (Taylor, Garner, & Hunt, 1959, p. 169).

One fairly recent development in "what's next?" question-asking is the extension of the concept of a research team far beyond the confines of a single laboratory. It is quite common in the computer age for researchers on different campuses to communicate by way of electronic mail (e-mail). The digital conversations often include descriptions of a proposed method preceded by the famous question: "what do you think would happen if we did this?" Although separated by thousands of miles, researchers can nonetheless carry on the kind of informal discussion that leads to creative research. They can even drink coffee while communicating electronically.

Replication and Extension

Many studies that follow upon the heels of completed studies will be similar enough to be considered replications, but different enough so that they are not exact duplicates of prior research. In other words, a distinction can be made between replication and extension. As research psychologists use the term in general, **replication** refers to a study that duplicates some or all of the procedures of some prior study. **Extension**, on the other hand, resembles a prior study and usually replicates part of it, but goes further and adds at least one additional feature. Furthermore, in studies that are extensions, the term **partial replication** is often used to refer to that part of the study which replicates some earlier work. Sometimes the term "exact" or "direct" replication is used to describe a point for point duplication of some other study.

Exact replication was used as a training procedure in Pavlov's famous laboratory in Russia. Whenever new workers came into the lab, their first experiment would be to replicate some previous study. Thus, Pavlov had a continuous system of checking on results while new researchers developed the skills to carry on extensions of earlier findings. In general, however, exact replications seldom occur, for the simple reason that researchers don't get promoted and tenured if all they do is repeat what someone else has done. Normally, exact replications only occur when serious questions are raised about some finding. For instance, if several researchers are trying to extend some finding and their studies include a partial replication and the replication fails to come out as expected, it might be necessary to go back to the original study and do an exact replication to determine if it really was a reliable finding. And as you recall from the last chapter, failures to replicate sometimes lead to the discovery of scientific fraud.

A study by Marean, Werner, and Kuhl (1992) is a good example of how research can replicate and extend at the same time. These researchers were interested in whether infants as young as 2 months could categorize different vowel sounds. The study was an extension of earlier work showing that 6-month olds had the ability. Marean et al. wondered if the ability developed even earlier than age 6. Their study tested 2- and 3-month-old children and as a partial replication, included 6-month olds as well. Basically, the study showed that as young as 2 months, children would show different reactions to two different vowels spoken by the same person, but would not react differently to two different persons speaking the same vowel. That is, they were discriminating by the general category of a vowel sound, not by the individual acoustic features of two different voices.

Reviewing the Literature

Research projects do not develop in a vacuum. The psychologists involved in a program of research are thoroughly familiar, not just with the work of their own lab, but also with the work done in other labs doing similar research. Those deriving experiments from theory are likewise familiar with the research concerning the theory in question. Even the experimenter who gets an idea for a study after making a casual observation often makes that observation within the context of some related knowledge or some problem at hand. How is a knowledge of the literature acquired?

One answer would be for you, as researcher-in-training, to go regularly to the library and read the articles in the current journals of psychology. The impossibility of this strategy becomes immediately apparent to one who tries, however. There are hundreds of different journals that publish psychology-related material and the APA publishes more than 20 different journals itself. In 1991, there were more than 34,000 different items listed in *Psychological Abstracts*, with each item being a journal article, technical report, doctoral dissertation, book, or chapter from an edited book. So the brute force method of systematically plowing through everything clearly fails.

Alternatively, you could organize a more intelligent search of the literature, and this section of the chapter describes some of the tools available to you. They include the *Thesaurus of Psychological Index Terms*, *Psychological Abstracts*, and various computerized databases from PsycINFO Services.

The Thesaurus of Psychological Index Terms

The *Thesaurus of Psychological Index Terms* (1994) was first published in 1974 and is in its seventh edition as of this writing. It provides an extensive cross-referencing of terms found in the subject index of *Psychological Abstracts* and which serve as key terms for computerized database searches. To see how it works, refer to Figure 3.4, which reproduces a portion of page 190 of the 1991 *Thesaurus*. Suppose you are doing a project on schizophrenia. The first thing to notice is that "Schizophrenia" is printed in boldface, while some other terms, such as "Schizophrenia (Disorganized Type)" are not. Boldfacing identifies terms as "postable," meaning they will be found as subject headings in *Psychological Abstracts*. One advantage of the *Thesaurus*, then, is that it saves you from finding out the hard way that a term you're looking up in an *Abstract* subject index isn't used.

```
Schizophrenia 87
PN  13140                                        SC  45440
    UF    Chronic Schizophrenia
          Dementia Praecox
          Process Schizophrenia
          Pseudopsychopathic Schizoprenia
          Reactive Schizophrenia
          Schizophrenia (Residual Type)
          Simple Schizophrenia
    B     Psychosis 87
    N     Acute Schizophrenia 73
          Catatonic Schizophrenia 73
          Childhood Schizophrenia 87
          Hebephrenic Schizophrenia 73
          Paranoid Schizophrenia 87
          Undifferentiated Schizophrenia 73
    R     Anhedonia 86
          Catalepsy 73
          Expressed Emotion 91
          Fragmentation (Schizophrenia) 73
          Schizoid Personality 73
          Schizotypal Personality 91
Schizophrenia (Disorganized Type)
    Use   Hebephrenic Schizophrenia
Schizophrenia (Residual Type)
    Use   Schizophrenia
Schizophreniform Disorder
    Use   Acute Schizophrenia
```

FIGURE 3.4   Portion of p. 190 from a Thesaurus.

Notice that the listing for schizophrenia includes several other terms that are classified with the abbreviations **UF**, **B**, **N**, and **R**. The latter three abbreviations refer to other postable listings that are **B**roader, **N**arrower, and **R**elated to the postable term of schizophrenia. This gives you several places besides just schizophrenia to look at in subject indexes. The UF means Used For and the terms in the category are all nonpostable. So if you looked up chronic schizophrenia in a subject index you wouldn't find it. Note that if a term is classified as UF, the term is also listed in the Thesaurus, but it is not boldfaced. The person looking up "Schizophrenia (Residual Type)" in the *Thesaurus* is told to "Use Schizophrenia."

The *Thesaurus* provides two advantages, then. First, you are prevented from wasting time looking up nonpostable terms in a subject index or asking a computerized data base for terms it doesn't have. Second, you acquire a full listing of postable terms before you begin systematically looking through the abstracts or start a computer search.

Psychological Abstracts

To continue with the example of schizophrenia, suppose after looking at the *Thesaurus* you decide to concentrate on "Paranoid Schizophrenia." Your next step is to begin searching either *Psychological Abstracts*, which are hard bound and on the shelves of your library, or a computerized database. If you are using the *Abstracts*, your first step is to find one of the volumes labeled "Subject Index." In 1991, there are two of these, one for postable terms from A through L, and the other for the rest. In this second index volume, you would find "Paranoid Schizophrenia" listed on page 1415, part of which is duplicated in Figure 3.5. As you can see, there are a number of separate studies listed, each described briefly in two or three lines—not very much information, but enough to help you decide if you want to investigate further. Each of these listings has a number after it, which is its assigned abstract number. The actual abstracts are assigned in this numerical sequence. From the subject index, you should create a list of abstract numbers you wish to examine further.

Suppose the item about "fear of AIDS,. . .," abstract number 12784 (highlighted in Figure 3.5), is on your list. You now turn to the actual volumes holding the abstracts (there are three for 1991) and find 12784. This will be found on page 1,276, part of which is reproduced in Figure 3.6. As you can see, the abstract listing includes further information about the study, including the reference and a summary, which is an exact duplicate of the abstract that is printed at the beginning of the article published in the journal *Psychopathology*.

There's a lot of work involved in doing a search through the *Abstracts*, but there are some strategies that will save you some time. First, always start with the most

---

Paranoid Schizophrenia

affect in early memories, 20–60 yr olds with borderline personality disorder vs paranoid schizophrenia vs neurotic character pathology, 15360

auditory discrimination & attention & memory & learning in dichotic listening procedure, paranoid schizophrenic 16–55 yr olds, 1397

auditory EP P300 & quantitative EEG & SPECT findings, 19 yr old female with chronic paranoid schizophrenia, 30568

azepine derivative, psychotic symptomatology, 24–64 yr olds with paranoid schizophrenia, 16377

clozapine & cimetidine vs rantidine, plasma clozapine & gastrointestinal side effects, 24 yr old male with paranoid schizophrenia, case report, 19324

clozapine induced neuroleptic malignant syndrome, female 26 yr old with paranoid schizophrenia & bulimia & anorexia nervosa, case report, 25269

content & frequency of delusions & hallucinations, cocaine abusing vs paranoid schizophrenic 18–62 yr olds, 33267

cortisol vs epinephrine vs norepinephrine vs testosterone vs free thyroxine levels, patients with paranoid schizophrenia vs bipolar manic disorder, diagnostic implications, 24467

dantrolene, lethal catatonia, 57 & 63 yr old females with bipolar disorder or paranoid schizophrenia, 19305

drug therapy, 27 yr old paranoid schizophrenic male with history of neuroleptic malignant syndrome, case report, 28345

DSM-II vs DSM-III-R prognosis, paranoid vs nonparanoid schizophrenic patients, 18551

episodic water intoxication & stereotypic behavior changes, 46 yr old male with paranoid schizophrenia, case report, 24392

fear of AIDS, paranoid schizophrenic 23 yr old male, Israel, case report, 12784

Grave's disease, male paranoid schizophrenic 57 yr old, case report, 18655

onset of delusions of substitution concurrent with detection of diabetes mellitus, 62 yr old male with chronic paranoid schizophrenia, case report, 27423

FIGURE 3.5   Portion of p. 1415—subject index of Abstracts.

12784. Spivak, Baruch; Mester, R.; Babur, I.; Mark, M. et al. (Geha Psychiatric Hosp, Beilinson Medical Ctr, Petach-Tikva, Israel) **Prolonged fear of AIDS as an early symptom of schizophrenia.** *Psychopathology*, 1990(May–Jun), Vol 23(3), 181–184.—Fear of acquired immune deficiency syndrome (AIDS) is becoming a symptom of a wide range of psychiatric disorders. A case is presented of a 23-yr-old Israeli male who developed a pathological preoccupation with having AIDS and underwent various unnecessary medical procedures until he was diagnosed as having a paranoid schizophrenic disorder. The S refused all blood tests and, at follow-up, was still living in fear and social isolation. With the high media profile that AIDS has achieved in recent years, it is expected that AIDS has become the object of psychopathological processes. Discussion focuses on diagnostic questions and on issues related to primary and secondary psychiatric prevention.

FIGURE 3.6   Portion of p. 1276—Abstracts.

recent years and work backwards. Second, be on the lookout for listings in the subject index that include the word "review." This will be an article that summarize lots of other articles. Take special note of articles in the journal *Psychological Bulletin* and chapters in the book series *Annual Review of Psychology*. Both publish long literature reviews that are potential gold mines for you because they will themselves contain extensive reference lists. In general, once you begin finding good articles on your topic of choice, you can put away the *Abstracts* and use the reference sections of the articles themselves as a means of further search. A third strategy is to use the author index. If you know that a specific researcher is active in the area you're searching (remember, researchers conduct programs of research), you could look for additional references to him or her in the author index.

Finally, abstracts from some general topic areas are compiled four times a year and published separately under the name of "PsycSCAN." There are separate quarterly *PsycSCAN* publications in the areas of clinical, applied, and developmental psychology, psychoanalysis, learning disorders and mental retardation, and applied experimental and engineering psychology.

Computerized Databases

In recent years, it has become possible to speed up literature searches considerably by using computerized databases. Even if your library doesn't have the ones I'll be describing, it probably has some general purpose ones that you have used. *Academic Abstracts* and *InfoTrac* are two common examples.

The American Psychological Association has compiled all of its search capabilities under the general umbrella of what are called "PsycINFO Services." These include the print publications of the *Thesaurus*, *Psychological Abstracts*, and *PsycSCAN*, and several different methods of conducting computerized searches: *PsycINFO*, *PsycLIT*, *PsycFILE*, and *PASAR*.

PsycINFO is an on-line service, meaning that the information in the database is

TABLE 3.1 *Comparing PsycINFO Services*

	PsycINFO	PsycLIT	PsycFILE
Format	On-line	CD-ROM	On-Line
Main coverage	journals, books, book chapters, dissertations, technical reports	journals, books, book chapters	journals
Coverage dates	1967–present	journals, 1974–present books 1987–present	1974–present
Updates	monthly	quarterly	quarterly
Availability	vendors (BRS, DIALOG/ Data-Star, etc.)	subscription, (e.g., Silver Platter, CD Plus, EBSCO)	human resource information network
Cost	variable	fixed	variable
Equipment needed	terminal or PC, modem + software	CD-ROM drive, PC or Macintosh	terminal or PC, modem + software

Source: PsycINFO services brochure, American Psychological Association.

not physically in your library but is accessed through a telephone linkage between your library's computers and *PsycINFO*. To use it requires that you tell the system to use specific search terms; in particular you will need to use postable terms again. Thus, as was the case for an *Abstracts* search, your first step should be to use the *Thesaurus*. *PsycINFO* will print out full references to articles it finds for you as well as the abstracts for those articles. In covers the literature found in over 1,300 journals.

PsycLIT does not cover quite as many sources as *PsycINFO* (it omits unpublished doctoral dissertations for instance), but it provides virtually the same searching capability and it is more convenient. It is in a different format, however. *PsycLIT* information is stored on CD-ROM discs located on site in your library. *PsycLIT* is better costwise if a lot of searches are being done—it comes at a fixed cost, whereas *PsycINFO* charges per search. *PsycFILE* is a specialized database for those in human resource management and covers areas such as personnel management, employee selection, and organizational behavior. It is a subset of *PsycINFO*. Table 3.1 summarizes the features of these three services.

Most schools will subscribe to either *PsycINFO* or *PsycLIT*. However, if your school has neither, you can have a search completed for you through *PASAR* (**P**sycINFO **A**ssisted **S**earch **A**nd **R**etrieval). You simply fill out a form and the *PASAR* staff will do a search for you (not out of the kindess of their hearts, of course; plan on spending about $60 to $80 per search.)

One final service that *PsycINFO* provides is called *PsycSOURCE*, which will send you the full text of any document that will be found in the *PsycINFO* database since January 1988. This will run you about $10 per document (you can probably do better through your library's interlibrary loan program though).

Your instructor will be able to tell you what is available within the psychology department or in the library and your librarians will be glad to help you as well. Happy searching!

You are now in a position to (a) discover what research is available in any area of psychology, and (b) develop some ideas for doing research in psychology. The next chapter introduces you to some of the basics about the data you will encounter in psychological research.

Chapter Review

Glossary Fill-Ins

1. An example of _____ research would be a study designed to determine how different levels of illumination in the work environment influence worker productivity.

2. According to Aronson, an experiment with _____ realism has greater value than one that only has _____ realism.

3. Near the end of Chapter 1, you learned how Skinner produced his first extinction curves when the food magazine broke; this illustrates _____.

4. Hypotheses are derived from theories through the logical process of _____.

5. A dog's escape behavior could be the result of trial and error learning or it could be an example of a form of sophisticated reasoning on the part of the dog. The first explanation is more _____ than the second.

6. A researcher is trying to design a study that would rule out the idea that a horse was capable of solving problems in mathematics. This is an example of what Popper would call a _____ strategy.

Multiple Choice

1. Compared with field research, which of the following is true about laboratory research?
   a. Laboratory research achieves greater mundane realism.
   b. Laboratory research achieves greater experimental realism.
   c. Laboratory research achieves a greater degree of control over the conditions of the experiment.
   d. Because all laboratory research is basic research, it is often criticized for being artificial.

2. A researcher interested in studying frustration creates a situation in which children play with desirable toys for a time, then a barrier is placed between them and the toys. The children's behaviors are videotaped and later analyzed. Which of the following is true?

    a. The procedure represents the researcher's attempt to operationally define frustration.

    b. This is a good example of why operational definitions cannot be created for unobservable constructs like frustration.

    c. This is a good example of converging operations.

    d. Asking how children will respond to frustration is not an empirical question.

3. One of the predictions from learned helplessness theory is that if animals have prior experience with successful escape, they will be less susceptible to showing the typical helplessness behavior after they encounter inescapable shock. Suppose you did a study to test this idea. Which of the following outcomes is an example of the fallacy of affirming the consequent?

    a. Dogs with prior escapes don't show helplessness later; therefore the theory is proven.

    b. Dogs with prior escapes don't show helplessness later; this outcome supports the theory.

    c. Dogs with prior escapes do show helplessness later; this outcome disproves the theory.

    d. Dogs with prior escapes do show helplessness later; this outcome supports the theory.

4. Exact replications

    a. Never occur.

    b. Are sometimes triggered by repeated failures of a partial replication.

    c. Are illustrated in the chapter by a study concerning infants' vowel identification.

    d. Are quite common; nobody really believes a study until it has been replicated several dozen times.

5. Why would you want to use the *Thesaurus of Psychological Index Terms?*

    a. You wouldn't; with computerized searches, there's no need for it any more.

    b. It gives you references to major reviews of the literature.

    c. It enables you to improve your writing by giving you synonyms for words.

    d. It gives you a full set of "postable" terms that could be broader than, narrower then, or related to the term you have in mind.

Applications Exercises

Exercise 3.1.—What's Next?

Go to the library and find the most recent copies of journals reporting research in psychology. Find an article that looks interesting, read it, and answer the following:

1. What were the basic findings of the study?
2. Given these findings, think of two different ideas that you could present to a hypothetical research team that would answer the following questions:
   a. Given the results of this study, what should be investigated in the next one?
   b. What do you think would happen if we did this ("this" = one of the two ideas)?

Exercise 3.2.—Creating Operational Definitions

For the following proverbs, decide how you might operationalize each of the key constructs in order to investigate whether the proverbs are true or not. Of course, your first step is to decide what the general meaning of each proverb is (i.e., don't take them literally).

1. Birds of a feather flock together.
2. Too many cooks spoil the broth.
3. A stitch in time saves nine.
4. Opposites attract.
5. Out of sight, out of mind.

Exercise 3.3.—Using the *Thesaurus* and the *Abstracts*

Go to the *Thesaurus of Psychological Index Terms* and *Psychological Abstracts* and do the following:

a. Identify some topic that is of interest to you and is a postable term.
b. Identify any other postable terms that are **R**, **B**, or **N** terms.
c. Use the subject index of the most recent *Abstracts* you can find and search for five articles that cluster around a single subtopic.
d. Find the five abstracts and write down the references using APA format (this is described in Appendix A and/or can be inferred from the references at the end of this book).

Exercise 3.4.—Confirmation Bias

We've seen in this chapter that one strategy used by scientists is to arrive at some empirical conclusion by ruling out or *falsifying* alternative explanations. But this strategy is difficult to develop as the following exercise from Wason and Johnson-Laird (1972, pp. 172–73) shows.

Imagine that you are holding four cards; each has a letter printed on one side and a number printed on the other. As you look at the cards, this is what you see:

E   K   4   7

You must decide which cards have to be turned over in order to determine whether the following rule is true or not:

If a card has a vowel on one side, then it has an even number on the other side.

Which cards would you turn over?
In falsification terms, which cards, if turned over, would falsify the statement?

CHAPTER 4

Measurement, Sampling, and Data Analysis

Chapter Overview

- ### What to Measure — Varieties of Behavior

  The behaviors measured in psychological research range from overt actions to self-reports to physiological recordings; the measures chosen for a particular study will depend on the manner in which the study's constructs are operationally defined. In many areas of psychological research, standard measures have developed over the years (e.g., reaction time).

- ### Evaluating Measures

  High-quality measures of behavior are both reliable and valid. To be reliable is to be repeatable and low in measurement error. Measures are valid if they actually measure what they are supposed to measure. Confidence in validity increases if a measure makes sense (face validity) and predicts future outcomes well (predictive validity). Construct validity accrues when a research program investigating relationships between the construct being measured and related phenomena result in consistent and predictable outcomes.

- ## Scales of Measurement

  Data for psychological research can be classified into four different scales of measurement: nominal, ordinal, interval, and ratio. In a nominal scale, numbers are category labels and the frequency of scores per category is the main interest. Ordinal scales occur when events are placed in rank order. Interval and ratio scales both assume equal intervals between quantitatively increasing scores; only ratio scales have a true zero point, however.

- ## Who to Measure — Sampling

  If the goal of research is to learn something about a specific population, then the sample selected for study should be representative of that population and should be formed through some type of probability sampling: simple random sampling, stratified sampling, or cluster sampling. For most research in psychology, however, the goal is to identify systematic relationships between variables and nonprobability sampling is both customary and adequate. Most psychological research uses a form of nonprobability sampling called convenience sampling.

- ## Statistical Analysis

  Statistical analysis is an essential tool for understanding the meaning of research outcomes. Descriptive statistics are calculated for the sample of participants in a particular study. They provide a summary of results and include measures of central tendency, variability, and association. Inferential statistics allow decisions about whether the results are due to chance factors or appear to reflect some genuine relationship that can be applied to the larger population.

All research in psychology involves measuring the actions of individuals participating in the study. In this chapter, we'll look at what kinds of events are measured in psychological research, the factors determining whether these measures are of any value, the different scales of measurement, and the methods for selecting the individuals who will provide these measures through their participation in a study. This chapter also presents the important distinction between descriptive and inferential statistics, and the logic of hypothesis testing.

What To Measure — Varieties of Behavior

The variety of behaviors measured by experimental psychologists is virtually unlimited. What is measured ranges from overt behaviors such as running through a maze to verbal reports by means of questionnaires to recordings of physiological activity while performing some task. To illustrate the rich variety of behaviors measured in psychological research, consider these recent examples.

1. A study of "Span of apprehension in schizophrenic patients as a function of distractor masking and laterality" (Elkins, Cromwell, & Asarnow, 1992) investigated attention span limitations in schizophrenic patients. Compared with nonschizophrenic controls, they did poorly when asked to identify target letters appearing in an array of distracting letters. The behavior measured was whether or not they could accurately name the target letters in different circumstances.

2. A study on "Differential calculation abilities in young children from middle- and low-income families" (Jordan, Huttenlocher, & Levine, 1992) tested these children on a variety of math problems and found that children from middle-income families outperformed others when problems were presented verbally, but the two groups performed the same on nonverbal problems. Two kinds of behaviors were measured: the children's responses to the math problems and the strategies they used. The children were observed solving the problems and scorers recorded whether the behaviors included such strategies as counting on fingers.

3. A study on "Perceived social support, social skills, and quality of relationships in bulimic women" (Grissett & Norvell, 1992) gave bulimic and nonbulimic women a battery of self-report tests to complete. The behaviors measured were their responses to these surveys (e.g., the Perceived Support Scale). Subjects were also put into a brief conversation with a confederate that was taped and rated by observers. The women's verbal and nonverbal behaviors during the conversation were scored on a measure of "social effectiveness." Bulimic women did not believe they received much support, and they were not rated very highly on social effectiveness.

4. A study asking "Does a cognitive map guide choices in a radial-arm maze?" (Brown, 1992) answered "maybe not." Radial-arm mazes, which feature a central platform and alleyways radiating from it in all directions, are among the more popular modern mazes. They are often used to study a rat's spatial memory (cognitive map) and the study by Brown investigated the rats' ability to avoid traveling down already-visited pathways. The behaviors measured were "macrochoices," operationally defined as occurring whenever a rat so much as stuck its nose into a pathway, and "microchoices," defined as orienting toward a pathway but not going down it (all this confirmed by videotape from a camera looking down on the maze).

Developing Measures from Constructs

From these examples, you can see that researchers measure behavior in many ways. But how do they decide what to measure? Where do they get the idea to measure calculation strategies by observing finger counting, microchoices by observing bodily orientation, or attention by seeing which letters are selected from an array?

In part, they know what to measure because they know the literature in their area of expertise and so they know what measures are typically used by other investigators. They also develop ideas for new measures by modifying commonly-used measures. Third, they develop measures out of the process of refining the constructs of interest in the study. Let me elaborate.

TABLE 4.1   *Sample Constructs and How They Are Measured*

Construct	Behavior to Measure the Construct
Span of apprehension	Letter identification
Calculation ability	Problems done correctly
Calculation strategy	Finger counting, etc.
Perceived social support	Score on self-report test
Social effectiveness	Observer ratings of social interaction
Rat macrochoice	Entering arm of radial maze
Rat microchoice	Orienting toward arm of radial maze

When researchers plan a study, they must first define the constructs to be used in the project as precisely as possible. Sound familiar? It should, because we are talking about operational definitions again. Part of the design for any study involves taking the constructs of interest, which by definition are not directly observable, and deciding which behaviors will adequately reflect those constructs. So in the previous examples, each researcher is faced with the task of taking some phenomenon and turning it into a manageable experiment by carefully defining the constructs in terms of measurable behaviors. Table 4.1 summarizes the four studies in terms of the constructs studied and how they were operationalized into specific behaviors.

One thing you might notice is that none of these constructs (attention, calculation ability, etc.) are directly observable—each must be inferred from the measures used to investigate them. This process is repeated over and over again in psychology and allows the research psychologist to ask some empirical questions that might seem to be impossible to answer at first glance. Let's consider in greater detail two specific examples of procedures frequently used to investigate the kind of question that might seem difficult if not impossible to answer empirically, such as:

Do infants understand the basic concept of gravity?
Can you demonstrate that people use visual images?

The measures used to study these seemingly nonempirical questions are as simple as recording (a) how long an infant looks at something and (b) how long it takes people to make decisions. Read on.

Case Study 1 — Habituation

Do infants have a concept of gravity? How could you find out? You cannot ask them directly of course, but the question can be asked indirectly, by way of a technique in which the amount of time a baby spends looking at different stimuli is measured. This so-called habituation procedure involves showing an infant the same stimulus over and over again, then changing to a new stimulus. From other research it is known that infants prefer novelty (Spelke, 1985), so if the same stimulus is repeatedly presented, they lose interest (i.e., they stop looking). The term *habituation* is defined as a gradual decrease in responding to repeated stimuli. If a new stimulus is presented *and* it is recognized as something new or unusual, the infant will increase the time spent looking at the new stimulus. So if looking time decreases and decreases and then suddenly increases, you can infer that the infant has noticed something new.

With this in mind, consider a delightful study by Kim and Spelke (1992). They compared 5- and 7-month olds and concluded that some type of basic understanding of gravity develops sometime during that period of infancy. The infants were shown repeated films of balls rolling up or down inclined planes, as depicted in the top two frames of Figure 4.1. During the habituation trials, subjects saw either a ball rolling down the plane while speeding up (condition 1) or the ball

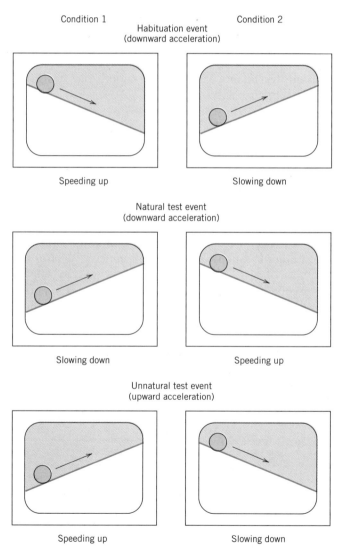

FIGURE 4.1 Stimulus items from Kim and Spelke's (1992) habituation study.

rolling up the plane while slowing down (condition 2). These events reflect the natural effects of gravity on balls rolling down and up hills. After habituation occurred (i.e., looking time decreased significantly after repeated trials), subjects were given either a "natural test event" (middle frames) or an "unnatural test event" (lower frames). Notice that in each of the two conditions, the natural test event differs from the habituation event in two ways (direction and speed), while the unnatural event differs in just one way (direction). In terms of how much the test event differed from the habituation event, it seems reasonable to expect the infants to perceive the natural event as novel and to look longer at it than at the unnatural one. Indeed, the 5-month olds did just that. The 7-month-old infants, however, looked at the *unnatural* event more, presumably because it violated what gravity dictates, whereas the natural event continued to be consistent with the laws of gravity displayed in the habituation events. Hence, the younger infants noticed changes in simple stimulus dimensions while the older children noticed changes violating the law of gravity. From the measures of preferential looking, then, Kim and Spelke inferred that infants, at least the 7-month olds, possessed some understanding of the concept of gravity!

Case Study 2—Reaction Time

Do we use visual images as part of our cognitive processing? How could you find out? Of course, you could ask, but if someone says, "yes, I'm using images," how could you be sure about what they were doing? That is, you would be confronting the same problem that brought about the demise of introspection as a method— its lack of objectivity. You could, however, ask people to perform some task that would produce one type of behavior if images were being used and a different type of behavior if images weren't being used. This is the strategy behind a well-known series of studies by Shepard and his colleagues of what is termed *mental rotation.*

Look at the two pairs of geometric objects in Figure 4.2. For each right-hand object of each pair, could it be the same as the left-hand object, but merely rotated to a different position? Or is it a different configuration altogether? How did you decide? Shepard and Metzler (1971) asked subjects to make these kinds of decisions but went one step further and recorded *how long it took* for subjects to make their decisions. Their reasoning was that if subjects solve these problems by taking the left-hand object and mentally turning it until it overlaps with the right-hand object, then the rotation process will take a certain amount of time. Furthermore,

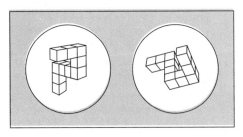 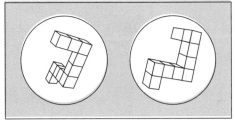

FIGURE 4.2   Stimulus items from Shepard and Metzler's (1971) mental rotation studies.

the more mental rotation required to reach the overlap point, the more time the process should take. I think you can see where this is going. Shepard and Metzler systematically varied the degree of rotation and found that as the angle increased, so did the amount of time to make the decision. From these measures of reaction time, then, they inferred that mental imagery was occurring in the task.

Reaction time is one of psychology's oldest and most enduring methods, but the rationale for its use has changed over the years. For more on its origins and evolution as a tried and true method in experimental psychology, see Box 4.1.

Box 4.1

ORIGINS— *Reaction Time: From Mental Chronometry to Mental Rotation*

The use of reaction time in psychology can be traced to the work of F. C. Donders, a Dutch physiologist, who argued that times for mental events could be determined by calculating the differences between the reaction times for different kinds of tasks (Boring, 1950). His idea ushered in a flood of research on what became known as "mental chronometry." Researchers would measure the time for a simple reaction (SRT): a single response made as quickly as possible after perceiving a single stimulus, a red light for instance. The task could then be complicated by displaying one of two stimuli, and telling the person to respond only to one of them. This was called discrimination reaction time (DRT) because the person had to discriminate between the two stimuli, such as a red and a green light, and then respond. DRT includes SRT plus the mental event of "discrimination," so subtracting SRT from DRT was believed to produce the time for discrimination:

$$DRT = SRT + discrimination$$
$$\therefore discrimination = DRT - SRT$$

The procedure could be elaborated even more, with additional mental events subtracted out, and it generated a great deal of excitement at the end of the nineteenth century, because psychology was trying to establish itself as a science, and what could be more scientific than to have mental events measured to the fraction of a second? The procedure was especially popular in Wundt's laboratory at Leipzig and was quickly imported to the United States, as you can see from Figure 4.3, which shows a reaction time experiment in progress at Clark University in the early 1890s.

Unfortunately, it soon became apparent that serious problems existed with the procedure. In particular, some reaction times would be faster than predicted from the complication logic, others slower. Oswald Külpe, one of Wundt's students, pointed out the fatal flaw—mental events don't just combine in a simple additive fashion to form more complicated events. Rather, a complex mental event has a quality all its own that is more than the sum of simpler events.

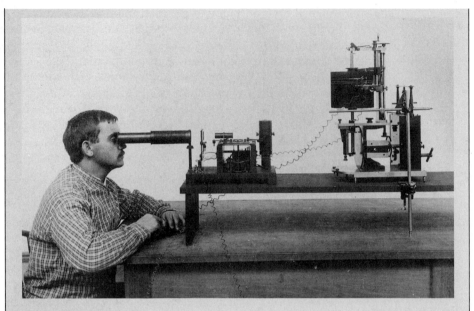

FIGURE 4.3   Reaction time study in progress at Clark University, circa 1892.

Although Külpe's arguments effectively ended mental chronometry and reaction time as a method declined in use during the heyday of behaviorism (roughly 1930–1950), it subsequently enjoyed a resurgence in several areas of cognitive psychology. The idea is no longer to measure the precise times of mental events, but to test predictions from cognitive theories. The mental rotation studies are a good example of this. Shepard predicted that if mental rotation occurs in the minds of subjects, then this mental activity should take a certain amount of time. Larger degrees of rotation should take greater amounts of time, and as you've seen, this indeed occurred.

Evaluating Measures

How can you tell if a measure of behavior is a good one? What accounts for the confidence with which psychologists use such things as preferential looking, reaction time, IQ tests, surveys of perceived social support, and so on? To answer the question requires a discussion of two key factors: reliability and validity.

Reliability

In general, a measure of behavior is said to be **reliable** if its results are repeatable when the behaviors are remeasured. Reaction time is a good example; its high reliability is one reason for its popularity over the years. Someone responding to a red light in 0.18 seconds on one trial will almost certainly respond within a few hundredths of a second of 0.18 on other trials and practically all the trials will be in the general vicinity of 0.18 seconds. Similarly, scores on the Graduate Record Exam (GRE) are reasonably reliable. Someone with a combined score of 850 on the GRE general test would probably score close to that a second time, and would be very unlikely to reach a score of 1,350.

From these two examples, I think you can see why reliability is essential in any measure. Without it, there is no way of determining what a score on a particular measure *means*. Presumably, in reaction time, you're trying to determine how fast someone is. If their reaction times vary wildly, there is no way to answer the question. Likewise, if GRE scores bounced four or five hundred points from one testing to another, the numbers would be of no use whatsoever to graduate schools because they would have no way of estimating the student's real score.

A behavioral measure's reliability is a function of the amount of **measurement error** said to be present. If there is a great deal of error, reliability is low, and vice versa. No behavioral measure is perfectly reliable, so there is some degree of measurement error that occurs with all measurement. That is, every measure is some combination of a hypothetical "true" score plus some measurement error. Ideally, measurement error is low enough so that an observed score is close to the true score.

The reaction time procedure provides a good illustration of how measurement error works and how it affects reliability. As in the previous example, suppose a person takes 0.18 seconds on a reaction time trial. Is this a true measure of speed? Probably not, a conclusion easily reached when you notice that for the following five trials this same person's reaction times are

0.16 sec   0.15 sec   0.19 sec   0.17 sec   0.19 sec

These scores vary because some amount of measurement error contributes to each trial. This error is caused by several possible factors, some which operate randomly from trial to trial. For example, on a particular trial the person might respond faster than the true score by guessing that the stimulus was about to be presented, or slower because of a momentary lapse of attention. Also, some systematic amount of error could occur if, for example, the experimenter signaled the subjects to get ready just before turning on the stimulus and the amount of time between the ready signal and the stimulus was constant. Then the subjects could learn to anticipate the stimulus and produce reaction times that would be systematically faster than the true ones.

Despite the presence of a small degree of measurement error, the above scores do cluster together reasonably well and the reaction times certainly would be judged more reliable than if the scores following the 0.18 seconds were

0.11 sec   0.25 sec   0.19 sec   0.09 sec   0.31 sec

With scores ranging from less than a tenth of a second to nearly a third of a second, it is difficult to determine the person's real speed.

When scores are reliable then, the researcher can assign some meaning to the magnitude of the scores. Reliability also allows the researcher to make more meaningful comparisons with other sets of scores. For example, comparing the first set of scores with the following ones reveals a clear difference in basic reaction time:

0.23 sec   0.26 sec   0.21 sec   0.22 sec   0.24 sec

It is probably fair to say that this second person is a bit slower than the person described earlier.

There are ways of calculating reliabilities, but this is seldom done in experimental research. Rather, confidence in the reliability of a measure develops over time, a benefit of the replication process. The habituation and reaction time procedures have been used often enough and yielded consistent enough results for researchers to be highly confident about their reliability.

Reliability *is* assessed more formally in research that evaluates any type of psychological test. These are instruments designed to measure such constructs as personality factors, abilities (e.g., IQ), and attitudes. They are usually paper-and-pencil tests in which a person responds to questions or statements of some kind. In the study mentioned earlier on bulimia, subjects filled out several of these measures, including one called the "Perceived Support Scale." Analyses designed to establish the reliability of this kind of test require the use of correlational procedures. For example, the test could be given on two occasions and the similarity in the two sets of results could be determined. Unless there are some dramatic changes taking place in a person's life, scores on two measurements with the Perceived Support Scale should be similar. The degree of similarity is expressed in terms of a correlation (high similarity = strong correlation). The specifics of this kind of analysis, especially as it relates to the whole area of psychological testing, will be explained more fully in Chapter 8 on correlational analysis.

Validity

A behavioral measure is considered **valid** if it measures what it has been designed to measure. A measure of perceived social support should truly measure the amount of support that people believe they have and not be a measure of some different construct. A test of intelligence should truly measure intelligence and not something else.

Sometimes a measure is assumed to have a degree of validity simply because it makes sense. As a measure of intelligence, a test with problems requiring some thinking makes more sense than a test in which people have to ride a bicycle accurately between two white lines. That is, problem solving and reasoning have more **face validity** as measures of intelligence than does bike riding (which has face validity as a measure of balance). Of course, face validity is not sufficient by itself; a test can seem to make sense and still not be a valid test. Most of the surveys found in popular magazines probably fit into this category.

A more critical test of validity is called **predictive validity**, which concerns whether the measure can accurately forecast some future event. If a test will be useful as an IQ test, for example, it should predict how well a child will do in school. Likewise, if a test is going to be effective for selecting employees, then high scorers should do well on the job. As is the case with reliability estimates, predictive validity research is correlational in nature and occurs primarily in research on psychological testing; you'll see it again in Chapter 8.

Another type of validity, **construct validity**, is especially relevant to experimental research. It concerns two issues at the same time: whether the construct being measured by a particular tool is a valid construct and whether the particular tool is the best one for measuring the construct. It is closely tied to the nature of theory, the deduction of research hypotheses from theory, and the evaluation of theories following the outcomes of research. As such, construct validity is never established or destroyed with a single study and is never proven for the same reason that theories are never proven. Rather, confidence in construct validity accumulates gradually and inductively as research produces supportive results.

As we've seen, psychology is loaded with constructs that cannot be observed directly—things like hunger, anxiety, intelligence, depression, perceived social support, span of apprehension, and so on. Because these constructs are hypothetical, their presence can only be inferred from the measures designed for them. Research measuring a construct in a particular way that yields predictable research outcomes serves to validate both the construct itself and the tool used to measure the construct.

Case Study 3—Construct Validity

To see how construct validity builds, consider a series of studies by the personality psychologist Walter Mischel and his colleagues. Mischel was interested in the problem of impatience in children. That is, children sometimes want things right now; they have difficulty waiting. Mischel devised a construct he called "delay of gratification" and set about trying to develop an adequate measure of it. The research program he developed showed both that delay of gratification is valid as a construct that fits into a general cognitive-social learning theory of personality and that the measures he developed were good ones.

One simple measure devised by Mischel was to ask children to choose between a small reward that was available immediately and a larger reward that would only be given to them after a delay. Mischel reasoned that if the inability to delay gratification was characteristic of young children, then older children should be more willing to wait for the larger reward than younger ones. This led to the obvious study (cited in Mischel, 1981), in which children completed a brief task, and then were told

> I would like to give each of you a piece of candy, but I don't have enough of these (indicating the larger, more preferred reinforcement) with me today. So you can either get this one (indicating the smaller, less preferred reinforcement) right now, today, or, if you want to, you can wait for this one (indicating), which I will bring back next Wednesday [one week later]. (Mischel, 1981, pp. 164–165)

The results confirmed Mischel's prediction: the immediate reward was chosen by 81% of 7-year olds, 48% of 8-year olds, and 20% of 9-year olds.

Of course, this one study was not sufficient to establish delay of gratification as a valid construct; nor did it establish his measure as a valid tool. So Mischel continued developing a series of studies, exploring the ways in which the evolving construct related to other already established constructs. For instance, he found that children willing to delay gratification were also more emotionally mature, more achievement oriented, less likely to be delinquent, and more likely to be socially responsible (Mischel, 1981). Thus, delay of gratification became accepted as a valid construct because of the accumulated research that came out as expected.

This discussion of construct validity has centered on research that attempts to develop and evaluate measures for certain constructs, but construct validity can also be considered in a broader sense as a way of evaluating the adequacy of particular experiments. This approach to construct validity will be elaborated in the next chapter after I lay out the defining features of an experiment in psychology.

Reliability and Validity

For a measure to be of any value in psychological research, it must have some degree of both reliability and validity. Reliability is important because it enables one to have some confidence that the measure taken is close to the "true" measure. Validity is important because it tells you if the measure actually measures what you hope it does. Note that validity assumes reliability, but the converse is not true. Measures can be reliable but not valid; valid measures must be reliable, however.

A simple example can illustrate this. In the last chapter you learned something about nineteenth-century phrenology, a popular theory claiming that you could measure a person's "faculties" by examining skull contour. From the above discussion of reliability, you should recognize that phrenological measures of the skull were indeed highly reliable—the distance between a point two inches above your left ear and two inches above your right ear is not going to change very much if measured on two separate occasions. However, to say the measure is an indication of the faculty of "destructiveness" is quite another matter. We know the skull contour measurement is not a valid measure of destructiveness because it doesn't make a whole lot of sense to us today (face validity), fails to predict aggressive behavior (predictive validity), and does not fit well with other research on constructs relating to destructiveness such as impulsiveness or with research on brain function (construct validity).

The issues of reliability and validity have ethical implications, especially when measures are used to make decisions about people's lives. Students are accepted or not accepted into college or graduate school, job applicants are hired or not hired, and people are given a psychiatric diagnosis and treatment, all on the basis of measurements of ability or behavior. If you were applying for a job and your score on some test was to be the determining factor, you would be justifiably upset to learn the test was not very reliable or valid.

Scales of Measurement

Whenever a behavior is measured, it means that numbers are assigned in some fashion. We say that someone responded in 3.5 seconds, scored 120 on an IQ test, or finished third best in a maze test. We also talk of placing X number of individuals into categories as a consequence of what they do or some characteristic they possess. These examples illustrate four different ways of assigning numbers to events, four different **measurement scales**. A clear understanding of these scales is an important prelude to a discussion of statistics because different types of statistical analyses will be completed depending on the type of measurement scale being used.

Nominal Scales

Sometimes the number we assign to events serves only to classify them into one group or another. When this happens, we are using what is called a **nominal scale** of measurement. In this case, the numbers assigned mean no more than a category label (e.g., 1 = males, 2 = females). Studies using these scales typically assign people to categories and count the number of people falling into them. We use nominal scales when we ask empirical questions like these:

✓ Comparing male and female joggers, who is more likely to run during the day and who is more likely to run in the evening?

✓ If you divide mentally disturbed people into those who are shy and those who are outgoing, will introverts be more likely to be suffering from anxiety disorders than extroverts?

✓ If you divide people into those expecting to experience severe shock and those not expecting it, will it affect their "affiliative" tendencies?

This last example was the empirical question asked in a well-known experiment in social psychology by Stanley Schachter (1959). He told half of his female subjects that the experiment they were about to begin would measure their physiological reactions to intense electrical shock; remaining subjects were told the shocks would be very mild and feel like a tickling sensation. After informing the women of each group about the forthcoming shock, Schachter told them to wait for 10 minutes while the equipment was being set up and asked whether they preferred to wait by themselves or with others (no preference was a third option). How they answered this question was Schachter's real interest and the study ended after the subjects expressed their preference.

Schachter was investigating the effects of anxiety on a construct called "affiliation" (the tendency to want to be with others). The results? Those expecting severe shock preferred to wait with others, while those expecting mild shock generally showed no preference. The study illustrates the use of a nominal scale because Schachter organized the data by counting up the number of people who fell into six different categories, depending on (a) what kind of shock they were expecting and (b) how they responded to the key question. The number of people (sometimes called a "frequency count") in each of these categories can be seen in Table 4.2. The data are also converted into percentages.

TABLE 4.2   *Using Nominal Scales: Schachter's Study of Affiliation*

	Number of People Expressing These Preferences		
	Wait Alone	Wait with Others	Don't Care
Those expecting severe shock	3 (9%)	20 (63%)	9 (23%)
Those expecting mild shock	2 (7%)	10 (33%)	18 (60%)

Source: Schachter (1959).

Ordinal Scales

Ordinal scales of measurement are basically sets of rankings. College transcripts, for example, usually list a student's general class rank: first, second, third, fiftieth, and so on. From these rankings, you can infer that one student had higher grades than another. Relative position is the only thing you know, however. Ed, Fred, and Ted would be ranked 1, 2, and 3 in each of the following cases, even though Ed is clearly superior to Fred and Ted only in the second case:

<table>
<tr><td align="center">***Case 1:***</td><td align="center">***Case 2:***</td></tr>
<tr><td>Ed's GPA   = 4.0</td><td>Ed's GPA   = 4.0</td></tr>
<tr><td>Fred's GPA = 3.9</td><td>Fred's GPA = 3.6</td></tr>
<tr><td>Ted's GPA = 3.8</td><td>Ted's GPA = 3.5</td></tr>
</table>

Studies using ordinal scales ask questions like:

✓   If a child ranks five toys and is given the one ranked third, will the ranking go up or down after the child has played with the toy for a week?

✓   Do male and female students rank textbook authors in the sciences and in the humanities differently if they are made aware of the gender of the writers?

✓   How do young and old people rank ten movies that vary in the levels of sex and aggression found in them?

A recent example of the use of an ordinal scale is a study by Korn, Davis, and Davis (1991). Historians of psychology and department chairpersons were asked to list, in rank order from 1 to 10, the psychologists they considered to be the most important. Two sets of rankings were solicited: one for the top ten of "all time" and the second for a "contemporary" top ten. The returns were then summarized to yield a picture of eminence in psychology. Who topped the chart? B. F. Skinner was considered the most eminent contemporary psychologist by both historians and chairpersons. Chairpersons also ranked Skinner number 1 all time; historians, who tended to select psychologists from earlier periods for their all-time list, dropped Skinner to number 8 and put Wundt on top.

Interval Scales

Most research in psychology uses interval or ratio scales of measurement. **Interval scales** extend the idea of rank order to include the concept of equal intervals between the events that are ordered. Research using psychological tests of personality, attitude, and ability are the most common examples of studies that are usually considered to involve interval scales. Scores on intelligence tests, for example, are usually assumed to be arranged this way. Someone with a 120 IQ is believed to be "more intelligent" (granting for the sake of illustration that IQ measures intelligence in some way) than someone else with a 110 IQ. Furthermore, and this is the defining feature of an interval scale, the difference in intelligence between people with IQs of 120 and 110 is assumed to be the same as the difference between people with IQs of 110 and 100. In other words, each single point of increase in an IQ score is believed to represent the same amount of increase in intelligence—the intervals are equal. Note the word *assumed*, however; some psychologists prefer to consider IQ scores (and scores on most personality tests as well) as an example of an ordinal scale, arguing that it is difficult if not impossible to be sure about the equal interval assumption. Most accept the inclusion of IQ as an example of an interval scale though, partly for a practical reason: Psychologists prefer to use interval and ratio scales generally because data on those scales allow for more sophisticated statistical analyses.

The brief description earlier of the study of bulimia used several measures (e.g., Perceived Support) that illustrate interval scales. Also, take a look at Box 4.2, which describes a classic set of studies in which interval scales were used in an attempt to show that our body type influences the kind of person we become.

Ratio Scales

In a **ratio scale**, the concepts of order and equal interval are carried over from ordinal and interval scales, but in addition, the ratio scale has a *true zero point*. That is, for ratio scores, a score of zero means the complete absence of the attribute being measured. Ratio scales are found in studies in which subjects are asked to perform tasks in which such things as the number of errors made or the number of words recalled are measured. Also, physical measures like height, weight, and time are measured on a ratio scale. The studies at the beginning of the chapter on habituation and reaction time both illustrate the use of a ratio scale.

One of the reviewers for this text suggested a creative way to distinguish between these scales through the example of a single event. Imagine the Kentucky Derby. The numbers assigned to the horses are on a nominal scale, their finishing positions are ordinal, the time of day from the beginning (e.g., 4:00 P.M.) to the end of the race (e.g., 4:02 P.M.) is an interval scale, and the total amount of time for the winner to run the race is a ratio scale.

Box 4.2

CLASSIC STUDIES—Measuring Somatotypes: When 7-1-1 met 1-1-7

You've already learned that phrenologists speculated about the relationship between some physical characteristic (skull contour) and what a person was like. Phrenology seems almost quaint to us today, but the idea of a relationship between physical characteristics and personality is an enduring one. A more systematic attempt to explore the connection was made by William Sheldon (1940, 1942).

What is striking about Sheldon's work is the attempt to define physique in terms of a precise scale of measurement. After examining about 4,000 photos of naked college men, he and his research team developed a system of classifying physiques in terms of three 7-point interval scales. Each scale reflected the degree to which the men displayed three prototypical body types: endomorphy (fat), mesomorphy (muscular), and ectomorphy (thin). Everyone was assumed to have some degree of each of the physiques, with one of them usually predominant. Thus, an extremely round person might be labeled a 7-1-1, while a very thin person would be a 1-1-7, and Arnold Schwarzenegger would be a 1-7-1. A 4-4-4 would be a perfectly balanced person. The set of numbers applied to a particular man was called his "somatotype."

After measuring somatotypes, Sheldon set out to measure personality types. These he believed also fell into three categories that could be measured on 7-point interval scales that would summarize the results of several personality tests. He labeled the

Who To Measure—Sampling

In addition to the decisions about which measures to use when doing research in psychology, the investigator must decide who will be asked to participate as subjects and have their behaviors measured. There are two general approaches taken: probability sampling and nonprobability sampling.

Probability Sampling

This strategy is used whenever the goal is to learn something specific about an identifiable group of individuals. As a group, those individuals are called a **population**; any subgroup of them is called a **sample**. Sometimes it is possible to study all members of a population. For example, if you wanted to learn the attitudes of all the people in your experimental psychology class about the issue of animal experimentation, you could survey everyone in the class. In this case the size of the population would be the size of your class. As you might guess, however, the popula-

categories viscerotonia, somatotonia, and cerebrotonia. Generally, viscerotonics were sociable, fun-loving, slow-moving, even tempered, and very interested in food. Somatotonics were aggressive, self-centered, and risk taking, and cerebrotonics were shy and secretive, preferred to be alone, and tended to pursue intellectual tasks. Sheldon's final step was to see if somatotypes related to personality types. You'll not be surprised to learn that these pairs occurred together most often:

endomorph—viscerotonia
mesomorph—somatotonia
ectomorph—cerebrotonia

Sheldon believed that someone's body type caused him to develop a certain personality, but critics pointed out that the relationships were not that strong and could be accounted for in several ways. Being an endomorph could cause someone to like food, but couldn't a strong liking of food create an endomorph?

The issues surrounding Sheldon's theory were complex, but for our purposes, the study is a classic example of trying to quantify human character and relate it to what the person looks like on some measurable scale of physique, an interval scale in this case. Incidentally, you might have noticed the absence of gender neutral language in this description of Sheldon's work, with personal pronouns like "his" and "him" being used. This is because Sheldon only studied males. Why? Recall that his procedure involved examining photographs of 4,000 naked men. Apparently, he gave some thought to replicating the study with women, but demurred because of "conventional sanctions against the necessary photographing of nude female [college students]" (Bavelas, 1978). You'll be reading about "convenience" samples shortly; some samples are more convenient than others.

tion of interest to a researcher is usually too large for every member in it to be tested. Hence, a subset of that population, a sample, must be selected.

Even though the entire population might not be tested in a study, the researcher wishes to draw conclusions about this broader group, not just the sample. Thus, it is important for the sample to reflect the population as a whole. When this happens, the sample is said to be **representative**; if it doesn't happen, the sample is said to be **biased** in some fashion. If you wish to investigate student perceptions of college life, it would be a serious mistake to select subjects from a list that included only those living in college residence halls. Because off-campus residents and commuter students might have very different attitudes from on-campus residents, the results of your survey would be biased in favor of the latter (you'll be learning more about the details of survey research procedures in Chapter 11).

Perhaps the most famous historical example of biased sampling occurred during political polling in the 1936 presidential election. As it had been doing with reasonable success for several previous elections, the *Literary Digest* tried to predict the election outcome by sending out about 10 million simulated ballots to subscribers and to others selected from a sample of phone books from around the country and from motor vehicle registration information (Sprinthall, 1982). About 25% of the ballots were returned to the magazine; of them, 57% preferred the Republican candidate Alf Landon, and 40% chose the incumbent president, Franklin Roosevelt. In the actual election, Roosevelt won in a landslide with more than 60% of the vote. Can you guess why the sample was biased?

Although the editors of *Literary Digest* were aware that their own subscribers tended to be upper-middle class and Republican, they thought they were broadening the sample and making it more representative by adding people from phone books and car registrations. In fact, they were simply selecting more Republicans. In the midst of the Great Depression, practically the only people who could afford phones and cars were members of the upper-middle and upper classes, who were unlikely to be Democrats. So in the survey the magazine actually was asking Republicans how they were going to cast their votes.

You might have noticed another flaw in the *Literary Digest* survey. A large number of ballots were returned, and the magazine was quite confident in its prediction of a Landon victory because the data reflected the views of a substantial number of people—almost 2.5 million. Note, however, that not only does the total represent only one-fourth of the ballots originally sent out, but the returns were from those who *chose* to send them back. So those responding to the survey tended to be not just Republicans, but Republicans who wished to make their views known (in light of which the 57% preferring Landon actually looks rather small, don't you think?)

This **self-selection** problem is a common one in surveys that appear in popular magazines and in requests by people like Ann Landers for readers to let her know about some issue. A survey will appear, then a month or so later the results of those who returned the survey will be reported, usually in a way implying that the results are valid. The person reporting the survey will try to impress you with the total number of returns, rather than representativeness of the sample. A recent example of this ploy is a report on female sexuality (Hite, 1987), which claimed, among other things, that more than 90% of married women felt emotionally abused in their relationships. When criticized because the survey was only sent to a select group of women's organizations and that only 4.5% of 100,000 people returned the surveys, the author simply pointed out that 4,500 people were enough for her (just like 2.5 million people were enough for *Literary Digest*).

As a scientific thinker, you should be very skeptical about claims made on the basis of these kinds of sampling procedures. The lesson of course is that if you want to make a statement about a specific population with some accuracy, you must use a sample that reflects that population accurately and you must select the sample directly, not rely simply on who decides to return the survey.

Random Sampling

The most fundamental type of probability sampling is to take a **simple random sample**. In essence, all this means is that each member of the population has an equal chance of being selected as a member of the sample. To select a random sample of 100 students from your school, for instance, you could place all of their names in a large hat and pick out 100. In actual practice, the procedure is a bit more sophisticated than this, however, usually involving a random number table such as the one found in Appendix C. To learn the essence of the procedure, work

TABLE 4.3 *Selecting a Random Sample Using a Table of Random Numbers*

Task: Select a random sample of 5 individuals from a population of 20 individuals.

Step 1. Assign numbers from **01** to **20** to the individuals who make up your population.

Step 2. Go to a table of random numbers. Here's a portion of one:

2	2	1	7	6	8	6	5	8	4	6	8	9	5
1	9	3	6	1	7	5	9	4	6	1	3	7	9
1	6	7	7	2	3	0	2	7	7	0	9	6	1
7	8	0	3	7	6	7	1	6	1	2	0	4	4
0	3	2	8	1	2	2	6	0	8	7	3	3	7

Step 3. Pick a spot to begin searching through the table. This can be anywhere; just be sure that you don't begin any two searches in the same place. Let's suppose you begin with the top number in the third column. It's a **1**. You will need to consider pairs of numbers together because the population is comprised of people who numbered from **01** through **20**. Hence you must use the **1** and the **7** next to it as your starting point.

Step 4. So your search for a sample of 5 begins with number 17, which falls within the range of **01** through **20**. The first person in your sample, therefore, is person **17**.

Step 5. Continue down the double column until you've found five individuals with numbers between **01** to **20**. Here's the table again. The 5 selected numbers are underlined, the section of the table that needed to be searched is boldfaced, and arrows indicate the direction of search.

2	2	**1**	**7**	6	8	6	5	8	4	6	8	9	5
1	9	**3**	**6**	1	7	5	9	4	6	1	3	7	9
1	6	**7**	**7**	2	3	0	2	7	7	0	9	6	1
7	8	**0**	**3**	7	6	7	1	6	1	2	0	4	4
0	3	**2**	**8**	1	2	2	6	0	8	7	3	3	7

Thus the sample consists of population members numbered **17, 3, 12, 2,** and **8**. Notice that the numbers larger than **20** (e.g., **36**) are bypassed and if a number repeats itself (**17**), it is not selected a second time.

through the example in Table 4.3, which shows you how to use random numbers to select a sample of five individuals from a 20-member population.

Simple random sampling is often an effective, practical way to create a representative sample. It is sometimes the method of choice for ethical reasons as well. In situations in which only a small group can receive some benefit or must incur some cost and there is no other reasonable basis for decision making, random sampling is the fairest method to use. A famous example occurred in 1969 in the midst of the Vietnam war, when a draft lottery system was established. For obvious reasons of fairness, each of the 365 days of the year was to have an equal chance of being selected first, second, third, and so on. Unfortunately, the actual procedure had some bias to it (Kolata, 1986). Capsules, one per day of the year, were placed in a large drum 1 month at a time. The January capsules went in first, then February, and so on. The drum was rotated to mix the capsules, but apparently this did not succeed completely because when the dates were drawn, those capsules entering the drum last tended to be the first to be picked. This was not a good time to have a birthday in December.

There are two problems with simple random sampling. First, there may be some systematic features of the population that you might like to have reflected in your sample. Second, the procedure may be impractical if the population is extremely large. How could you get a list of everyone in the United States in order to select a simple random sample of Americans? The first problem is solved by using stratified sampling; cluster sampling solves the second difficulty.

Stratified Sampling

Suppose you wanted to measure the attitudes about abortion on your campus and the school's population is 5,000, of whom 4,000 are women. You decide to sample 100 students. If you take a simple random sample, there are almost certainly going to be more women than men in your sample, but the proportions in the sample probably won't match those in the population. Your goal is to make the sample truly representative of the population, and on a question like abortion, there might be important differences of opinion between males and females. Therefore, if your sample is overrepresented with males it might not truly portray campus attitudes. In a situation like this, it would be a good idea to decide ahead of time that if 80% of the population is female, then exactly 80% of the sample will also be female. That is, just as the population has these two layers (or "strata"), so should the sample.

In a **stratified sample**, then, the *proportions* of important subgroups in the population are represented precisely in the sample. In the previous example, 80 females would be randomly sampled from the complete list of females, and 20 males would be selected from the list of males.

Note that some judgment is required here: The researcher has to decide just how many layers to use. In the case of the abortion survey, males and females were sampled in proportion to their overall numbers. Should each of the four undergraduate classes be proportionately represented also? What about Protestants and Catholics? What about left- and right-handers? Obviously, the researcher has to draw the line somewhere. Some characteristics (religion) are more critical than others (handedness) in deciding how to stratify the sample. Based on what has occurred in prior research, or the goals of the particular study at hand, it's up to the researcher to use some good sense.

Cluster Sampling

Stratified sampling is an effective procedure, but it still doesn't solve the problem encountered when trying to sample from a huge population: It is often impossible to acquire a complete list of individuals in the population. **Cluster sampling**, a procedure frequently used by national polling organizations, solves the problem.

With this approach the researcher randomly selects a cluster of people all having some feature in common. A campus survey at a large university might be done this way. If a researcher wanted a cross-section of students and stratified sampling was not feasible, an alternative would be to get a list of required classes. Each class would be a cluster and would include students from a variety of majors. If there were 40 core classes being offered, the researcher might randomly select 10 of them, then administer the survey to all students in each of the selected classes.

If the selected clusters are too large, the researcher can sample a smaller cluster within the larger one. Suppose you wanted to find out how students liked living in the high-rise dorms on your campus, which you've defined operationally as any dorm with eight floors or more. Suppose fifteen of these buildings exist on your campus, housing a total of 6,000 students. Using cluster sampling, you could first select six of the buildings (each building = a cluster), then for each building randomly select three floors, then sample all of the residents (about forty per floor, let's say) of the selected floors in the selected dorms. This would give you an overall sample size of 720 ($40 \times 3 \times 6$). Notice that you also could combine some elements of stratified sampling here. If ten of the dorms house women and the remaining five house men, you might select your first clusters to reflect these proportions: four female dorms and two male dorms.

Nonprobability Sampling

From what you've just read, you might think that a failure to use probability sampling results in an inferior study. This is certainly the case if the goal of the project is to describe specific features of a defined population accurately by investigating just a segment of it. However, most research in psychology is not like this. Rather, the goal is usually to study relationships between variables: Using imagery improves memory, observing aggression leads to aggression, as the number of bystanders increases, helping behavior decreases, and so on. Of course, the hope is that the results of these studies will extend beyond the subjects participating in it, but the researcher assumes that if the relationship studied is a powerful one, it will occur for most subjects within a particular population, regardless of how they are chosen. Naturally, whether this assumption turns out to be true depends on the normal processes of replication and extension discussed in Chapter 3. So in a study on the capacity limits of short-term memory in adults, it is not necessary to select a random sample: Virtually any group of reasonably fluent adult subjects will do.

Convenience Sampling

This is the most frequent (and yes, the most convenient) type of nonprobability sampling. In a **convenience sample**, the researcher simply requests volunteers from a group of available people who meet the general requirements of the study. Most typically, they are college freshmen and sophomores taking general psychology and being asked to participate in a study or two; you might have been in that boat yourself once.

Sometimes the convenience sampling approach is taken, but there is a specific type of person who is recruited for the study (this is sometimes called "purposive" sampling). For instance, when Stanley Milgram first recruited participants for his obedience studies, he placed ads in the local newspaper asking for volunteers. He deliberately (i.e., purposely) avoided using college students because he was concerned that they might be "too homogeneous a group . . . he wanted a wide range of individuals drawn from a broad spectrum of class backgrounds" (Milgram, 1974, p. 14). He could have tried a more sophisticated stratified or cluster sampling approach, but even if he did, there was no guarantee that the people he selected would be willing to come into the lab. Besides the fact that not all research needs a sample that is precisely representative of a population, Milgram's procedure shows that nonprobability sampling is often chosen for practical reasons.

Statistical Analysis

The first sentence in a well-known self-help book called *The Road Less Traveled* (Peck, 1978) is "Life is difficult" (p. 15). This is a belief that seems to be shared by many students taking a course in statistics, who readily identify with the character in Figure 4.4. I won't try to convince you that doing statistics compares with lying on a Florida beach in February, but I hope you'll come to see that part of the excitement of doing research in psychology comes from completing an analysis of the data you've painstakingly collected and finding out whether or not something *actually* happened in the study. I've seen mature, responsible adults writhing in agony while waiting for the results of some statistical analysis to print out, then reduced to anguish or raised to levels of ecstasy moments after looking at the magic numbers on the printout. So if you develop a passion for doing research in psychology, much of your emotion will be invested in dealing with the subtleties of statistical analysis.

My goal here is to introduce you to statistical thinking and the kinds of statistical analysis that you'll encounter when doing research in psychology. Ideally, you've al-

FIGURE 4.4   A common perception of statistics.

ready taken a course in statistics. If you haven't, you should take one as soon as possible, especially if you have any desire to go to graduate school in psychology. I'll be covering some of the essentials, but there is no substitute for a full course.

You will find a discussion about how to decide on the appropriate statistical analysis and how to actually carry out some of the more common ones in Appendix B. You also will find some discussion of statistical topics popping up at regular intervals for the rest of the book, for the simple reason that designing research in psychology cannot be separated from the analysis of that research. In this chapter, you will learn about the difference between descriptive and inferential statistics and about the logic of hypothesis testing.

Descriptive and Inferential Statistics

The most fundamental distinction between types of statistics is between "descriptive" and those referred to as "inferential." The difference parallels what you learned earlier about samples and populations. Simply put, **descriptive statistics** summarize the data collected from the sample of subjects participating in your study and **inferential statistics** allow you to draw conclusions about your data that can be applied to the broader population.

Descriptive Statistics

In essence, descriptive statistical procedures enable you to turn a large pile of numbers that cannot be comprehended at a glance into a very small set of numbers that can be more easily understood. Descriptive statistics include measures of central tendency, measures of variability, and measures of association, presented both numerically and visually (e.g., in graphs). In this chapter, we'll consider the more common procedures for measuring central tendency and variability. Measures of association (coefficients of correlation) will be covered in Chapter 8.

To illustrate measures of central tendency and variability, consider some sample data from a hypothetical memory study in which 20 subjects study and try to recall a list of 25 words. Each number in the following set represents the number of words recalled by each of the 20 participants.

S#	Recall	S#	Recall	S#	Recall	S#	Recall
1	16	6	18	11	19	16	19
2	17	7	19	12	15	17	21
3	14	8	16	13	15	18	17
4	17	9	20	14	17	19	15
5	18	10	17	15	18	20	18

You can easily see that communicating the results of this study requires something more than just showing someone this large pile of numbers. Instead, you could try to identify a *typical* score or what is called a "measure of central tendency." The most common measure of central tendency is the **mean**, or average, which is found simply by adding the scores together and dividing by the total number of scores. Thus,

$$\overline{X} = \Sigma X/N, \text{ where}$$
$$\overline{X} = \text{the mean (pronounced ``ex-bar'')}$$
$$\Sigma X = \text{the sum of the individual scores}$$
$$N = \text{the number of scores in the sample}$$

For the memory data:

$$\overline{X} = \Sigma X/N = (16 + 17 + 14 + \ldots 18)/20 = 346/20 = 17.30$$

Two other measures of central tendency are the median and the mode. The **median** is the score in the exact middle of a set of scores. Half the scores will be higher and half will be lower. The median is sometimes used when a set of scores includes one or two that are very different from the rest; in this situation, the mean gives a distorted view of the typical score. For instance, suppose the IQ scores of the five teachers in your psychology department were 93, 81, 81, 95, and 200 (probably the person teaching the research methods course). The mean IQ score of 110 gives a false impression that the psychology faculty as a whole is well above average. The median gives a better estimate of a typical IQ in this case, and it is found by lining up the scores from lowest to highest and finding the middle score. Thus:

$$81 \quad 81 \quad \mathbf{93} \quad 95 \quad 200$$
$$\uparrow$$
$$\text{median}$$

The **mode** is the score occurring most frequently in a set of scores. It is 81 in the previous example. The median and the mode for the hypothetical memory scores are both 17 (you should verify this).

Another way to organize a set of scores is to create a picture of them by using what is called a **frequency distribution**. This is a graph that plots the number of times each score occurs. The distribution of scores for the memory study is plotted in Figure 4.5. There are several things to note.

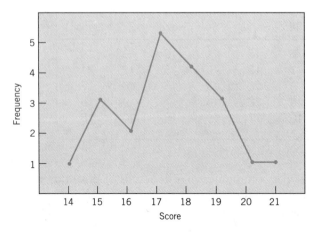

FIGURE 4.5 A frequency distribution of scores on a memory test.

First, the graph is created by counting the number of times (i.e., frequency) each score occurs. Thus,

Score	Frequency	Frequency as asterisks
14	1	★
15	3	★★★
16	2	★★
17	5	★★★★★
18	4	★★★★
19	3	★★★
20	1	★
21	1	★

Plotting the graph is easy once this table of frequencies has been created. You might have noticed that taking the pattern of asterisks and rotating it 90°F results in the equivalent of Figure 4.5.

The second thing to note about the frequency distribution is that it bulges near the middle and is relatively flat at each end. This is a pattern that approximates what would probably happen if you created a distribution of scores for the entire population, not just for the twenty people in the sample described here. Such a population distribution is the familiar bell-shaped curve known as the **normal curve** or normal distribution. You've seen it before; it looks like this:

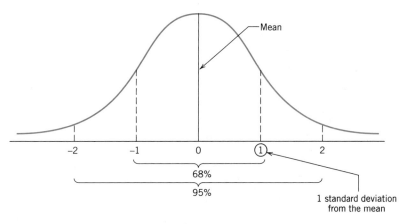

FIGURE 4.6   The normal curve.

The normal curve is a frequency distribution just like Figure 4.5, except that instead of being an *actual* distribution of sample scores, it is a *hypothetical* distribution of what all the scores in the population should be like if everyone is tested. The mean score, as well as the median and the mode, is in the exact middle of a normal distribution.

In the normal curve in Figure 4.6, two standard deviations on either side of the mean are marked. From the mathematical properties of the curve, it is possible to know that about two-thirds of all scores (68%, or 34% + 34%) in a population fall within a single standard deviation on either side of the mean. Furthermore, 95% of all scores fall within two standard deviations on either side of the mean. Obviously, scores that fall beyond two standard deviations are rare; they occur only 5% of the time. You might even describe such events as significant, as in "statistically significant." Keep this concept in mind; we'll return to it shortly.

The **standard deviation** for a set of *sample* scores is a measure of the average amount that the scores in the sample distribution deviate from the mean score. Two methods for calculating the size of a standard deviation are shown in Table 4.4. The first follows directly from the definition; the second is a computational approach, easier to complete with a calculator. For the scores in the hypothetical memory study, one standard deviation is equal to 1.81 words.

Just as there is more than one measure of central tendency, additional measures of variability exist; the simplest is the **range**, which is the difference between the largest and the smallest sample score. For the memory scores, the range is 7 (21 − 14). A final measure is the **variance**, which is the number calculated during the standard deviation calculation just prior to taking the square root (3.27 for the memory scores).

Means and standard deviations are the descriptive statistics most frequently encountered in psychological research. *Both* are needed to describe a set of scores ad-

---

TABLE 4.4   *Calculating Standard Deviations*

If you are using a statistics package like SPSS or SAS, standard deviations will be printed out as part of the analysis you complete. Likewise, most calculators include some basic statistical functions and the standard deviation will be one of them. Thus, you might actually avoid having to do the calculation. However, you might have a cheap calculator or a concerned professor (or both) who shares my belief that doing these things by hand provides a better grasp of their meaning.

There are two ways to calculate a standard deviation. The first uses a *deviation formula*. Working through it gives you the best insight into the nature of a standard deviation, which is by definition an approximate measure of the average amount that each score deviates from the mean. Here's how to do it for the 20 memory scores:

Step 1.   Calculate the mean score as follows:

$$\bar{X} = \Sigma X/n = 17.3$$

Step 2.   Calculate deviation scores, square each one, and add them up. Each deviation score (small x) is found by subtracting the mean from each individual score (big X). That is, $x = X - \bar{X}$. Squaring gets rid of the negative numbers.

X	$\bar{X}$	x	x^2
16	17.3	−1.3	1.69
17	17.3	−0.3	0.09
14	17.3	−3.3	10.89
•	•	•	•
18	17.3	0.7	0.49

$$\Sigma x^2 = \mathbf{62.20}$$

TABLE 4.4 *Calculating Standard Deviations* (continued)

Step 3. Calculate standard deviation, s

$$s = \sqrt{\Sigma x^2/(n-1)}$$
$$= \sqrt{62.2/(20-1)}$$
$$= \sqrt{3.27}$$
$$= \mathbf{1.81}$$

The deviation formula works fine, but it is a bit awkward for the calculator. A simpler method is to use *computational formula*, which is mathematically identical to the deviation formula. The formula is

$$s = \sqrt{\frac{\Sigma X^2 - (\Sigma X)^2/n}{n-1}}$$

and the calculation goes like this:

Step 1. Calculate ΣX^2 and $(\Sigma X)^2$

$$\Sigma X^2 = 16^2 + 17^2 + 14^2 + \cdots 18^2$$
$$= 256 + 289 + 196 + \cdots 324$$
$$= \mathbf{6048}$$

$$(\Sigma X)^2 = (16 + 17 + 14 + \cdots 18)^2$$
$$= 346^2$$
$$= \mathbf{119,716}$$

Step 2. Calculate $\Sigma X^2 - (\Sigma X)^2/n$

$$= 6048 - (119,716)/20$$
$$= 6048 - 5985.80$$
$$= \mathbf{62.2}$$

Step 3. Divide the result of Step 2 by $(n-1)$

$$= 62.2/19$$
$$= \mathbf{3.27}$$

Step 4. To get the standard deviation, take the square root of the result of Step 3

$$s = \sqrt{3.27}$$
$$s = \mathbf{1.81}$$

equately, a principle you can verify by considering the following sets of scores and calculating the mean for each set.

Set A:	23	24	27	21	25
Set B:	18	31	25	34	12

For both sets of scores the mean is 120/5 or 24, yet the two sets are clearly different from each other. The difference is in the variability of the scores for each set.

Box 4.3

ETHICS—Lying with Statistics

We've all been exposed to the deceptive and potentially unethical use of statistical information. As I am writing this, I've just survived the 1992 presidential campaign in which Arkansas was described as either a model state (Bill Clinton's numbers) or a dark and sinister wasteland unfit for human habitation (George Bush's numbers). Although politicians might be the worst offenders, with authors of aspirin commercials perhaps a close second, statistics are abused frequently enough that most people tend to be skeptical about them and you often hear people say things like: "Statistics don't really tell you anything useful—you can make them do anything you'd like." Is this really true?

Certainly, there are decisions to be made about how to present data and what conclusions to draw from them. You can be reasonably confident that articles published in reputable journals, having gone through a tough peer review process, are reporting statistical analyses that lead to defensible conclusions. What you need to be careful about are the uses of statistics in the broader public arena or by people determined to convince you of the truth of their tenaciously held beliefs.

Being informed about the proper use of statistics will enable you to identify these questionable statistical practices. Some things to be careful about were first described in Darrell Huff's 142-page "How to Lie with Statistics" (1954). It begins with a famous quote attributed to the British politician Benjamin Disraeli: "There are lies, damned lies, and statistics" (p. 2).

Here's an example of how to lie with statistics that relates specifically to the visual portrayal of data—graphs. Suppose you read about a study of reaction time comparing males and females that includes the following graph:

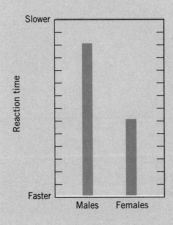

FIGURE 4.7   A bar graph showing hypothetical M-F reaction time differences with an unlabeled *Y*-axis.

This is a type of graph that Huff called a "Gee Whiz" graph, for obvious reasons. When you first looked at it, didn't you find yourself saying, "Gee whiz, what a big difference!"? The problem, however, is that the difference has been grossly exaggerated by fiddling with the vertical or Y-axis. You'll notice it is not labeled. If it was, the labels might look like the left-hand graph below. A more reasonable labeling of the Y-axis yields the graph on the right, which gives you a more "truthful" picture of what a statistical analysis would probably confirm—no significant difference exists.

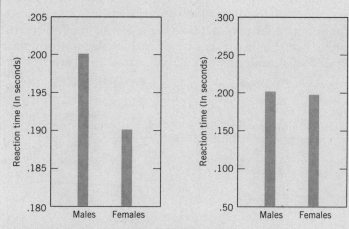

FIGURE 4.8 Bar graphs showing (*a*) a repeat of Figure 4.7, with Y-axis labeled and (*b*) the same data as in 4.7., but with Y-axis realistically labeled.

The moral is obvious: beware the Y-axis. Be especially skeptical about graphs that seem to show large differences with a Y-axis that is not labeled at all or labeled ambiguously.

The standard deviations are 2.24 for set A and 9.08 for set B (What are the ranges and variances for each set?). Hence, presenting an accurate picture of the data requires reporting measures of both central tendency and variability.

In articles describing research outcomes, descriptive statistics are reported three ways: First, if there are just a few numbers to report, they are sometimes worked into the narrative description; second, they might be presented in a table; and third, they might be placed into the visual form of a graph. Descriptions of how to construct tables and graphs that conform to the guidelines of the American Psychological Association and avoid the problems illustrated in Box 4.3 can be found in the sample research report in Appendix A. Chapter 7 also includes some information on graph making.

Inferential Statistics

Like most people, researchers have a need to be liked and admired by others. One way to accomplish this goal is to produce interesting research outcomes, results that apply beyond just the data collected in the study. That is, although a study looks at merely a small *sample* of all the data that could be collected, the researcher's hope is to arrive at a conclusion that will apply to the wider *population*. After all, the idea of the whole research enterprise is to arrive at general laws of behavior.

To illustrate what an inferential analysis tries to accomplish, let's consider a hypothetical maze learning study comparing rats fed immediately after reaching the end of a complicated maze with rats fed 10 seconds after reaching the end of the maze. Thus, the empirical question concerns whether immediate reinforcement is important for maze learning. Suppose the following results occurred for five rats in each group. Each score is the number of trials it takes for the rat to learn the maze; learning is operationally defined as two consecutive errorless runs through the maze.

Rat #	Immediate Food	Rat #	Delayed Food
1	12	6	19
2	13	7	20
3	16	8	16
4	11	9	18
5	14	10	15

Notice that the scores within each column are not all the same, a result of slight differences between the five rats in each group and perhaps some other random factors. Despite the lack of absolute uniformity, however, it appears that the rats given immediate reinforcement learned the maze faster (i.e., fewer trials).

Of course, we need more than a general impression resulting from a quick glance at the numbers. The first step is to calculate some descriptive statistics such as the mean and standard deviation. They are:

	Immediate	Delayed
Mean	13.2	17.6
Standard Deviation	1.9	2.1

On the average then, for this sample, maze learning required more trials when the food reward was delayed. Also, the variability of the scores within each set, as reflected in the standard deviations, is fairly low. Can we conclude *in general* that immediate reinforcement speeds up maze learning? Not yet. What is needed is an inferential analysis of the data that in this case involves what is called hypothesis testing.[1]

Hypothesis Testing

The first step in testing hypotheses is to make the assumption that there is *no* difference in performance between the different conditions that you are studying, in this case between immediate and delayed rewards. This assumption is called the **null hypothesis** (null = nothing), symbolized H_0 and pronounced "h sub oh." The research hypothesis, the outcome you are *hoping* to find (fewer trials for immediate reward), is called the **alternative hypothesis** or H_1. Thus, in your study, you hope to be able to disprove or reject H_0, thereby supporting (not proving) H_1, the hypothesis close to your heart.

If this language sounds odd to you, think of it as analogous to what happens in a court of law. There, the accused person is "presumed innocent." That is, the assumption is that the defendant has done nothing (null-thing). The job of the prosecution is to convince the jury of its alternative hypothesis, namely, that the defendant committed the crime. Like the prosecutor, the researcher's task is to show that something indeed happened, namely, that the reinforcement delay influenced learning, in the case being examined here.

There can only be two outcomes to any inferential analysis. The differences you find between the two groups of rats could be due to some genuine, real, honest-to-goodness effect or they could be due to chance. That is, the sample differences might mirror a true difference, or they might not. Hence, an inferential statistical analysis yields only two results—you can either reject H_0 or fail to reject it. Failing to reject H_0 means that any differences you've found (and studies almost always find *some* differences between groups) were most likely chance differences—you have failed to find a genuine effect that can be generalized beyond your sample. Rejecting H_0 means that you believe that an effect truly happened in your study and the results can be generalized. In the maze example, rejecting H_0, that is, finding a statistically significant difference, means that it really does seem to be a general rule that immediate reinforcement aids maze learning.

The researcher's hypothesis (H_1) is never "proven" to be true in an absolute sense, just as defendants are never *absolutely* proven guilty: Guilt is said to be proven only "beyond a reasonable doubt." Rather, H_0 can only be rejected (and at the same time H_1 supported) with some degree of confidence, which is set by what is called the **alpha (α) level**. Technically, alpha refers to the probability that you will reject H_0 by mistake (i.e., you think you have found a real effect, but there really isn't one in the population). By convention, alpha is set at .05 ($\alpha = .05$), but it can be set at other levels as well (e.g., $\alpha = .01$). If H_0 is rejected when alpha equals .05, it means that you believe the probability is very low (5 out of 100) that your research outcome is the result of chance factors.

---

[1] A second category of inferential analysis is called "estimation;" it involves estimating population values from sample scores.

The choice of .05 relates to the earlier discussion of the characteristics of the normal curve. Remember that for a normal distribution of scores, the probability is low, 5% or less, that a given score will be more than two standard deviations from the mean. Such an event is rare. Similarly, when comparing two sets of scores, as in the maze study, one asks about the probability of the obtained difference between the means occurring if the truth was that no real difference existed. If that probability is low enough, we reject H_0 and decide that some real difference must be occurring. The "low enough" is the probability of 5%, or .05. Another way to put it is to say that the obtained difference between the means would be so unexpected (i.e., rare) if H_0 were true that we just cannot believe that H_0 is true. We believe that something else happened, so we reject H_0 and conclude that a "statistically significant" difference exists.

Clear from this information is the fact that when you decide whether or not to reject H_0, you could be wrong. Actually, there are two kinds of errors you could make. First, you might reject H_0 and support H_1, get all excited about making some new breakthrough discovery, but be wrong. Rejecting H_0 when H_0 is in fact true is called a **Type I error**. The chance of this happening is equal to the value of alpha. That is, setting alpha at .05 and rejecting it means there is a 5% chance of making a Type I error—a 5% chance of thinking you have a real effect, but being wrong. Type I errors are sometimes suspected when a result fails several attempts at replication.

The other kind of mistake you could make is called a **Type II error**. This happens when you fail to reject H_0, but you are wrong. That is, you don't find a significant effect in your study, naturally feel depressed about it, but are in fact in error. There really is a true effect in the population, you just haven't found it in the sample you studied. Type II errors sometimes occur when the measurements used aren't very reliable or aren't sensitive enough to detect differences between conditions. As you will see in Chapter 9, this sometimes happens in program evaluation research. A program might indeed have a significant but small effect on those in it, but the measures used are too weak to pick up the subtle effects.

Table 4.5 summarizes the four possible outcomes of an inferential statistical analysis comparing two conditions of an experiment. As you can see, correct decisions result from rejecting H_0 when it is false and not rejecting H_0 when it is true. Erroneously rejecting H_0 produces a Type I error; a failure to reject H_0 when H_0 is false is a Type II error. If it makes it easier to understand the terminology, you can make the following substitutions in Table 4.5:

> For "Fail to Reject H_0," substitute:
> — "You did the study, you went through all the proper analyses, and what you came up with was zilch, nothing, zippo, no significant differences, and yes, you have good reason to be distraught, especially if this is your senior thesis project!"
> For "Reject H_0," substitute:
> — "You did the study, you went through all the proper analyses, and the difference came out significant at the .05 level, and yes, your life now has meaning and you'll be able to impress your friends and especially

TABLE 4.5   *Statistical Decision-Making: Four Possible Outcomes of a Study Comparing Two Conditions,* X *and* Y

		The True State of Affairs	
		H_0 is true: There should be no difference between X and Y	H_0 is false: There really is a difference between X and Y
Your Statistical Decision	**Fail to reject H_0:** In my study, I found no significant difference between X and Y, so I cannot reject H_0	Correct decision	Type II error
	Reject H_0: In my study, I found a significant difference between X and Y, so I reject H_0	Type I error	Correct decision {experimenter heaven}

your thesis director because you went through all this work and you *actually found something!*"

For "H_0 is true," substitute:

— "regardless of what might have occurred in your study, no true difference exists."

For "H_1 is true," substitute:

— "regardless of what might have occurred in your study, a true difference does exist."

With the substitutions in mind, correct decisions mean either (a) no real difference exists, which is OK because you didn't find one anyway, or (b) a real difference exists, and you found it (yes!!). A Type I error means there's no real difference, but you think there is because of the results of your particular study. A Type II error means there really is a difference, but you missed it in your study.

An inferential statistical decision to reject or not reject the null hypothesis in a study like the maze learning study depends on analyzing two general types of variability in the data. The first refers to the differences in the "number of trials to reach criterion" scores for the two groups of rats. These differences are caused by some combination of what is called (a) systematic variance and (b) error variance. **Systematic variance** is the result of some identifiable factor, either the variable of interest (reinforcement delay) or some factor that you've failed to control adequately.[2] **Error variance** is nonsystematic variability due to individual differences

---

[2]These uncontrolled factors are called *confounds*, and they will be examined in depth in the next chapter.

between the rats in the two groups and any number of random, unpredictable effects. Error variance also occurs within each group and accounts for the differences found there.

Mathematically, many inferential analyses will calculate some form of ratio that takes this form

$$\frac{\text{inferential}}{\text{statistic}} = \frac{\text{variability between conditions}}{\text{variability within each condition}}$$

The ideal outcome is to find that variability between conditions is huge, and variability within each condition is relatively small.

As you can see for yourself, this outcome occurs for the maze data; the differences between the two groups are substantial, while the scores within each group cluster fairly close together. The particular inferential test you would probably use in this case is called a *t* test for independent groups. Appendix B describes how you would actually do one.

Armed with some of the basics of how psychologists think about data, you are now ready to tackle the first of three chapters dealing with the experimental method, psychology's most powerful tool for trying to understand the intricacies of human behavior and mental processes. We'll begin with a general introduction to the experimental method, then consider some control problems that occur with such research; last, we'll examine the features of the most common types of experimental designs.

Chapter Review

Glossary Fill-Ins

1. In a _____ procedure, the researcher measures the amount of time an infant spends looking at a stimulus that is shown several times in succession.

2. If there is a great deal of _____, then reliability will be low.

3. The goal of random sampling is to select a group that will be _____ of the population as a whole.

4. A(n) _____ scale of measurement is used when research participants study and then recall a list of twenty words.

5. _____ statistics are used to answer the question: What was the typical performance of subjects on the color blindness test?

6. A researcher finds a significant difference in map-reading skill between males

and females. Nobody else can replicate the difference. The researcher may be making a _____ error.

Multiple Choice

1. For the recent studies described at the beginning of the chapter, which construct was measured by asking subjects to fill out a survey?
   a. Calculation abilities
   b. Span of apprehension
   c. Perceived support
   d. Macrochoices

2. Which of the following is true about the reliability of a measure?
   a. A measure is reliable if it seems to "make sense" as a measure of some construct (e.g., problem solving seems reasonable as a measure of intelligence).
   b. In experimental research, reliability is routinely assessed via correlational procedures.
   c. The higher the measurement error, the higher the reliability.
   d. The phrenologist's skull measurements would score high on a test for reliability.

3. The construct "delay of gratification" achieved construct validity because
   a. Children scoring high on Mischel's "delay" measure behaved as predicted on tasks that should have been related to delay of gratification.
   b. Children scoring high on Mischel's "delay" measure scored high on an already existing and accepted measure of "impulsiveness."
   c. The task used by Mischel made a great deal of sense as a way to measure impulsiveness.
   d. Children who showed a willingness to delay gratification once were likely to do the same thing when retested.

4. What is the advantage of cluster sampling over simple random sampling and stratified sampling?
   a. Unlike the others, cluster sampling is an example of probability sampling.
   b. With cluster sampling, it is not necessary to begin with a complete list of the population.
   c. Cluster sampling allows you to represent subgroups of the population (e.g., males and females) accurately.
   d. Cluster sampling is the only one that could be called "convenience" sampling.

5. Which of the following is accurately paired?
   a. Interval—numbers assigned to houses as street addresses.
   b. Ratio—temperature in Celsius (not Fahrenheit).
   c. Nominal—how long babies look at novel stimuli.
   d. Ordinal—college student deciding that professor X is the toughest grader, professor Y is next, and so on.

Applications Exercises

Exercise 4.1 — Sampling

1. Use the table of random numbers in Appendix C to select a simple random sample of students from your experimental psychology class; your instructor will provide a class list and indicate sample size.

2. Repeat the exercise but select a stratified sample that reflects the male-female proportions of your experimental psychology class.

Exercise 4.2 — Scales of Measurement

For each of the following studies, indicate which scale of measurement is being used for the behavior being measured.

1. Sally wishes to discover whether the children of Republicans and Democrats are more likely to major in the sciences, humanities, or business.

2. Fred decides to investigate whether rats who have learned one maze will learn a second one faster than naive rats.

3. Jim hypothesizes that children will rank different TV shows higher if they are in color, but that adults rankings won't be affected by color.

4. Nancy believes that somatotype changes with age so she proposes to use Sheldon's scale to measure somatotypes for a group of people on their tenth, fifteenth, and twentieth birthdays.

5. Susan is interested in helping behavior and believes the chances of someone helping are greater on sunny than on cloudy days.

6. John wishes to determine which of five new varieties of beer will be liked best by the patrons of his bar.

7. Ellen is interested in how students perceive the safety of various campus buildings. She asks a sample of students to arrange a deck of cards, each containing the name of a campus building, in a pile with the safest building on top and the least safe building on the bottom.

8. Pat believes that those with obsessive-compulsive disorders will make fewer formatting errors on APA-style lab reports that those without the disorder.

Exercise 4.3 — H_0, H_1, Type I errors, and Type II errors

For each of the following studies, (a) identify the null hypothesis, (b) make your best guess about the alternative hypothesis (that is, what would you expect to happen in this study), (c) describe an outcome that would be a Type I error, and (d) describe an outcome that would be a Type II error.

1. In a study of how well people can detect lying, male and female subjects will try to detect deception in films of females lying in some parts of the film and telling the truth in other parts.

2. In a perception study, infants will be habituated to slides of normal faces, then shown faces with slight irregularities to see if they can detect the differences.

3. Depressed and nondepressed patients will be asked to predict how they will do in negotiating a human maze.

4. Some athletes are given training in a new imaging procedure that they are to use just prior to shooting foul shots; they are compared with other athletes not given any special training.

Exercise 4.4 — Descriptive Statistics

Create two hypothetical sets of data for 20 trials of a simple reaction time task. Arrange it so that both sets have the same mean, but different medians, and different standard deviations. Draw a frequency distribution for each.

Exercise 4.5 — Inferential Statistics

Following the example in Appendix B, complete a *t* test for the hypothetical maze learning study described in this chapter. What do you conclude? Do the rats learn faster if given immediate rewards?

CHAPTER 5

Introduction to Experimental Research

Chapter Overview

- ## Essential Features of Experimental Research

  An experiment in psychology involves establishing independent variables, controlling extraneous variables, and measuring dependent variables. Independent variables refer to the creation of experimental conditions or comparisons that are under the direct control of the researcher. Extraneous variables are factors that are not of interest to the researcher; failure to control them leads to a problem called confounding. Dependent variables are the behaviors that are measured in the study; they must be defined precisely.

- ## Manipulated versus Subject Variables

  Some research in psychology compares groups of subjects who differ from each other in some way before the experiment begins (e.g., gender, age, intelligence). When this occurs, the independent variable is said to be selected by the experimenter rather than directly manipulated and it is called a subject variable. Research in psychology frequently includes both manipulated and subject variables. In a well-controlled study, conclusions about cause and effect can be drawn when using manipulated variables, but not when using subject variables.

• The Validity of Experimental Research

There are four ways in which psychological research can be considered valid. Valid research uses statistics properly (statistical conclusion validity), meaningfully defines independent and dependent variables (construct validity), generalizes its results beyond the particular experiment just completed (external validity), and is free of confounding variables (internal validity).

• Threats to Internal Validity

The internal validity of an experiment can be threatened by a number of factors. History, maturation, testing, instrumentation, and regression are confounding factors especially likely to occur in studies that include comparisons between pretests and posttests or studies lacking adequate control groups. Selection problems can occur when comparisons are made between groups of subjects who differ from each other in some systematic fashion. Selection problems also can interact with the other threats to internal validity, creating further difficulties with the interpretation of results. Problems with attrition occur when significant numbers of subjects drop out during the course of the study.

When Robert Sessions Woodworth published his *Experimental Psychology* in 1938, the book's content was already well-known among psychologists. As early as 1909, Woodworth was giving his Columbia University students copies of a mimeographed handout called "Problems and Methods in Psychology," and a companion handout called "Laboratory Manual: Experiments in Memory, etc." appeared in 1912. By 1920, the manuscript filled 285 pages and was called *A Textbook of Experimental Psychology*. After a 1932 revision, still in mimeograph form, the book finally was published in 1938. By then Woodworth's former students were using it to teach their own students and it was so well known that the publisher's announcement of its publication said simply "The Bible Is Out" (Winston, 1990).

The so-called Columbia Bible was encyclopedic, with more than 823 pages of text and another 36 pages of references. After an introductory chapter, it was organized into 29 different research topics such as "memory," "maze learning," "reaction time," "association," "hearing," "the perception of color," and "thinking." Students using the text would learn about the methods used in each content area, and they would also learn virtually everything there was to know in 1938 about each topic.

The impact of the Columbia Bible on the teaching of experimental psychology has been incalculable. Indeed, the teaching of experimental psychology today, and to some degree the structure of the book you're now reading, is largely cast in the mold set by Woodworth. In particular, he took the term experiment, until then loosely defined as virtually any type of empirical research, and gave it the definition it has today. Specifically, he contrasted it with correlational research, a distinction now taken for granted.

The defining feature of the experimental method was the manipulation of what Woodworth called an "independent variable," and this variable would have its effects on what he called the "dependent variable." In his words, the experimenter "holds all the conditions constant except for one factor which is his 'experimental factor' or his 'independent variable.' The observed effect is the 'dependent variable' which in a psychological experiment is some characteristic of behavior or reported experience" (Woodworth, 1938, p. 2). Although the terms were not invented by Woodworth, he was the first to use them as they are used today.

While the experimental method manipulates independent variables, the correlational method, according to Woodworth, "[m]easures two or more characteristics of the same individuals [and] computes the correlation of these characteristics. This method . . . has no 'independent variable' but treats all the measured variables alike" (Woodworth, 1938, p. 3). You'll learn more about correlational research in Chapter 8. For this and the next two chapters, however, the focus is on the experimental method, the researcher's most powerful tool for identifying cause and effect relationships.

Essential Features of Experimental Research

Since Woodworth, psychologists have thought of an **experiment** as a systemic research study in which the investigator directly varies some factor (or factors), holds all else constant, and observes the results of the systematic variation. The factors under the control of the experimenter are called independent variables, the variables being held constant are referred to as extraneous variables, and the behaviors measured are called dependent variables. Let's consider each of these characteristics in more detail.

Establishing Independent Variables

Any experiment can be described as a study that investigates the effect of *X* on *Y*. The *X* is Woodworth's **independent variable**—it is the factor of interest to the experimenter, the one that is being studied to see if it will influence behavior. It is sometimes called a "manipulated" factor, because the experimenter has complete control over it and is creating the situations that research participants will encounter in the study. As you will see, the concept of an independent variable can also extend to what are called nonmanipulated or subject variables, but for now let us consider only those independent variables that are under the experimenter's total control.

Independent variables must have a minimum of two "levels." That is, at the very least an experiment involves a comparison between two situations (or "conditions"). For example, suppose a researcher is interested in the effects of different dosages of marijuana on reaction time. In such a study, there has to be at least two different dosage levels in order to make a comparison. This study would be described as an experiment with "amount of marijuana" as the independent variable and "dosage 1" and "dosage 2" as the two levels of the independent variable. Of course, independent variables can have more than two levels. In fact, there are distinct advantages to adding levels beyond the minimum of two, as you'll see in Chapter 7 on experimental design.

Experimental research can be either basic or applied in its goals, and it can be conducted either in the laboratory or in the field (see Chapter 3 for an elaboration of these distinctions). Experiments that take place in the field are sometimes called **field experiments**. The term **field research** is a broader term for any empirical research outside of the laboratory, including both experimental studies and studies using nonexperimental methods.

Varieties of Independent Variables

The range of factors that can be used as independent variables is limited only by the creative thinking ability of the researcher. However, independent variables that are manipulated in a study tend to fall into three somewhat overlapping categories: situational variables, task variables, and instructional variables.

Situational variables are different features in the environment that subjects might encounter. For example, in a helping behavior study, the researcher interested in studying the effect of the number of bystanders on the chances of help being offered might create a situation in which subjects encounter a person in need of help. Sometimes the subject is alone with the person needing aid; other times the subject and the victim are accompanied by a group of either three or six bystanders. In this case, the situational independent variable would be the number of potential helpers on the scene with the subject and the levels would be 0, 3, and 6 bystanders.

Sometimes experimenters vary the type of task performed by subjects. One way to manipulate **task variables** is to give groups of subjects different kinds of problems to solve. For instance, research on the psychology of reasoning often involves giving subjects different kinds of logical problems to determine the kinds of errors people tend to make. Similarly, mazes can differ in the degree of complexity, different types of illusions could be presented in a perception study, and so on.

Instructional variables are manipulated by asking different groups of subjects to perform a particular task in different ways. For example, subjects in a memory task who are all shown the same list of words might be given different instructions about how to memorize the list. Some might be told to form visual images of the words, others might be told to form associations between adjacent pairs of words, and yet others might be told simply to repeat the words three times as each is presented.

Of course, it is possible to combine several types of independent variables in a single study. First, a study of the effects of crowding, task difficulty, and motivation on problem-solving ability could have subjects placed in either a large or small room, thereby manipulating crowding through the situational variable of room size. Second, some subjects in each type of room could be given difficult crossword puzzles to solve and others less difficult ones; this illustrates a task variable. Third, an instructional variable could manipulate motivation by telling subjects that they will earn either one dollar or five dollars for completing the puzzles.

Control Groups

In some experiments, the independent variable is whether or not some treatment is administered. The levels of the independent variable in this case are essentially 1 and 0: Some subjects get the treatment and others don't. In a study of the effects of TV violence on children's aggressive behavior, for instance, some children might be shown a violent TV program, while others don't get to see it. The term **experimental group** is used as a label for this first situation, in which the treatment is present. Those in the second type of condition, in which treatment is withheld, are said to be in the **control group**. Ideally, the subjects in a control group are identical to the experimental group subjects in all ways except that they do not get the experimental treatment. In essence, the control group provides a baseline measure against which the experimental group's behavior can be compared. Think of it this way: Control group = comparison group.

Varieties of Control Groups

Besides the typical control group situation in which a group is left untreated, there are three other types of control groups worth mentioning here: placebo controls, waiting list controls, and yoked controls.

A placebo is a substance that appears to have a some specific effect, but in fact is inactive. Sometimes patients will feel better when given a placebo but told it is drug X, simply because they believe the drug will make them better. In research, members of a **placebo control group** are led to believe that they are receiving some treatment when in fact they aren't. You can see why this would be necessary. Suppose you wished to determine if alcohol slows down reaction times. If you used a simple experimental group that was given alcohol and a second group that received nothing to drink, then gave both groups a reaction time test, the reactions might be slower for the first group. Can you conclude that alcohol slows reaction time? No—subjects might *think* that alcohol will slow them down, and their reactions might just reflect that bias. To solve the problem, you should include a group given a drink that seems to be alcoholic (and cannot be distinguished in taste from the true alcoholic drink) but isn't. This group is the placebo control group. Should you eliminate the straight control group (no drinks at all)? No—these subjects yield a simple baseline measure of reaction time. Suppose you use all three groups and get these average reaction times:

Experimental group → 0.32 seconds
Placebo control → 0.22 seconds
Straight control → 0.16 seconds

You could conclude that what subjects expect about the effects of alcohol slows reaction time somewhat (from 0.16 to 0.22), but that alcohol by itself also has an effect beyond people's expectations (0.22 to 0.32).

Waiting list control groups are often found in program evaluation research (Chapter 9), or in studies on the effectiveness of psychotherapy. In this case, the subjects in the experimental group are in a program because they are experiencing

Box 5.1

ETHICS—*Control Groups and Cancer Research*

In a study on human memory, in which an experimental group gets special instructions to use visual imagery while a control group is just told to learn the word lists, the question of who is assigned to the control group does not create an ethical dilemma. However, things are not so simple when an experiment is designed to evaluate the effectiveness of some program or treatment, which, if effective, would clearly benefit people by prolonging their lives. For example, in a well-known study of the effects of personal control on health (Langer & Rodin, 1976), some nursing home residents were given increased control over their daily planning, while control group residents had their daily planning done for them (for the most part) by nursing staff. On the average, residents in the first group were healthier, mentally and physically, and were more likely to be alive when the authors came back and did an 18-month follow-up study (Rodin & Langer, 1977). If you discovered that one of your relatives had been assigned to the control group, do you think you would be concerned?

In a similar vein, there has recently been some controversy over the assignment of subjects to control groups in psychological research with cancer patients (Adler, 1992). The research concerns the effects of support groups on the psychological well-being and physical health of women with breast cancer. The findings indicate that women in these groups recover more quickly and even live longer than women

some problem that the program is supposed to alleviate. For instance, a college might develop a program for treating students suffering from severe test anxiety. Anxiety before and after the program would be measured for the participants, but it would not be a good idea to compare their anxiety with the anxiety of just any other sample of students. Rather, it is better to use as a control group a sample of other subjects who are experiencing test anxiety also, but are on a waiting list for the program. If the program lasts from October 1 to October 30, then both groups could be assessed on both dates, but only the experimental group would get the program in October. Assuming the program is judged to be effective, the waiting list controls would get it in November.

Providing the opportunity for the waiting list subjects to benefit from the program also satisfies the ethical need to provide a service to students with problems that could hurt them in school, but it creates pressures on the researcher to use this control procedure only for brief-duration therapies or programs. In fact, some might argue that it is unethical to put people into a waiting list control group because they won't receive the program's benefits right away. This issue can be especially problematic when research evaluates life-influencing programs. Read Box

in control groups. Some researchers have argued that the data don't reflect the benefits of support groups as much as the harm done to those in the control group who might feel left out or rejected. This could create stress and it is known that stress can harm the immune system, leading to a host of health-related problems. So can being in a control group kill you?

Defenders of the traditional control group approach to evaluating programs make three arguments. First, they point out that hindsight is usually perfect. It is easy after the fact to say that "a program as effective as this one ought to be available to everyone." The problem is that *before* the fact it is not so obvious that a program would be effective. The only way to tell is to do the study. Prior to Langer and Rodin's nursing home study, for example, one could have predicted that the experimental subjects would be unnecessarily stressed by the added responsibilities and drop like flies. Similarly, those defending the cancer studies point out that when these studies began, few women expressed any preference about their assignment to either an experimental or a control group and some actually preferred to avoid the support groups (Adler, 1992). Hence, it was not likely that control group subjects really felt left out or deprived.

Second, researchers point out that in research evaluating some new treatment, the comparison is seldom between the new treatment and no treatment, it is usually between the new treatment and the current form of treatment. So for control group members, available services are not really being withheld.

Third, treatments cost money and it is certainly worthwhile to spend the bucks on the best treatment. That cannot be determined without well-designed research on program effectiveness. In the long run, then, programs with empirically demonstrated effectiveness serve the general good.

5.1 for an examination of this issue and a defense of the use of control groups in research.

A third type of control group is the **yoked control group**. It is used when subjects in the experimental group, for one reason or another, participate for varying amounts of time or are subjected to different types of events in the study. Each member of the control group is matched or "yoked" to a member of the experimental group so that for the two groups as a whole, the time spent participating or the types of events encountered is kept constant. A good example of a yoked control group is a study by Weiss (1977), which examined the relationship between control of stress and health. A group of experimental rats were exposed to occasional mild shocks to their tails but could turn them off (i.e., control them) by turning a small wheel with their paws (see Figure 5.1). A second group (straight control) was never shocked. A third group was a yoked control group. Each rat in this group was "yoked" to (paired with) a rat in the experimental group so that it received the same number of shocks, but could not control them. On a given trial, if rat A in the experimental group was shocked for two seconds before turning the wheel, the yoked rat would also be shocked for exactly two seconds on that trial.

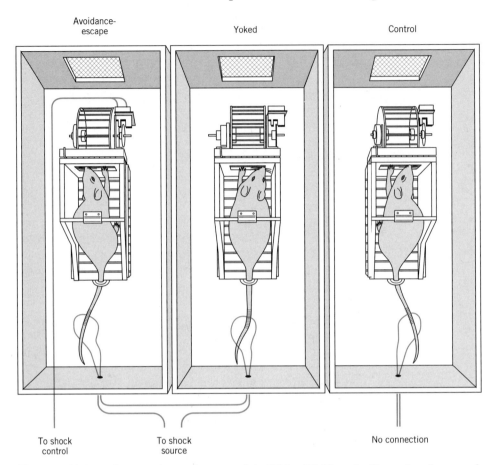

Avoidance-escape   Yoked   Control

To shock   To shock   No connection
control   source

FIGURE 5.1   The experimental set-up of the Weiss (1977) study, illustrating the use of a yoked control group.

Thus, the rats in the two groups received exactly the same degree of aversiveness. Weiss concluded that having control over the shock helped the rats avoid some of the unhealthful consequences of stress—the yoked rats developed ulcers, but rats in the other two groups didn't.

You might recognize the Weiss design as being the same as that used by Seligman to study learned helplessness. If you'll look back to the Chapter 3 discussion of falsification (p. 74), you'll find a description of a yoked control procedure, although I didn't use the term at that point.

Controlling Extraneous Variables

The second feature of the experimental method is that the researcher tries to control what are called **extraneous variables**. These are any uncontrolled factors that are not of interest to the researcher. As long as these are held constant, they present no danger to the study. If they are not adequately controlled, however, they might influence the behavior being measured in a systematic way. The result is called confounding. That is, a **confound** is any uncontrolled extraneous variable that covaries with the independent variable and could provide an alternative explanation of the results. Because a confounding variable changes at the same time that the independent variable changes, its effects cannot be separated from the effects of the independent variable. Hence, when a study has a confound, the results could be due to the effect of *either* the confound or the independent variable (or both), and there is no way to decide between the alternatives.

To illustrate some obvious confounding, consider a verbal learning experiment in which a researcher wants to show that students who try to learn a large amount of material all at once don't do as well as those who spread their learning over several sessions. That is, "massed" practice (cramming?) is predicted to be inferior to "distributed" practice. Three groups of students are selected, and each is given the same five chapters in a general psychology text to learn. Subjects in the first group are given 3 hours on Monday to study the material. Subjects in a second group are given 3 hours on Monday and 3 hours on Tuesday, and those in the final group get three hours on Monday, Tuesday, and Wednesday. On Friday, all of the groups are tested on the material (see Table 5.1 for the design). The results show that group 3 scores the highest, followed by group 2. Group 1 does not do well at all and the researcher concludes that distributed practice is superior to massed practice. Do you agree?

You probably don't agree with the conclusion, because there are at least two serious confounds in this study, both easy to spot. The subjects certainly differ in how their practice is distributed (1, 2, or 3 days), the *also* differ in how much total practice they get (3, 6, or 9 hours). This is a perfect example of a confound—it is impossible to tell if the results are due to one factor (distribution of practice) or the other (total practice hours); the two factors perfectly covary. The way to describe this situation is to say that "distribution of practice is confounded with total study hours." The second confound is retention interval. The test is on Friday for everyone, but different amounts of time have elapsed between study and test for each group. Perhaps group 3 did the best because they studied the material most recently and forgot the least amount. In this experiment then, distribution of practice is confounded with total study hours and with retention interval. Each confound by itself could account for the results, and the factors may also have interacted with each other in some way to provide yet another interpretation.

TABLE 5.1   *Confounding in a Hypothetical Distribution of Practice Experiment*

	Monday	Tuesday	Wednesday	Thursday	Friday
Group 1	3	—	—	—	*exam*
Group 2	3	3	—	—	*exam*
Group 3	3	3	3	—	*exam*

Note: The 3 in each cell equals the number of hours studying five chapters of a general psychology text.

TABLE **5.2** *Identifying Confounds*

Levels of IV Distribution of Practice	EV 1 Study Hours	EV 2 Retention Interval	DV Retention Test Performance
1 day	3 hours	3 days	lousy
2 days	6 hours	2 days	average
3 days	9 hours	1 day	great

IV = independent variable.
EV = extraneous variable.
DV = dependent variable

Look at Table 5.2, which gives you a convenient way to identify confounds. In the first column are the levels of the independent variable and in the final column are the results. The middle columns are extraneous variables that should be held constant. If they are not (as is the case here), then a confound exists. As you can see, the results could be explained by the variation in any of the first three columns, either individually or in some combination. To correct the problem, you simply need to insure that the middle two columns are constant instead of variable.

In the Applications Exercises at the end of the chapter, you will be identifying confounds. You'll find the task easier if you fit the problems into the Table 5.2 format. Take a minute and redesign the distributed practice study. How could you eliminate the confounding from these extraneous variables?

Learning to be aware of potential confounding factors and building appropriate ways to control for them are two of the scientific thinking skills that are most difficult to develop. Not all confounds are as obvious as the massed/distributed practice example. We'll encounter the problem often in remaining chapters and address it again shortly in the context of a discussion of what is called the internal validity of a study.

Measuring Dependent Variables

The third part of any experiment is measuring some behavior that is presumably influenced by the independent variable. The term **dependent variable** is used to describe those behaviors that are the measured outcomes of experiments. If, as mentioned earlier, an experiment can be described as the effect of X on Y and X is the independent variable, then Y is the dependent variable. In a study of the effects of TV violence on children's aggressiveness, the dependent variable would be some measure of aggressiveness. In the distribution of practice study, it would be a measure of exam performance.

The credibility of any experiment and its chances of discovering anything of value depend partly on the decisions made about what behaviors to measure as dependent variables. We've already seen that empirical questions cannot be answered unless the terms are defined with some precision. You might take a minute and review the section on "asking empirical questions" in Chapter 3 (pp. 63–65). It will remind you about the concepts of operational definitions and converging operations.

One final point. It is important to realize that a particular construct could be an independent, extraneous, or dependent variable, depending on the problem at hand. An experiment might manipulate a particular construct as an independent variable, try to control it as an extraneous factor, or measure it as a dependent variable. Consider the construct of anxiety, for instance. It could be a manipulated independent variable by telling subjects that they will be experiencing shock levels that will be either moderate or painful and then asking subjects if they prefer to wait by themselves or with others. It could also be a factor needing to be held constant in some experiments. For instance, if you wanted to evaluate the effects of a public-speaking workshop on the ability of students to deliver a brief speech, you wouldn't want to videotape those in one group without also taping the students in the other group. If everyone is taped, then the level of anxiety created by that factor is held constant. Anxiety could also be a dependent variable in a study of the effects of different types of exams (e.g., multiple choice vs essay) on the perceived test anxiety of students during final exam week. Some physiological measures of anxiety might be used in this case. Anxiety could also be considered a personality characteristic, with some people having more of it than others; this last possibility leads to the next topic.

Manipulated versus Subject Variables

Up to this point, the term independent variable has meant some factor manipulated directly by the researcher. An experiment compares one condition created by and under the control of the experimenter with another. In many studies, however, comparisons are also made between groups of people who differ from each other in ways other than those manufactured by the person designing the study. These comparisons are made between factors that are referred to variously as ex post facto variables, natural group variables, non-manipulated variables, or **subject variables**, which is the term I will use hereafter. They refer to already-existing characteristics of the subjects participating in the study, such as gender, age, intelligence, physical or psychiatric disorder, and any personality attribute you can name. When using subject variables in a study, the researcher cannot manipulate them directly but must *select* subjects for the different conditions by virtue of the characteristics they already have.

To illustrate the differences between manipulated and subject variables, consider a hypothetical study of the effects of anxiety on human maze learning. You could *manipulate* anxiety directly by creating a situation in which one group is made anxious (told they'll be performing in front of a large audience perhaps), while a second group is not (no audience). In that study, any subject who volunteers could potentially wind up in one group or the other. To do the study using a *subject* variable, on the other hand, you would select two groups differing in their characteristic levels of anxiety and ask each to try the maze. The first group would be those who were anxious types of people (as determined ahead of time by a personality test for anxiety proneness). The second group would include more relaxed types of people. Notice the major difference between this and the case of a manipulated variable. With anxiety as a subject variable, volunteers coming into the study cannot be placed into either of the conditions, but must be in one group or the other, depending on attributes they already possess. Anxious-all-the-time-Fred cannot be put into the "low-anxiety" group.

Some researchers, true to Woodworth's original use of the term, prefer to reserve the term independent variable for those variables directly manipulated by the experimenter. Others are willing to include subject variables as examples of a particular type of independent variable, on the grounds that the experimenter has some degree of control over them by virtue of the decisions involved in selecting them in the first place. I take this latter position and will use the term independent variable in the broader sense. However, whether the term independent variable is used broadly (manipulated + subject) or narrowly (manipulated only) is not important providing you understand the difference between a manipulated and a nonmanipulated or subject variable.

A study using only *manipulated* independent variables can be called an experiment in the strictest sense of the term; it is sometimes called a "true" experiment (which sounds a bit pretentious and carries the unfortunate implication that other studies are "false"). Studies using independent variables that are *subject* variables are occasionally called ex post facto studies or quasi-experiments ("quasi" meaning "to some degree" here).[1] Sometimes (often, actually) studies will include both manipulated and subject independent variables. Being aware of the presence of subject variables is important because they affect the kinds of conclusions that can be drawn from the study's results.

Drawing Conclusions when Using Subject Variables

Put a little asterisk next to this section—it's very important. Recall from Chapter 1 that one of the goals of research in psychology is to discover explanations for behavior. That is, we wish to know what caused some behavior to occur. Simply put, with manipulated variables, conclusions about the causes of behavior can be made; with subject variables, they cannot. The reason why has to do with the amount of control held by the experimenter in each case.

With manipulated variables, the experiment can meet the criteria listed in Chapter 1 for demonstrating efficient causality. The independent variable precedes the dependent variable, covaries with it, and assuming there are no confounds present, can be considered the most reasonable explanation for the results. In other words, if you vary some factor and successfully hold all else constant, the results

---

[1]The term "quasi-experimental" design is actually a broader term referring to any type of design in which subjects cannot be randomly assigned to the groups being studied (Cook & Campbell, 1979). These designs are often found in applied research and are elaborated in Chapter 9.

can only be attributed to the factor varied. In an experimental study with two groups, these groups will be equal to each other in all ways except for the manipulated factor.

When using subject variables, however, the experimenter can vary some factor (i.e., select subjects having certain characteristics) but cannot hold all else constant. Selecting subjects who are high or low on some definition of "anx. ty-proneness" does not guarantee that the two groups will be equivalent in othe. ways. In fact, they might be different from each other in several ways (self-confidence perhaps) that could influence the outcome of the study. When a difference between the groups occurs in this type of study, we cannot say that the differences were *caused* by the subject variable. In terms of the conditions for causality, while we can say that the independent variable precedes the dependent variable and covaries with it, we cannot eliminate alternative explanations for the relationship because extraneous factors cannot be controlled. When subject variables are present, all we can say is that the groups performed differently on the dependent measure.

An example from social psychology might help to clarify the distinction. Suppose you were interested in altruistic behavior and wanted to see how it was affected by the construct of "self-esteem." The study could be done in two ways. First, you could vary self-esteem directly by first giving subjects a bogus personality test. By providing different kinds of false feedback about the results of the test, positive and negative, self-esteem could be raised or lowered temporarily. Subjects could then be asked to do some volunteer work to see if those feeling good about themselves would be more likely to help.[2] A second way to do this study is to give subjects a valid personality test for level of self-esteem and select those who score in the upper 25% and lower 25% on the measure as the subjects for the two groups. Self-esteem in this case is a subject variable. As in the first study, these two types of people could be asked to do some volunteer work.

In the first study, differences in volunteering can be traced *directly* to the self-esteem manipulation. If all other factors are properly controlled, the temporary feeling of increased or decreased self-esteem is the *only* thing that could have produced the differences in helping. In the second study, however, you cannot say that high self-esteem is the direct cause of the helping behavior; what you can say is that people with high self-esteem are more likely to help than those with low self-esteem. All you can do is speculate about the reasons why this might be true because these subjects may differ from each other in other ways unknown to you. For instance, high self-esteem types of people might have had prior experience in volunteering and this experience had the joint effect of raising or strengthening their self-esteem and increasing the chances that they will volunteer in the future. Or they might have greater expertise in the specific volunteering tasks (e.g., public-speaking skills). As you will see in Chapter 8, this difficulty in interpretation is exactly the same problem encountered in correlational research.

Before moving on to the discussion of the validity of experimental research, read Box 5.2. It identifies the variables in a classic study that you probably recall

---

[2]Manipulating self-esteem raises ethical questions that were considered in a study by Sullivan and Deiker (1973). See Chapter 2, pp. 41–42.

Box 5.2

CLASSIC STUDIES — Bobo Dolls and Aggression

Ask any student who has just completed a course in child, social, or personality psychology (perhaps even general psychology) to tell you about the Bobo doll studies. The response will be immediate recognition, and a brief description along the lines of "Oh, yes, the studies showing that children will punch out an inflated doll if they see an adult doing it." A description of one of these studies is a good way to further clarify the differences between independent, extraneous, and dependent variables. The study was published by Albert Bandura and his colleagues in 1963 and is entitled "Imitation of Film-Mediated Aggressive Models" (Bandura, Ross, & Ross, 1963).

Establishing Independent Variables

The study included both manipulated and subject variables. The major manipulated variable was the type of experience that preceded the opportunity for aggression. There were four levels that included three experimental groups and a control group.

Experimental group 1: real life aggression (children directly observed an adult model aggressing against the Bobo doll)

Experimental group 2: human film aggression (children observed a film of an adult model aggressing against Bobo)

Experimental group 3: cartoon film aggression (children observed a cartoon of "Herman the Cat" aggressing against a cartoon Bobo)

Control group: no exposure to aggressive models

The nonmanipulated subject variable was gender. Male and female children from the Stanford University Nursery School (mean age = 52 months) were the subjects in the study. (Actually, there was also another manipulated variable — subjects in groups 1 and 2 were exposed to either a same-gender or opposite-gender model.) The basic procedure of the experiment was to expose the children to some type of aggressive model (or not, for group 4), then put them into a room full of toys (including Bobo), thereby giving them the opportunity to be aggressive themselves.

Controlling Extraneous Variables

Several possible confounds were nicely avoided. For example, in groups 1 and 2, the adults aggressed against a *5-foot* Bobo doll. When given a chance to pummel Bobo themselves, the children were put in a room with a *3-foot* Bobo doll. This kept the size relationship between person and doll approximately constant. Second, subjects in all four conditions were mildly frustrated before being given a chance to aggress. They were allowed to play for a few minutes with some very attractive toys, then told by the experimenter that the toys were special and were being reserved for some other children. Thus, for *all* the subjects, there was an equivalent (presumably) increase in their degree of emotional arousal just prior to the time when they were given the opportunity to be aggressive. Thus, any differences in aggressiveness could be attributed to the imitative effects and not emotional differences between the groups.

Measuring Dependent Variables

Several measures of aggression were used in this study. Aggressive responses were categorized as imitative, partially imitative, or nonimitative, depending on how closely they matched the model's behavior. For example, imitative aggressive behaviors included striking the doll with a wooden mallet, punching it in the nose, and kicking it. Partially imitative included hitting something else with the mallet and sitting on the doll but not hitting it. Nonimitative aggression included shooting darts from an available dart gun at targets other than Bobo and acting aggressively toward other objects in the room.

Briefly, the results of the study were that children in groups 1, 2, and 3 showed significantly more aggression than those in the control group, but the same amount of overall aggression occurred regardless of the type of modeling. Also, boys were more aggressive than girls in all conditions. Some gender differences also occurred in the style of aggression: The girls "were more inclined than the boys to sit on the Bobo doll but refrained from punching it" (Bandura, Ross, & Ross, 1963, p. 9). Figure 5.2 summarizes the results.

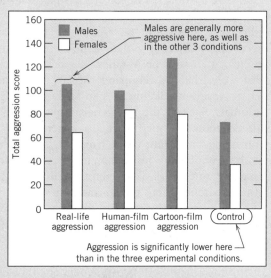

FIGURE 5.2 Data from Bandura, Ross, and Ross's Bobo study (1963) of the effects of imitation on aggression.

from your general psychology course—one of the so-called Bobo experiments that first investigated imitative aggression. Working through the example will help you apply your knowledge of independent, extraneous, and dependent variables, and to see how manipulated and subject variables are often used in the same study.

The Validity of Experimental Research

Chapter 4 introduced the concept of validity in the context of measurement. The term also applies to experiments as a whole—just as a measure is valid if it measures what it is supposed to measure, psychological research is said to be valid if it provides the understanding about behavior that it is supposed to provide. This section of the chapter introduces four different types of validity, following the scheme outlined by Cook and Campbell (1979) for research in field settings, but applicable to any experimental research. The four types of validity are statistical conclusion validity, construct validity (again), external validity, and internal validity.

Statistical Conclusion Validity

The last chapter introduced you to the use of statistics in psychology. In particular, you learned about measurement scales, the basic distinction between descriptive and inferential statistics, and the basics of hypothesis testing. **Statistical conclusion validity** concerns the extent to which the researcher uses statistics properly and draws the appropriate conclusions from the analysis.

The statistical validity of a study can be reduced in several ways. First, researchers might do the wrong analysis or violate some of the assumptions required for performing a particular analysis. For instance, the data for a study might be arranged on an ordinal scale, thereby requiring the use of a particular type of analysis. The researcher, however, mistakenly uses an analysis that is only appropriately for interval or ratio data. Second, the researcher might selectively report some analyses that came out as predicted, but not report others (guess which ones), a practice that borders on being fraudulent (see Chapter 2, pp. 49–52). This is similar to the third problem, in which the researcher might go "fishing." That is, the study has produced a massive amount of data, open to numerous combinations and types of analysis, and the researcher keeps trying different analyses until something significant emerges. Unfortunately, performing multiple analyses increases the chances of falsely thinking there is a significant effect. That is, the null hypothesis will be mistakenly rejected—a Type I error.

The final example of a factor that reduces the statistical validity of a study concerns the reliability of the measures used. If the dependent measures are not reliable, there will be a great deal of error variability, which reduces the chances of finding a significant effect. If there is a true effect (i.e., the null hypothesis should be rejected), but low reliability results in a failure to find it, the outcome would be a Type II error.

The careful researcher plans the statistical analysis at the same time the experimental design is being planned. In fact, no experiment should ever be designed without thought being given to how the data will be analyzed.

Construct Validity

The last chapter described construct validity in the context of measuring psychological constructs: It refers jointly to whether a test truly measures some hypothetical construct (e.g., delay of gratification) and whether the construct truly exists. In experimental research, **construct validity** has a related but slightly different meaning. It refers to the adequacy of the definitions for both the independent and dependent variables used in the study. In a study of the effects of TV violence on children's aggression, questions about construct validity could be (a) whether the programs chosen by the experimenter are the best choices to contrast violent versus nonviolent television programming, and (b) whether the measures of aggression used are the best ones that could be chosen. If the study used violent cartoon characters (e.g., Elmer Fudd shooting at Bugs Bunny) compared to nonviolent characters (e.g., Winnie the Pooh), someone might argue that children's aggressive behavior is unaffected by cartoons; hence, a more valid manipulation of the independent variable called "level of filmed violence" would involve showing children realistic films of people that varied in the amount of violence portrayed.

Similarly, someone might criticize the appropriateness of a measure of aggression used in a particular study. This is fact has been a problem in research on aggression. For rather obvious ethical reasons, you cannot design a study that results in subjects punching each other's lights out. Instead, aggression has been defined operationally in a variety of ways, some of which might seem to you to be more valid (e.g., angered subjects believing they are delivering shocks to another subject) than others (e.g., horn honking by frustrated drivers). As was true for the discussion of construct validity in the last chapter when the emphasis was on valid measurement, the validity of the choices about exactly how to define independent and dependent variables develops over time as accumulated research fits into a coherent (and converging) pattern.

External Validity

Experimental psychologists have been criticized for knowing a great deal about college sophomores and white rats and very little about anything else. This is in essence a criticism of **external validity**, which refers to the degree to which research findings generalize beyond the specific context of the experiment being conducted. For research to achieve the highest degree of external validity, its results should generalize in three ways—to other populations, to other environments, and to other times.

Other Populations

The comment about rats and sophomores fits here. As we've seen in Chapter 2, part of the debate over the appropriateness of animal research has to do with how well animal research provides explanations that are relevant for human behavior. Concerning sophomores, recall that Milgram deliberately avoided using college students; he selected adults from the general population as subjects for his obedience studies. The same cannot be said of most social psychologists, however. A survey by Sears (1986) of research in social psychology found that 75% of research published in 1980 in that field used undergraduates. When Sears repeated the survey for research published in 1985, the number was 74%. Sears argued that the characteristics of college students as a population could very well bias the general conclusions about social phenomena. Compared to the general population, for instance, college students are more able cognitively, more self-centered, more susceptible to social influence, and more likely to change their attitudes on issues. To the extent that research investigates issues related to those features, results from students might not generalize to other groups, according to Sears. He suggested that researchers expand the database and replicate important findings on a variety of populations. However, he also pointed out that many research areas (e.g., perception) produce outcomes relatively unaffected by the special characteristics of college students.

The "college sophomore problem" is only one example of a concern over generalizing to other groups. Another has to do with gender. Some of psychology's most famous research has been limited by using only males (or, less frequently, only females) and drawing conclusions as if they apply to everyone. Perhaps the best-known example is Lawrence Kohlberg's research on children's moral development. Kohlberg (1964) asked adolescent boys (aged 10–16) to read and respond to brief accounts of various moral dilemmas. On the basis of the boys' responses, Kohlberg developed a six-stage theory of moral development that became a fixture in developmental psychology texts. At the most advanced stage, the person acts according to a set of universal principles based on preserving justice and individuals rights.

In recent years, Kohlberg's theory has been criticized on external validity grounds. For example, Carol Gilligan (1982) has argued that Kohlberg's model overlooks important gender differences in thinking patterns and in how moral decisions are made. Males may place the highest value on individual rights, but females tend to value the preservation of individual relationships. Hence, females responding to some of Kohlberg's moral dilemmas might not seem to be as "advanced" morally as males, but this is due to a biasing of the entire model because Kohlberg sampled only males, according to Gilligan.

Other Environments

Besides generalizing to other types of individuals, externally valid results are applicable to other stimulus settings. This problem is the basis for the occasional criticism of laboratory research—it is said to be artificial and too far removed from "real life." Recall from the discussion of basic and applied research in Chapter 3 that the laboratory researcher's response to criticisms about artificiality is to use Aronson's concept of experimental reality. The important thing is that subjects be involved in the study; mundane reality is secondary.

Nonetheless, important developments in many subareas of psychology have resulted from attempts to study psychological phenomena in real-life settings. Such research is said to have **ecological validity**. The everyday memory research described in Chapter 1 (e.g., John Dean's memory, remember?) is an example of how concern over the limitations of laboratory research, in this case, memory experiments in the Ebbinghaus memorize-a-list-of-words tradition, led to a new direction.

Other Times

The third way in which external validity is sometimes questioned has to do with the longevity of results. One of the most famous series of experiments in all of psychology are the conformity studies done by Solomon Asch in the 1950s (e.g., Asch, 1956). These experiments were completed during a historical period when conservative values were dominant in the United States, the "red menace" of the former Soviet Union was a force to be feared, and conformity and obedience to authority were valued in society. In that context, Asch found that college students were remarkably susceptible to conformity pressures. Would the same be true today? Would the factors that Asch found to influence conformity (e.g., group consensus) operate in the same way today? In general, research concerned with more fundamental processes (e.g., cognition) stands the test of time better than research involving social factors that may be embedded in some historical context.

In summary, the external validity of some research finding increases as it applies to other people, places, and times. But must researchers design studies that include many different groups of people, take place in several settings, and get repeated every decade? Of course not. External validity is not determined by an individual research project; rather, this is another case of demonstrating the importance of the processes of replication and extension. For the researcher designing a study, the considerations of external validity pale compared to the importance of our next topic.

Internal Validity

The final type of experimental validity described by Cook and Campbell (1979) is called **internal validity**—the degree to which an experiment is methodologically sound and confound free. In an internally valid study, the researcher feels confident that the results, as measured by the dependent variable, are directly associated with the independent variable and not the result of some other, uncontrolled factor. In a study with confounding factors, as we've already seen in the massed/distributed practice example, the results may be uninterpretable. The outcome could be the result of the independent variable, the confounding variable(s), or some combination of both, and there is no clear way to decide between the different interpretations.

Threats to Internal Validity

Any uncontrolled extraneous factor can reduce a study's interval validity, but there are a number of problems that require special notice (Cook & Campbell, 1979).

These so-called threats to internal validity are especially dangerous when control groups are absent, a problem that sometimes occurs in program evaluation research (Chapter 9). Most of these problems occur in studies that extend over a period of time during which several measures are taken. For example, subjects might receive a pretest, an experimental treatment of some kind, then a posttest. Ideally, the treatment should produce some positive effect that can be assessed by observing changes from the pretest to the posttest. A second general type of threat occurs when comparisons are made between groups that are said to be "nonequivalent." These so-called subject selection problems can interact with the other threats.

Pretest-Posttest Studies

Do students learn general psychology better if the course is self-paced and computerized? If a college institutes a program to reduce test anxiety, can it be shown that it works? If you train people in various mnemonics strategies, will it improve their memories? These empirical questions all ask whether people will change as the result of some experience (a teaching method, an anti-anxiety program, memory training). To judge whether change occurred, one typical procedure is to evaluate people prior to the experience with what is known as a **pretest**. Then after the experience, some **posttest** measure is taken. The ideal outcome for the examples I've just described is that on the posttest, people (a) know general psychology better than they did at the outset, (b) are less anxious in test taking than they were before, or (c) show improvements in their memory ability. The typical research design compares experimental and control groups, with the latter not experiencing the treatment:

Experimental::	pretest	<u>treatment</u>	posttest
Control::	pretest		posttest

In the absence of a proper control group, there are several threats to the interval validity of research using pretests. Suppose we are trying to evaluate the effectiveness of a college's program to help students who suffer from test anxiety (i.e., they have decent study skills and tend to know the material, but they are so anxious during exams that they don't perform well on them). During freshman orientation, students fill out several questionnaires, including one that serves as a pretest for test anxiety. Let's assume the scores can range from 20 to 100, with higher scores indicating greater anxiety. Incoming students who score high are asked to participate in the college's test anxiety program, which includes relaxation training and other techniques. Three months later they are assessed again for test anxiety, and the results look like this:

pretest	<u>treatment</u>	posttest
90		70

Thus, the average pretest score of those selected for the program is 90 the average posttest score is 70. Assuming that the difference is statistically significant, what would you conclude? Did the treatment program work? Was the change due to the treatment or could other factors have been involved?

History and Maturation

Sometimes an event occurs between pre- and posttesting that produces large changes unrelated to the treatment program; when this happens, the study is confounded by **history**. For example, suppose the college in the previous example decided that grades are counterproductive to learning and that all courses would henceforth be graded on a pass/fail basis. Furthermore, suppose this decision came after the pretest for test anxiety and in the middle of the treatment program for reducing the anxiety. The posttest might show a huge drop in anxiety, but it could very likely be due to the historical event of the college's change in grading policy rather than to the program. Wouldn't you be a little more relaxed about this research methods course if grades weren't an issue?

In a similar fashion, the program for test anxiety involves first-semester freshmen, so prepost changes could also be the result of a general **maturation** of these students as they become accustomed to college life. As you probably recall, first-semester freshman year is a time of great change in one's life. Maturation is always a concern whenever a study extends over some period of time.

Notice of course that if a control group is used the experimenter can account for the effects of both history and maturation. These effects can be ruled out and the test anxiety program deemed effective if these results occurred:

Experimental::	pretest	<u>treatment</u>	posttest
	90		70
Control::	pretest		posttest
	90		90

On the other hand, either history or maturation or both would have to be considered as explanations for the changes in the experimental group if the control group scores dropped to 70 on the posttest.

Regression

To regress is to go back, in this case in the direction of a mean score. Hence, the phenomenon I'm about to describe is sometimes called **regression to the mean**. In essence, it refers to the fact that if score 1 is an extreme score, then score 2 will be closer to whatever the mean for the larger set of scores is. This is because, for a large set of scores, most will cluster around the mean and only a few will be far removed from the mean (i.e., extreme scores). Imagine you are selecting some score randomly from the normal distribution in Figure 5.3. Most of the scores center around the mean, so if you make a random selection, you'll most likely choose a score near the mean (X in the left-hand side of Figure 5.3). However, suppose you just happen to select one that is far removed from the mean (i.e., an extreme score — Y). If you then select randomly again, are you most likely to pick:

a. The exact same extreme score again?

b. A score even more extreme than the first one?

c. A score less extreme (i.e., closer to the mean) than the first one?

My guess is that you've chosen alternative c, which means you that understand the basic concept of regression to the mean! To take a more concrete example (refer to

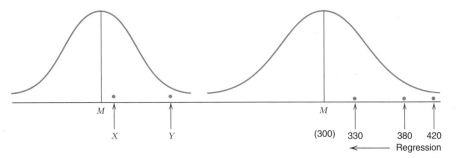

FIGURE 5.3   Regression to the mean.

the right-hand side of Figure 5.3), suppose you know that on the average (based on several hundred throws) Ted can throw a baseball 300 feet. Then he throws one 380 feet. If you are betting on his next throw, where would you put your money?

a.   380 feet

b.   420 feet

c.   330 feet

Again, I imagine you've chosen c, further convincing yourself that you get the idea of the regression phenomenon. But what does this have to do with our pretest/posttest study?

In a number of pre- and post studies, subjects are selected for some treatment because they've made an extreme score on the pretest. Thus, in the test anxiety study, subjects were picked because on the pretest they scored very high for anxiety. On the posttest their anxiety scores might improve, but the improvement could be a regression effect rather than the result of the anxiety reduction program. Once again, a control group of equivalent high-anxiety subjects would enable the researcher to spot a possible regression effect. For instance, the following outcome would suggest that some regression might be involved,[3] but the program nonetheless had an effect over and above regression. Can you see why this is so?

	pretest	treatment	posttest
Experimental::	90		70
Control::	pretest		posttest
	90		80

Regression effects can cause a number of problems and were probably the culprit in some early studies that erroneously questioned the effectiveness of the well-known Head Start program. That particular example will be taken up in Chapter 9 as an example of some of the problems involved in assessing large-scale federally supported programs.

---

[3]Notice that the sentence reads "might be involved," not "must be involved." This is because it is also possible that the control group change from 90 to 80 could be due to one of the other threats. Regression would be suspected if these other threats could be ruled out.

Testing and Instrumentation

Testing is considered to be a threat to internal validity when the mere fact of taking the pretest has an effect on posttest scores. There could be a practice effect of repeated testing or some aspects of the pretest could sensitize subjects to something about the program. For example, if the treatment program is a self-paced, computerized general psychology course, the pretest would be some test of knowledge. Subjects might be sensitized by the pretest to topics about which they seem to know nothing. They could then pay more attention to those topics during the course and do better on the posttest as a result.

Instrumentation is a problem when there are changes in the measurement instrument from pre- to posttest. In the self-paced general psychology course just mentioned, the pre- and posttests wouldn't be the same but would presumably be equivalent in level of difficulty. However, if the posttest happened to be easier as a test, it would produce improvement that was more apparent than real. Instrumentation is sometimes a problem when the measurement tool involves observations. Those doing the observing might get better at it with practice, making the posttest instrument essentially different from the pretest instrument.

Like the problems of history, maturation, and regression, the possible confounds of testing and instrumentation can be accounted for by including a control group. The only exception is that in the case of pretest sensitization, the experimental group might have a slight advantage over the control group on the posttest because the knowledge gained from the pretest might enable the experimental subjects to focus on specific weaknesses during the treatment phase, while control subjects would not have that opportunity.

Evaluating Pretests — the Solomon Design

Sometimes the effects of pretesting can be evaluated using a design called the Solomon 4-group design (Solomon, 1949), which looks like this:

Experimental 1::	pretest	treatment	posttest
Experimental 2::		treatment	posttest
Control 1::	pretest		posttest
Control 2::			posttest

Comparing the two experimental groups allows one to determine if the pretest is interacting with the treatment to produce changes in the posttest. Similarly, comparing the control groups tests whether the pretest by itself affects posttest performance. The ideal outcome of a Solomon design to evaluate the test anxiety program would be as follows:

Experimental 1::	pretest 90	treatment	posttest 70
Experimental 2::		treatment	posttest 70
Control 1::	pretest 90		posttest 90
Control 2::			posttest 90

On the other hand, an outcome suggesting that the low anxiety on the posttest was due to a pretesting effect would be this:

Experimental 1::	pretest	<u>treatment</u>	posttest
	90		70
Experimental 2::		<u>treatment</u>	posttest
			90
Control 1::	pretest		posttest
	90		70
Control 2::			posttest
			90

The Solomon design provides a nice way to evaluate the effects of pretesting, but is rather costly to implement. Compared to the simple experimental plus control group design, more subjects will be needed and two separate treatment programs might have to be run.

Subject Problems

Threats to internal validity can also arise from concerns over the subjects participating in the study. In particular, Cook and Campbell (1979) identified two problems.

Subject Selection Effects

One of the defining features of an experimental study with a manipulated independent variable is that subjects in the different conditions are equivalent to each other in all ways except for the independent variable. In the next chapter, you will learn how these equivalent groups are formed through random assignment and matching. If groups are not equivalent, then **subject selection** effects might occur. For example, suppose there are two sections of general psychology being offered and a researcher wants to compare a traditional lecture course with one combining lecture and discussion groups. School policy (a) prevents the researcher from randomly assigning students to the two courses, and (b) requires full disclosure of the nature of the courses. Thus, students can sign up for either section. I think you can see the difficulty here. If students in the lecture plus discussion outperform students in the straight lecture course, what caused the difference? Was it the nature of the course (the discussion element) or was it something about the students who *chose* that course? Maybe they were more articulate (hence, interested in discussion) than those in the lecture course. In short, there is a confound due to the selection of subjects for the two groups being compared.

Selection effects can also interact with other threats to internal validity. For example, in a study with two groups, some historical event might affect one group but not the other. Similarly, two groups might mature at different rates, respond to testing at different rates, be influenced by instrumentation in different ways, and show different degrees of regression.

One of psychology's classic studies is (unfortunately) a good example of a selec-

Box 5.3

CLASSIC STUDIES—Selection Problems and Executive Monkeys

The April 1958 issue of *Scientific American* included an attention-getting article called "Ulcers in 'Executive' Monkeys." It described several studies by Joseph V. Brady of the Walter Reed Army Institute of Research. Motivated partly by an Army study showing a relationship between gastric secretion by soldiers during a physical exam and the subsequent development of ulcers, Brady set out to investigate the relationships between emotionality and physical disorder by studying emotional behavior in rhesus monkeys. Much to his chagrin, many of his animals died, and autopsies revealed that most suffered from ulcers. In particular, those with ulcers tended to be animals in an avoidance conditioning procedure in which the monkeys were kept in restraining chairs and could respond by pressing a lever to escape from or avoid electric shock to the feet.

Brady reasoned that the ulcers could have resulted either from the repeated shock or from the stress associated with being in an avoidance conditioning procedure. Using good falsification thinking, Brady set up an experiment to rule out the possibility that shock alone caused the ulcers. He did this by putting two monkeys in adjoining restraint chairs that were physically alike in every way. One monkey, the "executive" (note the obvious reference to the stereotype of the hard-driving stressed-out business executive), could avoid the shocks that were programmed to occur every 20 seconds by pressing a lever at any time during the interval. For the control monkey, the lever didn't work and the animal was shocked every time the executive monkey let the 20 seconds go by and was shocked. Thus, both monkeys were shocked equally often, but only one monkey had the ability to control the shocks (at this point, it should occur to you that this is another example of a yoked control procedure). These contingencies were in effect for 6 hours followed by a 6-hour rest period. In a 24-hour period then, the monkeys had two 6-hour work sessions and two 6-hour rest sessions (the monkeys never left the restraining chairs, however).

Twenty-three days later (!) the executive monkey died and was found to have an ulcer. No ulcers were found in the control monkey. Brady then replicated the experiment with a second pair of monkeys and found the same result. He eventually reported data on four pairs of animals (Brady, Porter, Conrad, & Mason, 1958), concluding that the psychological stress of being in charge, not just of one's own fate but also that of a subordinate could lead to health problems, ulcers in this case. Can you see why the Army funded this research?

The study was widely reported in introductory psychology texts and publication in *Scientific American* gave it an even broader audience. However, a close examination of Brady's procedure showed that a subject selection confound occurred. Specifically, Brady did not randomly place the monkeys in the two groups. Rather, all eight of them started out as "executives" in the sense that they were pretested on how quickly they would learn an avoidance conditioning procedure. Those responding most quickly were placed in the executive condition for the experiment proper. Although Brady didn't know it at the time, animals differ in their characteristic levels of emotionality and the more emotional ones respond most quickly to shock. Thus, he unwittingly placed highly emotional animals (i.e., ulcer prone) in the executive condition and more laid back animals in the control condition.

The first to point out this problem was Weiss (1968), whose better-controlled studies with rats (e.g., Weiss, 1977) produced results the *opposite* of Brady's. As you recall from the discussion of yoked control groups earlier in this chapter, Weiss found that those with control over the shock in fact develop *fewer* ulcers than those with no control over the shocks.

One final aspect of the Brady research that probably occurred to you is that a modern-day ethics committee would require substantial changes in his procedures. Studying the relationship between stress and physical disease is vital, but as Weiss showed, it can be studied without the draconian procedure of keeping rhesus monkeys tightly restrained and relatively immobile for weeks at a time.

tion effect. It has come to be known as the "ulcers in executive monkeys" study and it is a pioneering investigation in the area of health psychology. For a close examination of this methodologically flawed research and its aftermath, read Box 5.3.

Attrition

Subjects do not always complete the experiment. Some studies may extend over a period of time and people move away, lose interest, and even die. In some studies, subjects might become uncomfortable and exercise their right to be released from further testing. Hence, for any number of reasons, there may be 100 subjects at the start of the study and only 60 at the end. This problem sometimes is called subject mortality, but I'll avoid the unfortunate connotations of that term and use the term **attrition** instead. Attrition is a problem because if particular types of people are more likely to drop out than others, the result is that the group finishing the study is on the average made up of different types of people than the ones starting the study. In essence then, this is similar to the selection problem because the result is that the group beginning the study is not equivalent to the group completing the study.

This concludes our introduction to the experimental method. The next two chapters will elaborate—Chapter 6 begins with a distinction between between-subjects designs and within-subjects (or repeated measures) designs and describes a number of control problems in experimental research. In particular, it looks at the problems of creating equivalent groups in between-subjects designs, controlling for sequence effects in within-subjects designs, and the biasing effects that result from the fact that both experimenters and subjects are humans. Chapter 7 looks at a variety of research designs, ranging from those with a single independent variable to those types of studies using what are called factorial designs.

Chapter Review

Glossary Fill-Ins

1. One of the defining features of an experiment in psychology is that _____ variables are carefully controlled

2. Age, gender, and socioeconomic status are all examples of _____ variables.

3. Sometimes athletes get their pictures on the cover of *Sports Illustrated* because they have done something spectacular. Then their performance declines and your roommate claims this is another example of the famous *Sports Illustrated* "jinx." More than likely, however, the performance decline following a spectacular performance is an example of _____.

4. Concern over _____ has led memory researchers to investigate such things as the reasons why we forget our keys and our ability to recognize people from old high school yearbook photos.

5. Professor Jones believes that Pat has really benefited from 4 years of a liberal arts education. Compared to freshman year, Pat is now better at critical thinking and is more tolerant of frustration. College may be the cause of this change, but another possible explanation is _____.

6. Failing to acknowledge that _____ has made the results uninterpretable, a researcher is excited because even though subject 23 is the only survivor of a long-term evaluation of a new type of therapy for paranoia, subject 23 seems to be genuinely cured of paranoid tendencies!

Multiple Choice

1. Schachter's study of how people expecting severe shock prefer to wait with others, described in Chapter 4 as an example using a nominal scale, might be criticized because all of the subjects were female. This would be a criticism of the study's
   a. Construct validity
   b. External validity
   c. Internal validity
   d. Ecological validity

2. One year prior to retirement, 50 people volunteer for an exercise program to reduce hypertension. One year after retirement, all 50 people remain in the program and their blood pressure is down. It is difficult to interpret these data because of what threat to internal validity?
   a. Attrition
   b. Maturation
   c. Instrumentation
   d. History

3. In a memory study, a researcher wishes to show that using visual imagery en-

hances recall. Some subjects are told to create images, others are told to repeat each word two times. Because forming images takes longer than repeating, those in the imagery group are shown the words at a slower presentation rate (4 sec/item) than those in the repetition group (2 sec/item). Which of the following is true about this study?

    a. Presentation rate is confounded with the instructional variable.

    b. Presentation rate is the independent variable.

    c. It has internal validity but lacks external validity.

    d. It is a nicely designed study with an instructional variable as the manipulated independent variable.

4. Which of the following is true of the famous Bobo doll study?

    a. All of the independent variables were manipulated variables.

    b. They controlled the "Bobo" factor by using the same inflatable doll for both the adults and the children.

    c. Children only imitated the models when the models were portrayed as cartoons.

    d. The manipulated independent variable was an example of a situational variable.

5. A researcher gives some subjects very easy puzzles, but tells them the puzzles are hard. Other subjects are given very hard puzzles, but are told they are easy. The purpose of this is to affect the subjects' self-confidence. Which of the following is true?

    a. Puzzle difficulty is confounded with instructions.

    b. The study is using the subject variable called "level of self-confidence."

    c. Self-confidence is a manipulated independent variable in this study.

    d. Self-confidence is the dependent variable in this study.

Applications Exercises

Exercise 5.1. — Identifying Variables

For each of the following, identify the independent variable(s), the levels of the independent variable(s), and the dependent variable(s). For independent variables, identify whether they are manipulated variables or subject variables. For dependent variables, indicate the scale of measurement being used.

1. In a cognitive mapping study, freshmen are compared with seniors in their ability to point accurately to campus buildings. Some of the buildings are in the center of the campus, along well-traveled routes; other buildings are on the periphery of campus. Besides pointing to the buildings, subjects are asked to indicate (on a scale of 1–5) how confident they are about their pointing.

2. In a study of the effectiveness of a new drug for treating panic disorders, some patients receive the drug while others only think they are receiving it. A third

group is not treated. After the program is completed, physiological responses to several stressful stimuli are taken. Six months later, all subjects are evaluated by a clinical psychologist as either suffering from panic disorders or not.

3. In a Pavlovian conditioning study, hungry animals are conditioned to salivate to the sound of a tone by pairing the tone with food. For some animals, the tone is turned on and then off again before the food is presented. For others, the tone remains on until the food is presented. For still others, the food precedes the tone.

4. In a study of developmental psycholinguistics, 2-, 3-, and 4-year old children are shown dolls and asked to act out several scenes to determine if they can use certain grammatical rules. Sometimes each child is asked to act out a scene in the active voice (Ernie hit Bert); other times each child acts out a scene in the passive voice (Ernie was hit by Bert). Children are judged by whether or not they act out the scene accurately and by how quickly they begin acting out the scene.

5. In a study of maze learning, some rats are fed after reaching the end of the maze during the course of 30 trials; others aren't; still others are not fed for the first 15 trials, but are fed for each of the 15 trials thereafter; a final group is fed for the first 15 trials and not fed for the last 15. The researcher makes note of any errors (wrong turns) made and how long it takes the animal to reach the goal.

Exercise 5.2. — Spot the Confound(s)

For each of the following, identify independent and dependent variables, and find at least one extraneous variable that has not been adequately controlled (i.e., that is creating a confound). Use the format illustrated in Table 5.2.

1. A testing company is trying to determine if a new type of driver (club 1) will drive a golf ball greater distances than three competing brands (clubs 2−4). Twenty male golf pros are recruited. Each golfer hits 50 balls with club 1, then 50 more with club 2, then 50 with club 3, then 50 with club 4. To add realism, the experiment takes place over the first four holes of an actual golf course—the first set of 50 balls is hit from the first tee, the second 50 from the second tee, and so on. The first four holes are all 410 yards or longer, and each is a par 4 hole.

2. A researcher is interested in the ability of schizophrenic patients to judge different time durations. It is hypothesized that loud noise will adversely affect their judgments. Subjects are tested two ways. In the "quiet" condition, some subjects are tested in a small sound-proof room that is used for hearing tests. Those in the "noisy" condition are tested in a nurse's office that has a stereo, which is playing music at a constant (and loud) volume. Because of scheduling problems, locked ward (i.e., slightly more dangerous) patients are available for testing *only* on Monday and open ward (i.e., slightly less dangerous) patients are available for testing *only* on Thursday. Furthermore, hearing tests are scheduled for Thursdays, so the sound-proof room is only available on Monday.

3. An experimenter is interested in whether memory can be improved if people use visual imagery. Subjects (all females) are placed in one of two groups—some are trained in imagery techniques, other are trained to use rote repetition. The imagery group is given a list of 20 concrete nouns (easier to form images than abstract nouns) to study and the other group is given 20 abstract words (ones that are especially easy to pronounce, so repetition will be easy), matched with the concrete words for frequency of general usage. To match the method of presentation with the method of study, subjects in the imagery group are shown the words visually (on a computer screen). To control for any "compu-phobia," rote subjects also sit at the computer terminal, but for them the computer is programmed to read the lists to them. After hearing their respective words lists, subjects have 60 seconds to recall as many words as they can, in any order that occurs to them.

CHAPTER 6

Control Problems in Experimental Research

Chapter Overview

- ### Between-Subjects Designs

  In between-subjects designs, a subject participates in just one of the experiment's conditions. Such a design is necessary when subject variables (e.g., gender) are being studied, or when participating in one condition of the experiment changes subjects in ways that make it impossible for them to participate in another condition. With between-subjects designs, the main difficulty is creating groups that are equivalent to each other on all factors except for the independent variable.

- ### The Problem of Creating Equivalent Groups

  The preferred method of creating equivalent groups in between-subjects designs, especially if the number of available subjects is large, is random assignment. If few subjects are available, if some factor (e.g., intelligence) correlates with the dependent variable, and if that factor can be assessed before the experiment begins, then equivalent groups can be formed by using a matching procedure.

- ## Within-Subjects Designs

    When each subject participates in all of the study's conditions, the study is using a within-subjects or repeated-measures design. For these designs, participating in one condition might affect how subjects behave in other conditions; that is, sequence effects can occur. Sequence effects include carryover effects and order effects.

- ## The Problem of Controlling Sequence Effects

    Sequence effects are controlled by various counterbalancing procedures, all of which insure that the various conditions are tested in more than one sequence. Different counterbalancing procedures are used, depending on whether subjects will be serving in each condition of the study once or more than once.

- ## Control Problems in Developmental Research

    In developmental psychology, the major independent variable is age, a subject variable. If age is studied between subjects, the design is referred to as a cross-sectional design. It has the advantage of efficiency, but cohort effects can occur, a special form of the nonequivalent groups problem. If age is a within-subjects variable, the design is called a longitudinal design and attrition can be a problem.

- ## Problems with Biasing

    The results of research in psychology can be biased by experimenter expectancy effects. These can lead the experimenter to treat subjects in various conditions in different ways, making the results impossible to interpret. Such effects can be reduced by automating the procedures and using double blind techniques. Subject bias also occurs. Participants might confirm the researcher's hypothesis if demand characteristics suggest to them the true purpose of a study.

In his landmark experimental psychology text, just after introducing his now famous distinction between independent and dependent variables, R. S. Woodworth emphasized the importance of control in experimental research. As he put it, "[w]hether one or more independent variables are used, it remains essential that all other conditions be constant. Otherwise you cannot connect the effect observed with any definite cause. The psychologist must expect to encounter difficulties in meeting this requirement . . ." (Woodworth, 1938, p. 3). We've already seen some of these difficulties. The general problem of confounding and the specific threats to internal validity discussed in the last chapter are basically problems of controlling extraneous factors. In this chapter, we'll look at some other aspects of maintaining control: the problem of creating equivalent groups in experiments involving separate groups of participants, the problem of sequence effects in experiments in which participants are tested several times, and problems resulting from bias.

Recall that an independent variable must have a minimum of two levels. At the very least, an experiment will compare condition A with condition B. Subjects who participate in the study might be placed in level A, B, or both. If they receive either A *or* B, but not both, the design is a **between-subjects design**, so-named because the comparison of levels A and B will be a contrast *between* two different groups of people. On the other hand, if each participant receives both levels A *and* B, you could say that both levels exist *within* each subject; hence, this design is called a **within-subjects design**. Let's examine each approach.

Between-Subjects Designs

Between-subjects designs are sometimes used out of necessity. If the independent variable is a subject variable, for instance, there is no choice. A study comparing introverts and extroverts or males and females requires comparing different groups of people. Using a between-subjects design is also unavoidable in some studies that use certain manipulated independent variables. Consider an experiment of the effects of physical attractiveness on criminal sentence lengths by Sigall and Ostrove (1975), for example. They gave college students descriptions of a crime and asked them to recommend a jail sentence for the woman convicted of it. There were two separate between-subjects manipulated independent variables. One was the type of crime, either a burglary in which "Barbara Helm" broke into a neighbor's apartment and stole $2,200, or a swindle, in which Barbara "ingratiated herself to a middle-aged bachelor and induced him to invest $2,200 in a nonexistent corporation" (Sigall & Ostrove, 1975, p. 412). The other manipulated variable was Barbara's attractiveness. Some participants saw a picture of her in which she was very attractive; others saw a photo of an unattractive Barbara, and a control group did not see any photo. The interesting result was that when the crime was burglary, attractiveness paid off. Attractive Barbara got a *lighter* sentence (2.8 years) than unattractive (5.2) or control (5.1) Barbara. However, the opposite happened for the swindle. Apparently thinking that Barbara was using her good looks to commit the crime, subjects gave attractive Barbara the swindler a harsher sentence (5.5 years) than the unattractive (4.4) or control (4.4) woman.

I think you can see why it was necessary to run this study with between-subjects variables. For those participating in the Attractive-Barbara-Swindle condition, for example, the experience would certainly affect them and make it impossible for them to "start fresh" in, say, the Unattractive-Barbara-Burglary condition. In some studies, participating in one condition makes it impossible for the same person to be in a second condition. Sometimes, it is essential that each condition include "naive" participants only.

While the advantage of a between-subjects design is that each subject enters the study fresh, and naive with respect to the procedures to be tested, the prime disadvantage is that large numbers of subjects may need to be recruited, tested, and debriefed. Hence, the researcher invests a great deal of energy in this type of design. My doctoral dissertation on memory involved five different experiments requiring between-subjects factors; more than 600 students trudged in and out of my lab before the project was finished!

Another disadvantage of between-subjects designs is that differences between the conditions could be due to the independent variables, but they might also be due to differences between the two groups of people. To deal with this potential confound, deliberate steps must be taken to create what are called **equivalent groups**. These are groups that are essentially equal to each other in all ways except for the independent variable. The number of equivalent groups in a between-subjects study corresponds exactly to the number of different conditions in the study.

The Problem of Creating Equivalent Groups

There are two common techniques for creating equivalent groups in a between-subjects experiment. The ideal approach is to use random assignment. A second strategy is to use a procedure called *matching*.

Random Assignment

First, be sure you understand that random assignment and random selection are not the same thing. Random selection, described in Chapter 4, is a procedure for getting subjects to come into your study. Random assignment is a method for placing these subjects, once selected, into the different groups. When **random assignment** is used, every subject volunteering for the study has an equal chance of being placed in each of the groups being formed.

By randomly assigning, individual difference factors that could bias the study get spread evenly throughout the different groups of subjects. Suppose you're comparing two presentation rates in a memory study. Let's further suppose that anxious subjects won't do as well on memory tasks as nonanxious subjects, but you are unaware of that fact. Some subjects are shown the words at a rate of 2 seconds/word; others at 4 seconds/word. The prediction is that recall will be better for the 4-second group. Here's some hypothetical data that such a study might produce. Each number refers to the number of words recalled out of a list of 30. After each subject number, I've placed an A or an R in parentheses as a way of telling you which subjects are anxious types of people and which are relaxed. Data for the anxious subjects are shaded.

If you look carefully at these data, you'll see that the three anxious subjects in

S#	2-sec rate	S#	4-sec rate
S1 (R)	15	S9 (R)	23
S2 (R)	15	S10 (R)	19
S3 (R)	16	S11 (R)	18
S4 (R)	18	S12 (R)	20
S5 (R)	20	S13 (R)	25
S6 (A)	10	S14 (A)	16
S7 (A)	12	S15 (A)	14
S8 (A)	13	S16 (A)	16
M	15	*M*	19
(*SD*)	(3.23)	(*SD*)	(3.72)

each group did worse than their five relaxed peers. However, because there are an equal number of anxious subjects in each group, the dampening effect of anxiety on recall is about the same for both groups. Thus, the main comparison of interest, the difference in presentation rates (the 4-second rate yields better recall, $19 > 15$), is preserved.

Random assignment won't guarantee placing an equal number of anxious subjects in each group, but in general the procedure has the effect of spreading potentially confounding factors equally throughout the different groups. This is especially true when there are large numbers of subjects being assigned to each group. In fact, the greater the number of subjects involved, the greater the chance that random assignment will work to create equivalent groups. If groups are equivalent, and if all else is adequately controlled, then you are in that enviable position of being able to say that your independent variable was responsible for the results of the study.

You might think that the actual process of random assignment would be fairly simple—just use a table of random numbers to assign each arriving subject to a group, or in the case of a two-group study, flip a coin. Unfortunately, however, the result of such an approach is that your groups will almost certainly have different numbers of people in them. In the worst-case scenario, imagine you are doing a study using 20 subjects divided into two groups of 10. You decide to flip a coin as each subject arrives: Heads, they're in group A; tails, group B. But what if the coin comes up heads all 20 times?

To complete a random assignment of subjects to conditions in a way that insures an equal number of subjects per group, a researcher might use **block randomization**, a procedure insuring that each condition of the study has a subject randomly assigned to it before any condition is repeated a second time. Each "block" contains all of the conditions of the study in a randomized order. Table 6.1

TABLE 6.1   *Block Randomization*

As a procedure for creating equivalent groups, block randomization forms blocks containing each of the conditions in the study. Within each block, the conditions are randomly arranged. Here's how it would work in a study comparing the effectiveness of four different presentation rates on memory for a word list.

Step 1.   Decide how many subjects you would like to test. If you wish to test an equal number of subjects per condition, the number must be a multiple of the total number of conditions (four in this case). Let's say you need 80 subjects, 20 for each presentation rate.

Step 2.   Designate the four conditions by the numbers 1, 2, 3, and 4. Each block is defined as some random sequence of those four numbers.

Step 3.   Go to a table of random numbers and work your way down the columns or across the rows looking for the numbers 1–4. Select each of the numbers once before selecting any of them a second time. For example, suppose a portion of the random numbers table looked like this and you began with the second row, reading across:

2	2	1	7	6	8	6	5	8	4	6	8	9	5
→ 1	9	3	6	1	7	5	9	4	6	1	3	7	9
1	6	7	7	2	3	0	2	7	7	0	9	6	1
7	8	0	3	7	6	7	1	6	1	2	0	4	4
0	3	2	8	1	2	2	6	0	8	7	3	3	7

I've underlined the sequence of random numbers that you would select in this case. Thus your first block would be 1-3-4-2. The 1, 3, and 4 are determined by the table; once those three are selected, the fourth number has to be a 2, so there's no need to look for it in the table. The second block is 1-3-2-4, the third is 3-2-1-4, and so on. You'll need to select 20 blocks of 4 to cover the total of 80 subjects.

Step 4.   Create a master sheet with all of the sequences on it.★ As each subject completes the experiment, cross off one of the 80 numbers on the master sheet. A portion of master sheet might look like this after the first six participants have been tested:

Block 1.   1—3—4—2
Block 2.   1—3—2 4
Block 3.   3   2   1   4
             .   .
             .   .
             .   .
Block 20.   2   4   3   1

★Never test a single subject until you have set up some kind of a master sheet that identifies exactly how each participant is to be treated.

shows you how this could be accomplished by hand; in actual practice, researchers often rely on a simple computer program to generate a sequence of conditions meeting the requirements of block randomization.

Matching

When there is just a small number of subjects in each condition of an experiment, random assignment can fail to create equivalent groups. The following example shows you how this might happen. Let's take the same study of the effects of presentation rate on memory used earlier and assume that the data you examined reflects an outcome in which random assignment happened to work. That is, there was an exact balance of five relaxed and three anxious people in each group. However, it is *possible* that random assignment could place *all six* of the anxious subjects in one of the groups. This might be unlikely, but it could occur (just as it's remotely possible for a perfectly fair coin to come up heads ten times in a row). If it did, this might happen:

S#	2-sec Rate	S#	4-sec Rate
S1 (R)	15	S9 (R)	23
S2 (R)	17	S10 (R)	20
S3 (R)	16	S11 (A)	16
S4 (R)	18	S12 (A)	14
S5 (R)	20	S13 (A)	16
S6 (R)	17	S14 (A)	16
S7 (R)	18	S15 (A)	14
S8 (R)	15	S16 (A)	17
M	17	*M*	17
(SD)	(1.69)	*(SD)*	(3.07)

This outcome of course is totally different from the first example. Instead of concluding that recall was better for a slower presentation rate (as in the earlier example), the researcher in this case could not reject the null hypothesis and would wonder what happened. After all, subjects were randomly assigned and the researcher's prediction about better recall for a slower presentation rate certainly makes sense. So what went wrong?

What happened was that random assignment inadvertently created two decidedly nonequivalent groups—one made up of entirely relaxed people and one dominated by anxious people. A 4-second rate probably does produce better recall, but the true difference was wiped out in this study because the mean for the 2-second group was inflated by relatively high scores from the relaxed subjects, and the 4-second group's mean was suppressed because of the anxiety effects. Another way of saying this is that the failure of random assignment to create equivalent groups probably led to a Type II error (presentation rate really does affect recall; this study just failed to find the effect).

To deal with the problem of equivalent groups in a situation like this, a matching procedure could be used. In **matching**, subjects are paired together on some trait such as anxiety level; then one member of each pair is randomly assigned to one of the groups. In this case, "anxiety level" would be called a **matching variable**. Matching often is used when:

a. The number (N) of subjects is small, so random assignment is risky and might yield unequal groups.

b. The matching variable is expected to affect the results in some predictable fashion (i.e., the matching variable correlates with the dependent variable).

c. There is some reasonable way of measuring subjects on the matching variable.

Of these three criteria, the first is true most of the time (matching sometimes occurs with large *N*), but the second and the third are essential. In the case of the memory study for instance, matching would be used only if the researcher had good reason to suspect that anxiety would affect recall and if there was some reasonable way of identifying each subject's typical anxiety level prior to the assignment of subjects to conditions. As you might guess, the latter is a requirement that sometimes makes matching impractical. When the procedure is feasible and appears to be needed, however, the steps in carrying it out are fairly straightforward. As an illustration of how it is done, work through the example in Table 6.2.

In the Chapter 4 discussion of stratified sampling, I pointed out that researchers using the procedure face the problem of how many "strata" to use. Matching cre-

---

TABLE 6.2   *How to Use a Matching Procedure*

In a study on problem solving requiring two different groups, a researcher is concerned that the subject's academic skills might correlate highly with performance on the problems to be used in the experiment. The subjects are college students, so the researcher decides to match the two groups on Grade Point Average (GPA). That is, deliberate steps will be taken to insure that the two groups are equal to each other in academic ability, as reflected by the students' GPA. Here's how the researcher does it:

Step 1.   Get a score for each subject on the matching variable. That's easy in this case because it simply means getting a list of GPAs from the Registrar. (Matching often requires pretesting the subjects on the matching variable; this can mean bringing subjects to the lab twice, which often makes it difficult to recruit participants, which is another reason why researchers prefer random assignment.) Let's suppose that there will be ten subjects in this study, five per group. Here are the GPAs for ten students:

TABLE 6.2   *How to Use a Matching Procedure* (**continued**)

S1: 3.24	S6: 2.45
S2: 3.91	S7: 3.85
S3: 2.71	S8: 3.12
S4: 2.05	S9: 2.91
S5: 2.62	S10: 2.21

Step 2.   Arrange the GPAs in ascending order.

S4: 2.05	S9: 2.91
S10: 2.21	S8: 3.12
S6: 2.45	S1: 3.24
S5: 2.62	S7: 3.85
S3: 2.71	S2: 3.91

Step 3.   Create five pairs of scores, with each pair consisting of adjacent GPA scores.

Pair 1: 2.05 and 2.21
Pair 2: 2.45 and 2.62
Pair 3: 2.71 and 2.91
Pair 4: 3.12 and 3.24
Pair 5: 3.85 and 3.91

Step 4.   For each pair, randomly assign one subject to group 1 and the other to group 2. Here's one possible outcome:

	Group 1	*Group 2*
	2.05	2.21
	2.62	2.45
	2.91	2.71
	3.12	3.24
	3.85	3.91
Mean GPA:	**2.91**	**2.90**

Now the study can proceed with the assurance that the two groups will be equivalent to each other (2.91 = 2.90) in terms of overall academic ability. (If more than two groups are being tested, the matching procedure is the same up to and including Step 2. In Step 3, instead of creating pairs of scores, the researcher creates clusters equal to the number of groups needed. Then in Step 4, the subjects in each cluster are randomly assigned to the groups.)

ates a similar dilemma for the investigator. In a memory study, should I match the groups for anxiety level? What about intelligence level? What about education level? I think you can see that some judgment is required here, for matching is difficult to accomplish with more than one matching variable. In fact, the problems of deciding on and measuring matching variables is one reason why research psychologists generally prefer to make the effort to recruit enough subjects to randomly assign, even when they might suspect that some variable correlates with the dependent variable. In memory research, for instance, researchers are seldom concerned about their subjects' anxiety levels, intelligence, or educational level. They simply make the groups large enough so that random assignment will distribute these potentially confounding factors evenly throughout the conditions of the study.

Within-Subjects Designs

As mentioned at the start of the chapter, each participant is exposed to each level of the independent variable in a within-subjects design. Because everyone in this type of study is measured several times, you will sometimes see this procedure described as a "repeated-measures" design (e.g., see Chapter 7). One practical advantage of this design should be obvious—fewer subjects need to be recruited. If you have a study comparing two conditions and you want to test 20 people in condition 1, you'll need to recruit 40 people for a between-subjects study but only 20 for a within-subjects study.

Within-subjects designs are sometimes the only reasonable choice. Experiments in areas like physiological psychology and sensation and perception often make comparisons between conditions that require just a brief amount of time to test but might demand extensive preparation (e.g., surgery). For example, a perceptual study using the Müller–Lyer illusion might vary the orientations of the lines to see if the illusion is especially strong when presented vertically (see Figure 6.1). The task might involve showing the illusion on a computer screen and asking the subject to press a certain key that changes the length of one of the lines. Participants are told to adjust the two lines until they seem to be the same length. Any trial of this procedure might take no more than 5 seconds, so it would be absurd to make the "illusion orientation" variable a between-subjects factor and use a subject for a fraction of a minute. Instead, it makes more sense to make the orientation variable a within-subjects factor and give each participant a sequence of trials to cover all levels of the variable (and perhaps duplicate each level several times).

A within-subjects design might also be necessary when subjects are scarce be-

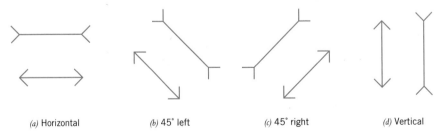

(a) Horizontal   (b) 45° left   (c) 45° right   (d) Vertical

FIGURE 6.1   Set of four Müller–Lyer illusions: horizontal, 45° left, 45° right, vertical.

cause the entire population of interest is small. Studying astronauts or people with multiple personalities are just two examples. Of course, there are times when even with a limited population, the design may require a between-subjects manipulation: Evaluating the effects of a new therapy for multiple personalities might require comparing those in therapy with others in a control group not being treated.

Besides convenience, the advantage of using within-subjects designs has to do with the elimination of the equivalent groups problem that occurs with between-subjects designs. Recall from Chapter 4 that an inferential statistical analysis comparing two groups examines the variability between experimental conditions with the variability within each condition. Variability between conditions could be due to (a) the independent variable, (b) other systematic variance resulting from confounding, and/or (c) nonsystematic error variance. A significant portion of the error variance in a between-subjects design results from individual differences between subjects in the different groups. But in a within-subjects design, any between-condition individual difference variance disappears. Let's look at a concrete example.

Suppose you are comparing two golf balls for distance. You recruit ten professional golfers and randomly assign them to two groups of five. After warming up, each golfer hits one ball or the other. Here are the results:

Pros in First Group	Golf Ball #1	Pros in Second Group	Golf Ball #2
pro 1	255	pro 6	269
pro 2	261	pro 7	266
pro 3	248	pro 8	260
pro 4	250	pro 9	270
pro 5	245	pro 10	257
M	253	*M*	265
(SD)	(5.26)	*(SD)*	(5.19)

There are several things to note here. First, there is some variability within each group, as reflected in the standard deviation for each group. This is error variance due to individual differences within each group and to other random factors. Second, there is apparently an overall difference between the groups. The pros in the second group hit their ball farther than the pros in the first group. Why? There are four possibilities:

a. Chance; perhaps this is not a statistically significant difference, and even if it is, there's a 5% chance that it is a Type I error.

b. The golf ball; perhaps the brand of golf ball hit by the second group simply goes farther (this, of course, is the research hypothesis).

c. Some confound (e.g., the wind changed for the second group).

d. Individual differences; maybe the golfers in the second group are stronger or more skilled.

The chances of the fourth possibility being a major problem are reduced by the procedures for creating equivalent groups described earlier. Using random assignment or matching allows you to be reasonably sure that the second group of golfers is about equivalent to the first group in ability, strength, and so forth. Despite that, however, it is still possible that *some* of the difference between the two groups can be traced back to the individual differences between the two groups. This problem simply does not occur in a within-subjects design. Suppose you repeated the previous study, but used just the first five golfers, and each pro hits ball 1, then ball 2. The table looks like this:

Pros in the Only Group	Golf Ball 1	Golf Ball 2
pro 1	255	269
pro 2	261	266
pro 3	248	260
pro 4	250	270
pro 5	245	257
M (*SD*)	**253** (5.26)	**265** (5.19)

Of the four possible explanations for the differences in the first set of data, explanation 4 can be eliminated for the second set. In the first set, the difference in the first row between the 255 and the 269 could be due to chance, the difference between the balls, a confound, or individual differences between the two groups. In the second set, there is no second group, so the fourth possibility is gone. Thus, in a within-subjects design, individual differences are eliminated from the estimate of the amount of variability between conditions. Statistically, this means that in a within-subjects design, an inferential analysis will be more sensitive to small differences between means than will be the case for a between-subjects design.

But wait. Are you completely satisfied that in the second case, the differences between the first set of scores and the second set could *only* be due to (a) chance factors, (b) the superiority of the second ball and/or (c) a confound? Are you thinking that perhaps pro 1 actually changed in some way between hitting ball 1 and hitting ball 2? Although it's unlikely that the golfer will add 20 pounds of muscle between swings, what if there was some kind of practice or warm-up effect operating? Or perhaps the pro detected a slight malfunction in his swing at ball 1 and corrected it for ball 2. In short, in a within-subjects design, a major problem is that once a subject has completed part A of a study, the experience or altered circumstances could influence performance in part B, C, and so forth, of the study. The problem is referred to as a **sequence effect**, and it can operate in several ways.

First, trial 1 might affect the subject in a way that improves trial 2's performance, as in the examples of a practice effect or a swing correction. On the other hand, sometimes repeated trials produce fatigue or boredom and performance steadily declines from trial to trial. These two effects can both be referred to as **carry-over** effects. Also, some particular sequences might produce effects that are different from other sequences; these could be called **order** effects. For example, suppose you are doing a cognitive mapping study and asking people to point as accurately as they can to several geographical locations. Assume for the moment that the study is being conducted in Chicago and that the locations being pointed to are Los Angeles, San Francisco, New York, St. Louis, and Pittsburgh. If subjects are asked to point to Los Angeles and then San Francisco, their accuracy in pointing to the latter might be different than if they pointed first to New York and then San Francisco. Pointing to two consecutive places that are in the same general direction might produce effects different from pointing to two consecutive places from opposite directions. In short, the order in which the conditions are presented, independently of any practice or fatigue effects, might influence the outcome.

The Problem of Controlling Sequence Effects

The typical way to control sequence effects is to use more than one sequence, a strategy known as **counterbalancing**. There are two general categories, depending on whether participants are tested in each experimental condition just one time or are tested more than once per condition.

Testing Once per Condition

In some experiments, subjects will be tested in each condition, but only tested once per condition. Consider, for example, an interesting study by Reynolds (1992) on the ability of chess players to recognize the level of expertise in other chess players. He recruited 15 chess players of different degrees of expertise from various clubs in New York City and asked them to look at six different chess games that were said to be in progress (i.e., about 20 moves into the game). On each trial, the players examined the board of an in-progress game (they were told to assume the pair of players of each game were of equal ability) and estimated the skill level of the players according to a standard rating system. The games were deliberately set up to reflect different levels of player expertise. Reynolds found that the more skilled of the 15 subjects made more accurate estimates of the ability re-flected in the board setups they examined than less–skilled subjects.

You'll recognize the design of the Reynolds study as including a within–subjects variable. Each of the 15 subjects examined all six games. Also, you can see that it made sense for each game to be evaluated just one time by each player. Hence, Reynolds was faced with the question of how to control for any sequence effects that might be present. He certainly didn't want all 15 subjects to see the six games in exactly the same order. How might he have proceeded?

Complete Counterbalancing

Whenever subjects are tested once per condition in a within–subjects design, one solution to the sequence problem is to use **complete counterbalancing**. This means that every possible sequence will be used exactly once. The total number of sequences needed can be determined by calculating $X!$, where X is the number of conditions, and ! stands for the mathematical calculation of a factorial. For exam-ple, if a study has three conditions, there are six possible sequences that can be used:

$$3! = 3 \times 2 \times 1 = 6$$

The six sequences in a study with conditions A, B, and C would be

ABC	BAC
ACB	CAB
BCA	CBA

The problem with complete counterbalancing is that as the number of condi-tions increases, the possible sequences that will be needed increase exponentially. There are six sequences needed for three conditions, but simply adding a fourth condition creates a need for 24 sequences ($4 \times 3 \times 2 \times 1$). As you can guess, com-plete counterbalancing was not possible in Reynolds study unless he recruited many more than 15 chess players as subjects. In fact, with six different games (i.e., conditions), he would need 720 (6!) players. Clearly, a different strategy is needed.

Partial Counterbalancing

Whenever a subset of the total number of sequences is used, the result is called **partial counterbalancing**. This was Reynolds' solution; he simply took a random sample of the 720 possible sequences by insuring that "the order of presentation [was] randomized for each subject" (Reynolds, 1992, p. 411). Sampling from the population of sequences is a common strategy whenever there are fewer subjects available than possible sequences or when there are a large number of sequences.

Reynolds sampled from the total number of sequences, but he could have cho-sen another approach that is frequently used—the balanced **Latin square**. It gets its name from an ancient Roman puzzle about arranging Latin letters in a matrix so that each letter appears only once in each row and each column (Kirk, 1968). The Latin square strategy is more sophisticated than simply choosing a random subset of the whole. With a perfectly balanced Latin square, you are assured that (a) each condition of the study occurs equally often in each sequential position, and (b) each condition precedes and follows each other condition exactly once. Work through Table 6.3 to see how to construct the following 6 × 6 Latin square. Think of each letter as one of the six games inspected by Reynolds' chess players.

A	B	F	C	E	D
B	C	**A**	D	F	E
C	D	B	E	**A**	F
D	E	C	F	B	**A**
E	F	D	**A**	C	B
F	**A**	E	B	D	C

TABLE 6.3   *Building a Balanced Latin Square*

In a balanced Latin square, each condition of the study occurs equally often in each sequential position and each condition precedes and follows each other condition exactly once. Here's how to build a 6 × 6 square.

Step 1.   Build the first row. It is fixed according to this general rule:

A B "X" C "X − 1" D "X − 2" E, "X − 3", F, and so on

where A refers to the first condition of the study and "X" refers to the letter symbolizing the final condition of the experiment. To build a 6 × 6 square, this first row would substitute

$$X = \text{the sixth letter of the alphabet} \rightarrow F$$
$$X - 1 = \text{the fifth letter} \rightarrow E$$

Therefore, the first row would be

A   B   **F** (subbing for "X")   C   **E** (subbing for "X − 1")   D

Step 2.   Build the second row. Directly below each letter of row 1, place in row 2 the letter that is next in the alphabet. The only exception is the F. Under that letter, return to the first of the six letters and place the letter A. Thus

A	B	F	C	E	D
B	C	A	D	F	E

Step 3.   Build the remaining four rows following the step 2 rule. Thus the final 6 × 6 square is

A	B	F	C	E	D
B	C	A	D	F	E
C	D	B	E	A	F
D	E	C	F	B	A
E	F	D	A	C	B
F	A	E	B	D	C

Step 4.   Take each of the six conditions of the study and randomly assign them to the letters A through F to determine the actual sequence of conditions for each row. Assign an equal number of subjects to each row.

I've boldfaced condition **A** (game A) to show you how the square meets the two requirements listed in the preceding paragraph. First, condition A occurs in each of the six sequential positions (first in the first row, third in the second row, etc.). Second, A is followed by each of the other letters exactly one time. From the top row to the bottom, (1) A is followed by B, D, F, nothing, C and E, (2) A is preceded by nothing, C, E, B, D, and F. The same is true for each of the other letters. To use the 6 × 6 Latin square, one randomly assigns each of the six conditions of the experiment, different chess games for Reynolds, to one of the six letters, A through F.

When using Latin squares, it is necessary for the number of subjects to be equal to or a multiple of the number of rows in the square. The fact that Reynolds had 15 subjects in his study tells you he didn't use a Latin square. If he added three more chess players, he could have randomly assigned three players to each of the six rows of the square (3 × 6 = 18).

Testing More Than Once Per Condition

In the Reynolds study it made no sense to ask the chess players to look at any of the six games more than once. Similarly, if subjects in a memory experiment are asked to study and recall four lists of words, with the order of the lists determined by a 4 × 4 Latin square, there's no need to ask them to study and recall any particular list a second time. However, in many studies, subjects experience each condition more than one time. This often happens in research in sensation and perception for instance. A look back at Figure 6.1 provides an example.

Suppose you were conducting a study to see if subjects would be more affected by the illusion when it was presented vertically than when shown horizontally or at a 45° angle. With the four conditions of the study randomly assigned to the letters A–D,

$$A = \text{horizontal}$$
$$B = 45° \text{ to the left}$$
$$C = 45° \text{ to the right}$$
$$D = \text{vertical}$$

Subjects in the study are shown the illusion on a computer screen and have to make adjustments until they perceive that the parallel lines are equal. The four conditions could be presented to subjects according to one of two basic procedures.

Reverse Counterbalancing

When using **reverse counterbalancing**, the experimenter simply presents the conditions in one order, then presents them again in the reversed order. In the illusion case, the order would be A-B-C-D-D-C-B-A. If the researcher desires to have the participant perform the task more than twice per condition, this sequence could be repeated as many times as necessary.

The principle of reverse counterbalancing can also be applied in a slightly different way in a within-subjects design in which subjects only see each condition

FIGURE 6.2 Nine-dot problem. The problem is to connect all the dots with exactly four straight lines. Once you begin drawing the first line, you cannot lift the pencil until all four lines have been drawn.

once. For example, in a study of the well-known 9-dot problem (see Figure 6.2), Lung and Dominowski (1985) were interested in whether skill resulting from practice with other dot problems, all requiring similar strategies, would transfer to the 9-dot problem. Subjects were given practice on the six problems found in Figure 6.3. As determined randomly, half the subjects given practice saw the problems in the order A through F; the remaining saw the reversed sequence, F through A.

By the way, you'll notice that I've solved the first three of the practice problems for you. Why not take a minute here and see if you can figure out the remaining three. Then see if solving the practice problems helps you to solve the famous 9-dot problem. If it does, you will have replicated part of Lung and Dominowski's study!

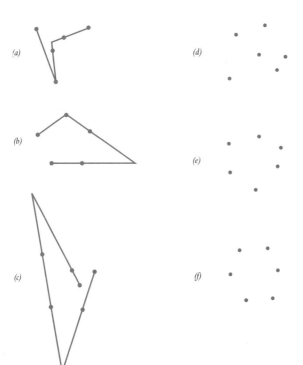

FIGURE 6.3 Practice dot problems from the Lung and Dominowski (1985) study, three solved and three unsolved. The problems must be solved by connecting all the dots with three straight lines.

Block Randomization

A second way to present a sequence of conditions when each condition is presented more than once is to use **block randomization,** the same procedure outlined earlier in the context of how to randomly assign subjects to groups in a between-subjects experiment. The basic rule is that every condition occurs once before any condition is repeated for a second time. Within each block, the order of conditions is randomized. This strategy eliminates the possibility that subjects could successfully predict what is coming next, a problem that can occur with reverse counterbalancing.

To use the illusion example again, subjects would receive all four conditions in a randomized order, then all four again, but in a block with a new randomized order, and so on for as many blocks of four as needed. Whereas a reverse counterbalancing would look like this:

A B C D   D C B A

a block randomization procedure might produce this:

B C D A   C A D B

To give you a sense of how block randomization works in an actual within-subjects experiment employing many trials, consider one of a series of mental rotation studies (see Chapter 4, pp. 94–95 for a description of the logic of this type of study) by Koriat and Norman (1984). They used the four Hebrew letters reproduced in Figure 6.4 (their subjects were fluent in Hebrew) and manipulated the following within-subjects factors:

1. Angle of orientation of the target letter (six levels: 0°, 60°, 120°, 180°, 240°, and 300°, rotated clockwise);

2. Angle of orientation of the target letter on the previous trial (same six levels—they were predicting that performance on a given trial would be affected by performance on the preceding trial);

3. Whether the target letter was normal or reversed (i.e., whether the answer was yes or no; two levels); and

4. Whether the target letter on the previous trial was normal or reversed (two levels).

Combining all of these levels produces 144 different types of trials ($6 \times 6 \times 2 \times 2$). After warm-up trials, Koriat and Norman asked subjects to complete four randomized blocks of trials, a total of 144×4 or 576 trials. Why four blocks? Because four different letters were being used, and Koriat and Norman wanted to insure that the "four letters were randomly assigned to each of the trials with the con-

FIGURE 6.4   Letters from the Hebrew alphabet used in Koriat and Norman's (1984) mental rotation study.

straints that each letter appeared equally often in both formats (normal and reversed), and that over the four blocks each of the four letters appeared once in each of the 144 combinations" (Koriat and Norman, 1984, p. 423).

Koriat and Norman found further evidence that subjects mentally rotate objects in order to make the correct decisions on the rotation task. They also found some evidence that instead of always rotating the letter back to vertical, subjects occasionally rotate the letter back to the position of the letter on the previous trial.

Problems with Counterbalancing

The various counterbalancing procedures help reduce sequence effects, but some may do so imperfectly because counterbalancing requires an assumption that sequential effects are linear and this might not always be true. To see why this can be a problem, consider the following hypothetical example.

Suppose you were doing a human maze learning experiment comparing two types of mazes like those in Figure 6.5, a sequential maze (A) requiring a series of left–right turns and a more spatial arrangement (B) like the Hampton Court maze. In a study with mazes like these, you would be blindfolded and told to work your way through the maze by moving a stylus or a pencil through the grooves that make up the pathways.

In the study, assume a within-subjects design is being used. Half of the subjects learn maze A followed by maze B; the remainder learn B, then A. This is complete counterbalancing. Assuming the entire session lasts an hour and that participants become more tired or bored as the time passes, performance on the second maze might suffer. But it is reasonable to assume this increase in boredom over the hour is a steady or *linear* increase. Hence, counterbalancing, which results in each maze being tested first and second an equal number of times, will balance out the effects

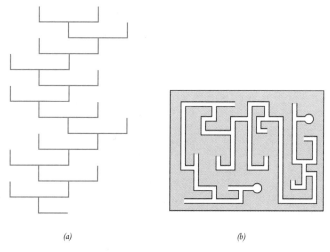

(a) *(b)*

FIGURE 6.5 Human stylus mazes of two types: a sequential maze (A) and a spatial maze (B).

of boredom. Let's say that boredom adds three errors to a score and that maze B (producing an average of 15 errors) is harder than maze A (10 errors). For the sequences A : B and B : A, this might happen:

	Errors Due to		
	Difficulty	Boredom	Total
Maze A	10	0	**10**
then			
Maze B	15	+3	**18**
Maze B	15	0	**15**
then			
Maze A	10	+3	**13**

With the two sequences combined, boredom contributes equally to mazes A and B and its effect washes out. The overall error scores are an average of 11.5 for maze A [(10 + 13)/2] and 16.5 [(18 + 15)/2)] for the more difficult maze B.

On the other hand, sequence effects sometimes occur in ways that counterbalancing won't cure. Suppose for example that solving maze A gives people an insight about solving mazes in general, but the same insight does *not* result when solving maze B. If this happened, then in the sequence A : B, learning A first will produce a great deal of transfer to maze B. On the other hand, learning B first will not produce much if any transfer to A in the sequence B : A. Another way of saying this is that the two sequences produce **asymmetric transfer** (Poulton, 1982). That is, one sequence produces a particular outcome that is not matched by the counterbalanced sequence. In the maze example, let's assume that learning A first has the effect of making B very easy; specifically, it reduces the total errors in B by 10. On the other hand, learning B first produces no transfer to A. Thus,

	Errors Due to			
	Difficulty	Transfer	Boredom	Total
Maze A	10	n/a	0	**10**
then				
Maze B	15	−10	+3	**8**
Maze B	15	n/a	0	**15**
then				
Maze A	10	0	+3	**13**

With the two sequences combined, the boredom effect still balances out, but the asymmetrical transfer effect doesn't. The final error scores are an average of 11.5 for *both* maze A [(10 + 13)/2] and the supposedly more difficult maze B [(8 + 15)/2]. The transfer problem would result in a finding of no difference between the mazes, undoubtedly an unpleasant surprise for the researcher. If one suspects asymmetrical transfer, it is wise to switch to a between-subjects design.

Control Problems in Developmental Research

As you have learned, the researcher must weigh several factors when deciding whether to use a between-subjects design or a within-subjects design. There are some additional considerations for researchers in developmental psychology, where two specific varieties of these designs occur — cross-sectional and longitudinal designs.

You've seen these terms before if you've had a course in developmental or child psychology. Research in these areas includes age as the prime independent variable — after all, the name of the game in developmental psychology is to discover how we change as we grow older. A **cross-sectional study** takes a between-subjects approach. A cross-sectional study comparing the language performance of 3-, 4-, and 5-year old children would use three different groups of children. A **longitudinal study**, on the other hand, studies a single group over a period of time; it takes a within-subjects or repeated–measures approach. The same language study would measure language behavior in a group of 3-year olds, then study these same children when they turned 4 and 5.

The obvious advantage of the cross-sectional approach to the experiment on language is time; such a study might take a month to complete. If done as a longitudinal study, it would take 3 years! However, a potentially serious difficulty with some cross-sectional studies is a special form of the problem of nonequivalent groups and involves what are known as **cohort effects**. A cohort is a group of people born about the same time. If you are studying three age groups, they differ not just in chronological age but also in terms of the environments in which they were raised. The problem is not especially noticeable when comparing 3-, 4-, and 5-year olds, but what if you're interested in whether intelligence declines with age and decide to compare a group of 20-somethings with groups of 40- and 60-somethings? You might indeed find a decline with age, but does it mean that intelligence gradually decreases with age, or might the differences relate to the very different life histories of the three groups? For example, the 60-year olds went to school during the Great Depression, the 40-somethings were educated during the post-WWII boom, and the 20-year olds were raised on TV. These factors could bias the results. Indeed, this outcome has occurred. Early research on the effects of age on IQ suggested that significant declines occurred, but these studies were cross-sectional. Subsequent longitudinal studies revealed a very different pattern (Schaie, 1988). For example, verbal abilities show very little decline, especially if the person remains verbally active (use it or lose it).

While cohort effects can plague cross-sectional studies, longitudinal studies

Box 6.1

CLASSIC STUDIES—The Record for Repeated Measures

In 1921, psychologist Lewis Terman (1877–1956) began what become the longest-running repeated–measures design in the history of psychology. A precocious child himself, Terman was always interested in studying so-called gifted children. His doctoral dissertation, supervised by Edmund Sanford at Clark University in 1905, was his first serious investigation of giftedness; he compared "bright" and "dull" local school children to see which tests might best distinguish between them (Minton, 1987). This early interest in giftedness and mental testing foreshadowed Terman's two main contributions to psychology. First, he took the intelligence test created by Alfred Binet of France and transformed it into the still-popular Sanford–Binet IQ test. Second, he began a longitudinal study of gifted children that was still going strong long after Terman himself died.

Terman was motivated by his belief, shared by most mental testers of the era, that America should become a meritocracy. That is, positions of leadership should be held by those most *able* to lead. You can see how this belief led to his interests in IQ and giftedness. To bring about a meritocracy there must be ways to recognize (i.e., measure) talent and nurture it.

Unlike his dissertation, which studied just 14 children, Terman's longitudinal study of gifted children was a mammoth undertaking. Through a variety of screening procedures, he recruited 1,470 children (824 boys and 646 girls). Most were in elementary school, but a sample of 444 were in junior or senior high school (sample numbers from Minton, 1988). Their average IQ score was 150, which put the group roughly in the top 1% of the population. Each child was given an extensive battery of tests and questionnaires by the team of graduate students assembled by Terman. By the time the initial testing was complete, each child had a file of about 100 pages (Minton, 1988)! The result of the first analysis of the group was published in more than 600 pages as the *Mental and Physical Traits of a Thousand Gifted Children* (Terman, 1925).

also have problems, most notably with attrition. If a large number of subjects drop out of the study, the group completing it might be very different from the group starting it. Referring to the age and IQ example, if people stay healthy, they might remain more interested in the intellectual life than if they are sick all the time. If they are chronically ill, they may die before a study is completed, leaving a group that might be generally more intelligent than the group starting the study.

In trying to balance cohort and attrition problems, some researchers use a strategy that combines cross-sectional with longitudinal studies. For instance, a series of studies by K. Warner Schaie (1983), known as the Seattle Longitudinal study, se-

Terman intended to do just a brief follow-up study, but the project took on a life of its own. The sample was retested in the late 1920s (Burks, Jensen, & Terman, 1930), and additional follow-up studies during Terman's lifetime were published 25 (Terman & Oden, 1947) and 35 (Terman & Oden, 1959) years after the initial testing. Following Terman's death, the project was taken over by Robert Sears, a member of the gifted group and a well-known psychologist in his own right. Between 1960 and 1986, Sears produced five additional follow-up studies of the group, and he was preparing a volume to be called *The Gifted in Later Maturity* when he died in 1989 (Cronbach, Hastorf, Hilgard, & Maccoby, 1990). In the forward to the 35-year follow-up, Sears wrote: "On actuarial grounds, there is considerable likelihood that the last of Terman's Gifted Children will not have yielded his last report to the files before the year 2010!" (Terman & Oden, 1969, p. ix).

There are two points worth making about this megalongitudinal study. First, Terman's work shattered the stereotype of the gifted child as someone who was brilliant but socially retarded and prone to burnout early in life. Rather, his group as a whole were both brilliant and well-adjusted and they became successful as they matured. By the time they reached maturity, "the group had produced thousands of scientific papers, 60 nonfiction books, 33 novels, 375 short stories, 230 patents, and numerous radio and television shows, works of art, and muscial compositions" (Hothersall, 1990, p. 353). Second, Terman's follow-up studies are incredible from the methodological standpoint of a longitudinal study's nemesis—attrition. The following figures (taken from Minton, 1988) are the percentages of living subjects who participated in the first three follow-ups:

After 10 years → 92%
After 25 years → 98%
After 35 years → 93%

These are remarkably high numbers, and they reflect the intense loyalty that Terman and his group had for each other. Members of the group referred to themselves as "Termites," and some even wore termite jewelry (Hothersall, 1990). Terman corresponded with hundreds of his subjects, and there was a genuine caring on Terman's part for these special people. After all, the group represented the type of person Terman believed held the key to America's future.

---

lected a new cohort every 7 years (starting in the 1950s) and retested cohorts every 7 years. This reduces the cohort effect by using groups only differing by seven years of age, and reduces problems of attrition by adding new subjects at regular intervals. Any one particular cohort might have a high rate of attrition, but with lots of cohorts, at least some of the groups remain relatively intact for an extended period of time.

The length of Seattle project is impressive, but the world's record for perseverance in a repeated–measures study occurred in what is arguably the most famous longitudinal study of all time. Before continuing, read Box 6.1, which chronicles the epic tale of Lewis Terman's study of gifted children.

Problems with Biasing

Because human beings are always the experimenters and usually the participants in research in psychology, there is the chance that the results of a study could be influenced by some "bias," a preconceived expectation about what is to happen in an experiment. These biases take several forms but fall into two broad categories: those affecting experimenters and those affecting subjects. These two forms of bias often interact.

Experimenter Bias

The Clever Hans case (Box 3.3, p. 75) is often used to illustrate the influence of **experimenter bias** on the outcome of some study. Hans's trainer, knowing the outcome to the question "What is 3×3?," sent subtle head-nodding cues that were read by the allegedly intelligent horse. Similarly, experimenters testing hypotheses sometimes might inadvertently do something that leads subjects to behave in ways that confirm the hypothesis. Although the stereotype of the scientist is that of an absolutely objective, dispassionate, even mechanical person, we've seen that researchers in fact become rather emotionally involved in their research. It's not difficult to see how a desire to confirm some strongly held hypothesis might lead an unwary experimenter to behave in such a way as to influence the outcome of the study.

For one thing, biased experimenters might treat the research participants in the various conditions differently. One procedure demonstrating this was developed by Robert Rosenthal. Subjects in some of his studies (e.g., Rosenthal & Fode, 1963a) are shown a set of photographs of faces and asked to make some judgment about the people pictured in them. For example, they might be asked to rate each photo on how successful the person seems to be, with the interval scale ranging from -10 (total failure) to $+10$ (totally successful). All subjects see the same photos and make the same judgments. The independent variable is experimenter expectancy. Some experimenters are led to believe that most subjects will give people the benefit of the doubt and rate the pictures positively; other experimenters are told to expect negative ratings. Interestingly enough, the experimenter's expectancies typically produce differences in the subjects' rating behavior, even though the pictures are identical for both groups. How can this be?

According to Rosenthal (1966), experimenters innocently communicate their expectancies in a number of subtle ways. For instance, on the person perception task, the experimenter holds up a picture while the subject rates it. If the experimenter is expecting a -8 and the subject says "$+9$," how might the experimenter act—with a slight frown perhaps? How might the subject read the frown? Might the subject try a "-7" on the next trial to see if this could elicit a smile or a nod from the experimenter? In general, could it be that experimenters in this situation, without even being aware of it, are subtly shaping the responses of their subjects? Does this remind you of Clever Hans?

Rosenthal has even shown that experimenter expectancies can be communicated to subjects in animal research. For instance, rats learn mazes faster for experimenters who *think* their animals have been bred for maze-running ability than those expecting their rats to be "maze-dull" (Rosenthal & Fode, 1963*b*). The rats of course are randomly assigned to the experimenters and should be equal in ability. The key factor here seems to be that experimenters expecting their rats to be "maze-bright" treat them better; for example, they handle them more, a behavior known to affect learning.

It should be noted that some of the Rosenthal research has been criticized on statistical grounds and for interpreting the results as being due to expectancy when they may have been due to something else. For example, Barber (1976) raised questions about the statistical conclusion validity of some of Rosenthal's work. In at least one study, according to Barber, 3 of 20 experimenters reversed the expectancy, getting data the opposite of the expectancies created for them. Rosenthal omitted these subjects from the analysis and obtained a significant difference for the remaining 17 experimenters. With all 20 experimenters included in the analysis, however, the difference disappeared. Barber also contended that in the animal studies, some of the results occurred because experimenters simply fudged the data (e.g., misrecording maze errors). Another difficulty with the Rosenthal studies is that his procedures don't match what normally occurs in experiments; most experimenters test all the subjects in all conditions of the experiment, not just those participating in one of the conditions. Hence, Rosenthal's results might overestimate the amount of biasing that occurs.

Despite these reservations, the experimenter expectancy effect cannot be ignored; it has been replicated in a variety of situations and by researchers other than Rosenthal and his colleagues (e.g., Word, Zanna, & Cooper, 1974). Furthermore, experimenters can be shown to inadvertently influence the outcomes of studies in ways other than through their expectations. The behavior of subjects can be affected by the experimenter's race and gender, as well as by demeanor, friendliness, and overall attitude (Adair, 1973). A recent example of the latter is a study by Fraysse and Desprels-Fraysse (1990), who found that preschoolers' performance on a cognitive classification task could be influenced by experimenter attitude. The children performed better with "caring" than with "indifferent" experimenters.

Controlling for Experimenter Bias

It is probably impossible to eliminate experimenter effects completely. Experimenters cannot be turned into machines. However, one strategy to reduce bias is to automate procedures as much as possible. For instance, it's not hard to remove a frowning or smiling experimenter from the person perception task. With modern computer technology, subjects could be shown photos on a screen and asked to make their responses with a key press while the experimenter is in a different room entirely.

Similarly, procedures for testing animals automatically have been available since the 1920s, even to the extent of eliminating human handling completely. E. C. Tolman didn't wait for computers to come along before inventing "a self-recording maze with an automatic delivery table" (Tolman, Tryon, & Jeffries, 1929). The delivery table was so-called because it "automatically delivers each rat into the entrance of the maze and 'collects' him at the end without the mediation of the experimenter. Objectivity of scoring is insured by the use of a device which automatically records his path through the maze" (Tryon, 1929, p. 73). Such automation is routine today. Recall from Chapter 4 the study of rats in the radial maze, in which rat "macrochoices" and "microchoices" were verified by videotaping each animal's performance (Brown, 1992). Furthermore, computers make it easy to present instructions and stimuli to subjects, while also keeping track of data.

A second approach to controlling for experimenter bias is to use a **double blind** procedure. This means simply that experimenters are kept in the dark (blind) about what to expect of subjects in a particular testing session (neither experimenters nor subjects know which condition is being tested, hence, the designation "double"). This can be accomplished when the principal investigator sets up the experiment but a colleague (usually a graduate student) actually collects the data. Double blinds are not always possible of course, as illustrated by the Dutton and Aron (1974) study you encountered in Chapter 3. As you recall, experimenters arranged to encounter subjects either on a suspension bridge swaying 230 feet over a river or on a solid bridge 10 feet over the same river. It would be a bit difficult to prevent those experimenters from knowing which condition of the study was being tested! On the other hand, many studies lend themselves to a procedure in which experimenters are blind to which condition is in effect. In a study comparing genuine "maze-bright" and "maze-dull" rats, it's easy to prevent experimenters from knowing which rats are being tested. In fact, in that particular case, the experimenters testing the rats probably wouldn't even know the study had to do with rat intelligence.

Subject Bias

People participating in psychological research cannot be expected to respond like machines. Rather, they are humans who *know* they are in an experiment. Presumably they have been told about the general nature of the research during the informed consent process, but in deception studies, they also know they haven't been told everything. Furthermore, even if there is no deception in a study, subjects may not believe it—after all, they are in a "psychology experiment" and aren't psychologists always trying to "psychoanalyze people?" In short, **subject bias** can occur in several ways, depending on what subjects are expecting and what they believe their role should be in the study. When behavior is affected by the knowledge that one is in an experiment and is therefore important to the study's success, the phenomenon is sometimes called the **Hawthorne effect**, after a famous series of studies of worker productivity. To understand the origins of this term, you should read Box 6.2 before continuing. You may be surprised to learn that most historians believe the Hawthorne effect has been misnamed and that the data of the original study were seriously distorted for political reasons.

Most research participants, in the spirit of trying to help the experimenter and contribute meaningful results, take on the role of the **good subject**, first described by Orne (1962). There are exceptions, of course, but in general subjects tend to be very cooperative, to the point of persevering through repetitive and boring tasks, all in the name of psychological science. Furthermore, if participants can figure out the hypothesis, they might try to behave in such a way that confirms it. Orne used the term **demand characteristics** to refer to those aspects of the study that reveal the hypotheses being tested. If these features are too obvious to participants, they no longer act naturally and it becomes difficult to interpret results. Did sub-

Box 6.2

ORIGINS—Productivity at Western Electric

The research that led to naming the "Hawthorne effect" took place at the Western Electric Plant in Hawthorne, Illinois, over a period of about 10 years, from 1924 to 1933. According to the traditional account, the purpose of the study was to investigate the factors influencing worker productivity. Numerous experiments were completed, but the most famous series became known as the Relay Assembly Test Room study.

In the Relay Assembly experiment, six female workers were selected from a larger group in the plant. Their job was to assemble relays for the phone company. Five workers did the actual assembly and the sixth supplied them with parts. The assembly was a time-consuming, labor-intensive, repetitive job requiring the assembly of some 35 parts per relay. Western Electric produced about 7 million relays a year (Gillespie, 1988), so naturally they were interested in making workers as productive as possible.

The first series of relay studies extended from May 1927 through September 1928 (Gillespie, 1988). During that time, several workplace variables were studied (and confounded with each other, actually). At various times, there were changes in the scheduling of rest periods, total hours of work, and bonuses paid for certain levels of production. The standard account has it that productivity for this small group quickly reached high levels and stayed there even when working conditions were worsened. The example always mentioned is during the infamous "12th test period," when workers were informed that the work week would increase from 42 to 48 hours per week, and that rest periods and free lunches would be discontinued. Virtually all textbooks describe the results something like this:

> . . . no matter what changes were made—whether there were many or few rest periods, whether the workday was longer or shorter, and so on—the women tended to produce more and more telephone relays. (Elmes, Kantowitz, & Roediger, 1992, p. 205)

Supposedly, workers remained productive because they believed they were a special group and the focus of attention—they were part of an experiment. This, of course, is the origin of the concept called the *Hawthorne effect*, the tendency for performance to be affected because people know they are being studied. The effect may be genuine, but whether it truly happened at Western Electric is uncertain.

A close look at what actually happened reveals some interesting alternative explanations. First, although accounts of the study typically emphasize how delighted the women were to be in this "special" testing room, the fact is that of the five original assemblers, two had to be removed from the room for insubordination and low output. One was said to have "gone Bolshevik" (Bramel & Friend, 1981). (Remember, the now former Soviet Union was brand new in the 1920s, and the "red menace" was a threat to industrial America, resulting in things like a fear of labor unions.) Of the two replacements, one was especially talented and enthusiastic and quickly became the group leader. She apparently was selected because she "held the record as the fastest relay-assembler in the regular department" (Gillespie, 1988, p. 122). Her efforts contributed mightily to the high levels of productivity.

A second problem with interpreting the relay data is a statistical one. In the famous twelfth period, productivity was recorded as output/week rather than output/hour, yet workers were putting in an extra 6 hours per week compared to the previous test period. If the more appropriate output/hour is used, productivity actually *declined* slightly (Bramel & Friend, 1981). Also, the women were apparently angry about the change, but afraid to complain lest they be removed from the test room, thereby losing their bonus money.

Historians argue that events must be understood within their entire political/economic/institutional context, and the Hawthorne studies are no exception. Painting a glossy picture of workers unaffected with specific working conditions but more concerned with being considered special ushered in the human relations movement in industry and led corporations to emphasize the "humane management" of employees to create one big happy family of labor and management. However, such a picture also helps to maintain power at the level of management and impede efforts at unionization, which some historians (e.g., Bramel & Friend, 1981) believe were the true motives of the studies completed at Western Electric.

jects behave as they normally would or did they figure out the hypothesis and behave so as to make it come true?

Orne demonstrated how demand characteristics can influence a study's outcome by recruiting subjects for a so-called sensory deprivation experiment (Orne & Scheibe, 1964). He assumed that subjects told they were in such an experiment would expect the experience to be stressful and might respond accordingly. This indeed occurred. Subjects who sat for 4 hours in a small but comfortable room showed signs of stress *only* if (a) they signed a form releasing the experimenter from any liability in case anything happened to them and (b) the room included a "panic button" which could be pressed if they felt too stressed by the deprivation. Control subjects were given no release form to sign, no panic button to press, and no expectation that their senses were being deprived; they did not react adversely.

The possibility that demand characteristics are operating has an impact on decisions about whether to opt for between- or within-subjects designs. Subjects serving in all of the conditions of a study have a greater opportunity to figure out the hypothesis(es). Hence, demand characteristics are potentially more troublesome in within-subjects designs than in between-subjects designs. For both types of designs, demand characteristics are especially devastating if they affect some conditions but not others, thereby introducing a confound.

Besides being good subjects (i.e., trying to confirm the hypothesis), participants also wish to be perceived as competent, creative, emotionally stable, and so on. The belief that they are being evaluated in the experiment produces what Rosenberg (1969) called **evaluation apprehension.** Subjects wish to be evaluated positively, so they may behave as they think the ideal person should behave. This concern over how one is going to look and the desire to help the experimenter often produce the same behavior among subjects, but sometimes the desire to create a favorable impression and the desire to be a good subject conflict. For example, in a helping behavior study, astute participants might guess they are in a condition of the study designed to reduce the chances that help will be offered. On the other hand, altruism is a valued, even heroic, behavior. The pressure to be a good subject and support the hypothesis pulls the subject toward nonhelping, but evaluation apprehension makes the subject want to help. At least one study has suggested that when faced with the option of confirming the hypothesis and being evaluated positively, the latter is the more powerful motivator (Rosnow, Goodstadt, Suls, & Gitter, 1973).

Controlling for Subject Bias

The primary strategy for controlling subject bias is to reduce demand characteristics to the minimum. One way of accomplishing this of course is through deception. As we've seen in Chapter 2, the prime purpose of deception is to induce participants to behave more naturally than they otherwise might. A second strategy, normally found in drug studies, is to use the placebo control group (see p. 131). This procedure allows for a comparison between those actually getting some treatment (e.g., a drug) and those who think they are getting the treatment but aren't. If subjects in both groups behave identically, the effects can be attributed to subject expectations of the treatment's effects.

A second way to check for the presence of demand characteristics is to do what is sometimes called a **manipulation check**. This can be accomplished during debriefing by asking subjects in a deception study to indicate what they believe the true hypothesis to be (of course, the "good subject" might feign ignorance). It can also be done during the study. Sometimes a random subset of subjects in each condition is stopped in the middle of an experiment and asked about the clarity of the instructions, what they think is going on, and so on. Manipulation checks are also used to see if some procedure is producing the effect it is supposed to produce. For example, if some procedure is supposed to make people feel anxious (e.g., telling subjects to expect shock), a sample of subjects might be stopped in the middle of the study and assessed for level of anxiety.

A final way of avoiding demand characteristics is to conduct field research. If subjects are unaware they are in a study, they are unlikely to spend any time thinking about research hypotheses. Of course, field studies have problems of their own as you recall from the discussion of informed consent and privacy invasions in Box 3.1 (p. 63).

Although I stated earlier that most research participants play the role of "good subjects," this is not uniformly true and some differences exist between those who truly volunteer and are interested in the experiment and those who are more reluctant volunteers and less interested. For instance, true volunteers tend to be slightly more intelligent and to have a higher need for social approval (Adair, 1973). Differences between volunteers and nonvolunteers can be a problem when college students are asked to serve as subjects as part of a course requirement. For ethical reasons, instructors are obligated to provide nonaversive alternatives for those who choose not to participate, thus insuring that research participants are volunteers, at least technically. However, some students are more enthusiastic volunteers than others. Furthermore, there can be a "semester effect" operating. The true volunteers sign up earlier in the semester. Therefore, if you ran a study with two groups and group 1 was tested in the first half of the semester and group 2 in the second half, differences found could be due to the independent variable, but they also could be due to differences between true volunteers who sign up first and the reluctant volunteers who wait as long as they can. Can you think of a way to control for this problem? If the concept "block randomization" occurs to you, and you say to yourself "this will distribute the conditions of the study equally through the duration of the semester," then you've accomplished something in this chapter. Well done.

To close out the chapter, read Box 6.3, which concerns the ethical obligations

---

Box 6.3

ETHICS — Research Participants Have Responsibilities Too

The APA ethics code spells out the responsibilities that researchers have to those who participate in their experiments. Participants have a right to expect that the guidelines will be followed and if not, there should be a clear process for registering complaints. But what about the participants? What are their obligations?

An article by James Korn in the journal *Teaching of Psychology* lists five basic responsibilities of those who volunteer for research. In his words, they are as follows:

1. Participants have the responsibility to listen carefully to the experimenter and ask questions in order to understand the research.

2. [Participants should b]e on time for the research appointment.

3. Participants should take the research seriously and cooperate with the experimenter.

4. When the study has been completed, participants share the responsibility for understanding what happened.

5. Participants have the responsibility for honoring the researcher's request that they not discuss the study with anyone else who might be a participant. (Korn, 1988, p. 77)

The assumption underlying this list is that research should be a collaborative effort between experimenters and participants. Korn's suggestion that participants take a more assertive role in making research more informative is a welcome one. An experimenter who simply "runs a subject" and records the data is ignoring valuable information.

of those participating as subjects in psychological research. The list of responsibilities you'll find there is based on the assumption that research should be a collaborative effort between experimenters and subjects. We've seen that experimenters must follow the APA ethics code. In Box 6.3, you'll learn that participants have responsibilities too.

In the last two chapters, you've learned about the essential features of experimental research and the particular control problems that must be faced by those who wish to do research in psychology. We've now completed the necessary groundwork for introducing the various kinds of experimental designs used to test the effects of independent variables. So . . . Let the designs begin!

Chapter Review

Glossary Fill-Ins

1. In a taste test, Joan is asked to evaluate diet drinks as follows: Diet Coke, Diet Pepsi, Diet Pepsi, Diet Coke. The investigator is using the control method of _____.

2. Concern over _____ effects might cause a developmental psychologist to opt for a longitudinal study rather than a cross-sectional one.

3. Random assignment and matching are two procedures used for the purpose of trying to create _____.

4. Although this does not appear to be what really happened at Western Electric, the concept of the _____ effect has come to mean that subjects' behaviors are influenced by the simple fact that they know they are in an experiment.

5. _____ procedures are often used in drug studies to avoid both subject and experimenter biasing effects.

6. Using the control method of _____, a researcher trying to use all possible sequences of four lists of words in a memory test would need 24 different sequences.

Multiple Choice

1. The primary advantage of between-subjects designs over within-subjects designs is that between-subjects designs
   a. Require fewer subjects.
   b. Avoid, by definition, the problem of equivalent groups.
   c. Reduce the amount of error variance between conditions.
   d. Avoid, by definition, the problem of sequence effects.

2. Block randomization is used
   a. As a method to accomplish random assignment while insuring that an equal number of subjects are assigned to each group.

    b. As a means of counterbalancing when subjects are tested more than once per condition in a within-subjects design.

    c. Both alternatives a and b.

    d. None of the above.

3. Matching is most likely to be used for creating equivalent groups whenever

    a. It is clear that some characteristic of the subjects correlates with the dependent variable.

    b. The number of subjects is very large.

    c. Counterbalancing is not feasible.

    d. All of the above.

4. When asymmetric transfer effects occur,

    a. It means that complete counterbalancing must be used.

    b. Then matching must be used as the method for creating equivalent groups.

    c. Then counterbalancing may not be successful in eliminating sequence effects.

    d. Then partial rather than complete counterbalancing must be used.

5. Experimenter expectancy effects

    a. Have been found in research with human subjects but not in animal research.

    b. Won't occur as long as subjects are unaware of the hypothesis being tested.

    c. Can be reduced by automating the procedure as much as possible.

    d. Have never been replicated after Rosenthal's research, so they probably aren't a real problem.

Applications Exercises

Exercise 6.1. — Between-Subjects or Within-Subjects?

Think of a study that might test each of the following hypotheses. In particular, indicate whether you think the independent variable should be a between- or a within-subjects variable or whether either approach would be reasonable. Explain your decision in each case.

1. A neuroscientist hypothesizes that damage to the primary visual cortex is more permanent in older animals.

2. A sensory psychologist predicts that it is easier to distinguish slightly different shadings of grays under daylight than under fluorescent light.

3. A clinical psychologist thinks that phobias are best cured by repeatedly exposing the person to the feared object and not allowing the person to escape until they realize the object really is harmless.

4. A social psychologist believes people will solve problems more creatively when in groups than when alone.

5. A developmental psychologist predicts cultural differences in moral development.

Exercise 6.2. — Constructing a Balanced Latin Square

A memory researcher wishes to compare long-term memory for a series of word lists as a function of whether the person initially studies either four or eight lists. Help the investigator in the planning stages of this project by constructing the two needed Latin squares, using the procedure outlined in Table 6.3.

Exercise 6.3. — Using Block Randomization

An experimenter wishes to test the hypothesis that victim status will influence how people judge a rapist. Subjects are given a description of an assault and are asked to recommend a sentence for the attacker who has been found guilty. Victim status is manipulated by telling different groups of subjects the 21-year-old victim was a prostitute, a pregnant mother of two, a college student without sexual experience, or just a 21-year-old woman (control group). Ten subjects will be tested per condition. Use a block randomization procedure to assign subjects to the four groups and produce a sheet that lists what condition each of the 40 subjects will encounter.

Exercise 6.4. — Random Assignment and Matching

A researcher is investigating the relative effectiveness of two different weight loss programs. Subjects will be assigned to the two groups and to a waiting list control group. To insure that the people in one group aren't significantly heavier than in any other group at the start of the study, it is decided to match the three groups on their starting weight. Here are the weights for the 15 participants, in pounds.

156	167	183	170	145
143	152	145	181	162
175	159	169	174	161

First, randomly assign subjects to the three groups using a block randomization procedure (think of each column as a block). Then use the matching procedure. Compare these two approaches by calculating two sets of mean weights for the three groups, one for each method of creating equivalent groups. Compare your results to those of the rest of the class. What do you conclude?

CHAPTER 7

Experimental Design

Chapter Overview

- ### One Factor — Two Levels

  The simplest experimental designs have a single independent variable and two levels of that variable. These designs can include between-subjects variables or within-subjects variables. Between-subjects variables can be directly manipulated or they can be selected as subject factors. The single factor design is often used when an experimental treatment of some kind is compared with a control condition.

- ### One Factor — More Than Two Levels

  When comparing only two levels of some experimental variable, the results always will appear to be linear, because a graph of the results will only have two points. Some relationships are nonlinear, however, and they can be discovered by adding more than two levels to an independent variable. Like the two level case, these multilevel designs can be either between- or within-subjects.

• More Than One Factor — Factorial Designs

Factorial designs are experiments with more than one independent variable. All of the variables can be between-subjects factors, or all can be within-subjects factors. A mixed factorial design includes at least one factor of each type (between and within). The main advantage of a factorial design over studies with a single independent variable is that factorials allow for the possibility of discovering interactions between factors. Person $\times$ environment interactions can occur in studies which include both manipulated and subject factors. When P $\times$ E interactions occur, they show how stimulus situations affect one type of person one way and a second type of person another way.

I like to cook. I'm not very good at it, however, so I am more or less tied to the procedures specified in cookbooks. Nonetheless, my meals are passable and being an experimental psychologist at heart, I occasionally try two tablespoons of soy sauce instead of one. My wife, on the other hand, is an extraordinary cook who seldom relies on the dictates of printed recipes. I can get by and avoid serious errors, but her efforts are exquisite by comparison and she seems to have an unerring sense of how to design and produce a meal.

The contrast between my wife and I as cooks is a bit like the comparison between an experienced research psychologist and a novice. For the accomplished researcher, the decisions about which independent variables to use, how many levels of each should be included, whether they should be between- or within-subjects factors, how to create equivalent groups or control for sequence, how to avoid confounds, and what statistical analysis will be required become routine. They seem to flow automatically from the empirical question at hand. The creative effort goes into developing some unusual variation on procedure, creating a new measuring tool, developing a brand new hypothesis, or testing some existing hypothesis in an innovative fashion. For the novice, however, all the decisions routinely made by the expert have to be worked through deliberately. Consequently, the beginner's designs may be methodologically sound but not especially inspiring (somewhat like my lasagna). With time and experience, however, designs become more elegant, creativity becomes more of a factor, and the researcher becomes more like the true chef.

In a certain sense, this chapter is like a cookbook. Along with the earlier chapters, especially the last two, it outlines some recipes for the fledgling research psychologist. You'll find the details of the most common experimental designs in this chapter, along with numerous examples of actual experiments illustrating those designs. The information here should enable you to design an experiment that is sound if not elegant, nutritious if not exquisite.

The first decision to be made about design follows directly from the empirical question at hand and concerns whether there will be one or more than one independent variable. If the answer is "one," the study is a **single-factor design**. These have single independent variables with two or more levels; they are the focus of the first two sections of the chapter. The chapter's last and most substantial section concerns factorial designs, which occur whenever more than one independent variable is used.

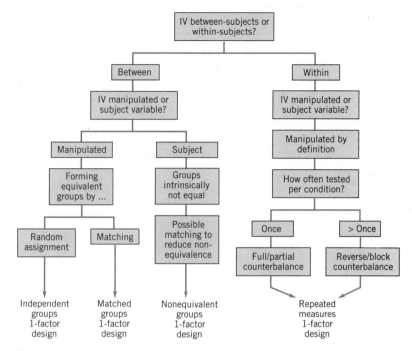

FIGURE 7.1   Decision Tree — Single Factor Designs.

One Factor — Two Levels

The simplest of all experimental designs uses one independent variable with two levels. As you can see from the decision tree in Figure 7.1, there are four possible designs fitting this definition, and they result from a series of decisions about the independent variable being investigated. First, this variable can be tested between- or within-subjects. If it is tested between-subjects, it could be either a manipulated or a subject variable. If the independent variable is manipulated, the design will either be called an **independent groups** design if random assignment is used to create equivalent groups, or a **matched group** design, if matching is needed. If a subject variable is being investigated, the groups are by definition comprised of different categories of subjects (e.g., males and females), and the design is called a **nonequivalent groups** design. Because groups are made up of different types of individuals in this type of design, researchers using them sometimes use a matching procedure to reduce the nonequivalence as much as possible, or they might simply insure that the subjects selected are similar in such variables as age, year in college, or socioeconomic class.

One final single-factor design is the **repeated-measures** design, used when the independent variable is tested within subjects. That is, each subject in the study experiences each level of the independent variable (i.e., is measured "repeatedly").

TABLE 7.1   *Attributes of Four Single-Factor Designs*

Type of Design	Minimum Levels of Independent Variable?	Independent Variable Between or Within?	Independent Variable Type?	Creating Equivalent Groups
Independent groups	2	between	manipulated	random assignment
Matched groups	2	between	manipulated	matching
Nonequivalent groups	2	between	subject	matching may reduce nonequivalence
Repeated measures	2	within	manipulated	n/a

The major attributes of each of the four main types of design are summarized in Table 7.1. Let's look at some specific examples.

Between-Subjects, Single-Factor Designs

Single-factor studies using only two levels are not as common as you might think. Most researchers prefer to use more complex designs, which usually produce more elaborate and more intriguing outcomes. Also, few journal editors are impressed with single-factor two-level designs. Nonetheless, there is a certain beauty in simplicity and nothing could be simpler than a study comparing just two conditions. The following are case examples of three such experiments.

Case Study 1 — Independent Groups

An example of an independent groups designs using a single factor with two levels is a well-known study by Blakemore and Cooper (1970). They were interested in the effects of experience on the development of the visual system. Two-week old cats were randomly assigned to the two levels of a manipulated independent variable that could be called "visual environment." The cats were to be raised in a setting dominated either by horizontal or vertical stripes. I think you can see why this had to be a between-subjects rather than a within-subjects design; it wouldn't make sense to raise a kitten in a vertical environment, *then* in a horizontal environment. In studies like this one, subjects experiencing one level of the independent variable are in essence "used up"; the experience makes it impossible for them to "start over" in the experiment's other condition.

Figure 7.2 shows Blakemore and Cooper's sketch of the apparatus for the "vertical" condition. The cat is standing on plexiglass and the stripes extend above and

FIGURE 7.2 Apparatus for Blakemore and Cooper's (1970) experiment on the effects of experiencing only horizontal or vertical environments.

below the surface. The wide collar around the cat's neck keeps the animal visually focused on the walls of the chamber. Over a period of several months, the cats were exposed either to the vertical or the horizontal world for five hours per day; they were kept in a darkened environment otherwise.

At the end of the study, Blakemore and Cooper tested the animals both behaviorally and by measuring the activity of neurons in their visual cortex. In terms of their general behavior, the cats quickly recovered from the deprivation. After "10 h[ours] of normal vision they . . . would jump with ease from a chair to the floor" (Blakemore & Cooper, 1970, p. 477). However, the cats raised in a vertical environment apparently could not perceive horizontal events very well; horizontally raised cats had problems with vertical stimuli:

> The differences were most marked when two kittens, one horizontally and the other vertically experienced, were tested simultaneously with a long black or white rod. If this was held vertically and shaken, the one cat would follow it and play with it. Now if it was held horizontally the other cat was attracted and its fellow ignored it. (Blakemore & Cooper, 1970, p. 478)

Obviously, early experience can profoundly affect how the brain develops.

Case Study 2—Matched Groups

Creating equivalent groups through matching occurs frequently in research evaluating the effects of some therapy or intervention program. Some subjects are exposed to the treatment while others are in a control group. The groups might be matched on variables like age, intelligence, severity of the problem for which therapy is sought, and so on. One example is a study by Fletcher and Atkinson (1972), who evaluated a program for teaching first graders to read by adding Computer Assisted Instruction (CAI) to their normal instruction. Fifty pairs of students were selected. Because Fletcher and Atkinson believed that both (a) gender differences in reading and (b) different levels of reading readiness would correlate with their dependent variables (e.g., standardized reading tests), they used matching to create equivalent groups of subjects. The subjects were matched for gender and readiness (using a standardized reading readiness test). Besides matching on these two factors, the investigators tried "to insure that both members [of each pair] were drawn from comparable classrooms with teachers of equivalent ability" (Fletcher & Atkinson, 1972, p. 598).

In addition to normal instruction, students assigned to the experimental CAI group were given computer instruction for 8–10 minutes per day during the second half of the first grade school year; control group subjects were given normal reading instruction. At the end of the school year, the CAI group was ahead of the control group in reading. Computer instruction has come a long way in the last 25 years, but this early study by Fletcher and Atkinson shows that even with a modest application of computer technology, gains can be made.

Case Study 3 — Nonequivalent Groups

Stimulated perhaps by Terman's megalongitudinal study of gifted children (see Box 6.1, p. 178), considerable research over the years has attempted to shed light on the gifted child. A study by Knepper, Obrzut, and Copeland (1983) asked whether gifted children might be adept at social and emotional problem solving, in addition to their normal advantages over average children in cognitive problem solving. Their experiment nicely illustrates a nonequivalent groups design. The independent variable was a subject variable, degree of giftedness, and two levels were compared, gifted (operationally defined as IQ ≥ 130) and average (IQ ≥ 90 and ≤110) students. The mean IQs for the groups were 136.9 and 102.9, respectively. A specific matching procedure was not used, but age was controlled by using only sixth graders. All were given a test called the Means–Ends Problem Solving Test, which measures the quality of solutions to interpersonal (social) and intrapersonal (emotional) problems. The gifted children indeed outperformed the average children on these tests of social and emotional problem solving, a finding consistent with Terman's conclusion that gifted children are not just "brains," but also have some social skills.

One important caution. Recall from Chapter 5 that conclusions about cause and effect cannot be drawn when subject variables are involved. Thus, it would be inappropriate to say that giftedness somehow causes an increase in the ability to solve social and emotional problems. All that can be said is that gifted and nongifted children seem to differ in how well they solve such tasks.

Within-Subjects, Single-Factor Designs

As you already know, any within-subjects design (a) requires fewer subjects, (b) is more sensitive to small differences between means, and (c) requires counterbalancing to control for sequence conditions. A within-subjects design with a single independent variable and two levels will counterbalance in one of two ways. If subjects participate in each condition just once, complete counterbalancing will be used. Half of the subjects will experience condition A, then B, and the rest will get B then A. If subjects are tested more than once per condition, reverse counterbalancing (ABBA) can be used. This route was taken by J. Ridley Stroop in the first two of three studies he reported in 1935. This study is high on anyone's "top ten

Box 7.1

CLASSIC STUDIES—Psychology's Most Replicated Finding?

Reverse counterbalancing was the strategy used in a study first published in 1935 by J. Ridley Stroop. The study is so well known that the phenomenon it first demonstrated is now called the "Stroop effect." In an article accompanying a recent reprinting of the original paper, Colin MacLeod called the Stroop effect the "gold standard" of measures of attention, and opened his essay this way:

> In 1992, it would be virtually impossible to find anyone in cognitive psychology who does not have at least a passing acquaintance with the Stroop effect. Indeed, this generalization could probably be extended to all those who have taken a standard introductory course, where the Stroop task is an almost inevitable demonstration. (MacLeod, 1992, p. 12)

MacLeod went on to argue that the Stroop effect is one of psychology's most replicated and most frequently cited findings. What did Stroop do?

The original study summarized three experiments, completed by Stroop as his doctoral dissertation. We'll focus on the first two because they each illustrate a within-subjects design with one independent variable, tested at two levels, and using reverse counterbalancing. In the first experiment, 14 male and 56 females performed two tasks. Both involved reading the names of colors. Stroop (1992, p. 16) called one condition RCNb (**R**eading **C**olor **N**ames printed in **b**lack). Subjects read 100 color names (e.g., GREEN) printed in black ink as quickly and as accurately as they could. The second condition Stroop (1992, p. 16) called RCNd ("**R**eading **C**olor **N**ames where the color of the print and the word are **d**ifferent"). In this case, the 100 color names were printed in colored ink, but the colors of the ink did not match the color name (e.g., the word GREEN would be printed in red ink). The subjects' task was to read the word (e.g., correct response is "green").

As a good researcher, Stroop was aware of the problems with sequence effects, so he used reverse counterbalancing (ABBA) to deal with the problem. After subdividing each of the stimulus lists into two sets of 50 items, Stroop gave some subjects the sequence RCNb-RCNd-RCNd-RCNb, and an equal number of subjects the sequence RCNd-RCNb-RCNb-RCNd. Thus, each subject read a total of 200 color names.

classic studies" list. For a close look at it (and to learn more about swastikas than you probably know at the moment), read Box 7.1 before continuing.

Another counterbalancing strategy for a study with just two conditions, with each being tested many times, is simply to alternate the conditions (ABAB . . .). Such an approach was taken in the following case study.

Stroop's experiment found no difference in performance between the RCNb and RCNd conditions. The average amount of time to read 100 words of each type was 41.0 seconds and 43.3 seconds, respectively. Reading the color names in the RCNd condition, then, was unaffected by having the words printed in contrasting colors.

It was in experiment 2 that Stroop found the huge difference that eventually made his name so well known. Using the same basic design, this time the response was *naming the colors* rather than reading color names. In one condition, NC (**N**aming **C**olor test), subjects named the colors of square color patches. In the second and key condition, NCWd (**N**aming **C**olor of **W**ord test where the color of the print and the word are **d**ifferent), subjects saw the same material as in the RCNd condition of experiment 1, but this time instead of reading the color name they were to name the color in which the word was printed. If the letters of the word Green were printed in red ink, the correct response this time would be "*red*," not "green." Subjects in 1935 had the same difficulty experienced by subjects today. Because reading is such an overlearned and automatic process, it interferes with the color naming, resulting in errors and slower reading times. Stroop found that the average color naming times were 63.3 seconds for condition NC and a whopping 110.3 seconds for the NCWd condition. I've taken the four different outcomes, reported by Stroop in the form of tables, and drawn a bar graph of them in Figure 7.3. As you can see, the Stroop effect is a robust phenomenon.

I mentioned previously that Stroop actually completed three experiments for his dissertation. The third demonstrated that subjects could improve on the NCWd task (the classic Stroop task) if given practice. An interesting aspect of this final study was that in the place of square color patches on the NC test, Stroop substituted color patches in the shape of swastikas, which "made it possible to print the NC test in shades which more nearly match[ed] those in the NCWd test" (Stroop, 1992, p. 18). Swastikas are ancient religious symbols, formed by bending the arms of a traditional Greek cross (+). Ironically, Stroop's study was published the same year (1935) that the swastika became officially adopted as the symbol for Nazi Germany.

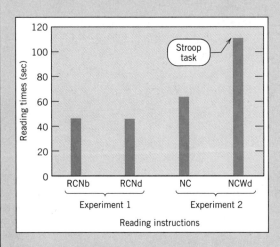

FIGURE 7.3 Combined data from the first two experiments of the original Stroop study (1935).

Case Study 4—Repeated Measures

In a study of motion perception and balance, Lee and Aronson (1974) tested some predictions from a theory of perception proposed by James Gibson, mentioned briefly in Chapter 1 as the husband of Eleanor Gibson. In particular, they were interested in how we maintain our balance in a moving environment. Seven children aged 13 to 16 months were placed in the apparatus pictured in Figure 7.4. When an infant was facing the back wall, the experimenter could move the walls and ceiling either forward or backward.

It was hypothesized that moving the room forward (Figure 7.5*a*) would create an "optic flow pattern" identical to the one produced if the infant's head was moving backwards (Figure 7.5*b*). This in turn would trigger a compensating tilt forward by the child. If so, then moving the room forward should cause the infant to lean forward or perhaps fall forward (Figure 7.5*c*). Just the opposite was predicted when the room was moved backward.

Unlike the study with the cats raised either in a vertical or horizontal world, there is no reason why Lee and Aronson's infants could not experience both experimental conditions: the room moving forward or backward. Hence, a within-subjects approach was taken: the design was a single-factor repeated-measures design. The independent variable was the direction of the room's movement, either forward or backward, and the infants' body lean or falling was measured as the dependent variable. Twenty repeated trials were completed per subject, with the room's movement alternating from trial to trial. Seven subjects were tested, but three of them became distressed, and for them the experiment was immediately terminated. The responses of the remaining four subjects were recorded by three observers (why would more than one observer be needed?). Some loss of balance in the predicted direction occurred on 82% of the trials. Loss of balance was cate-

FIGURE 7.4 Apparatus used in Lee and Aronson's (1974) "moving room" study.

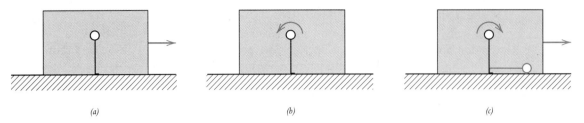

(a)   *(b)*   *(c)*

FIGURE 7.5   Predicted effects of moving the room forward in Lee and Aronson's (1974) experiment.

gorized by the observers as a sway (26% of the trials), a stagger (23%), or a fall (33%—ouch!).

One drawback to a counterbalancing procedure that simply alternates between conditions A and B is that subjects can easily predict what condition is about to occur. However, Lee and Aronson correctly decided that this problem was unlikely to influence their results, given the age of their subjects.

Analyzing Single-Factor, Two-Level Designs

To determine whether the differences found between the conditions of a two-level design are significant or due simply to chance, some form of inferential statistical analysis is required. When interval or ratio scales of measurement are used in the experiment, the most common approach is to use one of two varieties of the *t* test, an inferential procedure mentioned near the end of Chapter 4 and illustrated in Appendix B. Other techniques are required when nominal or ordinal scales of measurement are used.

If participants in the study are randomly assigned to the groups, or if the variable being studied is a subject variable (e.g., males vs females), the groups are said to be independent of each other and a *t* **test for independent groups** is used. If the independent variable is a within-subjects factor, or if the two groups of people are formed in such a way that some relationship exists between them (e.g., subjects in group A are matched on intelligence with subjects in group B), a *t* **test for dependent groups** (sometimes called a *t* test for correlated groups) is used. For the four single-factor designs just considered, the following *t* tests would be appropriate:

- *t* test for independent groups
  - independent groups design
  - nonequivalent groups design
- *t* test for dependent groups
  - matched groups design
  - repeated–measures design

In essence, the *t* test examines the difference between two mean scores and determines (with some probability) whether this difference is larger than expected by chance factors alone. If it is larger, and if potential confounds can be ruled out, then the researcher can conclude with a high probability that the differences are real. See Appendix B for step-by-step instructions on how to carry out both varieties of *t* test.

One Factor — More Than Two Levels

When experiments include a single independent variable, using two levels is the exception rather than the rule. Most single-factor studies use three or more levels and for that reason they often are called **single-factor multilevel designs**. As was true for two-level designs, these include both between- and within-subjects designs, and can be of the same four types: independent groups, matched groups, nonequivalent groups, and repeated measures.

Between-Subjects, Multilevel Designs

The distinct advantage of multilevel designs is that they enable the researcher to discover **nonlinear effects**. To take a simple between-subjects example, suppose you were interested in the effects of caffeine dosage on reaction time. You set up an experiment that compares two dosage levels (1 mg and 3 mg), get the results in Figure 7.6, and conclude that as a stimulant, caffeine speeds up reaction time. As dosage increases, reaction time quickens in a straight-line (i.e., linear) fashion.

Now suppose another researcher does this study but uses a multilevel design that includes four dosages (1 mg, 2 mg, 3 mg, and 4 mg)—an example of replicating (1 mg and 3 mg) and extending (2 mg and 4 mg) your finding. This study might produce the results in Figure 7.7.

This outcome replicates your results for the 1-mg and 3-mg conditions exactly, but the overall pattern for the four conditions calls your conclusion into serious question. Instead of caffeine simply increasing reaction time, the conclusion now would be that (a) adding caffeine increases reaction time, but only after a level of 2 mg is reached, and (b) caffeine increases reaction time only up to a point, after which it begins to slow down reaction time. That is, the outcome is no longer a

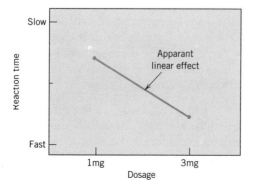

FIGURE 7.6   Hypothetical effects of caffeine on reaction time—two levels.

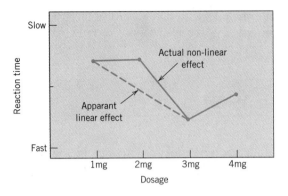

FIGURE 7.7   Hypothetical effects of caffeine on reaction time — four levels.

simple linear result, but a nonlinear one. In general, then, the advantage of multi-level designs is that they provide for more interesting outcomes than two-level designs.

Multilevel designs can also be used to test for specific alternative hypotheses and perhaps rule them out. This is a strategy you will recognize from the discussion in Chapter 3 of the merits of falsification. A perfect example is a study by Bransford and Johnson (1972).

Case Study 5 — Multilevel Independent Groups

Cognitive psychologists interested in how we comprehend new information have shown that understanding new ideas is easier if they are placed in some context. For example, understanding a textbook chapter is easier if you have already examined brief versions of its contents, an effect that occasionally leads textbook authors to put chapter summaries at the beginning of each chapter. The Bransford and Johnson (1972) study illustrates these context effects. In their study, subjects were asked to comprehend this paragraph. Try it:

> If the balloons popped, the sound wouldn't be able to carry, since everything would be too far away from the correct floor. A closed window would also prevent the sound from carrying, since most buildings tend to be well insulated. Since the whole operation depends on a steady flow of electricity, a break in the middle of the wire would also cause problems. Of course, the fellow could shout, but the human voice is not loud enough to carry that far. An additional problem is that a string could break on the instrument. Then there could be no accompaniment to the message. It is clear that the best situation would involve less distance. Then there would be fewer potential problems. With face to face contact, the least number of things could go wrong. (Bransford & Johnson, 1973, p. 392)

I imagine your reaction to this passage is "Huh"?, a response shared by many of the participants in the original study. However, Bransford and Johnson found that comprehension could be improved by adding some context. Here's what they did.

They designed a single-factor independent groups study with five levels of the independent variable. Subjects randomly assigned to a control group were asked to

FIGURE 7.8 Cartoon providing (a) context and (b) partial context for Bransford and Johnson's (1972) study.

do what I just asked of you. They read the paragraph and tried to recall as much as they could of the 14 idea units included in it. They recalled an uninspiring average of 3.6 ideas. A second group read the story twice to see if recall might improve with simple repetition. It didn't—they recalled 3.8 ideas. A third group was given a look at the cartoon in Figure 7.8*a*. Then they read and tried to recall the paragraph. They recalled 8.0 ideas out of 14. Clearly, the cartoon gave these participants an overall context within which to comprehend the sentences of the paragraph. But is it necessary to see the cartoon *first*, before reading the passage? Yes. The fourth condition of the study had subjects read the paragraph, *then* see the cartoon, then recall the paragraph. They recalled 3.6 ideas, just like the original control group. Finally, group 5 was given a partial context. Before reading the passage they saw the cartoon in Figure 7.8*b*. It contains all the elements of 7.8*a*, but rearranged. Subjects in this group recalled an average of 4.0 ideas. In graph form, the results looked like this:

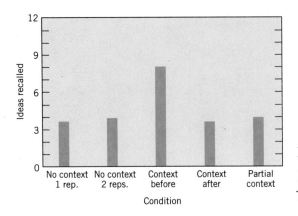

FIGURE 7.9   Data for the five conditions of Bransford and Johnson's (1972) study, in bar graph form.

Considering just two groups, "No Context-1 Repetition" and "Context Before," this study is reasonably interesting, showing a simple (linear) improvement in comprehension by adding some context in the form of the cartoon. However, adding the other conditions makes it a *really* interesting study by ruling out (i.e., falsifying) some alternative factors that might be thought to improve recall. Thus, context improves our understanding of something but *only* if that context occurs first. Because presenting the context after the reading doesn't help, it can be inferred that context improves recall by facilitating the initial processing of the information, not just its subsequent retrieval. Also, simple repetition doesn't help; neither does a partial context.

Within-Subjects, Multilevel Designs

Whereas a single-factor repeated-measures design with two levels has limited counterbalancing options, going beyond two levels makes all of these options available. If each condition is tested just once per subject, then both full or partial counterbalancing procedures are available. And when each condition is tested several times per subject, both reverse and block randomization procedures can be used.

As I've indicated before, repeated-measures designs occur frequently in perception and cognition research; a good example of a multilevel repeated–measures design is an interesting study on cognitive mapping and the use of spatial imagery by Kosslyn, Ball, and Reiser (1978).

Case Study 6—Multilevel Repeated Measures

Take a look at the map in Figure 7.10. If you participated in the Kosslyn et al. (1978) study, you would be asked to memorize it, paying special attention to the landmarks indicated by the letters (in the actual study they were marked with red dots). After demonstrating that you could draw the map accurately, the actual map would be removed. Then you would be asked to create a mental image of it and imagine that you were moving from one landmark to another. For example, on one trial you might be told to imagine yourself at the beach (point F). Five sec-

FIGURE 7.10   Map used by Kosslyn, Ball, and Reiser (1978), to study cognitive mapping.

onds later, the word "lake" (point C) would be presented, and you would be instructed to mentally "travel" there. This mental trip "was to be accomplished by imaging a little black speck zipping in the shortest straight line from the first object to the second. The speck was to move as quickly as possible, while still remaining visible" (Kosslyn et al., 1978, p. 52). Upon reaching the destination, you would hit a key, thereby yielding a reaction time measure, the dependent variable. There were 21 possible pairs of points, making this a study with a single independent variable ("distance between landmark points") with 21 levels. All subjects experienced all the pairs, making this a repeated measures design. Catch trials were also inserted (nonmap destinations, such as "bench") to prevent subjects from anticipating the destination and responding too early. For each of the nine participants, counterbalancing was accomplished by randomizing the sequence of trials, except that the same location was not allowed to occur twice within any three trials. Hence, this was an example of partial counterbalancing in which a random sample of sequences was selected.

If subjects perform this task by creating an image of the map and mentally scanning from one location to another on each trial, increasing the distance between the points should increase the reaction time, a prediction confirmed by the study. Figure 7.11 shows an almost a perfect linear increase in reaction time as the distance between the points increased.

Presenting the Data

One decision to be made when reporting the results of any research study is how to present the data. There are three choices. First, the numbers can be presented in sentence form, an approach that might be fine for reporting the results of experimental studies with just two levels, but that makes for tedious reading as the amount of data increases. You might have noticed this when reading about the re-

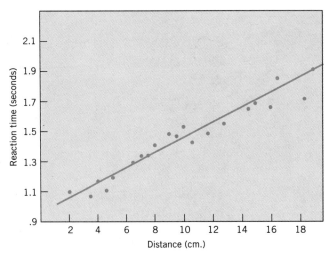

FIGURE 7.11   Data from the Kosslyn et al. (1978)
repeated–measures study.

sults of the five conditions of the Bransford and Johnson (1972) study. A second
approach is to construct a table of results. A table for the Bransford and Johnson
study might look like this:

TABLE 7.2   *The Bransford and Johnson (1972) Data
in Table Format*

**Mean Number of Idea-Units Recalled as a
Function of Different Learning and Recall Contexts**

Condition	Mean Score	Standard Deviation
No context		
One repetition	3.60	.64
No context		
Two repetitions	3.80	.79
Context		
before	8.00	.65
Context		
after	3.60	.75
Partial		
context	4.00	.60

Note: Maximum score is 14.

A third way to present the data is in the form of a graph, which would portray the
Bransford and Johnson study as you've already observed in Figure 7.9.
    Notice that in an experimental study, a graph always places the dependent vari-

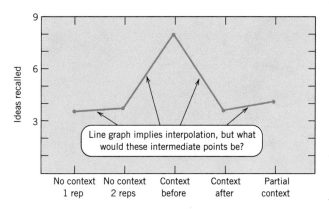

FIGURE 7.12 Bransford and Johnson (1972) data, inappropriately drawn as a line graph.

able on the vertical axis and the independent variable on the horizontal axis. The situation becomes a bit more complicated when using more than one independent variable, as you'll see in a few pages. Regardless of the number of independent variables, however, the dependent variable always goes on the vertical axis.

Deciding between tables and figures is often a matter of the researcher's preference. Graphs can be especially striking if there are large differences to report or if interactions occur (you'll be learning about these shortly). Tables are often preferred when there is so much data that a graph would be uninterpretable or when the researcher wishes to inform the reader of the precise values of the means; they may have to be guessed at with a graph. One rule you can certainly apply is that you should never present the same data both in table and graph form. In general, you should present data in such a way that the results you have worked so hard to obtain are shown most clearly.

Types of Graphs

You'll notice that I've presented the Bransford and Johnson data in the form of a bar graph. Why not present it as a line graph, as in Figure 7.12? Bad idea. The problem concerns the nature of the construct being used as the independent variable and whether its underlying dimension is continuous. A **continuous variable** is one for which an infinite number of values potentially exist. That is, the variable exists on a continuum. An example might be the dosage level of a drug. In a study comparing 3 mg, 5 mg, and 7 mg of some drug, dosage is a continuous variable. Presumably, we also could use 4-mg or 6-mg dosages if there was

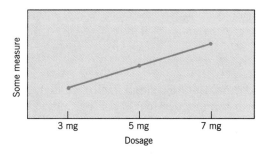

FIGURE 7.13 Appropriate use of a line graph with a continuous variable such as a drug's dosage level.

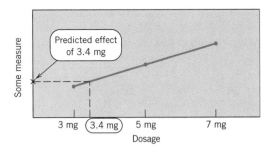

FIGURE 7.14 Interpolating between the points of a line graph.

a good reason for doing so. For continuous independent variables, it is appropriate to use a line graph to portray the results. That is, because it is reasonable to interpolate between the points of the graph to guess what the effects of intermediate values might be, the line can used for estimating these in-between effects. Thus, in the drug study, a graph could look like Figure 7.13, and the researcher would be on reasonably solid ground in predicting the effects of intermediate values of the drug, as illustrated by the point marked with an asterisk in Figure 7.14. Of course, interpolation can be problematic if a study uses two levels of the independent variable, if the two levels are far apart, and if the true relationship is nonlinear. Thus, in a drug study comparing 2-mg and 10-mg dosages producing the solid line in Figure 7.15, interpolating the effects of a 5-mg dosage would produce a large error if the true curve looked like the dotted line:

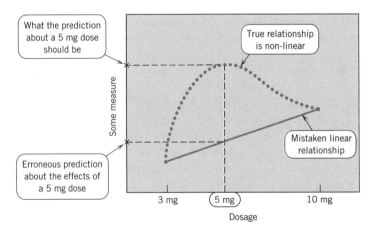

FIGURE 7.15 Problems with interpolation when there is a nonlinear effect and a wide range between levels of the independent variable.

This study would be a good candidate for a single-factor, multilevel design.

The situation is different if the independent variable is a **discrete variable**, in which each level represents a distinct category and no intermediate points can occur. Thus, no interpolation can be done, and to connect the points with a line is to imply that these intermediate points exist when in fact they don't. So when using discrete variables, as in the Bransford and Johnson study (see Figure 7.9), a bar graph is normally used. The basic rule is this:

If continuous → line graph preferred, bar graph OK

If discrete → bar graph preferred, line graph inappropriate (but see the description of interactions in the section on factorial designs for an exception)

Analyzing Single-Factor, Multilevel Designs

We've seen that in the case of single-factor, two level designs with the dependent variable measured on an interval or ratio scale, the null hypothesis can be tested with an inferential statistic called the *t* test. For a multilevel design such as the Bransford and Johnson study, you might think that the analysis would be a simple matter of completing a series of *t* tests between all of the possible pairs of conditions (e.g., context before vs context after). Unfortunately, things aren't quite that simple. The difficulty is that completing multiple *t* tests increases the risks of making a Type I error. That is, the more *t* tests you calculate, the greater are the chances of having one "accidentally" yield significant differences. In the Bransford and Johnson study, you would have to complete 10 different *t* tests to cover all the pairs of conditions.

The chances of making at least one Type I error when doing multiple *t* tests can be estimated by using this formula:

$$1 - (1 - \text{alpha})c$$
$$[c = \text{the \# of comparisons made}]$$

Thus, if all ten of the possible *t* tests are completed in the Bransford and Johnson study, there is a very good chance (4 out of 10) of making at least one Type I error:

$$1 - (1 - .05)^{10} = 1 - (.95)^{10} = 1 - .60 = .40$$

To avoid the problem of multiple *t* tests in single-factor designs, researchers use a procedure called a one-way analysis of variance or ANOVA (**AN**alysis **O**f **VA**riance). The "one-way" means one independent variable. In essence, a one-way ANOVA tests for the presence of some "overall" significance that could exist somewhere among the various levels of the independent variable. Hence, in a study with three levels, the null hypothesis is "level 1 = level 2 = level 3." Rejecting the null hypothesis does not identify exactly which of the " = 's" is really "≠," however. To determine precisely where the significance lies requires what is sometimes called "subsequent testing" or "post hoc (after the fact) analysis." In a study with three levels, subsequent testing would analyze each of the three pairs of comparisons, but only after the overall ANOVA has indicated that some significance exists. If the ANOVA does not find any significance, subsequent testing is normally not done.

The one-way ANOVA yields an "*F* score" or an "*F* ratio." Like the score from a *t* test, the *F* score examines the extent to which the obtained mean differences could be due to chance or some other factor (presumably the independent variable). The ANOVA is a basic tool widely used by experimental psychologists and if you aren't already familiar with its operation from taking a statistics course, you should work through the examples in Appendix B. You should also be aware that even though *t* tests are normally used when the independent variable has just two levels, a one-way ANOVA also could be used in that situation. Actually, the *t* test can be considered a special case of the analysis of variance, used when there is a single independent variable with just two levels.

More than One Factor — Factorial Designs

Suppose you are interested in memory and wish to find out if recall can be improved by training people to use visual imagery while memorizing. You could create a simple two-group experiment in which some people are trained in imagery techniques and some aren't. Suppose you also wonder about how memory is affected by a word list's presentation rate. Again, you could do a simple two-group study. Some subjects see the lists at 2 seconds per word, others at 4 seconds per word. In a factorial design, both of these studies could be done at the same time.

By definition, a **factorial design** is an experiment with more than one independent variable. In principle, this could involve dozens of variables, but in practice, factorial designs usually involve two or three factors, or at most, four. Let's stay with the memory example as a way of introducing a system for describing these designs.

Identifying Factorials

First, a factorial is described with a numbering system that simultaneously identifies the number of independent variables and the number of levels of each variable. Thus a 2×3 (reads as "two by three") factorial design has two independent variables; the first has two levels, the second has three. A $3 \times 4 \times 5$ factorial has three independent variables, with three, four, and five levels, respectively. The memory study would be a 2×2 design, with two levels of the "type of training" variable and two levels of the "presentation rate" variable.

Second, the conditions to be tested in a factorial study can be identified by looking at all combinations of the different levels of each independent variable. In the memory study, this produces a matrix, which looks like this:

		Presentation rate	
		2-sec/word	4-sec/word
Type of training	Imagery	imagery/2 sec	imagery/4 sec
	No Imagery	no imagery/2 sec	no imagery/4 sec

Before going on, there's something you should note very carefully. Up to this point, I have been using the concepts "conditions of the experiment" and "levels of the independent variable" as if they meant the same thing. These concepts indeed are interchangeable in single-factor experiments. In factorials, this is no longer the case. In all experimental designs, the term *levels* refers to the number of levels of the independent variable. In factorial designs, the term *conditions* equals the number of cells in the matrix like the one you just examined. Hence, the 2×2 memory study has *two* independent variables, each with *two* levels. It has *four* different conditions, however, one for each of the four cells. The number of conditions in any factorial can be determined simply by calculating the product of the numbers in the notation system. A 3×4 design has 12 conditions; a $2 \times 2 \times 4$ design has 16.

You can visualize a generalized 2×2 factorial matrix this way:

| | | Factor **B** | |
		Level **B1**	Level **B2**
	Level **A1**	condition **A1B1**	condition **A1B2**
Factor **A**			
	Level **A2**	condition **A2B1**	condition **A2B2**

It's important to be clear about this labeling system because if you are using a computerized statistics package, this is the language you will probably encounter. When the computer asks you for the data from cell A2B1 and you enter the data from A1B2 by mistake, the analysis will proceed and give you a nice printout, but the results will be completely wrong. Obviously, it is essential to enter the data in the proper cells. You will encounter this system if you work your way through the two-way ANOVA example in Appendix B.

Table 7.3 shows you how this system of laying out factorials works with a 2×4 and a $2 \times 2 \times 2$ design. Ignore the matrices with shaded cells for the moment; those will make sense after you finish reading the next section.

Main Effects

In the memory experiment we've been using as a model, the researcher is interested in the effects of two independent variables: type of training and presentation rate. In factorial designs, the term **main effect** is used to describe the overall effect of an independent variable. So in a study with two independent variables, there can be no more than two main effects. Determining the main effect of one

TABLE 7.3   *Sample Factorial Designs*

1. **2 × 4** factorial:

	B1	B2	B3	B4
A1	A1B1	A1B2	A1B3	A1B4
A2	A2B1	A2B2	A2B3	A2B4

Testing for the main effect of A (i.e., comparing A1 and A2)

	B1	B2	B3	B4
A1	A1B1	A1B2	A1B3	A1B4
A2	A2B1	A2B2	A2B3	A2B4

Testing for the main effect of B (i.e., comparing B1, B2, B3, and B4)

	B1	B2	B3	B4
A1	A1B1	A1B2	A1B3	A1B4
A2	A2B1	A2B2	A2B3	A2B4

2. A **2 × 2 × 2** factorial:

	C1			C2	
	B1	B2		B1	B2
A1	A1B1C1	A1B2C1	A1	A1B1C2	A1B2C2
A2	A2B1C1	A2B2C1	A2	A2B1C2	A2B2C2

Testing for the main effect of A (i.e., comparing A1 and A2)

	C1			C2	
	B1	B2		B1	B2
A1	A1B1C1	A1B2C1	A1	A1B1C2	A1B2C2
A2	A2B1C1	A2B2C1	A2	A2B1C2	A2B2C2

TABLE 7.3   *Sample Factorial Designs* (continued)

Testing for the main effect of B (i.e., comparing B1 and B2)

	C1			C2	
	B1	B2		B1	B2
A1	A1B1C1	A1B2C1	A1	A1B1C2	A1B2C2
A2	A2B1C1	A2B2C1	A2	A2B1C2	A2B2C2

Testing for the main effect of C (i.e., comparing C1 and C2)

	C1			C2	
	B1	B2		B1	B2
A1	A1B1C1	A1B2C1	A1	A1B1C2	A1B2C2
A2	A2B1C1	A2B2C1	A2	A2B1C2	A2B2C2

factor involves collapsing the data over all levels of the other factor(s). In the memory study, this can be illustrated as follows. The main effect of type of training is determined by collapsing the data for both presentation rates. Hence, all of the information in the lightly shaded cells would be combined and compared with the combined data in the heavily shaded cells:

		Presentation rate (B)	
		2-sec/word B1	4-sec/word B2
Type of training (A)	Imagery A1	imagery/2 sec A1B1	imagery/4 sec A1B2
	No Imagery A2	no imagery/2 sec A2B1	no imagery/4 sec A2B2

Similarly, the main effect of presentation rate is determined by collapsing the data for both types of training. In the following table, the effect of presentation rate would be evaluated by comparing all of the information in the lightly shaded cells with all of the data in the heavily shaded cells:

	Presentation rate (B)	
	2-sec/word B1	4-sec/word B2
Imagery A1	imagery/2 sec A1B1	imagery/4 sec A1B2
No Imagery A2	no imagery/2 sec A2B1	no imagery/4 sec A2B2

Type of training (A)

If you now take a second look at the matrices in Table 7.3, you'll see that I've used shading to indicate which cells combine during the various main effects analyses for the 2×4 and the $2 \times 2 \times 2$ designs.

Let's consider some hypothetical data that might be collected in a memory experiment like this. Assume that there are 25 subjects in each condition and that they are memorizing a list of 30 words. The average number of words recalled for each of the four conditions might look like this:

Type of training

	Presentation rate	
	2-sec/word	4-sec/word
Imagery	17	23
No Imagery	12	18

Does imagery training produce better memory? That is, is there a main effect of type of training? The way to find out is to compare all the "imagery" data with all the "no imagery" data. Specifically, this involves calculating what are called row means. The "imagery" row mean is **20** words [$(17 + 23)/2 = 40/2 = 20$], and the "no imagery" row mean is **15** words [$(12 + 18)/2 = 30/2 = 15$]. When asking if there is a main effect of training type, the question is, "Is the 20 significantly greater than the 15?"

In the same fashion, calculating the column means allows us to see if there is a main effect of presentation rate. For the 2 seconds per item column, the mean is **14.5** words; it is **20.5** words for the 4 second per item row. Putting all of this together yields:

	2-sec/word	4-sec/word	Overall
Imagery	17	23	**20.0**
No Imagery	12	18	**15.0**
Overall	**14.5**	**20.5**	

For these data, then, it appears that imagery improves memory ($20 > 15$) and that recall is higher if the words are presented at a slower rate ($20.5 > 14.5$). That is, there seem to be two main effects here (of course, it takes an ANOVA to determine whether the differences are real or due to chance).

Interactions

The distinct advantage of factorials over single-factor designs lies not in their ability to uncover main effects, but in their potential to show interactive effects. In a factorial design, an **interaction** is said to occur when the effect of one independent variable depends on the level of another independent variable. This is a moderately difficult concept to grasp, but it is of immense importance because interactions often provide the most interesting results in a factorial study. To start, consider a simple example. Suppose I believe that general psychology is best taught as a laboratory self-discovery course rather than as a straight lecture course, but I also wonder if this is generally true or true only for certain kinds of students. Perhaps science majors would especially benefit from the lab approach. To test the idea, I need to compare a lab with a lecture version of general psychology, but I also need to compare different types of students, perhaps science majors and humanities majors. This calls for a 2×2 design that would look like this:

		Course type	
		Lab emphasis	Lecture emphasis
	Science	Science students in a lab course	Science students in a lecture course
Student's major			
	Humanities	Humanities students in a lab course	Humanities students in a lecture course

In a study like this, the dependent variable would be some measure of learning; let's use a score from $1-100$ on a standardized test of knowledge of general psychology, given during final exam week. Suppose these results occurred:

	Lab emphasis	Lecture emphasis
Science	80	70
Humanities	70	80

Are there any main effects here? No—all the row and column means are the same: 75. So did nothing at all happen in this study? No—something clearly happened. Specifically, the science students did better in the lab course, but the humanities students did better in the lecture course. Or to put it in terms of the definition of an interaction, the effect of one variable (major) depended on the level of the other variable (course type). Hence, even if no main effects occur, an interaction can occur.

This teaching example also highlights the distinct advantage of factorial designs over single-factor designs. Suppose you completed the study as a single-factor, two-level design, comparing lab with lecture versions of general psychology. You would probably use a matched group design, and use student GPA and perhaps major as matching variables. In effect, you might end up with the same people who were in the factorial example. However, by running it as a single-factor design, your results would be:

Lab course → 75   Lecture course → 75

and you might conclude that it doesn't matter whether general psychology includes a lab or not. With the factorial design, however, you know that the lab indeed matters, but only for certain types of students. In short, factorial designs can be more informative than single-factor designs. To further illustrate the concept of interactions, consider the outcome of the following case study.

Case Study 7. An Interaction

There has been considerable research indicating that people remember something best if they are in the same location or context where they learned it in the first place. You might have experienced this if you were able to find your lost keys after putting yourself, either mentally or physically, back in the place where you last remembered seeing them.

The study winning the prize for the most creative test of this context-dependent learning hypothesis was carried out by Godden and Baddeley (1975). They used a 2×2 factorial in which subjects learned a list of 36 words in one setting, then recalled the list in either the same setting or a different one. What makes the experiment creative is the choice of settings. Members of a diving club were the subjects and they learned the lists either on the shore of a beach or in the water at a depth of 20 feet! The first independent variable was the location where learning took place and the two levels were "on land" and "under water." The second variable was where recall occurred and it also had the two levels of land and sea. Hence, there were four conditions to the study:

1. Learn on land—recall on land.
2. Learn on land—recall under water.
3. Learn under water—recall on land.
4. Learn under water—recall under water.

All divers eventually participated in all four conditions, making this a repeated-measures factorial design. The results, expressed as the average number of words recalled per list, are as follows:

		Where they recalled		
		On land	Under water	Overall
Where they learned	On land	13.5	8.6	**11.1**
	Under water	8.4	11.4	**9.9**
	Overall	**11.0**	**10.0**	

This outcome is similar to the pattern found in the hypothetical study about ways of teaching general psychology to science and humanities students. Row and column means are virtually identical, indicating an absence of significant main effects. Thus, for the experiment as a whole, the locations where the lists were learned didn't matter (the 11.1 was not significantly different from the 9.9) and the locations where they were recalled was likewise irrelevant (11.0 didn't differ from 10.0). But examining the four individual cell means shows that an interaction clearly occurred. When the divers learned on land, they recalled well on land (13.5) but poorly under water (8.6); when they learned under water, they recalled poorly on land (8.4) but did well when recalling while submerged (11.4). That is, learning was best when the learning context matched the recall context.

You might be interested in some of the control procedures developed for this study. The divers had difficulty hearing the tape-recorded words through the "diver underwater communication" gear, because of the noise produced by their breathing, so they had to learn to hold their breath for periods of six seconds at a time while the words were presented in clusters of three. Four-second "breathing" intervals occurred between the clusters of three words. The same procedures were simulated when the lists were presented on land. Also, all testing took place after divers had completed their normal diving routines for the day. Thus, "subjects began each session in roughly the same state, that is, wet and cold" (Godden & Baddeley, 1975, p. 327). If you're wondering about the "cold," thinking perhaps that the British researchers must have had the good sense to run this study in the Bahamas, the answer is that no, they weren't *that* creative (or well-financed, perhaps). The study was conducted on the west coast of *Scotland*.

Main Effects and Interactions

The example of context-dependent memory illustrates one type of outcome in a factorial design (an interaction, but no main effects), but there are many patterns of results. In a simple 2 × 2 design, for instance, there are eight possibilities:

1. A main effect for factor A only.
2. A main effect for factor B only.
3. Main effects for A and B only.
4. A main effect for A plus an interaction.
5. A main effect for B plus an interaction.
6. Main effects for both A and B plus an interaction.
7. An interaction only.
8. No main effects, no interaction.

Let's briefly consider several of these outcomes in the context of the earlier experiment on imagery, presentation rate, and memory. Before reading on, however, you should work carefully through Figure 7.16, which shows you how to translate the data in factorial matrix tables into graphs.

Ready? OK, for each of the examples starting on p. 220, I have constructed some hypothetical data that might result from the study on the effects of imagery instructions and presentation rate on memory for a 30-word list, translated the data into a graph, and given a verbal description of the results. I haven't tried to create all of the eight possibilities listed above; rather, the examples illustrate outcomes that might be likely to occur in this type of study.

Here's a simple method for creating a graph from a factorial matrix. Suppose a maze learning study has a 2 × 2 design. One variable is genetic strain: Mice are either maze-bright (bred for faster maze learning) or maze-dull (not so smart). The second variable is whether or not the food reinforcer at the end of the maze is given as soon as the mouse arrives (0 delay) or after a 5-second delay. The dependent variable is an error score.

Step 1.   Use the independent variable that constitutes the columns of the matrix and make that variable the label for the graph's horizontal axis. Label the vertical axis with the name of the dependent measure.

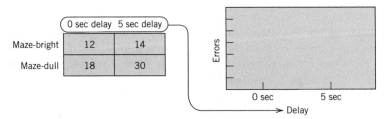

FIGURE 7.16   Transforming tables to graphs.

Step 2.   Take the data in the first row of the matrix and move it directly to the graph.

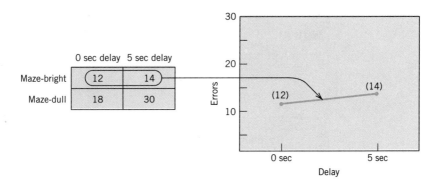

Step 3.   Do the same with the data in the second row of the matrix.

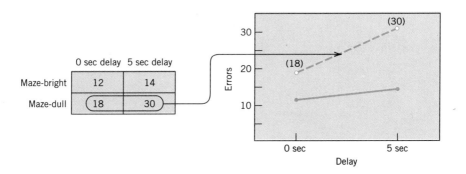

Step 4.   Create a legend that identifies the second independent variable as the one deriving from the rows of the matrix.

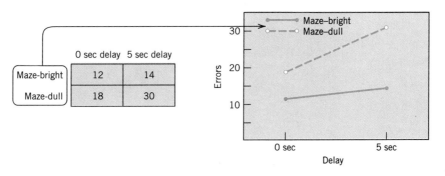

FIGURE 7.16 (continued)

Here's how the process would look with a 2 × 3 design, if a third level of the reinforcement delay were added:

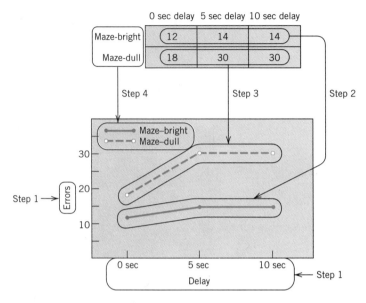

FIGURE 7.16 (continued)

1. Imagery instructions improve recall, regardless of presentation rate, which doesn't affect recall. That is, there is a main effect of factor A (imagery instructions) only.

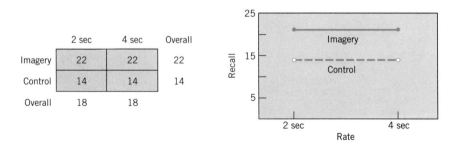

2. Recall is better with slower rates of presentation, but the imagery instructions were not effective in improving recall. That is, there is a main effect of factor B (presentation rate) only.

	2 sec	4 sec	Overall
Imagery	14	22	18
Control	14	22	18
Overall	14	22	

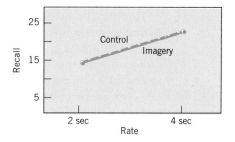

3. Recall is better with slower rates of presentation; in addition, the imagery instructions were effective in improving recall. In this case, main effects for both factors occur.

	2 sec	4 sec	Overall
Imagery	18	22	20
Control	14	18	16
Overall	16	20	

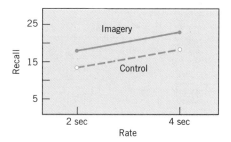

4. At a 2-second presentation rate, imagery training clearly improves recall; however, at the 4-second rate, recall is almost perfect regardless of how subjects are trained. That is, there is an interaction between type of training and presentation rate. In this case, the interaction has been produced by what is called a **ceiling effect**, a result in which the scores for different conditions are all so close to the maximum (30 words in this example) that no difference could occur.[1] Here, the imagery group recalls just about all the words, regardless of the presentation rate.

	2 sec	4 sec	Overall
Imagery	28	28	28
Control	12	28	20
Overall	20	28	

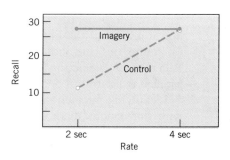

---

[1]It is also possible for scores in two conditions to be equal because they couldn't get any lower. Yes, these are called floor effects.

You may be wondering about the obvious main effects that occur in this example. Surely, the row and column means indicate an overall effect for both factors. Technically, yes, the analysis probably would yield statistically significant main effects in this example, but this is a good illustration of the fact that interactions sometimes take precedence over main effects. In this particular case, the main effects aren't really meaningful; the statement that imagery yields a general improvement in recall is not quite accurate. Rather, it only seems to improve recall at the faster presentation rate. Hence, the interaction is the key finding here. In any factorial study, if both main effects and interactions occur, the interactions should be interpreted first.

5. This is not to say that main effects never matter when an interaction exists. Consider this last example:

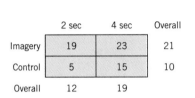

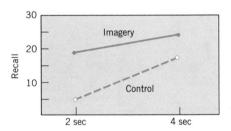

In this case, imagery training generally improves recall (i.e., there's a main effect for A; 21 > 10). Also, a slower presentation rate improves recall for both groups (i.e., a main effect for B also; 19 > 12). Both these outcomes are worth reporting. What the interaction shows is that slowing the presentation rate improves recall somewhat for the imagery group (23 is a bit better than 19), but improves recall considerably for the control group (15 is a lot better than 5). Another way of describing the interaction is to say that at the fast rate, the imagery training is especially effective (19 is a lot better than 5). At the slower rate, imagery training still yields better recall, but not by as much as the slow rate (23 is somewhat better than 15).

From examining these graphs, you might have noticed a standard feature of interactions. In general, if the lines on the graph parallel each other, then no interaction is present. If the lines are nonparallel, however, an interaction probably exists. Of course, this rule about parallel and nonparallel lines is only a general guideline. Whether an interaction exists (in essence, whether the lines are sufficiently nonparallel) is a statistical decision, to be determined by an analysis of variance.

Identifying interactions by examining whether lines are parallel or not is easier with line graphs than with bar graphs. Hence, the earlier guideline about line graphs being used only with continuous variables is sometimes ignored if the key finding is an interaction. For example, a study by Keltner, Ellsworth, and Edwards (1993) showed that when subjects are asked to estimate the likelihood of some bad event like a car accident occurring, there was an interaction between the emotion they were experiencing and whether the event was caused by a person or by circumstances. When subjects were experiencing sadness, they believed that events

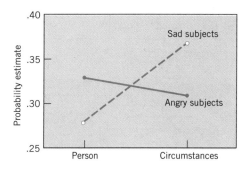

FIGURE 7.17   Using a line graph to highlight an interaction (from Keltner, Ellsworth, & Edwards, 1993).

produced by circumstances (e.g., wet roads) were more likely to occur than events produced by individual actions (e.g., poor driving). When subjects were angered, however, the opposite happened. As you can see from Figure 7.17, a line graph was drawn even though the X-axis uses a discrete variable. Keltner et al. (1993) wished to show the interaction as clearly as possible, so they ignored the guideline about discrete variables. To repeat a point made earlier, when presenting any data the overriding concern is to make the hard-earned results as clear as possible to the reader.

Varieties of Factorials

Like the decision tree in Figure 7.1 for single-factor designs, Figure 7.18 shows you the decisions involved in arriving at one of six possible factorial designs. You'll recognize that four of the designs mirror those in Figure 7.1, but two designs are unique to factorials. First, while the independent variable must be either a between-subjects or a within-subjects variable in a single-factor design, both types of variables can be present in a factorial design. When this happens, the design is called a **mixed factorial** design. Second, some between-subjects factorials include both a manipulated independent variable and a subject variable. Because these designs can yield an interaction between the type of person in the study and the situation created in the study, these designs can be called **P × E factorial** designs, or **P**erson by **E**nvironment designs, with environment defined broadly to include any manipulated independent variable. Figures 7.19 and 7.20 show the decisions to be made when using mixed and P × E designs. Let's consider examples of each of these in more detail.

Case Study 8 — A Mixed Factorial Design

For some mixed designs, order effects for the within-subjects variable are controlled through counterbalancing procedures. For other designs, however, the within-subjects factor involves a sequence of trials and the researcher is specifically looking for performance changes from one trial to another. With such a design, counterbalancing doesn't come into play.

An example of this latter situation occurs in memory research using a procedure called "release from PI" (Wickens, Born, & Allen, 1963). PI, or *proactive interference*, is a phenomenon in which the learning and recall of new information is hindered by the learning of old information. You might have experienced this if you found it difficult to remember a new phone number because your old one kept coming to

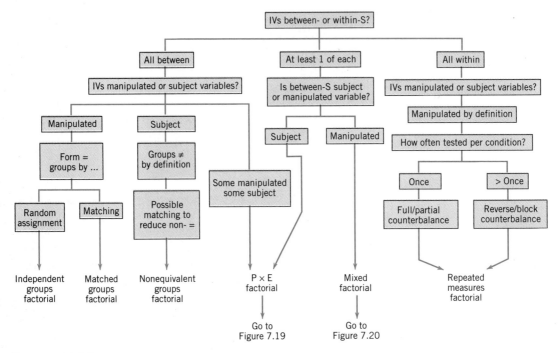

FIGURE 7.18   Decision tree—factorial designs.

mind. The amount of interference is expected to be especially bad if the old information is similar to the new information in some way. One way to test the idea that strength of PI is a function of item similarity is to have subjects study and recall a sequence of stimulus items that are similar, then switch to a different type of stimulus item. Presumably, PI should build up from trial to trial for the similar items, then "release" when the stimulus type changes. Behaviorally, this means that performance should gradually decrease, then increase again once the release trial occurs.

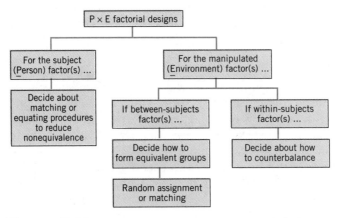

FIGURE 7.19   Decisions to be made with P × E designs.

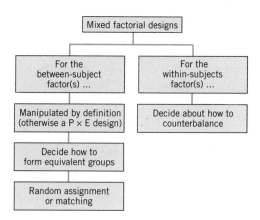

FIGURE 7.20 Decisions to be made with mixed designs.

Release-from-PI studies normally use words or nonsense syllables as stimuli, but a study by Gunter, Berry, and Clifford (1981) took a slightly different approach: They used items from television news shows in a series of experiments. We'll consider their experiment 1, which serves as a nice illustration of a mixed factorial design.

Subjects were told they would be seeing clips from a televised news broadcast and that they would be tested on the content of the news items. On each trial, they saw a sequence of three stories, then worked on a distractor task (a crossword puzzle) for a minute, then tried to recall as much as they could about the stories. Each subject experienced four such trials. Half of the subjects were randomly assigned to the release-from-PI condition; they went through three trials in which all the news was from a single general category (e.g., domestic political events), and a fourth ("release") trial with news from a different category (e.g., foreign political events). The remaining subjects were in a control group; all four of their trials were from the same category. Thus, the design was a 2 (release/no release) × 4 (trials) mixed factorial design. Whether or not subjects were in the release condition was the between-subjects factor and trials was the repeated-measures or within-subjects factor.

Figure 7.21 shows the results. That PI was operating is clear from the control

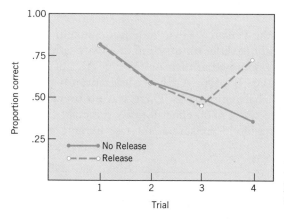

FIGURE 7.21 Release from proactive interference (data from Gunter, Berry, & Clifford, 1981).

group's scores; their recall scores steadily declined. Release from PI also occurred, as is evident from the recall scores of the experimental group.

One of the control features of this study is worth noting. One possible problem could be that performance on the release trial went up simply because the "foreign" items were easier than the "domestic" items. To eliminate the possibility, half of the subjects in the release group saw three domestic trials followed by a foreign trial; the other half saw three foreign trials followed by a domestic trial. Likewise, in the control group, half saw four domestic trials and the remainder saw four foreign trials. The order made no difference to the results.[2]

Case Study 9—A P × E Factorial Design

Over the past 20 years or so, there has been considerable interest in the so-called Type A behavior pattern (Friedman & Rosenman, 1974). Type A's are competitive, achievement oriented, and compulsive about many things, including time (they are often early, never late). They try to do too many things at once and seem to have a very high energy level. Type A's who combine these traits with a generally hostile attitude tend to develop coronary heart disease. That is, under certain circumstances, a Type A behavior pattern can be decidedly unhealthy.

Research on Type A behavior often uses a P × E factorial design. The P (subject) variable will be the behavior pattern—Type A or its antithesis, the more laid back Type B. Selection of subjects for each of these groups will be determined by scores on some test for Type A tendencies. The E variable will be some factor manipulated by the experimenter. For example, in a study by Holmes, McGilley, and Houston (1984), Type A and B college students were differentiated by their scores on a student version of the Jenkins Activity Survey, a test frequently used in research about Type A's. Three hundred and ninety-four students took the test, and the researchers recruited thirty high and thirty low scorers. Subjects in these two groups then were randomly assigned to one of three tasks, which differed in how challenging they were. Hence, the manipulated independent variable was task difficulty. The task was a "digit span" procedure borrowed from an IQ test in which subjects listened to a sequence of numbers (e.g., 3-4-8) and had to repeat them in reverse order (8-4-3). The three levels of difficulty were defined in terms of the number of digits read to subjects during the six trials completed by each of them: 2, 5, or 7. Arousal during the task, operationally defined in terms of several physiological measures, including systolic blood pressure, was the dependent variable.

Figure 7.22 shows the Person × Environment interaction that occurred. Arousal for Type A's and B's did not differ on easy and moderate tasks, but on very difficult tasks, systolic pressure continued to increase for Type A's, but leveled off for the B's. That is, compared to Type B's, Type A's showed significantly elevated systolic blood pressure, but only on challenging tasks. There was no overall main effect for personality type, but there was a main effect for task difficulty, as you can detect from the generally increasing blood pressure as the task became more difficult. In sum,

---

[2]Calling the design a 2 × 4 emphasizes the two important variables, but technically, this was a 2 × 2 × 4 mixed design, with the second 2 being the between-subjects factor of news category on trial 1, foreign or domestic.

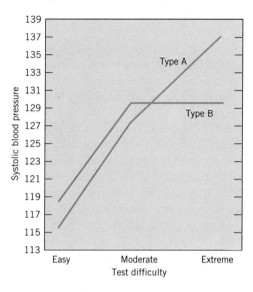

FIGURE 7.22   A **P**erson × **E**nvironment interaction: Type A personalities and task difficulty (from Holmes, McGilley, & Houston, 1984).

the study showed that "differences in arousal . . . between Type A and Type B persons are most likely to emerge at high levels of challenge" (Holmes et al., 1984, p. 1326), a finding consistent with the highly competitive, achievement focus of Type A persons.[3]

In terms of the language developed in Chapter 5, it is important to recognize that a P × E factorial is less than a "true" experiment, because the subject variables cannot be manipulated directly; subjects with already-existing characteristics can only be selected by the investigator. Hence, it is inappropriate to say that the Type A pattern *causes* significantly elevated blood pressure on difficult tasks. All that can be said is that the two types differ in how they react to challenging tasks.

Despite this limitation, some researchers believe these kinds of designs are ideal for studying human behavior. In a single study, it is possible to examine both individual differences in behavior (e.g., A's vs B's) and the effects of environmental factors (e.g., task difficulty). Finding a P × E interaction is an especially interesting outcome, for it illustrates how the environment affects different types of people in different ways.

Those advocating the use of P × E designs can trace their partiality to the work of Kurt Lewin (1890–1947), a pioneer in social and child psychology. The central theme guiding Lewin's work was that a full understanding of behavior required studying both the person and the situation. He expressed this idea in terms of the formula, B = f(P, E)—**B**ehavior is a joint **f**unction of the **P**erson and the **E**nvironment (Hothersall, 1990). P × E factorial designs, which derive their name from Lewin's formula, are perfectly suited for discovering the kinds of interactive relationships that Lewin believed characterized human behavior.

---

[3]In light of the earlier discussion about drawing graphs, should Holmes et al. have used a bar graph?

Analyzing Factorial Designs

We've already seen that multilevel, single-factor designs are analyzed with a one-way ANOVA. Similarly, factorial designs using interval or ratio data are analyzed with N-way ANOVAs, with N referring to the number of independent variables involved. Hence, the 2×3 factorial would be analyzed by a two-way ANOVA and a $2 \times 2 \times 2$ by a three-way ANOVA.

When doing a one-way ANOVA, just one F-ratio is calculated. Then there may be subsequent testing if the F is significant. For a factorial design, however, more than one F-ratio will be calculated. Specifically, there will be an F for each possible main effect and for each possible interaction. For example, in the 2×2 design investigating the effects of imagery training and presentation rate on memory, there will be an F-ratio calculated to examine the possibility of a main effect for type of training, another for the main effect of presentation rate, and a third for the potential interaction between the two. In an $A \times B \times C$ factorial, there will be *seven* F-ratios calculated: three for the main effects of A, B, and C, three more for the two-way interaction effects of $A \times B$, $B \times C$, and $A \times C$, plus one for the three-way interaction, $A \times B \times C$.

Subsequent testing may occur with factorial ANOVAs as well as with one-way ANOVAs. For example, in a 2×3 ANOVA, a significant F for the factor with three levels would trigger a subsequent analysis that compared the overall performance of levels 1 and 2, 1 and 3, and 2 and 3. Also, a factorial ANOVA is sometimes followed by what is called a **simple effects analysis**, a technique useful to examine the effects of an interaction or to test a specific prediction that compares one condition with another. For instance, consider the simplest of factorials, a 2×2:

The following simple effects could be analyzed in this case, depending on the nature of the interaction or whether the original hypotheses would require a specific comparison:

1. The effect of factor A at B1 : compares cells A1B1 with A2B1.
2. The effect of factor A at B2 : compares cells A1B2 with A2B2.
3. The effect of factor B at A1 : compares cells A1B1 with A1B2.
4. The effect of factor B at A2 : compares cells A2B1 with A2B2.

As a more concrete example, consider one of the hypothetical outcomes of the memory experiment described earlier in which an interaction between presentation rate and method of study occurred:

	2-sec (B1)	4-sec (B2)	Overall
Imagery (A1)	19 (A1B1)	23 (A1B2)	21.0
Control (A2)	5 (A2B1)	15 (A2B2)	10.0
Overall	12	19	

A simple effects analysis here would include the

1. Effect of study method (A) at the 2 second rate (B1):
    - Compares 19 with 5
2. Effect of study method (A) at the 4 second rate (B2):
    - Compares 23 with 15
3. Effect of presentation rate (B) for those using imagery (A1):
    - Compares 19 with 23
4. Effect of presentation rate (B) for those not using imagery (A2):
    - Compares 5 with 15

Before closing this chapter, let me make one final point about factorials and the analysis of variance. You've been looking at many factorial matrices in the second half of this chapter. They might vaguely remind you of farming. If so, it's no accident, as you can discover by reading Box 7.2, which tells you a bit about Sir Ronald Fisher, who invented the analysis of variance.

Box 7.2

ORIGINS—Factorials Down on the Farm

Imagine that you're in a small plane flying over Kansas. Looking out the window, you see mile after mile of farms, with their fields laid out in blocks. The pattern might remind you of the 2 × 2 and 3 × 3 boxes that you've encountered in the examples of factorial designs. This is because factorial designs and the ANOVA procedures for analyzing them were first devised by Sir Ronald Fisher, and they were developed in the context of agricultural research. The empirical question was, "what are the best possible conditions or combinations of conditions for raising crop X?"

Ronald Aylmer Fisher (1890–1962) was one of Great Britain's best known statisticians, equal in rank to the great Karl Pearson, who invented the correlation measure we now call Pearson's *r* (next chapter). Fisher was known for developing statistical procedures useful in testing predictions about genetics, and he is perhaps best known for creating the analysis of variance, which yields the *F* ratios that allow one to decide about the null hypothesis in experimental research. You can easily guess what the *F* represents.

For about a 15-year period beginning in 1920, Fisher worked at an experimental agricultural station at Rothamsted, England. While there, he was involved in research investigating the effects on crop yield of variables such as fertilizer type, rainfall levels, different planting sequences, and different genetic strains of various crops. He published articles with titles like "Studies in crop variation. VI. Experiments on the response of the potato to potash and nitrogen" (Kendall, 1970, p. 447). In the process, he invented analysis of variance as a way of analyzing the data. He especially emphasized the importance of using factorial designs, "for with separate [single-factor] experiments we should obtain no light whatever on the possible interactions of the different ingredients" (Fisher, 1951, p. 95). In the real world of agriculture, high crop yields resulted from complex combinations of factors and studying one factor at a time wouldn't allow a thorough evaluation of those interactive effects.

A simple 2 × 2 design in one of Fisher's experiments, with each block representing how a small square of land was treated, might look like this:

	Experimental fertilizer	No experimental fertilizer
Wheat: genetic strain I	wheat field A	wheat field B
Wheat: genetic strain II	wheat field C	wheat field D

As with any factorial, this design allows one to evaluate the main effects of fertilizer and type of wheat, as well as the interaction of the two. If we assume the shaded field produces significantly more wheat than the other three (which equal each other), then we would say that an interaction clearly occurred—the fertilizer was effective, but only for one strain of wheat.

This completes our cookbook of experimental designs. It's a chapter (along with Chapters 5 and 6) sure to require more than one reading and much practice with designs before you'll feel confident about your ability to create a methodologically sound experiment that is a good test of your hypothesis. I hope you'll find the information useful as a reference source that enables you to design experiments at least as well as I can cook.

Chapter Review

Glossary Fill-Ins

1. Blakemore and Cooper's study of perceiving horizontal and vertical perception required that different cats be used in the two conditions. That is, this study could not have been done as a _____ design.

2. A researcher predicts that introverts will do better on a problem-solving task if they do it by themselves rather than in front of an audience. Extroverts, however, are expected to do better with an audience than alone. The researcher will be using a _____ design.

3. If a graph has its points connected by straight lines, then the independent variable represented on a horizontal axis is most likely a _____ variable.

4. If a study has just one independent variable, adding more than two levels provides the opportunity to discover _____ effects.

5. In a study comparing two kinds of intellectual puzzles that differ in their level of complexity, the researcher is concerned that the IQs of the participants might be correlated with the dependent variable. For this single-factor study it would be wise to use a _____ design.

6. An example of a(n) _____ would be if Sir Ronald Fisher found that adding fertilizer helped wheat but hurt barley.

Multiple Choice

1. Children of four different age groups (5, 7, 9, 11) are tested on the Stroop task (using only the key condition that Stroop called NCWd) in order to see if experience in reading affects performance on the task. How would you describe the design?
   a. Independent groups, one factor, multilevel.
   b. Repeated-measures factorial.
   c. Nonequivalent groups, one factor, multilevel.
   d. Matched groups, one factor, two-level.

2. What do all repeated-measures designs have in common?
   a. They will always be factorial designs.
   b. Subjects will be tested in each condition of the study and tested more than once per condition.
   c. Matching will be the preferred method of creating equivalent groups.
   d. Every subject will be tested in at least two conditions of the study.

3. A 2 × 3 × 5 design has
   a. Three different independent variables.
   b. Thirty different levels.
   c. Thirty different independent variables.
   d. Dependent variables with two, three, and five levels, respectively.

4. A 2×2 mixed factorial design includes
    a. Two subject variables.
    b. A between-subjects and a within-subjects factor.
    c. A within-subjects variable and a repeated–measures variable.
    d. One factor with two levels and another factor with multiple levels.

5. In a maze learning experiment, 30 rats are tested with the lights on and 30 more with the lights off. Also, within each of the two groups, 10 rats receive reinforcement as soon as they reach the goal, 10 others are reinforced 5 seconds after they reach the goal, and the remaining 10 are fed 10 seconds after reaching the goal. What can you say about this design?
    a. Both independent variables are subject factors.
    b. It is best described as a 2×2 independent groups design.
    c. It is best described as a 2×3 mixed design.
    d. Six different conditions are being tested.

Applications Exercises

Exercise 7.1. — Identifying Designs

For each of the following descriptions of studies, identify the independent and dependent variables involved, the nature of the independent variable (between-subjects or within-subjects; manipulated or subject variable), and use Figures 7.1 and 7.17 to name the experimental design being used.

1. On the basis of scores on the Jenkins Activity Survey, three groups of subjects are identified: Type A, Type B, and intermediate. An equal number of subjects in each group is given one of two tasks to perform. One of the tasks is to sit quietly in a small room and estimate, in the absence of a clock, when 2 minutes have elapsed. The second task is to make the same estimate, except that while in the small room, the subject will be playing a hand-held video game.

2. In a study of how bulimia affects the perception of body size, a group of bulimic women and a group of same-aged and equally intelligent nonbulimic women are asked to examine a graded series of drawings of women of different sizes and asked to indicate which size best matches the way that they think they look.

3. College students in a cognitive mapping study are asked to use a direction finder to point accurately to three unseen locations that differ in distance. One is a nearby campus location, one is a nearby city, and the third is a distant city. Half of the subjects perform the task in a windowless room with a compass indicating the direction of north. The remaining subjects perform the task in the same room without a compass.

4. In a study of touch sensitivity, two-point thresholds are measured on ten different skin locations for an equal number of blind and sighted adults. Half of

the subjects use the psychophysics method of limits, and the remaining subjects use the method of constant stimuli.

5. Three groups of preschoolers from the same socioeconomic class and with the same general level of intelligence are put into a study of delay of gratification in which the size of the delay is varied. Children in all three groups complete a puzzle task. One group is told that as payment they can have a dollar now or three dollars tomorrow. The second group chooses between a dollar now or three dollars 2 days from now, and the third group chooses between a dollar now or three dollars 3 days from now.

Exercise 7.2. Main Effects and Interactions

For each of the following studies:

- Identify the independent variables and the levels of each, and the dependent variable.
- Place the data into the correct cells of a factorial matrix.
- Determine if main effects and/or interactions exist.
- Give a verbal description of each of the effects that occur.
- Draw a graph of the results.

For the purposes of the exercise, assume that a difference of 2 between any of the row or column means is a significant difference and that nonparallel = interaction.

1. A researcher is interested in the effects of ambiguity and number of bystanders on helping behavior. Subjects fill out a questionnaire in a room with zero or two other people who appear to be other subjects but aren't. The experimenter distributes the questionnaire and then goes into the room next door. After 5 minutes, there is a loud crash, possibly caused by the experimenter falling. For half of the subjects, the experimenter unambiguously calls out that he has fallen, is hurt, and needs help. For the remaining subjects, the situation is more ambiguous—the experimenter says nothing after the apparent fall. There are 20 subjects tested in each condition and the number who go to help the experimenter are as follows:

   - 0 bystanders; ambiguous   14
   - 2 bystanders; ambiguous   8
   - 0 bystanders; unambiguous   18
   - 2 bystanders; unambiguous   18

2. A researcher interested in maze learning hypothesizes that maze learning can be influenced by the size of the reinforcer and by the delay in reinforcement. Animals are given 40 learning trials in a maze, and the number of errors per trial is recorded. There are six conditions. At the end of the maze there is one of the following:

   a. 10-mg food pellet, and it is given to the animal immediately.
   b. 10-mg food pellet, but the animal has to wait 10 seconds in the goal box before the food is given.

    c. 10-mg food pellet, but the animal has to wait 20 seconds in the goal box before the food is given.

    d. 20-mg food pellet, and it is given to the animal immediately.

    e. 20-mg food pellet, but the animal has to wait 10 seconds in the goal box before the food is given.

    f. 20-mg food pellet, but the animal has to wait 20 seconds in the goal box before the food is given.

The average number of errors for animals in the six groups are

$$\text{a: } 10 \quad \text{b: } 40 \quad \text{c: } 60 \quad \text{d: } 10 \quad \text{e: } 30 \quad \text{f: } 50$$

Exercise 7.3. — Estimating Subject Needs

For each of the following, use the available information to determine how many research participants will be needed to complete the study (hint: one of these is unanswerable without more information):

1. A 3×3 mixed factorial; cell A1B1 needs ten subjects.

2. A 2×3 repeated–measures factorial; cell A1B1 needs 20 subjects.

3. A $2 \times 2 \times 2$ independent groups factorial; cell A1B1 needs five subjects.

4. A 2×4 mixed factorial; cell A1B1 needs eight subjects.

5. A 4×4 nonequivalent groups factorial, cell A1B1 needs five subjects.

CHAPTER 8

Correlational Research

Chapter Overview

- ### Psychology's Two Disciplines

  Along with experimental research, correlational research has been identified as one of psychology's two traditional approaches to science. Whereas experiments manipulate variables directly and observe the effects, correlational studies observe relationships between naturally occurring variables.

- ### Correlation and Regression—The Basics

  Two variables are said to be correlated when a reliable relationship exists between them. The relationship is a direct one in a positive correlation and an inverse one in a negative correlation. The strength of the relationship can be inferred from a scatterplot and from the size of the correlation coefficient. Knowing a correlation allows for predictions to be made, through a process called regression analysis.

- ## Interpreting Correlations

    A correlation between variables A and B does not allow the conclusion that A causes B. The directionality problem refers to the fact that causality could be in either of two directions, A → B or B → A. The third variable problem refers to the fact that for many correlations, the relationship results from one or some combination of uncontrolled variables that naturally covary with the variables of interest.

- ## Using Correlations

    Correlational procedures are often necessary when experiments cannot be carried out for practical or ethical reasons. The method is frequently used in research evaluating psychological tests, in research concerning individual differences in personality and psychopathology, and in twin studies and similar procedures for studying the relative contributions of heredity and environment to some trait.

- ## Multivariate Analysis

    Bivariate analysis studies the relationship between two variables. Multivariate analysis looks at the interrelationships between more than two variables. Made possible by the processing speed of modern computers, multivariate procedures like multiple regression and factor analysis are commonplace. Multiple regression predicts some outcome on the basis of two or more predictors. Factor analysis identifies clusters of factors underlying a large number of relationships.

Remember Robert Woodworth and the 'Columbia Bible', his precedent-setting text in experimental psychology (Chapter 5's opening paragraphs)? The book institutionalized the distinction we routinely make today between independent and dependent variables in experimental studies. The second distinction made by Woodworth, between experimental and correlational methods, likewise has had a profound effect on research in psychology. The experimental method manipulates variables, but the correlational method "[m]easur[es] two or more characteristics of the same individual [and] computes the correlation of these characteristics. . ." (Woodworth, 1938, p. 3).

Woodworth took pains to assure the reader that these two research strategies were of equal value. The correlational method was "[t]o be distinguished from the experimental method, [but] standing on a par with it in value, rather than above or below. . ." (Woodworth, 1938, p. 3). After making the assertion, however, Woodworth referred the reader elsewhere for information about correlational research and devoted the remaining 820 pages of his text to research illustrating the experimental method. The reader could be excused for thinking that correlational research was not quite as important as experimental research.

Psychology's Two Disciplines

The Woodworth text began a process of separation that led eventually to Lee Cronbach's 1957 presidential address to the American Psychological Association, entitled "The Two Disciplines of Scientific Psychology" (Cronbach, 1957). As you can guess, the two disciplines were correlational and experimental psychology. According to Cronbach, correlational psychology is concerned with investigating the relationships between naturally occurring variables and with studying individual differences. However, the experimental psychologist is not usually interested in individual differences, but is concerned with minimizing or controlling these differences in order to show that some stimulus factor influences every individual's behavior in some predictable way to some measurable degree. The correlationist observes variables and relates them; the experimentalist manipulates variables and observes the outcome. The correlationist looks for ways in which people differ from each other; the experimentalist looks for general laws that apply to everyone.

Cronbach was concerned that correlational psychology held second-class status in scientific psychology and expressed the belief that it was time for a synthesis to occur, for both approaches to be valued equally by advocates of each, and for research to encompass both strategies. As he put it,

> It is not enough for each discipline to borrow from the other. Correlational psychology studies only variance among organisms; experimental psychology studies only variance among treatments. A united discipline will study both of these, but it will also be concerned with the otherwise neglected *interactions between organismic variables and treatment variables.* (Cronbach, 1957, p. 681, italics added)

As the italicized phrase indicates, Cronbach was calling for an increase in designs like the P × E factorials (P = person or organism; E = environmental treatment) you learned about in Chapter 7. He was also calling for a renewed appreciation of the correlational method in general, an outcome that has occurred to some degree in the last 30 years. Aided by the enormous speed and capacity of modern computers, sophisticated correlational procedures like multiple regression and factor analysis are available and are in widespread use today. However, many experimental psychology textbooks continue the Woodworth tradition of paying little attention to the correlational method. This text is an exception, as you're about to discover. Before diving into the nuts and bolts of correlational research, however, you should read Box 8.1, which describes the origins of the correlational procedure in the attempts by Sir Francis Galton to study the inheritance of genius.

Correlation and Regression — The Basics

A correlation is said to exist whenever two variables are associated or related in some fashion. This idea is implied by the term itself: "co" for two and "relation" for, well, relation. In a direct or **positive correlation**, the relationship is such that a high score on one variable is associated with a high score on the second variable; similarly, a low score on one relates to a low score on the second. A **negative correlation**, on the other hand, denotes an inverse relationship. High scores

Box 8.1

ORIGINS—*Galton's Studies of Genius*

When you first encountered him in Chapter 1, Sir Francis Galton (1822–1911) was being portrayed as a bit of an eccentric (e.g., counting yawns to measure the quality of London theater). However, it would be a mistake to dismiss Galton as a crank. He was a pioneer in the empirical study of intelligence, among the first to make a strong case that genius is inherited and not the result of one's upbringing. Along the way, he invented correlations.

Galton was much impressed by Darwin's theory of evolution, especially the idea that individual members of a species vary from each other. Individual variations that are useful for survival are then "naturally selected" and passed on to offspring. Galton believed that intelligence was a trait on which people varied, that it was important for survival, and that it seemed to be inherited much like physical characteristics such as eye color and height. He set out to gather evidence for the idea that intelligence was inherited, and he produced two books on the subject: *Hereditary Genius* (1869) and *English Men of Science: Their Nature and Nurture* (1874), the latter introducing for the first time the now famous terms "nature" and "nurture." In his books, Galton noted the statistical tendency for genius and for skills in specific areas (e.g., chemistry, law) to run in families. He discounted the influence of the environment, however, and declared that genius was the result of inheritance. In part, his argument was based on the idea that intelligence was normally distributed in the population. Other traits (e.g., height) known to be influenced by heredity were also normally distributed, so Galton took this statistical fact to be an indication that heredity was involved (Fancher, 1990).

It wasn't until 1888 that Galton solved the problem of how to express the strength of a tendency for a trait like genius to run in families; he expressed his ideas in a paper called "Co-relations and their measurement" (cited in Fancher, 1990). First, Galton discovered that he could organize his data into row and column arrangements like the one in Figure 8.1. The numbers in each cell indicated how many people fell into the categories defined by the row and column headings. Hence, the largest number in those cells indicates that the sample included 14 children who were between 67 inches and 68 inches tall and whose parents' heights were also between 67 inches and 68 inches tall. As you will discover in a few pages, Galton's table is the origin of what are now called "scatterplots."

Second, Galton noticed that while the "co-relations" were imperfect, one regularity nonetheless occurred quite consistently. Taller than average parents had tall children, but they tended to be not quite as tall as Mom and Dad. Shorter than average parents had short children, but not quite as short. That is, the children's heights tended to drift back to, or regress to, the mean for the group. This "regression to the mean" phenomenon, which you already know can threaten a study's internal validity, is one of Galton's greatest discoveries.

> A third observation made by Galton was that a plot of the average of each column of his scatterplot yielded a more or less straight line. This in fact is a type of "regression line," another concept that you'll be encountering shortly. In sum, Galton discovered the main features of a correlational analysis.
>
> Shortly after reading about Galton's work, the young British statistician Karl Pearson continued developing the idea, eventually devising the modern formula for calculating coefficients of correlation. He named it "r" for "regression," in honor of Galton's discovery of the regression to the mean phenomenon. Also following Galton's lead, Pearson believed that correlational analysis supported the idea that many traits were inherited because they ran in families. A feature of correlations that you'll be learning about shortly is that drawing conclusions about causality from them, as both Galton and Pearson did, is a hazardous venture.

on one variable are accompanied by low scores on the second variable, and vice versa.

Positive and Negative Correlations

The relationship between study time and grades is a simple example of a positive correlation. If study time, operationalized as the total number of hours per week spent studying, is one variable and grade point average (GPA) ranging from 0.0 to

Children's heights (Mean = 68.0")

Parents' heights (Mean = 68.1")	63"	64"	65"	66"	67"	68"	69"	70"	71"	72"	73"
72"							1	2	2	2	1
71"					2	4	5	5	4	3	1
70"	1	2	3	5	8	9	9	8	5	3	
69"	2	3	6	10	12	12	2	10	6	3	
68"	3	7	11	13	14	13	10	7	3	1	
67"	3	6	8	11	11	8	6	3	1		
66"	2	3	4	6	4	3	2				
65"											
Mean height of parents in each column	67.2	67.3	67.4	67.6	67.9	68.2	68.4	68.8	69.1	69.3	

FIGURE 8.1　A table used by Galton to correlate the heights of parents and children—an original scatterplot [from Fancher, 1990].

4.0 is the second, you can easily see the positive correlation between the two in these hypothetical data from eight students:

	Study Hours	*GPA*
Student 1:	42	3.3
Student 2:	23	2.9
Student 3:	31	3.2
Student 4:	35	3.2
Student 5:	16	1.9
Student 6:	26	2.4
Student 7:	39	3.7
Student 8:	19	2.5

Spending a significant amount of time studying (e.g., 42 hours) is associated with a high GPA (3.3), while minimal study time (e.g., 16 hours) is paired with a poor GPA (1.9). An example of negative correlation might be the relationship between goof-off time and GPA. Goof-off time could be operationally defined as the number of hours per week spent in a specific list of activities that might include videogame playing, soap opera watching, and playing golf (of course, these same activities could be called "therapy" time). Here's some hypothetical data for another eight students. This time examine the inverse relationship between the number of hours per week goofing off and GPA.

	Goof-Off Hours	*GPA*
Student 1:	42	1.8
Student 2:	23	3.0
Student 3:	31	2.2
Student 4:	35	2.9
Student 5:	16	3.7
Student 6:	26	3.0
Student 7:	39	2.4
Student 8:	19	3.4

Notice that in a negative correlation, the variables go in opposite directions. Large amounts of goof-off time (e.g., 42) accompany a low GPA (1.8); less goof-off time (e.g., 16) relates to higher GPA (3.7).

The strength of a correlation is indicated by the size of a statistic known as the "coefficient" of correlation, which ranges from -1.00 for a perfect negative correlation, through 0.00 for no relationship, to $+1.00$ for a perfect positive correlation. The most common coefficient is the **Pearson's** r mentioned in Box 8.1, named for the British statistician who rivals Sir Ronald Fisher in stature. Pearson's r is calculated for data measured on either an interval or a ratio scale. Other kinds of correlations can be calculated for data measured on other scales. For instance, a correlation called Spearman's *rho* (rhymes with throw) is calculated for ordinal (i.e., rankings) data. Appendix B shows you how to calculate Pearson's r.

Like means and standard deviations, a coefficient of correlation is a descriptive statistic. The inferential analysis for correlations involves determining if a particular correlation is significantly greater than (or less than) zero. That is, in correlational research the null hypothesis (H_0) is that the true value of r is 0; the alternative hypothesis (H_1) is that $r \neq 0$. Rejecting the null hypothesis means deciding that a sig-

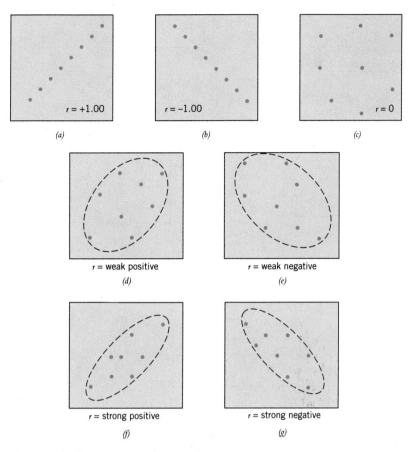

FIGURE 8.2   Varieties of scatterplots.

nificant relationship between two variables exists. Appendix B shows you how to determine if a correlation is statistically "significant."

Scatterplots

An indication of the strength of a correlation also can be discerned by examining the modern version of Galton's Figure 8.1 (see Box 8.1), what is now called a **scatterplot**; it graphs the relationship shown by a correlation. As shown in the examples in Figure 8.2, perfect positive (1a) and negative (1b) correlations produce points falling on a straight line, while a correlation of zero yields a scatterplot (1c) in which the points appear to be randomly distributed on the surface of the graph. Compared to relatively weak correlations (1d and 1e), the points fall closer to the straight line for relatively strong ones (1f and 1g).

Figure 8.3 shows you how a scatterplot is created from a set of data and Figure 8.4 shows you the scatterplots for the hypothetical GPA examples. They show a strong positive correlation between study time and GPA and a strong negative one between goof-off time and GPA. The actual correlations are +.88 and −.89, respectively.

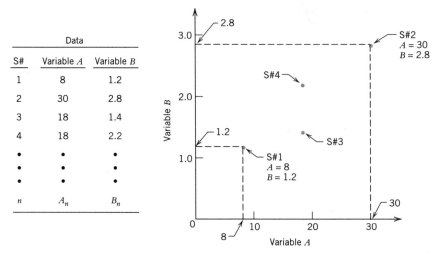

	Data	
S#	Variable A	Variable B
1	8	1.2
2	30	2.8
3	18	1.4
4	18	2.2
•	•	•
•	•	•
•	•	•
n	A_n	B_n

FIGURE 8.3   Creating a scatterplot from a data set.

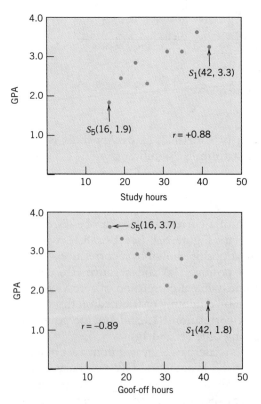

FIGURE 8.4   Scatterplots for some hypothetical GPA data.

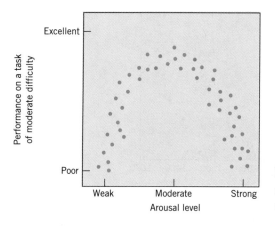

FIGURE 8.5　The curvilinear relationship between arousal level and performance.

Assuming Linearity

So far, the scatterplots you've examined contain points that vary to some degree from the straight line of a perfect correlation of −1.00 or +1.00. Some relationships are not linear, however, and applying Pearson's *r* to them will fail to identify the nature of the relationship. Figure 8.5 shows a hypothetical example, one of psychology's enduring findings: the relationship between arousal and performance. On tasks that are somewhat difficult, performance is good at moderate levels of arousal, but suffers if arousal is very low or very high (e.g., Anderson, 1990). At very low levels of arousal, the person doesn't have the energy to perform the task and at very high levels, the intense arousal interferes with the efficient processing of information necessary to complete the task. You can see from the scatterplot that points would fall consistently along this curved line, but trying to apply a linear correlational procedure would yield a Pearson's *r* of zero or very close to it. More specialized techniques beyond the scope of this text are needed for analyzing curvilinear relationships like the one in Figure 8.5.

Restricting the Range

When doing a correlational study, it is important to include individuals with a wide range of scores. **Restricting the range** of one (or both) of the variables lowers the correlation, an effect that you can see in Figure 8.6. Suppose you were investigating the relationship between SAT scores and success in college, the latter measured in terms of GPA at the end of the freshman year. Figure 8.6a shows what a scatterplot might look like for a sample of 25 students. The correlation is +.70. Suppose, however, that you decide to study this relationship, but only for students who score at least 1,200 on the SAT. Figure 8.6b highlights the points on the scatterplot for such students; these points can form their own scatterplot, as shown in Figure 8.6c. If you now examine 8.6a and 8.6c, it is clear that the correlation is lower on the right. In fact, the correlation drops to +.26.

　　This example has some interesting implications for colleges that decide not to consider students whose combined SAT scores fall below 1,200. Studies (e.g., Schrader, 1971) have shown the overall correlation between SAT scores and freshman year grades to be somewhere in the vicinity of +.40, statistically significant

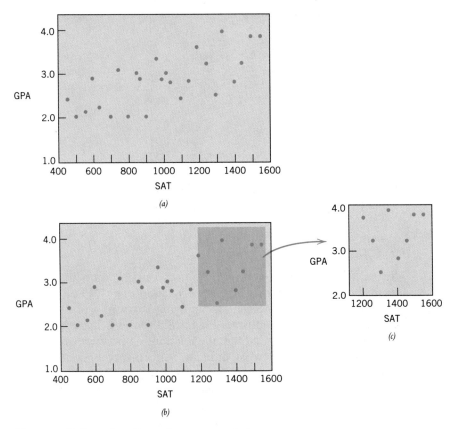

FIGURE 8.6   The effect of a range restriction.

but not huge. That correlation is calculated using students throughout the whole range of SAT scores, however. By restricting the range of SAT scores to those of 1,200 or above, the correlation will drop considerably. Procedures exist for "correcting" correlations to account for the restriction problem, but one has to be aware that restricting the range has direct effects on the ability to make predictions. Highly selective schools using an "SAT = 1,200" cutoff will certainly be getting lots of good students, but their ability to predict grades from SAT scores will not be as great as in a school without such a cutoff point. The correlation between SAT and academic success will be higher at the less restrictive school than it will be at the more restrictive school.

Regression Analysis—Making Predictions

As the previous example suggests, a major feature of correlational research is that predictions about human behavior can be made when strong correlations exist. If you know that two variables are correlated, then knowing a score on one of the variables enables you to predict a score on the other. You can see how this would work with the GPA example. Knowing of the strong relationship between study

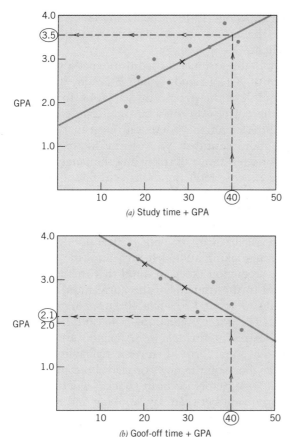

(a) Study time + GPA

(b) Goof-off time + GPA

FIGURE 8.7 Scatterplots with regression lines.

time and GPA, if I tell you that someone studies 40 hours per week, you could safely predict a relatively high GPA for that student. Similarly, a high GPA allows a prediction about study time. As you'll see later in the chapter, correlational research provides the foundation for using psychological tests to make predictions. Making predictions on the basis of correlational research is referred to as doing a **regression analysis**.

Figure 8.7 reproduces the scatterplots for (a) study time and GPA and (b) goof-off time and GPA, but this time each includes what is called a **regression line**. This line is used for making the predictions and is called a best-fitting line; it provides the best possible way of summarizing the points on the scatterplot.

The formula for the regression line is the same formula you learned in high school for creating a straight line on a graph with X and Y coordinates:

$$Y = a + bX$$

where a is the place where the line crosses the Y-axis (i.e., the Y-intercept) and b is the slope, the line's relative steepness. X is a known value and Y is the value you are trying to predict. The value of b can be calculated knowing (1) the size of the correlation and (2) the standard deviations for the variables being correlated, and "a" can be calculated knowing (1) the calculated value of b and (2) the mean scores for the variables being correlated. See Appendix B for details about how these values are calculated.

In a regression analysis, the formula is used to predict a value for Y (e.g., GPA) based on a given value of X (e.g., study time). Y is sometimes referred to as the criterion variable, and X as the predictor variable. In order to predict with confidence, however, the correlation must be significantly greater than zero. The higher the correlation, the closer the points on the scatterplot will be to the regression line, and the more confident you can be in the prediction you make. Thus, the problem mentioned above of restricting the range, which generally lowers correlations, has the effect of reducing the effectiveness of predictions.

From Figure 8.7, you also can see how a regression line aids in making predictions. Given the relationship between study time and GPA, one could ask what GPA could be expected from someone with 20, 30, or 40 study hours. As you can see, the process can be visualized by drawing vertical dotted lines from the X-axis to the regression line, then taking a 90° left turn until the Y-axis is encountered. The value on Y is the prediction (keep in mind that the confidence you have in the prediction is related to the strength of the correlation). Thus, a study time of 40 hours predicts a GPA of about 3.5, while 40 hours of goof-off time predicts a GPA of just under 2.1. The exact predictions, 3.48 and 2.13, respectively, can be calculated by using the regression formula (see Appendix B).

You can be certain that some form of regression analysis has occurred in much of the research you hear about on the news or read about in the popular press. For instance, a report about "risk factors for heart attacks" will be describing a study in which a significant correlation between, say, smoking and heart disease allows for the prediction that heavy smokers will be more likely to develop coronary problems than nonsmokers. That is, smoking predicts heart disease. Another study describing the "profile of a spouse abuser" might include the idea that such behavior is more likely to occur if the abuser is unemployed. Again, this follows from a correlation between unemployment and tendency to be abusive and allows for a prediction, via regression analysis, of the latter from the former.

One final point about a regression analysis is both procedural and ethical. In general, predictions should only be made for people who fall within the range of scores on which the correlation is based. For example, if a regression equation predicting college success is based on a study using middle-class suburban whites whose scores range from 1,000 to 1,400, then the equation should not be used to predict success for any applicant not within that range.

Interpreting Correlations

With its ability to predict, then, correlational research gives the researcher a powerful tool. However, great care must be taken in interpreting the results of correlational studies. Specifically, finding a correlation between two variables does not allow the conclusion that one of the variables is causing the other to occur. Unfortunately, a failure to appreciate this fundamental rule makes correlational research the method least understood by the general public. To illustrate, consider the research indicating that a certain type of baldness is a predictor of heart disease. I can remember when this story first appeared in winter 1993. All three networks highlighted the finding on their evening news programs on the same night (a slow news night?), each responsibly pointing out that the reason for the relationship was not clear. Nonetheless, within a few weeks, the multimillion dollar "let's not be bald anymore" industry started dropping some not so subtle hints that using their procedure for growing new hair might be beneficial for one's health (besides the normal outcome of the new hair attracting hordes of women). The implied message was that baldness leads to heart attacks; therefore, if baldness disappears, so will heart attacks.

If you can see the problem with this line of thinking, then you already have a sense of what is to follow. As you recall from Chapter 1, one of my goals is to help you become a more critical consumer of information. Understanding how to interpret correlational research properly will help you approach that goal, because drawing inappropriate conclusions from correlational research occurs quite frequently in popular descriptions of medical and psychological research.

Correlations and Causality

In an experimental study with a manipulated independent variable, we've already seen that cause and effect conclusions can be drawn. The variable of interest is manipulated, and if all else is held constant, the results can be attributed directly to the independent variable. With correlational research, the "all else is held constant" feature is missing, however, and this lack of control makes it impossible to conclude anything about cause and effect. Let's consider two specific ways in which interpretation problems can occur with correlations. These are referred to as the reversibility or directionality problem and the third variable problem (Neale & Liebert, 1973).

Directionality

If there is a correlation between two variables, *A* and *B*, it is *possible* that *A* is causing *B* to occur ($A \rightarrow B$), but it also could be that *B* is causing *A* to occur ($B \rightarrow A$). That the causal relation could occur in either direction is known as the **directionality problem**. The existence of the correlation, *by itself*, does not allow one to decide about the direction of causality.

Research on the relationship between TV watching and children's aggression typifies the directionality problem. Some of these studies are correlational and take the following general form. Some measure (variable *A*) of TV watching is made, the number of hours per week perhaps. For the same subjects, a second measure (variable *B*) of behavior is taken. It might be a combined score of teacher ratings of the aggressiveness for the children in the study. Suppose this study yields a correlation of +.58, which is found to be significantly greater than zero. What can be concluded?

One possibility, of course, is that watching large amounts of TV inevitably exposes the child to a great deal of violence, and we know that children learn by observation; thus, it would follow that a large dose of TV watching causes children to become aggressive; that is, $A \rightarrow B$.

But could causality be working in the reverse direction? Could it be that already-aggressive children simply like to watch TV more than their nonaggressive peers? Knowing that much of television involves violent programming, perhaps aggressive children choose to watch more of the things that really interest them. In short, perhaps being aggressive causes children to watch more TV; that is, B → A.

Solely on the basis of an existing correlation, then, choosing the correct causal direction is not possible. However, there is a way to deal with the directionality problem to some extent. It derives from the criteria for determining causality first described back in Chapter 1. As you recall, research psychologists are generally satisfied with attributing causality between *A* and *B* when they occur together, when *A* precedes *B* in time, when *A* causing *B* is consistent with some theory, and when other explanations for their co-occurrence can be ruled out.

For the TV and aggressiveness study, all we have is *A* and *B* occurring together and the fact that *A* causing *B* makes some sense from what is known about observational learning. However, using a procedure called a **cross-lagged panel correlation**, it is possible to increase one's confidence about directionality. In essence, this procedure investigates correlations between variables at several points in time. Hence, it is a type of longitudinal design. The following well-known example illustrates the procedure.

Case Study 1. TV and Aggression

Eron, Huesman, Lefkowitz, and Walder (1972) were interested in the same relationship between TV watching and aggression that I've been using as a hypothetical example. In particular, they measured (a) preference for watching violent television programs and (b) peer ratings of aggressiveness. The subjects were 875 third graders from a rural area of New York first studied in 1960; a modest but significant correlation of +.21 was found. What made the study interesting, however, was that Eron's team returned ten years later, found 427 of the same students (now arbitrarily labeled "thirteenth graders") and reassessed the same two variables. By measuring the two variables at two points in time, six correlations can be calculated. These correlations, as they occurred in the Eron et al. (1972) study, are displayed in Figure 8.8.

Of special interest are the diagonal or "cross-lagged" correlations because they

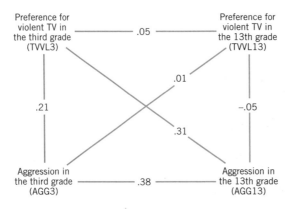

FIGURE 8.8   Results of a cross-lagged panel study of the effects of preferences for violent TV programs on later aggression [from Eron et al. (1972)].

measure the relationships between variables separated in time. If third-grade aggressiveness caused a later preference for watching violent TV ($B \rightarrow A$), then we would expect a fair-sized correlation between aggressiveness at time 1 and preference at time 2; in fact, the correlation is virtually zero (+.01). On the other hand, if an early preference for viewing violent TV programs led to a later pattern of aggressiveness ($A \rightarrow B$), then the correlation between preference at time 1 and aggressiveness at time 2 should be substantial. As you can see, this correlation is +.31, which is not large, but is significant. On this basis as well as some other indications in their study, Eron and his colleagues concluded that an early preference for watching violent TV is at least partially the cause of later aggressiveness.

Cross-lagged panel correlations must be interpreted cautiously, however. For one thing, if you examine the overall pattern of correlations in Figure 8.8, you will notice that the correlation of +.31 may be partially accounted for by the correlations of +.21 and +.38. That is, rather than there being a direct path from third-grade preference to thirteenth-grade aggression, perhaps the path is an indirect result of the relationship between preference for violent TV and aggression in the third grade and between the two measures of aggression. A child scoring high on preference for violent TV in the third grade might also be aggressive in the third grade and still be aggressive in the thirteenth grade. Alternatively, it could be that aggressiveness in the third grade produced both (a) a preference for watching violent TV in the third grade and (b) later aggressiveness. Thus, cross-lagged panel correlations help solve the directionality dilemma, but problems of interpretation remain. More generally, interpretation difficulties take the form of the "third variable" problem.

Third Variables

Let's begin with a completely absurd example (from Neale & Liebert, 1973). There is a positive correlation between the number of churches in a city and the crime rate in a city. The more churches there are, the higher the crime rate. Does this mean that increased "religiousness" causes increases in crime ($A \rightarrow B$)? Or does an increase in crime make people more religious ($B \rightarrow A$)? I think you can see that directionality is not an issue here: Neither alternative makes much sense. Rather, this is an example of a situation often found in correlational research. Because such research does not attempt to control extraneous variables, these variables might provide the basis for the correlation found. That is, rather than A causing B or B causing A, some unknown third variable, C, might be causing both A and B to happen. This is called the **third variable problem**, although it might be more appropriate to call it the third variables problem because it is often the case that more than one uncontrolled variable lies behind a correlation. What is the third variable behind the churches/crime rate example? How about "population size?"

Other examples are not so absurd and can easily mislead someone into making an unwarranted causal connection that could have some dramatic effects. In Box 8.1, you learned about Galton's and Pearson's belief that a positive correlation between parents and children proved that heredity was the prime cause of differences in level of intelligence. Both discounted the effects of the environment (e.g., intelligent parents providing a stimulating environment for their children) as the factor underlying the relationship between parents and children. Furthermore, both argued that because inheritance was the cause of intelligence, smart people should be encouraged to have lots of children. In fact, Galton is the founder of the eugenics movement, which advocated among other things that Great Britain take steps to improve the overall intelligence of its people through selective breeding. As Galton rather crassly put it, just as it is possible "to obtain by careful selection a permanent breed of dogs or horses with peculiar powers of running, . . . so it would be quite practical to produce a highly gifted race of men by judicious marriages during several consecutive generations" (Galton, 1869, cited in Fancher, 1990, p. 228). It isn't difficult to imagine the dark side of the eugenics movement, a recommendation that a group deemed "unfit" or "defective" be prevented from reproducing. Clearly, misinterpreting correlational research can have far-reaching consequences.

The relationship between watching violent TV programming and children's aggressiveness provides a more modern example of the third variable problem. As we've already seen, it is possible that watching TV violence increases aggression ($A \rightarrow B$), but that causality in the opposite direction could also occur ($B \rightarrow A$). Already-aggressive children might seek out and watch violent programming. The third possibility is that both A and B result from some third variable, C ($C \rightarrow A + B$). For instance, perhaps the parents are violent people. They cause their children to be violent by modeling aggressive behavior and they also cause their children to watch a lot of TV. The children might do this in order to "lie low" and avoid contact with parents who are always punishing them. Another third variable might be a lack of verbal fluency. Perhaps children are aggressive because they don't argue very effectively and they also watch lots of TV as a way of avoiding verbal contact with others.

Sometimes trying to identify third variables is a purely speculative affair. On other occasions, however, one might have reason to suspect that a particular third variable is operating. If so, and if it is possible to measure this third variable, its effects can be evaluated using a procedure called **partial correlation**, which attempts to control for third variables statistically. In effect, it is a *post facto* (after the fact) attempt to create at least semiequivalent groups. For example, suppose you know that the correlation between reading speed and reading comprehension is high, +.55 perhaps (example from Sprinthall, 1982). Furthermore, you might suspect that as a third variable, IQ might be contributing to this correlation. To complete a partial correlation, you would correlate (a) IQ and reading speed and (b) IQ and reading comprehension. Let's suppose they come out to be +.70 and +.72, respectively, high enough for you to be suspicious about IQ's influence. Calculating a partial correlation involves incorporating all three of these correlations (see Sprinthall for the exact procedure). What results is a partial correlation that measures the relationship between reading speed and reading comprehension with IQ "partialled out" or "controlled." In this case, the partial correlation is +.10. Thus, when IQ is partialled out, the correlation between speed and comprehension virtually disappears, which means that IQ is indeed an important third variable making a significant contribution to the original +.55 correlation between speed and comprehension.

Several partial correlations were calculated in the Eron et al. (1972) study to see if any important third variables might have been responsible for the relatively high correlation (+.31) between third-grade preference for violence and thirteenth-grade aggressiveness. Table 8.1 shows the results for 12 different potential third

TABLE 8.1 *Partial Correlations in Eron, Huesman, Lefkowitz, and Walder's (1972) Study of the Relationship Between a Preference for Watching Violent TV and Aggressive Behavior*

Controlled Variable	Partial Correlation between TVVL3 and AGG13*
None (original correlation)	.31
Third-grade variables	
peer-rated aggression	.25
father's occupational status	.31
child's IQ	.28
father's aggressiveness	.30
mother's aggressiveness	.31
punishment administered	.31
parents' aspirations for child	.30
parents' mobility orientation	.31
hours of television watched	.30
Thirteenth-grade variables	
father's occupational status	.28
subject's aspirations	.28
hours of television	.30

*TVVL3 = preference for watching violence on TV in the third grade.
 AGG13 = level of aggressiveness in the thirteenth grade.
Note: Adapted from Eron et al. (1972), Table 4.

variables (called "controlled variables" in the table). As you can see, the partial correlations range from +.25 to +.31, indicating that none of the 12 factors made a significant contribution to the original correlation of +.31. That is, even taking into account these other factors, the correlation between early preference for violent TV programs and later aggressiveness *remained close* to the +.31. The analysis strengthened their conclusion "that there is a probable causative influence of watching violent television programs in [the] early formative years on later aggression" (Eron et al., 1972, p. 263).

Structural Modeling

A more sophisticated technique called "causal modeling" or **structural modeling** has become popular in recent years for sorting out the causal paths between several variables (James, Mulaik, & Brett, 1982). The procedure considers both the directionality problem and the third-variable problems simultaneously. You can get the general flavor of this approach by considering a recent study about juvenile delinquency by Tremblay et al. (1992).

Longitudinal studies using cross-lagged procedures have shown that poor achievement in the early school years is associated with later delinquency. But it is also known that behavior problems correlate with poor school achievement in

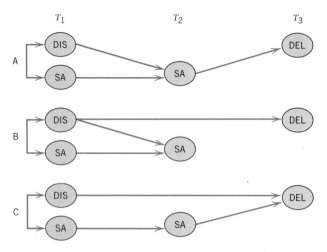

FIGURE 8.9   Models tested in the Tremblay et al. (1992) study of the predictors of delinquency, using structural modeling.

those early years. So, is the later delinquency the result of poor school performance or conduct problems or some combination of both? The Tremblay et al. (1992) study was designed to answer the question, which is of obvious importance because it determines whether one should attack the problem by trying to improve school performance or by working on the behavior problems. They measured disruptive behavior and achievement in the first grade, achievement in the fourth grade, and delinquent behavior in the eighth grade. Using what are called "linear structural equations," they tested the adequacy of the three different models portrayed in Figure 8.9. In model A, disruptive behavior and poor achievement in the first grade jointly cause poor achievement in the fourth grade, and this in turn causes the eighth-grade delinquency. Model B proposes that the delinquency is the direct result of the early disruptive behavior and is indirectly related to poor achievement in the first but not the fourth grade. Model C proposes two causal paths to delinquency: early disruptive behavior and poor achievement in the fourth grade (which, in turn, results from poor achievement in the first grade). In general, Tremblay et al. (1992) found support for model B, at least for boys, suggesting that an attack on the problem should focus more on early disruptive behavior than on school performance.

Correlations and Subject Variables

Finally, you should recognize that the interpretation problems occurring in correlational studies are exactly the same problems that exist in studies which include subject variables as independent variables. The last chapter described three such designs:

1. Single-factor, nonequivalent groups designs.
2. Factorial nonequivalent groups designs.
3. Factorial P × E designs.

Just as a significant correlation between TV watching and aggression doesn't allow a causal inference to be made, a significant difference in performance between Type A and Type B subjects on a challenging problem doesn't allow one either. Differences between A and B types still leaves open the question of how to interpret these differences (e.g., maybe Type A's are smarter than Type B's).

Using Correlations

Considering the pitfalls that exist when trying to interpret correlations, combined with the fact that those envied conclusions about cause and effect indeed can be made from so-called true experiments with manipulated independent variables, why not just do pure experimental studies? That is, why bother with correlational research in the first place?

The Need for Correlational Research

The answer has to do with both practical and ethical considerations. On practical grounds, some important research would not be feasible or may not even be possible as a pure experimental study. Studying gender differences in behavior, differences between age groups, or differences between personality types are major research areas in which it is not possible to randomly assign. A study looking for a correlation between severity of clinical depression and task perseverance has value in its own right even if subjects cannot be randomly assigned to "high-depression" and "low-depression" conditions. As Cronbach put it in his two-disciplines address, the correlational approach "can study what [we have] not learned to control or can never hope to control" (Cronbach, 1957, p. 672). Furthermore, some research is conducted with prediction as the major goal. For example, finding a correlation between certain personality attributes and success on job X allows personnel managers to predict who will succeed on the job while remaining not the least bit concerned about why the relationship exists.

Second, on rather obvious ethical grounds, there are some studies that simply cannot be done as experiments with manipulated variables. When nineteenth-century French physiologist Paul Broca discovered the brain's speech center, later named for him, he did it by noting a relationship between certain types of speech disorders and the extent of brain damage discovered upon a postmortem examination (Hothersall, 1990). *Experimental* evidence that the disorder was caused by the brain damage would require randomly assigning people to a "brain damage" group, which would have portions of their brain pulverized, or to a safer "control" group. Actually, you would also need a third group that could be called a "sham brain damage" group. They would go through most of the same surgical procedures as the brain damage group, except for the actual brain destruction. I think that you can appreciate the difficulty of recruiting human volunteers for this experiment. This is one reason why animals are used as subjects in experimental research investigating the relationship between brain and behavior.

Varieties of Correlational Research

Research using correlational procedures can be found in all areas of psychology. Correlations are especially prevalent in (1) research concerning the development of psychological tests, (2) research in personality and abnormal psychology, and (3) research in the Galton tradition that relates to the nature—nurture issue. These areas all emphasize ways in which people differ from each other. Let's look at some typical research from each of the three.

Case Study 2. Psychological Testing

In Chapter 4, you learned that for a measure to be of value, it must be both reliable and valid. Reliable measures are repeatable measures that are relatively free from measurement error. A measure is valid if it truly measures the trait in question. A reliable and valid measure of intelligence will yield about the same IQ score on two separate occasions and will be a true measure of intellectual ability and not a measure of something else. Research to establish reliability and validity depends heavily on correlations, as the following series of studies shows.

For measuring IQ scores in children, the big two are the Stanford-Binet IQ test and the Weschler Intelligence Scale for Children (WISC). Recently, however, a test called the Kaufman Assessment Battery for Children (K·ABC) has been making inroads (Kaufman & Kaufman, 1983). This test yields a "mental processing" score that is a composite of several subtests for "sequential processing" and "simultaneous processing." These are assumed to be basic mental abilities possessed by the child. In addition, there is a separate "achievement" score to reflect the kind of knowledge derived from school and elsewhere.

The Kaufmans evaluated the reliability of their test in several ways. For example, they used a procedure called a **split-half reliability**. This involves taking the items that make up a particular subtest, dividing them in half (e.g., even-numbered vs odd-numbered items), and correlating the two halves. The correlation should be high if the test is reliable—someone scoring high on one half should score high on the other half as well. A second type of reliability is called **test-retest reliability**, the relationship between two separate administrations of the test. Again, these reliabilities should be high—a reliable test yields consistent results from one testing to another. For the K·ABC, both split-half and test-retest reliabilities were high. What about the test's validity?

One indication of a test's validity is its **predictive validity**, the ability of the test to predict some future event. This validity is determined by correlating scores on the test in question (the K·ABC) with scores on some "criterion." The criterion is typically some other test or measurement that is conceptually related to the test in question. For an IQ test, criterion measures are often scores on tests relating to school performance, because IQ tests are designed to predict how well someone will perform in an academic environment. Scores on a valid test should correlate positively with criterion scores.

Numerous validity studies have been carried out with the K·ABC, using a wide range of criterion measures of school achievement (Kaufman & Kaufman, 1983). In general, the results are impressive; for instance, the test is known to be correlated with such criterion measures as the Iowa Tests of Basic Skills and the California Achievement Test, both well established as indicators of school success.

Implied in this K·ABC example is the importance of using good (i.e., reliable and valid) tests. After all, decisions that can affect lives often are made at least in part on the basis of these instruments. Children are placed into gifted programs, managers are promoted, college students get into medical school, and psychiatric patients get the correct diagnosis. All of these important decisions are made with the help of psychological tests. Hence, there are ethical issues related to the reliability and validity of these tools. Box 8.2 considers some of them and describes the APA guidelines for the development and use of tests.

Case Study 3. Research in Personality and Abnormal Psychology

The assessment of reliability and validity is also important when developing tests to measure normal and abnormal personality traits. Besides their use during test development, however, correlational procedures are important when investigating individual differences in personalities. For example, a study might select a large group of people, give them tests for several different traits, then correlate the scores. From this type of study, one might learn of a positive correlation between introversion and anxiety (introverts tend to be anxious) or of a negative correlation between introversion and sociability (introverts tend to avoid social contact). An example of this strategy is a study on explanatory style and depression by Seligman et al. (1988).

In Chapter 3, I introduced you to Seligman's work on learned helplessness as an illustration of how research is generated from theory and how theories evolve in the face of various research outcomes. You'll recall that Seligman began with a theory of learned helplessness based on some animal conditioning studies, then revised the theory to take "explanatory style" into account. People who are depressed have a history of learned helplessness and the resulting pessimistic explanatory style correlates with depression. The Seligman et al. (1988) study investigated the relationship between a pessimistic attributional style and the tendency to be depressed. They also wished to see if "cognitive therapy" could alleviate the depression and make the explanatory style more positive.

Those with a pessimistic explanatory style who experience a negative outcome of some kind blame themselves for the failure, assume it to be symptomatic of a more general inadequacy, and believe that failures will be the rule and not the exception in the future (Abramson, Seligman, & Teasdale, 1978). If so, it is easy to see how this way of thinking would also be accompanied by feelings of depression. In Seligman's study, an "Attributional Style Questionnaire" was used to measure explanatory style; depression was measured by means of an instrument called the Beck Depression Inventory. Briefly, what the researchers found was that the severity of depression correlated significantly with a pessimistic explanatory style, and this was true before therapy ($r = .+.56$), after therapy ($r = +.57$) and 1 year after therapy ($r = +.63$). The correlations remained about the same as the patients were improving in therapy because "[d]uring cognitive therapy, explanatory style and depression changed in lockstep from intake to termination, and as explanatory style became more optimistic, the patient became less depressed" (Seligman et al.,

Box 8.2

ETHICS—APA Guidelines for Psychological Testing

A glance back at Table 2.2 (p. 31) will show you that the 1992 revision of the APA ethics code includes a section called "Evaluation, Assessment, or Intervention." The ten standards listed there have to do with the development, use, and interpretation of psychological tests. Two standards in particular relate to research issues (American Psychological Association, 1992):

2.02. *Competence and Appropriate Use of Assessments and Interventions*
(a) Psychologists who develop, administer, score, interpret, or use psychological assessment techniques, interviews, tests, or instruments do so in a manner and for purposes that are appropriate in light of the research on or evidence of the usefulness and proper application of the techniques.

2.03. *Test construction*
Psychologists who develop and conduct research with tests and other assessment techniques use scientific procedures and current professional knowledge for test design, standardization, validation, reduction or elimination of bias, and recommendations for use.

From these standards and from the discussion of reliability and validity, it should be clear that there is considerably more to psychological testing than simply making up a questionnaire that seems to make sense. Yet that is the typical procedure used in developing most of the pseudoscientific tests you'll encounter in popular magazines. These tests appear to be scientific because they might include a scoring key ("if you scored between 0 and 25, it means . . ."), but the scales are essentially meaningless because there's never been any attempt to determine reliability or validity, or to standardize the test so that a specific score you obtain can be compared to some population data.

These tests are harmless as long as you understand that they aren't to be taken seriously. Armed with the appropriate attitude, then, you could explore the following:

✓ How tactful are you? [*Cosmopolitan*, January, 1993]
✓ Are you boring? [*Young and Modern*, June/July, 1992]
✓ Test yourself: How angry are you? [*Self*, January, 1993]
✓ Just a mood? Or real depression? Take our quiz [*Family Circle*, April 1, 1992]

To learn how *real* psychological tests are created and validated, take the tests and measurements course that I'm sure your psychology department offers.

1988, p. 17). That is, as their scores on explanatory style changed after being in therapy, their depression scores showed a corresponding change and as a result, the correlations stayed about the same. Because cognitive therapy is designed to change the way people think and hence how they explain to themselves what happens to them, the researchers believed their study yielded strong evidence for the idea that pessimistic explanations are at least one cause of depression and that an effective way to treat depression is to get people to change the way they think about events in their lives.

One of psychology's most famous series of studies is another example of using a correlational strategy to study personality, in this case the personality trait called "achievement motivation." Before reading on, take a look at Box 8.3, which describes a classic study from this tradition, a study suggesting that it might be wise for a culture to have high achievers as characters in the stories read by its children.

Case Study 4. The Nature–Nurture Issue

As you learned from Box 8.1, Sir Francis Galton was impressed by the tendency for genius to run in families. Studying family resemblances on various traits has become a major research strategy that bears on the issue of how heredity and environment contribute to various traits. The typical procedure is to measure some characteristic for each of many pairs of family members and to calculate the correlations between them. Heredity and environmental factors can be evaluated separately by comparing pairs differing in genetic similarity and in the similarity of their home environments. For example, identical twins reared together can be compared with identical twins separated at birth and reared in different environments, thereby keeping genetics constant and varying environmental similarity. Likewise, the environment could be kept more or less constant and genetics varied by comparing identical twins (genetically the same) reared together and fraternal twins (genetically not the same) reared together. Such research typically demonstrates the joint influence of both nature and nurture, as illustrated in Table 8.2, which summarizes the results from dozens of studies on the origins of intelligence (Bouchard & McGue, 1981). The higher the correlation, the more similar the IQ scores for the pair involved. Hence, the correlation of $+.86$ for identical twins means that if one twin has a high IQ, the other twin will also have a high IQ. Clearly, the size of the correlations declines as genetic similarity decreases, indicating the importance of heredity for intelligence. The environment is also critical, as indicated by the difference in correlations between identical twins raised together ($+.86$) and identical twins raised apart ($+.72$).

Historically, most twin studies have centered on the question of intelligence, but recently, there have been a number of studies demonstrating the heritability of personality and temperament traits, as well as work- and leisure-related interests (Bouchard, Lykken, McGue, Segal, & Tellegen, 1990). Even shyness appears to have some genetic basis. Emde et al. (1992) studied 200 pairs of 14-month old identical and fraternal twins (raised together) on a number of personality and cognitive factors. One variable was shyness, which was measured in several ways. First, it was

Box 8.3

CLASSIC STUDIES — The Achieving Society

Can you predict the achievement level of an entire society by analyzing the stories told to the children of that society? Yes, according to psychologist David McClelland's 1961 book, *The Achieving Society*, which documents an extraordinary attempt to extend the results of psychological research on achievement into the realm of historical explanation. Along with colleague John Atkinson, McClelland is a pioneer in the study of achievement motivation, the drive to take on challenges and succeed (McClelland, Atkinson, Clark, & Lowell, 1953). Together, they developed ways of measuring the achievement motive, completed countless studies on the correlates of achievement and the environments conducive to developing the need to achieve (hint: give your children lots of opportunities to be independent), and developed a theory of achievement motivation (Atkinson & Feather, 1966). Furthermore, by elaborating upon the "interaction between stable motives that characterize the personality and immediate situational influences, the theory of achievement motivation represent[ed] a step toward conceptual integration of 'the two disciplines of scientific psychology'" (Atkinson & Feather, 1966, p. 5) called for by Cronbach (1957) in his famous APA presidential address.

One way of measuring the need for achievement, or "nAch," is to use the Thematic Apperception Test (TAT), in which subjects look at ambiguous pictures and describe what they see in them (Murray, 1943). For instance, a drawing of a young boy staring at a violin might elicit a story about how he is dreaming of being a classical violinist. Someone writing such a story would get a higher score for nAch than someone who wrote a story about the child planning to take the violin and whack his sister over the head with it. Presumably, the stories that subjects create reflect the underlying motives important to them.

The idea that one could infer motives from stories led McClelland to wonder about the role that children's stories and a culture's myths and fables might have on the developing motives of young people. If these stories are loaded with achievement themes, won't the young children gradually develop the idea that achievement is important? Could it be that the overall level of nAch in a society could be inferred from an interpretation of children's literature, cultural myths, music, and plays? And if children are raised in an environment stressing achievement, will they achieve at a high level as adults?

Such speculation led to McClelland's classic research on achievement in society. He subjected children's literature to the same kind of analysis given TAT stories, then took various measures of societal economic health and correlated the two. What he found was a positive correlation; as achievement themes increased, actual achievement increased. Of particular interest was the fact that actual achievement lagged behind high levels of achievement in literature by about 50 years—just about the time it would take for children exposed to high-achievement literature to be old enough to have their high levels of nAch affect society.

TABLE 8.2 *Correlations Between IQ Scores for Pairs of Relatives Differing in Genetic Similarity and Home Environment*

	(No of Studies)	(No. of Pairs)	(r)
Identical twins reared together	34	4,672	.86
Identical twins reared apart	3	65	.72
Fraternal twins raised together	41	5,546	.60
Siblings reared together	69	26,473	.47
Siblings reared apart	2	203	.24
Cousins	4	1,176	.15

Note: The data reported are weighted averages of correlations from studies summarized by Bouchard and McGue, 1981.

considered to be an element of a general measure of "behavioral inhibition," which was assessed from videotapes of the infants responding when strangers entered a playroom. Avoiding a stranger while staying close to Mom produced a high score. Shyness was also measured by how the infant reacted to a home visit by the examiner and by the infant's behavior upon encountering the lab. Finally, parents filled out a survey that included a shyness scale. As with other twin studies, the correlations were calculated for identical and fraternal twins. Table 8.3 shows the resulting higher correlations for the twins who were closer genetically, hence supporting the hypothesis of a genetic component for shyness.

Multivariate Analysis

A bivariate approach investigates the relationships between any two variables. A multivariate approach, on the other hand, examines relationships between more than two variables (often many more than two). Up to this point in the chapter, we've been considering the bivariate case, except for the discussion of partial cor-

TABLE 8.3 *Correlations Between "Shyness" Scores for Pairs of Identical and Fraternal Twins*

	Pearson's r Value	
Shyness Measure	Identical Twins	Fraternal Twins
Behavioral inhibition	.57	.26
Shyness observations	.70	.45
Parent survey	.38	.03

Note: Adapted from Emde et al. (1992), Table 2.

relations and structural modeling, which evaluate the effects of third variables on the relationship between two others. Two additional popular multivariate procedures are multiple regression and factor analysis.

Multiple Regression

In the case of bivariate regression, there are two variables involved: the predictor variable and the criterion variable. If SAT scores are correlated with freshman year GPA, then this test can be used as a predictor for academic success. However, as you know from firsthand experience, phenomena like "success in college" are more complicated than this. SAT scores might predict success, but what about the influence of other factors like "motivation" or "high school grades" or "ability to select a no-brain major?"

Multiple regression solves the problem of there being more than one predictor of some outcome. In a **multiple regression** study, there is a criterion variable and a minimum of two predictor variables. The analysis enables you to determine not just the fact that these two or more variables predict, but the relative strengths of the predictions. These strengths are reflected in the multiple regression formula, which is an extension of the formula for simple regression:

$$\text{simple regression: } Y = a + bX$$

$$\text{multiple regression: } Y = a + b_1 X_1 + b_2 X_2 + \ \ldots \ b_n X_n$$

where each X is a different predictor variable, Y is the criterion, and the b's (called "beta weights") are the relative weightings given to each predictor.

The advantage of a multiple regression analysis is that by combining the influence of several predictor variables (especially if the predictors are not highly correlated with each other), prediction improves far beyond the bivariate regression case. High school grades by themselves predict college success, as do SAT scores. Together, however, they predict somewhat better than either by itself (Sprinthall, 1982).

To give you an idea of the range of studies using a multiple regression analysis, here are two recent examples:

1. A study predicting empathy from early childhood experiences (Barnett & McCoy, 1988): Empathic students tended to have experienced distressing childhood events that could have made them more sensitive to the trauma of others. The severity of the childhood trauma was weighted more heavily as a predictor than the total number of traumatic events.

2. A study predicting susceptibility to the common cold from negative life events, perceived stress, and negative affect (Cohen, Tyrell, & Smith, 1993): While you might think that getting a cold is the simple result of standing too close to that person who just sneezed all over your lunch, this study demonstrated that getting colds could be predicted from three variables related to stress. Those college students most likely to catch colds were those who (a) re-

cently experienced some stressful event(s), (b) were feeling that current demands on them were overwhelming, and (c) described their general emotional state as negative.

Factor Analysis

A second and widely used multivariate technique is called factor analysis. In this procedure, a large number of variables are measured and correlated with each other. It is then determined whether groups of these variables cluster together to form "factors." A simple example will clarify the idea. Suppose you gave a group of school-age children the following tasks:

- A vocabulary test (VOC)

- A reading comprehension test (COM)

- An analogy test (e.g., doctor is to patient as lawyer is to _____) (ANA)

- A geometry test (GEO)

- A puzzle completion test (PUZ)

- A rotated figure test (ROT)

Scores on these tests would all be correlated with each other, yielding what is called a correlation matrix. It might look like this:

	VOC	COM	ANA	GEO	PUZ	ROT
VOC	—	+.76	+.65	−.09	+.02	−.08
COM		—	+.55	+.04	+.01	−.02
ANA			—	−.07	−.08	+.09
GEO				—	+.78	+.49
PUZ					—	+.68
ROT						—

Notice how some of the correlations cluster together. Correlations between vocabulary, reading comprehension, and analogies are all high, as are those between geometry, puzzles, and rotation. Correlations between tests from one cluster with tests from the second cluster are essentially zero. This pattern suggests that the tests are measuring two fundamentally different mental abilities or "factors." We could probably call them "verbal fluency" and "spatial skills."

Factor analysis is a sophisticated statistical tool that identifies factors from sets of intercorrelations. It would undoubtedly yield the same two factors that we just reached by scanning the matrix. The analysis also determines "factor loadings." These in essence are correlations between each of the tests and each of the identified factors. In the above example, the first three tests would be "heavily loaded" on factor 1 (verbal fluency) and the second three tests would be heavily loaded on factor 2 (spatial skills). Of course, in real research, the correlations seldom cluster together as clearly as in the example I've used, and there is often some debate among researchers about whether the factors identified are truly separate from other factors. Also, there is occasional disagreement over the proper labels for the factors. Factor analysis itself only identifies factors; their naming is left entirely up to the researcher's judgment.

Factor analysis has been a tool in one of psychology's more enduring debates — whether intelligence is a unitary trait or not. Charles Spearman, who originated factor analysis in the early years of the twentieth century, believed that all tests for intelligence had significant loadings on a single factor that he called a general intelligence factor, or "*g*." Furthermore, each individual test would load heavily on a second factor that would include a skill specific to the test involved (e.g., math). These secondary or "special" factors he called "*s*." According to his "two-factor" theory, then, performance on IQ tests could be accounted for by the person's general intelligence (*g*) plus that person's special skills (*s*). He believed that *g* was inherited, but that the various *s* factors represented learning (Fruchter, 1954).

Other investigators, most notably Louis Thurstone, believed that intelligence was composed of a number of separate factors and that no unitary factor *g* existed. Again, on the basis of factor analysis, he believed there existed seven distinctly different factors; he called them "primary mental abilities" (Thurstone, 1938). These were verbal comprehension, word fluency, number skill, spatial skill, memory, perceptual speed, and reasoning.

The question of whether or not intelligence is unitary continues to perplex those who specialize in the measurement of intelligence. The important point for our purposes is that factor analysis can yield different outcomes. This is because (a) there are several varieties of factor analytic procedures that, in effect, make different decisions about how high the correlations must be before separate factors are identified, and (b) that different studies of the issue use different tests of intelligence. Consequently, researchers using alternative techniques and tests produce a range of outcomes. In short, like other statistical techniques, factor analysis is merely a tool; it cannot by itself resolve theoretical issues such as the nature of intelligence.

As you can tell from this brief introduction, correlational procedures contribute substantially to modern research in psychology. They are often necessary when experimental procedures cannot possibly be used, and with the development of some highly sophisticated multivariate procedures, questions of cause and effect can be addressed more directly than in the past when most correlational research was bivariate in nature.

Much correlational research takes place outside the laboratory. In the next chapter, we'll look more closely at applied research by outlining the details of several so-called quasi-experimental designs. We'll also look at program evaluation research as a specific example of applied research that is becoming increasingly important for the social service industry and for education.

Chapter Review

Glossary Fill-Ins

1. In a type of graph called a _____, the two axes represent the two variables being measured and correlated.

2. A researcher finds that aggressive children watch a lot of violence on TV. It could be that the continued exposure to violence is causing the aggression, but it could also be that naturally aggressive children prefer to watch programs that excite them. This example illustrates the _____ problem that occurs when interpreting correlations.

3. Determining test–retest reliability requires two administrations of a test; if a test can only be given once, _____ reliability can be calculated.

4. In the Eron et al. (1972) study, the relationship between third-grade TV preferences and thirteenth-grade aggression was not diminished when other factors were controlled statistically. The procedure used was to calculate _____.

5. When assessing the _____ validity of a creativity test, the criterion measure could be teacher ratings of the quality of student artwork.

6. In _____, the combined influence of several predictor variables is assessed.

Multiple Choice

1. For which of the following correlations is the relationship strongest?
   a. $+.81$
   b. $-.67$
   c. $-.86$
   d. $+1.04$

2. In correlational studies, extraneous variables are not controlled, resulting in the interpretation problem known as the
   a. Directionality problem
   b. Regression to the mean problem
   c. Range restriction problem
   d. Third variable problem

3. A graduate school decides to use a formula for making its acceptance decisions. Into the formula go the candidates' college grades over four years, grades in the major, and scores on the GRE. GRE scores are weighed most heavily,

then grades in the major. What procedure has been used to develop this formula?

   a. Multiple regression
   b. Bivariate regression
   c. Factor analysis
   d. Partial correlation

4. In the nineteenth century, many people believed that intelligence could be measured by determining brain size. Which of the following is true about this measure?

   a. It would have strong predictive validity.
   b. It would pass the reliability test.
   c. It would be neither reliable nor valid.
   d. It would be considered valid but not reliable.

5. A cross-lagged panel technique is sometimes used to help solve the_____ problem.

   a. Third variable
   b. Regression to the mean
   c. Negative correlation
   d. Directionality

Applications Exercises

Exercise 8.1. – Interpreting Correlations

Each of the following describes the outcome of a hypothetical bivariate correlational study. Describe at least two ways of interpreting each.

1. There is a positive correlation between the level of dominance shown by mothers and the level of shyness shown by children.
2. Whenever Emmitt Smith carries the football at least 20 times, the Dallas Cowboys win.
3. There is a negative correlation between depression and aerobic fitness level.
4. There is a positive correlation between the number of books to be found in the home and the college GPAs of the students coming from those homes.
5. Happily married couples tend to have more sex (with each other) than unhappy couples.
6. There is a negative correlation between grades and test anxiety.
7. People who watch old reruns of Hawaii 5-0 tend to get speeding tickets.

Exercise 8.2. — Constructing Scatterplots and Calculating Pearson's *r*

Create a scatterplot for the following data. After guessing what the correlation would be from looking at the plot, use the procedures described in Appendix B to calculate the actual Pearson's *r*. Finally, write a statement that describes the relationship.

1. Variable *A* = self-esteem
   - scores range from 0 to 50; higher scores indicate a higher level of self-esteem
2. Variable *B* = explanatory style
   - scores range from 0 to 75; higher scores indicate a negative or pessimistic way of interpreting life's bumps and bruises, and lower scores indicate a positive or optimistic way of interpreting these same outcomes.

Subject no.	Variable A	Variable B
1	42	32
2	22	34
3	16	65
4	4	73
5	46	10
6	32	28
7	40	29
8	12	57
9	28	50
10	8	40
11	20	50
12	36	40

Exercise 8.3. — Understanding Scatterplots

Draw scatterplots that would approximately illustrate the following relationships. Write a single statement that summarizes each relationship.

1. A correlation of +.48 between the sequential processing and the simultaneous processing subtests of the K·ABC.
2. A correlation of −.89 between GPA and scores on a test of "soap opera IQ."
3. A correlation of −.02 between intelligence and depression.
4. A correlation of +.90 between tendency to suffer from OCD (obsessive–compulsive disorder) and love of experimental psychology.

CHAPTER 9

Quasi-Experimental Designs and Applied Research

Chapter Overview

- ### Beyond the Laboratory

  The goal of applied research is to shed light on the causes of and solutions to real world problems. Like basic research, however, its outcomes also contribute to general theories about behavior. American psychologists have always been interested in applied research, partly because of institutional pressures to show that the "new" science of the late nineteenth century could be put to good use. Applied research can encounter ethical problems (e.g., with informed consent) and problems with internal validity (e.g., nonequivalent groups), but it is usually strong in external validity.

- ### Quasi-Experimental Designs

  Research with nonmanipulated independent variables is referred to as quasi-experimental. Nonequivalent control group designs are one example. They compare pretest/posttest changes in a group receiving some experimental treatment with changes in a control group that has been formed without random assignment. In a time series design, several measurements are taken both before and after the introduction of some treatment that is being evaluated. Time series analyses enable the researcher to evaluate the effects of trends. Sometimes a nonequivalent control group design and a time series design can occur together.

• Program Evaluation

The field of program evaluation is a branch of applied psychology that provides empirical data about the effectiveness of various human service and government programs. Needs assessment studies determine whether a new program should be developed. Whether a program is operating according to plan is determined by formative evaluations, and program outcomes are assessed by summative evaluations. Cost analyses help determine whether a program's benefits are worth the funds invested.

As I told you at the very beginning of this text, I would like nothing more than to see you emerge from this course with a desire to contribute to our knowledge about human behavior by becoming a research psychologist. My experience as a teacher in this course tells me that some of you indeed will become researchers, but that most of you won't. However, may of you *will* become professional psychologists of some kind, perhaps working as counselors or personnel specialists or in some other field in which your prime focus will be the delivery of psychological services. As such, you will encounter the worlds of applied research and program evaluation. You may discover you will need to be able to do things like

✓ Read, comprehend, and critically evaluate some research literature on the effectiveness of a program that your agency is thinking about implementing.

✓ Help in planning a new program by informing (tactfully) those who are completely ignorant about research design about the adequacy of the evaluation portion of their proposal.

✓ Participate in an agency self-study in preparation for some type of accreditation; and possibly, because your agency's director found out that you took this course,

✓ Design and be in charge of a study to evaluate some agency program.

In other words, this chapter is important whether or not you intend to do research in psychology ever again. We'll consider applied research in general and program evaluation in particular. The former is a general approach that was first encountered in Chapter 3 and will be elaborated here. The latter is the name given to a form of applied research that examines the effectiveness of programs designed to help people in various ways. The chapter also describes several so-called quasi-experimental designs that are frequently encountered in program evaluation/applied research.

Beyond the Laboratory

You first encountered the distinction between basic and applied research in the opening pages of Chapter 3. To review, the essential goal of *basic research* in psychology is to increase our core knowledge about human behavior. The knowledge might eventually have some application, but that possible outcome isn't the prime motivator; knowledge is valued as an end in itself. On the other hand, *applied research* is designed primarily for the purpose of increasing our knowledge about a particular real world problem, with an eye toward directly solving that problem. A second distinction between basic and applied research is that while basic research usually takes place within the confines of a laboratory on a college or university campus, applied research normally occurs outside of the academic setting, in clinics, in social service agencies, in jails, and in business settings. There are exceptions, of course.

To give you a sense of the variety of applied research, consider these article titles from recent issues of the *Journal of Applied Psychology*:

✓ Gender and the relationship between perceived fairness of pay or promotion and job satisfaction (Witt & Nye, 1992).
✓ Visual–spatial abilities of pilots (Dror, Kosslyn, & Waag, 1993).
✓ Using mug shots to find suspects (Lindsey, Nosworthy, Martin, & Martynuck, 1994).

These titles illustrate two features of applied research. First, following from the previous definition, the studies focus on easily recognizable problems. Second, the titles demonstrate that while the prime goal of applied research is problem solving, these studies also further our knowledge of basic psychological processes. In social psychology, for instance, a well-known theory about interpersonal relations is called "equity theory" (Adams, 1965). Its core premise is that when judging the quality of any interaction with another person, we weigh the relative contributions that we make with the relative gains that we receive. If the costs and benefits are somehow off-balance, we perceive the situation to be inequitable and are motivated to restore the balance. For example, in a marriage with both partners working full-time, the wife might perceive an inequity if household chores were unfairly distributed. She would then initiate various procedures (e.g., negotiation) to restore equity.

Most applied research has the dual function of addressing applied problems directly as well as providing evidence about basic psychological phenomena. Equity, for example, is frequently studied in applied research settings. The study on gender differences in perceived fairness in pay and in promotions deals with an important problem for industry (how to improve job satisfaction), but it also provides some data relevant to broader questions about the adequacy of equity theory. Another illustration of this point comes from the following case study, which evaluated a method for improving eyewitness identification.

Case Study 1. Applied Research

Remember the study with the Scottish diving club (Chapter 7), which showed that recall is best if both learning and recall occur in the same place (e.g., under water)? The importance of context for recall, combined with the generally known inaccuracies of eyewitness testimony, led Edward Geiselman and Ronald Fisher to develop a technique called the "cognitive interview." One of its several features is a principle they refer to as "event-interview similarity," in which the interviewer tries to "reinstate in the witness's mind the external (e.g., weather), emotional (e.g., feelings of fear), and cognitive (e.g., relevant thoughts) features that were experienced at the time of the crime" (Fisher, Geiselman, & Amador, 1989, p. 723). In short, the interview tries to get the witness to reinstate mentally the context of the event witnessed.

Fisher and his colleagues demonstrated the technique's effectiveness with college students who viewed a manufactured event in a controlled environment, but they were also interested in evaluating it "outside the friendly confines of the laboratory" (Fisher et al., 1989, p. 724). With cooperation from the robbery division of the Miami, Florida, police department, they trained seven detectives in the cognitive interview technique. Compared to the nine officers in a control group, those given the training elicited more reliable (i.e., corroborated with other information) facts during interviews with eyewitnesses. In Figure 9.1, you can see that both groups performed about the same on the pretest, which summarized a 4-month period, during which detectives recorded their interviews with witnesses; separate judges scored the records for factual content. After the experimental group completed training, both groups recorded several additional interviews, which were scored in the same fashion. As you can see, those trained to use the cognitive interview were able to elicit more information from witnesses.

In summary, the Fisher et al. (1989) study is an excellent illustration of how applied research can solve real problems while contributing to our knowledge about some fundamental psychological phenomenon. The study shows how a specific interview procedure can improve the efficiency of police work, while at the same time providing further evidence for the general importance of context on recall.

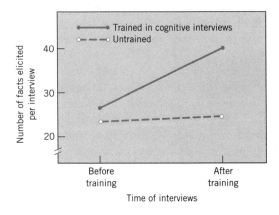

FIGURE 9.1   Effectiveness of the cognitive interview in an applied setting [data from Fisher, Geiselman, & Amador (1989)].

Applied Psychology in Historical Context

Because psychology in America developed in an academic setting, you might think that research in psychology has been traditionally biased toward basic research. Not so. From the time psychology emerged as a new discipline in the late nineteenth century, psychologists in this country have been interested in applied research. For one thing, institutional pressures in the early years of the twentieth century forced psychologists to show how their work could improve society. In order to get a sufficient piece of the academic funding pie at a time when psychology laboratories were brand new entities, psychologists had to show that their ideas could be put to use. As O'Donnell (1985) has shown, a major reason for the appeal of behaviorism as a dominant force in psychology was that it promised and delivered applications.

Psychologists trained as researchers, in addition to their prime focus on extending knowledge, found themselves frequently trying to apply the results of all kinds of research to solve problems in areas like education, mental health, and child rearing. In some cases, the attempts at application seem faintly ludicrous, as Figure 9.2 suggests. This photo is taken from E. W. Scripture's *Thinking, Feeling, Doing* (1895), perhaps the earliest deliberate attempt to show that basic laboratory phenomena such as reaction time could be applied to real-world situations.

A more lasting attempt to apply psychological principles can be found in the

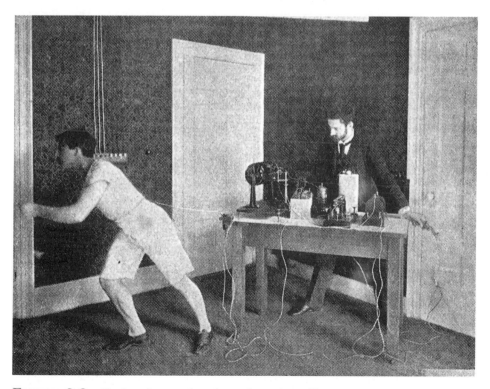

FIGURE 9.2 Testing the reaction time of a sprinter [from E. W. Scripture's *Thinking, Feeling, Doing* (1895)].

Box 9.1

ORIGINS—Hugo Münsterberg: Applied Psychologist Extraordinaire

That applied psychology would be a pivotal force in American psychology is not really surprising. After all, Americans are known for their abiding Yankee pragmatism. "What good is it?" is a sentence that comes naturally to us. Thus, it is surprising that Hugo Münsterberg (1863–1916), a native German, is considered one of the very first applied psychologists in America. When he arrived in this country to run the psychology laboratory at Harvard in 1892, he spoke barely a word of English. Yet by the time of his death he had written nearly 20 books in English and he was an acknowledged pioneer in industrial and forensic psychology and a contributor to clinical psychology.

Münsterberg's *Psychology and Industrial Efficiency*, published in 1913, is sometimes believed to mark the origins of industrial psychology (Hothersall, 1990). It included advice and summaries of research on such topics as the best way to select people for various jobs, the factors that most seriously affect worker productivity, and suggestions about marketing and advertising. He included some of his own research on developing tests for employee selection, using procedures now standard for validating such tools. For example, when asked to develop a selection system by the New England Telephone Company, Münsterberg analyzed the operator's job into the cognitive tasks involved (he identified 14 different ones), developed tests for each, and validated the tests by showing that those who scored highest became the best operators.

first clinic devoted to the treatment of psychological problems, founded by Lightner Witmer of the University of Pennsylvania. Witmer was trained as an experimental psychologist in Wundt's laboratory at Leipzig and was an avid experimentalist in the 1890s. In 1895, he even advocated that experimentalists secede from the fledgling APA and form their own organization because he felt the APA wasn't scientific enough (Goodwin, 1985). Yet in March 1896, when a schoolteacher brought a young boy with what we would now call a learning disability to Witmer's laboratory, it marked the origins of American psychology's first clinic (McReynolds, 1987). Witmer became devoted to applying all that was known about mental processes to the treatment of various psychological maladies, especially learning disorders related to school performance.

Psychology's interest in application also can be seen in the mental testing movement. I indicated in the last chapter that intelligence and personality testing are major industries in America; their roots can be found among the earliest psychologists. For example, James McKeen Cattell, like Witmer a product of Wundt's laboratory, invented the term "mental test" (1890) and developed an extensive (but fatally flawed—see Sokal, 1987) testing program in the 1890s at Columbia, which was

Münsterberg was also a pioneer in the area of forensic psychology—applying psychological principles to the law. His *On the Witness Stand*, which first appeared in 1908, includes a fascinating description of the perils of eyewitness testimony, anticipating the experimental work on the subject that began later in the century. Lacking direct experimental evidence of faulty eyewitness memory, he used his knowledge of such things as perceptual illusions to show how unreliable the human observer could be. He also argued that various physiological measures could be useful in detecting lying.

As often happens when an academician ventures into the public spotlight, however, Münsterberg was something of a controversial figure. Citing a study of problem solving in which group judgments were better than individual judgments, but only for male subjects, Münsterberg concluded that juries should not include females. His conclusion was reported widely in the press and earned him the ire that is reflected in this newspaper headline, cited in Hothersall (1990): "Angry at Münsterberg, Suffragists Say Women Fit for Jury."

More controversial was Münsterberg's attempts to portray the people of his native Germany in a favorable light. Unfortunately, he chose to do this in the years leading up to World War I, and his efforts earned him volumes of hate mail and accusations of being a German spy. According to Hothersall (1990), someone even offered Harvard 10 million dollars to fire him, but backed off when Münsterberg agreed to resign if the man would give 5 million to the university and 5 million to him! When Münsterberg died in 1916, just before the end of the war, he was one of America's villains. *The American Journal of Psychology*, which routinely published long obituaries for psychologists of much lesser light, failed even to mention his death. Consequently, his importance as an early pioneer and promoter of applied psychology was forgotten for years (Landy, 1992).

patterned after Galton's approach in Great Britain. In the early 1920s, he founded the Psychological Corporation, which exists today as a giant in the psychological testing industry (for example, it publishes all of the Weschler intelligence tests).

Finally, consider the career of Hugo Münsterberg, arguably the prototype of the applied psychologist in America. Like many of the early psychologists, he was trained as a research psychologist, but was renowned as an expert in applying psychological principles to business, to the clinic, and even to the courtroom. He was once also one of the more hated men in America, which is why he has been largely ignored in historical accounts of applied psychology, until recently. For more on someone who could claim the title of America's first true applied psychologist (even though he was German), read Box 9.1.

Psychologists at the end of the twentieth century are as interested in application as were their predecessors at the beginning of the century. Besides applying what is known about human behavior to the problems facing professional psychologists, they also conduct research that fits the previous definition of applied research. That is, they design and carry out studies in order to help create solutions to real-world problems, while at the same time contributing to the basic core knowledge of psychological principles. However, applied research projects encounter difficulties seldom found in the laboratory.

Design Problems in Applied Research

From what you've already learned in Chapters 2, 5, and 6, you should be able to anticipate most of the material in this section. The problems encountered in applied research include

✓ *Ethical dilemmas* (Chapter 2).
   A study conducted in the field might create problems relating to informed consent and privacy. Also, debriefing might not always be possible. Research done in an industrial or corporate setting might include an element of coercion if employees believe their job status depends on whether they volunteer to participate in a study.

✓ *A trade-off between internal and external validity* (Chapter 5).
   Because research in applied psychology often takes place in the field, the researcher loses varying degrees of control over the variables operating in the study. Hence, the danger of possible confounding reduces the study's internal validity. On the other hand, external validity is often high in applied research because the setting more closely resembles real life situations and the problems addressed by the research are everyday problems.

✓ *Problems unique to between-subjects designs* (Chapter 6).
   In applied research, it is often impossible to use random assignment to form equivalent groups. Therefore, the studies often must compare nonequivalent groups. This, of course, introduces the possibility of internal validity being threatened by selection problems or interactions between selection and other threats such as maturation. When matching is used to achieve a degree of equivalence, regression problems can occur (Chapter 5).

✓ *Problems unique to within-subjects designs* (Chapter 6).
   It is not always possible to counterbalance properly in applied studies using within-subjects factors. Hence, the studies might have uncontrolled sequence effects. Also, attrition can be a problem for studies that extend over a long period of time.

Before going much further in this chapter, you should look back at the appropriate sections of Chapters 2, 5, and 6 and review the ideas I've just mentioned. You also might review the section in Chapter 5 about the kinds of conclusions that can be drawn from manipulated and from subject variables.

Quasi-Experimental Designs

Strictly speaking, "true" experimental studies include manipulated independent variables and either equivalent groups for between-subjects designs or appropriate counterbalancing for within-subjects designs; anything less is quasi-experimental ("almost" experimental). In Chapter 5, the discussion of nonmanipulated variables centered on the use of subject variables as independent variables. In this chapter, the emphasis will broaden somewhat. In general, a **quasi-experiment** exists whenever causal conclusions cannot be drawn because there is less than complete control over the variables in the study. Thus far, we have seen several examples of designs that should be considered quasi-experimental:

- Single-factor, nonequivalent groups design, with two or more levels.
- Nonequivalent groups factorial designs.
- P × E factorial designs.
- All of the correlational designs.

In this chapter, we will consider two designs typically found in texts on quasi-experimental designs (e.g., Cook & Campbell, 1979). They are called nonequivalent control group designs and interrupted time series designs. Other quasi-experimental designs exist, but these are the two most frequently encountered.

Nonequivalent Control Group Designs

In this type of study, the purpose is to evaluate the effectiveness of some treatment program. Those in the program are compared with those in a control group who aren't treated. The design is used when random assignment is not possible for one reason or another, so in addition to the independent variable, the control group differs in other some way(s) from the treatment group. That is, the groups are not equivalent to each other at the outset of the study. You will recognize this as a specific example of the design labeled a nonequivalent groups design in Chapter 7, a type of design comparing nonequal groups, often selected with reference to a subject variable like age, gender, or some personality characteristic. In the case of a **nonequivalent control group design**, the groups are not equal to each other at the start of the study; in addition, they experience different events in the study itself. Hence, there is a built-in confound that can cloud the interpretation of these studies. Nonetheless, they can be effective designs for evaluating treatment programs when random assignment is impossible. Following the scheme first outlined by Campbell and Stanley (1963), the design can be symbolized like this:

$$\text{experimental group:} \quad O_1 \quad \mathbf{T} \quad O_2$$
$$\text{nonequivalent control group:} \quad O_1 \quad \quad O_2$$

where O_1 and O_2 refer to pretests and posttests, respectively, and T refers to the treatment that is being evaluated. Because the groups might differ on the pretest, the important comparison between the groups is not simply a test for differences on the posttest, but a comparison of the different amounts of *change* from pre- to posttest in the two groups. Hence, the statistical comparison is between the change scores (the difference between O_1 and O_2) for each group. Let's make this a bit more concrete.

Suppose the management of an electric fry pan company wants to institute a new flextime work schedule. Workers will continue to work 40 hours per week, but the new schedule allows them to begin and end each day at different times and to put all of their hours into 4 days if they wish to have a 3-day weekend. Management hopes this will increase productivity by improving morale and sets up a quasi-experiment to see if it does. The company owns two plants, one just outside of Pittsburgh and the other near Cleveland. Through a coin toss, managers decide to make Pittsburgh's plant the experimental group and Cleveland's plant the control group. Thus, the study is quasi-experimental for the obvious reason that workers cannot be randomly assigned to the two plants (imagine the moving costs; legal fees over union grievances, etc.). The independent variable is whether or not flextime is present and the dependent variable is some measure of productivity. Let's suppose the final design looks like this:

Pittsburgh plant: pretest → average productivity for 1 month prior to
                                        instituting flextime
                        treatment → flextime instituted for 6 months
                        posttest → average productivity during sixth month of flex-
                                        time

Cleveland plant: pretest → average productivity for 1 month prior to
                                        instituting flextime in Pittsburgh
                        treatment → none
                        posttest → average productivity during the sixth month that
                                        flextime is in effect in Pittsburgh

Outcomes

Figure 9.3 shows you four different outcomes of this quasi-experiment. All the graphs show improved productivity for the Pittsburgh plant. The question is whether the improvement was due to the program or to some other factor(s). Before reading on, try to determine which of the graphs provides the strongest evidence that introducing flextime increased productivity and try to identify the threats to internal validity, which make it difficult to interpret the other outcomes.

I don't imagine you found it difficult to conclude that in Figure 9.3a, something besides the flextime produced the apparent improvement. This graph makes the importance of some type of control group obvious, even if it has to be a non-equivalent control group. Yes, the Pittsburgh productivity increased, but the same thing happened in Cleveland. Therefore, the Pittsburgh increase cannot be attributed to the program, but could have been due to several of the threats to internal validity that you've studied. History and maturation are good possibilities. Perhaps a national election intervened between pre- and posttest and workers everywhere felt more optimistic, leading to increased productivity. Perhaps workers just showed improvement with increased experience.

Figure 9.3b suggests that productivity at Cleveland was high throughout the study and that at Pittsburgh, productivity began at a very low level but improved due to the flextime program. However, there are two dangers here. First, the Cleveland scores might reflect a *ceiling effect* (see Chapter 7). That is, their productivity level is so high to begin with that no further improvement could possibly be shown. If an increase could be seen (i.e., if scores on the Y-axis could go higher), you might see two parallel lines, as in Figure 9.3a. The second problem is that be-

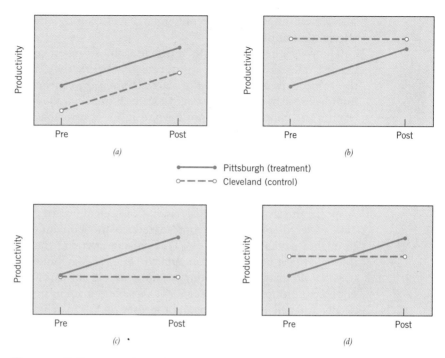

FIGURE 9.3 Hypothetical outcomes of a nonequivalent control group design.

cause Pittsburgh started so low, the increase there might be a regression effect rather than a true one.

Figure 9.3c seems at first glance to be the ideal outcome. Both groups start at the same level of productivity, but the group with the program (Pittsburgh) is the only one to improve. This may indeed be the case, and such an outcome generally makes applied researchers happy, but a problem can exist nonetheless. Because of the nonequivalent nature of the two groups, it is conceivable that subject selection could interact with some other influence. That is, some factor such as history or maturation could affect one plant but not the other. For example, it's not hard to imagine a selection by history problem here—some event affects the Pittsburgh plant but not the Cleveland plant. Perhaps the knowledge that they are participating in a study motivated the Pittsburgh workers (remember Hawthorne?). Perhaps between the pretest and the posttest, the Steelers won a Super Bowl; because workers in Pittsburgh are such avid sports fans, their general feeling of well-being could improve morale and therefore productivity. A selection by maturation effect might also account for the differences, although it would require that zero maturational change occurred at the Cleveland plant.

You've probably noted the similarity of Figures 9.3c and Figure 9.1 from the cognitive interview study. Fisher et al. (1989) did not randomly assign detectives to the training and nontraining group, but believed the two groups to be roughly equivalent nonetheless, based on a matching procedure using "information gathered in . . . preliminary interviews and the recommendations of the detectives' commanding officer" (Fisher et al., 1989, p. 724). Hence, they believed that the results shown in Figure 9.1 represented a real training effect and that any selection effects were minimal.

The outcome in Figure 9.3*d* provides the strongest support for program effectiveness. Here, the treatment group begins below the control group, yet surpasses the controls by the end of the study. Regression can be ruled out as causing the improvement because one would expect regression to raise the scores only to the level of the control group, not beyond it. Of course, selection problems and interactions between selection and other factors cannot be excluded completely, but this type of crossover effect is generally considered to be good evidence for program effectiveness (Cook & Campbell, 1979).

Regression and Matching

A special threat to the internal validity of nonequivalent control groups designs occurs when there is an attempt to reduce the nonequivalency of diverse groups through a matching procedure. This did not occur in the example we just worked through, but it often occurs in applied research. Matching was described in Chapter 6 as an alternative to random assignment, and it works reasonably well to create equivalent groups if the independent variable is manipulated and subjects can be randomly assigned after being paired together on the matching variable (see Chapter 6, to review matching). However, it can be a problem in nonequivalent control group designs when the two groups are sampled from populations that are significantly different from each other on the matching variable. If this occurs, then using a matching procedure can enhance the influence of a **regression effect** and make it appear that a successful program has failed. Let's look at a hypothetical example.

Suppose you are developing a program to improve the reading skills of disadvantaged youth. You advertise for volunteers to participate in an innovative reading program and select those most in need. To create a control group that controls for socioeconomic class, you recruit additional volunteers from similar neighborhoods in other cities. Your main concern is with equating the groups for initial reading skill, so you decide to match the two groups on this variable. You administer a reading skills pretest and use it to form two groups *that will have the same average score*. Let's say the test scores range from 0 to 50. You select children for the two groups so that the average score is 25 for both groups. The treatment group then gets the program, and the control group doesn't; the design is a typical nonequivalent control group design:

group 1:   pretest   reading   posttest
                              program
group 2:   pretest   —   posttest

Naturally, you're excited about the prospects of this study because you really believe the reading program is unique and will help lots of children. Hence, you're shocked when these reading scores occur:

group 1:   pre = 25   treatment   post = 25
group 2:   pre = 25   —   post = 29

Not only did the program not seem to work, but it appears that it even hindered the development of reading skills—the control group improved! What happened?

A strong possibility here is that regression effects resulting from the matching procedure overwhelmed any possible treatment effect. Remember that group 1 was formed from those with the greatest need for the program because their skills were so weak. If the reading pretest were given to *all* children who fall into this category (i.e., the population), the average score might be quite low, say, 17. When using the matching procedure, however, you were forced to select children who scored much higher than the average child from this population of "poor readers." At least some of those children scored higher than they should have on the pretest because no test is perfectly reliable—some degree of measurement error is likely to occur. Therefore, on a posttest, many of these children will score lower simply due to regression to the mean. Let's suppose the program truly was effective and should add an average of 4 points to the reading score. However, if the average regression effect was a loss of 4 points, this would account for the apparent lack of change from pre- to posttest:

$$[25] + [+4] + [-4] = [25].$$

For subjects in the control group, just the opposite might have occurred. Maybe their population score was much higher than 25 (35 perhaps). Maybe they were pretty good readers to begin with (i.e., from a different population than the other group). Selecting subjects who scored much lower than their population mean, in order to produce matching pretest scores, could result in a regression effect producing higher posttest scores. For these children, the posttest score would result from the same 4-point regression effect used previously. Thus,

$$[25] + [0] + [+4] = [29]$$

In sum, the program might actually have been a good idea, but the matching procedure caused a regression effect that masked its effectiveness.

This type of regression artifact apparently occurred during the first large-scale attempt to evaluate the effectiveness of Head Start, one of the cornerstone programs of President Lyndon Johnson's "Great Society" initiative in the 1960s (Campbell & Erlebacher, 1970). The program originated in 1965 as an ambitious attempt to give underprivileged preschool children a "head start" on school by teaching them various school-related skills and getting their parents involved in the process. By 1990, about 11 million children had participated (Horn, 1990), and Head Start is now recognized as perhaps the most successful social program run by the federal government. Yet in the early 1970s, it was under attack for its "failure" to produce lasting effects, largely on the basis of what has come to be known as the Westinghouse study (because the study was funded by a grant to the Westinghouse Learning Corporation and Ohio University), conducted by Victor Cicirelli and his colleagues (1969).

The Westinghouse study documented what it called "fade-out effects"—early gains by children in Head Start programs seemed to fade away by the third grade. The implication, of course, was that perhaps federal dollars were being wasted on ineffective social programs, a point made by President Nixon in an address to Congress, in which he explicitly referred to the Westinghouse study. Consequently, funding for Head Start came under attack during the Nixon years. At the same time, the basis for the criticism, the Westinghouse study, was being assaulted by social scientists.

Because Head Start was well underway when the evaluation project began, children couldn't be randomly assigned to treatment and control groups. Instead, the Westinghouse group selected a group of Head Start children and matched them for cognitive achievement with children who hadn't been through the program. However, in order to match the groups on cognitive achievement, Head Start children selected for the study were those scoring well above the mean for their overall group and control children were those scoring well below their mean. This is precisely the situation just described in the hypothetical case of a program to improve reading skills. Hence, the Head Start group's apparent failure to show improvement in the third grade was at least partially the result of a regression artifact caused by the matching procedure (Campbell & Erlebacher, 1969).

In fairness to the Westinghouse group, it should be pointed out that they would have disagreed vehemently with politicians who wished to cut the program. Cicirelli (1984) insisted that the study *"did not conclude that Head Start was a failure"* (p. 915, italics in the original), that more research was necessary, and that "vigorous and intensive approaches to expanding and enriching the program" (p. 916) be undertaken. More recently, Cicirelli (1993) pointed out that a key recommendation of the Westinghouse study was "not to eliminate Head Start but to try harder to make it work, based on encouraging findings from full-year programs" (p. 32).

Nonequivalent control group designs do not always produce the type of controversy that engulfed the Westinghouse study. Consider the following case study of earthquakes and nightmares.

Case Study 2. A Nonequivalent Control Group Design

Chapter 3 described a number of ways to develop ideas for research projects. Sometimes a study develops when a rare, unlikely-to-be-repeated event provides an opportunity to learn something about behavior. Such an event was the 1989 San Francisco earthquake, which occurred just prior to the beginning of a World Series game at 5:04 on October 17. To James Wood and Richard Bootzin of the University of Arizona, the event suggested an idea for a study about nightmares, a topic of interest to them (Wood & Bootzin, 1990). Along with several colleagues from Stanford University (located closer the quake's epicenter than San Francisco), they quickly designed a study to see if the experience of such a traumatic event would affect dream content in general and nightmares in particular (Wood, Bootzin, Rosenhan, Nolen-Hoeksema, & Jourden, 1992). By necessity, they used a nonequivalent control group design.

The experimental group consisted of students from Stanford and San Jose State University, who experienced the earthquake. Control subjects were also college students, recruited from the University of Arizona. They did not experience the quake, of course, but they were exposed to the extensive media accounts of it. Within days of the earthquake, subjects for both groups were recruited and began keeping a daily record of their dreams. As a control measure, subjects were not told that they would be recording dreams and nightmares until after they agreed to participate. This reduced the chances of the study attracting students who might be prone to report lots of nightmares, even if they didn't really experience them. Naturally, subjects were free to leave the study after it began.

The results were intriguing. Over the 3 weeks of the study, approximately 40% of those who experienced the quake had at least one nightmare; only 5% of the control subjects did. Of the nightmares experienced by the first group, roughly one fourth were about earthquakes. Virtually none of the control group's nightmares were about quakes. Furthermore, the frequency of nightmares correlated significantly with how anxious subjects reported they were during the time of the earthquake.

In the manner of careful researchers everywhere, Wood et al. (1992) acknowledged some of the problems in interpreting their results. For example, they recognized the dangers inherent in making comparisons between nonequivalent groups. Perhaps the nightmare frequencies resulted from aftershocks that would be experienced by one group but not the other. Also, lacking any pretest ("prequake") information about nightmare frequency for their subjects, they couldn't "rule out the possibility that California residents have more nightmares about earthquakes than do Arizona residents even when no earthquake has recently occurred" (Wood et al., 1992, p. 222). If one lives in California, perhaps earthquake nightmares are a normal occurrence. However, relying partly on their general expertise in the area of nightmare research, the authors argued that the nightmare frequency was exceptionally high in the California group and was likely to be the result of their recent traumatic experience. On balance, the study is a nice demonstration that experiencing an emotionally trying event leads to bad dreams about that event.

Interrupted Time Series Designs

If Wood and his colleagues could have foreseen San Francisco's earthquake, they might have started collecting nightmare data from their subjects for several months leading up to the quake and then for several months after the quake. That would enable them to determine (a) if the quake truly increased nightmare experiences for the subjects in the quake zone and (b) if the nightmare frequency peaked shortly after the quake, then returned to baseline. Of course, not even talented research psychologists can predict earthquakes yet, so Wood and his coworkers did the best they could and designed a nonequivalent control group study. If they had been able to take measures for an extended period before and after the critical event, their study would have been called an **interrupted time series design**.

Using the system in Campbell and Stanley (1963) again, the basic time series study can be symbolized like this:

$$O_1 \; O_2 \; O_3 \; O_4 \; O_5 \; \mathbf{T} \; O_6 \; O_7 \; O_8 \; O_9 \; O_{10}$$

where all the O's represent measures taken before and after T, which is the point where some treatment program is introduced or some event (like an earthquake) occurs. T is the "interruption" in the interrupted time series. Of course, the number of measures taken before and after T will vary from study to study and are not limited to a total of five each.

Outcomes

The main advantage of a time series design is that it allows one to evaluate **trends**, which are predictable patterns of events that occur with the passing of time. For example, suppose you were interested in seeing the effects of a two-month anti-smoking campaign on the number of teenage smokers in a community. The pro-

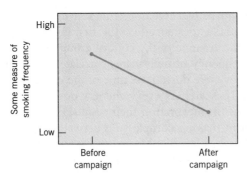

FIGURE 9.4 Incidence of smoking behavior just before and just after a hypothetical antismoking campaign.

gram might include some persuasion techniques, peer counseling, showing the teens a smoked-out lung or two, and so on. Assuming that you had a good measure of the smoking behavior, you could take the measure a few months before and a few months after introducing the program and perhaps get the results in Figure 9.4.

Did the program work? There certainly is a reduction in smoking, but it's hard to evaluate it in the absence of a control group. Yet even without a control group, it might be possible to see if the campaign worked if not one but several measures were taken both before and after the program was put in place. Consider the possible outcomes in Figure 9.5., which shows the effects of the antismoking campaign

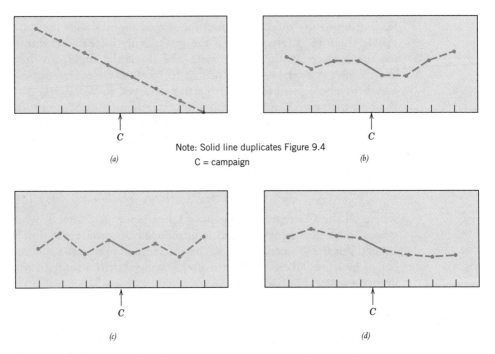

FIGURE 9.5 Hypothetical antismoking campaign evaluated with an interrupted time series design—several outcomes.

by measuring smoking behavior every 3 months for a year before and a year after the program.

Figure 9.5*a* is a good illustration of how an interrupted time series can identify trends. In this case, the reduction that looked so good in Figure 9.4 is shown to be nothing more than part of a general trend toward reduced smoking. This demonstrates an important feature of interrupted time series designs—they can serve to rule out (i.e., falsify, remember?) alternative explanations of an apparent change from pre- to posttest.

Two other outcomes that raise questions about the program's effectiveness are in Figures 9.5*b* and 9.5*c*. In 9.5*b*, smoking behavior was fairly steady before the campaign, then dropped, but just briefly. In other words, if the antismoking program had any effect, it was short-lived. In 9.5*c*, the decrease after the program was part of another general trend, this time a periodic fluctuation between higher and lower levels of smoking. The ideal outcome is shown in Figure 9.5*d*. Here, the smoking behavior is at a steady and high rate before the program begins, drops after the antismoking program has been put into effect, and remains low for some time after. Note also in 9.5*d* that the relatively steady baseline prior to the campaign enables the researcher to rule out regression effects.

Case Study 3. An Interrupted Time Series Design

An actual example of an outcome like this last one can be found in a study of worker productivity completed at an iron foundry by Wagner, Rubin, and Callahan (1988). They were interested in the effect of instituting an incentive plan that featured treating workers not as individuals but as members of small groups, each responsible for an entire production line. Productivity data were compiled over a period of about 10 years, 4 years prior to introducing the incentive plan and 6 years after. As you can see from their time series plot in Figure 9.6, productivity was fairly flat and not very impressive prior to the plan, but increased steadily after the plan was implemented.

This study also illustrates how those conducting interrupted time series designs try to deal with potential threats to internal validity. Figure 9.6 certainly appears to show that the incentive plan worked wonders, but the changes could have been influenced by other factors, including history, instrumentation, and selection. The authors argued that history did not contribute to the change, however, because they carefully examined as many events as they could in the period before and after the change and could find no reason to suspect that some unusual occurrence led to the increase in productivity. In fact, some events that might be expected to hurt productivity (e.g., recession in the automobile industry, which affected sales of iron castings) didn't. The researchers also ruled out instrumentation, which could be a problem if the method for recording worker productivity changed over the years. It didn't. Third, although we normally think of subject selection being a potential confound only in studies with two or more nonequivalent groups, it can occur in a time series if significant worker turnover occurred around the time of the new plan. It didn't. In short, designs like this one are susceptible to several threats to internal validity, but these threats often can be ruled out by carefully examining available information, as Wagner and his colleagues did.

Sometimes the conclusions from an interrupted time series design can be

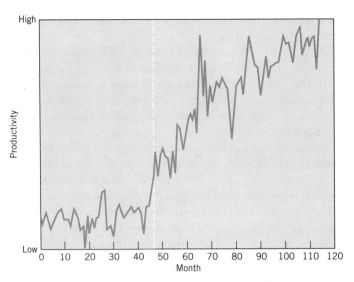

FIGURE 9.6   Interrupted time series design; effect of an incentive plan on worker productivity in an iron foundry [from Wagner, Rubin, & Callahan (1968)].

strengthened if a control comparison can be made. In essence, this procedure amounts to combining the best features of the nonequivalent control group design (a control group) and the interrupted time series design (long-term trend analysis). The design looks like this:

$$O_1 \; O_2 \; O_3 \; O_4 \; O_5 \; \mathbf{T} \; O_6 \; O_7 \; O_8 \; O_9 \; O_{10}$$
$$O_1 \; O_2 \; O_3 \; O_4 \; O_5 \qquad O_6 \; O_7 \; O_8 \; O_9 \; O_{10}$$

Furthermore, it is sometimes possible to find a second experimental condition in which the treatment is introduced earlier or later than is the case for the first experimental group. When this occurs, the second experimental group is sometimes referred to as a "switching replication," and the design as a whole looks like this:

$$O_1 \; O_2 \; O_3 \; O_4 \; O_5 \; \mathbf{T} \; O_6 \; O_7 \; O_8 \; O_9 \; O_{10}$$
$$O_1 \; O_2 \; O_3 \; \mathbf{T} \; O_4 \; O_5 \; O_6 \; O_7 \; O_8 \; O_9 \; O_{10}$$
$$O_1 \; O_2 \; O_3 \; O_4 \; O_5 \qquad O_6 \; O_7 \; O_8 \; O_9 \; O_{10}$$

The advantage of a switching replication is that it helps evaluate a general history threat because such an effect should bring about change in both groups at a single point in time. External validity is also enhanced because a program can be shown to be effective in two different places at two different times. An example of this strategy is the following case study by West, Hepworth, McCall, and Reich (1989).

Case Study 4. An Interrupted Time Series with Controls

The study evaluated the effects of a program to deal with one of society's more difficult problems—drunk driving. The state of Arizona enacted a tough drunk driving law in the summer of 1982. The Driving While Intoxicated (DWI) law provided for mandatory jail sentences, stiff fines, and license suspension, even for first-time offenders. West et al. (1989) designed an interrupted time series study to see if the law reduced traffic fatalities and DWI citations for one of Arizona's major cities, Phoenix. Two other (nonequivalent) cities, El Paso, Texas, and San Diego, California, were used for comparison purposes. Both cities were similar to Phoenix in climate and size and all three cities were from the same general geographic region (southwest). El Paso was the nonequivalent control group; during the time of the study there were no changes in the drunk driving law there. San Diego was chosen as a switching replication because the city was affected by a change in California law 6 months prior to the change in Arizona law. California's DWI law changed in January 1982; Arizona's in the following July. In both cases, the law moved in the direction of increased strictness.

Data on traffic fatalities and DWI citations were collected from the three cities between 1976 and 1984. Qualitative data in the form of interviews with judges and other professionals in the judicial system were included also. Figure 9.7 shows the results. Each point represents the mean number of fatalities over a 5-month

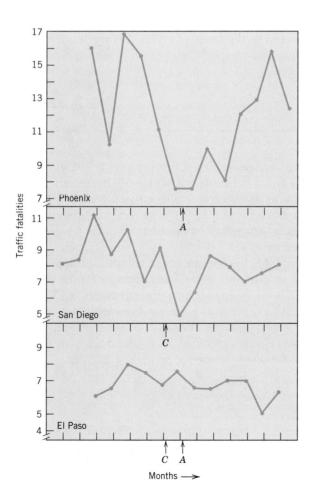

FIGURE 9.7 Interrupted time series with a nonequivalent control and a switching replication; short-term effects of changing drunk driving laws on traffic fatalities [adapted from West et al. (1989)].

block, and the approximate point when the laws changed are indicated by the A (Arizona) and the C (California). Compared with El Paso, which showed a steady fatality rate that was unaffected by the changes going on in Arizona and California, both Phoenix and San Diego showed a significant drop in fatalities. Unfortunately, in both cities, the drop seemed only temporary. West et al. (1989) were encouraged by the outcome, however, arguing that the "rate of decay of the effectiveness of the Arizona and California laws was much slower than has typically been found in previous evaluations of the effectiveness of harsher penalties for drunk driving" (p. 1233).

One other finding of note was that if you look at the Phoenix data you will notice that the drop in fatalities seemed to occur even before the law was implemented. It could be that some publicity from the new California law had an effect, but a more likely explanation was increased media coverage in Phoenix. For 6 months prior to the enactment of the new law, there was a large boost in media coverage of drunk driving and the fact that the new law in Arizona would represent a major crackdown.

Incidentally, the way this increase in media coverage was documented also gives you a hint of what it is like to be a graduate student. West reported that "[s]everal research assistants [guess who?] identified and measured in square inches the total amount of space devoted to the issues of drunk driving . . . in the highest circulation Phoenix morning newspaper" for a period of several months (p. 1217).

Program Evaluation

The attempt to assess changes in drunk driving laws is just one example of a type of applied research known as program evaluation. This research area developed in the 1960s in response to the need to evaluate social programs like Head Start, but it is concerned with much more than just answering the question "Did program X work?" More generally, **program evaluation** includes (a) procedures for determining if a true need exists for a particular program and who would benefit from implementing the program, (b) assessments of whether an implemented program is being run according to plan and if not, what changes can be made to facilitate its operation, (c) methods for evaluating program outcomes, and (d) cost analyses to determine if program benefits justify the funds expended. Let's consider each in turn. First, however, you should read Box 9.2, which highlights a paper by Donald Campbell (1969) that is always included at or near the top of the list of the "most important papers in the young history of program evaluation."

Planning for Programs

Agencies begin programs because administrators believe a need exists that would be met by the program. How is that need determined? Clearly, more is required than just an administrative decision that a program seems to make sense. An exercise program in a retirement community sounds quite reasonable, but if none of

Box 9.2

CLASSIC STUDIES — Reforms as Experiments

The 1969 article by Campbell, entitled "Reforms as Experiments," is notable for three reasons. First, it argues forcefully that we should have an experimental attitude about social reform. In the opening sentence, Campbell argued for applying the scientific way of thinking by writing that we

. . . should be ready for an experimental approach to social reform, an approach in which we try out new programs designed to cure specific social problems, in which we learn whether or not these programs are effective, and in which we retain, imitate, modify, or discard them on the basis of apparent effectiveness. (p. 409).

Second, Campbell's article describes several studies that have become classics in the field of program evaluation and prototypical examples of designs like the interrupted time series and the time series with controls. Pehaps the best known example is his description of a study to evaluate an effort to reduce speeding in Connecticut (Campbell & Ross, 1968). Following a year (1955) with a record number of 324 traffic fatalities, Governor Abraham Ribicoff instituted a statewide crackdown on speeding, making the reasonable assumption that speeding and traffic fatalities were correlated. The following year, the number of deaths fell to 284. This statistic was sufficient for Rubicoff to declare that with "the saving of 40 lives in 1956, a reduction of 12.3% from the 1955 . . . death toll, we can say that the program is definitely worthwhile" (quoted in Campbell, 1969, p. 412). Was it?

I hope you're saying to yourself that other interpretations of the drop are possible. For example, history could be involved; perhaps the weather was better and the roads were drier in 1956. Even more likely is regression — the 324 is a perfect example of an extreme score that would normally be followed by regression to the mean. Indeed, Campbell argued that regression contributed to the Connecticut results, pointing out that "[r]egression artifacts are probably the most recurrent form of self-deception in the experimental social reform literature" (p. 414). Such effects frequently occur in these studies because interventions like a speeding crackdown often begin right after something especially bad has happened. Purely by chance alone, things are not likely to be as bad the following year.

Was regression all that was involved here? Probably not. By applying an interrupted time series design with a nonequivalent control (nearby states without a crackdown on speeding), Campbell concluded that the crackdown probably did have some effect, even if it was not as dramatic as believed by the governor. You can see the results for yourself in Figure 9.8.

The third reason why the Campbell article is so important is that it gave researchers some insight into the political realities of doing research on socially

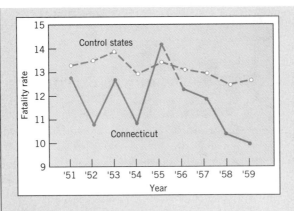

FIGURE 9.8 The Connecticut speeding crackdown; a classic example of an interrupted time series with a nonequivalent control [from Campbell (1969)].

relevant issues. Politicians often propose programs they believe will be effective, and while they might say they're interested in a thorough evaluation, they tend not to be too interested if the evaluation is negative. After all, by backing the program, they have a stake in its success and its continuance, especially if the program benefits the politician's home state or district. For this reason, politicians and the administrators hired to run programs seldom push for rigorous evaluation and are willing to settle for favorable research outcomes even if they come from flawed designs. For example, Governor Ribicoff was willing to settle for looking at no more than traffic fatalities immediately before and right after the crackdown on speeding.

Campbell recommended an attitude change that would shift emphasis from stressing the importance of a particular *program* to acknowledging the importance of the *problem*. This would lead politicians and administrators alike to think of programs as experimental attempts to solve the problem; different programs would be tried until one was found to work. As Campbell put it in the article's conclusion,

> *Trapped administrators* have so committed themselves in advance to the efficacy of the reform that they cannot afford an honest evaluation. . . . *Experimental administrators* have justified the reform on the basis of the importance of the problem, not the certainty of their answer, and are committed to going on to other potential solutions if the first one tried fails. They are therefore not threatened by a hard-headed analysis of the reform. (1969, p. 428, italics in the original)

the residents will participate, much time and money will be wasted. Before any project is even planned in any detail, some type of needs assessment should be completed.

Needs assessment is a procedure for predicting whether a population of sufficient size exists that would benefit from the proposed program and whether members of this population would actually use the program. Several systematic methods exist for estimating need, and it is important to rely on at least some of these techniques because it is easy to overestimate need. All it takes is several highly publicized cases of children being abandoned by vacationing parents for a call to be made for new programs to fix the problem somehow. Also, needs can be overestimated by those in a position to benefit (i.e., keep their jobs) from the existence of a particular program.

As outlined by Posavac and Carey (1985), there are several ways to identify the potential need for a program. These include

✓ *Census Data.* If your proposed program is aimed at the elderly, it's fairly obvious that its success will be minimal if there are very few seniors living in the community. Census data can provide basic demographic information about the number of people fitting into various categories. Furthermore, the information is fine-grained enough for you to determine such things as the number of single mothers under age 21, the number of people with various disabilities, or the number of elderly people below the poverty line.

In addition to census data, organizations might have some archival data available. For instance, a corporation thinking of starting a worksite day care center can examine its own files to estimate the number of employees who are working parents of young children. Finally, published research can also provide important information about need. Studies showing long-term decreases in IQ for children raised in impoverished environments provide strong evidence of a need for enrichment programs.

✓ *Surveys of Existing Programs.* There's no reason to begin a "meals on wheels" program if one already exists in the community and is functioning successfully. Thus, one obvious step in a needs assessment is to create an inventory of existing services. Part of the inventory will be an estimate of how many people are receiving existing services. You might discover, for example, that an existing meals on wheels program has such a limited budget that it is meeting no more than 10% of the need. In that case, developing a second program to cover a different part of town would be worthwhile.

✓ *Surveys of Residents.* A third needs assessment strategy is to administer a survey within the community, either to a broadly representative sample or to a target group identified by census data. Those participating could be asked whether they believe a particular program is needed. More importantly, the survey might enable the planner to estimate just how many people would actually use the proposed program.

An example of a thorough assessment of need is a project completed by the Du Pont Company prior to starting a program designed to promote healthy behaviors in the workplace (Bertera, 1990). The plan called for implementing a series of changes that would affect over 110,000 employees at 100 worksites. The obvious cost of putting such an ambitious plan into effect made it essential that need be demonstrated clearly.

The Du Pont needs assessment included an analysis of existing data on the frequency of various types of employee illnesses, on employee causes of death, and on the reasons for employee absence and disability over a 15-year period. One unanticipated result was that employees making the least amount of money and in the lowest-ranking jobs were the highest on all major categories of illness. That finding told the evaluators that this subgroup of workers needed special attention.

Additional indicators that the health promotion program was needed came from an audit of existed company programs for enhancing health (there were only a few) and surveys of employees to determine their knowledge of health-enhancing behaviors, their intentions to change things like eating habits, their self-assessments of whether their own behaviors were health enhancing or not, and their preferences for a range of health programs. On the basis of all of this information, Du Pont developed a comprehensive series of programs aimed at improving the health of its workers.

Once the needs assessment is complete and the decision is made to proceed, details of the program can be planned and the program begun. Once the program is underway, the second type of evaluation activity starts.

Monitoring Programs

Programs often extend over a considerable period of time. To wait a year or so before doing a final evaluation of program effectiveness might be nice and clean from a strict methodological point of view, but what if it is clear in the first month that problems exist that could be corrected easily? That is, rather than waiting until the program's completion, why not carefully monitor the progress of the program while it is in progress? This monitoring is called a **formative evaluation**. Recent analysis suggests that it is the most common form of evaluation activity (Sechrest & Figueredo, 1993).

A formative evaluation can include several components. For one thing, it determines if the program is being implemented as planned. For example, suppose a local crisis hotline decides to develop a new program aimed at the needs of young children who are home alone after school while their parents are still working. One important piece of the implementation plan is to make the new phone number available and well-known. A formative evaluation would determine whether the planned ads were actually placed in the newspapers at appropriate times and whether mass mailings of stickers with the number went out as planned. Also, a sample of residents could be called and asked if they'd heard of the new hotline for kids. There's no point in trying to evaluate the effectiveness of the program if people don't even know about it.

A second general function of the formative evaluation is to provide clear and continuing data on how the program is being used. Borrowing a term from accounting, evaluators sometimes refer to this procedure as a **program audit**. Just as a corporate auditor might look for inconsistencies between the way inventories are supposed to be managed and the way they are actually managed, the program auditor examines whether the program as described in the agency's literature is the same as the program that is actually being implemented.

Evaluating Outcomes

Politically, formative evaluations are less threatening than **summative evaluations**, which are overall assessments of program effectiveness. Formative evaluation is aimed at program improvement and is less likely to call into question the very existence of a program. Summative evaluation, on the other hand, can do just that. If the program isn't effective why keep it, and by extension, why continue to pay the program's director and staff (see what I mean about "threatening?") As Sechrest and Figueredo (1993) stated it,

> summative evaluation and even the rationale for doing it all call into question the very reasons for the existence of the organizations involved. Formative evaluation, by contrast, simply responds to the question 'How can we be better?' without strongly implying the question 'How do [we] know [we] are any good at all?' (p. 661)

Despite this political difficulty, summative evaluations are the core of the evaluation process and are an essential feature of any program funded by the federal government. Any agency wishing to spend tax dollars to develop a program is obligated to show that those dollars are being used effectively.

The actual process of performing summative evaluations involves applying some of the techniques you already know about, especially those having to do with quasi-experimental designs. However, more rigorous experiments with random assignment are possible sometimes, especially when evaluating a program that has more people desiring it than space available. In such a case, random assignment in the form of a lottery (random winners get the program; others get a waiting list) is not only methodologically ideal, it is also the only fair procedure to use.

One problem that sometimes confronts the program evaluator is how to interpret a failure to find significant differences between experimental and control groups. That is, the statistical decision is "fail to reject H_0." Such an outcome can be difficult to interpret. It could be that there just isn't any difference, yet there's always the possibility of a Type II error (see Chapter 4) being committed, especially if the measuring tools are not very sensitive or very reliable. The program might indeed have produced some small but important effect, but the analysis failed to discover it.

Although a finding of no difference can be problematic, most researchers believe that such a finding (especially if replicated) contributes important information for decision making, especially in applied research. For instance, someone advocating the continuation of a new program is obligated to show how the program is better than something already in existence. Yet if differences between experimental and control subjects cannot be shown, then perhaps it is wise to discontinue the new program (especially if it is expensive). Indeed, as Yeaton and Sechrest (1986) demonstrated, there may be life and death issues involved. They cite a study comparing different treatments for breast cancer that varied in the degree of surgical invasiveness. Survival rates for women undergoing minimally invasive procedures were *not* significantly different from the rates for women subjected to radical mastectomies. Such an outcome is an example of "failing to reject H_0." Should the results be ignored because no significant differences were found? Of course not. If the same outcome occurs with a less traumatic treatment procedure, why take the more radical step? Of course, the confidence one has in decisions made on the basis of a finding of "no difference" is directly related to how often such a finding has been replicated. A recommendation to rely on minimal surgical procedures only follows from repeated failures to find a difference between major and minor procedures.

A "fail to reject H_0" decision also can help evaluate excessive claims made by proponents of some new "miracle cure." Someone claiming to cure some serious mental disorder with a "revolutionary" new technique, for example, has the burden of showing that those given the procedure show significantly more improvement than those treated more conventionally.

As implied in these "failure to reject H_0" examples, a finding of no difference has important implications for decision making for reasons having to do with cost, and this brings us to the final type of program evaluation activity.

Weighing Costs

Suppose a researcher is interested in the question of worker health and fitness and is comparing two health-enhancement programs. One includes opportunities for exercising on company time, educational seminars on stress management, and a smoking ban. The second plan is a more comprehensive (and more expensive) program of evaluating each worker and developing an individually tailored fitness program, along with bonus incentives for things like reducing blood pressure and cholesterol levels. Both programs are implemented on a trial basis in two plant locations; a third plant is used as a control group. Hence, the design is a nonequivalent control group design with two experimental groups instead of just one. A summative evaluation finds no differences between the two experimental groups in terms of improved worker health, but both show improvements compared to the control group. That is, a health program works, but the Chevy version works just as well as the Cadillac version. If two programs producing the same outcome differ in cost, why bother with the expensive one?

This corporate fitness example illustrates one type of **cost-effectiveness analysis**, that is, monitoring the actual costs of a program and relating those costs to the effectiveness of the program's outcomes. If two programs with the same goal are equally effective, but the first costs half as much as the second, then it is fairly obvious that the first program should be used. A second type of cost analysis takes place during the planning stages for a program. Estimating costs at the outset helps determine whether a program is even feasible and provides a basis for comparison later between projected costs and actual costs.

A study by Erfurt, Foote, and Heirich (1992) provides an illustration of a cost-effectiveness analysis. They compared several "worksite wellness programs" at four automobile manufacturing plants. One of their findings was that "[t]he addition of a physical fitness facility (Site B) did not produce any incremental benefit in reducing [health] risks, as compared with health education classes (Site A) . . ." (p. 5). Because the cost per employee at Site A was $17.68, compared with $39.28 for Site B, it appeared that the fitness facility was either a bad idea (i.e., not worth the money), or was not being used properly.

Estimating costs with reference to outcomes can be a complicated process, often requiring the expertise of a specialist in cost accounting. Thus, a detailed discussion of the procedures for relating costs to outcomes is beyond the scope of this chapter, an opinion shared by my wife, who happens to be a cost accountant and finds my rudimentary knowledge amusing. Some of the basic concepts of a cost analysis can be discovered by reading Chapter 11 of Posavac and Carey's (1985) fine introduction to program evaluation. However, even these experts felt it necessary to caution the reader that learning the techniques involved with a cost analysis require considerable training.

As first mentioned in the discussion of external validity in Chapter 5, research in psychology is sometimes criticized for avoiding so-called real-world investigations. This chapter on applied research should make it clear that the criticism is without merit. Indeed, concern over application and generalizability of results is not far from the consciousness of all psychologists, even those committed primarily to basic research. It is evident from psychology's history that application is central to American psychology, if for no other reason than the fact that Americans can't help it. Looking for practical applications is as American as apple pie.

The next chapter introduces a slightly different tradition in psychological research—an emphasis on the intensive study of individuals. As you'll see, just as the roots of applied research can be found among psychology's pioneers, experiments with $N = 1$ also trace to the beginnings of the discipline.

Chapter Review

Glossary Fill-Ins

1. In order to determine if a new program for improving the literacy of unemployed adults was successful, the local agency running the program decided to conduct a _____ evaluation.

2. Early program evaluations of Head Start seemed to show that gains made by Head Start children were short lived; by the third grade, no differences existed between those who had been in the program and those who hadn't been in it. However, this outcome might have been the result of a _____ effect brought about by the matching procedure used to form the groups.

3. Because measurements are taken for such a long period of time, an interrupted time series design allows the researcher to evaluate the influence of _____.

4. A comparison of worker productivity at two plants, after an incentive program has been introduced at one of them, is most likely to involve a(n) _____ design.

5. Doing a survey of existing programs is an important part of the program evaluation procedure called _____.

6. A(n) _____ design is the best way to evaluate the effects of changing the drinking age on the number of alcohol-related fatalities.

Multiple Choice

1. As a general rule, applied research
   a. Is most likely to take place outside the laboratory.

  b. Is a recent development in the history of American psychology.

  c. Produces results that are irrelevant for testing general theories of behavior.

  d. Is synonymous with program evaluation research.

2. Which of the following is *not* one of problems encountered by applied research?

  a. Informed consent of the participants.

  b. The results seldom help to understand fundamental psychological phenomena.

  c. Reduced internal validity.

  d. Creating equivalent groups.

3. In a nonequivalent control group design,

  a. It is essential that both groups score the same on the pretest.

  b. Subjects should be randomly assigned if the experimental program only can accommodate a few people but many people are available.

  c. The important measure is usually the amount of change between the pretest and the posttest.

  d. A selection × history confound can be ruled out.

4. Suppose Ohio decides to implement a child restraint seatbelt law and wishes to evaluate its effectiveness with a time series design. It compares itself with Pennsylvania, which instituted essentially the same law 1 year earlier than Ohio. The Pennsylvania data is called

  a. A switching replication

  b. A nonequivalent control

  c. An equivalent control

  d. A trend

5. A family service agency implements a new program for debt counseling. A program evaluator periodically sits in on and assesses a debt counseling session to see if the plan is being followed. What type of program evaluation procedure is this?

  a. Needs assessment

  b. Summative evaluation

  c. Cost analysis

  d. Formative evaluation

Applications Exercises

Exercise 9.1 — Identifying Threats to Internal Validity

Threats to internal validity are common in quasi-experimental studies. What follows is a list of some threats that you've encountered in this chapter and in Chapter 5. For each of the hypothetical experiments that are described, identify which of these treats is most likely to provide a reasonable alternative explanation of the outcome.

Some Threats to Internal Validity

- History
- Regression
- Attrition
- Maturation
- Selection
- Selection × History

1. A college dean is upset about the so-called attrition rate—the percentage of freshman who return to the college as sophomores. Historically, the rate has been around 75%, but in the academic year just begun, only 60% of last year's freshmen return. The dean puts a tutoring program into effect and then claims credit for its effectiveness when the following year's attrition rate is 71%.

2. Two nearby colleges agree to cooperate in evaluating a new computerized instructional system. College A gets the program, and college B doesn't. Midway through the study, college B announces that it has filed for bankruptcy. One year later, computer literacy is higher at college A.

3. Twelve women who ask to be considered for a home birthing program are compared with a random sample of other pregnant women who undergo normal hospital procedures for childbirth. Women in the first group spend an average of 6 hours in labor, while those in the control group spend an average 9 hours in labor.

4. A 6-week program in managing test anxiety is developed and given to a sample of first-semester college freshmen. Their anxiety levels are significantly lower at the conclusion of the program than they were at the start.

5. A teacher decides to use an innovative teaching technique in which all students will proceed at their own pace throughout the term. The course will have ten units and each student goes to unit N after completing unit N-1. Once all ten units have been completed, the course is over and an A has been earned. Of the initial 30 students enrolled in the class, the final grade distribution looks like this:

$$A \rightarrow 16 \qquad F \rightarrow 2 \qquad W \rightarrow 12$$

The instructor considers the new course format a success.

Exercise 9.2 — Interpreting Nonequivalent Control Group Studies

A wheel bearing manufacturer owns two plants, both in Ohio. She wishes to see if money for health costs can be reduced if a wellness program is instituted. One plant (E) is selected to be given a year-long experimental program that includes health screening and individually tailored fitness activities. The second plant (C) is the control group. Absentee-due-to-sickness rates, operationally defined as the number of sick days per year per 100 employees, are measured at the beginning and end of the experimental year. What follows are four sets of results. Construct a graph for each and decide which (if any) provide evidence of program effectiveness. For those outcomes not supporting the program's effectiveness, provide an alternative explanation for the experimental group's apparent improvement.

Outcome 1.   E: pretest = 125   posttest = 90
                C: pretest = 125   posttest = 120
Outcome 2.   E: pretest = 125   posttest = 90
                C: pretest = 90   posttest = 90
Outcome 3.   E: pretest = 125   posttest = 90
                C: pretest = 110   posttest = 110
Outcome 4.   E: pretest = 125   posttest = 90
                C: pretest = 140   posttest = 105

Exercise 9.3 — Interpreting Time Series Studies

Imagine a time series study evaluating the effects of a helmet law on head injuries among hockey players. Injuries were significantly lower in the year the law was passed than in the immediately preceding year. Construct three time series graphs, one for each of the following patterns of results.

a. The helmet law worked!
b. The helmet law seemed to work initially, but its effects were temporary.
c. The helmet law had no effect; the apparent drop was probably a regression effect.
d. The helmet law didn't really work; the apparent drop seemed to reflect a general trend toward reduced violence in the sport.

Exercise 9.4 — Planning a Needs Assessment

You are the head of a five-person psychology department at a liberal arts college. One day, the Dean says to you, "Why don't you develop a Master's program in counseling psychology?" The college already has an MBA program and another Master's program in biology. Because you've read this chapter, you respond that a thorough needs assessment should be done. The dean tells you to go ahead and even approves a modest budget for the project. Explain how you would conduct the needs assessment.

CHAPTER 10

Small N Designs

Chapter Overview

- ### Research in Psychology Began with Small N

  Before the advent of sophisticated statistical tools, research in psychology featured studies using a single participant or at most a small number of subjects; the experimenter was usually one of the participants. In studies with more than one subject, the additional participants served the purpose of replication. That is, their data were presented individually; it was seldom summarized as an "average" score for a group of subjects.

- ### Reasons for Small N Designs

  Modern advocates of research featuring one or just a few subjects argue that grouping data can obscure individual performance and can mislead the researcher about the phenomenon being investigated. Second, large numbers of subjects may not be available when studying certain phenomena (e.g., a rare mental disorder). A third argument derives from B. F. Skinner's belief that the best way to understand, predict, and control behavior is to study single individuals intensively. He argued that if environmental circumstances are controlled sufficiently, then predictable behavior will occur and can be measured.

• Small N Designs in Applied Research

Applied behavior analysis is the name given to the application of behavioral principles to change human behavior, often in a clinical setting. The most common approach is to use some form of withdrawal design, in which a baseline measure of behavior is taken before a treatment program is introduced. After a time the therapy is removed (withdrawn) and then reinstated. Evidence for the effectiveness of the treatment is inferred if the behavior to be changed is affected by these reversals. Other designs include multiple baseline designs, used when reversals aren't feasible; alternating treatment designs, which compare different treatments within the same individual; and changing criterion designs, which gradually shape some target behavior.

• Psychophysics

In addition to research in the operant tradition, there are other varieties of small N research. The best example is psychophysics, the study of relationships between the physical stimulus and the perceptual reaction to it. Psychophysics research examines the factors influencing our ability to detect the presence of stimuli and our ability to distinguish between similar stimuli. Research in psychophysics dates from the very beginnings of psychology's history.

One of the goals for my course in experimental psychology is for students to gain some experience reading and interpreting actual studies as they appear in the literature. Two or three times a semester, my students pick a journal article and write a brief summary of it. To give them some scientific thinking experience (another course goal), I also ask them to propose some ideas for a "next study." Recently, one of my students came across an article about children and gas masks that used a design quite different from those you've read about thus far in this text.

The article was called "The effects of a parent-implemented crisis intervention: A real-life emergency involving a child's refusal to use a gas mask," and it described a procedure for changing the behavior of an Israeli preschooler who refused to wear a gas mask during Scud missile attacks by Iraq in the Gulf War of 1991 (Klingman, 1992). The child's reluctance was understandable considering the discomfort involved, but the mask was essential because there were realistic fears that some of the missiles landing haphazardly in Israel were armed with chemical weapons.

The article describes how a "cognitive-behavioral-oriented" (p. 73) approach was used to help the child. After a "baseline" period, during which the child's behavior was observed when parents made their normal (and futile) requests for him to don the mask, an intervention period began. It consisted of (a) story-telling about a bear who refused to use a gas mask, (b) a game in which the child was placed in charge of convincing a stuffed bear to wear the mask in an emergency situation, and (c) direct reinforcement for mask wearing. The procedures seemed to work—the child began using the mask on request and continued doing so when assessed in a follow-up.

The most obvious thing worth noticing about this study is that only one subject was used and he was studied rather intensively. Up to this point in the text, the designs you've encountered typically have involved several or many subjects, specific methodological problems like creating equivalent groups or avoiding sequence effects have been dealt with, mean scores have been calculated, inferential analyses like ANOVA have been completed, and general conclusions (e.g., main effects) about the effects of independent variables have been drawn.

In this chapter, you will encounter many studies like the gas mask study. They are often called single-subject designs, because the behavior of each research subject is considered individually, but they can also be called "small N designs," because these studies sometimes use several subjects. The data for these subjects *might* be combined statistically, but more often the data for each of the additional subjects are described individually and used for replication purposes.

This small N strategy is most frequently associated with B. F. Skinner, who you first encountered in Chapter 1. However, it is important to realize that Skinner was not the first to focus on individual subjects. Rather, small N designs have a long history; in fact, the first experimental psychologists used this approach all the time.

Research in Psychology Began with Small N

When psychology emerged as a new science in the second half of the nineteenth century, statistical analysis was also in its infancy. Galton was just beginning to conceptualize correlations, and inferential techniques like ANOVA did not yet exist. Widespread use of large N designs and inferential statistics only occurred after Fisher's work on the analysis of variance appeared in the 1930s (see Chapter 7, Box 7.2). Before this time, small N was the rule.

Some of psychology's pioneers used the smallest N possible—they studied their own behavior or the behavior of a single individual. In Chapter 1, you learned about the most famous example of this—Hermann Ebbinghaus's exhaustive study of his own ability to learn and recall lists of nonsense syllables. Another pioneering example is Charles Darwin's study of child development, accomplished by keeping a detailed diary of his own son's childhood. It was published as "A Biographical Sketch of an Infant" in the British Journal *Mind* in 1877 (Hothersall, 1990). A third example is Watson and Rayner's infamous Little Albert experiment (1920; see Chapter 2, Box 2.1).

In Wundt's laboratory at Leipzig, small N designs were also the dominant strategy. Students pursuing the doctorate were assigned specific research topics that typically took a year or so to complete. The studies normally involved a very small number of research participants, with the investigator often serving as one of the subjects. The additional subjects usually were other doctoral students. For instance, the bulk of James McKeen Cattell's dissertation research on reaction time included data from just two people—Cattell and his friend and fellow student Gustav Berger (Sokal, 1981). Clearly, the separation in role (and status) that exists today between Experimenter with a capital E and subject with a small s was not in evidence in those days. In fact, while in the 1890s participants were sometimes called subjects, they were just as likely to be called "observers," a term that suggests a higher status and a more active role than "subject." Whether to use the term subject or observer was an issue as late as 1930 (Danziger, 1985).

Pioneer experimental psychologists sometimes crudely summarized data (e.g., reporting means) from several observers, but more often they reported the data for each person participating. A good illustration of this is a study from the laboratory at Clark University, completed in the early 1890s. It was a study of what was called "facial vision," the ability to detect the presence of nearby objects even when they cannot be seen. At one time, blind people were believed to have developed this as a special sense to compensate for their loss of vision. However, F. B. Dressler (1893) was able to show that the skill had more to do with hearing than with vision.

Figure 10.1 is a photo of the actual experimental setup, one of a series of photos showing research in progress at Clark in 1892. As you can see, a blindfolded subject would be seated next to a panel made up of four 1-foot squares. From left to right, the squares were either open or filled with (a) wood in a latticed design, (b) wood in a solid panel, or (c) wire screening. The panel hung from the ceiling and could be moved by the experimenter (it's Dressler in the photo) so that each of the squares could be placed next to the subject's face. The task was to identify which surface was next to one's face; the participants were Dressler and two other graduate student colleagues.

Remarkably, all three participants learned to distinguish between pairs of surfaces, as shown in Table 10.1, reproduced from the original article. The data represent the number of right ("R.") or wrong ("W.") responses. For example, when comparing the latticed surface with the solid one, F. B. D. (guess who that was) was

FIGURE 10.1 Dressler's apparatus for studying facial vision, 1892.

TABLE 10.1   *Data from Dressler's Study of Facial Vision*

Subject	Open and Lattice				Lattice and Solid				Solid and Wire			
	R.	W.	R.	W.	R.	W.	R.	W.	R.	W.	R.	W.
J. A. B.	65	15	59	25	58	2	56	0	45	0	46	2
O. C.	72	47	74	46	33	13	28	14	21	4	14	9
F. B. D.	53	24	58	17	69	1	70	4	73	0	77	2

correct 69 times and wrong just once when the correct answer was "lattice" and correct 70 out of 74 times when the correct answer was "solid." Similar results occurred for the other two subjects.

Notice that while data for all three subjects are presented, there are no summary statistics combining the three data sets. This is because the strategy was to show the phenomenon occurring reliably for each subject, not for the "average" subject. That is, Dressler tested two additional subjects to serve the purpose of *replicating* the initial finding twice. This strategy is frequently used today in small N designs.

Do the results of Dressler's study mean that facial vision as a separate sense truly exists? No. As a good research psychologist, Dressler looked for a more parsimonious explanation and for a way to rule out (falsify) the existence of the special facial sense. He found it by making a small procedural change—he plugged everyone's ears. The result was clear: Their "power to distinguish [the panels] was lost entirely" (Dressler, 1893, p. 349). Hence, facial vision turned out to be the ability to detect slight differences in reflected sound waves.[1]

Studies like Dressler's, featuring data from one or just a few subjects, can be found throughout the early years of experimental psychology, but large N studies were not completely absent. For example, some could be found in educational psychology and in child study research (Danziger, 1985). Such studies would feature empirical questions like "What do elementary school children fear?," and they would summarize questionnaire results from hundreds of children (e.g., Hall, 1893). However, as indicated earlier, it wasn't until the 1930s and Sir Ronald Fisher that psychologists routinely began to collect data from large numbers of subjects and perform the kinds of descriptive and inferential statistics that are widely used today.

One final example of an early small N design is worth describing in some detail. Because the research is an important historical antecedent of B. F. Skinner's work on operant conditioning and was a foreshadowing of the coming of behaviorism when it was completed nearly a hundred years ago, it is deservedly considered a "classic" study. It also shows that good science can be done with a meager budget (and talent) for apparatus construction.

---

[1]Given this result, what would you as experimenter do next? For example, what if you varied the distance between the panels and the subject?

Box 10.1

CLASSIC STUDIES—Cats in Puzzle Boxes

You briefly encountered Edward L. Thorndike (1874– 1959) in Box 1.2. Using mazes crudely constructed by placing books on end, he studied maze learning in chicks at about the same time that Small was adapting the Hampton Court maze for rats. He is best remembered, however, for studying how cats escape from puzzle boxes (Thorndike, 1898). The research is important for several reasons: It shows how psychology's pioneers relied on the detailed study of individual subjects, it is a good example of how to use parsimonious explanations for behavior, and it is an early example of the kind of research that paved the way for the development of behaviorism, especially the Skinnerian variety.

Studying Individual Cats

To investigate learning in cats, Thorndike built 15 puzzle boxes, each with its own unique escape mechanism. Quite by accident, photos of the actual boxes were discovered in the papers of Robert Yerkes by historian John Burnham (1972), and two of them are reproduced in Figure 10.2. Clearly, Thorndike was not very talented as an apparatus builder. In fact, his mechanical aptitude was so minimal that he never learned how to drive a car (Hothersall, 1990). There is an important lesson here though: Consequential research can be done without highly sophisticated equipment. The quality of the idea for the study is more important than the bells and whistles.

Cats were studied individually, and Thorndike described his results cat by cat. The cats learned to escape from the boxes through a trial and error process and according to what Thorndike named the "Law of Effect." The cats' actions were initially random and only occasionally successful. Behaviors that worked tended to be repeated ("stamped in" was the phrase Thorndike used), while unsuccessful behaviors were gradually eliminated ("stamped out"). The progress of one of Thorndike's cats (number 10, in Box C) can be seen in Figure 10.3.[2]

Using Parsimonious Explanations

Thorndike's Law of Effect challenged prevailing ideas about the thinking abilities of animals and provided a more parsimonious explanation of problem solving abilities. He argued there was no reason to attribute reasoning to animals if their behavior can be explained by a simpler process (i.e., trial and error learning). Thorndike had little patience with animal researchers who uncritically attributed higher mental processes to animals, an attitude shaped by Lloyd Morgan, whose famous canon of parsimony (see Chapter 3) appeared about this time. Thorndike was familiar with Morgan's work and probably heard the Englishman give an invited address on animal learning when Morgan visited Harvard in 1896 (Jonçich, 1968).

[2]Thorndike did not label the *X*-axis on his graphs, except to note when a significant period of time passed between his otherwise consecutive trials. In Figure 10.3, for example, an unmarked vertical line meant a day, a 2 was 2 days, 1h was an hour, and 78 was 78 hours.

FIGURE 10.2 Two of the puzzle boxes (C and D) built and used by Thorndike in his classic study of cats in puzzle boxes [from Burnham (1972)].

Anticipating Skinner

The final point worth noting about Thorndike's puzzle box research is that it represented an experimental approach to the study of learning that paved the way for other behavioral researchers. It also provided a model for learning that eventually took the form of B. F. Skinner's experimental analysis of behavior, which you will encounter shortly. Skinner (1953) acknowledged his debt to Thorndike by referring to the latter's work as being among "the first attempts to study the changes brought about by the consequences of behavior" (p. 59).

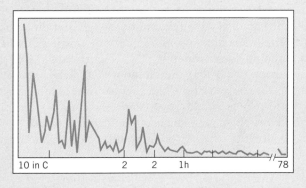

FIGURE 10.3 A record of cat 10 learning to escape from Box C [from Thorndike (1911)].

Reasons for Small N Designs

Despite the popularity of large N designs in modern psychology, studies using one or just a few subjects have made and continue to make important contributions to our knowledge of behavior. As you will soon discover, these studies cover the entire range from laboratory to field studies and from basic to applied research. There are several reasons why small N designs are used.

Misleading Results from Grouped Data

The process of summarizing data from large groups of individuals sometimes yields results that characterize no single individual who participated in the study. This was a central theme in Murray Sidman's *Tactics of Scientific Research* (1960), considered to be the classic text on small N methodology by advocates of the approach. Because group averages are "contaminated" by individual differences between subjects, Sidman argued, "[g]roup data may often describe a process, or a functional relation, that has no validity for any individual" (p. 274).

More importantly, Sidman's concern was that averaging data could produce a result supporting theory X when perhaps it shouldn't do so. Consider an example from a concept learning experiment with young children as subjects. They are shown a long series of stimulus pairs and have to guess which is "correct." If they make the right choice, they are rewarded. The stimuli are in the form of simple geometric objects; Figure 10.4 shows what the stimulus pairs might be for seven of the trials. The plus sign refers to the stimulus in each pair that will be reinforced (with an M & M perhaps). As you can see, the stimuli vary in shape (triangle or square or circle), color (red or green), and position (on the left or right). The correct concept in the example is "red" and to accumulate a large pile of M & Ms, the child must learn that shape and position are irrelevant stimulus dimensions. In the language of concept learning research, color is the "relevant dimension" and red is the "relevant value" on that dimension. The task is considered to be learned when the child reaches some "criterion" score, perhaps 10 consecutive correct choices.

An old controversy in the concept learning literature concerns the manner in which this type of task is learned (Manis, 1971). According to a "continuity" theory, learning is a gradual process of accumulating habit strength. Each reinforced trial strengthens the "tendency" to respond to the relevant dimension and weakens responses to the irrelevant dimensions. A graph of this hypothesized incremental learning process should look something like Figure 10.5*a*. On the other hand, "noncontinuity" theory held that the children were actively trying out different hypotheses during the early trials. While they were searching for the correct hypothesis, their performance would be at chance level (50%), but once they hit on the correct hypothesis, their performance would zoom up to 100% accuracy and stay there. Noncontinuity theory predicts that performance should look like Figure 10.5*b*.

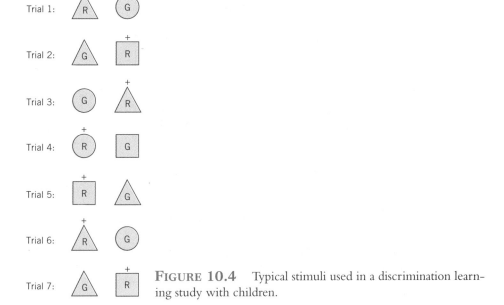

FIGURE 10.4 Typical stimuli used in a discrimination learning study with children.

The history of this issue is long and complicated and general conclusions are subject to many qualifications, but part of the resolution hinges on how the data are handled. If data from many subjects are grouped together and plotted, the result indeed looks something like Figure 10.5*a*, and continuity theory is supported. However, a picture more like Figure 10.5*b*, which supports a noncontinuity theory, emerges when one looks more closely at individual performance. Examining

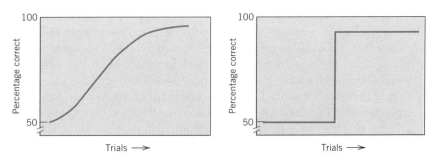

FIGURE 10.5 Concept learning data as predicted by (a) continuity and (b) noncontinuity theory.

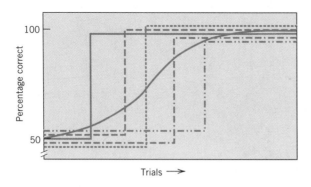

FIGURE 10.6   How group-
ing data from individual children
in a concept learning experiment can produce a smooth but
deceptive curve.

performance on trials just prior to when a solution is achieved reveals that accuracy is about 50% (e.g., Trabasso, 1963). After criterion, performance is virtually
perfect. That is, subjects perform at chance level up to a point when they hit on
the correct solution, then their performance improves dramatically. So how does
the individual performance illustrated in 10.5*b* end up as 10.5*a* when the data are
summarized?

The key has to do with how long it takes for each child to hit on the correct
solution; some figure it out quickly, others take longer. This situation is portrayed
in Figure 10.6. As you can see, a series of individual curves, when combined, could
easily yield the smooth curve of 10.5*a*. This is a clear instance of how grouped data
can create an impression that is not confirmed by examining the behavior of individual participants. As a general rule, any researcher using large N, especially in research where learning is involved, should examine at least some of the individual
data to see if it mirrors the grouped data.

Practical Problems with Large N Designs

Small N designs are sometimes necessary because potential subjects are difficult to
find. This can happen in clinical psychology for example, when a researcher wants
to study people with a particular disorder. Suppose a clinician wishes to test the effectiveness of a new type of therapy for those suffering from obsessive–compulsive
disorders (OCD). The simplest large N design would compare two groups of subjects, with perhaps 20 per group. Matching would almost certainly be required,
probably for characteristics like gender, intelligence, and economic status. To produce these two matched groups could require a relatively large initial sample of
people suffering from OCD, perhaps more than a hundred. Yet OCD is a rare disorder, affecting only about 2% of the population of psychiatric patients. According
to one estimate, even at the large psychiatric hospital, "it would take up to two
years to accumulate a series of obsessive compulsives for study" (Bergin & Strupp,
1972, cited in Barlow & Hersen, 1984, p. 15).

A related problem occurs in some animal research, especially if surgery is involved; the surgical environment will be expensive, and the procedures will be

time-consuming. The animal colony itself can be difficult to maintain, with costs in these days of animal rights activism including the expense of a security system. In some cases, the species being studied might be hard to obtain, prohibitively expensive, or require long training. For example, the research on teaching sign language to chimpanzees and other apes requires hundreds of hours per animal and the studies typically extend over many years. In a study teaching sign language to a lowland gorilla (Patterson & Linden, 1981), the ape knew more than 400 different signs at age ten; the study began when the ape was just a year old.

The Experimental Analysis of Behavior

Thus, large N designs might occasionally fail to reflect the behaviors of individuals and they may not be feasible even if they are desired. However, there are also philosophical reasons for preferring small N designs, and those reasons were best articulated by the most famous advocate of this approach, B. F. Skinner (1904–1990). As you may recall from Chapter 4, Skinner was rated the most eminent contemporary psychologist in a recent survey of historians and heads of psychology departments (Korn, Davis, & Davis, 1991).

Skinner believed passionately that if psychology was to achieve its goals of predicting and controlling behavior, it must study individual organisms intensively and derive general principles only after exhaustive study of individual cases. That is, psychology should be an inductive science, reasoning from specific cases to general laws of behavior. Indeed, Skinner once said that the investigator should "study one rat for a thousand hours" rather than "a thousand rats for an hour each, or a hundred rats for ten hours each" (Skinner, 1966, p. 21). The goal is to reduce error variance by achieving precise control over the experimental situation affecting the single subject. As Skinner put it, "I had the clue from Pavlov: control your conditions and you will see order" (1956, p. 223). He called his system the "experimental analysis of behavior," and while you should look elsewhere for a thorough discussion of his ideas, the essentials are worth mentioning here because they provide the philosophical underpinning for the research designs in applied behavior analysis.

Selection by Consequences

Skinner is best known for his research on **operant conditioning** a "process in which the frequency of occurrence of a bit of behavior is modified by the consequences of the behavior" (Reynolds, 1968, p. 1). That is, when some behavior occurs in a particular situation, it will be followed by some consequence. If the consequence is positive, the behavior will tend to recur when the individual is in the same situation again. Negative consequences, on the other hand, decrease the future probability of some behavior occurring. If a child's tantrum behavior works (i.e., results in a toy), it will tend to recur; if it doesn't, it won't.

Thus, the behaviors that characterize our lives are controlled by the environments in which we live. According to Skinner, the positive and negative consequences that we experience in a sense "select" the typical behaviors that define us.

To predict and control behavior, all that is needed is to be able to "specify three things: (1) the occasion upon which a response occurs, (2) the response itself, and (3) the reinforcing consequences. The interrelationships among them are the 'contingencies of reinforcement'" (Skinner, 1969, p. 7).

Note that the above definition of operant conditioning includes the phrase "frequency of occurrence." Skinner believed that in an experimental analysis of behavior, the only dependent variable worth studying was the **rate of response**. If the goals of psychology are to predict and to control behavior, and for Skinner those were the only ones, then all that matters is whether a behavior occurs or doesn't occur and how frequently it occurs per unit of time.

Operant Procedures

In the laboratory, operant conditioning is most often studied using an apparatus called an operant chamber, or Skinner box. Figure 10.7 shows a typical one designed for rats. When the lever protruding from the wall is depressed, a food pellet is released into the food cup. Rats are trained to bar press for the food reinforcer using a procedure called *shaping*. They are reinforced by the experimenter for gradually approximating a bar press and finally for the bar press itself. Eliminating the bar pressing behavior can be accomplished by withholding the reinforcement, a procedure called *extinction*.

Once bar pressing is established it can be brought under the environmental control of stimuli such as the light you can see just above the bar. If food pellets follow bar presses only when the light is on, the animal quickly learns a simple *dis-*

FIGURE 10.7   An operant chamber with cumulative recorder, as used by rats.

crimination: Press when the light is on, but don't bother if the light is off. In Skinner's contingencies of reinforcement language, the light being on in the chamber constitutes the "occasion upon which a response occurs," the "response itself" is the bar press, and the food pellet is the "reinforcing consequence."

The rate of bar pressing is recorded continuously with an apparatus called a **cumulative recorder**; Figure 10.8*a* shows one in operation. As the paper is fed out at a constant rate of speed, thereby producing time on the *X*-axis, a pen moves across the paper by a fixed distance every time the animal presses the bar. When a response is followed by a reinforcer, the pen is programmed to create a short diagonal marking line. When the pen reaches the top of the paper, it returns to the baseline to start over. The second pen keeps track of events like the light going on and off. Response rate can be assessed very simply by looking at the slope of the cumulative record. In the cumulative record in Figure 10.8*b*, the rat is bar pressing

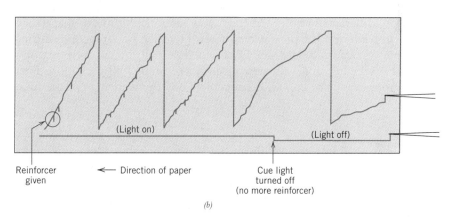

(Light on)   (Light off)

Reinforcer given   ← Direction of paper   Cue light turned off (no more reinforcer)

(b)

FIGURE 10.8 (*a*) The basic operation of a cumulative recorder and (*b*) a hypothetical cumulative record showing both a high and low rate of responding.

very rapidly in the initial portion of the record (the cue light in the box is on, and it signals that bar pressing produces food), but is hardly pressing at all in the second half (light off).

A classic illustration of the operant approach can be found in the encyclopedic *Schedules of Reinforcement* (Ferster & Skinner, 1957). Its importance to the experimental analysis of behavior is elaborated in Box 10.2. Be sure to read it before you encounter the schedules discussed in case study 1.

The major publication for basic research in operant conditioning is the *Journal of the Experimental Analysis of Behavior*. These recent titles will give you a sense of what you might encounter there:

✓ Effects of fixed and variable ratios on human behavioral variability (Tatham, Wanchisen, & Hineline, 1993).

✓ Effects of delayed reinforcement on infant vocalization rate (Reeve, Reeve, Brown, Brown, & Poulson, 1992).

✓ Low-response-rate conditioning history and fixed-interval responding in rats (LeFrancois and Metzger, 1993).

Case Study 1. An Experimental Analysis

The third study is an excellent example of the type of basic research encountered in the experimental analysis of behavior. LeFrancois and Metzger (1993) were interested in one of behaviorism's fundamental questions: How does prior learning history influence current behavior? All behaviorists believe that knowing one's learning history is essential in order to predict current behavior, but there is disagreement about whether present-day behavior is affected *primarily* by present-day contingencies of reinforcement or by earlier contingencies. If behavior is adaptive, then one might expect present-day contingencies to have the greater effect. However, it could be argued that an especially powerful reinforcement schedule early in life could have effects that carry over to the present day.

LeFrancois and Metzger tested these two possibilities in an operant experiment with six rats. All rats began by being trained to a DRL-20s schedule. "DRL" stands for "**d**ifferential **r**einforcement of **l**ow rates," and it means that the animals were reinforced for a bar press *only* if it was preceded by 20 seconds during which *no* bar presses occurred. After the DRL schedule, half the rats were put on a fixed interval (FI) schedule and half were given a fixed ratio (FR) schedule. Finally, the second group was placed on an FI schedule. Thus, the sequence for the two groups was:

(1) DRL   → FI
(2) DRL → FR → FI

That is, all rats wound up on the FI schedule, but some experienced one type of learning history (DRL) and others a different type (DRL, then FR). Would the present-day FI control the behavior, yielding no differences between the groups, or would prior history affect the FI? The answer can be seen in Figure 10.9, which compares the cumulative records for one of the rats in each group. Quite clearly, when DRL was followed immediately by FI (10.9*a*), response rate was low during FI. However, when an FR schedule intervened, it dramatically affected the response rate on FI, producing many more responses (10.9*b*). Thus, performance on

Box 10.2

CLASSIC STUDIES — Schedules of Reinforcement

Schedules of Reinforcement (Ferster & Skinner, 1957) is not a book meant to be read. Rather, it is a book to have on the shelves, so that if someone asks you how a "fixed ratio" schedule affects behavior, you can open to the fixed ratio chapter, and say "Here, see for yourself." That is, the 739-page book is more of an "atlas" (Skinner's term) than a summer-reading page turner.

Co-authored with Skinner's student and colleague Charles Ferster, the book is a remarkable achievement, arguably Skinner's most important research contribution, and perhaps the ultimate example of a purely inductive approach to science. It is filled with example after example of descriptions and cumulative records that illustrate dozens of different types of reinforcement contingencies. Something of Skinner's work ethic can be seen from his description of the process of compiling the book:

> Thousands of hours of data meant thousands of feet of cumulative records. . . . We worked systematically. We would take a protocol and a batch of cumulative records, dictate an account of the experiment, select illustrative records, and cut and nest them in a few figures. In the end, we had more than 1,000 figures, 921 of which went into the book. (Skinner, 1984, p. 109).

The 921 (!) cumulative records in Ferster and Skinner's book showed how behavior was affected by various schedules of reinforcement. A schedule is said to be in effect "[w]henever the environment reinforces some but not all occurrences of a response emitted by the organism" (Reynolds, 1968, p. 59). Few behaviors are reinforced every time they occur, and some behaviors (gambling, for example) are reinforced very infrequently. Yet partial reinforcement produces behaviors that can be very resistant to extinction (same example).

Two common types of schedules are called interval and ratio schedules. On a fixed interval (FI) schedule, for instance, behavior is reinforced only after a certain fixed amount of time has passed. A variable interval (VI) schedule also reinforces behavior after certain amounts of time, but the times vary from reinforcer to reinforcer. Ratio schedules depend not on time but on the amount of behavior produced. A fixed ratio (FR) schedule reinforces the individual for producing a certain number of responses. Analogous to the VI schedule, a variable ratio (VR) schedule reinforces after a certain number of responses, but the number keeps changing. Ratio schedules produce relatively high response rates, because the amount of reinforcement earned depends on how often the behavior occurs. Interval schedules usually produce low rates of responding, although you are about to learn of an exception to this in case study 1.

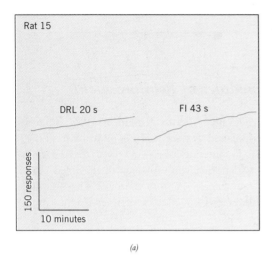
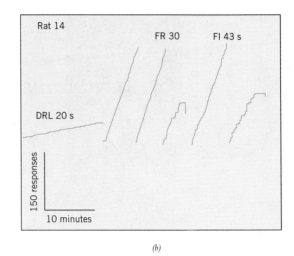

FIGURE 10.9 Cumulative records from rats experiencing either (*a*) DRL → FI or (*b*) DRL → FR → FI [from LeFrancois & Metzger (1993)].

the FI schedule was most influenced by what immediately preceded it. DRL influenced behavior only if it reflected the animal's *recent* past (first rat). LeFrancois and Metzger concluded that "responses of laboratory animals are sensitive to immediate history, and are relatively insensitive to a history of low-rate conditioning [DRL] when it is followed by high-rate conditioning [FR]" (1993, p. 543).

You might be thinking that this experiment sounds a bit like the "grouped data" experiments that you encountered in earlier chapters. However, while there are indeed two groups of three rats in the study, no summary statistics were presented and you'll find no inferential statistics in the journal article. Rather, the behavior of each of the six animals was described and six cumulative records were included. This strategy is of course identical to the one used by Dresler in the 1890s when he studied facial vision—the phenomenon is demonstrated on a single individual and replicated on others.

Applied Behavior Analysis

As historian Laurence Smith (1992) has pointed out, a distinction can be made between two broad categories of scientist type. Those representing the "contemplative ideal" focus their attention on trying to understand the basic causes of events in the natural world. Those reflecting the "technological ideal" look for ways to use science to control and change the world. Skinner was firmly in the latter group. Although most of his own research was pure laboratory work, he was always interested in applying the results of an experimental analysis of behavior to real-world problems, and he made important contributions to education, industry, child rearing, and behavior therapy. His ideas even contributed directly to the NASA space program; on at least two space flights, chimpanzees were given complex op-

Box 10.3

ETHICS—*Controlling Human Behavior*

In Chapter 1, the goals of psychology were described as description, prediction, explanation, and control. You might have felt a bit uneasy about "control," because it suggests a deliberate attempt to manipulate behavior, perhaps against a person's "will." Because of this implication, behaviorists from Watson to Skinner have been accused of seeking dictatorial control via conditioning. When "Cliff Notes" summarized Skinner's *Walden Two*, a fictional account of a community established on operant principles, it compared the community to Orwell's nightmare world of *Nineteen Eight-Four* (Todd & Morris, 1992). The perception of behaviorist as Big Brother overstates the case, but it is strengthened when one encounters chapters in Skinner's books with headings like "Designing a Culture" (1953) or superficially reads some of Skinner's statements, usually taken out of context.

The notion that one can and perhaps should act to alter behavior follows from the behaviorist's dictum that our behavior is conditioned by our surroundings. If the environment will shape behavior *anyway*, why not insure that productive behaviors are shaped? This attitude is clearly reflected in two famous quotes. The first is John Watson's claim:

Give me a dozen healthy infants, well-formed and my own specified world to bring them up in and I'll guarantee to take any one at random and train him to become any type of specialist I might select—doctor, lawyer, artist, merchant—chief, and yes, even the beggarman and thief, . . . (1924, p. 82)

The second quote is from Skinner's *Walden Two*. Through the voice of the community's founder and perhaps with Watson's dozen infants quote in mind, Skinner wrote:

"What remains to be done?" he said, his eyes flashing. "Well, what do you say to the design of personalities? Would that interest you? The control of temperament? Give me the specifications, and I'll give you the man!". (1948/1976, p. 274)

For Skinner, the controversy over behavior control was a nonissue. It is not a question of deciding whether to control behavior or not, he believed. Behavior *was* controlled by its consequences. Given that basic fact, he believed it followed that some effort should be made to create contingencies that would yield productive rather than nonproductive behaviors. Critics remained unconvinced and asked who would be the person deciding which behaviors should be shaped. Skinner believed his critics were missing the point.

One particular manifestation of the controversy over control exists in the psychology clinic, where the behavioral procedures you are about to study have been quite successful in helping people. One especially controversial procedure has been the use of punishment, including electric shock, to alter the behavior of disturbed children. For example, in a study by Kushner (1970), a severely retarded 7-year-old child (mental age of 2) was treated with electric shock for handbiting. The child frequently bled after biting his hand and he had suffered serious infections. Attempts to curb the behavior by having him wear boxing gloves or elbow splints failed. The treatment consisted of placing electrodes on the child's thigh and immediately shocking him every time his hand reached his mouth. The result was an almost immediate decline in the behavior that lasted even when the electrodes were removed.

When procedures like this are used in a study evaluating their effectiveness, has the ethical principle of not harming research participants been violated? Defenders of the use of punishment argue that other procedures often don't work with behaviors like self-biting. As long as appropriate safeguards are in place (e.g., other procedures have been tried unsuccessfully, informed consent from guardians has been obtained), the courts have upheld the use of shock "in extraordinary circumstances such as self-destructive behavior that [is] likely to inflict physical damage" (Kazdin, 1978, p. 352).

Researchers also contend that it is essential to investigate the procedures empirically, even if this means manipulating the level and the frequency of punishment, in order to discover the optimal procedure. This could mean that some children in a study will be punished at a higher level than is later determined necessary to alter the behavior, but the ideal therapy procedure (i.e., minimum punishment that still solves the problem) can never be known without the research being conducted. With the ultimate goal being finding the best way to help these terribly disturbed children, research evaluating the use of punishment seems to be not only justified but essential.

erant tasks to learn while being sent into space. One psychologist involved in the project stated that "[e]very technique, schedule, and programming and recording device we used then and subsequently can be traced to [Skinner] or his students" (Rohles, 1992, p. 1533).

Finally, Skinner was not shy about calling for the redesign of society based on operant principles, a recommendation that made him a controversial figure. To some, his prescriptions for improving the world seemed ominous, and he was accused of trying to turn everyone into rats in Skinner boxes. This issue of control is elaborated in Box 10.3, and you should read it carefully and see if you agree with its conclusion before going on to the descriptions of how conditioning principles can be used to solve a variety of applied behavior problems.

The "applications" side of the experimental analysis of behavior is sometimes called **applied behavior analysis**. It includes any procedure that uses behavioral, especially operant, principles to solve real-life problems. To get a sense of the range of environments in which these principles are used, consider the following recent titles from the *Journal of Applied Behavior Analysis*:

✓ Musical reinforcement of practice behaviors among competitive swimmers (Hume & Crossman, 1992).

✓ Analysis of a simplified treatment for stuttering in children (Wagaman, Miltenberger, & Arndorfer, 1993).

✓ Behavior change in the funny papers: Feedback to cartoonists on safety belt use (Mathews & Dix, 1992).

The designs that we'll be examining in the next section are most frequently applied to clinical settings, but as you can see from this list, the earlier mention of Skinner's applied work, and the designs that follow, operant principles are used in an assortment of circumstances.

Small N Designs in Applied Behavioral Research

Near the end of their research report on fear conditioning in the Little Albert experiment, Watson and Rayner (1920) described several ways in which the fear might be removed. Although they never tried any of these on Little Albert, the attempt to reduce fear using behavioral methods was made a few years later in a pioneering study by Mary Cover Jones (1924). Taking a 34-month-old boy named Peter who was afraid of rabbits, Jones succeeded in eliminating the fear. Her strategy was to give Peter his favorite food while placing the rabbit at a distance from him and gradually moving the animal closer, a technique similar to modern-day *systematic desensitization* procedures.

Behavioral approaches to therapy did not immediately flourish following Jones's successful treatment of Peter, but they did become popular, beginning in the fifties and especially in the sixties. The impetus was provided by some additional demonstrations of the effectiveness of procedures based on learning principles, along with a developing skepticism of traditional approaches to therapy, especially those relying on Freudian methods. In the 1960s, several journals featuring behavioral approaches to therapy appeared, including *Behavior Research and Therapy* (1963) and the *Journal of Applied Behavior Analysis* (1968). From that point on, research began to appear regularly that included designs attempting to demonstrate that a particular method produced a specific behavioral change in a "single subject."

Elements of Single-Subject Designs

The essential logic of single-subject designs is quite simple. Because there are usually no control groups in these studies, the behavior of a single individual must be shown to change as a result of the treatment being applied and not as a result of some confounding factor. At the very minimum, this requires three elements. First, the target behavior must be operationally defined. It's not sufficient to say simply that an attempt will be made to reduce a child's disruptive classroom behavior. Rather, the behavior must be defined in terms of easily recorded events, such as speaking out in class while someone else is already speaking. In the example that opened the chapter, the main target behavior involved getting the young Israeli child to put on and wear a gas mask, but the researchers also measured what they called "passive disruptive" behavior, "defined as ignoring requests [to put on the mask] or pretending not to hear" (Klingman, 1992, p. 72).

The second feature of any single-subject design is to establish a **baseline** level of responding. This means the behavior in question must be observed for a period of time prior to treatment to determine its typical frequency. It is against this baseline level of responding that the effects of a treatment program can be assessed. The third element is to begin the treatment and continue to monitor the behavior. Congratulations if you've noticed this sounds just like the logic of the interrupted time series design of the last chapter. In both cases, the goal is to evaluate some treatment against an established baseline.

The simplest single-subject design is sometimes referred to as an **A–B design**, with A standing for baseline and B for treatment. The ideal outcome is for the behavior to change when A changes to B, which as you recall is exactly what happened in the gas mask study. From your knowledge of threats to internal validity, however, I suspect you may be thinking that the A–B design is a weak one. You're right—a change in behavior might be the result of treatment, but it could also result from a variety of confounding factors, including history, maturation, and even regression. To reduce the chances of alternative explanations like this, the withdrawal design was developed.

Withdrawal Designs

If a treatment goes into effect and behavior changes but the change is due perhaps to maturation, then it is unlikely for the behavior to change back again to its original form if the treatment is subsequently removed or withdrawn. However, if the treatment is withdrawn and the behavior does return to its baseline level, then it is likely that the behavior is being affected by the treatment and not maturation. This is the logic behind the use of a **withdrawal** design (sometimes referred to as a "reversal" design), the simplest of which is an **A–B–A** design. As you might guess, this design begins just like the A–B design, but after the treatment has been in effect for a while, it is withdrawn (the second A).

If behavior changes correlate precisely with the introduction and removal of treatment, confidence is increased that the treatment is producing the change. That confidence is further strengthened if reintroducing the treatment brings about another change in behavior. For this reason, researchers prefer an **A–B–A–B** design over the A–B–A design. In effect, the treatment program is evaluated twice. The A–B–A–B design also has the ethical advantage of finishing the experiment with treatment in place. Its ideal outcome is illustrated in Figure 10.10. Note that in order for the treatment to be considered successful, the behavior must return to baseline (or close to it) after the withdrawal and it must change again when treatment is reinstated. When such a result occurs, it is difficult to interpret it in any way other than as the successful application of a treatment program. As an example of how this very common design is actually used, consider the following case study

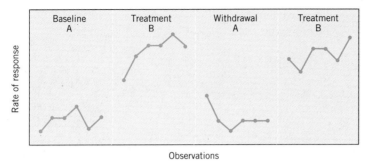

FIGURE 10.10 Ideal outcome of an A−B−A−B withdrawal design.

of competitive swimmers.

Case Study 2. An A−B−A−B Design

The study, by Hume and Crossman (1992), was designed to improve the practice behaviors of five 12- to 16-year-old male members of a swim club during "dryland training periods" (p. 665), those times when the boys were not in the water but were nonetheless supposed to be doing certain things to improve their swimming performance. "Productive" behaviors included things like exercising (e.g., doing situps) or demonstrating techniques to another swimmer. "Nonproductive" behaviors included inappropriate exercise (e.g., doing handstands), distracting activities (e.g., stealing other swimmers' goggles), and off-task discussions (e.g., about girls). As you might guess, especially considering the age of the boys, the baseline level of nonproductive behaviors was quite high and a source of some irritation to the coaches, who apparently forgot about once being age 12–16 themselves.

Three trained observers recorded behavior during a baseline period (A) of about a dozen practice sessions. Then the reinforcement program was introduced (B) for several sessions, withdrawn (A) for several more, and introduced (B) again. Three of the boys were assigned to a "contingent reinforcement" group; the remaining pair were in a "noncontingent reinforcement" group. The reinforcement consisted of playing music, already known to be popular with the boys, during practice time. The three boys in the contingent reinforcement group each had to reach a certain level of productive behavior during their out-of-pool time in order for music to be played (for all five boys) during the immediately following session.

As is customary for small N designs in the operant tradition, the results for each swimmer were presented individually. Figure 10.11 shows you what happened for one of the swimmers in the contingent reinforcement group; the program seemed to work quite well for him. During baseline, nonproductive behaviors were dominant for all but one practice session, but this changed quickly during the intervention; productive behaviors were now more frequent. Withdrawing and then reinstating treatment also produced effects consistent with the idea that making music contingent on behavior improved the quality of the practice sessions.

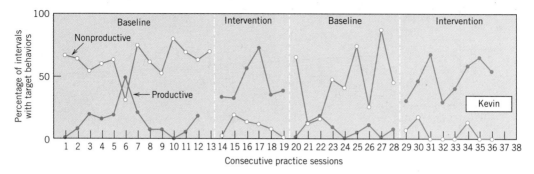

FIGURE 10.11 Data from an A–B–A–B design used by Hume and Crossman (1992) to increase the productivity of swimming practice.

Multiple Baseline Designs

Sometimes a withdrawal design simply isn't feasible. For example, if the treatment program involves teaching a particular skill, that skill will remain "learned" even if the program is terminated. That is, when the treatment is withdrawn, the behavior will not return to baseline but will remain high. A withdrawal design may also present ethical problems, especially if the behavior being changed is self-destructive. If an autistic child is systematically banging his head against the wall and an operant procedure manages to stop the behavior, withdrawing the procedure to see if the head banging resumes is probably not justified. Multiple baseline designs solve these types of practical and ethical difficulties.

In a **multiple baseline** design, baseline measures are established and treatment then is introduced *at different times.* There are three varieties. Baselines can be established (1) for the same type of behavior in two or more individuals, (2) for two or more different behaviors within the same individual, or (3) for the same behavior within the same individual, but in two or more different settings. The logic is the same in all cases. Consider for example a situation in which the goal is to change three different behaviors in the same individual. The ideal outcome is shown in Figure 10.12. As you can see, the study begins by establishing the usual baseline for each of the three behaviors. Then treatment is begun for one behavior, but not the other two. If the treatment is effective, it should change the first behavior only. Similarly, when the treatment is extended to behavior 2, it should begin to affect that behavior but not behavior 3. At time 3, the third behavior should change. Hence, the effectiveness of the treatment program is inferred from the fact that as it is introduced at different times, the behavior responds only at that time and not before. On the other hand, if all three, or two of the three, behaviors change after treatment occurs at time 1, then it becomes difficult to attribute the changes to the treatment.

Multiple baseline studies are among the most frequently encountered in the literature. A good example is a study by Wagaman, Miltenberger, and Arndorfer (1993), who used a multiple baseline design to evaluate a program to help children with a stuttering problem.

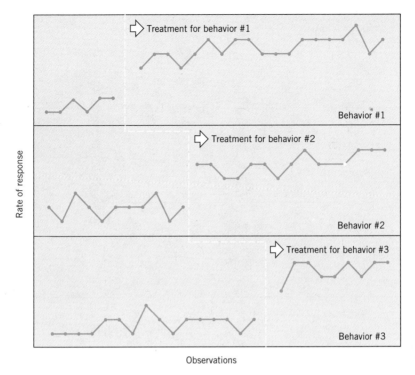

FIGURE 10.12   Ideal outcome of a multiple baseline design.

Case Study 3. Multiple Baselines Across Subjects

The study illustrates the first type of multiple baseline described above; the goal was to change the same type of behavior in several individuals. The behavior was stuttering and the individuals were eight school children (six males, two females) ranging in age from 6 to 10. The treatment was a simplified form of a procedure called "regulated breathing," in which the children were taught to reduce stuttering by trying to produce most of their speech while exhaling instead of while inhaling. The children were taught at home; parents were also taught the technique. The program also included elements of social reinforcement (from parents) and awareness training, in which both parents and children were taught to quickly identify every type of speech problem.

This latter feature of the program brings into focus a question that may have occurred to you: How was stuttering defined? Obviously, a program to train full awareness of stuttering must begin with clear behavioral definitions of the phenomenon. Wagaman et al. (1993) developed specific criteria to identify four categories of stuttering: "(1) word repetitions, (2) part-word repetitions, (3) prolongation of a sound, and (4) blocking or hesitation before the completion of a word" (p. 55). To insure the reliability of their measures, they tape recorded all sessions and had multiple raters evaluate the tapes. Agreement among raters was high.

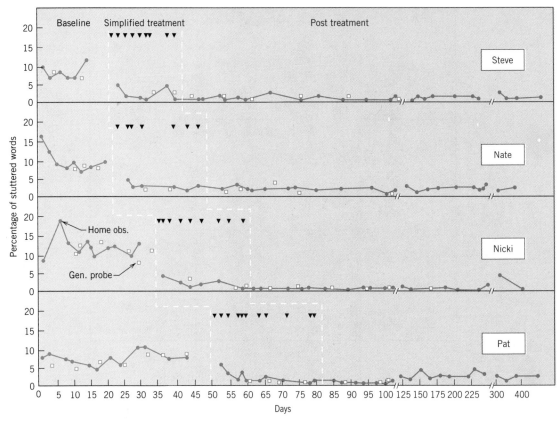

FIGURE 10.13   Decreasing stuttering behaviors in a multiple baseline study by Wagaman et al. (1989).

Figure 10.13 shows what happened for four of the children (curves for the other four were virtually identical). Several points are worth noting. First, as in all single-subject designs, the study begins by establishing a baseline level of performance. Second, as is characteristic of multiple baseline studies, the treatment program began at different times. In general, you can usually spot a multiple baseline study by looking for several graphs piled on top of each other, with a dotted line moving down from one curve to the next in a step-wise fashion. Third, the stuttering behavior for each child clearly responded to treatment.

If you count the tiny arrowheads above the treatment portions of the curves, you'll notice that they aren't equal. "Steve," for example, had nine treatment sessions, while "Nate" had just seven (the names are fictitious of course). From what you learned in earlier chapters, you might be wondering if there is a control problem here. Shouldn't the number of training sessions be held constant? Keep in mind, however, that a key element in the philosophy of the small N approach is a focus on the individual. Wagaman et al. (1993) were more concerned with insuring that each child reached a certain level of performance than with keeping the total number of sessions "under control." Thus, training for each child continued until each child "consistently achieved the criterion level of stuttering (<3% stuttered words) (p. 57).

Research in the small N tradition is sometimes criticized on the grounds that the results don't generalize beyond the experimental situation and because there is a lack of follow-up. The Wagaman et al. (1993) study addressed both of these problems. First, notice that most of the points in Figure 10.13 are filled circles, but some are open squares; one of them is labeled "gen. probe," for "generalization probe." These squares represent times when the researchers assessed the children's stuttering in the school setting. The circles ("home obs.") refer to sessions in the home. Clearly, even though training took place at home, the results generalized to the school. Second, notice that an extensive follow-up (10–13 months) was done for each child, as indicated by the right-hand sections of Figure 10.13. Hence, the program not only worked in the short term; its effects lasted.

Alternating Treatments Designs

A third major category of single-subject design is called an **alternating treatment** design (Barlow & Hersen, 1984). The procedure is used when comparing the effectiveness of more than one type of treatment for the same individual. It has become a popular procedure because of its ability to evaluate more than a single treatment approach within the same study. After establishing the usual baseline, treatments are alternated several times; this is done randomly to reduce any sequencing effects that might occur (you'll recognize this as another example of counterbalancing). The design is nicely demonstrated in a study of social behaviors in developmentally delayed preschoolers by Chandler, Fowler, and Lubek (1992).

Case Study 4. Alternating Treatments

The research article describes two studies designed to evaluate various combinations of different variables, each known by itself to be a factor affecting peer interactions for preschool children. We'll consider just study 2. It included four 3- to 4-year-old girls in a day care center who "were considered at risk for developmental delays" (p. 256).

Following baseline measurements of social interactions with peers, three consecutive interventions occurred, each comparing two alternating treatments. Chandler and her colleagues evaluated four different types of treatment:

1. *Standard.* In this condition, the teacher was absent, play materials were limited, and the peer who was present was known to be skilled at peer interactions. Prior research had shown each of these three factors to be effective by itself for encouraging interactions. Chandler et al. (1992) were interested in their combined effects.

2. *Contrast.* This was the opposite of the standard condition. The teacher was present, the room was filled with play materials, and the peer was unskilled.

3. *Standard / Social Prompts.* This was similar to the standard condition (i.e., limited play materials, skilled peer) except that the teacher was present in the room and was instructed to prompt the subject to make peer interactions.

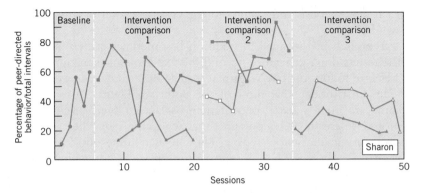

FIGURE 10.14   Data from an alternating treatments design to evaluate different ways of improving peer interactions [from Chandler et al. (1992)].

4.   *Contrast/Social Prompts.* This was similar to the contrast condition (teacher present, lots of play materials, unskilled peer) except that as in treatment 3, the teacher prompted for peer interactions.

The results for "Sharon" can be seen in Figure 10.14. The first comparison was between the Standard (■) and the Contrast (▲) treatments, the second is between Standard and Standard/Social (□) prompts, and the third between Contrast and Contrast/Social (△) prompts. Overall, the highest frequency of "peer-directed behavior" for Sharon occurred during the standard condition. This was especially true during intervention 1. Intervention 2 suggests that it isn't necessary for the teacher to prompt the students to interact and in fact the prompting seems to reduce peer interactions. Teacher prompts can be effective, however, if the conditions are otherwise not conducive to interaction (unlimited play materials and an unskilled peer), as is shown in the final intervention comparison. A similar pattern of results occurred for the other three children.

Other Designs

The A–B–A–B withdrawal, multiple baseline, and alternating treatment designs are not the only ones used in applied behavior analyses. Depending on the problem at hand, many researchers combine elements of the main designs, modify the designs slightly, or create a new design. An example of a modification of the A–B–A–B design is called the **A–B–C–B** design. It is often used for situations in which the treatment program involves the use of contingent reinforcement. That is, during treatment (B) the target behavior is reinforced immediately after it occurs and reinforcement occurs at no other time. During C reinforcement is provided, but it is not made contingent on the target behavior. Thus, reinforcement is given at both B and C, but depends on the behavior being performed only during B. The design helps to control for placebo effects by demonstrating that the behavior change occurs not just because the subject is pleased about getting reinforcers, happy about being attended to, and so on, but because of the specific reinforcement contingencies.

Another example of a modified A−B−A−B design is one that is used in evaluating the effectiveness of some drug treatment for a single subject. Several differences sequences have been used, but a common one is an $A-A_1-B-A_1-B$ design (e.g., Liberman, Davis, Moon, & Moore, 1973). A is the normal baseline and A_1 is a second baseline during which the subject receives a placebo. The real drug is given during B.

A final example of a single-subject design is called the **changing criterion** design, inspired by the operant procedure of shaping. In this design, the target behavior is too difficult for the subject to accomplish initially; it must be shaped in small increments. The procedure begins by establishing the usual baseline, then a treatment is begun and continued until some criterion has been reached. Then the criterion is made increasingly more stringent until the final target behavior has been shaped. Physical fitness programs are good candidates for this strategy (e.g., DeLuca & Holborn, 1992). The program begins by reinforcing minimal physical activity and gradually increases the amount of activity per reinforcement.

Evaluating Single-Subject Designs

The designs we've been considering have been enormously helpful in assessing the effectiveness of operant and other conditioning approaches to behavior change. They all derive from the Skinner/Pavlov dictum that if conditions are precisely controlled, then orderly and predictable behavior will follow. Small N behavioral designs are not without critics, however.

The most frequent complaint concerns external validity, the extent to which results generalize. If a particular form of behavior therapy is found to be effective for a single subject in a specific situation, how do we know the therapy is generally effective for other people with the same disorder? Maybe there was something very unusual about the individual who was the subject in the study. Maybe treatment effects that occur in one setting won't generalize to another.

Advocates reply that generalization is indeed evaluated directly in some studies; the Wagaman et al. (1993) multiple baseline study is a good example. Second, although conclusions from single-subject studies are certainly weak if the results aren't replicated, replication and extension are common features of this approach. For instance, the use of "differential attention" to shape behavior (e.g., parents attending to their child's desired behaviors and ignoring undesired behaviors) is now a well-established phenomenon, thanks to dozens of small N studies demonstrating its effectiveness for a variety of behaviors. Considering just the population of young children, for example, Barlow and Hersen (1984) provide a list of 65 studies on the use of differential attention, all published between 1959 and 1978.

Single-subject designs are also criticized for not using statistical analyses but relying instead on a simple visual inspection of the data. To some extent, this reflects a philosophical difference between those advocating large and small N. Defenders of small N argue that conclusions are only drawn when the effects are large enough to be obvious to anyone. It is worth noting, however, that some statistical analyses are beginning to be found in research reports of single-subject designs. For example, some studies have used time series analyses to separate treatment effects from trend effects (Junginger & Head, 1991). Time series analyses also help with the problem of relatively unstable baselines (as in Figure 10.14), which can make a visual inspection of a single-subject graph difficult to interpret.

Statistical analyses have even begun to creep into the *Journal of the Experimental Analysis of Behavior*, traditionally the purest of the pure Skinnerian journals. One operant researcher lamented that in a survey of the articles in the 1989 volume of *JEAB*, he found that nearly one third of the articles used inferential statistics in one form or another and that no more than 10% of the articles included cumulative records (Baron, 1990).

A third criticism of single-subject designs is that they cannot adequately test for interactive effects. As you recall from Chapter 7 on experimental design, one of the attractive features of the factorial design is its ability to identify the interactions between two or more independent variables. Interactive designs for small N studies exist, but they are exceedingly cumbersome. For example, a study by Leitenberg et al. (1968, cited in Barlow & Hersen, 1984) used an A–B–BC–B–A–B–BC–B design to compare two therapy techniques (B and C) plus their combined effect (BC). Notice, however, that technique C never occurred by itself. This required a replication on a second subject, which took the form A–C–BC–C– A–C–BC–C.

One especially interesting interaction that you learned about in Chapter 7 can result from the $P \times E$ design, which includes both a subject (P) and a manipulated (E) variable. One type of $P \times E$ interaction occurs when the manipulated factor affects one type of person one way but affects others in a different way. The subject variables in $P \times E$ designs are, of course, between-subjects variables by definition, but except for some multiple baseline studies, single-subject designs are within-subjects designs. Thus, $P \times E$ interactions analogous to the one just described can only be found in single-subject designs through extensive and complicated replications in which it is found that (a) treatment 1 works well with person type 1 but not with person type 2, and (b) treatment 2 works well with person type 2 but not with person type 1.

A final criticism of small N designs in the operant tradition concerns their exclusive reliance on frequency of response as the dependent variable. This approach excludes research using reaction times, whether or not a word is recalled correctly, amount of time spent looking (as in a habituation study), and a number of other variables that shed important light on human behavior. The response rate is certainly a crucial variable, but it is difficult to discount the value of the other dependent measures.

Small N designs are by no means confined to operant research and applied behavior analysis. One of psychology's earliest small N research strategies involved studying sensory thresholds using the methods of psychophysics.

Psychophysics

In the opening paragraph of this book, I made reference to Wilhelm Wundt's 1874 text as a landmark in establishing psychology as a scientific discipline. Experimental psychology preceded Wundt, however, most obviously in the person of

Gustav Fechner (1801–1887), whose 1860 book, *Elements of Psychophysics*, is occasionally considered the first real text in experimental psychology. His research established **psychophysics**, the study of the relationship between the physical stimulus and the sensation of it.

You can get a thorough dose of research in psychophysics by taking a course in sensation and perception. Here, you will receive a brief overview of the type of research found in psychophysics, and you will learn how the research is another example of the small N approach.

Thresholds

Research in psychophysics concerns two related skills: the ability to detect the presence of a stimulus and the ability to distinguish between slightly different stimuli. The problem of detection originally concerned identifying what Fechner called an **absolute threshold**, the stimulus intensity just sufficient for us to be aware of a stimulus. Every time you take a hearing or a visual acuity test, you are in an experiment about absolute thresholds. More commonly, because it is recognized that absolute thresholds are seldom if ever "absolute" cut-off points, detection research takes the form of identifying (a) the factors that affect our abilities to detect stimuli and (b) how the process of deciding whether to say the stimulus has been detected can be influenced by factors like incentive and fatigue.

The second type of threshold studied in psychophysics concerns discrimination and is called the **difference threshold**, or "just noticeable difference" (jnd). If you are looking at two lights that differ slightly in intensity but they look identical to you, then a difference threshold has not yet been reached. If the intensity of one of the lights is increased until you now just barely notice a difference, then you've achieved a difference threshold. Difference thresholds can become more finely tuned with practice, as is obvious from the differences between professional piano tuners, wine tasters (and in the nineteenth century, wool sorters), and the rest of us.

Methods of Psychophysics

Fechner described three basic psychophysical methods, which continue to be used today. To illustrate each, imagine you are taking a hearing test. You are sitting in a soundproof booth wearing earphones, and your instructions are to press a button every time you hear a tone. The examiner sounds a tone that you can easily hear, then one that is a bit softer, then softer still, until you cannot hear it any more. After a time, you begin to think that you can hear the tone again, then there's one that is a bit louder, and so on. The examiner in this case is using the **method of limits**, which alternates what are called descending and ascending trials. On a descending trial, the first stimulus is well above threshold; subsequent stimuli gradually decrease in intensity until they are no longer detected. On ascending trials, the first stimulus is below threshold, and with subsequent stimuli the intensity is gradually increased. Overall threshold is determined by averaging the intensity level at which the tone is just barely detected during ascending trials and just barely lost on descending trials.

Two other ways of establishing thresholds are the method of constant stimuli and the method of adjustment. In a hearing test using the method of constant stimuli, the intensity of a stimulus on any given trial is determined randomly. This procedure avoids some of the guessing and anticipating that can occur with the method of limits. In the method of adjustment, the subject controls the stimulus intensity directly and is told to adjust it until the stimulus is just barely detectable or just barely different from a second stimulus.

Finally, operant methods have been used to study thresholds in animals. For instance, discrimination procedures can be used. If an animal can learn to bar press when hearing tone 1 but not to press when hearing tone 2, then it must be able to distinguish between the tones. If it cannot learn the discrimination, it probably cannot tell the difference between the tones.

Psychophysics and Small N

If you think about these methods for a minute, you'll see why psychophysics research almost always uses a small number of subjects. First, few subjects are required in most psychophysics studies because most people have very similar sensory systems. Because individual differences are so small, results found with just a few subjects can be easily generalized to others. As always, of course, replication confirms the verdict.

The second reason for using small N designs in psychophysics relates back to the distinction between within-subjects and between-subjects factors. Establishing thresholds requires the use of a within-subjects design in which each person is exposed to a large number of stimulus intensities. It makes no sense to give one subject stimulus 1, another subject stimulus 2, and so on, and then calculate some average threshold for a large group of people. Rather, thresholds need to be established within single individuals and they can only be established by taking large numbers of trials over a range of stimuli for a single individual. Thus, rather than taking a few measurements for many individuals, psychophysics researchers take many measurements for just a few individuals. Furthermore, there's no point wasting a subject's time by presenting only one or a few stimuli per person; a single trial only takes a few seconds. Who wants to do a study that requires 5 minutes to set up the equipment, another 5 minutes to instruct the subject, perhaps 10 minutes to debrief the subject, and 30 *seconds* to actually collect data?

A third and related reason why psychophysics research uses small N has to do with control. Most threshold research is done under highly controlled laboratory conditions. Thus, on each trial, the data obtained will be less affected by error variance than might be the case, say, in a social psychology experiment on helping behavior. This, of course, is reminiscent of Skinner again: If conditions are controlled, order will follow.

This chapter has introduced you to a tradition of research in psychology that has deep roots and vigorous advocates. It is an approach ideally suited for some circumstances such as for studying the effects of reinforcement contingencies on behavior and for determining sensory thresholds. It may be less suited for other situations that might require between-subjects designs or be interested in a wider range of dependent measures. The next chapter completes our survey of method by examining approaches that are primarily descriptive.

Chapter Review

Glossary Fill-Ins

1. The first step in any applied behavior analysis to establish a _____ level of responding.
2. During a hearing test exam using the psychophysics method of _____, Joel was told to turn a dial that decreased the loudness of a tone. He was told to stop turning when he could no longer hear the tone.
3. The study in which the Israeli child was induced to wear a gas mask utilized an _____ design.
4. The _____ design is the applied behavior analysis strategy that most resembles the operant procedure of shaping.
5. In a Skinnerian experimental analysis of behavior, the preferred dependent measure is _____.
6. To change an autistic child's self-stimulation behavior, a reinforcement plan is put into effect in three different settings, but staggered so that the contingencies are introduced in one setting at a time. The researcher is using a _____ design.

Multiple Choice

1. Which of the following is true about Dressler's study of facial vision?
    a. It shows that grouping the data from several subjects can produce a result that does not reflect the behavior of any single subject.
    b. It is an early example of a small N design in which the additional subjects served the purpose of replication.
    c. It is an example of the psychophysics method of limits.
    d. It is an exception to the fact that in psychology's early years, small N designs were the rule.
2. All of the following are arguments typically made by those in favor of using small N designs *except*
    a. Because of individual differences, inferential statistics are needed to determine if the independent variable is responsible for changes in the dependent variable.
    b. Sometimes when data from many subjects are averaged, the picture that emerges does not reflect the behavior of any single individual.

    c.   Research on relatively rare psychological phenomena may not be possible except by using a small N design.

    d.   If the precise control of conditions yields orderly behavior, then the emphasis should be on controlling environmental conditions for single organisms rather than achieving statistical control.

3.   When is a multiple baseline design preferred over an A-B-A-B design?

    a.   When the target behavior cannot be reached all at once.

    b.   When the goal is to compare two different treatment strategies in the same subject.

    c.   When withdrawing treatment is not feasible for some reason.

    d.   When the goal is to study more than a single individual.

4.   A researcher in an institution for retarded children wishes to develop and evaluate a treatment program that would get the children to make their beds properly each morning. Two approaches are recommended by the staff, one involving a token economy system in which points can be earned and traded in for other reinforcers and a second that relies on the use of staff attention as a reinforcer, in which bed making is reinforced by giving the child extra attention. To evaluate the effectiveness of these strategies, what would be the best design to use?

    a.   Alternating treatments design

    b.   Withdrawal design

    c.   Multiple baseline design

    d. $A-A_1-B-A_1-B$ design

5.   Why is an $A-B-A-B$ design preferred over an $A-B-A$ design?

    a.   It isn't; the $A-B-A$ design is more efficient because it takes less time.

    b.   Because it includes a withdrawal of treatment.

    c.   Because it compares contingent with noncontingent reinforcement.

    d.   Because it evaluates the treatment effect twice rather than once.

Applications Exercises

Exercise 10.1 — Designing Self-Improvement Programs

Design a changing criterion program for one of the following self-improvement projects. For each project, be sure to define the target behavior(s) carefully, identify what you would use as reinforcement, and indicate what each successive criterion would be.

1.   Increase productive study time.

2.   Develop an exercise program.

3.   Change to healthier eating behaviors.

4.   Improve time management.

Exercise 10.2 — Hypothetical Outcomes of Applied Behavior Analyses

For each of the following, sketch hypothetical graphs that illustrate each of the alternative outcomes.

1. $A-A_1-B-A_1-B$ design:
   a. The drug worked.
   b. Cannot tell if the drug worked or not; could have been a placebo effect.

2. $A-B-C-B$ design:
   a. Reinforcement works, but only if it is made contingent upon specific behaviors.
   b. Reinforcement works regardless of whether or not it is made contingent upon specific behaviors.

3. Multiple baseline across three settings:
   a. The program works.
   b. Cannot discount a history or maturation effect.

4. $A-B-A-B$ design
   a. The program works.
   b. Hard to tell if the program brought about the change or if some other factor such as maturation brought about the change.

Exercise 10.3 — Depicting the Results of Applied Behavior Analyses

For each of the following descriptions and data sets, prepare a graph that would accurately portray the results.

1. An $A-B-A-B$ design was used to reduce the number of interruptions made in class by a child whose behavior was disrupting his second-grade class. During treatment, the teacher was instructed to ignore the child's interruptions and to pay special attention to the child when he was behaving productively (e.g., doing classwork). The number of interruptions per 1-hour recording session were as follows:
   1. During first A: 12, 12, 7, 6, 6, 9, 8, 10, 9, 11
   2. During first B: 9, 8, 9, 4, 3, 2, 2, 1, 4, 2
   3. During second A: 4, 2, 3, 4, 4, 1, 5, 2, 14, 12
   4. During second B: 9, 9, 2, 1, 1, 1, 0, 3, 4, 1

2. A multiple baseline across persons design was used to improve the foul shooting percentage of three basketball players during practices. A system was used in which successful shots earned points that could later be used to obtain more substantial reinforcers. Each of the following numbers represents the number of foul shots made for each 50 attempted. The numbers that are italicized are baseline data.
   Player 1.
   32, 29, 38, 31, 33, 44, 36, 37, 44, 41, 40, 38, 45, 42, 40, 44
   Player 2.
   30, 32, 28, 30, 30, 40, 39, 42, 43, 38, 40, 45, 44, 44, 42, 44
   Player 3.
   22, 28, 19, 21, 26, 18, 22, 26, 29, 21, 23, 20, 35, 39, 40, 39

CHAPTER 11
Other Research Methods

Chapter Overview

- ## Observational Research

  The goal of providing accurate qualitative and quantitative descriptions of behavior can be accomplished by using basic observational methods. In naturalistic observation, the observer is separate from those being observed and the
  subjects of the study are either accustomed to or unaware of the observer's
  presence. The observer becomes an active member of the group being studied
  in participant observation studies. Observation studies vary in the amount of
  structure imposed by the researcher. Lack of control, observer bias, and subject
  reactivity are three methodological problems with observational research. The
  researcher also must confront the ethical dilemmas of informed consent and
  invasion of privacy.

- ## Survey Research

  The primary purpose of survey research is to gather descriptive information about people's attitudes, opinions, and self-described behaviors. Surveys can be administered in face-to-face interviews, by means of written tests, or over the phone. Constructing reliable and valid surveys is a major task, and survey data can be affected by the expectations and response biases of those taking them. Conclusions drawn from survey research can be invalidated if the group sampled does not reflect the population targeted by the survey.

- ## Case Studies

  Case studies are in-depth descriptions and analyses of individual persons or events. Case histories of individuals serve to highlight the backgrounds and current features of individuals fitting into defined categories (e.g., those diagnosed as suffering from specific psychological disorders) or to provide a close analysis of extraordinary individuals. Case histories of events occur when researchers either have the opportunity to collect data about some significant current event (e.g., an earthquake) or investigate a type of event (e.g., stage hypnotism) that is of interest for some reason.

- ## Archival Research

  When research uses information that has already been collected for some other purpose or as part of the public record, it is called archival research. Archival information is often an essential part of program evaluation research, especially interrupted time series studies. Archival research projects can be designed to answer empirical questions, but the results are limited by what information is available and there is no guarantee that the data will be representative.

As you can tell from the overall chapter structure of the text, center stage has been occupied by the experimental method. It was the direct focus of attention in Chapters 5, 6, and 7, and the earlier chapters, especially Chapter 3, led up to it. As you recall, the starring role for the experiment derives from its potential for yielding cause and effect conclusions. In the last three chapters, you have encountered methods that some traditionalists might relegate to supporting role status because the conclusions drawn from them are weaker than those drawn from experiments. However, we've seen that while drawing casual conclusions from correlational, quasi-experimental, and small N studies can be problematic, these methods are essential if we are to fully understand human behavior. The same can be said of the methods you're about to encounter in this chapter. Each one has weaknesses, but they are indispensable members of the cast.

In this next-to-last chapter, we'll be examining methods for doing research in psychology that could collectively be called descriptive. That is, their major purpose is to provide accurate descriptions of the interrelationships between individuals and their environments. They are often the only approach that circumstances permit and in general, they are a rich source of hypotheses for further study. They often rely on qualitative analysis of the phenomena being studied, but they can also include sophisticated quantitative analysis.

Observational Research

As you know from the discussion of psychology's goals in Chapter 1, human behavior cannot be predicted, controlled, or explained unless it is first described accurately. The major purpose of observational research is to contribute this descriptive information; these studies provide in-depth accounts of individuals or groups of individuals as they behave naturally in some specific setting.

Varieties of Observational Research

Observational research with the goal of describing behavior can be classified along two dimensions. First, studies vary in terms of the degree of experimenter involvement with subjects. Sometimes the researcher does not interact in any substantial way with the group being observed; at other times, the researcher might even become a member of the group being studied. These studies are called *naturalistic observation* and *participant observation,* respectively. Second, observational researchers impose varying degrees of structure on the setting being observed. This can range from "zero," when the researcher simply enters some environment and observes behavior, to "quite a bit," when the researcher creates a structured setting and observes what occurs in it. Differing degrees of structure can exist in both naturalistic and participant observation studies.

Naturalistic Observation

In a **naturalistic observation** study, an attempt is made to study the normal behaviors of people or animals as they act in their everyday environments. Settings for naturalistic observation studies range from preschools to the African rainforest, and the subjects observed have included humans of all ages and animals of virtually every species. In some cases, semiartificial environments are sufficiently "natural" for the research to be considered a naturalistic observation. Studying animal behavior in modern zoos, which often simulate the animals' normal environment to a remarkable degree, is an example.

In some naturalistic studies, the observer is hidden from those being observed. In a study of sharing behavior among preschoolers, for example, observers might be in the next room, viewing the children through a one-way mirror (the observers can see through it; to the child it appears as a mirror). In a mall, an observer studying the mating rituals of the suburban adolescent could be sitting on a bench in a strategic location. In other studies, the observer might not be present at all—increasingly, naturalistic observation studies are being conducted with the aid of videorecorders. The films are viewed later and scored for the behaviors being investigated.

In naturalistic observations of animals, it is often impossible for the observer to remain hidden—the animals quickly sense the presence of an outsider. Under these circumstances, the observer typically makes no attempt to hide. Rather, it is hoped that after a period of time, the animals will become so habituated to the observer that they will behave normally. This is a strategy borrowed from the field

Box 11.1

CLASSIC STUDIES—When Prophecy Fails

One of the social psychology's dominant theories in the 1960s and 1970s was the theory of cognitive dissonance, developed by Leon Festinger. In general, it held that when we experience thoughts that contradict each other, we will be uncomfortable (i.e., we will experience cognitive dissonance) and we will be motivated to reduce the dissonance by convincing ourselves that everything is fine. One prediction derived from the theory is that if we exert a tremendous effort in some way, and the outcome is not what we initially expected, we will need to convince ourselves that the effort was nonetheless worthwhile. Festinger got the chance to test the prediction after encountering a news story with the following headline (Festinger, Riecken, & Schachter, 1956, p. 30):

> "Prophecy From Planet. Clarion Call to City: Flee That Flood. It'll Swamp Us On Dec. 21, Outer Space Tells Suburbanite"

The story described how a certain Mrs. Keetch had predicted a flood that would destroy most of North America in late December. How did she know? She was in direct contact with aliens from a planet called Clarion who had been visiting Earth in their flying saucers and had seen fault lines that were about to rupture and open the floodgates. Mrs. Keetch headed a small group of followers, in effect a religious cult, and they were devoted to convincing the world to repent their sins before it was too late (and time was running out; the story appeared just 4 months before the predicted catastrophe).

Festinger guessed the flood would not occur, so he became interested in how Mrs. Keetch and the group would react during the aftermath of a failed prophecy. He decided to see firsthand. Over the next several weeks, along with two colleagues

of anthropology, in which field workers spend long periods of time living among native members of remote cultures.

Participant Observation

Ocassionally, the researcher will join a group being observed, thus making the study a **participant observation**. Its chief virtue is its power to get the investigator as close to the action as possible. Being a participating member of the group can give the researcher first-hand insights that remain hidden to a more remote observer.

One of psychology's classic studies involved participant observation. In it, a small group of social psychologists joined a religious cult in order to examine the

and five hired observers, Festinger joined the group as a participant observer. What transpired is described in a delightful book (Festinger et al., 1956) with the same title as this box. There are several points worth noting from a methodological standpoint.

First, recording the data created a number of problems. The observers did not want to reveal their true purpose, so they could hardly take notes during the meetings at Mrs. Keetch's house. Hence, they found it necessary to rely on memory more than they would have liked. The problem was overcome to some degree when they hit on the idea of using the bathroom as a place to write down as much of their narrative data as they could. A second problem was reactivity. At no point did they believe their true purpose was known to the group, but they were very concerned that their presence strengthened certain of the group's beliefs. Because so many new people seemed to be joining the group over a short period of time, Mrs. Keetch believed (and therefore the group believed) that the mass joining was a "sign from above" that the flood prophecy was correct. Two observers were believed by the group to have been " 'sent' by the Guardians" (p. 242), the residents of Clarion, and one observer was actually believed to be *from* Clarion. Hence, the participant observers probably strengthened the convictions of Mrs. Keetch's small group, the effects of which are difficult to assess. This reactivity also poses an ethical dilemma. By strengthening the group's convictions, it could be argued that Festinger and his colleagues contributed to their "pathology."

As you know because you're reading this now, the world didn't end that December 21. It was not the only failed prophesy. Mrs. Keetch also told the group that the Guardians would send a spaceship that would land in the back yard that afternoon to carry them to safety. Of course, the ship didn't arrive and the world didn't end 4 days later. Did the group become discouraged, give up, call Mrs. Keetch insane, and return to their normal lives? No, in fact most of them became even *more* vigorous in their proselytizing. Apparently, in order to justify their efforts, they convinced themselves that their work had *prevented* the catastrophe—the group "spread so much light that God had saved the world from destruction" (p. 169). Hence, rather than quitting after a prophecy fails, one's commitment can actually be strengthened.

kinds of thinking that characterized its members. In particular, they examined this empirical question: If you publicly prophesize the end of the world, and the world fails to end, how do you deal with your failed prophecy? The answer was surprising enough that it contributed to the development of one of social psychology's best-known theories—the theory of cognitive dissonance. To learn more of this classic study of what happens when prophecy fails, take a look at Box 11.1.

Evaluating Observational Methods

The researcher using observational methods must be prepared to counter several problems, including an absence of control, the possibilities of observer bias and subject reactivity, and the ethical dilemmas associated with the issues of invasion of privacy and informed consent.

Absence of Control

Some degree of control occurs in observational studies that are structured (see case study 2), but in general the observational researcher must take what circumstances provide. Because of this lack of control, the conclusions drawn from observational studies must be drawn very carefully. If an observer records that child A picks up a toy and shortly thereafter child B picks up a duplicate of the same toy, does it mean that B is imitating A? Perhaps, but other interpretations are possible, the most obvious one being that the toy is simply an attractive one. When reading accounts of observational research, you won't encounter sentences like "X caused Y to occur."

On the other hand, observational research can often serve the purpose of falsification, an important strategy for theory testing. An observation consistent with theoretical expectations provides useful inductive support, but an observation that contradicts a theory is even more informative. As you know from Chapter 3, one contradiction won't disprove a theory, but it can certainly call it into question. For example, an influential theory of animal aggression in the 1960s, (Lorenz, 1966) held that fighting between members of the same species (except for humans) was hardly ever fatal to the combatants. For years, those studying aggression argued over the reasons why human aggression seemed to be so different from and so much worse than animal aggression. However, explaining the difference presupposes that the difference truly exists; observational research, however, has raised serious questions about the alleged nonfatality of animal aggression. In conflicts over territory among chimpanzees, for example, something analogous to "border wars" have been observed (Goodall, 1978). If a lone chimp from one group encounters several chimps from another group, the lone chimp will almost certainly be attacked and killed. Such a finding raises serious questions about Lorenz's claim that nonhuman aggression is seldom if ever fatal.

In a more recent example, Boesch–Achermann and Boesch (1993) observed several instances of parent chimpanzees teaching their offspring how to use tools (a hammer/anvil operation) to successfully open several varieties of nuts (see Figure 11.1). This is an important finding that questions earlier beliefs. As the researchers put it:

> Recent critical reviews of animal learning processes have denied that animals have the ability to imitate, but the teaching instances we observed would have no functional role if the chimpanzees did not have an imitative capacity. Many people still consider pedagogy one of the uniquely human attributes; our observations of chimpanzees indicate otherwise. (p. 20)

Despite control difficulties then, observational research can provide significant information. It can call some ideas into question, and it can also be a fruitful source of hypotheses for further study. Hence, the Boesch-Achermann and Boesch study questioned prior claims about the teaching abilities of chimps; it also could lead to further research on the teaching capacities of nonhuman primates. Could

FIGURE 11.1 Chimpanzees using tools: An adult female eating a nut, which she has just cracked with a stone hammer while her son inspects the nut shell. Mother chimpanzees share many of their cracked nuts with their offspring. Through this sharing, mother chimpanzees teach their offspring how to use tools to open nuts [from Boesch-Achermann and Boesch (1993)].

chimpanzees in captivity who have learned an operant task teach it to their offspring?

Observer Bias

A second problem for those doing observational research comes in the form of experimenter bias. In Chapter 6, you learned that when experimenters expect certain outcomes to occur, they might act in ways that could bring about such a result. In observational research, **observer bias** means having preconceived ideas about what will be observed and having those ideas color one's observations. For instance, consider what might happen if someone is studying aggression in preschoolers and believes from the outset that little boys will be more aggressive than little girls. For that observer, the exact same ambiguous behavior could be scored as aggressive if a boy did it but not aggressive if performed by a girl. Similarly, in an animal study, observers with different beliefs about whether animals can be altruistic might interpret certain ambiguous behaviors differently. Biasing can also occur because observational studies can potentially collect huge amounts of information. Deciding what to observe invariably involves reducing this information to a manageable size, and the choices about what to select can be affected by preconceived beliefs.

Biasing effects can be reduced significantly if the behaviors being observed are defined precisely enough and if observers have some training in identifying target behaviors. When actually making the observations, **behavior checklists** are often used. These are lists of predefined behaviors that observers are trained to spot. For example, when studying how preschoolers play, Bakeman and Brownlee (1980) distinguished between several types of play, including "solitary" play, in which a child plays alone, with toys that other children are not playing with, and ignores other children, and "parallel" play, in which the child plays with the same toys as adjacent children, but does not interact with those children. From videotaped recordings of the children, observers coded behaviors according to the type of play seen.

Arriving at a clearly defined target behavior is not always as simple as it might seem. Consider a study about gender differences in the tendency to interrupt another speaker. Who is more likely to interrupt, a male or a female?[1] Defining "interruption" might not seem too difficult until you think about it for a moment. What exactly constitutes an interruption event? Does it only occur when person A begins to speak while person B is already speaking? What about the case when B finishes a sentence but perhaps has more to say? If A speaks at that point, is it an interruption? If so, exactly what is the minimum time that must elapse between any two of B's sentences before A's intervening sentence would be considered a noninterruption? It is always possible to arrive at operational definitions, but it is important to recognize that they might be arbitrary. A subsequent failure to replicate a study could result from just a slight difference in defining the behavior being observed.

A second way to control for observer bias is to have several observers and see if their records agree. This you might recognize as a form of reliability; in this case, it is called **interobserver reliability**, usually measured in terms of the percentage of times that observers agree. Of course, both observers could be biased in exactly the same way, but a combination of checklists, observer training, and agreement among several observers generally controls bias. Bias also can be reduced to the extent that procedures are mechanized. We've already seen that videotaping allows for increased objectivity.

Finally, bias can be reduced by introducing various sampling procedures for systematically selecting a subset of the available information for observation and analysis. For example, a procedure called **time sampling** is sometimes used in observational studies. Rather than trying to maintain a continuous record of everything occurring, behavior is sampled at predefined times and only during those times. These times can be selected according to some rule, or they might be randomly selected. Similarly, **event sampling** selects only a specific set of events for observation; others are ignored. These procedures were used in case study 1.

Subject Reactivity

Think about all of the things you do in a typical day. Would you do all of them in exactly the same way if you knew you were being observed? Probably not. In all likelihood, you would show **reactivity**; that is, your behavior would be influenced by the knowledge that it was being recorded. Obviously, this problem can occur in observational research and is the reason for the popularity of devices like two-way mirrors. The problem also exists when animals are the subjects of observation and the observers cannot hide. As mentioned earlier, researchers assume that after a pe-

---

[1]Quick answer—males, a result well-known to all females, but a surprise to most males, who don't usually have much insight into their tendency to interrupt.

riod of time the animals will become accustomed to the presence of outsiders, but it is difficult to evaluate the extent to which this actually occurs.

Reactivity can be reduced by using **unobtrusive measures**. These are any measures taken of behavior, either directly or indirectly, when the subject is unaware of the measurement being made. Direct unobtrusive measures include hidden video or audiorecordings or behavior samples collected by hidden observers. Indirect unobtrusive measures record events and outcomes that one assumes have resulted from certain behaviors even though the behaviors themselves have not been observed. Webb et al. (1981) describe a number of these indirect measures and they can be quite creative. Here's just a sample:

✓ Contents of trash, to study eating and drinking habits

✓ Smudges on the glass casings of museum exhibits, to measure popularity (and the height of smudges allows inferences about the age of those viewing the exhibit)

✓ Degree of wear on floor coverings placed in strategic locations, to study foot traffic patterns

Ethics

As I am sure you have already recognized, reducing reactivity inevitably raises the ethical problems of invading privacy and a lack of informed consent. Wouldn't you be a bit disturbed to discover that researchers were hiding under the bed in your dorm, keeping track of everything you said and did? Believe it or not, that study already has been done (Henle & Hubbell, 1938), although quite clearly it would not gain IRB approval today.

In Box 3.1, you saw that some researchers are hesitant to conduct research in the field because of concerns over the privacy of potential subjects. However, observational research is generally condoned by the American Psychological Association's ethical code (1992), provided that certain safeguards are in place. For example, informed consent of participants is not considered essential if behavior is studied in public environments (as opposed to the privacy of one's dorm room). The standards that relate to observational research are reprinted in Table 11.1.

To conclude this section, consider the following two observational studies that illustrate the second dimension described at the beginning of this section—the degree of structure created by the researcher. The first is more purely observational, without any intervention on the part of the researchers; the second is more structured.

Case Study 1. 'Touching' Observations

When males and females are together in public places, they often are observed touching each other. Who is more likely to initiate the touching, males or females? Are there gender differences in the types of touching that occur? Are there age differences in touching? These and other questions were investigated by Hall and Veccia (1990), using naturalistic observations of couples in public places. Their work nicely illustrates the complexities of running a naturalistic observational study.

TABLE 11.1 *APA Ethical Code and Observational Research*

In addition to the general guidelines for research, the following standards from the American Psychological Association's 1992 code of ethics are especially relevant to observational research:

- **Standard 1.14 Avoiding Harm**

  Psychologists take reasonable steps to avoid harming their . . . research participants . . . and to minimize harm where it is foreseeable and un-avoidable

- **Standard 5.03 Minimizing Intrusions on Privacy**

  (a) In order to minimize intrusions on privacy, psychologists include in written and oral reports, consultations, and the like, only information germane to the purpose for which the communication was made.

  (b) Psychologists discuss confidential information . . . or evaluate data concerning . . . research participants . . . only for appropriate scientific or professional purposes and only with persons clearly concerned with such matters.

- **Standard 5.08 Use of Confidential Information for Didactic or other Purposes**

  (a) Psychologists do not disclose in their writings, lectures, or other public media, confidential, personally identifiable information concerning their . . . research participants . . . unless [they have] consented in writing or unless there is other ethical or legal authorization for doing so.

  (b) Ordinarily, in such scientific and professional presentations, psychologists disguise confidential information concerning such persons . . . so that they are not individually identifiable. . . .

- **Standard 6.12 Dispensing with Informed Consent**

  Before determining that planned research (such as research involving only anonymous questionnaires, naturalistic observations, or certain kinds of archival research) does not require the informed consent of research participants, psychologists consider applicable regulations and institutional review board requirements, and they consult with colleagues as appropriate.

- **Standard 6.13 Informed Consent in Research Filming or Recording**

  Psychologists obtain informed consent from research participants prior to filming or recording them in any form, unless the research involves simply naturalistic observations in public places and it is not anticipated that the recording will be used in a manner that could cause personal identification or harm.

Source: American Psychological Association, 1992.

Hall and Veccia trained five observers to make detailed yet unobtrusive records of mixed-sex and same-sex touching in a variety of public places ranging from airports to subways to malls, all in the Boston area. As in any observational study, they first had to face definitional problems. What exactly constitutes a touch? When should recording begin and end? Exactly what should be recorded in each observation?

Observers were equipped with a hand-held tape recorder for their descriptions and a small timing device that beeped every 10 seconds. To prevent others from hearing these signals (i.e., to remain unobtrusive), observers listened through earphones. The interval between beeps was considered a recording interval, during which several things were observed about a specific couple in view. First, their ages (by decade) were noted; then it was noted whether or not they were touching at the beginning of the interval, whether touching commenced during the interval, or whether no touching at all occurred. If touching occurred, the body parts involved and the form of touching (e.g., hand-holding) were described. Finally, the person initiating the touch was identified. For mixed-sex pairs, touches were coded as being initiated either by males (MF touch) or females (FM). This was not always possible, especially for touches already in progress at the start of an interval, but interobserver reliability was high (91% agreement).

When the subjects being observed were in motion (e.g., moving through a mall), the observers used a time sampling technique to select subject pairs. Once an initial pair was selected and their behavior recorded during a 10-second recording interval, another 10 seconds was allowed to pass before another couple would be selected. A form of event sampling was also used; the couple selected after the end of 10 seconds was the one closest to a predefined landmark.

Based on some earlier research, Hall and Veccia thought that in mixed-sex pairs, males would be more likely to initiate touches than females, perhaps because of a gender difference in the need for power or control. To their surprise, they found no differences: MF touches equaled FM touches overall. A closer analysis yielded some interesting outcomes, however. For example, Table 11.2 shows a large age effect. For younger couples, especially those under age 30, MF touches were indeed more frequent. In older couples, however, the female was more likely to initiate the touch. The effect is open to several interpretations, but one possibility suggested by Hall and Veccia is that males might feel a greater need to assert power and control in the early stages of a relationship; older couples are more likely to have been in a relationship for a longer time. (Of course, it could be that in older

TABLE 11.2 *Age Differences in Touching in Mixed-Sex Pairs*

Age of Dyad	No. of Touches		% of Touches	
	MF	FM	MF	FM
teens	16	6	73	27
20s	58	46	56	44
30s	28	29	49	51
40+	7	26	21	79

Note: MF = male-initiated touch; FM = female-initiated touch
Source: Adapted from Hall and Veccia (1990), Table 6.

couples, the FM touching amounts to an elbow to the ribs, resulting from the male's wistful observing of the touching among younger couples.)

Another interesting difference found by Hall and Veccia concerned the form of the touching. Although there were no significant gender differences in touches initiated with the hand, there were differences for the touches defined as "arm around" and "armed linked." As you might guess, males were more likely to use the former and females the latter.

Case Study 2. Observing Altruism in Children

A study by Peterson, Ridley-Johnson, and Carter (1984) is an interesting example of an observational study that adds a structured element to a naturalistic observation. They were studying helping behavior in school children, a phenomenon that was estimated from prior observations to occur spontaneously no more than once or twice per hour. Because it occurs so infrequently, the researchers decided to create a situation in which helping behavior would be more likely to occur. Thus, one reason to introduce greater structure in an observational study is to increase the frequency of otherwise rare events.

The structure was created by telling the children they would each have a turn wearing a "supersuit," a "smock of royal blue with a red satin star in the middle of the chest" (p. 237). It was fastened with one large button at the back of the neck; pretesting showed that buttoning it usually required the help of a second person. During free play periods, children took turns wearing the suit, with the order determined by drawing names from a jar. Each child had about 4 minutes with the supersuit.

The observations were videotaped, and two observers independently rated the tapes for helping behavior. Interobserver reliability was high: They agreed more than 90% of the time. The coding scheme for operationally defining the behaviors broke them into two general categories: The "donor" behaviors exhibited by potential helpers, and the "recipient" behaviors of those wearing the suit. An example of a donor behavior was "*spontaneous helping*—without any direct verbal or physical prompt, the donor offers verbally or physically to fasten the button on the supersuit" (Peterson et al., 1984, p. 237, italics in the original). An example of a recipient behavior was "*requesting help*—recipient verbally asks for help . . . or approaches the donor, turns so the button at the back is toward the potential donor, and gestures toward it" (Peterson et al., 1984, p. 238, italics in the original).

The results? Of 56 opportunities for help, spontaneous helping occurred 32 times and prompted helping occurred 13 times. More interesting, however, was the way in which recipients responded to being helped. Surprisingly, Peterson et al. (1984) found that children rarely reinforced others for helping. In fact, "more child recipients actually gave negative consequences (e.g., 'go away' and a shove in response to another child's attempt to help fasten the suit) than positive consequences for helping" (p. 238)! Also, very little reciprocal help (child A helps child B and B subsequently helps A) was observed.

Peterson et al. (1984) also asked each child to rate the social competence of classmates, and it was determined that most of the helping was done by the most socially competent children. This rating procedure is an example of how an observational study can add elements of other methods. In this case, the added element involved a type of survey, which brings us to that topic.

Survey Research

Survey research is based on the simple idea that if you want to find out what people think about some topic, just ask them. That is, a **survey** is a structured set of questions or statements given to a group of people in order to measure their attitudes, beliefs, values, or tendencies to act. Over the years, people have responded to surveys assessing everything from one's political preferences to one's favorite type of sexual activity.

Unlike most of the methods described in this text, surveying usually requires careful attention to sampling procedures. As you recall from Chapter 4 [and a quick review of the section there on sampling is a good idea], researchers sometimes try to estimate some specific feature (e.g., political preference) of a large category of people (the population) based on the data collected from just a small number of people (the sample). This is precisely the goal of survey research. In order for survey results to be valid, the sample must reflect the same properties as the population; that is, the sample must be "representative." Hence, with the survey method, the adequacy of the conclusions drawn depends in part on the quality of the sampling procedures.

Varieties of Survey Methods

There are three major techniques for collecting survey data. Each has its own strengths and weaknesses, both in terms of sampling and otherwise.

Interviews

You have undoubtedly heard of the Kinsey report, perhaps the most famous sex survey of all time. Completed in the years following World War II, it resulted from detailed face-to-face interviews with thousands of men and women and yielded two large books on sexual behavior in America, one for men (Kinsey, Pomeroy, & Martin, 1948) and one for women (Kinsey, Pomeroy, Martin, & Gebhard, 1953). Although you might think that Kinsey's **interview survey** format might have inhibited subjects from describing the intimate details of their sexual attitudes and behaviors, especially considering the historical era in which the studies were done, this apparently did not occur. In fact, conservative postwar America was shocked by the revelations of premarital sex, masturbation, and adultery. The books, although written in dry academic prose and loaded with tables and bar graphs, nonetheless reached best-seller status and made Kinsey a controversial figure. Accused by some of contributing to a moral decline and even of being a

Communist, he was regarded by others as a pioneer in the scientific study of an important aspect of human behavior (Christenson, 1971).

The interview format for surveying has the advantages of being comprehensive and of yielding highly detailed information. Even though the interviewer typically asks a standard set of questions, the skilled interviewer is able to elicit considerable information through follow-up questions or probes. Having an interviewer present also reduces the problem of questions being unclear; the interviewer can clarify on the spot. Sampling is seldom a major problem, although in some cases sizable segments of the population may not be included because they refuse to be interviewed, cannot be located, or live in an area that the interviewer would prefer to avoid. For example, the poor and the homeless are usually underrepresented in national surveys.

The major problems with the interview approach are cost, logistics, and interviewer bias. Interviewers need to be hired and trained, travel expenses can be substantial, and interviews might be restricted to a fairly small geographic area because of the logistical problems of sending interviewers long distances. And despite training, there is always the possibility that interviewer bias can affect the responses given in the face-to-face setting. For example, cross-race bias might exist, resulting in systematic differences between interviews with members of one's own race and members of other races.

Written Surveys

The second type of survey format is the paper-and-pencil test or **written survey**. These are found in a number of formats but usually involve asking subjects whether they agree or disagree with a series of statements or questions. When questions are asked, they can either be open-ended or closed. An **open-ended question** requires a response that must have more than just a yes or no answer; subjects must provide descriptive information. A **closed question** can be answered with a yes or a no or by choosing a single response from several alternatives. To illustrate the difference, consider these two ways of asking about school financing:

Open: How do you think we should finance public education?
Closed: Do you think that property taxes should be used to finance public education?

Written surveys with closed questions often use an interval scale of measuring the responses. As you recall from Chapter 4, with an interval scale there is no true zero point, but the intervals between points on the scale are assumed to be equal. The most common type of interval scale used in surveys is the so-called Likert scale (after the person who invented it, Rensis Likert). A typical Likert scale has anywhere from 5 to 9 distinct points on it, with each point reflecting a score on the continuum. For example, on a survey of attitudes toward televised coverage of news, subjects might be asked to indicate how much they agree with a series of statements according to a five point scale. A sample item might look like this:

The person anchoring a news show should have at least 5 years of experience as a professional journalist.

SD   D   U   A   SA

Respondents circle the point on the scale that indicates what they believe. SD stands for "strongly disagree," D for "disagree," U for "undecided," and so on. These points could then be converted to a 5-point scale (SD = 1, D = 2, etc.), and scores from several items dealing with the same issue could be combined.

Written surveys can be sent through the mail, as you know, because you've probably thrown a few away, or they can be administered in a group setting. Obviously, the return rate, the percentage of people filling out and handing in the survey, will be higher with the latter procedure, and this is a problem for surveys sent through the mail. Although there are no generally agreed-upon guidelines for acceptable return rates with mailed surveys, those done under federal contracts usually aim for at least 75% (Fowler, 1993). This can be a rather difficult standard to meet; return rates lower than 20% have been reported for published surveys. Obviously, a low rate makes it difficult to draw conclusions because such an outcome almost certainly means that the final sample will not be a representative one.

The best chance for a decent return rate for a mail survey occurs if (a) the survey is brief, easy to fill out, and includes mostly closed questions, with open-ended questions included only as options, (b) nonresponse triggers a second mailing and perhaps even a phone request to fill out the form, (c) the entire package is professional in appearance, and (d) the recipient has no reason to think the survey is merely step one in a sales pitch. Also, rates can be improved by including a small gift or token amount of money (Fowler, 1993). With adequate return rates and a well-designed written survey, this method can be more efficient and less expensive than interviews, while still yielding valuable data.

Phone Surveying

The third way to conduct a survey is to pick up the phone and call subjects. You might recall from Chapter 4 that sampling from phone books caused a problem for *Literary Digest's* prediction about the 1936 presidential election; not everyone could afford phones then. Today, however, phones are found in more than 90% of American homes. What about unlisted numbers? No problem: A common procedure used in phone surveying is called "random-digit dialing," which makes it possible for any phone number to be dialed.

Phone surveying has an obvious advantage in cost over interviews and written surveys. It also combines the efficiencies of a mail survey with the personal contact of an interview. A clear advantage over the interview is logistical; many more interviews can be completed per unit of time. Furthermore, the phone interviewer is not likely to be assaulted, a problem that sometimes occurs when field interviewers venture into high crime areas. The downside of phone interviewing is that the surveys must be brief because subjects can lose patience; this restriction also tends to cut down on open-ended questioning. A related problem is response rate. Although you might think that response rate would be quite high with phone surveying, this is not the case. For one thing, the increase in two-income families means that phone surveyors reach more answering machines than people during the day. Thus, many calls go unanswered, including repeat calls to the same number. This has led researchers to concentrate their activities during the early evening hours. Unfortunately, this is also the time when telemarketers call with fabulous deals on new credit cards or "free" vacations to Orlando. Compounding the problem is the fact that many telemarketers, unconcerned with ethics, begin their pitch by making the call sound like a survey. It's not clear how many people have hung up on legitimate surveyers, thinking they are hearing just another sales pitch.

The three techniques of interviewing, giving written surveys, and doing phone surveys are not mutually exclusive. Each can stand alone of course, but they are often combined. Interviewers might ask some open-ended questions verbally, then ask subjects to fill out a written questionnaire; written notice and a preliminary description of a survey might be sent just prior to phone surveying; or phone surveying might follow up on either interviews or written surveys. Each particular research project creates separate demands on the researcher, often requiring a certain amount of creativity in order to achieve the goals of study.

Evaluating Survey Research

Surveys have become an established means of collecting data and have a well-earned reputation for yielding valuable information about human behavior. Nonetheless, four major problems can occur. The first has to do with sampling considerations, as described earlier. Obviously, a biased sample can produce very misleading results. The second problem concerns response bias, the most common of which is called a **social desirability** bias. Sometimes, people respond to a survey question in a way that reflects not how they truly feel or what they truly believe, but how they think they should respond. That is, they attempt to create a positive picture of themselves—one that is socially desirable. The social psychology literature has a long history of research showing that the attitudes people express do not always correlate with their behavior. Thus, the results of survey research have to be interpreted with response bias in mind and conclusions can be strengthened to the extent that other research provides converging results.

A third major problem in survey research concerns the content of the items contained in the survey. Questions might be ambiguous, as when people are asked whether they agree with statements like this:

> Visiting relatives can be fun.

The questions might also be in the form of what a lawyer would call a leading question. Here are two examples that would almost certainly yield different response patterns.

> Given the importance to future generations of preserving the environment, do you believe the Clean Air Act should be strengthened, weakened, or left alone?
> Given the fact that installing scrubbers at utility plants could increase electricity bills by 25%, do you believe the Clean Air Act should be strengthened, weakened, or left alone?

Other questions might be so loaded that they will badly misrepresent opinions. Would you be surprised if a lot of people agreed with this statement, even those who believe a woman has the right to have an abortion?

Do you believe in killing babies?

Sometimes survey writers try to include too much, resulting in an item that actually asks two questions at once. For example, subjects might be asked whether they agree with this:

> I don't mind if female patrons in bars swear and buy drinks for men who are unknown to them.

The responder who agrees with the swearing part but disagrees with the drink-buying part would find it impossible to answer if forced to respond on a Likert scale.

These are just a few examples of the problems that occur when creating survey items. For more detailed guidance on survey construction, several excellent guides exist (e.g., Converse & Presser, 1986; Fowler, 1993).

A final problem with surveys is not methodological but ethical. Decisions affecting people's lives are sometimes made with the help of survey data, and if the surveys are flawed in some way, people can be hurt. Although professional psychologists operating within the ethics code are unlikely to use surveys inappropriately, abuses nonetheless can occur. The problem is recognized by the judicial system, which has established a set of standards for the use of survey data in courts of law (Morgan, 1990). The standards amount to this: If you are going to collect and use survey data, do it as a professional psychologist would. That is, be careful about sampling, survey construction, and data analysis. For an interesting and rather disturbing example of how survey methods can be misused, refer to Box 11.2, which examines the case of a female journalist who was fired from her news anchor job, partly on the basis of a rigged survey.

Survey methods have become quite complex in recent years. With the advent of computers and sophisticated multivariate statistical procedures such as multiple regression and factor analysis (Chapter 8), the results from a large survey can provide an enormous amount of information. As an example of a study that used part of a longer and more detailed survey, and to illustrate the features of a well-done survey, consider the following case study of the predictors of marital happiness in older couples.

Case Study 3. Being Happily Married

There's a long history of research on what contributes to a happy and productive marriage. What makes this study by Ward (1993) a bit different is that he focused on the state of marriage in the later years, at a time when children have left the house and when retirement becomes a major transition point in one's life. Ward was especially interested in the question of how marital happiness was related to perceived fairness in the way household tasks are distributed. For example, when a spouse retires and is hanging around the house all the time, how does that affect the marital relationship?

The data for analysis were part of a larger survey, the National Survey of Families and Households, conducted in 1987–1988 and sampling 9,643

Box 11.2

ETHICS — Using and Abusing Surveys

In early 1981, station KMBC of Kansas City hired Christine Craft, a news journalist from California, to co-anchor their evening news. Less than a year later, she was demoted from that position. The station claimed incompetence, but Ms. Craft sued, arguing that she was hired for her journalistic talent, not her youthful good looks, yet was fired for the latter reason. She won.

On the surface of it, the station appeared to act prudently, basing their decision not merely on whim but on data collected in a professional survey of viewers. However, this case illustrates not the use of survey research, but its misuse. According to Beisecker (1988), the study had several major flaws.

First, although the use of a "survey" conveys the impression of objectivity, the research was hopelessly biased from the start. One major problem was that the firm doing the research also served as paid consultants to the station and those doing the research already knew what decision the station wanted. The resulting bias was reflected in the wording of a phone survey that was used. One purpose of the survey was to compare Ms. Craft with other local news anchors, yet the questions were stacked against her. For example, she did poorly, compared to other anchors, on a question regarding which news anchor "knows Kansas City best" (p. 23), not surprising when one considers that (a) at the time of the survey, Ms. Craft had been with the station for 6 months and the other anchors had all been at their stations at least a year, and (b) in her early months with KMBC, Ms. Craft had been vigorously pro-

Americans aged 19 or older (Sweet, Bumpass, & Call, 1988, cited in Ward, 1993). Of this larger group, Ward selected the responses from 1,353 married couples, with all subjects aged at least 50 (they ranged from 50 to 95). Eighty percent of the couples had been married 30 years or more.

Information was collected both in the interview and written formats. The variables that were measured included the degree of satisfaction with the marriage, the degree of participation by each partner in household tasks, and the perceived fairness of the way these tasks were distributed. Some of the actual survey items included (p. 430):

1. "Taking all things together, how would you describe your marriage?" (7-point Likert scale ranging from 1 = very unhappy, to 7 = very happy).

2. "How often in the last year have you had open disagreements about household tasks?" (6-point scale from 1 = never to 6 = almost every day).

3. "If a husband and wife both work full-time, they should share household tasks equally." (5-point scale from 1 = strongly agree to 5 = strongly disagree).

moted as "a fresh new face from California" (p. 23). Also, much of the survey dealt with questions about attractiveness and appearance; very little of it concerned journalism.

In addition to the bias that characterized the project from the start, there were statistical problems serious enough for Beisecker (1988) to conclude that "the research firm did not employ any recognizable statistical tests or principles of statistical inference to justify its generalizations from the sample data" (p. 25). In other words, while the consultant firm reported simple *descriptive* statistics summarizing the survey results, they did not conduct the proper *inferential* statistics that would allow conclusions about the significance of the results. For example, it was reported that among 25- to 34-year-olds in the survey who were asked which channel's news had declined in quality, 30% said KMBC and 16% said a competing channel, KCMO. Much was made of this "2–1 margin" and it was attributed to the alleged detrimental effects of Ms. Craft's presence. However, the year before (1980), when Ms. Craft was still in California, the *same* question on another survey by the *same* firm yielded 26% for KMBC and 15% for KCMO. An inferential analysis surely would have shown no difference between the numbers for the 2 years. Not only was the analysis not done, the consultant/researchers conveniently omitted the 1980 data from the 1981 results.

Clearly, survey research can be done well and its results interpreted meaningfully. In the case of Christine Craft, though, the research was not done in the spirit of Standard 1.06 of the APA's ethics code (American Psychological Association, 1992):

> Psychologists rely on scientifically and professionally derived knowledge when making scientific or professional judgments or when engaging in scholarly or professional endeavors.

Couples were also asked to respond to the degree of fairness they perceived in the way household tasks were actually distributed in their own marriages. The results were complicated, but in general Ward found that:

a. Overall level of happiness was very high. On item 1, 57% circled the 7 and another 23% answered 6. Very few disagreements were reported as well. These results aren't too surprising—couples miserable with each other seldom last 30 years.

b. The spouses also strongly agreed that household chores should be distributed equally, but when the actual amount of time devoted to these tasks was estimated by each spouse, guess what? Women said they spent an average of 37 hours per week, men reported 15. Women were more likely than men to perceive the actual difference as unfair.

c. Concerning fairness and marital happiness, Ward reported that "perceived fairness of household labor [was] related to marital happiness, but only for wives" (p. 427). That is, if tasks were distributed unfairly, it lowered marital satisfaction for wives. An unfair distribution, even if perceived as such by the

> ## Box 11.3
>
> ### *CLASSIC STUDIES—The Mind of a Mnemonist*
>
> Case histories often document lives that are classic examples of particular psychological types. In abnormal psychology, for example, the case history approach is often used to understand the dynamics of specific disorders by detailing individual examples of them. Case histories also can be useful in experimental psychology, however, shedding light on basic psychological phenomena. A classic example of such a history is the one compiled by Alexander Romanovich Luria (1902–1977), a Russian physiologist/psychologist famous for his studies of Russian soldiers brain-injured during World War II and for his work on the relationship between language and thought (Brennan, 1991).
>
> The case involved S. V. Sherashevsky, or S. as Luria referred to him, whose remarkable memory abilities gave him a career as a stage mnemonist (yes, people actually paid to watch him memorize things), but also caused him considerable distress. The case is summarized in Luria's *The Mind of a Mnemonist* (1968). Luria studied S. for more than 20 years, documenting both the range of S.'s memory and the accompanying problems of his being virtually unable to forget anything.
>
> Luria first discovered that there seemed to be no upper limit on how much information S. could memorize; more astonishing, the information did not seem to decay with the passage of time. He could easily memorize lists of up to 70 numbers and could recall them in either a forward or reverse order. Also, "he had no difficulty reproducing any lengthy series . . . whatever, even though these had been presented to him a week, a year, or even many years earlier" (Luria, 1968, p. 12).

husbands, did not affect *their* perceptions of marital happiness—understandable when one considers that husbands usually end up on the winning end of inequities when it comes to sharing household tasks.

Case Studies

At the beginning of the last chapter, when pointing out that psychology began with small N designs, I briefly mentioned Darwin's detailed analysis of his son's early years. This can be considered an example of a **case study**, defined broadly as an in-depth analysis of a single case. The "case" is usually a person; if so, the method is occasionally referred to as a "case history" because it involves a close analysis of the history of that person's life or a major portion of it. The approach is

This is an unbelievable performance, especially considering that most people cannot recall more than seven or eight items on this type of task and that forgetting is the rule rather than the exception. As a student, you might be wondering what the down side to this could possibly be. After all, it would seem to be a wonderful "problem" to have, especially during final exam week.

Unfortunately, S.'s extraordinary memory skills were accompanied by severe deficits in other cognitive areas. For example, he found it almost impossible to read for comprehension. This was because every word evoked strong visual images that interfered with the overall organization of the idea conveyed by the sentence. Similarly, he was an ineffective problem solver, found it difficult to plan and organize his life, and was unable to think abstractly. The images that produced his remarkable memory interfered with everything else.

Is S. anything more than an idle curiosity, a bizarre once-in-a-lifetime person who doesn't really tell us anything about ourselves? No. In fact, the case sheds important light on normal memory. In particular, it provides a glimpse into the functional value of the limited capacity of short-term memory. We sometimes curse our inability to recall something that we were thinking about just a few minutes before, but the case of S. shows that forgetting allows us to clear the mind of information that might be useless (e.g., there's no reason to memorize most of the phone numbers we look up) and enables us to concentrate our energy on more sophisticated cognitive tasks. Because S. couldn't avoid remembering things, he was uable to function at higher cognitive levels.

One final point: It turns out that S. was not a once–in–a–lifetime case. Another person ("VP") with a similarly remarkable memory was studied by American psychologists Hunt and Love (1972). Oddly enough, VP grew up in a city in present-day Latvia that was just a short distance from the birthplace of Luria's S.

common in clinical work, in which the case of someone with a particular disorder is used to illustrate the factors that lead to and influence it. The most famous practitioner of this type of case study was Sigmund Freud, who built his theories on the basis of detailed case examples of his patients.

Case histories have also been completed by experimental psychologists, and one of the best known examples is Alexander Luria's fascinating account of a man who seemed unable to forget anything. The classic study is detailed in Box 11.3, and if you think that having a near perfect memory would solve many of your problems, you'll soon have second thoughts after reading about Luria's S.

A case study is not limited to the investigation of a single person, however. The term is also applied to the analysis of a single event or a single class of events that illustrates some phenomenon. For example, although the Festinger study of cults was described in Box 11.1 as a famous example of participant observation, the study could also be considered a case study of a cult. Case studies of events are often completed when a rare event or an event of historic importance occurs. For example, researchers have done case studies of how nearby residents reacted to the nuclear accident at Three Mile Island in Pennsylvania in 1979 (Aronson, 1992) and whether people retained accurate "flashbulb" memories of where they were and what they were doing when President Kennedy was assassinated (Yarmen & Bull, 1978).

Case Study 4. Being Hypnotized on Stage

Besides chronicling the effects of rare and extraordinary occurrences, case studies can also investigate common yet intriguing events like staged displays of hypnotism, in which ordinary people seem to be willing to do some very unusual things. Such was the focus of a case study by Crawford, Kitner-Triolo, Clarke, and Olesko (1992). They interviewed 22 college students who had participated on stage during a campus performance by a stage hypnotist, in order to study the aftereffects of such an experience. Being hypnotized was enjoyable for most students, but a small minority found it annoying, embarrassing, or even frightening. Somewhat surprising was the finding that a substantial proportion of the group experienced posthypnotic amnesia. Of the 22, 8 agreed with the statement "After I left the stage, I could not remember some things I did," and 6 agreed that "The next day I could not remember some things I did." One subject who was especially disturbed by the amnesia likened it to an alcoholic blackout. Also surprising was the report that 5 of the 22 believed the hypnotist to have total control over their actions. These levels of amnesia and perceptions of control aren't normally found in follow-up studies of participants in laboratory studies of hypnosis. Hence, this case study yielded important information about the effects of hypnotism that would not have been apparent from more controlled studies.

On the basis of their analysis, Crawford et al. (1992) made several recommendations about on-campus hypnotism shows, including "screening out participants who are in therapy or counseling, correcting misperceptions about hypnosis among the participants before the hypnosis begins, . . . removing all amnesia suggestions and reviewing the events at the end of the hypnotic experience, and remaining available afterward for further questions" (p. 666).

Finally, the term case study can be used when referring to an especially good example of some phenomenon, which is how I've been using the term since Chapter 4. Beginning there and including the hypnotism example you just read, you've encountered numerous case studies—relatively in-depth descriptions of studies that I chose because they seemed to be good illustrations of particular methods or experimental designs.

Evaluating Case Studies

At first glance, it might appear that the description of a single case would not be very informative. External validity is the most obvious weakness—how much can be generalized from a single example? Of course, as is true in all research, confidence in external validity only accumulates gradually, as the findings are replicated.

This can occur with cases studies just as it can with other varieties of research. While it might be difficult to replicate a spectacular event like the 1989 San Francisco earthquake, it isn't difficult to see if the same effects occur with other kinds of natural disasters.

A second difficulty with the case study is that ample opportunity exists for the biases of the researcher to color the case description. Is it all that surprising to find unending discussions of unresolved Oedipal complexes and various other sexually based problems in case histories written by Freudians? To illustrate, during a recent session using *PsychLit* to fish for research examples for this chapter, I encountered a study called "Ph.D. Envy: A Psychoanalytic Case Study" (Behr, 1992). It described the case of a woman with a "profound and debilitating anxiety around not being able to finish her Ph.D. dissertation. . . . [Her] contempt for those without Ph.D.s and the intense envy of those who possessed them led to the psychical equivalence of Ph.D. envy and penis envy" (p. 99). Would her case be described differently by a non-Freudian? Almost certainly.

A third problem concerns memory. Because subjects of case histories of individuals are often required to recall events from the past, a whole range of memory problems introduce themselves. As researchers such as Elizabeth Loftus have shown repeatedly, our memories for the events of our lives are often distorted by circumstances that intervene between the target event and the later recall of it. Take, for example, a Floridian who experienced the devastating Hurricane Andrew in 1992. If asked to describe the experience as part of a case study a year later, some of the information would undoubtedly be accurate. After all, someone is not likely to forget the roof being blown off the house. However, during the intervening year, the person has (a) experienced the event; (b) seen videos, new stories, TV recreations, and photographs of the event; (c) listened to countless hurricane stories from friends and neighbors; and (d) probably dreamt of the event a few times. As Loftus has demonstrated (e.g., Loftus & Hoffman, 1989), our subsequent memories are often "constructions" of the event itself and these later occurrences. That is, we now have a memory that incorporates many elements, only one of which is the actual event itself.

Despite the difficulties, case histories can be quite informative. First, because of the level of detail, they can provide insights into behavior that cannot occur in larger N studies that collect limited amounts of data per subject. Luria's study not only details S.'s extraordinary memory capacity, but shows how it affected other aspects of the poor man's life. Luria's S. also illustrates a second point: Some individuals are so rare that a case study approach is the only feasible one. Third, like all descriptive research, case studies can be a useful source of empirical questions for future investigation. As you've seen, Crawford et al. (1992) were surprised that about one third of the college students participating in the hypnotism show experienced some degree of amnesia for what happened on stage and almost as many believed the hypnotist to be in complete control. Is there some important personality or cognitive factor that differentiates these students from others? In what ways are posthypnotic and postalcohol amnesias alike and different? Would those students who believed the hypnotist was in control also be more likely to develop learned helplessness than other students?

Besides providing hypotheses for further research, case studies, like observational research, can sometimes serve the purpose of falsification. That is, if a strong assertion is made about some psychological phenomenon, a single disconfirming case can raise serious questions about it. You already know about one famous example (See Box 3.3). Claims made about Clever Hans' math skills were effectively falsified when the case was investigated by the psychologist Pfungst.

A second example comes from the field of parapsychology, which investigates phenomena like extrasensory perception. You've undoubtedly read about "psychics" who claim to have special abilities to read minds, predict the future, and to influence events (e.g., make a spoon bend) through mind power. These claims can be questioned by describing case studies in which a person, usually a professional magician, is able to repeat every phenomenon demonstrated by the psychic, yet makes it clear that nothing but the ordinary deceptions of the professional magician are involved (e.g., Randi, 1982). Defenders of parapsychology might argue that psychics produce their results mentally and magicians produce theirs physically, but the more parsimonious explanation is that both outcomes occur the same way (i.e., physically).

In sum, case studies are susceptible to biases and their results may not generalize easily, but like observation studies they can be useful in generating new research, they can help falsify weak theories, and at times they can be the only way to document an extraordinary person or event.

Archival Research

Researchers sometimes take advantage of information that is already available in order to test hypotheses. When this occurs, the approach is called **archival research**, with the term "archives" referring both to the records themselves and to the places where the records are stored. Archival data range from public information such as census data, court records, genealogical data, corporate annual reports, and patent office records, to more private information such as credit histories, health history data, educational records, personal correspondence, and diaries. "Archives" as locations refer to places like university libraries, government offices, and computerized databases. You can begin to get a sense of the topics that can be studied using archival data from the following titles of research articles:

✓ Perceived equity, motivation, and final-offer arbitration in major league baseball (Bretz & Thomas, 1992)

✓ The institutionalization of premarital cohabitation: Estimates from marriage license applications, 1970 and 1980 (Gwaltney–Gibbs, 1986)

✓ Attributions in the advice columns: Actors and observers, causes and reasons (Schoeneman & Rubanowitz, 1985)

Varieties of Archival Research

Archival research is often a component of a larger research effort that includes other methods. Program evaluation research is a good example. As you recall from Chapter 9, program evaluation research includes needs assessment studies, formative and summative evaluations, and cost analyses. All of these can include archival information. Needs assessments usually examine census data, and both agency records and statistical data from other programs can contribute to evaluations and cost analyses. Furthermore, at least one of the methods you encountered in Chapter 9, the interrupted time series design, invariably includes archival information, such as traffic accident data, in order to chart trends.

Sometimes, archival research will require not just the selection and statistical analysis of records, but a **content analysis**, which can be defined as any systematic examination of materials that organizes qualitative information in terms of predefined categories. Any type of record can be content analyzed, and while most content analyses examine verbal materials like text or interview data, nonverbal material can be analyzed as well. For example, in a study by Brantjes and Bouma (1991), the drawings of patients suffering from Alzheimer's disease were content analyzed, correlated with the degree of mental deterioration, and compared to drawings of non-Alzheimer's subjects of the same age.

As with observational research when checklists of target behaviors are developed ahead of time, it is important to have clearly defined categories of content in mind before beginning a content analysis. It is also a good idea to have more than one person doing the analysis, so as to check on the reliability of the analysis. If possible, in order to avoid any biasing effects, scorers should be blind to the hypothesis being tested.

The effective use of a content analysis of verbal materials is illustrated in a study by Lau and Russell (1980). To investigate how people explain their successes and failures in sports, they examined newspaper accounts of major sporting events for comments by players, coaches, and sportswriters about why they (or the team they were writing about) either won or lost. Explanations were coded into two broad categories, depending on whether a win or a loss was blamed on internal (it was our responsibility entirely) or external (an excuse of some type) factors. In general, they found that winners were more likely to give internal explanations for their success; after losing, there was about an equal proportion of internal and external explanations.

Although by their nature archival studies do not allow the direct manipulation of independent variables, they often involve sophisticated attempts to control for potential confounding factors. A clever example of this is a study by Ulrich (1984), who demonstrated that recovery from surgery could be influenced by having a room with a pleasant view of the outside world.

Case Study 5. A Room with a View

One of the more interesting areas of research that has developed in psychology within the past 15 years concerns the relationship between mental and physical well-being. Health psychologists study such problems as the link between stress and illness, the doctor–patient relationship, and in the case of the Ulrich study,

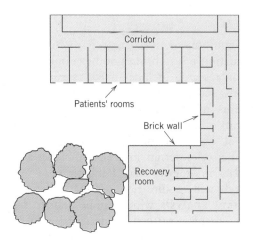

FIGURE 11.2 Floor plan of hospital used in archival study of recovery from surgery, showing rooms facing either a group of trees or a brick wall [from Ulrich (1984)].

whether such a seemingly minor factor as hospital architecture can affect patient health.

Ulrich (1984) examined patient records over a period of about 10 years in a suburban Pennsylvania hospital. He was interested in whether recovery from surgery could be affected by the type of room in which the patient spent postoperative time. In particular, he compared rooms with windows facing a brick wall with rooms with windows that provided a pleasant view of a small group of trees (see Figure 11.2 for a floor diagram). All the rooms were the same size and in each room the beds were arranged so that patients could easily look out the windows.

Because the study was archival, Ulrich could not randomly assign patients to the rooms, but he did everything possible to make the two groups of patients comparable. First, he only used patients recovering from a common type of gall bladder surgery and omitted those under the age of 20 and over 69. Second, he created two similar groups using a variety of matching variables including age, gender, smoking history, and weight. Thus, he examined records for two groups of patients who were roughly equivalent to each other; the only major difference was the view they had out their windows—bricks or trees.

From the archival records, Ulrich examined length of postoperative hospitalization, whether and in what amounts patients requested medication for pain and/or anxiety, the frequency of minor complications such as headache or nausea, and nurses' notes about the patients. What he found was a clear advantage for those recovering in a room with a view. They spent an average of one less day in the hospital after surgery (7.96 vs 8.70 days), they requested less pain medication, and when they did request it, they asked for lower doses than patients staring at the bricks. A content analysis of nursing records determined that those looking out on the park-like setting were more likely to elicit positive rather than negative comments from the nurses (but maybe the nurses were affected by the trees too!). The groups did not differ in their requests for antianxiety medication; nor were there differences in postoperative minor complications.

The Ulrich study is one of a growing number that show how physical health can be influenced by a myriad of nonmedical factors. The study also illustrates how health psychology has become a multidisciplinary field: At the time of the study's publication, Ulrich taught in the Department of *Geography* at the University of Delaware.

Evaluating Archival Research

There are several advantages inherent to archival research. The most obvious one is that the amount of information available in late twentieth century is virtually unlimited and the possibilities for archival research are restricted only by the creativity of the investigator. A second strength is that archival research can converge with the results of laboratory research, thereby increasing external validity. McClelland's research on achievement motivation is an example. The studies that you read about in Box 8.3 used archival information such as children's literature and patent information in different historical eras in order to show that achievement themes in the literature predicted later technological achievement. The results were consistent with other laboratory research on the relationship between the achievement needs of individuals and their achieving behavior. A third advantage is that archival information is nonreactive; because the information already exists, collecting it eliminates the possibility of subject reactivity.

The fact that archival data already exists also creates problems for researchers. Despite the vast amount of data available, some information vital to a researcher might be missing or the available data might not be a representative sample. In the study listed earlier that examined the content of advice columns, for example, Schoeneman and Rubanowitz (1985) had to contend with the fact that what eventually is printed in an advice column is just a small proportion of the letters written to advice columnists. Who can say what factors determine the selection of letters for publication?

A final problem with archival research is the one common to all the strategies described in this chapter—experimenter bias. In archival research, this can take the form of selecting only those records that support one's hypothesis or interpreting content in a way that is biased by one's expectations. The problem can be difficult to avoid completely because the researcher doing archival research is typically faced with much more information than can be used and the information can often be open to several interpretations.

Of course, the judicious researcher can reduce the effects of bias by developing a clear plan ahead of time that includes a carefully worked out procedure, operational definitions for all the pertinent variables, criteria for selecting materials, and so on. In Ulrich's hospital recovery study, for example, only patients hospitalized between May 1 and October 20 of a given year had their records scrutinized. Why were those months the only ones selected? Because during the rest of the year, there was no foliage on the trees and his goal was to compare patients who were looking at brick walls with those looking at fully bloomed and presumably more aesthetically pleasing trees.

In sum, archival studies are an effective way to use information about events that have already occurred and therefore enable the researcher to test hypotheses when variables aren't available for direct experimental manipulation. Considering the vast amount of information out there, and its increased availability (e.g., via

Internet), archival research is an approach that promises to become even more visible in the years ahead.

With this chapter on descriptive methods, the cast of characters for the production called "research in psychology" is complete. What remains is to return to a theme introduced back in Chapter 1—the excitement of doing research in psychology. One more brief chapter to go.

Chapter Review

Glossary Fill-Ins

1. If an observational study uses just one observer to record behavior, then _____ cannot be determined.

2. _____ is likely to occur when people know they are being observed and their behavior is being recorded.

3. "Do you think a course in statistics should be required of psychology majors?" is an example of a(n) _____ question.

4. Competition from telemarketing is a major problem for _____.

5. Someone would perform a _____ in order to determine if the transcript of an interview included a large number of self-references ("I," "me," etc.).

6. Freud's preferred method for collecting data was the _____.

Multiple Choice

1. Becoming so involved with a group that one loses objectivity is most likely to occur in which type of study?
   a. Researchers joining a cult.
   b. Observing chimpanzee behavior in the wild.
   c. Observing patterns of touching among teenagers.
   d. Observing sharing in a structured preschool setting.

2. In a naturalistic observation, how does one deal with the problem of reactivity?
   a. Subjects never know they are being observed.
   b. Subjects always know they are being observed and give informed consent.
   c. Observers are hidden or subjects are habituated to the observer's presence.
   d. The observer becomes a member of the group.

3. The major advantage of interviews over written and phone surveys is that interviews
   a. Yield more comprehensive information.
   b. Are less expensive.
   c. Never experience sampling problems.

      d. Avoid the problem of bias.

4. Which of the following empirical questions would be best answered by using an archival study?

      a. Which species of tropical fish most vigorously defends its territory?

      b. How do most Americans feel about the concept of national health insurance?

      c. Are natural disasters given greater news coverage if they occur in popular tourist locations?

      d. At a movie theater, are overweight patrons more likely to buy the "bucket" of popcorn while normal weight patrons buy the "cup" of popcorn?

5. Which of the following is true of the case study as a method?

      a. Case studies of events are easily replicated.

      b. It can be an in-depth analysis of the occurrence of an unusual event.

      c. It is the method of choice when a representative sample is needed.

      d. External validity is seldom a problem.

Applications Exercises

Exercise 11.1. — Improving Poor Survey Items

Following are several examples of items that could be found on surveys. Some are in the form of closed questions, others in the form of agree/disagree statements. For each item, (a) identify what is wrong and (b) rewrite it so as to solve the problem.

      a. Have you had an upset stomach lately?

      b. Highly prejudiced people are usually hostile and not very smart.

      c. Do you agree with most people that violations of seat belt laws should result in harsh penalties?

      d. Most doctors have a superior attitude.

      e. People who are overweight lack willpower and are usually unhappy.

      f. In your opinion, how tall is the average professional golfer?

Exercise 11.2. — Defining Behaviors for Observational Research

Imagine that you are in the beginning stages of an observational research study and have to arrive at clear operational definitions for the behaviors you'll be observing. How would you define the behaviors to be recorded in studies with the following hypotheses:

      a. Men interrupt women more than women interrupt men.

      b. Male and female college students carry their books differently.

      c. In a free play situation, older children play cooperatively, but younger children engage in parallel play.

    d. While in the college library, most students spend less than half their time actually studying.

    e. Teenagers patrolling malls follow clearly defined routes, which they repeat at regular intervals.

Exercise 11.3. — Deciding on Descriptive Methods

For each of the hypotheses listed below, identify the best methodological approach from the following possibilities. Indicate the reason(s) for your choice.

- naturalistic observation
- written survey
- participant observation
- interview survey
- case study
- phone survey
- archival study

    a. Fraternities and sororities represent well-ordered cultures that reward conformity to unwritten norms for behavior.

    b. When respondents are given the opportunity and encouragement to explain their opinions on controversial issues, their ideas are usually based on anecdotal evidence.

    c. A national sample (2,000 people) is chosen for a consumer survey on preferred snack foods.

    d. For 1 month after a highly publicized suicide, there will be an increase in driver fatalities in which the driver is alone in the car and the accident does not involve other drivers.

    e. After a near-disastrous landing in which the landing gear failed and passengers had to be evacuated, most of the people who flew on Flight 304 will experience mild to severe anxiety problems that will interfere with sleep.

    f. When college students enter the cafeteria, males are more likely to be unaccompanied than females, and this is especially true for the dinner meal.

CHAPTER 12

Epilogue: Doing Research in Psychology

Chapter Overview

- ### Psychological Science and Pseudoscience
  It is important to distinguish legitimate scientific inquiry from pseudoscience. The latter is characterized by a deliberate attempt to associate itself with true science, by a reliance on anecdotal evidence and theories that cannot be adequately tested, by developing elaborate modifications to defeat legitimate falsification, and by a tendency to explain complicated phenomena with overly simplistic concepts.

- ### The Excitement of Psychological Research (Part 2)
  Life as a researcher in psychology is continually challenging and rewarding, and the best researchers have a passion for their work. Unlimited opportunities await those excited by the prospect of making discoveries about human behavior.

Talk about an unyielding devotion to research. On July 14, 1893, Lightner Witmer,[1] then a young experimental psychologist at the University of Pennsylvania, wrote to his colleague at Harvard, Hugo Münsterberg. The letter was mostly a "what I did on my summer vacation" exercise, but it displays the lengths to which some scientists will go to study human behavior. Witmer was apparently interested in the psychological experience of pain. As he wrote to Münsterberg, he was using a novel approach:

> . . . I let a horse throw me from his back, allowing me to drop on my shoulder and head. I showed a beautiful case of loss of consciousness. . . . I not only do not remember mounting the horse and running, but I almost forgot everything that happened. . . . [F]rom the time I got up in the morning till I regained consciousness about 11 o'clock, I can form no continuous series of events. My head was bad for a while but is all right now, but my arm has served the purpose of quite a number of experiments as it still continues quite painful at times. . . . The psychological side of my afflictions will form the basis of at least three lectures next fall. (Witmer, 1893)

I don't know if you'll become as "personally involved" with research as Lightner Witmer did, but I hope that as you reach the end of this course on research methods, you have come to appreciate the value of doing research in psychology. In this final chapter, you will encounter some additional evidence that doing research in psychology can be rewarding, exciting, and fun. First, however, we begin by distinguishing between true scientific research in psychology and work that claims to apply scientific methods and appears to increase our understanding of human behavior, but does neither.

Psychological Science and Pseudoscience

Because everyone is interested in human behavior, it is not surprising that many claims are made about its causes and inner workings. Many of those claims are based on legitimate scientific inquiry, of course, following the rules of the game that you have learned about in this text. That is, we know much about human behavior as a result of relying on the kinds of thinking and the specific methods you've learned. However, many claims are made in the name of psychological science using methods and ways of thinking that are *not* truly scientific, but merely pseudoscientific. In general, the term **pseudoscience** is applied to any field of inquiry that appears to use scientific methods and tries hard to give that impression, but is actually based on inadequate or unscientific methods and yields results that are not valid. An important goal of this course in research methods is to enable you to differentiate legitimate scientific activity from pseudoscience. As the Sidney Harris cartoon in Figure 12.1 suggests, pseudoscience is not unpopular.

---

[1]Witmer is a good example of someone trained as an experimental psychologist but with strong interests in application. Chapter 9 mentions the fact that in the late 1890s, he founded American psychology's first clinic.

FIGURE 12.1   The popularity of pseudoscience.

Recognizing Pseudoscience

If you lived in the early 1880s, you could send away to the New York firm of Fowler and Wells for a "Symbolic Head and Phrenological Map" for 10¢. For another $1.25, the head and map could be accompanied by a copy of *How to Read Character: A New Illustrated Handbook of Phrenology and Physiognomy* (Anonymous Advertisement, 1881). Thus equipped, you would then be in a position to "scientifically" measure character through an analysis of the shape of the skull.

If you lived in the early 1980s, you could send away to the Edmund Scientific Company and order, for $11.50, a "Biorhythm Kit," complete with a precision "Dialgraf Calculator" (Gardner, 1981). To help interpret these biorhythms, you could add a copy of *Biorhythm: A Personal Science* (Gittelson, 1975). Thus equipped, you would then be able to "scientifically" analyze the influence of biological rhythms in your life.

As these examples suggest, people will pay for self-knowledge, especially if the methods appear to be scientific and are easy to implement and understand. Both nineteenth-century phrenology and twentieth-century biorhythm theory are now considered pseudosciences; there are important differences between the two, but in general they both serve to exemplify the main features of pseudoscientific approaches to knowledge.

Associate with True Science

Pseudosciences do everything they can to associate themselves with legitimate science. In some cases, the origins of a pseudoscience can be found in true science; in other instances, the pseudoscience confuses its concepts with legitimate scientific ones. Phrenology illustrates the former, biorhythms the latter.

Phrenology originated in legitimate attempts to demonstrate that different parts of the brain had identifiably different functions; it can be considered one of the first systematic theories about the localization of brain function (Bakan, 1966). It was created in the late eighteenth century by Franz Joseph Gall (1758–1828), a highly respected Viennese physician. His lifelong belief in the relationship between personality and bodily structure[2] culminated in what he called "craniometry," the doctrine asserting that (a) different personality and intellectual attributes were associated with different parts of the brain, (b) particularly strong attributes would result in larger brain areas, and (c) skull measurement would yield size estimates for the different areas of the brain. Therefore, by measuring skulls, one could identify personality and intelligence. Gall spent a significant part of his life trying to accumulate cases in support of his grand idea. By the midnineteenth century the theory was well-known in Europe and America and was called "phrenology."

One criterion of a good theory is that it should generate research, and that was certainly true of phrenology. Legitimate scientific research tested its limits, developing important research procedures in the process. By any reasonable scientific standard, the theory failed. For example, in a brilliant series of animal studies, the French physiologist Pierre Flourens showed that certain parts of the brain claimed by phrenologists to have function X in fact served function Y (Hothersall, 1990). After Flourens, few legitimate scientists continued to believe in the value of phrenology; for them, the theory was falsified.

Despite Flourens, however, phrenology refused to die, partly due to the aggressive marketing of firms like the one mentioned above, headed by Fowler and Wells. By the second half of the nineteenth century, phrenology as big business flourished: Phrenological societies were formed, popular journals were established, and phrenological analysis was used for everything from choosing a career to picking an honest servant. Character descriptions in terms of phrenological categories can be found in the writings of many famous nineteenth-century authors (e.g., Edgar Allen Poe). Even if a theory is discredited within the scientific community, then, it can still find favor with the public. This creates special problems for psychology as a science because it isn't difficult for virtually any type of theory about human nature to have some appeal.

The progression in phrenology's history is from legitimate science to pseudoscience. On the other hand, biorhythm theory was of questionable validity from its start. It developed near the end of nineteenth theory with the concept of "vital periodicity," promoted by Wilhelm Fleiss (1858–1928), a somewhat shadowy figure who for time was a close confidant of Sigmund Freud. Fleiss believed that all humans were bisexual: Everyone had a male and female side. Furthermore, the bisexuality was related to two different cycles, one female and one male. The female cy-

---

[2]You read about a more recent example of this idea in Box 4.2.

cle was 28 days and the male cycle was said to be 23 days. Why 28 and 23? The 28 was the average time between menstrual cycles for women, and the 23 was the average time between the end of one menstrual cycle and the beginning of another (it's not clear how the latter translates to "male cycle").

Fleiss tried to make the connection to legitimate science by tying these cycles to the 28-day lunar cycle and invoking Darwinian evolution. He argued that (a) Darwin demonstrated that some organisms living near the shore were affected by the cyclical changes in the tides and therefore by the moon because the moon influences tides, (b) the evolutionary history of humans includes a time when ancestors were creatures of the sea, and (c) therefore buried deeply in our genetic past were rhythmic influences related to the lunar cycle (Sulloway, 1979). Fleiss believed that 28 and 23 were almost magical numbers and that various mathematical combinations of these numbers enabled predictions about the future. For instance, he showed that several famous persons died on "critical" days—multiples of 23 or 28 or sums of other numbers plus 23 or 28. Freud was so taken by the Fleissian mathematical gymnastics that for a time he was apparently convinced that he would die at age 51, the sum of the two key numbers (Palmer, 1982)!

Modern biorhythm theory developed in the 1930s when a Swiss engineering professor named Alfred Teltscher believed his students showed intellectual cycles of 33 days. With some obvious gender stereotyping, he renamed Fleiss's female and male cycles, calling them "emotional" and "physical," respectively, and produced a theory claiming that the three basic cycles, intellectual, emotional, and physical, accounted for much that happened in one's life.

According to the Swiss model, all three cycles begin at the moment of birth, when they are at some baseline level. Day by day, each ascends to some maximum level, drops to a low point, ascends again, and so on. Because the cycles are of different lengths, they will intersect at times and they will reach high and low points on different days. Good things happen at high points in a given cycle, bad things at low points, and especially bad things at points where a cycle passes the baseline. These are called "critical days," and the problems occur because the cycles are "unstable" during those days. Especially dangerous are "double critical" days when two cycles hit baseline; even more ominous are the occasional "triple critical" days, when it is wise to just stay in bed and hope for the best. According to the theory, knowing one's biorhythms helps explain past events and by allowing predictions of the future, enables one to plan appropriately. For example, Gardner (1981) reported that in some Swiss hospitals, doctors scheduled surgery only after checking the biorhythmic charts of patients to see if their physical cycles were high (no word on whether the doctors checked their own charts).

The biorhythm theory popular in the 1970s and 1980s deliberately associated itself with genuine biological research. For example, writers (e.g., Gittelson, 1975) frequently referred to biological studies of periodicity, such as the legitimate work on circadian rhythms, the well-known daily cycles of biological activity (e.g., the cyclical fluctuations in body temperature). They also tried to create the illusion of being scientific by being mathematical. Seemingly complicated calculators were used to chart one's cycles on a day-to-day basis. Yet like phrenology before it, biorhythm theory (a) failed all legitimate scientific tests and (b) prospered anyway, at least for a time.

Rely on Anecdotal Evidence

A second feature of pseudoscience, and one that helps explain the popularity of theories like phrenology and biorhythms, is the heavy reliance on and uncritical acceptance of anecdotal evidence. Thus, Gall's evidence consisted mostly of a catalogue of examples to support his theory: a thief with a large area of "acquisitiveness," a priest with an overdeveloped bump for "reverence," a prostitute with excessive "amativeness." Biorhythm advocates use the same approach. Their literature is filled with examples of good and bad things happening as predicted by the cycles. Such evidence has immediate appeal to the uncritical reader. There tends to be an "Oh, wow!" reaction to reports that several presidents died on critical days and that President Kennedy's intellectual cycle was at a critical point when he made the not so smart decision to ride in a Dallas motorcade with the top down (Palmer, 1982).

There is nothing wrong with accumulating evidence inductively to support a theory; even anecdotal examples like the ones mentioned above are not automatically disqualified. The problem occurs when one relies *exclusively* on anecdotes, or makes more of them than is warranted. The difficulty is that anecdotal evidence is selective evidence. Examples that don't fit aren't considered. Yes, there may be some thieves with a particular skull shape, but in order to evaluate a specific relationship between skull configuration X and thievery, one must know (a) how many thieves do *not* have configuration X, and (b) how many people with configuration X *aren't* thieves. Without knowing these latter two pieces of information, there is no way to determine if there is anything unusual about a particular thief with skull shape X.

The identical problem occurs with biorhythms. When Arnold Palmer won the British Open in 1962, all three cycles were high. Yet if one looked at Arnold Palmer's entire golfing career, would his successes and failures be predictable via biorhythms? Surely not, if similar research on the true predictability of biorhythms is any indication. Biorhythms have been found incapable of predicting accident rates, baseball batting averages, mood swings, performance on tests, and a host of other behaviors (Hines, 1979). Studies claiming to show that biorhythmic analysis accurately predicts events have been shown to be methodologically inadequate or statistically flawed (Hines, 1979).

A modern variation on the theme of only noticing confirmations occurs when people claim to have ESP because on a couple of occasions, "I was thinking about Mom, and she called!" Of course, they never record all of the times when (a) "I was thinking about Mom, but she didn't call!" and (b) "I wasn't thinking about Mom, yet she called!" They also fail to recognize that if they talk to Mom about every 2 weeks, their frequency of "thinking about Mom" will increase near the end of the 2-week interval, thereby increasing the chances of a "hit." You'll recognize this latter interpretation as an example of an alternative explanation that is more *parsimonious* than the ESP explanation for the coincidence.

Deny Falsification

As you recall from Chapter 3, one of the hallmarks of a legitimate scientific theory is that it is precise enough to be put to the sternest test of all—the test of falsification. That is, to be acceptable, a theory must be structured so that specific predictions can be made and experiments can yield outcomes counter to predictions. We know, of course, that single failures never cause a theory to be tossed out completely, but the fact remains that theories must be capable of disproof, at least in principle. In pseudoscience, this does not occur, even though on the surface it would seem that both phrenology and biorhythms would be easy to disprove. Indeed, within the scientific community, it is generally recognized that disproof has occurred.

Advocates of pseudosciences such as phrenology and biorhythms have had to confront claims of disproof and the accompanying skepticism of legitimate scientists. Not all thieves have bumps in just the right places, and not all critical days produce disasters. Apologists respond to these threats rather creatively. Instead of allowing an apparent contradiction to hurt the theory, they "rearrange" the theory a bit, or add some additional elements, in order to accommodate the anomaly. Hence, the apparent disproof winds up being touted as further proof of the strength of the theory! For example, if a known pacifist nonetheless had a large area of destructiveness, a clever phrenologist would find even larger areas of cautiousness, benevolence, and reverence, and these would be said to offset the apparent violent tendencies. Likewise, if nothing went wrong on a critical day, it could be shown that the danger was balanced by one of the cycles being in an especially strong phase. Thus, for pseudoscience, any possible outcome can be explained (or more accurately, explained away). Yet as we know, a theory that explains all possible outcomes fails as a theory, because it can never make specific predictions. If it cannot be tested, it cannot be falsified. If it cannot be falsified, it is useless as a theory.

Reduce Complexity to Simplicity

A final characteristic of pseudoscience worth noting is that these doctrines take what are actually very complicated phenomena and reduce them to overly simplistic concepts. This, of course, has great consumer appeal, especially in psychology. Trying to figure out human behavior is a universal human activity and if the process can be simplified, either by measuring someone's head, reading a biorhythm chart, determining someone's astrological sign, or interpreting one's handwriting, then many people will be taken in by the apparent ease of the explanations.

In sum, pseudoscience is characterized by an association with true science, a misuse of the rules of evidence by relying on anecdotes and avoiding a true falsification test, and an oversimplification of complex processes. Perhaps because of our enormous interest in human behavior, pseudoscientific approaches to psychology are not hard to find in any historical era and many people seem to have difficulty seeing the inherent weaknesses in pseudoscientific doctrines. As a scientific thinker, however, you have been developing the skills to distinguish valid psychological science from what pretends to be. More generally, you are now in a position to be skeptical when you hear people say things like:

- "OK, so there's evidence that smoking is harmful, but my uncle smoked three packs a day from the time he was 13, and he lived to be 89."

——conclusion: therefore it is OK to smoke.

——problem: anecdotal evidence; emphasis on confirmation only (what about your aunt, who died at age 40 of lung cancer, possibly from second-hand smoke?).

- "That's the third time recently that I've seen a story about a plane crash; it just goes to show that bad things come in threes."

  ——conclusion: here is a proven theory that allows us to understand the universe better.

  ——problem: anecdotal evidence; no prior definition of the length of time that includes the three events; therefore falsification cannot occur because any outcome can be made to fit the "theory"; complexity reduced to simplicity.

Psychological Science and Human Bias

Does the foregoing analysis mean that "true" psychologist/scientists are immune from the foibles that characterize pseudoscientific thinking? Are scientists merely objective processors of information, revising theories purely on the basis of data, completely unbiased in the way they do science? Are they never guilty of trying to discount evidence that contradicts their own ideas? Do they never modify their theories to account for anomalies? The answers, of course, are all no; after all, psychologist/scientists are human beings. They want their experiments to come out in certain ways and get angry or depressed when they don't. They have a strong attachment to theory X, try to find evidence to support it, and get upset with researcher Smith whose study calls X into question. They then try to show that Smith did something wrong or that Smith's study was a fluke. Smith may not react too well to this and the result could be a continuing controversy over some research issue.

Is this bad? It certainly can be counterproductive, as when James Mark Baldwin and E. B. Titchener became enmeshed in a controversy over the proper use of introspection as a method in the late 1890s. The details need not concern us, but what is interesting about the case is that although it began rationally, it did not end that way. As the analysis by historian David Krantz in Figure 12.2 shows, the contents of the published papers in the debate began by concentrating on theory and data. Before long, however, personal invective characterized the discussion. There's nothing wrong with questioning a piece of research or someone's interpretation of it, but science is seldom advanced by comments like this from Baldwin: "I cannot help thinking that Professor Titchener sometimes allows the dust of his machinery to obscure his vision" (cited in Krantz, 1969, p. 11).

Fortunately, most debate in psychology is not like the Baldwin–Titchener controversy (at least not in print). In general, the outcome of disagreements among researchers is that the science progresses. If one takes the long view and assumes that the scientific approach rigorously applied by many researchers in different labs will ultimately yield valid and useful information about human behavior, then individual unwillingness to give up a pet idea is not necessarily bad. For one thing, it means that ideas won't be abandoned hastily. Theories need strong, stubborn, opin-

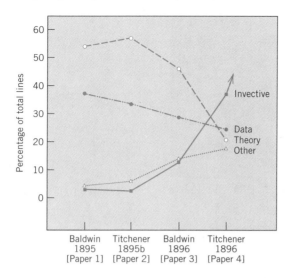

FIGURE 12.2 A content analysis of the Baldwin–Titchener controversy, showing a gradual decrease in substantive discussion and an increase in personal attacks [from Krantz (1969)].

ionated, dogmatic, hard-headed advocates if they are to be tested adequately. As historian of science Thomas Kuhn has argued, being dogmatically attached to one's pet theories assures that they will not be given up just because an experiment or two has flopped. In his words,

. . . Preconception and resistance seem the rule rather than the exception in mature scientific development. . . . [T]hey are community characteristics with deep roots in the procedures through which scientists are trained for work in their profession. Strongly held convictions . . . often seem to be a precondition for success in the sciences. (Kuhn, 1970, p. 357)

Ironically, to be absolutely objective, dispassionate, ruled only by data, and unemotional about research is not only impossible for the human being in us, but such an approach might not be the best for the advancement of psychological science. Rather, being a vigorous advocate for a theory guarantees that it will be pushed to its limits.

The Excitement of Psychological Research (Part 2)

In Chapter 1, you briefly met two such vigorous advocates for their ideas, Eleanor Gibson and B. F. Skinner, and you learned something about the excitement of making important discoveries by doing psychological research. I tried to make the point that perhaps the best reason for doing research is because it is great fun, despite the occasional frustrations, setbacks, and long hours. That lesson is repeated over and over again through the lives of the men and women who are leaders among today's generation of psychological researchers. Two good examples are

FIGURE 12.3 Robert Sternberg.

Bob Sternberg of Yale University and Elizabeth Loftus of the University of Washington.

Robert Sternberg

For some people, experiences early in life set the tone for what follows. Such is the case for Bob Sternberg (see Figure 12.3), whose varied interests include the psychology of love and the psychology of creativity, but who is best known for his research into the varieties of human intellectual behavior. He traces this interest to grade school, where he "really stunk on IQ tests" (Trotter, 1986, p. 56), mainly because of severe test anxiety. He overcame the problem, invented his own mental test as a seventh-grade science project, and the rest, as they say, is history.

Sternberg (1988) originated what he calls a "triarchic" theory of intelligence, which proposes the existence of three different aspects of human intelligence. The first is similar to the traditional concept of IQ and emphasizes the cognitive skills involved in analytical thinking; Sternberg calls it the *componential* aspect. The second variety of intelligence Sternberg calls *experiential* and it is related to creative thinking. The person strong in experiential intelligence generates lots of innovative and effective ideas. Third, some people are especially skillful at adapting to their varied environments. They possess a kind of practical intelligence, which Sternberg calls a *contextual* intelligence.

Sternberg's work as a research psychologist is a good illustration of the idea elaborated in Chapter 3 that much research derives from everyday observations. For Sternberg, these observations are his principle source of inspiration:

> All of my ideas (almost) come from watching people—myself, students I work with, my kids, my relationships with people, other people's relation-

ships, and so on. . . . The point is that in psychology, there is no better data source than the people around you. I've never found books or lectures or labs as good as real experience for getting ideas. . . . I've always found that I do my best work on problems that I find exciting, so I try to deal with such problems, whether or not they are in vogue. (R. J. Sternberg, personal communication, May 18, 1993)

Like every psychologist with a major research program, Sternberg attracts a dedicated group of students to his research team. It is easy to understand why students would want to work for him. In contrast with some laboratories where the director identifies projects that are then assigned to students, Sternberg tries to give his students ownership of their work, thereby giving them a chance to generate their own enthusiasm for a project:

The most important thing is to *help students find projects that really excite them.* Thus, I don't just have students do my own research—I try to help them find topics and approaches that really turn them on, and then follow them. . . . You do better by following your students than by having them follow you. (R. J. Sternberg, personal communication, May 18, 1993, italics added)

Elizabeth Loftus

The work of Elizabeth Loftus (see Figure 12.4) is a perfect blend of the ideas of basic and applied research, as described in Chapter 3. She has contributed much to

FIGURE 12.4 Elizabeth Loftus.

our knowledge of the fundamental processes of human memory, while at the same time showing how these principles apply to real-world memory phenomena such as eyewitness memory. Loftus herself identifies this mixture as the most interesting aspect of her work as a research psychologist: "I get to make interesting scientific discoveries and at the same time apply these and other psychological discoveries to the lives of real people" (personal communication, May 18, 1993).

Loftus is arguably the world's leading expert on the phenomenon of eyewitness memory, part of her broader interest in the factors affecting long-term memory. As a result of her recognized expertise, she has testified in more than 100 court cases in which eyewitness testimony was a crucial element (Loftus, 1986). As you recall, her research was mentioned briefly in the last chapter as a caution against relying on the accuracy of case history information when it depends on memory of the distant past. Loftus and her colleagues and research team have completed dozens of studies of the ways in which past memories become distorted by information intervening between the time of the event to be recalled and the time of recall. Most of this research has focused on direct eyewitness recall, but recently, she has taken on the empirical question of whether memories of childhood sexual abuse can be accurate when remembered many years later. She argues that serious distortions can and do occur.

Loftus's enthusiasm for her research in memory was sparked near the end of her graduate school career at Stanford. Her doctoral dissertation was a basic research project: "An Analysis of the Structural Variables that Determine Problem-Solving Difficulty on a Computer-Based Teletype." If your eyes are glazing over as you read the title, Loftus would not be offended. As the project neared its end, she was also "a bit bored with the whole thing" (Loftus & Ketcham, 1991, p. 5). Luckily, she took a social psychology course from Jon Freedman and he sparked her interest in some of the more practical aspects of memory. As Loftus described it:

> In my last six months of graduate school, I spent every free moment in Freedman's lab, setting up the experimental design, running subjects, tabulating the data, and analyzing the results. As the project took shape and [we] realized that we were on to something, that we were actually discovering something new about how the brain works, I began to think of myself as a *research psychologist*. Oh, those were *lovely* words—I could design an experiment, set it up, and follow it through. I felt for the first time that I was a scientist, and I knew with ultimate clarity that it was exactly what I wanted to be doing with my life. (Loftus & Ketcham, 1991, p. 6, first italics in the original; second italics added)

There is a common thread that weaves together the work of Gibson and Skinner (as described in Chapter 1) and that of Sternberg, Loftus, and other psychological researchers, including our favorite pain researcher, Lightner Witmer. It is difficult to place a label on this common feature, but it is emotional, and "passion" is not a bad descriptor. You can detect it if you read carefully the quotes I've chosen, both in chapter 1 and here. In each of the Gibson, Skinner, and Witmer quotes, for example, the concept of beauty appears. For Gibson, the first tentative studies with the visual cliff "worked *beautifully.*" When Skinner returned to his jammed pellet dispenser, he found "a *beautiful* curve." Witmer described his adventure with pain as "a *beautiful* case of loss of consciousness." Similarly, when Sternberg described his desire to help his students find research projects "that really *excite* them" and when Loftus referred to her self-identity as a research psychologist as "*lovely* words," that same intensity of feeling was being expressed.

There are enormous gaps in our knowledge of human behavior. Hence, there is ample space available for those with the kind of passion displayed by people like Gibson, Skinner, Sternberg, Loftus, and countless others. What could be better than to have a career that is continually exciting and rewarding? The invitation is open.

Chapter Review

Glossary Fill-Ins

1. Compared to true science, _____ misuses the rules of evidence.

2. Fred claims he has ESP because he sometimes thinks about his mother just before she calls on the phone. Fred's evidence is called _____ evidence.

Multiple Choice

1. The primary difference between phrenology and biorhythm theory is that
   a. Phrenology is more recent.
   b. Phrenology was disproven; biorhythm theory has found strong empirical support.
   c. Phrenology originated in legitimate science.
   d. Phrenology has withstood the test of time and is still with us; biorhythms was a fad that lasted just 2–3 years.

2. What do all pseudosciences have in common?
   a. They begin as legitimate science, but soon they degenerate.
   b. They try to separate themselves from true science in order to be more accessible to the general public.
   c. Those promoting them are only interested in defrauding the general public.
   d. The theories cannot be falsified.

3. According to Kuhn, what is the consequence of a researcher's unwillingness to give up a theory?
   a. The researcher is quickly recognized as a fraud.
   b. The theory won't be abandoned until it is fully tested.
   c. The researcher's work will be considered pseudoscience.
   d. The researcher's perseverance will pay off and others will be convinced.

Applications Exercise

Exercise 12.1. — Graphology

You have probably seen full-page advertisements advocating the "science" of handwriting analysis. You will be told to send in a sample of your own handwriting and for a fee, you will be sent a personality description. The basic idea behind graphology is that the way you form your letters as you write them is a reflection of the type of person you are.

a. Consider each of the main aspects of pseudoscience. How might each apply in the case of graphology?

b. Design an experiment that would be a true test of graphology's claim.

APPENDIX A

Communicating the Results of Research in Psychology

In this Appendix, you will learn how to:

- Prepare and write an APA-style laboratory report
- Prepare a professional presentation of your research either as a
  - Paper to be read
  - Poster to be written and organized

Research Reports, APA Style

You are about to enter the world of the obsessive–compulsive. As you begin to learn about APA-style lab reports, it will seem to you that the anguish over every omitted comma, every word not printed in caps when it should be, and every F or t not underlined will be symptomatic of something very seriously wrong with your instructor. The format will seem impossible to master. Take heart, however. The rules have an important purpose and the procedures for preparing a lab report can be learned; furthermore, the APA (1994) publishes an easy-to-use *Publication Manual* (*PM*) that has answers to any of your format questions. With the *PM* by your side, it really isn't necessary to memorize the rules about commas and underlining.

If you don't already own a copy of the *PM* and expect to take some additional courses in psychology, you should obtain one immediately. This appendix will help you learn how to communicate results; but at just over 300 pages, the manual is the ultimate weapon against a botched report.

There are two main reasons for the rules that dictate a consistent format for reporting the results of empirical research in psychology. First, research outcomes accumulate external validity as they are repeated in different labs with different subjects and perhaps with slightly varied procedures. In order to replicate a study exactly, or to make a systematic variation in some procedure, the reader must know precisely what was done in the original study. By reading the results of a study written in a known and predictable format, the replication process is made easier. Second, a consistent format makes the review process more efficient. Thousands of research articles are submitted to dozens of psychological research journals every year. Typically, each article is screened by an editor, then sent to two or three other researchers with expertise in the article's topic. These "peer reviewers" read the article and send the editor a written critique that includes a recommendation about whether the article should be published (most journals reject 70%–80% of submitted articles). In the absence of an agreed-upon format, the work of the editor and reviewers would be hopelessly complicated. For the purposes of the methods course you are now taking, having a regular format makes it easier for your instructor to grade your report fairly.

General Guidelines

One of my beliefs is that the only way to learn how to do research in psychology is to actually do some research. The same principle applies to writing. It is a skill like any other, and it improves with practice, assuming that one's efforts are followed by feedback of some kind. Thus, the most basic recommendation I can make is for you to write whenever you can and ask others to read what you've written. When writing a lab report, I would suggest you find someone who has already completed the research methods course *and* earned a decent grade. As you are writing your report, ask this person to read your work and critique it.

Writing Style

The laboratory report is not the Great American Novel. Therefore, some literary devices that might enhance a creative writing exercise, such as deliberately creating an ambiguity to hold the reader's attention, or omitting details to arouse curiosity,

Calvin and Hobbes

by Bill Watterson

FIGURE A.1   Academic writing?

are out of place in scientific writing. Rather, one should always strive for perfect clarity and simplicity of expression. This is easier said than done, of course, but despite the grain of truth in Figure A.1, academic writing is not necessarily stuffy and difficult to follow.

All good writing begins with a knowledge of correct grammatical usage. Grammatical errors automatically create ambiguity and awkwardness, so your first step in learning to write a lab report is to be sure that you know the basic rules of sentence structure. Numerous English usage guides are available and the *PM* includes a number of guidelines specifically targeted for the kinds of sentences found in scientific writing.

In addition to grammatical errors, beginning writers of APA lab reports often use some common words inappropriately. For example, although the term "significant" generally means important or meaningful, the writer using the term in this fashion in a lab report might mislead the reader. This is because in a lab report, significant implies "statistically significant," which has a technical definition relating to the rejection of H_0. A reader encountering the word in a lab report might assume the technical definition is being used even if the writer didn't mean it that way. To eliminate ambiguity, never use the term in the lab report except when it clearly refers to statistical significance.

Two other common problems with word usage concern the confusion between "affect" and "effect," and the use of some plural nouns such as "data." These problems are elaborated in Tables A.1 and A.2.

Word Processing Tools

Chances are you have already discovered that word processing can significantly improve the quality of your writing. This is due primarily to the ease with which changes can be made, but quality word-processing software also includes additional features to make your writing life easier. The most obvious example is a spelling checker, which can help you avoid the embarrassment of misspelling "psycology."

TABLE A.1   *Effectively Using the Terms Affect & Effect*

One of the most common errors found in student lab reports is the failure to distinguish between the different meanings of the words "affect" and "effect."

affect as a noun means an emotional state; thus
    —Because of the pressure of a rapid presentation rate, subjects showed increased *affect*.
affect as a verb means to influence; thus
    —Increasing the presentation rate *affected* recall.
effect as a noun means the result of some event; thus
    —The *effect* of increasing the presentation rate was a decline in recall.
effect as a verb means to bring about or accomplish some result; thus
    —We *effected* a change in recall by increasing presentation rate.

A common error is to use *effect* as a verb when *affect* should be used; thus

Incorrect: Changing to a fixed ratio schedule *effected* the rat's behavior.
Correct: Changing to a fixed ratio schedule *affected* the rat's behavior.

A second common error is to use *affect* as a noun when *effect* should be used; thus

Incorrect: Changing to a fixed ratio schedule had a major *affect* on the rat's behavior.
Correct: Changing to a fixed ratio schedule had a major *effect* on the rat's behavior.

TABLE A.2   *Plurals of Words with Latin or Greek Origins*

The plural forms of many words found in scientific writing derive from their origins in Latin and Greek. A failure to recognize the plural form can lead to a grammatical error of disagreement between noun and verb. The most common example is the word **data**, which refers to more than one piece of information, and is the plural of **datum**. Although the term is sometimes found in common usage as a singluar noun, the *PM* (p. 37) suggests that it be used only in the plural form.

Incorrect: The *data was* subjected to a content analysis.
Correct: The *data were* subjected to a content analysis.

Other examples:

Singular form	Plural form
analysis	analyses
criterion	criteria
hypothesis	hypotheses
phenomenon	phenomena
stimulus	stimuli

Spelling checkers don't substitute for careful proofreading, however, because they will find nothing wrong with this:

The too subjects where asked two respond of the light was read.

These errors would be detected by a good grammar checker, though, another feature of some word processors. Besides spotting grammatical flaws, grammar checkers also detect sentences that are too long and awkward and let you know if too many of your sentences are written in the passive rather than the active voice. Generally, using the active voice adds to clarity and simplifies sentences. To illustrate,

Passive: An investigation of sleep deprivation was done by Smith (1992).
Active: Smith (1992) investigated sleep deprivation.

A third word-processing feature to improve writing is the search function, which scans the manuscript for specific words or phrases. This allows the writer to determine if some terms or concepts are being overused, a common first-draft problem. Once repeated words are discovered, or any other time the writer wishes to express a concept in a different way, another word-processing add-on is available—the thesaurus. Of course, the tool existed in book form long before word-processing originated, and it is indispensable for the writer looking for an alternative word for "indispensable" (my electronic thesaurus suggests the following options: necessary, essential, imperative, required, and requisite).

A final word-processing tool is the style sheet, a set of instructions that automatically formats some portion of text. These can be quite useful for documents that have a consistent format; laboratory reports are an obvious example.

Gender-Neutral Language

For years, linguists and psychologists interested in language use have investigated the connections between language and thinking. Although there is much disagreement over the nature of this relationship, there is consensus that using language in certain ways can reinforce and perpetuate certain concepts, including stereotypes about people. One example that is specifically addressed in the *PM* is language considered to be sexist because it implies inequalities between males and females. The APA first developed guidelines for nonsexist or "gender-neutral" language in 1977. Authors submitting their manuscripts to an APA journal must use nonsexist language.

Language that is gender neutral avoids two kinds of problems. The first is referred to as a problem of designation. These are instances when terms include only masculine terminology but are supposed to refer to both males and females. The most common example is the use of "man" when "person" is intended, as in "Man has long been interested in the causes of mental illness." Some research has shown that even though the intent might be truly nonsexist when using such language, readers often interpret the language in ways that exclude females. For example, a study by Kidd (1971) found that when subjects read sentences using "man" or "his" in a supposed nonsexist fashion, they perceived the sentences as referring to men 86% of the time.

Here are some examples of sentences with problems of designation, along with suggested corrections. As you will see, problems can be solved fairly easily by re-wording, using plurals, or omitting gender designations altogether. The examples are taken directly from Table 1 of the *PM* (pp. 54–60).

1. The client is usually the best judge of the value of his counseling.
    <u>Better</u>:   Clients are usually the best judge of the value of the counseling they receive.

2. Man's search for knowledge.
    <u>Better</u>:   The search for knowledge.

3. Research scientists often neglect their wives and children.
    <u>Better</u>:   Research scientists often neglect their spouses and children.

In addition to problems of designation, some sexist language shows problems of evaluation. That is, the terms selected for males and females imply an inequality. For example, a writer describing high school athletes might refer to the men's basketball team and the girl's basketball team (better: women's team). Also, using phrases like "typically male" or "typically female" can promote stereotypical think-ing, as can using stereotypical descriptors for behaviors that may be identical for males and females (e.g., ambitious men, but aggressive women; cautious men, but timid women).

Although the guidelines for gender-neutral language are generally designed to correct problems harmful to women, at least one example addresses an inequality detrimental to men. This occurs when the term "mothering" is used to refer to any behavior involving some kind of supportive interaction between parent and child. Using mothering to refer to females and "fathering" to refer to the same be-havior in males doesn't work, because fathering has a different meaning altogether. Rather, APA recommends that the gender-neutral terms "nurturing" or "parent-ing" be used here, to recognize the fact that males perform these kinds of support-ive behaviors also.

Academic Honesty

In the Chapter 2 section on scientific fraud, the discussion centered on the falsifi-cation of data, but plagiarism[1] was also mentioned as a serious problem to be avoided, and you probably worked through the plagiarism exercise at the end of the chapter. Standard 6.22 of the 1992 ethics code specifically addresses plagiarism, stating that writers "do not present substantial portions or elements of another's work as their own . . ." (American Psychological Association, 1992).

The most obvious form of plagiarism is copying information directly from some source without using quotation marks and then failing to cite the source. The principle is clear: Don't do this under any circumstance. A second form of

---

[1]The term derives from the Latin word *plaga,* which was a snare or hunting net. The term was eventually applied to the capturing, snaring or kidnapping of children; thus plagiarism is like a "kidnapping" of someone's ideas (*Webster's Word Histories*, 1989).

plagiarism is more subtle, however, and students may not always realize that they are plagiarizing and that a citation is necessary. This occurs when students use their own words for concepts, but the concepts clearly belong to some other person. For example, although I composed the paragraph description of Sternberg's theory of intelligence in Chapter 12, a reference to his 1988 book was included because concepts like the componential, experiential, and contextual aspects of intelligence are his creations, and they belong to him. Any time you use an idea, term, theory, or research finding that seems to "belong" to another person, be sure to cite that person's work. To avoid plagiarism, then, either use direct quotes and clearly attribute the words to the original source or give credit to the creator of an idea, again by the use of a proper citation. (You'll encounter the APA guidelines for accurately citing sources presently.)

Miscellaneous

Although your instructor may have some specific additions to or deletions from the following checklist, the following APA formatting rules are designed to create a document that is physically easy to read.

- ✓ Double-space throughout the entire manuscript
- ✓ Make the margins (top, bottom, and sides) at least one inch throughout
- ✓ Use a paper clip, not a stapler, to join the pages
- ✓ Avoid **changing** the printing fonts
- ✓ Don't print in **boldface** or *italics* (items that would be italicized in a journal article are underlined in the manuscript; see the sample paper).
- ✓ Make a photocopy of the manuscript and turn in the original; if you are word processing, save your manuscript file.

Main Sections of the Lab Report

The APA-style lab report describing the outcome of an empirical study includes each of the following elements, in this order:

- Title page
- Abstract
- Introduction
- Method
- Results
- Discussion
- References

Following the references section, reports typically include separate pages for au-

TABLE A.3   *Top Twenty Formatting Errors*

- In the Title Page:
  1. Not right-justifying the short title and page number.
  2. Not left-justifying the running head.
  3. Not capitalizing all the letters of the running head.
  4. Capitalizing all the letters of the title.
  5. Capitalizing the "h" in "Running head."

- In the Abstract:
  6. Typing the word "abstract" all in caps.
  7. Indenting the first line as in a normal paragraph.
  8. Using more than a single paragraph.
  9. Writing more than 120 words.

- In the Introduction:
  10. Failing to start the section by repeating the exact title.
  11. Starting the section by labeling it "Introduction."
  12. Making referencing errors.

- In the Method Section:
  13. Failing to label the section properly ("Method" is centered between the margins).
  14. Failing to underlie subheadings (e.g., "Materials").
  15. Starting the section on a new page instead of continuing immediately after the end of the introduction.

- In the Results Section:
  16. Failing to label the section properly.
  17. Failing to use proper abbreviations for statistical concepts like the mean.
  18. Failing to report inferential statistical analyses properly.

- In the Discussion Section:
  19. Failing to label the section properly.
  20. Making referencing errors.

thor notes, other footnotes (if any), tables, a listing of figures, and the figures themselves. In some cases an appendix (listing the actual stimulus materials, for instance) might be included. What follows is a description of how to prepare each section of the lab report. As you are reading, refer to (a) Table A.3, which lists the most common (in my experience) formatting errors occurring in the report, and (b) the sample lab report included at the end of the appendix.

Title Page

The title page has a very precise format, as you can see from the sample paper. It includes the following elements:

The Short Title/Page Number

Found in the upper-right-hand corner, the short title is the first two or three words of the complete title. Immediately below and double-spaced is the number 1, which designates the title page as page 1 of the manuscript.[2] Both the short title and the page number are right-justified (i.e., they are flush with the right hand margin). Except for pages on which figures (e.g., graphs, diagrams, flow charts) are drawn, *every* page of the manuscript includes the short title and the page number. This helps to identify the manuscript if pages become separated for some reason.

Running Head

If you examine an article printed in any of the APA journals, you will find that after the first page, the top of every page includes a "header" that is either the author's name (even-numbered pages) or a brief version of the full title (odd-numbered pages). The latter is called the "running head," because it is found in a header and it runs throughout the printed article.

To fit into its assigned location, a running head must be brief, yet sufficiently informative to convey the sense of the title. Thus, the running head is not the same thing as the short title. The only time they might be identical is when the first two or three words of the title (i.e., the short title) just happen to provide a good description of the study's content.

The running head is printed at the top of the title page, just below the short title and page number, and flush with the left-hand margin. It is limited to 50 characters (i.e., letters, spaces between words, and punctuation marks). For the staged hypnotism study (case study 4 in chapter 11), which had a running head of 39 characters, the top of the title page of the submitted manuscript looked like this:

Running head: EXPERIENCES ACCOMPANYING STAGE HYPNOSIS

Title/Author/Affiliation

The title of the article, the name of the person writing the paper (or names, for papers with more than one author), and the author's college or university affiliation go below the running head, centered between left and right margins. The first letters of the primary words in the title are capitalized. Thus, for the hypnotism study, the title looked like this:

Transient Positive and Negative Experiences
Accompanying Stage Hypnosis

Give some thought to the wording of the article's title, which should range from 10 to 12 words. It should give the reader a clear idea of the article's content and preview the variables being investigated. For example, in an experimental study, a common title format is "The effect of X on Y," which enables the reader to identify the independent and dependent variables. Thus, a study entitled "The ef-

---

[2]Some word-processing software makes it difficult to have headers of more than one line. APA format allows for this: It is acceptable to place the short title five spaces to the left of the page number on the same line.

fect of landmarks and north orientation on directionality" tells the reader that subjects will be performing some kind of direction-finding task for the dependent measure and that two independent variables will be manipulated: whether or not landmarks are present and whether or not subjects are told the direction of north.

A second type of format is to write a declarative sentence that summarizes the main result. An example would be: "Helping behavior depends on situational ambiguity and the empathy levels of bystanders." This title tells the reader that the study includes a manipulated independent variable, whether or not the situation clearly calls for help, and a subject variable, whether or not bystanders are empathic individuals.

Abstract

This is the first text material to be read in a lab report, and the last to be written. It is also the *only* part of the article looked at by many readers, who are forced by the sheer mass of information to read the abstract first in order to determine if the entire article is worth examining in detail. It is reprinted in full in *Psychological Abstracts*.

The abstract contains elements of each of the remaining four sections and because it cannot exceed 960 characters (about 120 words) in a single paragraph, it must be very carefully prepared—every word counts. The abstract's opening statement is perhaps the most informative. It always includes a statement of the problem, and it usually informs the reader about the subjects tested and/or the variables under investigation. Here are some samples of the opening sentences of abstracts, taken from three of the case studies used in Chapter 11.

- To describe sex differences in interpersonal touch, observation was made of 4,500 dyads in their teens and older in public places (Hall & Veccia, 1990, p. 1155)

- Frequency of positive and negative experiences accompanying stage hypnosis was assessed in follow-up interviews with 22 participants of university-sponsored performances (Crawford et al., 1992, p. 663).

- Records on recovery after cholecystectomy of patients in a suburban Pennsylvania hospital between 1972 and 1981 were examined to determine whether assignment to a room with a window view of a natural setting might have restorative influences (Ulrich, 1984, p. 420).

In addition to the meaty opening sentence, an abstract will mention something about method, it will briefly summarize the key results (the second most important sentence), and it usually closes with a brief conclusion.

The abstract occupies page 2 and only page 2 of the lab report. You should begin a new page when starting the introduction.

Introduction

The introduction thoroughly describes the problem being studied and by reviewing the pertinent research literature, makes it clear what is known and what is not known about the problem. What is unknown or unclear provides the basis for one or more predictions, and these predictions form the hypotheses for the study. Thus, an introduction includes, in this order, a statement of the problem, a literature review, and one or more hypotheses to be tested in the study. In a well-written introduction, the hypotheses are found in the final paragraph and flow naturally from the earlier descriptions of the problem and the review of related research. In a poorly written introduction, the hypotheses just seem to pop out at the end of the section and don't seem to have any rational basis.

The introduction begins page 3 of the manuscript and is the only major section of the lab report that is not headed by its identifying label. Rather, the section is headed with the article's title.

APA Citation Format

When reviewing past research related to the problem at hand, you will need to provide citations for the studies mentioned; the *PM* provides a specific format for this. Sometimes the author's name will be part of the sentence you are writing. If so, the date of publication follows the name and is placed in parentheses. For example:

> No such effect was found in a study by Smith (1990).

If the author's name is not to be included in the sentence, the name, a comma, and the date are placed in the parentheses. For example:

> No such effect was found in the above-mentioned study (Smith, 1990).

If a direct quote is used, the page number is included. For example:

> The results were that "neither males nor females were affected by the instructional manipulation" (Smith, 1990, p. 23).
>   or
> The results of the study by Smith (1990) were that "neither males nor females were affected by the instructional manipulation" (p. 23).

Every work cited in the introduction (or any other part of the manuscript) must be given a complete listing at the end of the paper. You'll learn how that is accomplished below, in the description of the "References" section of the report.

The *PM* has a thorough guide to citations and can be consulted for virtually any question you might have. Also, you'll find the APA's format being used in most of your psychology texts, including this one; hence, you have several available models.

Method

The guiding principle of the method section is that it must be detailed enough for other researchers to read it and be able to replicate the study in their own laboratories. Notice that I've written "other researchers" and not "other people." Thus, some specialized knowledge of methodology can be taken for granted. It is enough to say that subjects were matched according to variables X, Y, and Z; explaining matching step by step is not necessary. Similarly, it is enough to describe the type of counterbalancing used (e.g., a 4×4 Latin square) without explaining the reason why such a control procedure is needed.

The method section includes several subsections, which vary depending on the particular study. One subsection always occurs, however, and it is labeled "Participants." This normally opens the method section and includes a description of the sample of people or animals participating in the study. The reader of the subsection should be able to determine how many participants there were, how many were placed in each condition, and how they were selected.

The description of research subjects is usually followed by a subsection called "Apparatus" if equipment was used or "Materials" if the experimenter used paper and pencil materials such as questionnaires or personality tests. Standard equipment usually can be described with reference to the manufacturer and model number. Apparatus created especially for the study should be described in more detail and perhaps drawn (see sample paper). Copyrighted surveys or personality questionnaires can simply be listed with the appropriate citation.

A third subsection is called "Procedure" or sometimes "Procedure and Experimental Design." It will be the longest portion of the method section. It lists and operationally defines all the variables, identifies the design of the study and all the control features, and describes exactly what happened to the research participants.

Unlike the introduction, the method section does not begin on a new page. It follows immediately after the end of the intro and is labeled with the word "Method," which is centered (refer to the sample paper for the formatting rules for the subsections). This same continuity rule applies to the results and discussion sections.

Results

This section of the report provides a concise yet complete verbal description of results, along with descriptive and inferential statistics. A typical paragraph in the results section includes a verbal description of some finding, accompanied by the relevant descriptive and inferential statistics supporting the verbal statement. No attempt is made to explain why some prediction succeeded or failed: Such interpretation belongs in the discussion section.

A good way to organize the results section is with reference to the sequence of hypotheses in the introduction. For instance, if the introduction ends with three hypotheses, the results section should have a paragraph devoted to each prediction, presented in the same order as in the intro.

Reporting the Data: Statistics

As you recall from Chapter 4, descriptive statistics summarize data and inferential statistics determine whether it is prudent to reject the null hypothesis(es). The most common descriptive statistics reported are means, standard deviations, and correlation coefficients. Typical inferential statistics includes t tests, F ratios from ANOVAs, and Chi square (X^2) Tests. Procedures for calculating all of these are presented in Appendix B. For now, be aware of three things: (1) there are standard abbreviations for statistical terms such as the sample mean (*M*) and standard deviation (*SD*), (2) at some point before reporting inferential statistics, identify the alpha level (usually .05 or .01) being used, and (3) the general rule in reporting statistics is to put the descriptive statistics before the inferential statistics in any given paragraph. A typical results section might have consecutive sentences like this:

. . . Subjects given the imagery instructions recalled a mean of 16.5 words ($SD = 2.3$), while those told merely to repeat the words recalled 12.3 words ($SD = 3.1$) on the average. The difference was significant, $F(1,18) = 12.8$, $p < .01$.

The shorthand method for reporting inferential statistics is basically the same for all types of analysis. The test is identified (e.g., *F*), the degrees of freedom are listed (1 and 18), the calculated value of the test is reported (12.8), and the probability of the outcome being due to chance (less than .01) is indicated.

Portraying the Data: Tables and Figures

Descriptive statistics, especially in factorial designs, are often complicated enough that a long paragraph description of them will be impossible to follow. To avoid the problem, data are often presented in tables and/or figures. Tables are row and column arrangements that typically present means and standard deviations or sets of correlations. Figures can be graphs, diagrams, flow charts, sketches of apparatus, or photos. Each has specific formatting rules, which can be seen in the sample paper.

It is sometimes difficult to decide whether to present the data either in a table or as a figure. In general, a table is preferred if it seems important to report the precise mean scores (on a graph the exact scores require some guessing) or if there is so much data that a graph would be hopelessly cluttered. On the other hand, graphs can often illustrate a point dramatically and they are especially useful for showing an interaction effect in a factorial study. One certainty is that it is inappropriate to present the same data two ways—both in a table and as a figure. If a graph is used, it can take several forms, but the most common are line graphs and bar graphs. As described and illustrated in Chapter 7, line graphs are used when the variable on the *X*-axis is a continuous variable; for discrete variables (e.g., gender), bar graphs should be used.

When using tables or figures, it is not sufficient just to present them. In the text of the results section, you must refer the reader to them and point out their important features. Some skill is involved here, because you don't want to write a detailed description that points out every aspect of a table or graph. Thus, in a graph showing a serial position curve in a memory experiment, you might encounter a sentence like this:

. . . As shown in Figure 1, recall was quite high for the first few words of the list, poor for middle words, and almost perfect for the final three words.

As you can tell from the sample paper, tables and figure are not placed in the middle of the text description. Rather, they are placed at the end of the report and insertion points are included in the manuscript at appropriate places.

Also from the sample paper, notice that the title for a table is included on the same page as the table but the figure titles (called "figure captions") are typed on a page that is separate from the figures themselves. This is not an arbitrary rule that is designed to lower your grade; rather, it is a rule that follows from the way a manuscript is to be transformed into a finished journal article. Tables are set in type like any other text, as are the figure captions. The figures themselves, however, are submitted as high-quality photographs and have to be fitted into their appropriate space (this is why the pages of figures don't include short titles and page numbers). Hence, the figures and their captions are submitted separately. If you have more than one figure, it is not necessary to create a separate figure caption page for each one; simply list all of the captions on a single page.

Discussion

This final section of text material serves to tie the entire report together. It begins by summarizing the main results with reference to the original hypothesis(es) and then proceeds with its major task—interpretation. This evaluation includes relating the results to any theoretical points raised in the introduction and trying to explain failed predictions (a common problem confronting student researchers). The discussion also addresses the problem of alternative explanations of results. As the author of the article, you will decide on an interpretation that seems the most reasonable, but sometimes other alternatives could be considered. You should mention these alternatives and then explain why you don't think they measure up to your explanation.

Finally, the discussion includes an important element of any research program: consideration of the "what's next?" question. That is, writers usually make suggestions about what the next study should be, given the outcome of the one just completed. This of course is a natural consequence of the fact that research always answers some questions but raises others.

References

Unlike the method, results, and discussion sections, this section starts a new page and includes a listing of all the items cited in the lab report. The *PM* includes a complete set of rules for virtually every type of citation; here are some examples of the most common ones:

1. *A journal article with one author*
   Loftus, E. F. (1986). Ten years in the life of an expert witness. <u>Law and Human Behavior, 10,</u> 241–263.

2. *A journal article with more than one author*
   Hall, J. A., & Veccia, E. M. (1990). More 'touching' observations: New insights on men, women, and interpersonal touch. <u>Journal of Personality and Social Psychology, 59,</u> 1155–1162.

3. *A book*
   Sternberg, R. J. (1988). <u>The triarchic mind: A new theory of human intelligence.</u> New York: Viking Penguin, Inc.

4. *A book that is not a first edition*

   Hothersall, D. (1990). <u>History of psychology</u> (2nd ed.). New York: McGraw-Hill.

5. *A chapter from an edited book*

   Kuhn, T. S. (1970). The function of dogma in scientific research. In B. A. Brody (Ed.), <u>Readings in the philosophy of science</u> (pp. 356–373). Englewood Cliffs, NJ: Prentice-Hall.

One final point: Before turning in a lab report, you should check to see that (a) every source mentioned in the text of your lab report is given a reference listing in this section of the paper, and (b) every reference listed in this section is referred to in the text of the paper.

Presentations and Posters

If you're lucky, you may find yourself in a position to present the results of some of your research publicly. This can range from a presentation to other psychology students as part of a course requirement to a more formal presentation at a professional conference. For example, some sessions for undergraduate research are scheduled at national meetings of the APA and APS (American Psychological Society) and at regional meetings (e.g., at MPA, the Midwestern Psychological Association). Recently, a number of conferences have developed specifically for the purpose of presenting undergraduate research.

The presentations at these meetings will take one of two forms: papers or posters. The paper is the more traditional format. In a typical 1-hour session (50 minutes, actually), several researchers will each read a paper describing their work. If this happens to you, here are some recommendations:

1. You will be given a strict time limit—stick to it. A typical limit is 12 minutes, which allows time for 4 papers in the session. If you take 20 minutes, the person who is scheduled to go last in the session will hate you forever.

2. Prepare a one-page handout that a friend can distribute to the audience just as you are being introduced. The handout should include your hypothesis(es), an abbreviated description of the design, and the results, usually as a table or graph. Many in the audience will be thinking about what session they are going to attend in the next hour, planning dinner, or rehearsing their own presentation rather than listening carefully to you, so your handout can be an effective way for them to take useful information away with them.

3. If audio–visual equipment is available, take advantage of it. For example, if the room where you give your presentation will have an overhead projector in it, prepare transparencies that duplicate the tables and graphs in your handout. Then show them at the appropriate spot in your presentation and point out the salient features.

4. Prepare a normal lab report, then adapt it to the form of a document to be presented orally. This means focusing on the essential points and avoiding

picky details. For example, although you should include the model name for some apparatus in the lab report, the generic name (e.g., operant chamber) is fine for a presentation. The listener should be clear about the purpose of your study, the essential elements of design and control, the results, and what your overall conclusions are. Your presentation style should be more conversational than it would be in the more formal lab report.

5. Practice your presentation in front of some friends; ideally, have it videotaped and then practice some more.

The second form of presentation, and one that is becoming increasingly popular, is the poster session. These resemble high school science fairs, and probably derived from them. If you do a poster, you will find yourself in a large room filled with row after row of $4' \times 6'$ bulletin boards. On the board you will arrange a display (see Figure A.2) that enables someone to understand what you have discovered in your research. You will also prepare multiple copies (usually 50) of a brief version of your paper to be given to those who wish to take one.

Poster sessions have the advantage of allowing the presentation of many more research projects per hour than the typical paper session, and they of course eliminate all of the public speaking anxiety that accompany a paper presentation (this could be a disadvantage; learning to speak in public is an important skill). They also increase the chances that you will meet people with research interests similar to yours. At an effective poster session, you will have half a dozen good conversations,

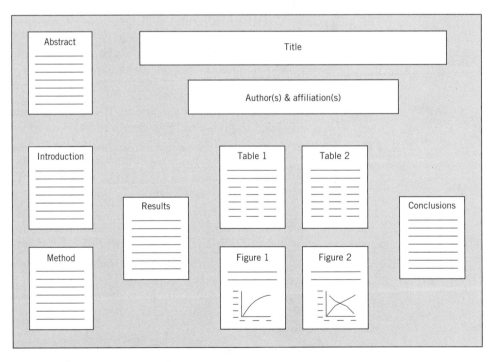

FIGURE A.2   Sample poster layout.

get some ideas for interpreting your results differently perhaps, and develop some answers to "what's next?" questions. If both you and the person you meet have an e-mail address, who knows? You might be co-authors some day.

A Sample Research Report

The following sample report is a revised version of a paper that three of my students authored and delivered to an undergraduate research conference. This report is shorter than and not as sophisticated as the articles you'll find in most journals, but it is closer to the kind of lab report that you will be preparing as you learn APA format, so you should find it helpful.

1. Short title and page number are right justified; title page is page 1. Alternatively, short title and page number can be placed on the same line, separated by five spaces and with the page number right justified.

2. Short title: first 2-3 main words of title.

3. Left-justified.

4. No cap here.

5. All caps; no more than 50 characters, including spaces; unlike the short title, the running head should be somewhat informative of the variables in the study.

6. Title, author(s), and affiliation are centered (your instructor might want you to add the date even though it is not in the APA format; for papers submitted to APA journals, the date will be on the cover letter sent by the author to the editor).

7. Title should begin to inform the reader about the variables to be encountered in the study.

Effects of North   1

3   2   1

Running head: ORIENTATION, DISTANCE, AND POINTING ACCURACY

4   5

The Effects of North Orientation and Target Distance on Accuracy   7

in Pointing to Geographic Locations

6   Aimee Faso, Theresa Yuncke, and Teresa Kottman

Wheeling Jesuit College

8. Center.

9. Double space (throughout the entire manuscript).

10. No paragraph indent here.

11. Maximum of 960 characters and spaces; about 120 words.

8   Abstract

10   The ability to point accurately toward fixed geographical targets was investigated in
9
a $2 \times 2 \times 6$ factorial design. Seventy-two subjects (36 male and 36 female) tried to

locate six different targets; three of these targets were within walking distance of

the laboratory and the remaining three were at least 70 miles from campus.

11   Half the subjects were oriented to the compass direction of noth; half were not. A

north orientation facilitated performance for the three distant targets, but did not

significantly improve performance for the three nearby targets. No gender

differences occurred.

12. Continue to right justify the short title and page numbers, but do not right justify the text of the article.

13. Do not include the label "Introduction;" instead, reproduce the title exactly as it is on the cover page.

14. Begin a new page for the introduction.

15. Opening paragraph introduces the topic area of the research and defines terms (cognitive maps).

16. Introduction describes some prior research, but only if it is relevant to your study. Here, the Evans and Pezdek study is described because it introduces the difference between two ways of developing cognitive maps.

17. When a reference like this is within parentheses, the ampersand (&) is used; when the reference is in the flow of a sentence, use the word "and."

Effects of North

3   12

The Effects of North Orientation and Target Distance on Accuracy   14

in Pointing to Geographic Locations

13

15   Cognitive maps are mental representations of spatial information (Ormrod,   17

Ormrod, Wagner, & McCallin, 1988). They enable us to know where we are in the

geographic environment and they help us navigate through the environment in

order to move efficiently from point A to point B. Researchers interested in cognitive

mapping have studied such topics as how the elements of these maps develop (e.g.,

Cohen, 1985), how they are structured (e.g., Sholl, 1987), how they are used for

navigation (e.g., Kaplan, 1976), and how accurate we are when using them for

making decisions about where things are located. This last topic was the focus of the

experiment described here.

16   Evans and Pezdek (1980) demonstrated that people rely on two methods of

developing cognitive maps. First, they use the results of direct experience in

navigating through the environment. Thus students become familiar with a campus

by moving around in it. They know for instance that to get to the library from the

gym, one takes a left at the campus shop and goes about 200 yards. A second type of

cognitive map knowledge is cartographic: people study maps. Even if we have never

visited Europe, we know that France is just to the south of England and separated

from it by the English Channel. Of course some cognitive map knowledge can result

both from direct experience and from studying maps.

Evans and Pezdek (1980) asked subjects to decide as quickly as possible if sets of

three target locations were in the correct spatial positions with reference to each

other. When the locations were states, subjects used cartographic information when

making their decisions. When the target locations were nearby on-campus locations,

however, subjects apparently relied on their direct experience.

18   Our study had two purposes. First, it was designed to measure how accurately

subjects could point toward locations that were either nearby or distant. If distant

targets (e.g., cities) are learned and thought of with reference to actual maps,

---

18. The last portion of the introduction describes the study's hypotheses and the basis for them. It isn't enough to say that you expect X to happen; you must make a case for X. This paragraph ends with a specific hypothesis; the sentences leading up to it build the case for that hypothesis.

19. If two or more works are cited within parentheses, separate them with a semicolon and place them in alphabetical order (with reference to the first author's name in a multi-authored article).

20. Do not begin the method section on a new page; continue to double space throughout.

21. Centered.

22. Method should be written so that another researcher could read it and repeat the study.

23. Subheadings are underlined and placed flush with left margin; the description follows in paragraph form.

24. If you begin a sentence with a number, the number must be spelled out completely. This sentence could not begin like this: "72 undergraduate. . . ."

25. "Figures" are usually graphs, but they can also be such things as photographs, maps, or in this case, a sketch of the apparatus.

Effects of North

4

then accuracy in pointing to these targets should be improved if subjects receive some specific cartographic information such as the direction of "North." If nearby targets are learned by moving through the local environment, however, rather than by using maps, then a north orientation might not be very helpful when pointing to them. On this basis, we hypothesized that when pointing at distant geographic targets, accuracy would be improved by giving subjects a north orientation. When pointing at local targets, however, north orientation was not expected to help.

The second purpose of the study was to explore possible gender differences in using cognitive maps. Some studies (e.g., Kozlowski & Bryant, 1977) have failed to find differences between males and females on a cognitive mapping task, but several

19 (e.g., Herman, Kail, & Siegel, 1979; Ward, Newcombe, & Overton, 1986) have found that males use spatial information more efficiently than females. On this basis, we expected that males might point more accurately to geographic targets than females.

20   Method   21

23 Participants

24   Seventy-two undergraduate volunteers (36 males and 36 females) from a small   22
private college took part in the study. Experimenters visited freshman and sophomore level classes, described the general procedure, and asked for volunteers. No course credit was given. None of the subjects were residents of the three distant target cities, but all were familiar with the cities. Participation required approximately 10 minutes. Subjects were tested individually.

Apparatus

Subjects pointed towards a series of targets by means of a goniometer (see   25
Figure 1), a device used by physical therapists for measuring angles (e.g., at the elbow). One arm of the goniometer was fixed to a board and the second was free to rotate through 360°. This second arm served as a pointer.

26

Insert Figure 1 about here

The experiment took place in a small classroom that had blackout curtains drawn to prevent subjects from seeing anything outside of the building. Subjects stood at a lab table with the goniometer lined up so that its fixed arm was pointing either (a) directly toward north or (b) approximately east/northeast. This latter direction was the result of lining up the goniometer so that the board on which it was fixed was flush with the edge of the lab table.

Procedure

27   The study used a $2 \times 2 \times 6$ factorial design. The first factor was the subject variable of gender. The second factor was whether or not subjects performed the task while knowing the direction of north. The 36 males and 36 females were randomly assigned to the two levels of this north orientation factor, with the restriction that an equal number of males and females were assigned to each group. Thus 18 males and 18 females were given a north orientation; the remaining 18 males and 18 females were not.

The third factor was the within-subjects variable of target location. Six different targets were used. Three were locations that were either on or within walking distance of the campus: the college's front entrance, a local bar, and a money machine. The remaining locations were distant geographic targets that were at least 70 miles from Wheeling: Pittsburgh, Cleveland, and Washington (DC). Target sequence was counterbalanced through the use of a 6×6 Latin square. Subjects were randomly assigned to a row of the square, with the restriction that equal numbers of males and females were assigned to each row.

26. The actual figures are drawn on separate pages and included at the end of the report. Place an insertion note like this to indicate about where the figure would appear in a published journal article. The insertion note should appear at the end of the paragraph in which the figure is first mentioned.

27. Notice that the order of describing the variables is maintained through the method and results sections. First gender is described, then orientation, then location.

Effects of North

6

Subjects were told they would be given a series of locations, some near and some far, and that they were to move the free arm of the goniometer so that it was pointing directly at each location. Subjects in the north orientation condition were told that the fixed arm of the goniometer was pointed toward north and they could use it as a reference point. Subjects in the control condition were told nothing about the orientation of the goniometer.

The primary dependent measure was accuracy of pointing. Experimeters determined the correct answers for each location with reference to reliable maps. This made it possible to determine the degree of error for each of the subject's responses. Whether the error was to the "left" or to the "right" of the target was ignored. Thus the error scores ranged from 0° to 180°. Subjects were also asked to describe any strategies they used when performing the task.

After completing all six trials and describing any strategies they used, subjects were debriefed. Those requesting final results were sent a brief summary at the conclusion of the study.

Results

The data were analyzed with a 2 (gender) × 2 (orientation) × 6 (target location) analysis of variance, with the level of alpha set at .05. The mean error across all conditions for males was 52.1° and for females it was 46.9°; the difference was not significant, $F(1, 68) < 1$. A main effect for orientation was found, however, ($F(1, 68) = 24.87$, $p < .01$). The average error for those given the north orientation was 33.2°; it was 65.9° for those in the control group. As shown in Table 1, the overall advantage for those given a north orientation occurred both for males and for females.

Insert Table 1 about here

---

28. Something about debriefing is usually mentioned, but it is not necessary to describe how you conformed to all aspects of the ethics code; it is assumed that you did. Authors submitting articles to APA journals are required to include a statement in their cover letter to the editor confirming that the guidelines were followed.

29. Do not begin the results section on a new page; continue to double space throughout.

30. Centered.

31. Report descriptive statistics; in this case some means are reported in the text, others in Table 1, and still others in graph form (Figure 2).

32. Report inferential statistics, in this case the results of the ANOVA; note that the format for reporting the ANOVA contains these elements:
- the name of the test, underlined: F
- the degrees of freedom, in parentheses (1, 68)
- the calculated value of the F ratio: 24.87
- the chances of making a Type I error, with p underlined: p < .01
- n.b. if the value of F is less than 1, just say so and omit the p value.

33. Never type tables into the text of the report. As with figures, place an insertion note at the end of the paragraph that first mentions a particular table. The table itself comes later.

There was no overall effect for target location ($\underline{F}$(5, 350) < 1), but there was a significant interaction between north orientation and target location, $\underline{F}$(5, 340) = 7.91, $\underline{p}$ < .01. A simple effects analysis of the effect of north orientation for each location found that those given the orientation had less error for all three distant locations ($\underline{p}$ < .01). For the closer targets, there were no differences between those given and those not given a north orientation ($\underline{p}$ < .05) for the first two locations (front entrance and bar), but the north orientation did facilitate performance for the third close location, a money machine just off campus ($\underline{p}$ < .05). This effect can be seen in Figure 2.

Insert Figure 2 about here

Neither the 2-way interaction between gender and location ($\underline{F}$(5, 350) < 1) nor the 3-way interaction between gender, orientation, and location ($\underline{F}$(5, 350) < 1) was significant.

34

36

Discussion   35

A significant main effect for north orientation occurred in the study, but the more important result is the interaction between north orientation and location. When pointing to distant targets, subjects clearly were aided by being told the direction of north; when the targets were nearby, a north orientation was not as helpful. However, the fact that the north orientation did provide an advantage for one of the three local targets suggests a need for some replication before the

37

interaction can be considered a reliable finding.

This outcome is consistent with the research of Evans and Pezdek (1980) in finding that cognitive mapping includes two types of knowledge. One type of

38

spatial knowledge results from the direct experience of moving to and from nearby locations. Such knowledge is perhaps organized in terms of local landmarks and direction changes with reference to those landmarks ("take a right at the

---

34. Do not begin the discussion section on a new page; continue to double space throughout.

35. Centered.

36. Recall from chapter 7 that when both main effects and interactions occur, the interaction should be interpreted first and sometimes the interaction is more important than the main effect (this is one of those times).

37. Results don't always come out as nicely as one would like; an outcome with a slight ambiguity calls for further research to determine if the effect is reliable.

38. Concentrate on the main finding and try to interpret what it means by relating it back to what was described in the introduction.

mailroom"). Hence pointing accurately to such targets is not as likely to be aided by reference to compass points. Indeed, when explaining their strategies, several subjects visualized the trip from the building where they were being tested to the location in question.

The second type of spatial knowledge is more oriented to the compass and results from our experience with maps, which are always oriented to north. When pointing to these locations, we apparently rely on images of the maps we have studied, an idea supported by subjects' comments. More than half said they tried to visualize a map when trying to decide about Pittsburgh, Cleveland, or Washington; no subject mentioned maps when referring to the close locations.

39　In addition to replicating our results, future research might extend the findings by examining the effects of local landmarks on pointing accurately toward nearby targets. Just as the current study found that cartographic information improved performance for distant targets more than for close ones, perhaps the opposite result would occur if subjects were given local landmarks instead of a north orientation. If navigating to nearby targets involves using these landmarks, then pointing accuracy might be improved for them but not for distant targets.

No gender differences were found, perhaps due to the nature of the task.
40　Although several studies have found a slight advantage for males, one study that failed to find a difference between males and females (Kozlowski & Bryant, 1977) also used a "point to X" procedure.

In summary, our knowledge of geographic locations results from direct
41　experience in traveling to those places and from a more abstract map knowledge. When asked to point to geographic targets, giving subjects a north orientation enhances their performance when pointing at targets learned with reference to maps; however, a north orientation does not help subjects point more accurately to nearby targets that are learned by the experience of visiting them.

39. This is a good place to show off some "what's next" thinking.

40. There is no need to go into an elaborate explanation about why some prediction failed, especially if there is no immediately obvious way to interpret the result. Something should be said about each hypothesis, however, whether it came out as expected or not.

41. Summarize your conclusion but try to avoid being repetitive.

42. Begin the references section on a new page.

43. Centered; if you only have a single reference, call this part of the report the "Reference" section.

44. Note the proper formatting: what is underlined; where the commas and periods are; what is capitalized.

45. The first line of a reference is indented with a normal paragraph indent; when the article is printed in a journal, this is converted to the "hanging indent" format, which has the first line flush to the left margin and subsequent lines indented 2–3 spaces.

46. N.B. Every item in the References section should be mentioned in the paper itself; likewise, every reference cited in the paper should be found in the References section.

42
45

43   References

Cohen, R. (1985). The development of spatial cognition. Hillsdale, NJ: Lawrence   44
Erlbaum Associates.

Evans, G. W., & Pezdek, K. (1980). Cognitive mapping: Knowledge of real world
distance and location information. Journal of Experimental Psychology: Human
Learning and Memory, 6, 13-24.

Herman, J. F., Kail, R. V., & Siegel, A. W. (1979). Cognitive maps of a college
campus: A new look at freshman orientation. Bulletin of the Psychonomic Society, 13,
183-186.

Kaplan, R. (1976). Way-finding in the natural environment. In G. T. Moore & R. G.
Golledge (Eds.), Environmental knowing (pp. 46-57). Stroudsburg, PA: Dowden,
Hutchinson, and Ross.

Kozlowski, L. T., & Bryant, K. J. (1977). Sense of direction, spatial orientation, and
cognitive maps. Journal of Experimental Psychology: Human Perception and
Performance, 3, 590-598.

Ormrod, J. E., Ormrod, R. K., Wagner, E. D., & McCallin, R. C. (1988).
Reconceptualizing map learning. American Journal of Psychology, 101, 425-433.

Sholl, J. (1987). Cognitive maps as orienting schemata. Journal of Experimental
Psychology: Learning, Memory, and Cognition, 13, 615-628.

Ward, S. L., Newcombe, N., & Overton, W. F. (1986). Turn left at the church, or
three miles north: A study of direction giving and sex differences. Environment and
Behavior, 18, 192-313.

46

47. Use a separate page for each table if you have more than one.

48. Continue to include short title and page number on pages with tables.

49. Note underlining and use of horizontal lines to organize the table; never use vertical lines.

50. Statistical symbols (e.g., <u>M, SD, t, r, F</u>) are always underlined.

51. Clarifies dependent measure; note underlining.

47

50

51

48

49

Effects of North

10

Table 1

<u>Error Scores as a Function of Gender and Whether North Orientation Was Given</u>

Gender		Orientation	
		With North	Without North
Male			
	<u>M</u>	30.7	63.2
	<u>SD</u>	(30.5)	(42.9)
Female			
	<u>M</u>	35.7	68.5
	<u>SD</u>	(29.1)	(42.8)

<u>Note.</u> The error score is measured as the difference in degrees between the correct response and the subject's actual response.

52. Call this "Figure Caption" if your report only has one figure.

53. Center.

54. Note underline.

55. Carry second line back to left margin.

56. These are the descriptions that will appear beneath the figures if your paper gets published in a journal.

Effects of North

11

52   Figure Captions   53

54   Figure 1. A goniometer. The fixed arm pointed toward north for half the subjects; the   56

55   arm free to rotate was used for pointing toward geographic targets.

Figure 2. Amount of error in pointing toward three nearby and three distant targets, both for those given a north orientation and those given no orientation.

57. Do not include the short title or page number on pages with figures (in pencil, print "top," "Figure 1" and the short title on the back of this page near the top left edge). Do the same for Figure 2 on the next page.

58. If you have more than one figure, use a separate page for each (all of the figure captions can be placed on a single page though).

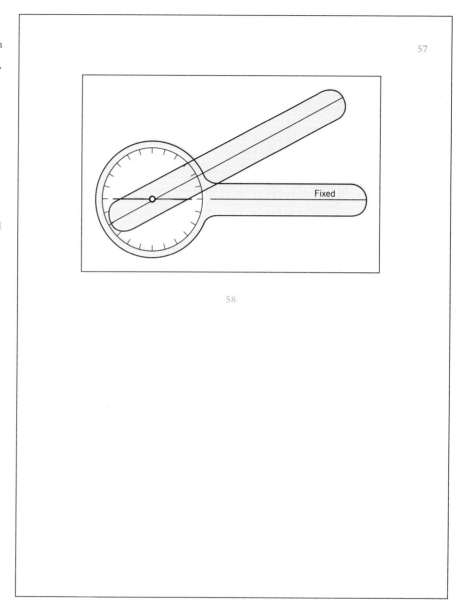

59. Carefully label the X and Y axes.

60. Place identifying key so that it fits somewhere below the high point on the Y axis and to the left of the most extreme point on the X axis.

61. If a numbered axis does not begin at zero, put in parallel slashes to indicate a break.

62. Why is this a bar graph and not a line graph?

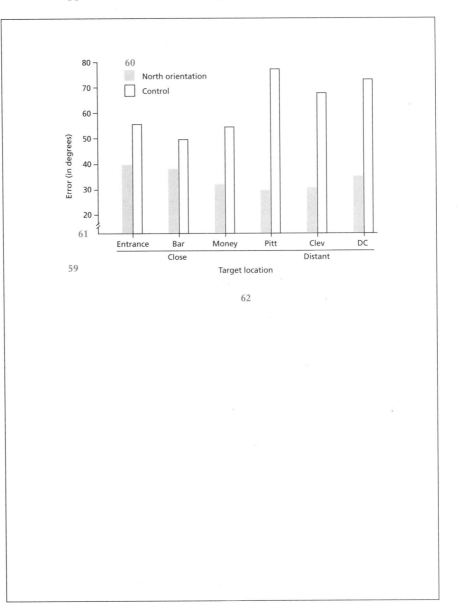

APPENDIX B

Using Statistics

In this Appendix, you will learn how to:

- Assess the degree of relationship between two variables by calculating the most common coefficient of correlation, Pearson's r
- Perform a simple regression analysis
- Calculate two varieties of the X^2 or chi-square test (the "chi" rhymes with "pie"), an inferential test for nominal data
- Calculate the most common inferential analyses for interval and ratio data
  - t test
  - analysis of variance

Making Intelligent Use of Statistics

Deciding on the proper statistical analysis is an essential skill for the psychological researcher. You already know part of the process from the descriptions in Chapters

4, 7, and 8. Chapter 4 introduced you to the different scales of measurement (nominal, ordinal, interval, and ratio) and the basic distinction between descriptive and inferential statistics. It also showed you how to calculate some of the fundamental descriptive statistics such as means and standard deviations and it introduced the logic of hypothesis testing. Chapters 4 and 7 introduced the use of *t* tests and the analysis of variance (ANOVA) for performing inferential analyses of experiments. In Chapter 8, correlation coefficients were described.

Here you will learn how to decide among the various types of analyses for your own data and research designs, how to carry out some of the more common analyses, and how to interpret the outcomes by referring to statistical tables. Ideally, you will be using a software package such as SPSS (Statistical Package for the Social Sciences), which will perform the analyses for the projects you'll be doing; however, working through the examples in this appendix can give you a better understanding of how these analyses are actually done.

The decisions about which statistical analyses to perform depend on several factors, including (a) whether the goal is to examine an association or make a comparison, (b) the scale of measurement being used, (c) certain aspects of the research design, such as whether an independent variable is tested between or within subjects, and in some cases, (d) sample size.

When the purpose of the analysis is to determine the degree of relationship between any two measured variables, then some form of correlation coefficient will be calculated. The most common is the Pearson's *r*, which is used whenever the data are measured on either interval or ratio scales. If an ordinal scale is used, you must calculate a Spearman's rho, symbolized r_s; it will give you a measure of the degree of relationship between two sets of ordinal rankings. A measure of association also exists for nominal data (the contingency coefficient, *C*). See below for an example of Pearson's *r*; consult a statistics text for how to perform r_s and *C*.

When the analysis is designed to compare the two or more conditions of a study to see if differences exist between or among them, a number of inferential procedures exist. The examples found below illustrate three of the most common tests: the chi-square test (X^2), the *t* test and the analysis of variance (ANOVA). The latter two tests both require that data be measured on either an interval or a ratio scale; X^2 is used with nominal data. Consult a statistics text for details about how to perform the tests (e.g., the Mann–Whitney *U*) that are available for evaluating differences with ordinal data.

Assessing Relationships

Example 1. *Pearson's r*

When both variables are measured on either an interval or a ratio scale, then the relationship between them can be calculated by using Pearson's *r*. For example, suppose a researcher is interested in determining the relationship between the amount of goof-off time that a student accumulates and the student's grade point average (G.P.A.). G.P.A. ranges from 0.0 to 4.0 and goof-off time is the number of hours spent per week in several specifically defined activities (e.g., soap opera watching). The data for eight students (same as on page 240 of Chapter 8) are as follows:

Student #	Goof-Off Hrs Variable X	X^2	G.P.A. Variable Y	Y^2	X times Y
1	42	1764	1.8	3.24	75.6
2	23	529	3.0	9.00	69.0
3	31	961	2.2	4.84	68.2
4	35	1225	2.9	8.41	101.5
5	16	256	3.7	13.69	59.2
6	26	676	3.0	9.00	78.0
7	39	1521	2.4	5.76	93.6
8	19	361	3.4	11.56	64.6
sum	231	7293	22.4	65.50	609.7

Formula for Pearson's r:

$$r = \frac{N\Sigma XY - \Sigma X \Sigma Y}{\sqrt{[N\Sigma X^2 - (\Sigma X)^2][N\Sigma Y^2 - (\Sigma Y)^2]}}$$

Step 1.   *Calculate Each Element*

$$N\Sigma XY = (8)(609.7) = 4877.6$$
$$\Sigma X \Sigma Y = (231)(22.4) = 5174.4$$
$$N\Sigma X^2 = (8)(7293) = 58344$$
$$(\Sigma X)^2 = (231)(231) = 53361$$
$$N\Sigma Y^2 = (8)(65.5) = 524$$
$$(\Sigma Y)^2 = (22.4)(22.4) = 501.76$$

Step 2.   *Fit Elements into the Formula for r and Solve*

$$r = \frac{4877.6 - 5174.4}{\sqrt{[58344 - 53361][524 - 501.76]}}$$

$$r = \frac{-296.8}{\sqrt{[4983][22.24]}}$$

$$r = \frac{-296.8}{\sqrt{[110821.9]}} = \frac{-296.8}{332.9} = -.89$$

Step 3. *Determine if the Calculated r is Significant (i.e., different from zero)*

This is accomplished by examining Table C.2 in Appendix C, which lists "critical values" (*cv*) for *r*. To use the table, first determine the degrees of freedom (*df*). In the case of Pearson's *r*, $df = N - 2$, where *N* refers to the number of pairs of scores. In our example, then, $df = 8 - 2 = 6$. In the table at the line for $df = 6$, you'll find two critical values, one for a significance level of .05 (*cv* = .707) and one for .01 (*cv* = .834). If the calculated value is *equal to or greater than* the critical value, then you may reject the null hypothesis that $r = 0$. That is, you can conclude that the correlation is statistically significant. In our case, the $-.89$ is significant at the .01 level because it exceeds the *cv* of .834. Thus, the probability is a very small .01 (1 in 100) that the obtained correlation of $-.89$ occurred by chance. Of course, whether the correlation is positive or negative doesn't matter; it is the absolute value of the calculated correlation that counts.

If you examine Table C.2 carefully, you will notice a basic fact about correlations. If you have just a few pairs (as in the above example), the correlation has to be quite high before it can be considered significant. It is fairly easy to arrive at a relatively high correlation purely by chance when there are only a few pairs. On the other hand, if there are a large number of pairs of scores, correlations that seem quite low can nonetheless be significant.

Example 2. *Regression Analysis*

In Chapter 8 you learned that correlations enable predictions to be made, using a procedure called a regression analysis. The analysis yields a regression line and this line in turn provides the basis for the predictions. Here's how it works with the example just completed about the relationship between goof-off time and GPA.

Formula for a regression line:

$$Y = a + bX$$

a = the *Y*-intercept
b = the slope of the line
X = a known value
Y = the value you are trying to predict

Step 1. *Calculate Each Element*

$$b = r\frac{s_y}{s_x}$$

r = Pearson's $r = -.89$

s = standard deviation (see Table 4.4, p 114 for calculations)

$$s_y = 0.63$$

$$s_x = 9.43$$

$$b = -.89 \; \frac{.63}{9.43} = (-.89)(.07) = -.06$$

$$a = \overline{Y} - b\overline{X}$$

$$\overline{Y} = \text{mean score for } Y = 2.80$$

$$\overline{X} = \text{mean score for } X = 28.88$$

$$a = 2.80 - (-.06)(28.88) = 4.53$$

Step 2. *Insert values for the Y-intercept and slope into the regression formula*

$$Y = a + bX = 4.53 + (-.06)X$$

$$Y = 4.53 - .06X$$

Step 3. *Use the formula for predictions*

If Pat has 40 goof-off hours, what is his predicted GPA?

$$Y = 4.53 - .06X$$

$$Y = 4.53 - (.06)(40)$$

$$Y = 4.53 - 2.40$$

$$Y = 2.13$$

If Pat has 20 goof-off hours, what is her predicted GPA?

$$Y = 4.53 - .06X$$

$$Y = 4.53 - (.06)(20)$$

$$Y = 4.53 - 1.20$$

$$Y = 3.33$$

Assessing Differences

Example 3. χ^2 — *Goodness of Fit*

When data are reported in terms of the number of times certain events fall into clearly defined categories, then a nominal scale of measurement is being used. To determine if the frequencies of these events reveal a systematic pattern, or are merely the result of chance, requires an inferential test for nominal data. Chi-square (χ^2) is such a test, certainly the most common statistical procedure used for nominal data. There are two varieties of χ^2, depending on whether one or more samples are used. The one-sample case is sometimes called χ^2 goodness of fit because it assesses whether the frequencies obtained in a study deviate from frequencies that would be expected either by chance or according to some predicted model.

As an example, suppose students suspect that their professor's multiple choice tests are biased in terms of how often each of five alternatives is the correct answer. That is, it seems to them that alternatives b, c, and d are correct more frequently than alternatives a or e. The professor is concerned and decides to evaluate all the previous semester's multiple choice tests. The number of times that each alternative is chosen is counted. If no bias is operating, the number of times that each alternative is the correct one should be about the same. Thus, the null hypothesis is that all the expected frequencies will be the same. There are 400 multiple choice items in the sample; thus, the expected frequency (E) for each alternative is equal to 400/5 or 80. The actual frequencies are:

Alternative a:	62
Alternative b:	85
Alternative c:	78
Alternative d:	111
Alternative e:	64
[Total:	400]

Formula for X^2—goodness of fit:

$$X^2 = \Sigma \frac{(O - E)^2}{E}$$

Step 1. *Calculate Each Element*

$$
\begin{aligned}
O - E: \quad & 62 - 80 = -18 \\
& 85 - 80 = +5 \\
& 78 - 80 = -2 \\
& 111 - 80 = +31 \\
& 64 - 80 = -16
\end{aligned}
$$

$$
\begin{aligned}
(O - E)^2: \quad & (-18)^2 = 324 \\
& (+5)^2 = 25 \\
& (-2)^2 = 4 \\
& (+31)^2 = 961 \\
& (-16)^2 = 256
\end{aligned}
$$

Step 2. *Fit Elements into the Formula for X^2 and Solve*

$$\chi^2 = \Sigma \frac{(O - E)^2}{E}$$

$$\chi^2 = \frac{324}{80} + \frac{25}{80} + \frac{4}{80} + \frac{961}{80} + \frac{256}{80}$$

$$\chi^2 = 4.05 + .31 + .05 + 12.01 + 3.20$$

$$\chi^2 = 19.62$$

Step 3. *Determine if the Calculated X^2 is Significant*

Table C.3 in Appendix C lists "critical values" for X^2. The degrees of freedom for a one sample X^2 is equal to the number of categories minus 1, or 4 $(5 - 1 = 4)$ in this particular case. In the table at the line for $df = 4$, you'll find two critical values, one for a significance level of .05 $(cv = 9.49)$ and one for .01 $(cv = 13.28)$. The calculated value exceeds both; hence, X^2 is significant at the .01 level. The professor would conclude that some bias does exist in the distribution of multiple choice alternatives; alternatives a and e indeed seem to be underused.

Example 4. X^2—*two samples*

For research in psychology, X^2 is most frequently used when more than one sample of frequencies exists. The most common case is when two different groups of subjects are used and each group is placed into two or more categories, depending on the topic of interest. For example, suppose a researcher wanted to know if there are gender differences in the choice of certain majors. The application forms of incoming students are examined (i.e., an archival procedure) to determine the number of males and females choosing psychology, biology, and math. The following table, called a contingency table, shows the results:

	Psychology	Biology	Math	Row Totals
Males	13	17	20	50
Females	24	16	10	50
Column Totals	37	33	10	100

The null hypothesis is that no gender differences exist in the choice of major. To test the null hypothesis for these frequency data, X^2 is calculated:

Formula for X^2—two samples:

$$\chi^2 = \Sigma \frac{(O - E)^2}{E}$$

Step 1. *Calculate Expected Frequencies (E)*

$$E = [(\text{row total})(\text{column total})]/\text{grand total}$$

- for the cell "males preferring psychology" (m,p):

$$E_{m,p} = [(50)(37)]/100 = 1850/100 = 18.5$$

- for the remaining cells:

$$E_{m,b} = [(50)(33)]/100 = 1650/100 = 16.5$$
$$E_{m,m} = [(50)(30)]/100 = 1500/100 = 15.0$$

$$E_{f,p} = [(50)(37)]/100 = 1850/100 = 18.5$$
$$E_{f,b} = [(50)(33)]/100 = 1650/100 = 16.5$$
$$E_{f,m} = [(50)(30)]/100 = 1550/100 = 15.0$$

Step 2. *Calculate $(O - E)^2$ for each cell:*

$$(O - E)^2: \quad \begin{aligned} \text{m,p} &\rightarrow (13 - 18.5)^2 = 30.25 \\ \text{m,b} &\rightarrow (17 - 16.5)^2 = .25 \\ \text{m,m} &\rightarrow (20 - 15.0)^2 = 25.00 \\ \text{f,p} &\rightarrow (24 - 18.5)^2 = 30.25 \\ \text{f,b} &\rightarrow (16 - 16.5)^2 = .25 \\ \text{f,m} &\rightarrow (10 - 15.0)^2 = 25.00 \end{aligned}$$

Step 3. *Fit Elements into the Formula for χ^2 and Solve*

$$\chi^2 = \Sigma \frac{(O - E)^2}{E}$$

$$\chi^2 = \frac{30.25}{18.5} + \frac{.25}{16.5} + \frac{25.00}{15.0} + \frac{30.25}{18.5} + \frac{.25}{16.5} + \frac{25.00}{15.0}$$

$$\chi^2 = 1.64 + .02 + 1.67 + 1.64 + .02 + 1.67$$

$$\chi^2 = 6.66$$

Step 4. *Determine if the Calculated χ^2 is Significant*

The degrees of freedom for a two sample χ^2 is equal to:

$$(\# \text{ rows} - 1)(\# \text{ columns} - 1) = (3 - 1)(2 - 1) = 2$$

In table C.3 at the line for $df = 2$, the critical values are 5.99 (.05 significance level) and 9.21 (01 level). The calculated value of 6.66 exceeds the first but not the second; hence χ^2 is significant at the .05 level but not at the .01 level. Gender differences did seem to occur in the choice of major: significantly more females than males expressed interest in majoring in psychology, the opposite was true for math, and males and females showed about equal preference for biology.

Example 5.   *t Test—Independent Groups*

In studies with a single independent variable and just two levels, the difference between the two sets of scores is often assessed with a *t* test.[1] As you recall from

---

[1]It is sometimes called the "Student's" *t*, not in your honor, but because that was the pseudonym chosen by the test's inventor, W. S. Gosset, when he first published a description of the test in 1908.

Chapter 7, there are two basic varieties, depending on whether the two sets of scores derive from independent groups of subjects or not. Independent groups occur when subjects are randomly assigned or when a subject variable such as gender or age is used. Such designs call for a *t* test for independent groups. A *t* test for dependent groups is used when the same subjects serve in both conditions or when the two different groups of subjects are related in some way, either through a matching procedure or some natural matching, as happens when parents are compared with children (see Example 6). Here's a simple way to calculate a *t* test for independent groups. It uses the variance, which you recall from Chapter 4 is an important measure of the variability in a set of scores; taking the square root of it yields the standard deviation. Refer back to Table 4.4 (p. 114) for the details.

Suppose a researcher is doing a simple memory experiment in which two groups of subjects are formed through random assignment. One group studies a list of 25 words at a presentation rate of 2 sec per item; the rate for the other group is 4 sec per item. Here are the number of words recalled by the 5 subjects in each group:

Subject #	2 sec/item (X_1)	Subject #	4 sec/item (X_2)
1	14	6	18
2	11	7	23
3	12	8	19
4	17	9	17
5	13	10	22
sum	67		99
n	5		5
mean	**13.4**		**19.8**
standard deviation	2.3		2.6
variance	5.3		6.7

The *t* test divides the differences between the two means obtained in the study by the "standard error of the difference," an estimate of how much the means should vary on the basis of chance or error. The researcher hopes for a large numerator and a small denominator and therefore a large value for *t*; when this happens the actual differences between the means are likely to be larger than those expected by chance.

The formula for the *t* test for independent groups:

$$t = \frac{\overline{X}_1 - \overline{X}_2}{\sqrt{\left[\dfrac{(n_1 - 1)s_1^2 + (n_2 - 1)s_2^2}{n_1 + n_2 - 2}\right]\left[\dfrac{1}{n_1} + \dfrac{1}{n_2}\right]}}$$

Step 1.   *Calculate Each Element*

$$\overline{X}_1 = \Sigma X_1/n_1 = 67/5 = 13.4$$

$$\overline{X}_2 = \Sigma X_2/n_2 = 99/5 = 19.8$$

$$s_1^2 = \frac{\Sigma X_1^2 - [(\Sigma X_1)^2/n_1]}{n_1 - 1} = 5.3$$

$$s_2^2 = 6.7$$

Step 2.   *Fit Elements into the Formula for t and Solve*

$$t = \frac{\overline{X}_1 - \overline{X}_2}{\sqrt{\left[\frac{(n_1 - 1)s_1^2 + (n_2 - 1)s_2^2}{n_1 + n_2 - 2}\right]\left[\frac{1}{n_1} + \frac{1}{n_2}\right]}}$$

$$t = \frac{13.4 - 19.8}{\sqrt{\left[\frac{(5 - 1)5.3 + (5 - 1)6.7}{5 + 5 - 2}\right]\left[\frac{1}{5} + \frac{1}{5}\right]}}$$

$$t = \frac{-6.4}{\sqrt{\left[\frac{21.2 + 26.8}{8}\right]\left[.2 + .2\right]}}$$

$$t = \frac{6.4}{\sqrt{[(6)(.4)]}} = -\frac{6.4}{1.55}$$

$$t = -4.13$$

Step 3.   *Determine if the Calculated t is Significant*

The degrees of freedom for a *t* test for independent groups is equal to:

$$(n_1 + n_2 - 2) = (5 + 5 - 2) = 8$$

Table C.4 lists the critical values for assessing the outcome of the *t* test. On the line for df = 8, the critical values are 2.31 (.05 significance level) and 3.36 (.01 level). The calculated value of 4.13 exceeds both (the minus sign doesn't matter); hence *t* is significant at the .01 level. It would be reasonable for the researcher to reject the null hypothesis and conclude that recall performance differed for subjects given different presentation rates.

Example 6.   *t Test—Dependent Groups*

As mentioned above, the *t* test for dependent groups is used for matched groups and repeated–measures designs when the independent variable has two levels. Each pair of scores will be related to some degree, because each pair comes from (a) subjects who are similar to each other in some way, or (b) the same subjects. Like the *t* test for independent groups, the one for dependent groups relates the actual difference between the means to the difference that would be expected by chance (i.e., the standard error of the difference). This involves calculating the correlation between the two sets of scores and working it into the formula for the *t* test. The following example accomplishes the same thing with a simpler formula that allows for a direct calculation of *t* without first calculating a Pearson's *r*.

Suppose a researcher is using a matched groups design to compare two ways of teaching computer literacy: a self-paced approach vs straight lecture. The 10 subjects in each group have been matched for previous GPA and general verbal intelligence. Thus, subject pair 1 (below) refers to two individuals with about the same GPA and intelligence. The dependent measure is a test score that can reach a maximum of 35. Here are the data, along with the preliminary calculations of D and D^2 for each paired set of scores.

Subject Pairs	Self-Paced	Lecture	D	D^2
1	26	18	8	64
2	31	22	9	81
3	26	21	5	25
4	28	20	8	64
5	22	17	5	25
6	22	15	7	49
7	23	21	2	4
8	29	20	9	81
9	24	19	5	25
10	24	23	1	1
sum	255	196	59	419
N = 10				
mean	**25.5**	**19.6**		

The formula for the *t* test for dependent groups:

$$t = \frac{\Sigma D}{\sqrt{\left[\dfrac{N\Sigma D^2 - (\Sigma D)^2}{N - 1}\right]}}$$

Step 1. *Calculate Each Element*

$$\Sigma D = 8 + 9 + ...1 = 59$$

$$(\Sigma D)^2 = (59)^2 = 3481$$

$$\Sigma D^2 = 64 + 81 + ...1 = 419$$

Step 2. *Fit Elements into the Formula for t and Solve*

$$t = \frac{\Sigma D}{\sqrt{\left[\dfrac{N\Sigma D^2 - (\Sigma D)^2}{N-1}\right]}}$$

$$t = \frac{59}{\sqrt{\left[\dfrac{(10)(419) - 3481}{9}\right]}}$$

$$t = \frac{59}{\sqrt{\left[\dfrac{709}{9}\right]}} = \frac{59}{\sqrt{78.8}} = \frac{59}{8.9}$$

$$t = 6.63$$

Step 3. *Determine if the Calculated t is Significant*

The degrees of freedom for a *t* test for dependent groups is equal to the number of pairs of scores minus 1; in this case $df = 10 - 1 = 9$. Use Table C4 again. On the line for $df = 9$, the critical values are 2.26 (.05 significance level) and 3.25 (.01 level). The calculated value of 6.63 exceeds both; hence, *t* is significant at the .01 level. It appears that the self-paced strategy worked better than the traditional lecture approach.

Example 7. *1-way ANOVA—Independent Groups*

A *t* test works fine when two conditions are being compared, but most experiments compare more than two conditions.[2] They might include a single independent variable with more than two levels, or they might include more than one independent variable (i.e., a factorial design). Consider first the case of a single variable with multiple levels. If the data are measured on an interval or ratio scale, then the 1-way ANOVA is the analysis of choice (n.b. 1-way = 1 independent variable, 2-way = 2 such variables, and so on).

As an example, consider a study in which three different groups of animals are taught a complex maze. The independent variable is the delay of reinforcement that occurs when they reach the goal box. Group 1 rats are reinforced immediately upon reaching the goal. Those in group 2 are reinforced 5 seconds after they reach the goal, and for those in group 3, reinforcement is delayed by 10 seconds. The dependent measure is the number of trials it takes the animals to learn the maze, with learning defined as two consecutive errorless trials.

Five rats are randomly assigned to each condition. Hence, there are three dis-

---

[2]If there is a single independent variable with two levels, a 1-way ANOVA will produce the same outcome as a *t* test. Indeed, the *t* test can be considered a special case of the analysis of variance.

tinct groups, and the proper analysis is a 1-way ANOVA for independent groups. Here are the results, along with some basic summary statistics.

	Group X_1		Group X_2		Group X_3
Subject #	No Delay	Subject #	5-sec Delay	Subject #	10-sec Delay
1	12	6	19	11	21
2	15	7	17	12	25
3	13	8	22	13	20
4	10	9	24	14	19
5	16	10	20	15	23
ΣX	66		102		108
$(\Sigma X)^2$	4356		10404		11664
n	5		5		5
$\overline{X}$	**13.2**		**20.4**		**21.6**
ΣX^2	894		2110		2356

The analysis of variance calculates a statistic called the F ratio. In the 1-way ANOVA for independent groups, basic formula for F divides the "mean square between groups" by the "mean square within groups" (also called the "mean square error"). In essence, this comparison between the variability between conditions and the variability within each condition is the same comparison made with the t test. The ANOVA formulas might seem rather daunting to you at first, but you'll find that there is a certain rhythm to them and that you will catch on quickly (really).

The formula for the F ratio in a 1-way ANOVA for independent groups is

$$F = \frac{MS_{BG}}{MS_{WG}} \text{ or } F = \frac{MS_{BG}}{MS_e}$$

Step 1. *Calculate Sums of Squares*

$$\text{total } SS = (\Sigma X_1^2 + \Sigma X_2^2 + \Sigma X_3^2) - \frac{(\Sigma X_1 + \Sigma X_2 + \Sigma X_3)^2}{N}$$

$$= 894 + 2110 + 2356 - \frac{(66 + 102 + 108)^2}{15}$$

$$= 5360 - 5078.4 = 281.6$$

$$SS_{BG} = \frac{(\Sigma X_1)^2}{n_1} + \frac{(\Sigma X_2)^2}{n_2} + \frac{(\Sigma X_3)^2}{n_3} - \frac{(\Sigma X_1 + \Sigma X_2 + \Sigma X_3)^2}{N}$$

$$= \frac{4356}{5} + \frac{10404}{5} + \frac{11664}{5} - \frac{(66 + 102 + 108)^2}{15}$$

$$= [871.2 + 2080.8 + 2332.8] - 5078.4$$

$$= 5284.8 - 5078.4 = 206.4$$

$$\text{total } SS = SS_{BG} + SS_{WG}$$
$$281.6 = 206.4 + SS_{WG}$$
$$SS_{WG} = 281.6 - 206.4 = 75.2$$

Step 2.   *Calculate degrees of freedom*

$$\text{total } df = (N - 1) = (15 - 1) = 14$$
$$df_{BG} = (\text{\# of conditions}) - 1 = 3 - 1 = 2$$
$$df_{WG} = (n_1 - 1) + (n_2 - 1) + (n_3 - 1)$$
$$= (5 - 1) + (5 - 1) + (5 - 1) = 12$$

Step 3.   *Calculate Mean Square Values*

$$MS_{BG} = SS_{BG}/df_{BG}$$
$$= 206.4/2 = 103.2$$
$$MS_{WG} = SS_{WG}/df_{WG}$$
$$= 75.2/12 = 6.3$$

(n.b. the MS_{WG} is also known as the "error term" or MS_e)

Step 4.   *Fit Mean Squares into the Formula for F and Solve*

$$F = \frac{MS_{BG}}{MS_{WG}}$$

$$F = \frac{103.2}{6.3} = 16.5$$

Step 5.   *Construct an ANOVA Source Table*

The essential components of the analysis of variance can be summarized in what is called a source table. It includes a listing of the sources of variance found in the study and for each source, the sums of squares, degrees of freedom, and mean square values; the *F* value is also included. For the maze study a source table would look like this:

Source	SS	df	MS	F
Amount of delay	206.4	2	103.2	16.5
Error	75.2	12	6.3	

Step 6.   *Determine if the Calculated F is Significant*

Table C.5 lists the critical values for assessing the outcome of the *F* test. The table is read by reading across the top of the table until you reach the correct *df* value for the numerator of the *F* ratio (2 in our example), then reading down until you reach the *df* value for the denominator of the *F* ratio (i.e., until you reach the values for *df* = 12). The critical values are 3.89 (.05 significance level) and 6.93 (.01 level). The calculated value of 16.5 exceeds both; thus, *F* is significant at the .01 level. It would be reasonable for the researcher to rejection the null hypothesis and conclude that some differences exist betwen the three groups.

Step 7.   *Perform Subsequent Analyses*

As you recall from the discussion in Chapter 7, when a 1-way analysis like the one just completed yields a significant effect, the question of the exact location of that effect remains unresolved. To solve the problem requires additional testing of each of the pairs of means (13.2 vs 20.4, 13.2 vs 21.6, and 20.4 vs 21.6), using one of several tests that have been developed for the purpose. For example, using a test called the Tukey HSD (stands for "honestly significant difference") test, the results would be that the 13.2 was significantly lower than the other two means, which did not differ from each other. These results would enable the researcher to conclude that delaying reinforcement significantly retards learning, but whether the delay is 5 or 10 seconds doesn't seem to matter. Consult a statistics text for the computation procedures for the Tukey HSD, or for other methods, including Scheffé's test, and the Newman–Keuls test.

Example 8.   *1-Way ANOVA—Repeated Measures*

Although the basic calculations are similar, the ANOVA is slightly different when the design is a within-subjects design (also referred to as a repeated-measures design). Because each subject serves in all of the study's conditions, there is a reduced amount of variance between the conditions. You can see why if you return for a second to the discussion of between- and within-subjects factors at the beginning of Chapter 6. In the golf ball example, you learned that when using a within-subjects design, the differences in distance between golf ball 1 and golf ball 2 cannot be attributed to individual differences because the same individuals are hitting both balls. As you will see from the following calculations, the mean square for the error term is lessened because it does not include variance attributed to individual differences. This variability is called "subject variance," and it is calculated separately from the error term.

   Although the repeated-measures ANOVA is designed for the within-subjects design, it is also used in between-subjects designs when matching is used to create related groups of subjects. This is because in a matched-groups design, the matching procedure reduces the variablity between the individuals assigned to the different conditions. It is not reduced as much as in the repeated-measures design, of course, but it is lowered enough to warrant using the repeated-measures ANOVA.

As an example of a repeated-measures ANOVA, consider a hypothetical longitudinal study examining the effect of age on logical thinking. Using a test of logic that yields scores ranging from 0 (bad) to 50 (good), a researcher compares the performance of seven individuals at three different times. The first assessment is at their 30th birthday. Their abilities are reassessed at age 45 and again at age 60. Here are the results, along with some basic summary statistics (including row totals).

Subject #	X_1 Age 30	X_2 Age 45	X_3 Age 60	ΣSs	ΣSs^2
1	32	27	25	84	7056
2	43	44	40	127	16129
3	23	27	18	68	4624
4	30	25	20	75	5625
5	45	41	37	123	15129
6	29	31	23	83	6889
7	19	23	15	57	3249
ΣX	221	218	178		
n	7	7	7		
$\overline{X}$	**31.6**	**31.1**	**25.4**		
ΣX^2	7529	7190	5072		
$\Sigma\Sigma Ss^2$					58701

The formula for the F ratio in a 1-way ANOVA for repeated measures:

$$F = \frac{MS_{BC}}{MS_e}, \text{ where } MS_{BC} \text{ refers to the mean square "between conditions"}$$

Step 1. *Calculate Sums of Squares*

$$\text{total } SS = (\Sigma X_1^2 + \Sigma X_2^2 + \Sigma X_3^2) - \frac{(\Sigma X_1 + \Sigma X_2 + \Sigma X_3)^2}{N}$$

$$= 7529 + 7190 + 5072 - \frac{(221 + 218 + 178)^2}{21}$$

$$= 19791 - 18128 = 1663$$

$$SS_{BC} = \frac{(\Sigma X_1)^2}{n_1} + \frac{(\Sigma X_2)^2}{n_2} + \frac{(\Sigma X_3)^2}{n_3} - \frac{(\Sigma X_1 + \Sigma X_2 + \Sigma X_3)^2}{N}$$

$$= \frac{(221)^2}{7} + \frac{(218)^2}{7} + \frac{(178)^2}{7} - \frac{(221 + 218 + 178)^2}{21}$$

$$= [6977.3 + 6789.1 + 4526.3] - 18128$$

$$= 18292.7 - 18128 = 164.7$$

$$SS_{subjects} = \frac{\Sigma\Sigma Ss^2}{\# \text{ conditions}} - \frac{(\Sigma X_1 + \Sigma X_2 + \Sigma X_3)^2}{N}$$

$$= \frac{58701}{3} - 18128$$

$$= 19567 - 18128 = 1439$$

$$\text{total } SS = SS_{BC} + SS_{subjects} + SS_e$$

$$1663 = 164.7 + 1439 + SS_e$$

$$SS_e = 1663 - 164.7 - 1439 = 59.3$$

Step 2. *Calculate degrees of freedom*

$$\text{total } df = (N - 1) = (21 - 1) = 20$$

$$df_{BC} = (\# \text{ of conditions}) - 1 = 3 - 1 = 2$$

$$df_{subjects} = (\# \text{ of subjects}) - 1 = 7 - 1 = 6$$

$$df_e = (df_{BC})(df_{subjects})$$

$$= (2)(6) = 12$$

Step 3. *Calculate Mean Square Values*

$$MS_{BC} = SS_{BC}/df_{BC}$$

$$= 164.7/2 = 82.4$$

$$MS_e = SS_e/df_e$$

$$= 59.3/12 = 4.9$$

(n.b. the MS and F ratio for "subjects" ordinarily is not calculated)

Step 4. *Fit Mean Squares into the Formula for F and Solve*

$$F = \frac{MS_{BC}}{MS_e}$$

$$F = \frac{82.4}{4.9} = 16.8$$

Step 5. *Construct an ANOVA Source Table*

The source table for a repeated measures ANOVA adds a line for "subjects" and it would look like this for the study on aging and logic:

Source	SS	df	MS	F
Age	164.7	2	82.4	16.8
Subjects	1439	6	—	—
Error	59.3	12	4.9	

Step 6. *Determine if the Calculated F Is Significant*

Refer to Table C.5 again for the critical values for assessing the outcome of the *F* test. Because the degrees of freedom happen to be the same as in the 1-way ANOVA for independent groups, the critical values are also the same: 3.89 (.05 significance level) and 6.93 (.01 level). The calculated value of 16.8 exceeds both; *F* is significant at the .01 level. The null hypothesis of no age differences can be rejected.

Step 7. *Perform Subsequent Analyses*

As in the earlier example, finding a significant *F* by itself doesn't tell you where the true differences lie. Subsequent testing is again required; by examining the means (31.6, 31.1, and 25.4) you can probably guess the outcome of this hypothetical study on age differences in logic ability.

Example 9. *2-Way ANOVA — Independent Groups*

A 2-way ANOVA is used for a factorial design with two independent variables. If both variables are between-subjects variables and subjects are randomly assigned to conditions, the appropriate analysis is an independent groups ANOVA. If both variables are testing within subjects, an analysis similar to the 1-way ANOVA for repeated measures is completed. Finally, if the design is a mixed one, involving both within-subjects and between-subjects factors, the analysis combines elements of an independent groups ANOVA and a repeated measures ANOVA. The following example is of the simplest case, a 2 × 2 ANOVA for independent groups. For details about other factorial ANOVAs, consult an advanced text in statistics.

To assess the effects of program content and level of anger on aggressive behavior, a researcher uses a 2 × 2 independent groups factorial design and randomly assigns five third-grade boys to each of the following conditions:

1. Violent content/subjects angered.
2. Violent content/subjects not angered.
3. Nonviolent content/subjects angered.
4. Nonviolent content/subjects not angered.

After experiencing one of these four conditions, each subject is given the opportunity to be aggressive. Assume a reliable and valid measure is used and it yields a score from 0–25, with higher numbers indicating greater aggression. For the following data, film content is factor A, with violent films being level A_1 and nonviolent films being level A_2. Factor B is whether or not subjects are made angry; for level B_1, subjects are angered and for B_2 they are not.

	B_1 (angry)	B_2 (not angry)	
A_1 (violent)	22	16	
	23	18	
	12	19	
	19	19	
	22	13	
	$\Sigma X_{A1B1} = 98$	$\Sigma X_{A1B2} = 85$	$\Sigma X_{A1} = 183$
	$n_{A1B1} = 5$	$n_{A1B2} = 5$	$n_{A1} = 10$
	$\overline{X}_{A1B1} = 19.6$	$\overline{X}_{A1B2} = 17.0$	$\overline{X}_{A1} = 18.3$
	$\Sigma X^2_{A1B1} = 2002$	$\Sigma X^2_{A1B2} = 1471$	$\Sigma X^2_{A1} = 3473$
A_2 (nonviolent)	14	10	
	13	12	
	20	15	
	15	11	
	17	9	
	$\Sigma X_{A2B1} = 79$	$\Sigma X_{A2B2} = 57$	$\Sigma X_{A2} = 136$
	$n_{A2B1} = 5$	$n_{A2B2} = 5$	$n_{A2} = 10$
	$\overline{X}_{A2B1} = 15.8$	$\overline{X}_{A2B2} = 11.4$	$\overline{X}_{A2} = 13.6$
	$\Sigma X^2_{A2B1} = 1279$	$\Sigma X^2_{A2B2} = 671$	$\Sigma X^2_{A2} = 1950$
	$\Sigma X_{B1} = 177$	$\Sigma X_{B2} = 142$	$\Sigma X_T = 319$
	$n_{B1} = 10$	$n_{B2} = 10$	$N = 40$
	$\overline{X}_{B1} = 17.1$	$\overline{X}_{B2} = 14.2$	
	$\Sigma X^2_{B1} = 3281$	$\Sigma X^2_{B2} = 2142$	$\Sigma X^2_T = 5423$

In a 2-way ANOVA, three separate F ratios are calculated, one for each of the two main effects and one for the interaction:

Main effect for factor A   *Main effect for factor B*   *Main effect for interaction*

$$F = \frac{MS_A}{MS_e} \qquad\qquad F = \frac{MS_B}{MS_e} \qquad\qquad F = \frac{MS_{A \times B}}{MS_e}$$

Step 1.   *Calculate Sums of Squares*

$$\text{total } SS = \Sigma X_T^2 - \frac{(\Sigma X_T)^2}{N}$$

$$= 5423 - \frac{(319)^2}{20}$$

$$= 5423 - 5088.1 = 334.9$$

$$SS_A = \frac{(\Sigma X_{A1})^2}{n_{A1}} + \frac{(\Sigma X_{A2})^2}{n_{A2}} - \frac{(\Sigma X_T)^2}{N}$$

$$= \frac{(183)^2}{10} + \frac{(136)^2}{10} - 5088.1$$

$$= [3348.9 + 1849.6] - 5088.1$$

$$= 110.4$$

$$SS_B = \frac{(\Sigma X_{B1})^2}{n_{B1}} + \frac{(\Sigma X_{B2})^2}{n_{B2}} - \frac{(\Sigma X_T)^2}{N}$$

$$= \frac{(177)^2}{10} + \frac{(142)^2}{10} - 5088.1$$

$$= [3132.9 + 2016.4] - 5088.1$$

$$= 61.2$$

$$SS_{A \times B} = \frac{(\Sigma X_{A1B1})^2}{n_{A1B1}} + \frac{(\Sigma X_{A1B2})^2}{n_{A1B2}} + \frac{(\Sigma X_{A2B1})^2}{n_{A2B1}} + \frac{(\Sigma X_{A2B2})^2}{n_{A2B2}} - \frac{(\Sigma X_T)^2}{N}$$

$$\quad - SS_A - SS_B$$

$$= \frac{(98)^2}{5} + \frac{(85)^2}{5} + \frac{(79)^2}{5} + \frac{(57)^2}{5} - 5088.1 - 110.4 - 61.2$$

$$= [1920.8 + 1445.0 + 1248.2 + 649.8] - 5088.1 - 110.4 - 61.2$$

$$= 4.1$$

$$\text{total } SS = SS_A + SS_B + SS_{A \times B} + SS_e$$

$$334.9 = 110.4 + 61.2 + 4.1 + SS_e$$

$$SS_e = 334.9 - (110.4 + 61.2 + 4.1)$$

$$= 159.2$$

Step 2.   *Calculate degrees of freedom*

$$\text{total } df = (N - 1) = (20 - 1) = 19$$

$$df_A = (\text{\# of levels of A}) - 1 = 2 - 1 = 1$$

$$df_B = (\text{\# of levels of B}) - 1 = 2 - 1 = 1$$

$$df_{A \times B} = (df_A)(df_B) = (1)(1) = 1$$

$$df_e = (n_{A1B1} - 1) + (n_{A1B2} - 1) + (n_{A2B1} - 1) + (n_{A2B2} - 1)$$
$$= (5 - 1) + (5 - 1) + (5 - 1) + (5 - 1) = 16$$

Step 3. *Calculate Mean Square Values*

$$MS_A = SS_A / df_A$$
$$= 110.4/1 = 110.4$$

$$MS_B = SS_B / df_B$$
$$= 61.2/1 = 61.2$$

$$MS_{AxB} = SS_{AxB} / df_{AxB}$$
$$= 4.1/1 = 4.1$$

$$MS_e = SS_e / df_e$$
$$= 159.2/16 = 9.9$$

Step 4. *Fit Mean Squares into the Formula for F and Solve*

Main effect for factor A   *Main effect for factor B*   *Main effect for interaction*

$$F = \frac{110.4}{9.9}$$ $$F = \frac{61.2}{9.9}$$ $$F = \frac{4.1}{9.9}$$

$$= 11.2$$ $$= 6.2$$ $$= .41$$

Step 5. *Construct an ANOVA Source Table*

The source table for a 2-way ANOVA for independent groups would look like this for the study on the effects of program content and anger on aggression:

Source	SS	df	MS	F
Content (A)	110.4	1	110.4	11.2
Anger (B)	61.2	1	61.2	6.2
Interaction (A × B)	4.1	1	4.1	.4
Error	159.2	16	9.9	

Step 6. *Determine if the Calculated F Values Are Significant*

Refer again to Table C.5. This time the degrees of freedom for all three *F* values are 1 for the numerator and 16 for the denominator. The critical values are 4.49 (.05 significance level) and 8.53 (.01 level). From the calculated values of *F*, it can be concluded that the study resulted in two main effects and no interaction. The main effect for factor A is significant ($p < .01$ level), as is the main effect for B ($p < .05$ level. The main effect for A means that the overall level of aggression when violent films are seen ($\overline{X}_{A1} = 18.3$) is greater than when nonviolent films are seen ($\overline{X}_{A2} = 13.6$). The effect for B means that aggression is higher when subjects are angered ($\overline{X}_{B1} = 17.7$) than when this doesn't happen ($\overline{X}_{B2} = 14.2$).

Step 7.   *Perform Subsequent Analyses*

As described in Chapter 7, subsequent testing in a factorial ANOVA can take two forms. If there is a significant main effect for a factor with more than two levels, then pairwise comparisons of the overall means would be done, perhaps using Tukey's HSD test again. If a significant interaction occurred, simple effects testing could be done. In the aggression example, neither of these situations occurs and no subsequent testing is needed.

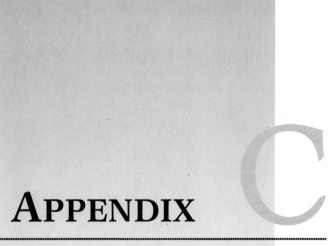

APPENDIX C

Statistical Tables

In this appendix, you will find these tables for statistical decision making:

TABLE C.1   *Random Numbers*

03	47	43	73	86	36	96	47	36	61	46	98	63	71	62	33	26	16	80	45	60	11	14	10	95
97	74	24	67	62	42	81	14	57	20	42	53	32	37	32	27	07	36	07	51	24	51	79	89	73
16	76	62	27	66	56	50	26	71	07	32	90	79	78	53	13	55	38	58	59	88	97	54	14	10
12	56	85	99	26	96	96	68	27	31	05	03	72	93	15	57	12	10	14	21	88	26	49	81	76
55	59	56	35	64	38	54	82	46	22	31	62	43	09	90	06	18	44	32	53	23	83	01	30	30
16	22	77	94	39	49	54	43	54	82	17	37	93	23	78	87	35	20	96	43	84	26	34	91	64
84	42	17	53	31	57	24	55	06	88	77	04	74	47	67	21	76	33	50	25	83	92	12	06	76
63	01	63	78	59	16	95	55	67	19	98	10	50	71	75	12	86	73	58	07	44	39	52	38	79
33	21	12	34	29	78	64	56	07	82	52	42	07	44	38	15	51	00	13	42	99	66	02	79	54
57	60	86	32	44	09	47	27	96	54	49	17	46	09	62	90	52	84	77	27	08	02	73	43	28
18	18	07	92	46	44	17	16	58	09	79	83	86	19	62	06	76	50	03	10	55	23	64	05	05
26	62	38	97	75	84	16	07	44	99	83	11	46	32	24	20	14	85	88	45	10	93	72	88	71
23	42	40	64	74	82	97	77	77	81	07	45	32	14	08	32	98	94	07	72	93	85	79	10	75
52	36	28	19	95	50	92	26	11	97	00	56	76	31	38	80	22	02	53	53	86	60	42	04	53
37	85	94	35	12	83	39	50	08	30	42	34	07	96	88	54	42	06	87	98	35	85	29	48	39
70	29	17	12	13	40	33	20	38	26	13	89	51	03	74	17	76	37	13	04	07	74	21	19	30
56	62	18	37	35	96	83	50	87	75	97	12	25	93	47	70	33	24	03	54	97	77	46	44	80
99	49	57	22	77	88	42	95	45	72	16	64	36	16	00	04	43	18	66	79	94	77	24	21	90
16	08	15	04	72	33	27	14	34	09	45	59	34	68	49	12	72	07	34	45	99	27	72	95	14
31	16	93	32	43	50	27	89	87	19	20	15	37	00	49	52	85	66	60	44	38	68	88	11	80
68	34	30	13	70	55	74	30	77	40	44	22	78	84	26	04	33	46	09	52	68	07	97	06	57
74	57	25	65	76	59	29	97	68	60	71	91	38	67	54	13	58	18	24	76	15	54	55	95	52
27	42	37	86	53	48	55	90	65	72	96	57	69	36	10	96	46	92	42	45	97	60	49	04	91
00	39	68	29	61	66	37	32	20	30	77	84	57	03	29	10	45	65	04	26	11	04	96	67	24
29	94	98	94	24	68	49	69	10	82	53	75	91	93	30	34	25	20	57	27	40	48	73	51	92
16	90	82	66	59	83	62	64	11	12	67	19	00	71	74	60	47	21	29	68	02	02	37	03	31
11	27	94	75	06	06	09	19	74	66	02	94	37	34	02	76	70	90	30	86	38	45	94	30	38
35	24	10	16	20	33	32	51	26	38	79	78	45	04	91	16	92	53	56	16	02	75	50	95	98
38	23	16	86	38	42	38	97	01	50	87	75	66	81	41	40	01	74	91	62	48	51	84	08	32
31	96	25	91	47	96	44	33	49	13	34	86	82	53	91	00	52	43	48	85	27	55	26	89	62

TABLE C.1   *Random Numbers* (continued)

66	67	40	67	14	64	05	71	95	86	11	05	65	09	68	76	83	20	37	90	57	16	00	11	66
14	90	84	45	11	75	73	88	05	90	52	27	41	14	86	22	98	12	22	08	07	52	74	95	80
68	05	51	18	00	33	96	02	75	19	07	60	62	93	55	59	33	82	43	90	49	37	38	44	59
20	46	78	73	90	97	51	40	14	02	04	02	33	31	08	39	54	16	49	36	47	95	93	13	30
64	19	58	97	79	15	06	15	93	20	01	90	10	75	06	40	78	78	89	62	02	67	74	17	33
05	26	93	70	60	22	35	85	15	13	92	03	51	59	77	59	56	78	06	83	52	91	05	70	74
07	97	10	88	23	09	98	42	99	64	61	71	62	99	15	06	51	29	16	93	58	05	77	09	51
68	71	86	85	85	54	87	66	47	54	73	32	08	11	12	44	95	92	63	16	29	56	24	29	48
26	99	61	65	53	58	37	78	80	70	42	10	50	67	42	32	17	55	85	74	94	44	67	16	94
14	65	52	68	75	87	59	36	22	41	26	78	63	06	55	13	08	27	01	50	15	29	39	39	43
05	26	93	70	60	22	35	85	15	13	92	03	51	59	77	59	56	78	06	83	52	91	05	70	74
07	97	10	88	23	09	98	42	99	64	61	71	62	99	15	06	51	29	16	93	58	05	77	09	51
68	71	86	85	85	54	87	66	47	54	73	32	08	11	12	44	95	92	63	16	29	56	24	29	48
26	99	61	65	53	58	37	78	80	70	42	10	50	67	42	32	17	55	85	74	94	44	67	16	94
14	65	52	68	75	87	59	36	22	41	26	78	63	06	55	13	08	27	01	50	15	29	39	39	43
17	53	77	58	71	71	41	61	50	72	12	41	94	96	26	44	95	27	36	99	02	96	74	30	83
90	26	59	21	19	23	52	23	33	12	96	93	02	18	39	07	02	18	36	07	25	99	32	70	23
41	23	52	55	99	31	04	49	69	96	10	47	48	45	88	13	41	43	89	20	97	17	14	49	17
60	20	50	81	69	31	99	73	68	68	35	81	33	03	76	24	30	12	48	60	18	99	10	72	34
91	25	38	05	90	94	58	28	41	36	45	37	59	03	09	90	35	57	29	12	82	62	54	65	60
34	50	57	74	37	98	80	33	00	91	09	77	93	19	82	74	94	80	04	04	45	07	31	66	49
85	22	04	39	43	73	81	53	94	79	33	62	46	86	28	08	31	54	46	31	53	94	13	38	47
09	79	13	77	48	73	82	97	22	21	05	03	27	24	83	72	89	44	05	60	35	80	39	94	88
88	75	80	18	14	22	95	75	42	49	39	32	82	22	49	02	48	07	70	37	16	04	61	67	87
90	96	23	70	00	39	00	03	06	90	55	85	78	38	36	94	37	30	69	32	90	89	00	76	33

Source: Fisher, R. A., & Yates, F. (1963). Statistical tables for biological, agricultural, and medical research (6th ed.).
Table XXXIII. Edinburgh: Oliver & Boyd.

TABLE C.2   *Critical Values for Pearson's r*

df	.05	.01	df	.05	.01
1	.997	1.00	16	.468	.590
2	.950	.990	17	.456	.575
3	.878	.959	18	.444	.561
4	.811	.917	19	.433	.549
5	.755	.875	20	.423	.537
6	.707	.834	25	.381	.487
7	.666	.798	30	.349	.449
8	.634	.767	35	.325	.418
9	.602	.735	40	.304	.393
10	.576	.708	45	.288	.372
11	.553	.694	50	.273	.354
12	.532	.661	60	.250	.325
13	.514	.641	70	.232	.302
14	.497	.623	80	.217	.283
15	.482	.606	90	.205	.267
			100	.195	.254

Source: Fisher, R. A., & Yates, F. (1963). *Statistical tables for biological, agricultural, and medical research* (6th ed.). Table VII. Edinburgh: Oliver & Boyd.

TABLE C.3   *Critical Values for Chi-Square (χ^2)*

df	.05	.01	df	.05	.01
1	3.84	6.64	16	26.30	32.00
2	5.99	9.21	17	27.59	33.41
3	7.82	11.34	18	28.87	34.80
4	9.49	13.28	19	30.14	36.19
5	11.07	15.09	20	31.41	37.57
6	12.59	16.81	21	32.67	38.93
7	14.07	18.48	22	33.92	40.29
8	15.51	20.09	23	35.17	41.64
9	16.92	21.67	24	36.42	42.98
10	18.31	23.21	25	37.65	44.31
11	19.68	24.72	26	38.88	45.64
12	21.03	26.22	27	40.11	46.96
13	22.36	27.69	28	41.34	48.28
14	23.68	29.14	29	42.56	49.59
15	25.00	30.58	30	43.77	50.89

Source: Fisher, R. A., & Yates, F. (1963). *Statistical tables for biological, agricultural, and medical research* (6th ed.). Table IV. Edinburgh: Oliver & Boyd.

TABLE **C.4**   *Critical Values for the t Distribution (two-tailed test)*

df	Alpha (α) Level		df	Alpha (α) Level	
	.05	.01		.05	.01
1	12.71	63.66	18	2.10	2.88
2	4.30	9.93	19	2.09	2.86
3	3.18	5.84	20	2.09	2.85
4	2.78	4.60	21	2.08	2.83
5	2.57	4.03	22	2.07	2.82
6	2.45	3.71	23	2.07	2.81
7	2.37	3.50	24	2.06	2.80
8	2.31	3.36	25	2.06	2.79
9	2.26	3.25	26	2.06	2.78
10	2.23	3.17	27	2.05	2.77
11	2.20	3.11	28	2.05	2.76
12	2.18	3.06	29	2.05	2.76
13	2.16	3.01	30	2.04	2.75
14	2.15	2.98	40	2.02	2.70
15	2.13	2.95	60	2.00	2.66
16	2.12	2.92	120	1.98	2.62
17	2.11	2.90	∞	1.96	2.58

Source: Fisher, R. A., & Yates, F. (1963). *Statistical tables for biological, agricultural, and medical research* (6th ed.). Table III. Edinburgh: Oliver & Boyd.

TABLE C.5   *Critical Values for the F Distribution*

		degrees of freedom (numerator)							
	1	*2*	*3*	*4*	*5*	*6*	*7*	*8*	*9*
1	161.4	199.5	215.7	224.6	230.0	234.0	236.8	238.9	240.5
	4052.40	**4999.5**	**5403**	**5625**	**5764**	**5859**	**5928**	**5981**	**6022**
2	18.51	19.00	19.16	19.25	19.30	19.33	19.35	19.37	19.38
	98.50	**99.00**	**99.17**	**99.25**	**99.30**	**99.33**	**99.36**	**99.37**	**99.39**
3	10.31	9.55	9.28	9.12	9.01	8.94	8.89	8.85	8.81
	34.12	**30.82**	**29.46**	**28.71**	**28.24**	**27.91**	**27.67**	**27.49**	**27.35**
4	7.71	6.94	6.59	6.39	6.26	6.16	6.09	6.04	6.00
	21.20	**18.00**	**16.69**	**15.98**	**15.52**	**15.21**	**14.98**	**14.80**	**16.66**
5	6.61	5.79	5.41	5.19	5.05	4.95	4.88	4.82	4.77
	16.26	**13.27**	**12.06**	**11.39**	**10.97**	**10.67**	**10.46**	**10.29**	**10.16**
6	5.99	5.14	4.76	4.53	4.39	4.28	4.21	4.15	4.10
	13.75	**10.92**	**9.78**	**9.15**	**8.75**	**8.47**	**8.26**	**8.10**	**7.98**
7	5.59	4.74	4.35	4.12	3.97	3.87	3.79	3.73	3.68
	12.25	**9.55**	**8.45**	**7.85**	**7.46**	**7.19**	**6.99**	**6.84**	**6.72**
8	5.32	4.46	4.07	3.84	3.69	3.58	3.50	3.44	3.39
	11.26	**8.65**	**7.59**	**7.01**	**6.63**	**6.37**	**6.18**	**6.03**	**5.91**
9	5.12	4.26	3.86	3.63	3.48	3.37	3.29	3.23	3.18
	10.56	**8.02**	**6.99**	**6.42**	**6.06**	**5.80**	**5.61**	**5.47**	**5.35**
10	4.96	4.10	3.29	3.48	3.33	3.22	3.14	3.07	3.02
	10.04	**7.56**	**6.55**	**5.99**	**5.46**	**5.39**	**5.20**	**5.06**	**4.94**
11	4.84	3.98	3.24	3.36	3.20	3.09	3.01	2.95	2.90
	9.65	**7.21**	**6.22**	**5.67**	**5.32**	**5.07**	**4.89**	**4.74**	**4.63**
12	4.75	3.89	3.20	3.26	3.11	3.00	2.91	2.85	2.80
	9.33	**6.93**	**5.95**	**5.41**	**5.06**	**4.82**	**4.64**	**4.50**	**4.39**
13	4.67	3.81	3.16	3.18	3.03	2.92	2.83	2.77	2.71
	9.07	**6.70**	**5.74**	**5.21**	**4.86**	**4.62**	**4.44**	**4.30**	**4.19**
14	4.60	3.74	3.13	3.11	2.96	2.85	2.76	2.70	2.65
	8.86	**6.51**	**5.56**	**5.04**	**4.69**	**4.46**	**4.28**	**4.14**	**4.03**
15	4.54	3.68	3.29	3.06	2.90	2.79	2.71	2.64	2.59
	8.68	**6.36**	**5.42**	**4.89**	**4.56**	**4.32**	**4.14**	**4.00**	**3.89**
16	4.49	3.63	3.24	3.01	2.85	2.74	2.66	2.59	2.54
	8.53	**6.23**	**5.29**	**4.77**	**4.44**	**4.20**	**4.03**	**3.89**	**3.78**
17	4.45	3.59	3.20	2.96	2.81	2.70	2.61	2.55	2.49
	8.40	**6.11**	**5.18**	**4.67**	**4.34**	**4.10**	**3.93**	**3.79**	**3.68**
18	4.41	3.55	3.16	2.93	2.77	2.66	2.58	2.51	2.46
	8.29	**6.01**	**5.09**	**4.58**	**4.25**	**4.01**	**3.84**	**3.71**	**3.60**
19	4.38	3.52	3.13	2.90	2.74	2.63	2.54	2.48	2.42
	8.18	**5.93**	**5.01**	**4.50**	**4.17**	**3.94**	**3.77**	**3.63**	**3.52**

Source: Pearson, E.S., & Hartley, H.O. (1966). *Biometrika tables for Statisticians* (3rd ed). Vol. I. London Cambridge Univ. Press.

N.B. In normal print are critical values for alpha = .05.

In boldface are critical values for alpha = .01.

TABLE C.5   *Critical Values for the F Distribution* (continued)

	degrees of freedom (numerator)									
10	*12*	*15*	*20*	*24*	*30*	*40*	*60*	*120*	*∞*
241.9	243.9	245.9	248.0	249.1	250.1	251.1	252.2	253.3	254.3
6056.90	**6106**	**6157**	**6209**	**6235**	**6261**	**6287**	**6313**	**6339**	**6366**
19.40	19.41	19.43	19.45	19.45	19.46	19.47	19.48	19.49	19.50
99.40	**99.42**	**99.43**	**99.45**	**99.46**	**99.47**	**99.47**	**99.48**	**99.49**	**99.50**
8.79	8.74	8.70	8.66	8.64	8.62	8.59	8.57	8.55	8.53
27.23	**27.05**	**26.87**	**26.69**	**26.60**	**26.50**	**26.41**	**26.32**	**26.22**	**26.13**
5.96	5.91	5.86	5.80	5.77	5.75	5.72	5.69	5.66	5.63
14.55	**14.37**	**14.20**	**14.02**	**13.93**	**13.84**	**13.75**	**13.65**	**13.56**	**13.46**
4.74	4.68	4.62	4.56	4.53	4.50	4.46	4.43	4.40	4.36
10.05	**9.89**	**9.72**	**9.55**	**9.47**	**9.50**	**9.29**	**9.20**	**9.11**	**9.02**
4.06	4.00	3.94	3.87	3.84	3.81	3.77	3.74	3.70	3.67
7.87	**7.72**	**7.56**	**7.40**	**7.31**	**7.23**	**7.14**	**7.06**	**6.97**	**6.88**
3.64	3.57	3.51	3.44	3.41	3.38	3.34	3.30	3.27	3.23
6.62	**6.47**	**6.31**	**6.16**	**6.07**	**5.99**	**5.91**	**5.82**	**5.74**	**5.65**
3.35	3.28	3.22	3.15	3.12	3.08	3.04	3.01	2.97	2.93
5.81	**5.67**	**5.52**	**5.36**	**5.28**	**5.20**	**5.12**	**5.03**	**4.95**	**4.86**
3.14	3.07	3.01	2.94	2.90	2.86	2.83	2.79	2.75	2.71
5.26	**5.11**	**4.96**	**4.81**	**4.73**	**4.65**	**4.57**	**4.48**	**4.40**	**4.31**
2.98	2.91	2.85	2.77	2.74	2.70	2.66	2.62	2.58	2.54
4.85	**4.71**	**4.56**	**4.81**	**4.33**	**4.25**	**4.17**	**4.08**	**4.00**	**3.91**
2.85	2.79	2.72	2.65	2.61	2.57	2.53	2.49	2.45	2.40
4.54	**4.40**	**4.25**	**4.10**	**4.02**	**3.94**	**3.85**	**3.78**	**3.69**	**3.60**
2.75	2.69	2.62	2.54	2.51	2.47	2.43	2.38	2.34	2.30
4.30	**4.16**	**4.01**	**3.86**	**3.78**	**3.70**	**3.62**	**3.54**	**3.45**	**3.36**
2.67	2.60	2.53	2.46	2.42	2.38	2.34	2.30	2.25	2.21
4.10	**3.96**	**3.82**	**3.66**	**3.59**	**3.51**	**3.43**	**3.34**	**3.25**	**3.17**
2.60	2.53	2.46	2.39	2.35	2.31	2.27	2.22	2.18	2.13
3.94	**3.80**	**3.66**	**3.51**	**3.43**	**3.35**	**3.27**	**3.18**	**3.09**	**3.00**
2.54	2.54	2.40	2.33	2.29	2.25	2.20	2.16	2.11	2.07
3.80	**3.67**	**3.52**	**3.37**	**3.29**	**3.21**	**3.13**	**3.05**	**2.96**	**2.87**
2.49	2.42	2.35	2.28	2.24	2.19	2.15	2.11	2.06	2.01
3.69	**3.55**	**3.41**	**3.26**	**3.18**	**3.10**	**3.02**	**2.93**	**2.84**	**2.75**
2.45	2.38	2.31	2.23	2.19	2.15	2.10	2.06	2.01	1.96
3.59	**3.46**	**3.31**	**3.16**	**3.08**	**3.00**	**2.92**	**2.83**	**2.75**	**2.65**
2.41	2.34	2.27	2.19	2.15	2.11	2.06	2.02	1.97	1.92
3.51	**3.37**	**3.23**	**3.08**	**3.00**	**2.92**	**2.84**	**2.75**	**2.66**	**2.57**
2.38	2.31	2.23	2.16	2.11	2.07	2.03	1.98	1.93	1.88
3.43	**3.30**	**3.15**	**3.00**	**2.92**	**2.84**	**2.76**	**2.67**	**2.58**	**2.49**

continued

433

TABLE C.5 *Critical Values for the F Distribution* (continued)

		degrees of freedom (numerator)								
		1	*2*	*3*	*4*	*5*	*6*	*7*	*8*	*9*
	20	4.35	3.49	3.10	2.87	2.71	2.60	2.51	2.45	2.39
		8.10	**5.85**	**4.94**	**4.43**	**4.10**	**3.87**	**3.70**	**3.56**	**3.46**
	21	4.32	3.47	3.07	2.84	2.68	2.57	2.49	2.42	2.37
		8.02	**5.78**	**4.87**	**4.37**	**4.04**	**3.81**	**3.64**	**3.51**	**3.40**
	22	4.30	3.44	3.05	2.82	2.66	2.55	2.46	2.40	2.34
		7.95	**5.72**	**4.82**	**4.31**	**3.99**	**3.76**	**3.59**	**3.45**	**3.35**
	23	4.28	3.42	3.03	2.80	2.64	2.53	2.44	2.37	2.32
		7.88	**5.66**	**4.76**	**4.26**	**3.94**	**3.71**	**3.54**	**3.41**	**3.30**
	24	4.26	3.40	3.01	2.78	2.62	2.51	2.42	2.36	2.30
		7.82	**5.61**	**4.72**	**4.22**	**3.90**	**3.67**	**3.50**	**3.36**	**3.26**
Degrees of freedom (denominator)	25	4.24	3.39	2.99	2.76	2.60	2.49	2.40	2.34	2.28
		7.77	**5.57**	**4.99**	**4.18**	**3.85**	**3.63**	**3.46**	**3.32**	**3.22**
	26	4.23	3.37	2.98	2.74	2.59	2.47	2.39	2.32	2.27
		7.72	**5.53**	**4.98**	**4.14**	**3.82**	**3.59**	**3.42**	**3.29**	**3.18**
	27	4.21	3.35	2.96	2.73	2.57	2.46	2.37	2.31	2.25
		7.68	**5.49**	**4.60**	**4.11**	**3.78**	**3.56**	**3.39**	**3.26**	**3.15**
	28	4.20	3.34	2.95	2.71	2.56	2.45	2.36	2.29	2.24
		7.64	**5.45**	**4.57**	**4.07**	**3.75**	**3.53**	**3.36**	**3.23**	**3.12**
	29	4.18	3.33	2.93	2.70	2.55	2.43	2.35	2.28	2.22
		7.60	**5.42**	**4.54**	**4.04**	**3.73**	**3.50**	**3.33**	**3.20**	**3.09**
	30	4.17	3.32	2.92	2.69	2.53	2.42	2.33	2.27	2.21
		7.56	**5.39**	**4.51**	**4.02**	**3.70**	**3.47**	**3.30**	**3.17**	**3.07**
	40	4.08	3.23	2.84	2.61	2.45	2.34	2.25	2.18	2.12
		7.31	**5.18**	**4.31**	**3.83**	**3.51**	**3.29**	**3.12**	**2.99**	**2.89**
	60	4.00	3.15	2.76	2.53	2.37	2.25	2.17	2.10	2.04
		7.08	**4.98**	**4.13**	**3.65**	**3.34**	**3.12**	**2.95**	**2.82**	**2.72**
	120	3.92	3.07	2.68	2.45	2.29	2.17	2.09	2.02	1.96
		6.85	**4.79**	**3.95**	**3.48**	**3.17**	**2.96**	**2.79**	**2.66**	**2.56**
	∞	3.84	3.00	2.60	2.37	2.21	2.10	2.01	1.94	1.88
		6.63	**4.61**	**3.78**	**3.32**	**3.02**	**2.80**	**2.64**	**2.51**	**2.41**

TABLE C.5   *Critical Values for the F Distribution* (continued)

degrees of freedom (numerator)									
10	*12*	*15*	*20*	*24*	*30*	*40*	*60*	*120*	*∞*
2.35	2.28	2.20	2.12	2.08	2.04	1.99	1.95	1.90	1.84
3.37	**3.23**	**3.09**	**2.94**	**2.86**	**2.78**	**2.69**	**2.61**	**2.52**	**2.42**
2.32	2.25	2.18	2.10	2.05	2.01	1.96	1.92	1.87	1.81
3.31	**3.17**	**3.03**	**2.88**	**2.80**	**2.72**	**2.64**	**2.55**	**2.46**	**2.36**
2.30	2.23	2.15	2.07	2.03	1.98	1.94	1.89	1.84	1.78
3.26	**3.12**	**2.98**	**2.83**	**2.75**	**2.67**	**2.58**	**2.50**	**2.40**	**2.31**
2.27	2.20	2.13	2.05	2.01	1.96	1.91	1.86	1.81	1.76
3.21	**3.07**	**2.93**	**2.78**	**2.70**	**2.62**	**2.54**	**2.45**	**2.35**	**2.26**
2.25	2.18	2.11	2.03	1.98	1.94	1.89	1.84	1.79	1.73
3.17	**3.03**	**2.89**	**2.74**	**2.66**	**2.58**	**2.49**	**2.40**	**2.31**	**2.21**
2.24	2.16	2.09	2.01	1.96	1.92	1.87	1.82	1.77	1.71
3.13	**2.99**	**2.85**	**2.70**	**2.62**	**2.54**	**2.45**	**2.36**	**2.27**	**2.17**
2.22	2.15	2.07	1.99	1.95	1.90	1.85	1.80	1.75	1.69
3.09	**2.96**	**2.81**	**2.66**	**2.58**	**2.50**	**2.42**	**2.33**	**2.23**	**2.13**
2.20	2.13	2.06	1.97	1.93	1.88	1.84	1.79	1.73	1.67
3.06	**2.93**	**2.78**	**2.63**	**2.55**	**2.47**	**2.38**	**2.29**	**2.20**	**2.10**
2.19	2.12	2.04	1.96	1.91	1.87	1.82	1.77	1.71	1.65
3.03	**2.90**	**2.75**	**2.60**	**2.52**	**2.44**	**2.35**	**2.26**	**2.17**	**2.06**
2.18	2.10	2.03	1.94	1.90	1.85	1.81	1.75	1.70	1.64
3.00	**2.87**	**2.73**	**2.57**	**2.49**	**2.41**	**2.33**	**2.23**	**2.14**	**2.03**
2.16	2.09	2.01	1.93	1.89	1.84	1.79	1.74	1.68	1.62
2.98	**2.84**	**2.70**	**2.55**	**2.47**	**2.39**	**2.30**	**2.21**	**2.11**	**2.01**
2.08	2.00	1.92	1.84	1.79	1.74	1.69	1.64	1.58	1.51
2.80	**2.66**	**2.52**	**2.37**	**2.29**	**2.20**	**2.11**	**2.02**	**1.92**	**1.80**
1.99	1.92	1.84	1.75	1.70	1.65	1.59	1.53	1.47	1.39
2.63	**2.50**	**2.35**	**2.20**	**2.12**	**2.03**	**1.94**	**1.84**	**1.73**	**1.60**
1.91	1.83	1.75	1.66	1.61	1.55	1.50	1.43	1.35	1.25
2.47	**2.34**	**2.19**	**2.03**	**1.95**	**1.86**	**1.76**	**1.66**	**1.53**	**1.38**
1.83	1.74	1.67	1.57	1.52	1.46	1.39	1.32	1.22	1.00
2.32	**2.18**	**2.04**	**1.88**	**1.79**	**1.70**	**1.59**	**1.47**	**1.32**	**1.00**

APPENDIX D

Answers to Student Review Questions and Selected Exercises

Chapter 1. Scientific Thinking in Psychology

Chapter Review Answers (relevant pages in parentheses)

A. *Fill–Ins*
1. tenacity (5)
2. authority (6)
3. a priori (6)
4. determinism (7)
5. introspection; objectivity (15; 8)
6. empirical question (9)

B. *Multiple Choice*
1. b (7)   2. c (8)   3. a (5)   4. a (17)   5. d (12)

Applications Exercises

Exercise 1.1 Asking Empirical Questions

Possible answers to 1:

- To what extent do people of different faiths believe in a "personal God" who is involved in their day to day living?
- Has the level of church attendance decreased for certain age groups in the last 20 years?

Possible answers to 2:

- Will people be less likely to donate to charity if they are told that all donations will be anonymous?
- If a child's teddy bear is in need of help, will younger children be more likely to help than older children?

Chapter 2. Ethics in Psychological Research

Chapter Review Answers

A. ***Fill-Ins***
1. dehoaxing; desensitizing (42)
2. critical incidents (30)
3. informed consent (36)
4. speciesism (46)
5. falsifying data (50)
6. subjects (32)

B. ***Multiple Choice***
1. b (29)   2. c (36)   3. d (36)   4. a (48)   5. c (50)

Applications Exercises

Exercise 2.1 Thinking Empirically about Deception

Possible answers to 1:

- Administer a survey on the extent to which psychologists are trusted; give it to
  - people who have never participated in a study
  - those who have signed up for a study but not yet participated
  - those who participated in a study with no deception
  - those who participated in a study with mild deception
  - those who participated in a study with severe deception

Exercise 2.3 Avoiding Plagiarism

Plagiarism can occur even when paraphrasing is used. The key factor is whether or not the original author has some degree of "ownership" over the idea in question. In this case, it is clear from the original that Ekman created the term "Othello error." The student should have quoted directly from Ekman or given Ekman credit for the idea. For instance, the third-to-last sentence could have been written like this:

Ekman (1985) has called this the "Othello error."

Also, the specific phrase "disbelieving-the-truth mistake" probably should be attributed to Ekman.

Chapter 3. Developing Ideas for Research in Psychology

Chapter Review Answers

A. *Fill-Ins*

1. applied (59)
2. experimental; mundane (62)
3. serendipity (66)
4. deduction (70)
5. parsimonious (76)
6. falsification (73)

B. *Multiple Choice*

1. c (61) 2. a (64) 3. a (71) 4. b (79) 5. d (80)

Applications Exercises

Exercise 3.2 Creating Operational Definitions

Possible answer to 1. Birds of a feather flock together.

- General meaning is that people with similar attitudes, likes and dislikes, and so on, will be more likely to form friendships than those who are dissimilar.

- To study this empirically could involve setting up a simulated dating service; prospective dating partners would fill out surveys indicating their general attitudes about a variety of things; the researcher could then pair together couples with differing degrees of similarity. "Similarity" (i.e., birds of a feather) could be operationally defined in terms the degree of agreement in survey answers. After the couple meets and goes out to dinner (researcher's expense of course), they could each be asked to indicate the chances that they will meet (i.e., flock together) again in the immediate future.

Exercise 3.4 Confirmation Bias

The correct answer is "E and 7"—these are the only cards that can falsify the statement (i.e., finding an odd number on the other side of the E or finding a vowel on the other side of the 7). A common response is "E and 4," but the choice of "4" shows a confirmation bias. Turning over a 4 and seeing a vowel indeed provides confirming data, but turning over the 4 and finding a consonant does not disconfirm the statement.

Chapter 4. Measurement, Sampling, and Data Analysis

Chapter Review Answers

A. *Fill-Ins*

1. habituation (92)
2. measurement error (97)
3. representative (105)
4. ratio (103)
5. Descriptive (111)
6. Type I (120)

B. *Multiple Choice*

1. c (91) 2. d (100) 3. a (99) 4. b (108) 5. d (101)

Applications Exercises

Exercise 4.2 Scales of Measurement

1. Nominal—categories are formed
2. Ratio—time
3. Ordinal—rank order
4. Interval—assuming that Sheldon's 7-point scales are interval scales
5. Nominal—assuming subjects will be classified as either helpers or non-helpers
6. Probably ordinal (if patrons rank the beers best to worst); possibly interval (why?)
7. Ordinal—rankings
8. Ratio—meaningful zero point (could be zero errors)

Exercise 4.3 H_0, H_1, Type I errors, and Type II errors

1. H_0: ability of males to detect deception = ability of females to detect deception
   H_1: ability of males to detect deception < ability of females to detect deception
   Type I error: females perform significantly better, but no true difference exists
   Type II error: no significant difference is found, but females truly are better at detecting deception

Chapter 5. Introduction to Experimental Research

Chapter Review Answers

A. *Fill-Ins*
   1. extraneous (134)
   2. subject (137)
   3. regression to the mean (147)
   4. ecological validity (144)
   5. maturation (147)
   6. attrition (152)

B. *Multiple Choice*
   1. b (143)   2. d (147)   3. a (135)   4. d (140)   5. c (129)

Applications Exercises

Exercise 5.1 Identifying Variables

1. IV 1. gender (subject); two levels (male and female)
   IV 2. building location (manipulated); two levels (central and peripheral)
   DV 1. pointing accuracy (probably degrees of error from true score) (ratio)
   DV 2. confidence ratings (interval)
2. IV 1. drug (manipulated); three levels (drug; placebo control; control)

DV 1. physiological responses to stress (ratio)
DV 2. diagnosis (nominal)

3. IV 1. pairing of tone with food (manipulated); three levels (three pairings)
   DV 1. amount of salivation (ratio)

4. IV 1. age (subject); three levels (2-, 3-, & 4-years old)
   IV 2. voice (manipulated); two levels (active, passive)
   DV 1. accuracy (nominal)
   DV 2. reaction time (ratio)

Exercise 5.2 Spot the Confound(s)

1. | *IV* | *EV 1* | *EV 2* | *DV* |
    |------|--------|--------|------|
    | driver type | golf hole | sequence | distance |
    | 1 | 1st hole | 1st 50 balls | |
    | 2 | 2nd hole | 2nd 50 balls | |
    | 3 | 3rd hole | 3rd 50 balls | |
    | 4 | 4th hole | 4th 50 balls | |

    —the four holes are probably quite different, even if they are all par four holes (e.g., uphill vs downhill)
    —from the 1st to the 200th ball, the golfers might tire

2. IV: whether or not there is noise
    confounds: room size, type of patient, day of week

3. IV: whether or not imagery training is given
    confounds: noun type, presentation method

Chapter 6. Control Problems in Experimental Research

Chapter Review Answers

A. *Fill-Ins*
   1. reverse counterbalancing (172)
   2. cohort (177)
   3. equivalent groups (160)
   4. Hawthorne (182
   5. Double blind (182)
   6. complete counterbalancing (170)

B. *Multiple Choice*
   1. d (159) 2. c (161; 174) 3. a (164) 4. c (176) 5. c (180)

Applications Exercises

Exercise 6.1 Between-Subjects or Within-Subjects?

1. Older animals must be compared with younger ones; therefore one IV will be the subject variable of age and it has to be a between-subjects variable. A second IV could be degree of brain damage, a manipulated variable, and it will also be tested between-subjects because each animal should have an intact brain at the start of the study.

2. Within-subjects
3. Probably between-subjects
4. Probably within-subjects
5. Between-subjects

Exercise 6.4 Random Assignment and Matching

Because there is small N, the matching procedure will probably yield three groups whose mean weights are closer together.

Chapter 7. Experimental Design

Chapter Review Answers

A. *Fill-Ins*
   1. repeated−measures (194)
   2. P × E factorial (223)
   3. continuous (207)
   4. nonlinear (201)
   5. matched groups (193)
   6. interaction (230)

B. *Multiple Choice*
   1. c (201)   2. d (193)   3. a (210)   4. b (223)   5. d (210)

Applications Exercises

Exercise 7.1 Identifying Designs

1. IV1: personality type (subject)(between)
   IV2: whether or not interval is filled (manipulated)(between)
   DV: time estimation
   2 × 3 P × E factorial design

2. IV1: with or without eating disorder (subject)(between)
   DV: size matching task
   Nonequivalent groups, 1-factor design

3. IV1: distance (manipulated)(within)
   IV2: with or without north (manipulated)(between)
   2 × 3 mixed factorial design

Exercise 7.2 Main Effects and Interactions

1.

	Ambiguous	Not Ambiguous	Row Means
0 bystanders	14	18	16
2 bystanders	8	18	13
Column means	11	18	

There are two main effects. More helping is offered when there are zero bystanders than when there are two bystanders (16 > 13). More helping is offered when the situation is unambiguous than when it is ambiguous (18 > 11).

However, the important effect here is an interaction. When the situation is not ambiguous, helping is the same and fairly high regardless of the number of bystanders (18 = 18), but when the situation is ambiguous, helping is more likely to occur with fewer bystanders (14 > 8).

Exercise 7.3 — Estimating Subject Needs

1. 30
2. 20
3. 40
4. Cannot tell (need to know which factor is between and which is within)
5. 80

Chapter 8. Correlational Research

Chapter Review Answers

  A. *Fill-Ins*
      1. scatterplot (241)   4. partial correlations (250)
      2. directionality (247)   5. predictive (254)
      3. split–half (254)   6. multiple regression (260)

  B. *Multiple Choice*
      1. c (240)   2. d (249)   3. a (260)   4. b (254)   5. d (248)

Applications Exercises

Exercise 8.1 Interpreting Correlations

1. Dominant mothers might not allow the child to have any experiences with self-determination and as a result produce a shy child; or, a naturally shy child might force a mother to become more dominant because the child never takes any initiative; or, because of a divorce, the mother is forced to become more assertive while at the same time the child becomes withdrawn because of the stress.

Exercise 8.2 Constructing Scatterplots & Calculating Pearson's *r*

The correlation is −.80. High scores on the self-esteem measure are associated with low scores on the attribution style measure. Because low scores on attribution style mean a more optimistic style, the correlation means that those with high self-esteem tend to have an optimistic attribution style.

Exercise 8.3 Understanding Scatterplots

1. Children who do well on the sequential processing subtest of the K•ABC also tend to do well on the simultaneous processing subtest.
2. Students who know a lot about soap operas tend to have poor grades.
3. Intelligence and depression are unrelated. Someone with a high (or a low) IQ may or may not be depressed; there's no way to predict.
4. If you know that someone is a research psychologist, there's a good chance the person is an obsessive–compulsive.

Chapter 9. Quasi-Experimental Designs & Applied Research

Chapter Review Answers

A. *Fill-Ins*
    1. summative (290)
    2. regression (278)
    3. trends (281)
    4. nonequivalent control group (275)
    5. needs assessment (288)
    6. interrupted time series (281)

B. *Multiple Choice*
    1. a (269)   2. b (274)   3. c (275)   4. a (284)   5. d (290)

Applications Exercises

Exercise 9.1 Identifying Threats to Internal Validity

1. Regression, possibly history.
2. Selection × history.
3. Selection.
4. Maturation, possibly history or regression.
5. Attrition.

Exercise 9.2 Interpreting Nonequivalent Control Group Studies

Outcome 1. The program seems to work, assuming that the equivalency in pretests scores was not created in such a way as to encourage a regression effect (as in Head Start). There is a slight drop in the control group, perhaps reflecting regression, history, or maturation, but the drop in the experimental group is much greater.

Outcome 2. The high score for the experimental group seems to have been an extreme score and its reduction to 90 was probably a regression effect.

Outcome 3. May be some regression operating, or an interaction between selection and some other factor, but this outcome is the one usually interpreted as showing program effectiveness.

Outcome 4. The decrease is the same for both groups, indicating some common factor producing both. Regression, history, or maturation are all potential candidates.

Chapter 10. Small N Designs

Chapter Review Answers

   A. **Fill–Ins**

      1. baseline (316)   4. changing criterion (323)
      2. adjustment (326)   5. rate of response (308)
      3. A–B (316)   6. multiple baseline (318)

   B. **Multiple Choice**

      1. b (300)   2. a (304)   3. c (318)   4. a (321)   5. d (316)

Applications Exercises

Exercise 10.2 Hypothetical Outcomes of Applied Behavior Analyses

1. a.

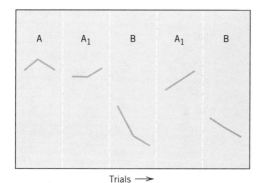

1. b.

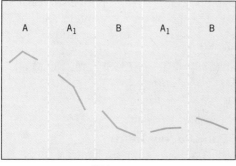

2.   a.

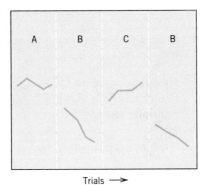

Trials →

2.   b.

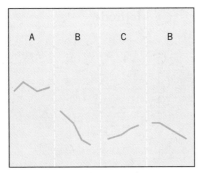

Trials →

Chapter 11. Other Research Methods

Chapter Review Answers

  A. **Fill-Ins**
  1.   interobserver reliability (338)   4.   phone surveys (345)
  2.   Reactivity (338)   5.   content analysis (355)
  3.   closed (344)   6.   case study (350)
  B. **Multiple Choice**
  1.   a (334)   2.   c (338)   3.   a (343)   4.   c (354)   5.   b (351)

Applications Exercises

Exercise 11.1 Improving Poor Survey Items
  a.   The concept of an upset stomach could be defined more precisely, but the

major problem is the "lately." A better way to ask this might be to list some consequences of an upset stomach and ask for frequency counts. For example:
For each of the following health problems, indicate how frequently they have occurred in the last two weeks:

- nausea without vomiting
- vomiting
- diarrhea
- stomach "queasiness" that produced loss of appetite

  b. This statement asks about two different attributes, hostility and intelligence. The solution is to divide them into two separate questions.

  c. This is a leading question, solved by eliminating the "do you agree with most people." However, the "harsh penalties" could be defined more precisely, perhaps by asking the question in a multiple choice format. Also, the item might be elaborated into more than one question, in order to evaluate responses to several types of seat belt violations (e.g., an adult not buckling up vs an adult failing to have children buckle up).

Exercise 11.3 Deciding on Descriptive Methods

  a. Participant observation has a slight advantage over naturalistic observation here; fraternities and sororities tend to be fairly closed to outsiders and may be difficult to observe from a distance.

  b. An interview survey would be a good way to elicit this information, although a written survey might also work.

  c. Because of the numbers of subjects involved, a phone survey is probably the most efficient approach.

  d. Do an archival study of police reports from a sample of cities.

  e. Use a case study analysis of the experiences of the passengers, perhaps using an interview survey format.

  f. Do a naturalistic observation.

Chapter 12. Epilogue: Doing Research in Psychology

Chapter Review Answers

  A. *Fill-Ins*
      1. pseudoscience (362)
      2. anecdotal (366)

  B. *Multiple Choice*
      1. c (364)   2. d (366)   3. b (369)

Glossary

A priori method A way of knowing proposed by Peirce in which a person develops a belief by reasoning and reaching agreement with others who are convinced of the merits of the reasoned argument.

A–A₁–B–A₁–B design A small N design for evaluating placebo effects; A₁ is a condition in the sequence in which a placebo treatment is given.

A–B design A small N design in which a baseline period (A) is followed by a treatment period (B).

A–B–A design A small N design in which a baseline period (A) is followed by a treatment period (B) followed by a period in which the treatment is reversed or withdrawn (second A).

A–B–A–B design Like an A–B–A design except that a second treatment period is established (second B).

A–B–C–B design A small N design that compares contingent reinforcement (B) with noncontingent reinforcement (C); allows the researcher to separate the effects of reinforcers and contingency.

Absolute threshold Stimulus intensity sufficient for subject to first detect the presence of a stimulus.

Alpha level The probability of making a Type I error; the significance level.

Alternating treatments design A small N design that compares, in the same study and for the same subject(s), two or more separate forms of treatment for changing some behavior.

Alternative hypothesis The researcher's hypothesis about the outcome of a study (H_1).

Anecdotal evidence Evidence from a single case that illustrates a phenomenon; when relied on exclusively, as in pseudoscience, faulty conclusions easily can be drawn.

ANOVA Short for **AN**alysis **O**f **VA**riance, the most common inferential statistical tool for analyzing the results of experiments when dependent variables are measured on interval or ratio scales.

Applied behavior analysis Research using various methods to evaluate the effectiveness of conditioning procedures in bringing about changes in the rate of response of some behavior.

Applied research Research with the goal of trying to solve some immediate real life problem.

Archival research A type of descriptive method in which already-existing records are examined to test some research hypothesis.

Asymmetric transfer Occurs when one sequence produces a transfer effect that is different from that produced by another counterbalanced sequence.

Attrition A threat to the internal validity of a study; occurs when subjects fail to complete a study, usually but not necessarily in longitudinal studies; subjects finishing the study may be nonequivalent to those who started it.

Authority A way of knowing proposed by Peirce in which a person develops a belief by agreeing with someone perceived to be an expert.

Baseline The initial stage of a single-subject design, in which the behavior to be changed is monitored to determine its normal rate of response.

Basic research Research with the goal of describing, predicting, and explaining fundamental principles of behavior.

Behavior checklists Lists of behaviors with predefined operational definitions that researchers are trained to use in an observational study.

Between-subjects design Any experimental design in which different groups of subjects serve in the different conditions of the study.

Biased sample A sample that is not representative of the population.

Bivariate Any analysis investigating the relationship between two variables.

Block randomization A procedure used to accomplish random assignment and insure an equal number of subjects in each condition; insures that each condition of the study has a subject randomly assigned to it before any condition has a subject assigned to it again; also used in within-subjects design as a counterbalancing procedure to insure that when subjects are tested in each condition more than once, they experience each condition once before experiencing it again.

Carry-over effect Form of sequence effect in which systematic changes in performance occur as a result of completing a sequence of conditions (e.g., warm-up effects, fatigue, boredom).

Case study A type of descriptive method in which an in-depth analysis is made of either a single individual, a single rare event, or an event that clearly exemplifies some phenomenon.

Ceiling effect Occurs when scores for two or more conditions are at or near the maximum possible for the scale being used, giving the impression that no differences exist between the conditions.

Changing criterion design A small N design in which the criterion for receiving reinforcement begins at a modest level and becomes more stringent as the study progresses; used to shape behavior.

Closed questions A type of question found on surveys that can be answered with a "yes" or a "no" or by marking a point on some scale.

Cluster sample A probability sample which randomly selects clusters of people having some feature in common (e.g., students taking history courses) and tests all people within the selected cluster (e.g., all students in three of the ten history courses available).

Cohort effect A cohort is a group of people born at the same time; cohort effects can reduce the internal validity of cross-sectional studies because differences between groups could result from the effects of growing up in different historical eras.

Complete counterbalancing Occurs when all possible orders of conditions are used in a within-subjects design.

Confound Any extraneous variable that covaries with the independent variable and could provide an alternative explanation of the results.

Construct A hypothetical factor (e.g., hunger) that cannot be observed directly but is inferred from certain behaviors (e.g., eating) and assumed to follow from certain circumstances (e.g., 24 hours without food).

Construct validity In measurement, it occurs when the type of measure being used accurately assesses some hypothetical construct; also refers to whether the construct itself is valid; in research, refers to whether the operational definitions used for independent and dependent variables are valid.

Content analysis A procedure used in descriptive research to systematically categorize the content of the behavior (often verbal behavior) being recorded.

Continuous variable Variable for which an infinite number of values potentially exist (e.g., a drug's dosage level).

Control A goal of science in which basic principles discovered through scientific methods are applied in order to solve a problem.

Control group A group not given a treatment that is being evaluated in a study; provides a means of comparison.

Convenience sample A nonprobability sample in which the researcher requests volunteers from a group of people who meet the general requirements of the study (e.g., teenagers); used in most psychological research, except when specific estimates of population values need to be made.

Converging operations Occurs when the results of several studies, each defining its terms with slightly different operational definitions, nonetheless converge on the same general conclusion.

Correlation matrix A table that summarizes a series of correlations between several variables.

Cost effectiveness analysis Form of program evaluation that evaluates program outcomes in terms of the costs involved in developing, running, and completing the program.

Creative thinking A process of making an innovative connection between seemingly unrelated ideas or events.

Criterion variable In a regression analysis, this is the variable that is being predicted from the predictor variable (e.g., college grades are predicted from SAT scores).

Critical incidents Method used by ethics committees which surveys psychologists and asks for examples of unethical behavior by professional psychologists.

Cross-lagged panel correlation Refers to a type of correlational research designed to deal with the directionality problem; if variables X and Y are measured at two different times and if X precedes Y, then X might cause Y, but Y cannot cause X.

Cross-sectional study In developmental psychology, a design in which age is the independent variable and different groups of people are tested; each group is of a different age.

Cumulative recorder Apparatus for recording the subject's cumulative rate of response in operant conditioning studies.

Data-driven Belief of research psychologists that conclusions about behavior should be supported by data collected scientifically.

Debriefing A postexperimental session in which the experimenter explains the study's purpose, reduces any discomfort felt by subjects, and answers any questions posed by subjects.

Deception A research strategy in which subjects are not told all of the details of an experiment at its outset; used for the purpose of avoiding demand characteristics.

Deduction Reasoning from the general to the specific; in science, used when deriving research hypotheses from theories.

Dehoaxing That portion of debriefing in which the true purpose of the study is explained to subjects.

Demand characteristic Any feature of the experimental design or procedure that increases the chances that subjects will detect the true purpose of the study.

Dependent variable Behavior measured as the outcome of an experiment.

Description A goal of psychological science in which behaviors are accurately classified, or sequences of environmental stimuli and behavioral events are accurately listed.

Descriptive statistics These provide a summary of the main features of a set of data collected from a sample of subjects.

Desensitizing That portion of debriefing in which the experimenter tries to reduce any distress felt by subjects as a result of their research participation.

Determinism An assumption made by scientists that all events have causes.

Difference Threshold Occurs when stimulus 1 is just noticeably different from stimulus 2.

Directionality problem In correlational research, this refers to the fact that for a correlation between variables X and Y, it is possible that X is causing Y, but it is also possible that Y is causing X; the correlation alone provides no basis for deciding between the two alternatives.

Discoverability An assumption made by scientists that the causes of events can be discovered by applying scientific methods.

Discrete variable Variable in which each level represents a distinct category that is qualitatively different from another category (e.g., males and females).

Double blind A control procedure designed to reduce bias; neither the subject nor the person conducting the experimental session knows which condition of the study is being tested; often used in studies evaluating drug effects.

Ecological validity Said to exist when research studies psychological phenomena in everyday situations (e.g., memory for where we put our keys).

Empirical question A question that can be answered by making objective observations.

Equivalent groups Groups of subjects in a between-subjects design that are essentially equal to each other in all ways except for the different levels of the independent variable.

Error variance Nonsystematic variability in a set of scores, due to random factors or individual differences.

Ethics A set of principles prescribing behaviors that are morally correct.

Evaluation apprehension A form of anxiety experienced by subjects that leads them to behave so as to be evaluated positively by the experimenter.

Event sampling A procedure in observational research in which only certain types of behaviors occurring under precisely defined conditions are sampled.

Experiment A research procedure in which some factor is varied, all else is held constant, and some result is measured.

Experimental group In a study with an identified control group, the experimental group is given the treatment being tested.

Experimental realism Refers to how deeply involved the subjects become in the experiment; considered to be more important than mundane realism.

Experimenter bias Occurs when an experimenter's expectations about a study affect its outcome.

Explanation A goal of science in which the causes of events are sought.

Extension Replicating some part of a prior study, but adding some additional features (e.g., additional levels of the independent variable).

External validity The extent to which the findings of a study generalize to other populations, other settings, and other times.

Extraneous variable Any uncontrolled factor that is not of interest to the researcher but could affect the results.

Face validity Granted when a measure appears on the surface to be a reasonable measure of some trait (e.g., as a measure of intelligence, problem solving has more face validity than hat size).

Factor analysis A multivariate analysis in which a large number of variables are intercorrelated; variables that correlate highly with each other form "factors."

Factorial design Any experimental design with more than one independent variable.

Falsification Research strategy advocated by Popper which emphasizes putting theories to the test by trying to disprove or falsify them.

Falsifying data Manufacturing or altering data in order to bring about a desired result.

Field experiment An experiment that is conducted outside of the laboratory; a narrower term than field research.

Field Research Research that occurs in any location other than a scientific laboratory.

Formative evaluation Form of program evaluation

that monitors the functioning of a program while it is operating to determine if it is functioning as planned.

Frequency distribution   A graph that depicts how frequently each score in a data set occurs.

Good subject role   A form of subject bias in which subjects try to guess the experimenter's hypothesis and then behave in such a way as to confirm it.

Hawthorne effect   Name often given to a form of subject bias in which behavior is influenced by the mere knowledge that the subject is in an experiment and is therefore of some importance to the experimenter.

History   A threat to the internal validity of a study; occurs when some historical event that could affect subjects occurs between the beginning of a study and its completion.

Hypothesis   An educated guess about a relationship between variables that is then tested empirically.

Independent groups design   A between-subjects design that uses a manipulated independent variable and has at least two groups of subjects; subjects are randomly assigned to the groups.

Independent variable   The factor of interest to the researcher; it can be directly manipulated by the experimenter (e.g., creating different levels of anxiety in subjects) or subjects can be selected by virtue of their possessing certain attributes (e.g., selecting two groups who differ in their normal levels of anxiousness).

Induction   Reasoning from the specific to the general; in science, used when the results of specific research studies are used to support or refute a theory.

Inferential statistics   Used to draw conclusions about the broader population on the basis of a study using just a sample of that population.

Informed consent   The idea that persons should be given sufficient information about a study in order to make their decision to participate as a research subject an informed and voluntary one.

Instructional variable   Type of independent variable in which subjects are given different sets of instructions about how to perform (e.g., given a list of stimuli, various groups might be told to process them in different ways).

Instrumentation   A threat to the internal validity of a study; occurs when changes to the measuring instrument occur from pretest to posttest (e.g., because of their experience with the instrument, experimenters might use it differently from pretest to posttest).

Interaction   In a factorial design, occurs when the effect of one independent variable depends on the level of another independent variable.

Internal validity   The extent to which a study is free from methodological flaws, especially confounding factors.

Interobserver reliability   The degree of agreement between two or more observers of the same event.

Interrupted time series design   Quasi-experimental design in which a program or treatment is evaluated by measuring performance several times prior to the institution of the program and several times after the program has been put into effect.

Interval scale   Measurement scale in which numbers refers to quantities and intervals are assumed to be of equal size; a score of "zero" is just one of many points on the scale and does not denote the absence of the phenomenon being measured.

Interview survey   A survey method in which the researcher interviews the subject face-to-face; allows for more in-depth surveying (e.g., follow-up questions and clarifications).

Introspection   Method used in early years of psychological science in which subjects would complete some task, then describe the events occurring in consciousness while performing the task.

Laboratory research   Research that occurs within the controlled confines of the scientific laboratory.

Latin square   Form of partial counterbalancing in which each condition of the study occurs equally often in each sequential position and each condition precedes and follows each other condition exactly one time.

Laws   Regular, predictable relationships between events.

Longitudinal study   In developmental psychology, a design in which age is the independent variable and the same group of people is tested repeatedly at different ages.

Main effect   Refers to whether or not statistically significant differences exist between the levels of an independent variable in a factorial design.

Manipulation check   In debriefing, a procedure to determine if subjects were aware of a deception experiment's true purpose; also refers to any procedure that determines if systematic manipulations have the intended effect on subjects.

Matched groups design   A between-subjects design that uses a manipulated independent variable and has at least two groups of subjects; before being randomly assigned to groups, subjects are matched on some variable that is assumed to affect the outcome.

Matching   A procedure for creating equivalent groups in which subjects are measured on some factor (a "matching variable") expected to correlate with the dependent variable; groups are then formed by taking subjects who score at the same level on the matching variable and randomly assigning them to groups.

Maturation A threat to the internal validity of a study; occurs when subjects change from the beginning to the end of the study simply as a result of maturational changes within them and not as a result of some independent variable.

Mean The arithmetic average of a data set, found by adding the scores and dividing by the total number of scores in the set.

Measurement error Produced by any factor that introduces inaccuracies into the measurement of some variable.

Measurement scales Ways of assigning numbers to events; see nominal, ordinal, interval, and ratio scales.

Median The middle score of a data set; an equal number of scores are both above and below the median.

Method of adjustment Psychophysics method in which the subject adjusts stimulus intensity until the stimulus is just barely detected or differences between two stimuli are just noticeably different.

Method of constant stimuli Psychophysics method in which stimulus intensities, either individually (absolute threshold) or in pairs (difference threshold) are presented in a random sequence.

Method of limits Psychophysics method that alternates ascending and descending series of stimuli; on ascending trials, the stimulus begins below threshold and is intensified until detected; on descending trials, the stimulus begins above threshold and is decreased until it is no longer detected.

Mixed factorial design A factorial design with at least one between-subjects factor and one within-subjects factor.

Mode The most frequently appearing score in a data set.

Multiple baseline design A small N design in which treatment is introduced at staggered intervals when trying to (a) alter the behavior of more than one individual, (b) alter more than one behavior in the same individual, or (c) alter the behavior of an individual in more than one setting.

Multiple regression A multivariate analysis which includes a criterion variable and two or more predictor variables; the predictors will have different weights.

Multivariate Any analysis investigating the relationships among more than two variables.

Mundane realism Refers to how closely the experiment mirrors real life experiences; considered to be less important than experimental realism.

Naturalistic observation Descriptive research method in which the behavior of people or animals is studied is it occurs in its everyday natural environment.

Needs assessment Form of program evaluation that occurs before a program begins and determines whether the program is needed.

Negative correlation A relationship between variables X and Y such that a high score for X is associated with a low score for Y and a low score for X is associated with a high score for Y.

Nominal scale Measurement scale in which the numbers have no quantitative value, but serve to identify categories into which events can be placed.

Nonequivalent control group design Quasi-experimental design in which subjects cannot be randomly assigned to the experimental and control groups.

Nonequivalent groups design A between-subjects design with at least two groups of subjects that uses a subject variable or that creates groups that are nonequivalent.

Nonlinear effects Any outcome that does not form a straight line when graphed; can only occur when independent variables have more than two levels.

Normal curve A hypothetical frequency distribution for a population; a bell-shaped curve.

Null hypothesis The assumption that no real difference exists between treatment conditions in an experiment or that no significant relationship exists in a correlational study (H_0).

Objectivity Exists when observations can be verified by more than one observer.

Observer bias Can occur when preconceived ideas held by the researcher affect the nature of the observations made.

Open-ended question A type of question found on surveys that requires more than a "yes" or "no" answer.

Operant conditioning Form of learning in which behavior is modified by its consequences; a positive consequence strengthens the behavior immediately preceding it and a negative consequence weakens the behavior immediately preceding it.

Operational definitions A definition of a concept or a variable in terms of precisely described operations, measures, or procedures.

Operationism Philosophy of science approach proposed by Bridgman which held that all scientific concepts should be defined in terms of a set of operations to be performed.

Order effect Form of sequence effect in which one particular order of conditions could produce one type of effect, while a different order could produce a different type of effect.

Ordinal scale Measurement scale in which assigned numbers stand for relative standing or rankings.

Parsimonious A characteristic of a good theory which means that it includes the minimum number of constructs and assumptions in order to adequately explain and predict.

Partial correlation A multivariate statistical procedure for evaluating the effects of known third variables; if the correlation between X and Y remains high, even after some third factor Z has been "partialed out," then Z can be eliminated as a third variable.

Partial counterbalancing Occurs when a subset of all possible orders of conditions are used in a within-subjects design (e.g., a random sample of all possible orders could be selected).

Partial replication Repeats a portion of some prior study; usually completed as part of a study that extends the results of the initial study.

Participant observation Descriptive research method in which the behavior of people is studied as it occurs in its everyday natural environment and the researcher becomes a part of the group being observed.

Pearson's r Measure of the size of a correlation between two variables; ranges from a perfect negative correlation of -1.00 to a perfect positive correlation of $+1.00$; if $r = 0$, then no correlation exists.

Phone survey A survey method in which the researcher asks questions over the phone.

Pilot study During the initial stages of research it is common for some data to be collected; problems spotted in this trial stage enable the researcher to refine the procedures and prevent the full-scale study from being flawed methodologically.

Placebo control group Control group in which some subjects believe they are receiving the experimental treatment, but aren't.

Plagiarism Deliberately taking the ideas of someone and claiming them as one's own.

Population All of the members of an identifiable group.

Positive correlation A relationship between variables X and Y such that a high score for X is associated with a high score for Y and a low score for X is associated with a low score for Y.

Posttest A measurement given to subjects at the conclusion of a study, after subjects have experienced a treatment or have been in a control group; comparisons are made with pretest scores to determine if change occurred.

Pretest A measurement given to subjects at the outset of a study, prior to their being given a treatment (or not treated, when subjects are in a control group).

Predictions A goal of psychological science in which statements about the future occurrence of some behavioral event are made, usually with some probability.

Predictive validity Occurs when some measurement accurately predicts some future event (e.g., an IQ has predictive validity if scores on it predict who will succeed in school).

Predictor variable In a regression analysis, this refers to the variable that is being used to predict the criterion variable (e.g., SAT scores are used to predict college grades).

Program audit An examination of whether a program is being implemented as planned; a type of formative evaluation.

Program evaluation A form of applied research that includes a number of research activities designed to evaluate programs from planning to completion.

Programs of research Series of interrelated studies in which the outcome of one study leads naturally to another.

Pseudoscience A field of inquiry that attempts to associate with true science, relies exclusively on selective anecdotal evidence, and is deliberately too vague to be adequately tested.

Psychophysics One of experimental psychology's original areas of research; investigates the relationship between physical stimuli and the perception of those stimuli; studies sensory thresholds.

P × E factorial design A factorial design with at least one subject factor (P = person) and one manipulated factor (E = environmental).

Quasi-experiment Occurs whenever causal conclusions about the effect of an independent variable cannot be drawn because there is less than complete control over the variables in the study.

Random assignment The most common procedure for creating equivalent groups in a between-subjects design; each subject volunteering for the study has an equal probability of being assigned to any one of the groups in the study.

Range In a set of scores, the difference between the score with the largest value and the one with the smallest value.

Rate of response The favored dependent variable of those researchers working in the operant tradition; refers to how frequently a behavior occurs per unit of time.

Ratio scale Measurement scale in which numbers refer to quantities, intervals are assumed to be of equal size; a score of "zero" denotes the absence of the phenomenon being measured.

Reactivity Occurs when subjects' behavior is influenced by the knowledge that they are being observed.

Regression analysis In correlational research, knowing the size of a correlation and a value for variable X, it is possible to predict a value for variable Y; this process occurs through a regression analysis.

Regression line Summarizes the points of a scatterplot and provides the means for making predictions.

Regression to the mean If a score on a test is extremely high or low, a second score taken will be closer to the mean score; can be a threat to the internal validity of a study when the pretest score is an extreme score and the posttest score changes naturally in the direction of the mean.

Reliability The extent to which measures of the same phenomenon are consistent and repeatable; measures high in reliability will contain a minimum of measurement error.

Repeated-measures design Another name for a within-subjects design; subjects are tested in each of the experiment's conditions.

Replication To repeat an experiment; exact replications are rare, occurring primarily when the results of some prior study are suspected to be erroneous.

Representative sample A sample with characteristics that match those same attributes as they exist in the population.

Research team A group of researchers (professors and students) working in the same laboratory, or in different locations but working together on the same research problem.

Restricting the range Occurs in a correlational study when only a limited range of scores for one or both of the variables is used; range restrictions tend to lower correlations.

Reverse counterbalancing Occurs in a within-subjects design when subjects are tested more than once per condition; subjects experience one sequence, then a second with the order reversed from the first (e.g., ABCCBA).

Sample Some portion or subset of a population.

Scatterplot A graph depicting the relationship shown by a correlation.

Science A way of knowing characterized by the attempt to apply objective, empirical methods when searching for the causes of natural events.

Self-selection problem In surveys, when the sample is composed of only those who voluntarily choose to respond; the result can be a biased sample.

Sequence effect Can occur in a within-subjects design when the experience of participating in one of the conditions of the study influences performance in subsequent conditions (see carry-over effect and order effect).

Serendipity The process of making an accidental discovery; finding X when searching for Y.

Simple effects analysis An analysis following an ANOVA that examines the effects of each independent variable at each of the levels of other independent variables; useful for examining interactions.

Simple random sample A probability sample in which each member of the population has an equal chance of being selected as a member of the sample.

Single-factor design Any experimental design with a single independent variable.

Single-factor multilevel design Any design with a single independent variable and more than two levels of the independent variable.

Situational variable Type of independent variable in which subjects encounter different environmental circumstances (e.g., large vs small rooms in a crowding study).

Social desirability bias A type of response bias in survey research; occurs when people respond to a question by trying to put themselves in a favorable light.

Speciesism For those who believe in animal rights, a form of prejudice said to characterize those who use animals as research subjects and therefore deprive them of their "rights."

Split-half reliability A form of reliability in which one half of the items (e.g., the even-numbered items) on a test are correlated with the remaining items.

Standard deviation A measure of the average deviation of a set of scores from the mean score; the square root of the variance.

Statistical conclusion validity Said to exist when the researcher uses statistical analysis properly and draws the appropriate conclusions from the analysis.

Statistical determinism An assumption made by research psychologists that behavioral events can be predicted with a probability greater than chance.

Stratified sample A probability sample that is random with the restriction that important subgroups are proportionately represented in the sample.

Subject Name given to a human or animal research participant.

Subject bias Can occur when the subjects' behavior is influenced by their beliefs about how they are supposed to behave in a study.

Subject selection effect A threat to the internal validity of a study; occurs when subjects participating in a study cannot be assigned randomly to groups; hence, the groups are nonequivalent.

Subject variable   A type of independent variable that is selected rather than manipulated by the experimenter; it refers to an already-existing attribute of the subjects chosen for the study (e.g., gender, age).

Summative evaluation   Form of program evaluation completed at the close of a program that attempts to determine its effectiveness in solving the problem for which it was planned.

Survey   A descriptive method in which subjects are asked a series of questions or respond to a series of statements about some topic.

Systematic variance   Variability that can be attributed to some identifiable source, either the systematic variation of the independent variable or the uncontrolled variation of a confound.

***t* test for dependent groups**   An inferential statistical analysis used when comparing two groups in either a matched groups design or a repeated–measures design.

***t* test for independent groups**   An inferential statistical analysis used when comparing two groups in either an independent groups design or a nonequivalent groups design.

Task variable   Type of independent variable in which subjects are given different types of tasks to perform (e.g., mazes that differ in level of difficulty).

Tenacity   A way of knowing proposed by Peirce in which a person maintains a biased view and refuses to alter it in the face of contradictory data.

Test-retest reliability   A form of reliability in which a test is administered on two separate occasions and a correlation between the two is calculated.

Testing   A threat to the internal validity of a study; occurs when the fact of taking a pretest influences posttest scores, perhaps by sensitizing subjects to the purpose of a study.

Theory   A set of statements that summarizes and organizes existing information about some phenomenon, provides an explanation for the phenomenon, and serves as a basis for making predictions to be tested empirically.

Third variable problem   Refers to the problem of drawing causal conclusions in correlational research; third variables are any uncontrolled factors that could underlie a correlation between variables X and Y.

Time sampling   A procedure in observational research in which behavior is sampled only during predefined times (e.g., every 10 minutes).

Trends   Predictable patterns of events that occur over a period of time; evaluated in time series studies.

Type I error   Rejecting the null hypothesis when it is true; finding a statistically significant effect when no true effect exists.

Type II error   Failing to reject the null hypothesis when it is false; failing to find a statistically significant effect when the effect truly exists.

Unobtrusive measures   Any measure of behavior that can be recorded without subjects knowing that their behavior has been observed.

Validity   In general, the extent to which a measure of X truly measures X and not Y (e.g., a valid measure of intelligence measures intelligence and not something else).

Variance   A measure of the average squared deviation of a set of scores from the mean score; the standard deviation squared.

Waiting list control group   Control group in which subjects aren't yet receiving treatment, but will eventually; used to insure that those in the experimental and control groups are similar (e.g., all seeking treatment for problem X).

Withdrawal design   Any small N design in which a treatment is in place for a time, then removed to determine if the behavior returns to baseline.

Within-subjects design   Any experimental design in which the same subjects serve in each of the different conditions of the study; also called a repeated-measures design.

Written survey   A survey method in which the researcher creates a written questionnaire that is filled out by subjects.

Yoked control group   Control group in which the treatment given a member of the control group is matched exactly with the treatment given a member of the experimental group.

References

ABRAMSON, L. Y., SELIGMAN, M. E. P., & TEASDALE, J. D. (1978). Learned helplessness in humans: A critique and reformulation. *Journal of Abnormal Psychology, 87,* 49–74.

ADAIR, J. G. (1973). *The human subject: The social psychology of the psychological experiment.* Boston: Little, Brown, & Co.

ADAMS, J. S. (1965). Inequity in social exchange. In K. Berkowitz (Ed.), *Advances in experimental social psychology.* New York: Academic Press.

ADLER, T. (1992, November). Trashing a laboratory is now a federal offense. *APA Monitor, 23,* 14.

ADLER, T. (1992, September). Debate: Control groups—bad for cancer patients? *APA Monitor, 23,* 34.

American Heritage Dictionary. (1971). New York: American Heritage Publishing Company.

American Psychological Association. (1953). *Ethical standards of psychologists.* Washington, DC: Author.

American Psychological Association. (1982). *Ethical principles in the conduct of research with human participants.* Washington, DC: Author.

American Psychological Association. (1994). *Publication manual of the American Psychological Association* (4th ed.). Washington, DC: Author.

American Psychological Association. (1994). *Thesaurus of psychological index terms* (7th ed.). Washington, DC: Author.

American Psychological Association. (1985). *Guidelines for ethical conduct in the care and use of animals.* Washington, DC: Author.

American Psychological Association. (1992). Ethical principles of psychologists and code of conduct. *American Psychologist, 47,* 1597–1611.

ANDERSON, C. A., LEPPER, M. R., & ROSS, L. (1980). Perseverance of social beliefs: The role of explanation in the persistence of discredited information. *Journal of Personality and Social Psychology, 39,* 1037–1049.

ANDERSON, J. E. (1926). Proceedings of the thirty-fourth annual meeting of the American Psychological Association. *Psychological Bulletin, 23,* 113–174.

ANDERSON, K. J. (1990). Arousal and the inverted-U hypothesis: A critique of Neiss's 'reconceptualizing arousal.' *Psychological Bulletin, 107,* 96–100.

Anonymous Advertisement. (1881, October). *Phrenological Journal, 73,* old series, 3–4.

ARONSON, E. (1992). *The social animal* (6th ed.). New York: W. H. Freeman.

ASCH, S. (1956). Studies of independence and conformity: A minority of one against a unanimous majority. *Psychological Monographs, 70,* (Whole No. 416).

ATKINSON, J. W., & FEATHER, N. T. (1966). *A theory of achievement motivation.* New York: John Wiley & Sons.

BAKAN, D. (1966). The influence of phrenology on American psychology. *Journal of the History of the Behavioral Sciences, 2,* 200–220.

BAKEMAN, R., & BROWNLEE, J. R. (1980). The strategic use of parallel play: A sequential analysis. *Child Development, 51,* 873–878.

BANDURA, A., ROSS, D., & ROSS, S. A. (1963). Imitation of film-mediated aggressive models. *Journal of Abnormal and Social Psychology, 66,* 3–11.

BARBER, T. X. (1976). *Pitfalls in human research.* New York: Pergamon Press.

BARLOW, D. H., & HERSEN, M. (1984). *Single case experimental designs: Strategies for studying behavior change* (2nd ed.). New York: Pergamon Press.

BARNETT, M. A., & MCCOY, S. J. (1989). The relation of distressful childhood experiences and empathy in college undergraduates. *Journal of Genetic Psychology, 150,* 417–426.

BARON, A. (1990). Experimental designs. *The Behavior Analyst, 13,* 167–171.

BAUMRIND, D. (1964). Some thoughts on ethics of research: After reading Milgram's 'Behavioral study of obedience.' *American Psychologist, 19,* 421–423.

BAVELAS, J. B. (1978). *Personality: Current theory and research.* Monterey, CA: Brooks/Cole Publishing Company.

BEAUCHAMP, T. L., & CHILDRESS, J. F. (1979). *Principles of biomedical ethics.* New York: Oxford University Press.

BEHR, W. A. (1992). Ph.D. envy: A psychoanalytic case study. *Clinical Social Work Journal, 20,* 99–113.

BEISECKER, T. (1988). Misusing survey research data: How not to justify demoting Christine Craft. *Forensic Reports, 1,* 15–33.

BERTERA, R. L. (1990). Planning and implementing health promotion in the workplace: A case study of the Du Pont Company experience. *Health Education Quarterly, 17,* 307–327.

BLAKEMORE, C., & COOPER, G. F. (1970). Development of the brain depends on the visual environment. *Nature, 228,* 477–478.

BOESCH-ACHERMANN, H., & BOESCH, C. (1993). Tool use in wild chimpanzees: New light from dark forests. *Current Directions in Psychological Science, 2,* 18–21.

BORING, E. G. (1950). *A history of experimental psychology* (2nd ed.). Englewood Cliffs, NJ: Prentice-Hall, Inc.

BOUCHARD, T. J., & McGUE, M. (1981). Familial studies of intelligence: A review. *Science, 212,* 1055–1059.

BOUCHARD, T. J., LYKKEN, D. T., McGUE, M., SEGAL, N. L., & TELLEGEN, A. (1990). Sources of human psychological differences: The Minnesota study of twins reared apart. *Science, 250,* 223–228.

BRADY, J. V. (1958, April). Ulcers in 'executive' monkeys. *Scientific American, 199,* 95–100.

BRADY, J. V., PORTER, R. W., CONRAD, D. G., & MASON, J. W. (1958). Avoidance behavior and the development of gastroduodinal ulcers. *Journal of the Experimental Analysis of Behavior, 1,* 69–72.

BRAMEL, D., & FRIEND, R. (1981). Hawthorne, the myth of the docile worker, and class bias in psychology. *American Psychologist, 36,* 867–878.

BRANSFORD, J. D., & JOHNSON, M. K. (1972). Contextual prerequisites for understanding: Some investigations of comprehension and recall. *Journal of Verbal Learning and Verbal Behavior, 11,* 717–726.

BRANTJES, M., & BOUMA, A. (1991). Qualitative analysis of the drawings of Alzheimer's patients. *The Clinical Neuropsychologist, 5,* 41–52.

BRENNAN, J. F. (1991). *History and systems of psychology.* Englewood Cliffs, NJ: Prentice-Hall.

BRETZ, R. D., JR., & THOMAS, S. L. (1992). Perceived equity, motivation, and final-offer arbitration in major league baseball. *Journal of Applied Psychology, 77,* 280–287.

BRIDGMAN, P. W. (1927). *The logic of modern physics.* New York: Macmillan.

BROWN, M. F. (1992). Does a cognitive map guide choices in the radial-arm maze? *Journal of Experimental Psychology: Animal Behavior Processes, 18,* 56–66.

BURKS, B. S., JENSEN, D. W., & TERMAN, L. (1930). *Genetic studies of genius, vol. 3. The promise of youth: Follow-up studies of a thousand gifted children.* Stanford, CA: Stanford University Press.

BURNHAM, J. C. (1972). Thorndike's puzzle boxes. *Journal of the History of the Behavioral Sciences, 8,* 159–167.

BYRNE, G. (1988, October 7). Breuning pleads guilty. *Science, 242,* 27–28.

CAMPBELL, D. T. (1969). Reforms as experiments. *American Psychologist, 24,* 409–429.

CAMPBELL, D. T., & ERLEBACHER, A. (1970). How regression artifacts in quasi-experimental evaluations can mistakenly make compensatory education look harmful. In J. Hellmuth (Ed.), *Compensatory education: A national debate.* New York: Brunner-Mazel.

CAMPBELL, D. T., & ROSS, H. L. (1968). The Connecticut crackdown on speeding: Time series data in quasi-experimental analysis. *Law and Society Review, 3,* 33–53.

CAMPBELL, D. T., & STANLEY, J. C. (1963). *Experimental and quasi-experimental designs for research.* Chicago: Rand-McNally.

CARNAP, R. (1966). *An introduction to the philosophy of science.* New York: Basic Books.

CATTELL, J. M. (1890). Mental tests and measurements. *Mind, 15,* 373–380.

CATTELL, J. M. (1895). Proceedings of the third annual meeting of the American Psychological Association. *Psychological Review, 2,* 149–172.

CHANDLER, L. K., FOWLER, S. A., & LUBEK, R. C. (1992). An analysis of the effects of multiple setting events on the social behavior of preschool children with special needs. *Journal of Applied Behavior Analysis, 25,* 249–263.

CHRISTENSEN, L. (1988). Deception in psychological research: When is its use justified? *Personality and Social Psychology Bulletin, 14,* 664–675.

CHRISTENSON, C. V. (1971). *Kinsey: A biography.* Bloomington, IN: Indiana University Press.

CICIRELLI, V. G. (1984). The misinterpretation of the Westinghouse study: A reply to Zigler and Berman. *American Psychologist, 39,* 915–916.

CICIRELLI, V. G. (1993). Head Start evaluation. *APS Observer, 6*(1), 32.

CICIRELLI, V. G., COOPER, W. H., & GRANGER, R. L. (1969). *The impact of Head Start: An evaluation of the effects of Head Start on children's cognitive and affective development.* Westinghouse Learning Corporation, OEO Contract B89-4536.

COHEN, S., TYRELL, D. A., & SMITH, A. P. (1993). Negative life events, perceived stress, negative affect, and susceptibility to the common cold. *Journal of Personality and Social Psychology, 64,* 131–140.

COILE, D. C., & MILLER, N. E. (1984). How radical animal activists try to mislead humane people. *American Psychologist, 39,* 700–701.

CONVERSE, J. M., & PRESSER, S. (1986). *Survey questions: Hand crafting the standardized questionnaire.* Newbury Park, CA: Sage Publications.

COOK, T. D., & CAMPBELL, D. T. (1979). *Quasi-experimental design and analysis issues for field settings.* Chicago: Rand-McNally.

COULTER, X. (1986). Academic value of research participation by undergraduates. *American Psychologist, 41,* 317.

CRAWFORD, H. J., KITNER-TRIOLO, M., CLARKE, S. W., & OLESKO, B. (1992). Transient positive and negative experiences accompanying stage hypnosis. *Journal of Abnormal Psychology, 101,* 663–667.

CRONBACH, L. J. (1957). The two disciplines of scientific psychology. *American Psychologist, 12,* 671–684.

CRONBACH, L. J., HASTORF, A. H., HILGARD, E. R., & MACCOBY, E. E. (1990). Robert R. Sears (1908–1989). *American Psychologist, 45,* 663–664.

DALLENBACH, K. M. (1913). The measurement of attention. *American Journal of Psychology, 24,* 465–507.

DANZIGER, K. (1985). The origins of the psychological experiment as a social institution. *American Psychologist, 40,* 133–140.

DARLEY, J. M., & LATANÉ, B. (1968). Bystander intervention in emergencies: Diffusion of responsibility. *Journal of Personality and Social Psychology, 8,* 377–383.

DELUCA, R. V., & HOLBORN, S. W. (1992). Effects of a variable-ratio schedule with changing criteria on exercise in obese and nonobese boys. *Journal of Applied Behavior Analysis, 25,* 671–679.

Department of Health and Human Services (1983). Federal regulations for the protection of human research subjects. In L. A. Peplau, D. O. Sears, S. E. Taylor, & J. L. Freedman (Eds.), *Readings in social psychology* (2nd ed.). Englewood Cliffs, NJ: Prentice-Hall.

DEWSBURY, D. A. (1990). Early interactions between animal psychologists and animal activists and the founding of the APA committee on precautions in animal experimentation. *American Psychologist, 45,* 315–327.

DONNERSTEIN, E. (1980). Aggressive erotica and violence against women. *Journal of Personality and Social Psychology, 39,* 269–277.

DRESSLER, F. B. (1893). On the pressure sense of the drum of the ear and 'facial-vision.' *American Journal of Psychology, 5,* 344–350.

DROR, I. E., KOSSLYN, S. M., & WAAG, W. L. (1993). Visual-spatial abilities of pilots. *Journal of Applied Psychology, 78,* 763–773.

DUTTON, D. G., & ARON, A. P. (1974). Some evidence for heightened sexual attraction under conditions of high anxiety. *Journal of Personality and Social Psychology, 30,* 510–517.

EBBINGHAUS, H. (1913). *Memory: A contribution to experimental psychology* (H. A. Ruger & C. E. Bussenius, Trans.). New York: Teachers College. (Original work published 1885).

EGELAND, B. (1975). Effects of errorless training on teaching children to discriminate letters of the alphabet. *Journal of Applied Psychology, 60,* 533–536.

EKMAN, P. (1985). *Telling lies: Clues to deceit in the marketplace, politics, and marriage.* New York: W. W. Norton and Co.

ELKINS, I. J., CROMWELL, R. L., & ASARNOW, R. F. (1992). Span of apprehension in schizophrenic patients as a function of distractor masking and laterality. *Journal of Abnormal Psychology, 101,* 53–60.

ELMES, D. G., KANTOWITZ, B. H., & ROEDIGER, H. L., III. (1992). *Research methods in psychology* (4th ed.). St. Paul, MN: West Publishing Company.

EMDE, R. N., PLOMIN, R., ROBINSON, J., CORLEY, R., DEFRIES, J., FULKER, D. W., REZNICK, J. S., CAMPOS, J., KAGAN, J., & ZAHN-WAXLER, C. (1992). Temperament, emotion, and cognition at fourteen months: The MacArthur longitudinal twin study. *Child Development, 63,* 1437–1455.

ERFURT, J. C., FOOTE, A., & HEIRICH, M. A. (1992). The cost-effectiveness of worksite wellness programs for hypertension control, weight loss, smoking cessation, and exercise. *Personnel Psychology, 45,* 5–27.

ERON, L. D., HUESMAN, L. R., LEFKOWITZ, M. M., & WALDER, L. O. (1972). Does television violence cause aggression? *American Psychologist, 27,* 253–263.

FADEN, R. R., & BEAUCHAMP, T. L. (1986). *A history and theory of informed consent.* New York: Oxford University Press.

FANCHER, R. E. (1990). *Pioneers of psychology* (2nd ed.). New York: Norton.

FECHNER, G. (1966). *Elements of psychophysics.* (H. E. Adler, Trans.). New York: Holt. (Original work published 1860).

FEINBERG, J. (1974). The rights of animals and unborn generations. In W. T. Blackstone (Ed.), *Philosophy and environmental crisis.* Athens, GA: University of Georgia Press.

FERNALD, D. (1984). *The Hans legacy.* Hillsdale, NJ: Lawrence Erlbaum Associates.

FERSTER, C. B., & SKINNER, B. F. (1957). *Schedules of reinforcement.* Englewood Cliffs, NJ: Prentice-Hall.

FESTINGER, L., RIECKEN, H. W., & SCHACHTER, S. (1956). *When prophecy fails.* Minneapolis: University of Minnesota Press.

FISHER, R. A. (1951). *The design of experiments* (6th ed.). New York: Hafner Publishing Company (Original work published 1935).

FISHER, R. A., & YATES, F. (1963). *Statistical tables for biological, agricultural, and medical research* (6th ed.). Edinburgh: Oliver & Boyd.

FISHER, R. P., GEISELMAN, R. E., & AMADOR, M. (1989). Field test of the cognitive interview: Enhancing the recollection of actual victims and witnesses of crime. *Journal of Applied Psychology, 74,* 722–727.

FLETCHER, J. D., & ATKINSON, R. C. (1972). Evaluation of the Stanford CAI program in initial reading. *Journal of Educational Psychology, 63,* 597–602.

FOWLER, F. J., JR. (1993). *Survey research methods* (2nd ed.). Newbury Park, CA: Sage Publications.

FRAYSSE, J. C., & DESPRELS-FRAYSSE, A. (1990). The influence of experimenter attitude on the performance of children of different cognitive ability levels. *Journal of Genetic Psychology, 151,* 169–179.

FRIEDMAN, M., & ROSENMAN, R. H. (1974). *Type A behavior and your heart.* New York: Knopf.

FRUCHTER, B. (1954). *Introduction to factor analysis.* Princeton, NJ: D. Van Nostrand.

FULERO, S. M., & KIRKLAND, J. (1992, August). *A survey of student opinions on animal research.* Poster presented at the annual meeting of the American Psychological Association, Washington, DC.

GALLUP, G. G., & BECKSTEAD, J. W. (1988). Attitudes toward animal research. *American Psychologist, 43,* 74–76.

GALLUP, G. G., & SUAREZ, S. D. (1985a). Animal research versus the care and maintenance of pets: The names have been changed but the results remain the same. *American Psychologist, 40,* 968.

GALLUP, G. G., & SUAREZ, S. D. (1985b). Alternatives to the use of animals in psychological research. *American Psychologist, 40,* 1104–1111.

GARDNER, G. T. (1978). Effects of federal human subjects regulations on data obtained in environmental stressor research. *Journal of Personality and Social Psychology, 36,* 628–634.

GARDNER, M. (1981). *Science: Good, bad, and bogus.* Buffalo: Prometheus Books.

GIBSON, E. J. (1980). Eleanor J. Gibson. In G. Lindsey (Ed.), *A history of psychology in autobiography: Vol. 7.* San Francisco: W. H. Freeman and Company.

GIBSON, E. J., & WALK, R. D. (1960). The 'visual cliff.' *Scientific American, 202,* 64–71.

GILLESPIE, R. (1988). The Hawthorne experiments and the politics of experimentation. In J. G. Morawski (Ed.), *The rise of experimentation in American psychology.* New Haven, CN: Yale University Press.

GILLIGAN, C. (1982). *In a different voice: Psychological theory and women's development.* Cambridge, MA: Harvard University Press.

GITTELSON, B. (1975). *Biorhythms: A personal science.* New York: Arco Publishing.

GODDEN, D. R., & BADDELEY, A. D. (1975). Context-dependent memory in two natural environments: On land and under water. *British Journal of Psychology, 66,* 325–331.

GOODALL, J. (1978). Chimp killings: Is it the man in them? *Science News, 113,* 276.

GOODWIN, C. J. (1985). On the origins of Titchener's Experimentalists. *Journal of the History of the Behavioral Sciences, 21,* 383–389.

GREEN, B. F. (1992). Exposé or smear? The Burt affair. *Psychological Science, 3,* 328–331.

GREENBERG, M. S. (1967). Role playing: An alternative to deception. *Journal of Personality and Social Psychology, 7,* 152–157.

GRISSETT, N. I., & NORVELL, N. K. (1992). Perceived social support, social skills, and quality of relationships in bulimic women. *Journal of Consulting and Clinical Psychology, 60,* 293–299.

GUNTER, B., BERRY, C., & CLIFFORD, B. R. (1981). Proactive interference effects with television news items: Further evidence. *Journal of Experimental Psychology: Human Leaerning and Memory, 7,* 480–487.

GWALTNEY-GIBBS, P. A. (1986). The institutionalization of premarital cohabitation: Estimates from marriage license applications, 1970 and 1980. *Journal of Marriage and the Family, 48,* 423–434.

HALL, G. S. (1893). *The contents of children's minds on entering school.* New York: Kellogg.

HALL, J. A., & VECCIA, E. M. (1990). More 'touching' observations: New insights on men, women, and interpersonal touch. *Journal of Personality and Social Psychology, 59,* 1155–1162.

HARRIS, B. (1979). Whatever happened to little Albert? *American Psychologist, 34,* 151–160.

HENLE, M., & HUBBELL, M. B. (1938). 'Egocentricity' in adult conversation. *Journal of Social Psychology, 9,* 227–234.

HILGARD, E. R. (Ed.). (1978). *American psychology in historical perspective.* Washington, DC: American Psychological Association.

HILGARTNER, S. (1990). Research fraud, misconduct, and the IRB. *IRB: A Review of Human Subjects Research, 12,* 1–4.

HINES, T. M. (1979). Biorhythm theory: A critical review. *The Skeptical Inquirer, 3,* 26–36.

HITE, S. (1987). *Women and love.* New York: Knopf.

HOBBS, N. (1948). The development of a code of ethics for psychology. *American Psychologist, 3,* 80–84.

HOLMES, D. S. (1976a). Debriefing after psychological experiments. I. Effectiveness of postdeception dehoaxing. *American Psychologist, 31,* 858–867.

HOLMES, D. S. (1976b). Debriefing after psychological experiments. II. Effectiveness of postexperimental desensitizing. *American Psychologist, 31,* 868–875.

HOLMES, D. S., MCGILLEY, B. M., & HOUSTON, B. K. (1984). Task-related arousal of Type A and Type B persons: Levels of challenge and response specificity. *Journal of Personality and Social Psychology, 46,* 1322–1327.

HORN, J. L. (1990, October). Psychology can help kids get a Head Start. *APA Monitor, 22,* 3.

HOTHERSALL, D. (1990). *History of psychology* (2nd ed.). New York: McGraw-Hill.

HUBEL, D. H. (1988). *Eye, brain, and vision.* New York: Scientific American Library.

HUFF, D. (1954). *How to lie with statistics.* New York: Norton.

HUME, K. M., & CROSSMAN, J. (1992). Musical reinforcement of practice behaviors among competitive swimmers. *Journal of Applied Behavior Analysis, 25,* 665–670.

HUNT, E., & LOVE, T. (1972). How good can memory be? In A. W. Melton & E. Martin (Eds.), *Coding processes in human memory.* Washington, DC: V. H. Winston & Sons.

JAMES, L. R., MULAIK, S. A., & BRETT, J. M. (1982). *Causal analysis: Assumptions, models, and data.* Newbury Park, CA: Sage Publications.

JONÇICH, G. (1968). *The sane positivist: A biography of Edward L. Thorndike.* Middletown, CN: Wesleyan University Press.

JONES, J. H. (1981). *Bad blood: The Tuskegee syphilis experiment.* New York: Free Press.

JONES, M. C. (1924). A laboratory study of fear: The case of Peter. *Pedagogical Seminary, 31,* 308–315.

JORDAN, N. C., HUTTENLOCHER, J., & LEVINE, S. C. (1992). Differential calculation abilities in young children from middle- and low-income families. *Developmental Psychology, 28,* 644–653.

JUNGINGER, J., & HEAD, S. (1991). Time series analyses of obsessional behavior and mood during self-imposed delay and response prevention. *Behavior Research and Therapy, 29,* 521–530.

KAUFMAN, A. S., & KAUFMAN, N. L. (1983). *K•ABC: Kaufman Assessment Battery for Children. Interpretive manual.* Circle Pines, MN: American Guidance Service, Inc.

KAZDIN, A. E. (1978). *History of behavior modification: Experimental foundations of contemporary research.* Baltimore: University Park Press.

KELTNER, D., ELLSWORTH, P. C., & EDWARDS, K. (1993). Beyond simple pessimism: Effects of sadness and anger on social perception. *Journal of Personality and Social Psychology, 64,* 740–752.

KENDALL, M. G. (1970). Ronald Aylmer Fisher, 1890–1962. In E. S. Pearson & M. G. Kendall (Eds.), *Studies in the history of statistics and probability.* London: Charles Griffin & Company.

KIDD, V. (1971). A study of the images produced through the use of the male pronoun as the generic. *Moments in Contemporary Rhetoric and Communication, 1,* 25–30.

KIM, K., & SPELKE, E. S. (1992). Infants' sensitiviy to effects of gravity on visible object motion. *Journal of Experimental Psychology: Human Perception and Performance, 18,* 385–393.

KINSEY, A. C., POMEROY, W. B., & MARTIN, C. E. (1948). *Sexual behavior in the human male.* Philadelphia: W. B. Saunders.

KINSEY, A. C., POMEROY, W. B., MARTIN, C. E., & GEBHARD, P. H. (1953). *Sexual behavior in the human female.* Philadelphia: W. B. Saunders.

KIRK, R. E. (1968). *Experimental design: Procedures for the behavioral sciences.* Belmont, CA: Brooks/Cole.

KLINGMAN, A. (1992). The effects of a parent-implemented crisis intervention: A real-life emergency involving a child's refusal to use a gas mask. *Journal of Clinical Child Psychology, 21,* 70–75.

KNEPPER, W., OBRZUT, J. E., & COPELAND, E. P. (1983). Emotional and social problem-solving thinking in gifted and average elementary school children. *Journal of Genetic Psychology, 142,* 25–30.

KOBERG, D., & BAGNALL, J. (1974). *The universal traveler.* Los Altos, CA: William Kaufman, Inc.

KOHLBERG, L. (1964). Development of moral character and moral behavior. In L. W. Hoffman & M. L. Hoffman (Eds.), *Review of child development research* (Vol. 1). New York: Sage Publications.

KOHN, A. (1986). *False prophets: Fraud and error in science and medicine.* Oxford, England: Basil Blackwell, Ltd.

KOLATA, G. B. (1986). What does it mean to be random? *Science, 231,* 1068–1070.

KORIAT, A., & NORMAN, J. (1984). What is rotated in mental rotation? *Journal of Experimental Psychology: Learning, Memory, and Cognition, 10,* 421–434.

KORN, J. H. (1988). Students' roles, rights, and responsibilities as research participants. *Teaching of Psychology, 15,* 74–78.

KORN, J. H., DAVIS, R., & DAVIS, S. F. (1991). Historians' and chairpersons' judgments of eminence among psychologists. *American Psychologist, 46,* 789–792.

KOSSLYN, S. M., BALL, T. M., & REISER, B. J. (1978). Visual images preserve metric spatial information: Evidence from studies of image scanning. *Journal of Experimental Psychology: Human Perception and Performance, 4,* 47–60.

KRANTZ, D. L. (1969). The Baldwin-Titchener controversy: A case study in the functioning and malfunctioning of schools. In D. L. Krantz (Ed.), *Schools of psychology: A symposium.* New York: Appleton-Century-Crofts.

KRUPAT, E. (1975). Conversation with John Darley. In E. Krupat (Ed.), *Psychology is social: Readings and conversations in social psychology.* Glenview, Illinois: Scott, Foresman and Company.

KUHN, T. S. (1970). The function of dogma in scientific research. In B. A. Brody (Ed.), *Readings in the philosophy of science.* Englewood Cliffs, NJ: Prentice-Hall.

KUSHNER, M. (1970). Faradic aversive controls in clinical practice. In C. Neuringer & J. L. Michael (Eds.), *Behavior modification in clinical practice.* New York: Appleton-Century-Crofts.

LANDY, F. J. (1992). Hugo Münsterberg: Victim or visionary? *Journal of Applied Psychology, 77,* 787–802.

LANGER, E. J., & RODIN, J. (1976). The effects of choice and enhanced personal responsibility for the aged: A field experiment in an institutional setting. *Journal of Personality and Social Psychology, 34,* 191–198.

LAU, R. R., & RUSSELL, D. (1980). Attributions in the sports pages. *Journal of Personality and Social Psychology, 39,* 29–38.

LEE, D. N., & ARONSON, E. (1974). Visual proprioceptive control of standing in human infants. *Perception and Psychophysics, 15,* 529–532.

LEFRANCOIS, J. R., & METZGER, B. (1993). Low-response-rate conditioning history and fixed-interval responding in rats. *Journal of the Experimental Analysis of Behavior, 59,* 543–549.

LIBERMAN, R. P., DAVIS, J., MOON, W., & MOORE, J. (1973). Research design for analyzing drug-environment-behavior interactions. *Journal of Nervous and Mental Disease, 156,* 432–439.

LINDSEY, R. C. L., NOSWORTHY, G. J., MARTIN, R., & MARTYNUCK, C. (1994). Using mug shots to find suspects. *Journal of Applied Psychology, 79,* 121–130.

LOFTUS, E. F. (1986). Ten years in the life of an expert witness. *Law and Human Behavior, 10,* 241–263.

LOFTUS, E. F., & HOFFMAN, H. G. (1989). Misinformation and memory: The creation of new memories. *Journal of Experimental Psychology: General, 118,* 100–104.

LOFTUS, E. F., & KETCHAM, K. (1991). *Witness for the defense: The accused, the eyewitness, and the expert who puts memory on trial.* New York: St. Martin's Press.

LOFTUS, E. F., & PALMER, J. C. (1974). Reconstruction of automobile destruction: An example of the interaction between language and memory. *Journal of Verbal Learning and Verbal Behavior, 13,* 585–589.

LORENZ, K. (1966). *On aggression.* New York: Harcourt, Brace, Jovanovich.

LUNG, C., & DOMINOWSKI, R. L. (1985). Effects of strategy instructions and practice on nine-dot problem solving. *Journal of Experimental Psychology: Learning, Memory, and Cognition, 11,* 804–811.

LURIA, A. R. (1968). *The mind of a mnemonist.* New York: Basic Books.

MACLEOD, C. M. (1992). The Stroop task: The 'gold standard' of attentional measures. *Journal of Experimental Psychology: General, 121,* 12–14.

MANIS, M. (1971). *An introduction to cognitive psychology.* Belmont, CA: Brooks/Cole.

MAREAN, G. C., WERNER, L. A., & KUHL, P. K. (1992). Vowel categorization by very young infants. *Developmental Psychology, 28,* 396–405.

MATHEWS, R. M., & DIX, M. (1992). Behavior change in the funny papers: Feedback to cartoonists on safety belt use. *Journal of Applied Behavior Analysis, 25,* 769–775.

McCLELLAND, D. C. (1961). *The achieving society.* Princeton, NJ: Van Nostrand.

McCLELLAND, D. C., ATKINSON, J. W., CLARKE, R. A., & LOWELL, E. L. (1953). *The achievement motive.* NY: Appleton-Century-Crofts.

McREYNOLDS, P. (1987). Lightner Witmer: Little-known founder of clinical psychology. *American Psychologist, 42,* 849–858.

MIDDLEMIST, R. D., KNOWLES, E. S., & MATTER, C. F. (1976). Personal space invasions in the lavoratory: Suggestive evidence for arousal. *Journal of Personality and Social Psychology, 33,* 541–546.

MILES, W. R. (1930). On the history of research with rats and mazes: A collection of notes. *Journal of General Psychology, 3,* 324–337.

MILGRAM, S. (1963). Behavioral study of obedience. *Journal of Abnormal and Social Psychology, 67,* 371–378.

MILGRAM, S. (1974). *Obedience to authority: An experimental view.* New York: Harper & Row.

MILLER, A. G. (1972). Role playing: An alternative to deception? *American Psychologist, 27,* 623–636.

MILLER, N. (1985). The value of behavioral research on animals. *American Psychologist, 40,* 423–440.

MINTON, H. L. (1987). Lewis M. Terman and mental testing: In search of the democratic ideal. In M. M. Sokal (Ed.), *Psychological testing and American society, 1890–1930.* New Brunswick, NJ: Rutgers University Press.

MINTON, H. L. (1988). Charting life history: Lewis M. Terman's study of the gifted. In J. G. Morawski (Ed.), *The rise of experimentation in American psychology.* New Haven, CT: Yale University Press.

MISCHEL, W. (1981). *Introduction to personality* (3rd ed.). New York: Holt, Rinehart, and Winston.

MORGAN, C. L. (1903). *Introduction to comparative psychology.* London: The Walter Scott Publishing Company.

MORGAN, F. W. (1990). Judicial standards for survey research: An update and guidelines. *Journal of Marketing, 54,* 59–70.

MOSES, S. (1991, July). Animal research issues affect students. *APA Monitor, 22,* 47–48.

MOWRER, O. H., & MOWRER, W. M. (1938). Enuresis— a method for its study and treatment. *American Journal of Orthopsychiatry, 8,* 436–459.

MURRAY, H. A. (1943). *Thematic apperception test.* Cambridge, MA: Harvard University Press.

MYERS, D. G. (1990). *Social Psychology* (3rd ed.). New York: McGraw-Hill.

MYERS, D. G. (1992). *Psychology* (3rd ed.). New York: Worth.

NEALE, J. M., & LIEBERT, R. M. (1973). *Science and behavior: An introduction to methods of research.* Englewood Cliffs, NJ: Prentice-Hall.

NEISSER, U. (1963). Decision-time without reaction-time. *American Journal of Psychology, 76,* 376–385.

NEISSER, U. (1978). Memory: What are the important questions? In M. M. Gruneberg, P. E. Morris, & R. N. Sykes (Eds.), *Practical aspects of memory.* London: Academic Press.

NEISSER, U. (1981). John Dean's memory: A case study. *Cognition, 9,* 1–22.

O'DONNELL, J. M. (1985). *The origins of behaviorism: American psychology, 1870–1920.* New York: New York University Press.

ORNE, M. T. (1962). On the social psychology of the psychology experiment: With particular reference to demand characteristics and their implications. *American Psychologist, 17,* 776–783.

ORNE, M. T., & SCHEIBE, K. E. (1964). The contribution of nondeprivation factors in the production of sensory deprivation effects. *Journal of Abnormal and Social Psychology, 68,* 3–12.

PALMER, J. D. (1982, October). Biorhythm bunkum. *Natural History,* 90–97.

PATTERSON, F. G., & LINDEN, E. (1981). *The education of Koko*. New York: Holt, Rinehart, & Winston.

PEARSON, E. S., & HARTLEY, H. O. (1966). *Biometrika tables for statisticians* (3rd ed.). Vol. I. London: Cambridge University Press.

PECK, F. S. (1978). *The road less traveled*. NY: Simon & Schuster.

PETERSON, L., RIDLEY-JOHNSON, R., & CARTER, C. (1984). The supersuit: An example of structured naturalistic observation of children's altruism. *Journal of General Psychology, 110,* 235–241.

POPPER, K. R. (1959). *The logic of scientific discovery*. New York: Basic Books.

PORSOLT, R. D., LePICHON, M., & JALFRE, M. (1977). Depression: A new animal model sensitive to antidepressant treatments. *Nature, 266,* 730–732.

POSAVAC, E. J., & CAREY, R. G. (1985). *Program evaluation: Methods and case studies* (2nd ed.). Englewood Cliffs, NJ: Prentice-Hall.

POULTON, E. C. (1982). Influential companions: Effects of one strategy on another in the within-subjects designs of cognitive psychology. *Psychological Bulletin, 91,* 673–690.

RANDI, J. (1982). *Flim flam! Psychics, ESP, unicorns, and other delusions*. Buffalo: Prometheus Books.

REEVE, L., REEVE, K. F., BROWN, A. K., BROWN, J. L., & POULSON, C. L. (1992). Effects of delayed reinforcement on infant vocalization rate. *Journal of the Experimental Analysis of Behavior, 58,* 1–8.

REYNOLDS, G. S. (1968). *A primer of operant conditioning*. Glenview, IL: Scott, Foresman, and Company.

REYNOLDS, R. I. (1992). Recognition of expertise in chess players. *American Journal of Psychology, 105,* 409–415.

RODIN, J., & LANGER, E. J. (1977). Long-term effects of a control-relevant intervention with the institutionalized aged. *Journal of Personality and Social Psychology, 35,* 897–902.

ROHLES, F. H., JR. (1992). Orbital bar pressing: A historical note on Skinner and the chimpanzees in space. *American Psychologist, 47,* 1531–1533.

ROMANES, G. J. (1886). *Animal intelligence*. New York: D. Appleton and Co.

ROSENBERG, M. J. (1969). The conditions and consequences of evaluation apprehension. In R. Rosenthal & R. L. Rosnow (Eds.), *Artifact in behavioral research*. New York: Academic Press.

ROSENTHAL, R. (1966). *Experimenter effects in behavioral research*. New York: Appleton-Century-Crofts.

ROSENTHAL, R., & FODE, K. L. (1963a). Three experiments in experimenter bias. *Psychological Reports, 12,* 491–511.

ROSENTHAL, R., & FODE, K. L. (1963b). The effect of experimenter bias on the performance of the albino rat. *Behavioral Science, 8,* 183–189.

ROSNOW, R. L., GOODSTADT, B. E., SULS, J. M., & GITTER, A. G. (1973). More on the social psychology of the experiment: When compliance turns to self-defense. *Journal of Personality and Social Psychology, 27,* 337–343.

SAMELSON, F. (1992). Rescuing the reputation of Sir Cyril [Burt]. *Journal of the History of the Behavioral Sciences, 28,* 221–233.

SANFORD, E. C. (1910, August 8). *Letter to E. B. Titchener*. Titchener Papers, Cornell University, Ithaca, New York.

SANFORD, E. C. (1914). Psychic research in the animal field: Der Kluge Hans and the Elberfeld horses. *American Journal of Psychology, 25,* 3–31.

SCHACHTER, S. (1959). *The psychology of affiliation*. Stanford, CA: Stanford University Press.

SCHAIE, K. W. (1983). The Seattle longitudinal study: A 21 year exploration of psychometric intelligence in adulthood. In K. W. Schaie (Ed.), *Longitudinal studies of adult psychological development*. New York: Guilford Press.

SCHAIE, K. W. (1988). Ageism in psychological research. *American Psychologist, 43,* 179–183.

SCHOENEMAN, T. J., & RUBANOWITZ, D. E. (1985). Attributions in the advice columns: Actors and observers, causes and reasons. *Personality and Social Psychology Bulletin, 11,* 315–325.

SCHRADER, W. B. (1971). The predictive validity of the College Board Admissions tests. In W. H. Angoff (Ed.), *The College Board Admissions Testing Program*. New York: College Entrance Examination Board.

SCHULTZ, D. P., & SCHULTZ, S. E. (1992). *A history of modern psychology* (5th ed.). New York: Harcourt, Brace, Jovanovich.

SCRIPTURE, E. W. (1895). *Thinking, feeling, doing*. Meadville, PA: Chautauqua-Century Press.

SEARS, D. O. (1986). College sophomores in the laboratory: Influences of a narrow data base on psychology's view of human nature. *Journal of Personality and Social Psychology, 51,* 515–530.

SECHREST, L., & FIGUEREDO, A. J. (1993). Program evaluation. In L. W. Porter & M. R. Rosenzweig (Eds.), *Annual Review of Psychology* (vol. 44). Palo Alto, CA: Annual Reviews, Inc.

SELIGMAN, M. E. P. (1975). *Helplessness: On depression, development, and death.* San Francisco: W. H. Freeman and Co.

SELIGMAN, M. E. P., & SCHULMAN, P. (1986). Explanatory style as a predictor of productivity and quitting among life insurance agents. *Journal of Personality and Social Psychology, 50,* 832–838.

SELIGMAN, M. E. P., CASTELLON, C., CACCIOLA, J., SCHULMAN, P., LUBORSKY, L., OLLOVE, M., & DOWNING, R. (1988). Explanatory style change during cognitive therapy for unipolar depression. *Journal of Abnormal Psychology, 97,* 13–18.

SHAKOW, D. (1930). Hermann Ebbinghaus. *American Journal of Psychology, 42,* 505–518.

SHELDON, W. H. (1940). *The varieties of human physique: An introduction to constitutional psychology.* New York: Harper & Row.

SHELDON, W. H. (1942). *The varieties of temperament: A psychology of constitutional differences.* New York: Harper & Row.

SHEPARD, R. N., & METZLER, J. (1971). Mental rotation of three-dimensional objects. *Science, 171,* 701–703.

SHERROD, D. R., HAGE, J. N., HALPERN, P. L., & MOORE, B. S. (1977). Effects of personal causation and perceived control on responses to an environment: The more control, the better. *Journal of Personality and Social Psychology, 13,* 14.

SIDMAN, M. (1960). *Tactics of scientific research.* New York: Basic Books.

SIGALL, H., & OSTROVE, N. (1975). Beautiful but dangerous: Effects of offender attractiveness and nature of the crime on juridic judgment. *Journal of Personality and Social Psychology, 31,* 410–414.

SILVERMAN, I. (1975). Nonreactive methods and the law. *American Psychologist, 30,* 764–769.

SINGER, P. (1975). *Animal liberation.* New York: Avon.

SKINNER, B. F. (1953). *Science and human behavior.* New York: The Free Press.

SKINNER, B. F. (1956). A case history in scientific method. *American Psychologist, 12,* 221–233.

SKINNER, B. F. (1966). Operant behavior. In W. K. Honig (Ed.), *Operant behavior: Areas of research and application.* New York: Appleton-Century-Crofts.

SKINNER, B. F. (1969). *Contingencies of reinforcement.* Englewood Cliffs, NJ: Prentice-Hall.

SKINNER, B. F. (1976). *Walden Two.* New York: Macmillan (Original work published 1948).

SKINNER, B. F. (1979). *The shaping of a behaviorist.* New York: New York University Press.

SKINNER, B. F. (1984). *A matter of consequences.* New York: New York University Press.

SMALL, W. S. (1900). An experimental study of the mental processes of the rat. *American Journal of Psychology, 11,* 80–100.

SMITH, L. D. (1992). On prediction and control: B. F. Skinner and the technological ideal of science. *American Psychologist, 47,* 216–223.

SMITH, S. S., & RICHARDSON, D. (1983). Amelioration of deception and harm in psychological research: The important role of debriefing. *Journal of Personality and Social Psychology, 44,* 1075–1082.

SOKAL, M. M. (1987). James McKeen Cattell and mental anthropometry: Nineteenth-century science and reform and the origins of psychological testing. In M. M. Sokal (Ed.), *Psychological testing and American society, 1890–1930.* New Brunswick, NJ: Rutgers University Press.

SOKAL, M. M. (1992). Origins and early years of the American Psychological Association, 1890–1906. *American Psychologist, 47,* 111–122.

SOKAL, M. M. (Ed.). (1981). *An education in psychology: James McKeen Cattell's journal and letters from Germany and England, 1880–1888.* Cambridge, MA: MIT Press.

SOLOMON, R. L. (1949). An extension of control group design. *Psychological Bulletin, 46,* 137–150.

SPELKE, E. S. (1985). Preferential looking methods as tools for the study of cognition in infancy. In G. Gottlieb & N. Krasnegor (Eds.), *Measurement of audition and vision in the first year of postnatal life.* Norwood, NJ: Ablex.

SPRINTHALL, R. C. (1982). *Basic statistical analysis.* Reading, MA: Addison-Wesley Publishing Company.

STERNBERG, R. J. (1988). *The triarchic mind: A new theory of human intelligence.* New York: Viking Penguin, Inc.

STROOP, J. R. (1992). Studies of interference in serial verbal reactions. *Journal of Experimental Psychology: General, 121,* 15–23. (Original work published 1935).

SULLIVAN, D. S., & DEIKER, T. E. (1973). Subject-experimenter perceptions of ethical issues in human research. *American Psychologist, 28,* 587–591.

SULLOWAY, F. J. (1979). *Freud, biologist of the mind.* New York: Basic Books.

TATHAM, T. A., WANCHISEN, B. A., & HINELINE, P. N. (1993). Effects of fixed and variable ratios on human behavioral variability. *Journal of the Experimental Analysis of Behavior, 59,* 349–359.

TAYLOR, D. W., GARNER, W. R., & HUNT, H. F. (1959). Education for research in psychology. *American Psychologist, 14,* 167–179.

TERMAN, L. M. (1925). *Genetic studies of genius, vol. 1. Mental and physical traits of a thousand gifted children.* Stanford, CA: Stanford University Press.

TERMAN, L. M., & ODEN, M. H. (1947). *Genetic studies of genius, vol. 4. The gifted child grows up: Twenty-five years' follow-up of a superior group.* Stanford, CA: Stanford University Press.

TERMAN, L. M., & ODEN, M. H. (1959). *Genetic studies of genius, vol. 5. The gifted group at mid-Life: Thirty-five years' follow-up of the superior child.* Stanford, CA: Stanford University Press.

THORNDIKE, E. L. (1898). Animal intelligence: An experimental study of the associative processes in animals. *Psychological Review Monographs, 2* (No. 8).

THORNDIKE, E. L. (1911). *Animal intelligence.* New York: Macmillan.

THURSTONE, L. L. (1938). Primary mental abilities. *Psychometric Monographs,* No. 1. Chicago: University of Chicago Press.

TITCHENER, E. B. (1916). *A textbook of psychology.* NY: MacMillan. (Original work published 1909).

TODD, J. T., & MORRIS, E. K. (1992). Case histories in the great power of steady misrepresentation. *American Psychologist, 47,* 1441–1453.

TOLMAN, E. C. (1959). Principles of purposive behavior. In S. Koch (Ed.), *Psychology: A study of a science: Vol. 2. General systematic formulations, learning, and special processes.* New York: McGraw-Hill.

TOLMAN, E. C., TRYON, R. C., & JEFFRIES, L. A. (1929). A self-recording maze with an automatic delivery table. *University of California Publications in Psychology, 4,* 99–112.

TOMAS, V. (Ed.). (1957). *Charles S. Peirce: Essays in the philosophy of science.* New York: The Liberal Arts press.

TRABASSO, T. (1963). Stimulus emphasis and all-or-none learning in concept identification. *Journal of Experimental Psychology, 65,* 398–406.

TREMBLAY, R. E., MASSE, B., PERRON, D., LeBLANC, M., SCHWARTZMAN, A. E., & LEDINGHAM, J. E. (1992). Early disruptive behavior, poor school achievement, delinquent behavior, and delinquent personality: Longitudinal analysis. *Journal of Consulting and Clinical Psychology, 60,* 64–72.

TROTTER, R. J. (1986, August). Three heads are better than one. *Psychology Today,* 56–62.

TRYON, R. C. (1929). The genetics of learning ability in rats: Preliminary report. *University of California Publications in Psychology, 4,* 71–89.

TULVING, E. (1966). Subjective organization and the effects of repetition in multi-trial free recall. *Journal of Verbal Learning and Verbal Behavior, 5,* 195–197.

ULRICH, R. S. (1984). View through a window may influence recovery from surgery. *Science, 224,* 420–421.

WAGAMAN, J. R., MILTENBERGER, R. G., & ARNDORFER, R. E. (1993). Analysis of a simplified treatment for stuttering in children. *Journal of Applied Behavior Analysis, 26,* 53–61.

WAGNER, J. A., III, RUBIN, P. A., & CALLAHAN, T. J. (1988). Incentive payment and nonmanagerial productivity: An interrupted time series analysis of magnitude and trend. *Organizational Behavior and Human Decision Processes, 42,* 47–74.

WARD, R. A. (1993). Marital happiness and household equity in later life. *Journal of Marriage and Family, 55,* 427–438.

WASON, P. C., & JOHNSON-LAIRD, P. N. (1972). *Psychology of reasoning: Structure and content.* Cambridge, MA: Harvard University Press.

WATSON, J. B. (1907). Kinesthetic and organic sensations: Their role in the reactions of the white rat to the maze. *Psychological Review Monograph Supplements, 8* (No. 33).

WATSON, J. B. (1924). *Behaviorism.* New York: Norton.

WATSON, J. B., & RAYNER, R. (1920). Conditioned emotional reactions. *Journal of Experimental Psychology, 3,* 1–14.

WEBB, E. J., CAMPBELL, D. T., SCHWARTZ, R. D., SECHREST, L., & GROVE, J. B. (1981). *Nonreactive measures in the social sciences* (2nd ed.). Boston: Houghton-Mifflin.

Webster's word histories. (1989). Springfield, MA: Merriam-Webster, Inc.

WEISS, J. M. (1968). Effects of coping response on stress. *Journal of Comparative and Physiological Psychology, 65,* 251–260.

WEISS, J. M. (1977). Psychological and behavioral influences on gastrointestinal lesions in animal models. In

J. D. Maser & M. E. P. Seligman (Eds.), *Psychopathology: Experimental models.* San Francisco: Freeman.

WEST, S. G., HEPWORTH, J. T., McCALL, M. A., & REICH, J. W. (1989). An evaluation of Arizona's July 1982 drunk driving law: Effects on the city of Phoenix. *Journal of Applied Social Psychology, 19,* 1212–1237.

WICKENS, D. D., BORN, D. G., & ALLEN, C. K. (1963). Proactive inhibition and item similarity in short-term memory. *Journal of Verbal Learning and Verbal Behavior, 2,* 440–445.

WINSTON, A. S. (1990). Robert Sessions Woodworth and the "Columbia Bible": How the psychological experiment was redefined. *American Journal of Psychology, 103,* 391–401.

WITMER, L. (1893, July 14). *Letter to Hugo Münsterberg.* Münsterberg Papers, Boston Public Library, Boston, MA.

WITT, L. A., & NYE, L. G. (1992). Gender and the relationship between perceived fairness of pay or promotion and job satisfaction. *Journal of Applied Psychology, 77,* 910–917.

WOOD, J. M., & BOOTZIN, R. R. (1990). The prevalence of nightmares and their independence from anxiety. *Journal of Abnormal Psychology, 99,* 64–68.

WOOD, J. M., BOOTZIN, R. R., ROSENHAN, D., NOLEN-HOEKSEMA, S., & JOURDEN, F. (1992). Effects of the 1989 San Francisco earthquake on frequency and content of nightmares. *Journal of Abnormal Psychology, 101,* 219–224.

WOODWORTH, R. S. (1938). *Experimental psychology.* New York: Henry Holt.

WORD, C. O., ZANNA, M. P., & COOPER, J. (1974). The nonverbal mediation of self-fulfilling prophecies in interracial interaction. *Journal of Experimental Social Psychology, 10,* 109–120.

WUNDT, W. (1904). *Principles of physiological psychology* (5th ed.) (E. B. Titchener, Trans.). New York: MacMillan. (Original work published 1874).

YARMEN, A. D., & BULL, M. P. (1978). Where were you when President Kennedy was assassinated? *Bulletin of the Psychonomic Society, 11,* 133–135.

YEATON, W. H., & SECHREST, L. (1986). Use and misuse of no-difference findings in eliminating threats to validity. *Evaluation Review, 10,* 836–852.

Photo Credits

Chapter 1: *Figure 1.2:* Carol Clayton. *Figure 1.3:* Harvard University News Office, Photo by Rick Stafford.

Chapter 2: *Figure 2.2: American Psychologist*, March 1990, p. 321 by Courtesy of Publishers of Life.

Chapter 3: *Figure 3.3:* Holt, Rinehart and Winston.

Chapter 4: *Figure 4.3:* Courtesy of Clark University Archives. *Figure 4.4:* ©Sidney Harris.

Chapter 7: *Figure 7.4:* Courtesy of Dr. David N. Lee, Department of Psychology, University of Edinburgh, Scotland.

Chapter 9: *Figure 9.2:* from Scrupture, E.W. (1895), *Thinking, feeling, doing.* Meadville, PA: Chautauqua-Century Press.

Chapter 10: *Figure 10.1:* Courtesy of Clark University Archives. *Figure 10.2:* Courtesy Yale University Library. *Figure 10.7:* Sybil Shelton/Monkmeyer Press Photo. *Figure 10.8a:* Courtesy of Gerbrands Corporation.

Chapter 11: *Figure 11.1:* Hedwige Boesch/Zoologisches Institut der Universitat Basel.

Chapter 12: *Figure 12.1:* ©Sidney Harris. *Figure 12.3:* Courtesy Robert Sternberg, Yale University. *Figure 12.4:* Courtesy Elizabeth Loftus, University of Washington.

Appendix: *Figure A.1:* Bill Watterson/Universal Press Syndicate.

Name Index

Subject Index

Text and Illustration Credits

Chapter 1 Pages 3 and 4: Myers, D. G., *Social Psychology, 3rd ed.* Copyright © 1990, p. 393, Worth Publishers. Reprinted with permission of McGraw-Hill. Page 14: Tolman, E. C., *Principles of Purposive Behavior.* Koch, S., (Ed.), p. 152. Copyright © McGraw-Hill, 1959.

Chapter 2 Page 28: Copyright © 1992 by the American Psychological Association. Reprinted by permission. Page 42: Sullivan, D. S., and Decker, T. E., *American Psychologist, 28*, p. 589. Copyright © 1973 by the American Psychological Association Reprinted by permission.

Chapter 3 Pages 66 and 67: From Hubel, D. H. *Eye, Brain, and Vision.* Copyright © 1988 by Scientific American Library. Reprinted with permission of W. H. Freeman and Company. Pages 67 and 68: Krupat, E. (Ed.), "*Conversation with John Darley.*" From *Psychology is Social: Readings and Conversations in Social Psychology*, pp 255–263 Copyright © 1975. Reprinted by permission of HarperCollins College Publishers. Page 69: Seligman, M. E. P., *Helplessness: On Depression, Development and Death.* Copyright © 1975 by Martin E. P. Seligman. Reprinted with permission of W. H. Freeman and Company. Page 81, Figure 3.4: Reprinted with permission from *Thesaurus of Psychological Index Terms*, American Psychological Association, all rights reserved. Copyright © 1994. Pages 81 and 82 and Figure 3.5: From *Psychological Abstracts*, Subject Index. Reprinted with permission from Psychological Abstracts. Copyright © 1991 by the American Psychological Association. Figure 3.6: From *Psychological Abstracts, 78.* Reprinted with permission from Psychological Abstracts. Copyright © 1991. American Psychological Association, all rights reserved. Table 3.1: Source: PsycINFO services brochure, reprinted with permission of the American Psychological Association. Copyright © 1992.

Chapter 4 Page 93, Figure 4.1: From Kim, K., and Spelke, E. S., Infant's sensitivity to effects of gravity on visual motion (pp. 385–393). *JEP: Human Perception and Performance, 18(2).* Copyright © 1992. Reprinted with permission from the American Psychological Association. Page 94, Figure 4.2: From Ulrich, R. S., Figure 1, Vol. 224, 1984, *Science*, pages 420–421. Copyright © 1984 by the AAAS. Page 99: Excerpt from *Introduction to Personality*, Third Edition, by Walter Mischel. Copyright © 1981 by Holt, Rinehart, and Winston, Inc., reprinted by permission of the publisher. Table 4.2: Adapted from *The Psychology of Affiliation*, by Stanley Schachter with the permission of the publishers, Stanford University Press. Copyright © 1959 by the Board of Trustees of the Leland Stanford Junior University.

Chapter 5 Figure 5.1: From *Psychopathology: Experimental Models* by Seligman and Maser. Copyright © 1977, Martin E. P. Seligman and Jack Maser. Reprinted with permission of W. H. Freeman and Company. Figure 5.2: From Bandura, A., Ross, D., and Ross, S. A., Imitation of film-mediated aggressive models (pp. 3–11). *Journal of Abnormal and Social Psychology, 66.* Copyright © 1963 by the American Psychological Association. Adapted by permission.

Chapter 6   Figure 6.3: From Lung, C-T., and Dominowski, R. L., Effects of strategy instructions and practice on nine-dot problem solving (pp. 804–811). *JEP: Learning, Memory, and Cognition, 11(4).* Copyright © 1985 by the American Psychological Association. Reprinted by permission. Figure 6.4: From Koriat, A., and Norman, J., What is rotated in mental rotation? (pp. 421–434). *JEP: Learning, Memory, and Cognition, 10(3).* Copyright © 1984 by the American Psychological Association. Reprinted by permission.

Chapter 7   Figure 7.2, page 195: From Blakemore, C., and Cooper, G. F., *Nature, 228,* p. 478. Copyright © 1970 by H. Holt-Macmillan. Reprinted by permission. Page 197: From MacLeod, C., The Stroop task: The 'gold standard' of attentional measures (pp. 12–14). *JEP: General, 121(1).* Copyright © 1992 by the American Psychological Association. Reprinted by permission. Figure 7.3: From Stroop, J. R., Studies of interference in serial verbal reactions (reprint of 1935 article) (pp. 15–23). *JEP: General, 121(1).* Copyright © 1992 by the American Psychological Association. Reprinted by permission. Page 202; Figures 7.9 and 7.12; Table 7.2: From Bransford, J. D., and Johnson, M. K., Contextual prerequisites for Understanding (pp. 717–726). *Journal of Verbal Learning and Verbal Behavior, 11.* Copyright © 1972 by Academic Press. Figures 7.10 and 7.11: From Kosslyn, S. M. et al., Visual images preserve metric spatial information (pp. 47–60). *JEP: Human Perception and Performance, 4(1).* Copyright © 1978 by the American Psychological Association. Reprinted by permission. Page 217: From Godden, D. R., and Baddeley, A. D., Context-dependent memory in two natural environments: On land and under water. *British Journal of Psychology, 66,* 325–331, adaptation of Table 1. Copyright © 1975 by the British Psychological Society. Figure 7.17: From Keltner, D., Ellsworth, P. C., and Edwards, K., Beyond simple pessimism: Effects of sadness (pp. 740–752). *Journal of Personality and Social Psychology, 64(5).* Copyright © 1993 by the American Psychological Association. Reprinted by permission. Figure 7.21: From Gunter et al., 1981, Proactive interference effects with television (pp. 480–487). *JEP: Human Learning and Memory, 7(6).* Copyright © 1981 by the American Psychological Association. Adapted by permission. Figure 7.22: From Holmes, D. S., McGilley, B. M., and Houston, B. K., 1984, Task-related arousal of Type A and Type B persons (pp. 1322–1327). *Journal of Personality and Social Psychology, 46(6).* Copyright © 1984 by the American Psychological Association. Reprinted by permission.

Chapter 8   Figure 8.1: From Fancher, R. E., *Pioneers of Psychology (2nd Ed.),* p. 231. Copyright © 1990 by W. W. Norton & Co. Figure 8.8 and Table 8.1: From Eron, L. D. et al., Does television violence cause aggression? (pp. 253–263). *American Psychological, 27.* Copyright © 1972 by the American Psychological Association. Reprinted by permission. Figure 8.9: From Tremblay, R. E. et al., Early disruptive behavior, poor school achievement (pp. 64–72). *Journal of Consulting and Clinical Psychology, 60(1).* Copyright © 1992 by the American Psychological Association. Reprinted by permission. Page 256: From APA, Standards 2.02 (a.

only), 2.03. Ethical Principles of Psychologists and Code of Conduct. Copyright ©
1992 by the American Psychological Association. Reprinted by permission. Table
8.2: From Bouchard, T. J., and McGue, M., Familial studies of intelligence: A review (pp. 1055–1059). *Science, 212.* Copyright © 1981 by the American
Association for the Advancement of Science. Adapted by permission. Table 8.3:
From Emde, R. N. et al., 1992, Temperament, emotion, and cognition at fourteen
months (pp. 1437–1455). *Child Development, 63.* Copyright © 1992 by the Society
for Research in Child Development, Inc. Adapted by permission of the University
of Chicago Press.

Chapter 9   Figure 9.1: From Fisher et al., Field test of the cognitive interview
(pp. 722–727). *Journal of Applied Psychology, 74(5).* Copyright © 1989 by the
American Psychological Association. Adapted by permission. Page 291: From
Sechrest, L., and Figueredo, A. J. 1993, Program evaluation. Reproduced with permission, from the *Annual Review of Psychology, Volume 44,* © 1993, by Annual
Reviews, Inc. Figure 9.6: From Wagner, J. A. et al., 1968, Incentive payment and
nonmarginal productivity (pp. 47–74). *Organizational Behavior and Human Decision
Processes, 42.* Copyright © 1988 by Academic Press. Reprinted by permission.
Figure 9.7: From West, S. G. et al., An evaluation of Arizona's July 1982 drunk dri-
ving law (pp. 1212–1237). *Journal of Applied Social Psychology, 19.* Copyright ©
1989 by V. H. Winston & Sons, Inc. Adapted by permission. Pages 287 and 288:
From Campbell, D. T., Reforms as experiments (pp. 409–429). *American
Psychologist, 24.* Copyright © 1969 by the American Psychological Association.
Reprinted by permission.

Chapter 10   Page 311: From Skinner, B. F., *A Matter of Consequences.* Copyright
© 1984 by New York University Press. Reprinted by permission. Page 313:
Watson, J. B., 1924, Behaviorism. Copyright © 1924 by W. W. Norton & Co.
Reprinted by permission. Figure 10.11: From Hume, K. M., and Crossman, J.,
Musical reinforcement of practice behaviors (pp. 665–670). *Journal of Applied
Behavior Analysis, 25.* Copyright © 1992 by the University of Kansas. Reprinted by
permission. Figure 10.13: From Wagaman, J. R., Miltenberger, R. G., and
Arndorfer, R. E., Analysis of simplified treatment for stuttering in children (pp.
53–61). *Journal of Applied Analysis, 26.* Copyright © 1993 by the University of
Kansas. Reprinted by permission. Figure 10.14: From Chandler et al., 1992, An
analysis of the effects of multiple setting events (pp. 249–263). *Journal of Applied
Behavior Analysis, 25.* Copyright © 1992 by the University of Kansas. Reprinted by
permission. Page 336: From Boesch-Acherman, H., and Boesch, C., Tool use in
wild chimpanzees (pp. 18–21). *Current Directions in Psychological Science, 2.*
Copyright © 1993. Reprinted with permission of Cambridge University Press.

Chapter 11   Table 11.1: From APA, Standards 1.14, 5.03, 5.08, 6.12, 6.13. Ethical
Principles of Psychologists and Code of Conduct. Copyright © 1992 by the
American Psychological Association. Reprinted by permission. Table 11.2: From
Hall, J. A., and Veccia, E. M., More 'touching' observations: New insights (pp.
1155–1162). *Journal of Personality and Social Psychology, 59(6).* Copyright © 1990 by
the American Psychological Association. Reprinted by permission. Page 349: From
APA, Standard 1.06. Ethical Principles of Psychologists and Code of Conduct.
Copyright © 1992 by the American Psychological Association. Reprinted by per-

mission. Page 348: From Ward, R. A., Marital happiness and household equity in later life (pp. 427–438). *Journal of Marriage and the Family, 55*. Copyright © 1993 by the National Council of Family Relations. Reprinted by permission. Figure 11.2: From Ulrich, R. S., 1984, View through a window may influence recovery from surgery (pp. 420–421). *Science, 224*. Copyright © 1984 by the American Association for the Advancement of Science. Reprinted by permission.

Chapter 12 Page 362: From Witmer, L. Copyright © 1893 by the Boston Public Library. Figure 12.2: From Krantz, D. L., Schools of Psychology: A Symposium, © 1969, p. 7. Reprinted by permission of Prentice Hall, Englewood Cliffs, New Jersey. Pages 370 and 371: From Sternberg, Robert J., Excerpts from letter to author. Copyright 1993 by Robert J. Sternberg. Reprinted by permission. Page 380: From APA, Guidelines for nonsexist language. Publication Manual. Copyright 1983 by the American Psychological Association. Reprinted by permission.

Appendix C Tables on pages 432–435: From Pearson, E. S., and Hartley, H. O., *Biometrika Tables for Statisticians, Vol. 1, 3rd Ed.* Copyright 1966 by Cambridge University Press. Reprinted by permission.